MODERN BRITISH PRIME MINISTERS FROM BALFOUR TO JOHNSON

Dick Leonard's *Modern British Prime Ministers from Balfour to Johnson* surveys the lives and careers of all the 24 Prime Ministers from Arthur Balfour to Boris Johnson in succinct, informative and entertaining chapters.

Bringing to life the political achievements and personal idiosyncrasies of Britain's rulers over the 20th and 21st centuries, the author recounts the circumstances which took them to the pinnacle of British political life, probes their political and personal strengths and weaknesses, assesses their performance in office and asks what lasting influence they have had. Along the way Leonard entertains and informs, revealing little-known facts about the private lives of each of the Prime Ministers, for example, which two Premiers, one Tory, one Labour, were taught by the same governess as a child? Who was thrashed at his public school for writing pornography and later donated one-fifth of his wealth to the nation? Who was awarded a fourth-class degree at Oxford and went on to father eight children? Who was described by his son as 'probably the greatest natural Don Juan in the history of British politics'?

This book can also form part of a two-volume set published by Routledge including the companion volume *British Prime Ministers from Walpole to Salisbury: The 18th and 19th Centuries*.

This book will be of key interest to scholars, students and readers of British political history, the Executive, government, and British politics.

Dick Leonard was a journalist, historian and Member of Parliament. He spent the last two decades writing biographies of all the British Prime Ministers from Walpole to Johnson. He was Assistant Editor of *The Economist* for 12 years, and also worked for *The Observer*, the BBC, and the Fabian Society. There is a detailed description of Dick Leonard's work, life and legacy available at www.markleonard.eu/dickleonard

"Dick Leonard is the doyen of the history of British premiership. No one has his grasp of the lives and records of the men and two women who have been Prime Minister. This book is a unique source of illumination and delight."

Anthony Seldon, *Former Vice-Chancellor of the University of Buckingham, UK*

"A great resource for students, scholars and the general public alike. It contains essential information on the prime ministers as leaders but also as people: how they ended up in the role, their character, achievements and weaknesses … as well as providing fascinating insights into the broader political issues of their time."

Oliver Daddow, *University of Nottingham, UK*

"Dick Leonard's book on British Prime Ministers is an excellent account of the changing role of the premiership in UK politics, and the twists and turns of political life. The book is of great interest to the general reader, but also a fantastic undergraduate and postgraduate teaching resource."

Patrick Diamond, *Queen Mary, University of London, UK*

"A terrific read and also a major contribution to public debate."

David Marquand, *University of Oxford, UK*

MODERN BRITISH PRIME MINISTERS FROM BALFOUR TO JOHNSON

Volume Two

Dick Leonard

LONDON AND NEW YORK

First published 2022
by Routledge
2 Park Square, Milton Park, Abingdon, Oxon OX14 4RN

and by Routledge
605 Third Avenue, New York, NY 10158

Routledge is an imprint of the Taylor & Francis Group, an informa business

© 2022 Dick Leonard

The right of Dick Leonard to be identified as author of this work has been
asserted by him in accordance with sections 77 and 78 of the Copyright,
Designs and Patents Act 1988.

All rights reserved. No part of this book may be reprinted or reproduced or utilised
in any form or by any electronic, mechanical, or other means, now known or
hereafter invented, including photocopying and recording, or in any information
storage or retrieval system, without permission in writing from the publishers.

Trademark notice: Product or corporate names may be trademarks or registered trademarks,
and are used only for identification and explanation without intent to infringe.

British Library Cataloguing-in-Publication Data
A catalogue record for this book is available from the British Library

Library of Congress Cataloging-in-Publication Data
Names: Leonard, R. L. (Richard Lawrence), author.
Title: Modern British Prime Ministers from Balfour to Johnson / Dick Leonard.
Description: Abingdon, Oxon; New York, NY: Routledge, 2022. | "Volume 2." |
Includes bibliographical references and index.
Identifiers: LCCN 2021023197 (print) | LCCN 2021023198 (ebook) |
ISBN 9780367469184 (hardback) | ISBN 9780367469177 (paperback) |
ISBN 9781003031963 (ebook)
Subjects: LCSH: Prime ministers–Great Britain–Biography. |
Great Britain–Politics and government–20th century. |
Great Britain–Politics and government–21sth century.
Classification: LCC DA566.9.A1 L46 2022 (print) |
LCC DA566.9.A1 (ebook) | DDC 941.082092/2–dc23
LC record available at https://lccn.loc.gov/2021023197
LC ebook record available at https://lccn.loc.gov/2021023198

ISBN: 978-0-367-46918-4 (hbk)
ISBN: 978-0-367-46917-7 (pbk)
ISBN: 978-1-003-03196-3 (ebk)

DOI: 10.4324/9781003031963

Typeset in Bembo
by Newgen Publishing UK

To the three generations of my family, to all of whom I owe so much: Irène (my wife), John and Marjorie (my brother and sister-in-law), Mark and Miriam (our children), Gabrielle and Phiroze (their partners), Jakob, Noa and Isaac (our grandchildren).

CONTENTS

List of plates	*ix*
About the author	*x*

Introduction	1
1 Arthur Balfour: Bob's your uncle	6
2 Henry Campbell-Bannerman: "A good, honest Scotchman"	16
3 H.H. Asquith: Not quite in the Gladstone mould	27
4 David Lloyd George: "A dynamic force"	40
5 Andrew Bonar Law: Tory puritan	55
6 Stanley Baldwin: "A man of the utmost insignificance"?	64
7 Ramsay MacDonald: An 'aristocrat' among plain men?	76
8 Neville Chamberlain: A family affair	89
9 Winston Churchill: His finest hour	101
10 Clement Attlee: Quiet revolutionary	112
11 Anthony Eden: Self-destruction of a Prince Charming	124

viii Contents

12 Harold Macmillan: Idealist into manipulator	135
13 Alec Douglas-Home: Right man, wrong century?	148
14 Harold Wilson: Master – or victim – of the short term	158
15 Edward Heath: Cheerleader for Europe	173
16 James Callaghan: Labour's conservative	186
17 Margaret Thatcher: Grocer's daughter to Iron Lady	198
18 John Major: "Thatcherism with a human face"	213
19 Tony Blair: Fallen idol	227
20 Gordon Brown: Dominant Chancellor, uncertain Premier	244
21 David Cameron: The accidental architect of Brexit	262
22 Theresa May: "A bloody difficult woman"?	285
23 Boris Johnson: Statesman or buffoon?	303
Index	*320*

PLATES

1   Arthur James Balfour
2   Sir Henry Campbell-Bannerman
3   Herbert Henry Asquith
4   David Lloyd George
5   Andrew Bonar Law
6   Stanley Baldwin
7   James Ramsay Macdonald
8   Neville Chamberlain
9   Winston Churchill
10 Clement Attlee
11 Sir Anthony Eden
12 Harold Macmillan
13 Sir Alex Douglas-Home
14 Harold Wilson
15 Sir Edward Heath
16 James Callaghan
17 Margaret Thatcher
18 Sir John Major
19 Tony Blair
20 Gordon Brown
21 David Cameron
22 Theresa May
23 Boris Johnson

ABOUT THE AUTHOR

Dick Leonard was involved in politics for all his adult life, briefly as a Labour MP, when he was PPS to Anthony Crosland, and for much longer as a political journalist in Westminster and Brussels. The author, or part-author, of some 20 books, he was for many years Assistant Editor of *The Economist*. He also worked for the BBC, *The Observer*, and the Fabian Society. He taught at the Universities of Essex and Brussels (ULB). His articles have appeared in *The Guardian*, *Financial Times*, *The Times* and *The New York Times* and have been syndicated in many other leading newspapers across the world. For the last 20 years he worked as a historian, writing acclaimed works on the rivalries between Gladstone and Disraeli, Fox and Pitt, as well as biographical portraits of all British Prime Ministers from Walpole to Johnson. He completed this book in May 2021 at the age of 90, a few weeks before he died. There is a detailed description of Dick Leonard's work, life and legacy available at www.markleonard.eu/dickleonard

Publications by Dick Leonard

British Prime Ministers from Walpole to Salisbury: The 18th and 19th Centuries
The Great Rivalry: Disraeli-Gladstone: A Dual Biography
Titans: Fox vs. Pitt (with Mark Garnett)
The Routledge Guide to the European Union (with Robert Taylor)
The Economist Guide to the European Union (10 editions)
Elections in Britain (5 editions)
Guide to the General Election
Paying for Party Politics
Crosland and New Labour (edited)
The Socialist Agenda: Crosland's Legacy (edited with David Lipsey)
World Atlas of Elections (edited with Richard Natkiel)
The Backbencher and Parliament (edited with Val Herman)
The Pro-European Reader (edited with Mark Leonard)
The Future of Socialism by Anthony Crosland (edited 50th anniversary edition)

INTRODUCTION

Fifty-three men and two women have held the post of Prime Minister (or, more formally, First Lord of the Treasury) since Robert Walpole was appointed by George I, in 1721. Over the last two decades I have made a close study of these 55 individuals. My aim has been to provide a succinct account of their political careers, assess their achievements and, where appropriate, draw conclusions as to their relevance to the present day.

This volume on the Prime Ministers of the 20th and 21st centuries follows on from my earlier volume, *British Prime Ministers from Walpole to Salisbury: The 18th and 19th Centuries*. In order to avoid repetition I begin this volume with Balfour because Salisbury was predominantly a 19th-century figure.

Historians argue about whether it is great men and women or social and economic forces which fashion events. No one studying the lives and careers in this book would doubt that it is a combination of the two. While many of the most fundamental changes would no doubt have occurred in any event, some at least were down to the judgement, force of character, and sometimes, indeed, errors of particular Prime Ministers. Here are a few of the more obvious examples:

- Salisbury's legacy: the dominance of the Conservative Party, through extending its appeal to new sections of the electorate.
- Asquith's failure to broaden the base of the Liberal Party, which allowed Labour to replace it as the main progressive party.
- Churchill's defiance of his party and much 'common-sense' opinion in continuing to fight a war which seemed lost.
- Attlee, overseeing the creation of a uniquely universalist welfare state, and ensuring that the end of the British Empire was achieved peacefully, at least as far as Britain was concerned.
- Heath, ensuring British entry into Europe – too late, but quite possibly rather earlier than any other Prime Minister would have done.
- Thatcher, like Salisbury before her, changing the rules of British politics, and entrenching Conservative economic ideology, so much so that Labour Prime Ministers such as Blair and Brown, at least to some extent, were still prisoners of her legacy.

DOI: 10.4324/9781003031963-1

2 Introduction

- Blair, overseeing a constitutional revolution, and perhaps reshaping the electoral politics of the 21st century.
- Cameron, whose agreement to hold referenda on Scottish independence and Britain's EU membership took Britain out of the EU and unleashed nationalist forces in Scotland, Northern Ireland and England that could eventually spell the end of the Union.

The 24 Prime Ministers in the 20th and 21st centuries came from a variety of backgrounds. Five of them (Salisbury, Balfour, Churchill, Eden and Douglas-Home) were aristocrats, while two others, Macmillan and Cameron, were married to aristocrats. Apart from Macmillan, six others (Campbell-Bannerman, Bonar Law, Baldwin, Chamberlain, Attlee and Blair) came from comfortable middle-class or professional families. Two more – Brown and May – were offspring of clergy. The remaining eight came from the working or lower middle classes, though four of them (Asquith, Wilson, Heath and Thatcher) effectively 'reclassed' themselves through graduating at Oxford University. Of those from 'humble homes', only Lloyd George, MacDonald, Callaghan and Major succeeded in climbing to the top of the 'greasy pole' without the benefit of a university education. (It is remarkable that of the Prime Ministers who were university graduates, 14 attended Oxford and three Cambridge. The only other universities represented were Glasgow (attended by Campbell-Bannerman, who was also to graduate at Cambridge) and Edinburgh (attended by Gordon Brown). It would be idle to maintain that the people discussed in this volume were the most able and distinguished British politicians of the century. The list includes a number of mediocrities and one or two rank failures, as well as some of the highest competence and perhaps two or three of outstanding quality. It would be easy enough to pick a dozen names of other leading politicians who might well have made it to 10 Downing Street and who would quite probably have outperformed many of those who actually did. On the Conservative side, the names of Joseph and Austen Chamberlain, R.A. Butler, Iain Macleod, Michael Heseltine and Kenneth Clarke spring to mind. A Labour list would include Ernest Bevin, Stafford Cripps, Aneurin Bevan, Hugh Gaitskell, Roy Jenkins and Tony Crosland. The uneven performance of those actually chosen to fill the highest political position in the land is at least partly explicable by the circumstances of their selection. In the early years of the century, party leaders, and hence Prime Ministers, were chosen (if not by the monarch) by their leading parliamentary colleagues, and their performances in the House of Commons were regarded as perhaps the most important criterion. The Labour Party, however, insisted from the outset in choosing its leader by a ballot of all its MPs, a practice soon copied by the Liberals and, much later (after 1964), by the Tories.

Later still, all three parties gave their rank-and-file members a direct role in electing the leader. Other qualities (sometimes conflicting) have become more important in assessing the rival claims of potential leaders, including their ideological position within the party, their support among party activists, and – perhaps most important – their appeal to the electorate as a whole. This has not precluded the choice of compromise candidates who have been pre-ferred to more dynamic but also more divisive contenders, and the choice has sometimes gone – apparently fortuitously – to somebody who just happened to be in the right place at the right time. It is the candidate who is the least offensive and is judged to have the 'safest pair of hands' who usually emerges at the end of the day.

There are, of course, exceptions, and these are liable to occur in unusual situations. Neither Churchill nor Attlee – perhaps the two most successful of 20th-century Premiers – would have been likely to have been chosen in 'normal circumstances': one was regarded as altogether too flamboyant, and the other as not nearly flamboyant enough. Churchill became Prime Minister, *in extremis*, in 1940, when the nation was staring military defeat in the face. Attlee had become leader of the Labour Party five years earlier, but only because all the more favoured candidates of his generation had lost their parliamentary seats in the 1931 general election, which put them temporarily out of the running. The conditions under which the different Prime Ministers have governed, and the extent of their responsibilities, have changed to a remarkable degree over the past 100 years, due largely to three factors – the great increase in the scope of government activities, the much more continuous involvement of heads of government in international affairs, and latterly in those of the European Union, and the tremendous development of the media and all forms of communication.

All these have contributed to a speeding up of the rhythm of prime ministerial lives and have made far greater demands on their stamina. Nevertheless, the core functions of the Prime Minister have not changed all that much over time. No job description was ever published, but one was effectively drawn up by officials in the Cabinet Office in the late 1940s. It was left to gather dust in their files, until a copy was exhumed from the archives of the Public Record Office by Professor Peter Hennessy in the 1990s. He summarised and expanded on it in his magisterial work *The Prime Minister: The Office and Its Holders since 1945*, published in 2000 (Hennessy, 2000, pp. 53–101). Hennessy identified 12 main official functions of the Prime Minister, which included handling the government's relations with the monarch, as Head of State, appointing and dismissing ministers, presiding over the Cabinet and its most important committees, arranging the membership and agenda of other committees, exercising overall control of the Civil Service, allocating functions between government departments and deciding on their creation and abolition, dealing with other heads of government and taking an especially close interest in foreign affairs and defence matters, and deciding on a wide range of top appointments, not only in the Civil Service, but in "many institutions of a national character". As Hennessy points out, this list refers only to the Prime Minister's official functions, and makes no mention of the considerable demands made on him or her as leader of the largest political party. These, since Lloyd George set the precedent in 1918, include deciding the date on which general elections are held (subject to the agreement of the Queen), although this was limited with the introduction of the Fixed Term Parliament Act in 2011. Nor does the list of responsibilities include the Prime Minister's role as the principal representative of the government in the House of Commons. This function, however, has diminished over the years. Prior to Lloyd George, the Prime Minister normally doubled up his post with being Leader of the House (unless he was a member of the House of Lords), which involved him spending many hours seated on the government benches. Recent Prime Ministers, notably Margaret Thatcher and Tony Blair, have, by contrast, spent very little time in the Commons, except when they were themselves making statements or answering Parliamentary Questions or, more rarely, participating in debates. By contrast, the amount of time and effort that Prime Ministers have devoted to addressing the general public, mainly of course through television, has grown enormously, and it is arguable that recent Premiers have suffered from overexposure, and that this has accelerated their 'sell by' dates.

"The office of the Prime Minister is what its holder chooses and is able to make of it", wrote Asquith in his memoirs, a sentiment with which most of his fellow Prime Ministers would probably have agreed. Nevertheless, some observers have seen it as an office which has grown inexorably in power, so that from being *primus inter pares* (first among equals) within the Cabinet, as the 19th-century Liberal politician John Morley defined the position, he/

4 Introduction

she has come totally to dominate it. Cabinet government in this view, which was argued for strongly by John Mackintosh (*The British Cabinet*, 1977) and Richard Crossman (Bagehot, 1964, pp. 37–57) in the 1960s, has given way to prime ministerial or even 'presidential' government. Others, notably Professor George Jones (King, 1985, pp. 195–220), attempted to refute this argument, pointing out the many constraints under which Prime Ministers still operate. My own view is that there has been a considerable increase in prime ministerial power, but that it has not been a linear one. Strong Prime Ministers have been followed by weaker ones, and the strength of a Prime Minister's position depends upon many factors other than his/her own will and innate abilities. These include the quality of their fellow Cabinet ministers and the limits to their deference, whether they are leading a coalition or a single party administration, the size of their parliamentary majority, their standing in their own political party, the state of the opinion polls and the run of by-election results, the length of time they have been in office and the effectiveness of the main opposition party.

One evident constraint upon future would-be strongmen or women is that two of the most domineering Prime Ministers of the 20th century – Lloyd George and Thatcher – were eventually unhorsed by their own followers, who despaired of their imperious ways.

No attempt has been made in the body of this book to put the Prime Ministers in any sort of rank order. At the very end of the 20th century, a BBC programme polled a small sample of historians, commentators and politicians and asked them to produce such a list, excluding the incumbent, Tony Blair. The result, published in *The Guardian* on 27 December 1999, was as follows:

1. Winston Churchill (Con, 1940–45, 1951–55)
2. David Lloyd George (Lib, 1916–22)
3. Clement Attlee (Lab, 1945–51)
4. Herbert Asquith (Lib, 1908–16)
5. Margaret Thatcher (Con, 1979–90)
6. Harold Macmillan (Con, 1957–63)
7. Marquess of Salisbury (Con, 1895–1902)
8. Stanley Baldwin (Con, 1923–24, 1924–29, 1935–37)
9. Sir Henry Campbell-Bannerman (Lib, 1905–08)
10. Harold Wilson (Lab, 1964–70, 1974–76)
11. Edward Heath (Con, 1970–74)
12. James Callaghan (Lab, 1976–79)
13. Andrew Bonar Law (Con, 1922–23)
14. Ramsay MacDonald (Lab, 1924, 1929–35)
15. Sir Alec Douglas-Home (Con, 1963–64)
16. Arthur Balfour (Con, 1902–05)
17. John Major (Con, 1990–97)
18. Neville Chamberlain (Con, 1937–40)
19. Sir Anthony Eden (Con, 1955–57)

There have been five Prime Ministers since the list was produced who are obviously not included. I myself would not strongly dissent from this overall assessment, but would probably have put Lloyd George and Thatcher rather lower, and Attlee, Campbell-Bannerman and Heath somewhat higher. It is my hope that readers of this book may find it some help in forming their own judgements of the achievements and shortcomings of those who guided our destinies during the past century.

Note on sources

The present volume is not based on a large amount of original research. So far as the first half of the book is concerned, my principal source has been a close reading of relevant historical works as well as the main biographies of the personalities involved. This is also true of the later period, but it has been increasingly supplemented by my own observations of the political scene, during the course of a long career as a political journalist, and a much shorter one as an active politician and Member of Parliament. In these capacities, I have had some personal contact with all but two of the Prime Ministers since Macmillan, though I knew only two of them – Wilson and Callaghan – at all well, and was not a close associate of either of them.

I may not, perhaps, have achieved the highest level of objectivity. Even though I have striven to avoid conscious bias, I cannot avoid unconscious ones, and it is right that the reader should be aware that mine come from a centre-left position. What I have tried to do is to judge the characters involved by the success or otherwise with which they have pursued their own declared objectives, rather than whether I personally approve of such objectives. I have also made a serious effort not to apply 21st-century standards to the careers of the earlier Prime Ministers who were operating according to the norms of the late 19th and early 20th centuries.

Short bibliographies are included at the end of each chapter. The following more general works have also been of assistance to the author:

Works consulted

Walter Bagehot, 1964, *The English Constitution*, Introduction by Richard Crossman, London, Watts.
F.W.G. Benemy, 1965, *The Elected Monarch*, London, Harrap.
Humphry Berkeley, 1968, *The Power of the Prime Minister*, London, Allen & Unwin.
Lord Blake, 1975, *The Office of Prime Minister*, London, Oxford University Press.
Peter Hennessy, 2000, *The Prime Minister: The Office and Its Holders since 1945*, London, Penguin.
Dennis Kavanagh and Anthony Seldon, 1999, *The Powers behind the Prime Minister*, London, HarperCollins.
Anthony King (ed.), 1985, *The British Prime Minister*, 2nd edition, Basingstoke, Macmillan (now Palgrave Macmillan).
John P. Mackintosh, 1977, *The British Cabinet*, 3rd edition, London, Stevens.
Anthony Seldon (with Jonathan Meakin and Ilias Thoms), 2021, *The Impossible Office: The History of the British Prime Minister*, Cambridge, Cambridge University Press.

1

ARTHUR BALFOUR

Bob's your uncle

The most civilised, and perhaps the most intelligent, of 20th-century Prime Ministers was Arthur Balfour. He was also, by common consent, one of the least effective. Cynics may conclude that there was a direct connection: that the rough-and-tumble of democratic politics is not designed for finer spirits. Yet Balfour successfully held high ministerial office, both before and after his premiership, and left his mark in several important areas of public policy. Indeed, it is a little-known fact that Balfour's career as a Cabinet minister was the longest in British history. He served under four very different Prime Ministers, a clear indication that his contribution was highly valued. Balfour's record, compared in length of years with other long-serving statesmen, is listed by his most recent biographer as follows: Balfour 27, Churchill 26, Liverpool 25, Gladstone 24, Palmerston 23, the Younger Pitt 22 (Mackay, 1985, p. 354).

Arthur James Balfour, later first Earl of Balfour (1848–1930), was born with a 'silver spoon' in his mouth – that was, in fact, the title of the first chapter in Kenneth Young's biography (Young, 1963, p. 1). He was the third child, and the eldest son, of James Maitland Balfour, a country landowner and local Tory MP who had inherited a large fortune and estate (Whittingehame in East Lothian) from his own father, who had made a fortune as a contractor in India. James Maitland Balfour died at the age of 36, when Arthur was only 7, and he was brought up by his strong-minded mother, Lady Blanche Balfour, sister of Lord Salisbury, who at the age of 31 was left with eight young children to raise. Lady Blanche devoted herself entirely to the educational and moral instruction of her children, widening their intellectual horizons, fostering their curiosity and giving them a firm basis of religious belief. Though a devoted evangelical Christian, she was no narrow sectarian, and brought up her children as members of both the Church of England and of Scotland, a membership which Balfour retained throughout his life.

Lady Blanche's declared intention, once she had completed the tuition of her eight surviving children, was to move to London's East End and devote herself to the poor, but this ambition was thwarted by her early death at 47. This left Arthur, whose education had continued at Eton and Cambridge, though without his achieving any particular distinction, as the head of the family. At 24, with a fortune probably exceeding £1 million (equal to at least

DOI: 10.4324/9781003031963-2

£75 million today), surrounded by an adoring family circle of brothers, sisters and cousins (several of them of high intelligence and intellectual distinction), he had the world at his feet. Handsome, clever, charming, witty, he was also immensely well connected (his Uncle Robert, the future Prime Minister, was a trustee of his estate and seems to have felt more affinity with the young Arthur than with any of his own large brood of children). His own family was supplemented by the interlocking Lyttelton and Gladstone families, with whom Balfour became associated through his Cambridge friendship with Spencer Lyttelton and his younger brother, Alfred. There were eight Lyttelton brothers and four sisters in all, and their Gladstone cousins with whom they were on intimate terms, were also numerous.

Both families were effectively co-opted to the Balfour circle. An unending carousel of visits ensued between Balfour's Whittingehame estate, and the country houses of Hagley Hall (Lytteltons) and Hawarden (Gladstones). The young Balfour much impressed William Gladstone, who seems to have regarded him as a possible future Liberal MP and a more than possible son-in-law, his daughter Mary being clearly enamoured of him. She became a close friend of Balfour's, but he evinced no romantic interest and she eventually married a local parson.

Surrounded by this large and admiring circle of intelligent and discriminating young people, who merged into a wider group of young and mostly aristocratic people of both sexes, known as "the Souls" on account of their love of elevated conversation, and of playing both physical and intellectual games, Balfour was the undoubted centre of attention, being known variously as "Prince Arthur" or "King Arthur". The absence of any struggle in his life, in contrast to his Uncle Robert who had fierce disputes with his father and had to work hard as a young man to earn his living, had a profound and not entirely positive effect on his temperament. He grew up as a wonderfully tolerant man, with an exceptionally open mind, a lively curiosity and a wide range of interests, but also prone to self-indulgence and a marked inability or unwillingness to commit himself.

This was very evident in his personal life. Balfour remained unmarried, the only bachelor Prime Minister of the 20th century apart from Edward Heath. There is absolutely no evidence that he was homosexual, despite his acquiring the nickname of "Pretty Fanny" at Cambridge, because of the alleged effeminacy of his artistic tastes. Balfour was, in fact, exceptionally fond of female company, and had a number of very close women friends, but few, if any, affairs.

The biggest tragedy in Balfour's life appears to have been the sudden death, aged 24, of May Lyttelton, the sister of his friends Spencer and Alfred, in March 1875. There had been no previous indication that they were romantically involved, but Balfour exhibited profound grief, sending her brother Edward an emerald ring which had belonged to his mother to put in May's coffin, and claiming that they had talked of marriage. If so, he had proved himself a hesitant and undemonstrative wooer.

Thereafter, he never seems to have contemplated marriage, though he had an intimate friendship over many years with a young married woman, Mary Wyndham, the wife of Lord Elcho, later Earl of Wemyss. They corresponded with each other for over 30 years, but the exact nature of their relationship is far from clear. One of Balfour's biographers, Kenneth Young, states bluntly that Mary Elcho was his mistress, and remained so for many years. This book caused great offence to the Wemyss family, who withdrew the Balfour-Elcho correspondence from the collection of Balfour papers in the British Museum, and later writers have doubted whether there was an actual physical relationship. Much later the correspondence was edited for publication by Jane Ridley and Clayre Percy, whose judgement is worth recording:

> Were they lovers? we wondered, as so many people have wondered at the time and since. At first we thought not. To begin with, the letters give little away. Then it became plain that something was going on; this was not a platonic friendship. But lovers in the conventional sense they were probably not. Which makes their relationship all the odder. It was an *amitié amoureuse* that lasted for well over thirty years. It never compromised Balfour's political career; and it did not threaten Mary Elcho's marriage. Yet for both of them it was the most important relationship in their lives.
>
> *(Ridley and Percy, 1992, p. viii)*

Whatever the truth, Balfour was notably circumspect in his correspondence. There is not one word of endearment in the several hundred letters which have survived, nor does he once address Mary Elcho by her Christian name.

This disinclination to commit himself is the key to both Balfour's strength and his weakness as a politician. On the one hand, he was exceptionally gifted as a drafter of memoranda, setting out with crystal clarity the pros and cons of any proposed line of action. This made him an extremely useful member of a Cabinet, a committee of inquiry or other public body. Yet his lack of passion precluded him from giving a decisive lead one way or the other, which was a fatal flaw in a Prime Minister, and was one reason why his government of 1902–05 broke up around him.

As a young man in his mid-twenties, Balfour was widely seen as no more than a gifted dilettante, as an anonymous poem preserved by Mary Elcho well illustrates:

> Playful little Arthur, he
> Plays with things so prettily
> To him everything's a game
> Win or lose it's all the same
> Plays with politics or war
> Trivial little games they are –
> Plays with souls and plays at golf –
> This must never be put off.
> Plays with deep philosophies,
> Faiths and minor things like these,
> Plays with praise and plays with blame
> Everything is but a game
> Win or lose, it's all the same.
> Playful little Arthur, he
> Cannot take things seriously.
> *(Ridley and Percy, 1992, p. 20)*

Yet, at times, Balfour did want to take things seriously. At Cambridge he had thought of giving up his inheritance to a younger brother, and devoting himself to philosophy. He had been dissuaded by his mother, who wrote to him: "You will have nothing to write about by the time you are 40" (Young, 1963, p. 10). When he was 26, his Uncle Robert came to his rescue, suggesting a political career. He provided him with a safe seat, close to his Hatfield estate, and Balfour was elected unopposed for Hertford in the 1874 election, which led to the formation of Disraeli's government.

Balfour was in no hurry to make his mark, waiting for two years before making his maiden speech, and remained a fairly obscure backbencher until 1878 when Salisbury again gave him a push up, taking him with him to the Congress of Berlin as his private secretary, an invaluable experience for a (much) later Foreign Secretary. In the short term, however, it did little to stimulate his political ambition. Instead, he resumed his earlier interest in philosophy, publishing, in 1879, *A Defence of Philosophic Doubt.*

When the Tories lost the 1880 election, Balfour belatedly began to play an active role in the House of Commons, associating himself with the so-called Fourth Party, a small group of freebooters who tried to inject a more vigorous opposition to Gladstone's first government than was provided by the lacklustre leadership of Sir Stafford Northcote, the Tory leader in the Commons. The dominant figure in the Fourth Party was Lord Randolph Churchill, and the only other members were John Gorst and Sir Drummond Wolff. Balfour was the most detached member of the four – largely because he soon detected in Churchill a likely rival to Uncle Robert as the future Conservative leader.

Yet his detachment probably owed as much to his regarding parliamentary tactics as a fascinating game, rather than having a deeper purpose. As Mackay writes: "He was motivated partly by genuine sympathy with the wish for a more lively opposition to the government and partly by his constant desire to improve his debating skills, as an end in itself rather than through ambition for ministerial office" (Mackay, 1985, p. 29). This desire paid off: from being an uncertain and hesitant speaker, Balfour progressed to being one of the most effective debaters in the House.

His languorous appearance and apparent frivolity still meant that few took him seriously, and his appointment as President of the Local Government Board by Lord Salisbury, when he formed his first government in June 1885, was uniformly attributed to family favouritism. The term "Bob's your Uncle" entered the English language around this time, almost certainly as an ironic explanation for Balfour's preferment. When Salisbury again became Prime Minister in July 1886, Balfour was appointed to the newly created post of Secretary for Scotland, becoming a member of the Cabinet a few months later. He did not serve for long: in March 1887 Sir Michael Hicks Beach resigned because of ill health from the far more important and controversial post of Chief Secretary for Ireland. To general amazement, the Prime Minister appointed his nephew in his place.

Few appointments had appeared more outlandish since Caligula made his horse a consul. That this dandyish, effete figure would match up to the demands of the toughest job in the government, which had broken the health of his predecessor, and only five years before had cost the life of Lord Frederick Cavendish, assassinated in Dublin's Phoenix Park, strained the bounds of credulity. The immediate reaction was one of hilarity, while the formidable Irish Party in the House of Commons, smarting from their recent setback over Home Rule, sharpened their sabres in the easy expectation of carving him up in parliamentary debate.

Only his uncle seemed to believe that Balfour had it in him to rise to the occasion, and he was not disappointed. Showing quite unexpected vigour, and the ability to work for long hours and apply himself to enervating detail, Balfour succeeded in calming down a potentially revolutionary situation in Ireland, while gaining the upper hand over the Irish parliamentary party in a series of blistering skirmishes. His twin objectives in Ireland were to restore law and order through a ruthless application of recently enacted coercive legislation, while seeking to remove the economic causes of discontent by Land Reform Acts forced through Parliament despite the opposition of Tory landowners. On the first count, he was largely successful, but not before three rioters had been shot dead by police at a mass demonstration in Mitchelstown, County Cork, which earned him the nickname of Bloody Balfour. His attempts to pacify Irish land hunger also led to a falling away of agitation, though the deceptive peace which descended on Ireland for 20 or so years after his stewardship ended perhaps owed as much to the decline and premature death of Charles Stewart Parnell. At best, he secured a respite while doing nothing to prevent the eventual resurgence of nationalist demands.

In 1891 Salisbury rewarded Balfour by making him Leader of the House of Commons, in succession to W.H. Smith, who had died. Unusually, he was also First Lord of the Treasury, as the Prime Minister did not need this title as he was already a Secretary of State as Foreign Secretary. He had also assigned 10 Downing Street, first to Smith and then to Balfour, preferring to live in his own houses in Arlington Street and Hatfield. On this occasion, nobody laughed and nobody uttered the word "nepotism". Balfour was acknowledged to have been the most capable and successful of the Tory ministers, and he was now widely seen as a future Prime Minister on his own merits. Yet Balfour did not shine – initially at least – in his new post. He lacked the patience to spend long hours attending to the minutiae of parliamentary debates, nor did he devote himself with conspicuous energy to the endless task of reconciling the views and prejudices of the various personalities and factions making up the House of Commons, in particular neglecting too often currents of opinion within his own party. While he had been Irish Secretary he had seen a clear purpose to his work, to which he felt totally committed. Playing party games in the House of Commons was a different matter, and he resented having to subordinate his other wide interests to the daily drudgery of leading the House. It may have been with some personal relief that he greeted the result of the election in July 1892 which brought the Liberals back to power. Although he subsequently devoted himself to leading the Tory opposition in the Commons, he also returned to his earlier love of philosophy, writing perhaps his most significant book, *The Foundations of Belief*, which appeared in 1895.

The collapse of Lord Rosebery's Liberal government in the same year saw Balfour's return as Leader of the House in Salisbury's third and final government. He again made heavy weather of the post, but gradually buckled down and became the ageing Salisbury's indispensable prop and partner, substituting for him on numerous occasions when he was indisposed. He was eventually seen as his uncle's inevitable successor, partly, it is true, because there was no obvious alternative. Lord Randolph Churchill had died in 1894, and neither Joseph Chamberlain nor the Duke of Devonshire, both Liberal Unionists, would have been readily acceptable at the head of a Tory government.

As Salisbury declined, Balfour took over more and more responsibility, providing much-needed leadership after the early disasters of the Boer War and taking personal charge of the highly controversial Education Bill which seemed doomed because of the strength and width of opposition, led by the Nonconformist churches which did not want public money to be spent on Anglican schools. It was finally enacted shortly after he replaced his uncle as Prime Minister in July 1902.

Balfour's inheritance in 1902 seemed to be full of promise. The return of peace after the hard-won victory in South Africa, and the succession of Edward VII to the throne, had created a new atmosphere of optimism. Moreover, the 'khaki' election of October 1900 had given the

Tories a crushing parliamentary majority, while the Liberals, torn apart by their differences over the Boer War, seemed hopelessly divided.

Yet there was one glaring gap. Balfour himself had no programme in mind for the government he was about to lead. Always in the past he had been guided by his uncle, and he had shown a high level of competence in carrying through the tasks which had been assigned to him. Now the onus of steering the ship of state was upon him, and – apart from completing the passage of the Education Bill – he had no particular destination in mind.

Others did know where they wanted to go – notably Chamberlain who had surprised both Salisbury and Balfour in 1895, when he had opted to become Colonial Secretary rather than Chancellor of the Exchequer. He retained this post under Balfour, and his belief in the importance of maintaining and expanding the British Empire was stronger than ever. Following a conference in August 1902, at which all the British colonies, notably Canada and South Africa, were represented, he became convinced that the best way of binding the Empire together was to give trade preferences to all its members. He therefore demanded, as a first step, that import duties on corn, imposed as a temporary measure under the last Salisbury government, should be retained, but remitted in the case of Empire suppliers. He saw this as the beginning of a process of 'Tariff Reform', which would be based on a generalised system of Imperial preferences.

Chamberlain's advocacy of Tariff Reform was resisted by a no less determined group within the Cabinet, who strongly believed in the virtues of free trade. They were led by the Chancellor of the Exchequer, C.T. Ritchie, and the veteran Duke of Devonshire, who as Lord Hartington had defected from the Liberal Party with the great majority of the Whig faction two decades earlier. Chamberlain had succeeded in converting a large section of the Tory Party to his views, and neither he – nor his free trade opponents – were in any mood to compromise.

In the circumstances, any Prime Minister would have had difficulty in holding the Cabinet together, and it was fairly predictable that one wing or the other would be driven to resignation. Balfour's achievement was to lose both of them. Four free trade ministers (Ritchie, Devonshire, Lord George Hamilton and his own cousin, Lord Balfour of Burleigh) resigned because they believed he was leaning too far in Chamberlain's direction, while Chamberlain himself left because he did not lean far enough.

In truth, Balfour had no strong views on the issue one way or the other, a position which was neatly summed up by a piece of doggerel composed by a Liberal MP, Sir Wilfred Lawson:

> I'm not for Free Trade, and I'm not for Protection.
> I approve of them both, and to both have objection.
> In going through life I continually find
> It's a terrible business to make up one's mind.
> So in spite of all comments, reproach and predictions,
> I firmly adhere to Unsettled Convictions.
> *(Quoted by Young, 1963, p. 214)*

Balfour's attempt at compromise was to seek to commit the government to a policy of 'retaliation'; that is that it should continue a general policy of free trade, while reserving the right to impose import duties against countries which pursued projectionist policies. Although he recognised the strength of support within the Tory Party for Chamberlain's views, he believed that Tariff Reform, which implied a tax on imported food, would be deeply unpopular in the country as a whole. He therefore concluded that it was not 'practical politics', at least in the short run. His rational approach was shared by few of his party colleagues. In the grip of ideological fervour, both sides continuously fuelled the dispute – uncannily foreshadowing the contortions over Europe of the Major government in the 1990s – and gravely damaging party unity.

A more tactically aware politician would have sought to divert the attention of his supporters by spectacular initiatives in other directions. Yet Balfour appeared to have no shots in his locker. He did not believe that social engineering was the business of government. Profoundly conservative in outlook, he would certainly have subscribed to the tenet that "he who governs least governs best". Despite his resourcefulness in pushing through the 1902 Education Act, and his backing for several earlier Bills designed to improve social conditions in Ireland, he did not in general believe in the virtues of legislation. If an Act of Parliament did no actual harm, that was a bonus in his view: most attempts to legislate only made matters worse.

Although devoted to the Conservative Party, Balfour had little understanding of its psyche and, unlike his Uncle Robert, was not prepared to immerse himself in matters of party organisation and patronage. Nor did he have any respect for the views of the party rank-and-file. "I would as soon be guided by the views of my valet as by the Conservative Party conference" he said on a famous occasion. This patrician indifference to the growing democratisation of British politics, which was even affecting the Conservative Party under the influence of Joe Chamberlain, made Balfour an inappropriate figure to lead a political party in the 20th century. Moreover, his own lack of raw ambition led him to under-estimate the ambitions of others. He remained on excellent personal terms with Chamberlain, and seemed never to have suspected that the latter was at least partly motivated by his own desire for the premiership, an aspiration which was only terminated by the massive stroke which he suffered in July 1906 and which incapacitated him for the remaining eight years of his life.

Balfour became increasingly exasperated by the disunity of his party, but made only fitful attempts to overcome it, tending to withdraw "to seek the solace of the golf course at North Berwick", as Mackay puts it. His government nevertheless lingered on for over two years after the resignations, by which time Balfour conceded that he had had enough. He was then guilty of a profound misjudgement. Instead of seeking a dissolution from the King, he meekly resigned on 5 December 1905, allowing a Liberal government, under Sir Henry Campbell-Bannerman, to take over in advance of a general election. This enabled the hitherto divided Liberals to present themselves as a united government, and combine the advantage of incumbency with the opportunity to blame the retiring government for all the current discontents. Balfour's private secretary, J.S. Sanders, attributed the stunning Liberal victory in the election which followed, in January 1906, to four causes: the swing of the pendulum, accentuated by the large Tory gains in 1900, the scandal over the importation of Chinese 'slave labour' into South Africa, the organisation of Labour and the Socialist vote, and Nonconformist campaigning against the 1902 Education Act (Mackay, 1985, p. 226).

Yet more important than any of these was probably the appalling picture of disunity presented by the Tories, and Balfour's maladroit handling of his own party. He himself was among the defeated candidates, but managed to get back to the Commons within two months when one of his supporters resigned a safe seat.

There was, however, more to Balfour's premiership than his failure to cope with the Tariff Reform issue. There were a number of achievements to his credit, many of which were of considerable long-term significance. Three, at least, stand out. The 1902 Education Act fell far short of matching the educational reforms in Germany which enabled its scientific and industrial development to exceed that of any of its European rivals. It did, however, put secondary education on a firm financial footing and opened up opportunities to a large number of (mostly lower middle-class) children.

Secondly, Balfour, acutely aware of military failings and poor co-ordination between the services during the Boer War, was instrumental in establishing, and presiding over, the Committee of Imperial Defence (CID). For the first time, this enabled long-term military planning to proceed and provided a forum for mediating between the designs of the War Office and the Admiralty. Balfour was an extremely active chairman, and continued to take a keen interest in its work even after ceasing to be Prime Minister, writing far-seeing memoranda at their request, and unofficially rejoining the Committee in 1914 at the invitation of the Prime Minister, Herbert Asquith.

Thirdly, Balfour took steps to ensure that Britain's foreign and defence policies were properly co-ordinated, which all too often they had not been in the past. He also presided over the ending of Britain's long-standing tradition of "splendid isolation", to use Salisbury's phrase. A treaty of alliance was signed with Japan, and the Anglo-French Entente was concluded in April 1904. This was not initially intended as a military alliance, but subsequent secret negotiations conducted by Asquith's Foreign Secretary, Sir Edward Grey, effectively converted it into one, making British participation in the First World War almost inevitable.

With the exception of Sir Alec Douglas-Home, who served as Foreign Secretary, Balfour was the only 20th-century Prime Minister who continued to have a substantial political career after the end of his premiership. He was leader of the opposition for six years after 1906, acquiescing in, if not initiating, the use of the House of Lords ("Mr Balfour's Poodle" in Lloyd George's words) to frustrate the passage of the 1909 'People's Budget'. After King George V had agreed, following the two general elections of 1910, to Asquith's demand to create as many Liberal peers as necessary to secure the passage of the 1911 Parliament Act, which clipped the wings of the Upper House, Balfour advised Tory peers to give up their die-hard opposition to the Act. A large number of them defied his advice, though not quite enough to prevent the Bill being passed. Balfour, in disgust, and already heartily sick of party political manoeuvring, threw in his hand. Not many in his party regretted his decision: they preferred a more partisan and less rational figure to lead them against the forces of radicalism and socialism which they saw closing in on them.

At that stage, Balfour almost certainly saw this as the end of his life in high politics, and joyfully returned to his study of philosophy, undertaking to give two major courses of lectures at the University of Glasgow. In the event, only one course had been given by August 1914, when Balfour, although a member of the opposition, was immediately recruited to help the war effort. He was co-opted to the CID (henceforth renamed the War Council), and became First Lord of the Admiralty, in succession to Winston Churchill, when a coalition government was formed in May 1915. In December 1916, when Lloyd George replaced Asquith as Prime Minister, he was appointed as Foreign Secretary, provoking the lasting hostility of Asquith who previously had been a personal friend. Balfour had not intrigued against Asquith, who, however, was affronted by the alacrity with which Balfour had moved, in Winston Churchill's words, "from one cabinet to another, from the Prime Minister who had been his Champion to the Prime Minister who had been his most severe critic … like a powerful and graceful cat walking delicately and unsoiled across a rather muddy street" (Churchill, 1937, p. 249).

14 Arthur Balfour

As Foreign Secretary, Balfour showed a sureness of touch which had eluded him as Prime Minister. His most significant contribution was in leading a mission to Washington, immediately after America's entry into the war in April 1917. He created an immensely favourable impression, and did much to persuade a still reluctant congress and administration to devote themselves wholeheartedly to the war effort.

The Balfour Declaration of November 1917, expressing British support for "the establishment in Palestine of a national home for the Jewish people", has undoubtedly become Balfour's greatest claim to posthumous fame. Although it resulted from a decision of the whole Cabinet (the one Jewish member, Edwin Montagu, being ironically the sole dissenter), it is unlikely that it would have seen the light of day without Balfour's enthusiastic advocacy. As a student of history, he had been fascinated by the survival over two millennia of this small and unimportant tribe, while great empires had perished. He had met with Chaim Weizmann 12 years earlier and had been deeply impressed by his Zionist convictions. In his later years he often said that, "looking back on his life in politics, he felt that what he had been able to do for the Jews was the thing most worth while" (Young, 1963, p. 386).

In general, however, Balfour seldom took the lead in Cabinet, and normally strongly supported the views of Lloyd George. Yet, on one occasion, his influence was probably decisive, and may indeed have had the unfortunate effect of helping to prolong the war. In September 1917, the Austrian Foreign Minister, Baron Von Kühlmann, had sent a message through the Spanish government proposing peace talks. The war was going badly for the allies, with the Russians on the brink of collapse and mutinies in the French army, and Lloyd George and others were tempted to follow up the Austrian approach and to see whether Germany also would be interested in a negotiated peace. Balfour, however, after having first proposed unsuccessfully that the Austrian feelers should be discussed with all the other allied powers, rallied the War Cabinet into fighting on without responding to Von Kühlmann's approach.

Balfour's last important task as Foreign Secretary was to attend the Versailles Peace Conference as Lloyd George's deputy. According to eyewitness accounts, the business was dispatched a great deal more expeditiously when he was substituting for his chief. In 1922 he accepted an earldom, but throughout most of the 1920s he continued as a Cabinet minister, as Lord President of the Council, representing Britain at the Washington Conference on naval limitation in 1921 and at the Imperial Conference in 1926. He continued to take a close interest in defence matters, being an assiduous attender of the CID, and took energetic steps to foster scientific and industrial research, creating the Committee of Civic Research, in 1925. Despite his age he remained one of the most influential members of the Cabinet, and Baldwin refused to allow him to resign, even when his health failed in 1928. He remained in office right up to the 1929 general election, when Baldwin was defeated, dying in the following year at the age of 81.

A long and distinguished political career thus came to an end, which contrasted sharply with his failure as Prime Minister. The simplest explanation is that he was lacking in leadership qualities, and that in particular he was deficient in man management. Despite his immense charm, and exceptionally wide range of friends and acquaintants, he did not find it easy to handle powerful and ambitious colleagues. His waspish wit was widely appreciated – except by its victims, who over the course of time became more and more numerous. On one occasion, for instance, he said of a Cabinet colleague, "if he had a little more brains he would be a half-wit" (Douglas Home, 1987, p. 170). His own lack of commitment not only prevented him from embracing political causes with enthusiasm, but blinded him from appreciating the passions and ambitions which drove many of his colleagues.

In human terms, his detachment undoubtedly had its redeeming features. In 1898, for example, when he was already number two in the Tory party and the probable next Prime Minister, he performed an extraordinary act of friendship towards Herbert Asquith. At the bidding of the latter's wife, Margot, he wrote a letter to her wealthy father, Sir Charles Tennant, asking him to settle a large income on Asquith so that he could afford to give up his practice at the bar and assume the leadership of the Liberal Party. Tennant refused, but it was remarkable that Balfour had exerted himself to facilitate the choice by his political opponents of a man who promised to be a most formidable rival.

Many politicians undoubtedly take politics and themselves too seriously. With Arthur Balfour, the opposite was the case. The anonymous poet quoted above was writing about a carefree young man in his mid-twenties. His perceptive analysis could equally apply to the 54-year-old who became Prime Minister in 1902: "Playful little Arthur, he/ Cannot take things seriously".

Works consulted

Winston Churchill, 1937, *Great Contemporaries*, London, Thornton Butterworth.
William Douglas Home, 1987, *The Prime Minister: Stories and Anecdotes from Number 10*, London, W.H. Allen.
Ruddock F. Mackay, 1985, *Balfour: Intellectual Statesman*, Oxford, Oxford University Press.
Jane Ridley and Clayre Percy, 1992, *The Letters of Arthur Balfour and Lady Elcho 1985–1917*, London, Hamish Hamilton.
Kenneth Young, 1963, *Arthur James Balfour*, London, Bell.

2

HENRY CAMPBELL-BANNERMAN

"A good, honest Scotchman"

In December 1898 Lord Tweedmouth, a former Liberal Chief Whip, travelled to Scotland to meet Sir Henry Campbell-Bannerman at his residence at Belmont Castle. His mission: to offer him the leadership of the Liberal Party. Tweedmouth was confident that C.B., as he was universally known, would decline the offer, which was made as a courtesy to a popular and highly regarded but indolent colleague, already 62, who was believed to be without any ambition beyond becoming Speaker of the House of Commons. Once this formality was out of the way, Tweedmouth and the party's top brass, on whose behalf the offer was made, could get down to the serious business of choosing the man who was to lead their party into the next century. There appeared to be four possibilities. Former Prime Minister Lord Rosebery and former Chancellor of the Exchequer William Harcourt, both of whom had petulantly resigned the leadership in the preceding three years, complaining of lack of support by their colleagues. Could one, or the other, be tempted back? Former Home Secretary Herbert Asquith had ruled himself out, on the grounds that he could not afford to relinquish his prodigious earnings at the bar. Could his arm be twisted? And there was John Morley, the former deputy leader, who had somewhat hastily bracketed his own resignation with that of Harcourt, and now showed signs of regretting it. Any of these would cut a more impressive figure than the amiable but dull C.B., it was thought, and there was general consternation when Tweedmouth reported back that he had accepted the offer.

This is a plausible – but not necessarily accurate – account of how C.B. became the leader of his party. It was recounted by Austen Chamberlain 14 years later, on the authority of two Liberal Cabinet ministers, and is accepted by C.B.'s biographer, John Wilson, as possibly true (Wilson, 1973, pp. 287–8). Whether or not the offer to C.B. was genuinely intended, it is apparent that his appointment was originally seen only as a stopgap measure in the expectation that the 46-year-old Asquith would inevitably succeed him within a very short period. It was not to work out quite like that.

C.B., like Clement Attlee half a century later, was a prime example of a politician with apparently modest attainments outdistancing far flashier rivals. He was born plain Henry Campbell on 7 November 1836, the second son of a wealthy and self-made Glasgow businessman and local Tory leader, Sir James Campbell. His mother – Janet Bannerman – was

DOI: 10.4324/9781003031963-3

the daughter of an equally wealthy Manchester merchant. Her own brother, Henry, was later to leave his nephew a life interest in his estate on condition that he "assumed my surname of Bannerman either alone or in addition to his usual surname, but so that the name of Bannerman shall be the last and principal name" (Wilson, 1973, p. 46).

The young Henry Campbell had a happy and stress-free childhood. His parents, an earlier biographer, J.A. Spender, noted: "had all the Scottish virtues: they were religious, dutiful, orderly and businesslike; in spite of their wealth, they lived simply and applied themselves seriously to the education of their children" (Spender, 1923, p. 7). At the age of 11 he was enrolled at Glasgow High School, and just before his 14th birthday he was sent with his elder brother and a cousin on a 10-month tour through Europe (an upper middle-class version of the Grand Tour). This left him with a lasting taste for continental travel, a good command of French, and a love of French life and literature. He subsequently studied at Glasgow University and at Trinity College, Cambridge, from which he emerged with a Third Class Honours degree in Classics. He was regarded as a pleasant and intelligent student, but indolent, and failed to make much of a mark.

On leaving Cambridge, aged 22, he joined the family firm of J. & W. Campbell, warehousemen and drapers, run by his father and Uncle William, becoming a partner two years later without unduly exerting himself. At about this time he surprised his father and elder brother, both passionate Tories, by his conversion to Liberalism, possibly influenced by Uncle William who had quit both the Tory Party and the Church of Scotland some years earlier to become a Free Churchman and a Liberal, while remaining on excellent terms with his brother who by then had become Lord Provost of Glasgow. C.B.'s own conversion was also accepted good-naturedly within the family, though it puzzled some of his later political colleagues. Augustine Birrell, for example, who was to be President of the Board of Education in C.B.'s government, wrote in his memoirs: "How C.B. became a Liberal I never knew. Certainly not by prayer or fasting or by a course of hard reading" (Wilson, 1973, p. 38).

C.B.'s earliest major biographer, J.A. Spender, suggests the credit might belong to Daniel Lawson, one of the 200 clerks working in the family firm,

> a man of original character who read strange books and talked Radical and Chartist politics. The two had long, earnest and stubborn talks, and it was whispered that 'old Daniel' was getting great influence over Mr Henry. In truth, he was rapidly becoming a Radical, not a Whig or Palmerstonian, but a really advanced politician.
>
> *(Spender, 1923, pp. 20–1)*

It was as a Radical that Henry Campbell contested a by-election in Stirling Burghs in April 1868 at the age of 31. It was an unusual contest: there was no Tory candidate and Campbell brashly offered himself in competition to the official Liberal nominee, a Whig. The Whig was victorious, but Campbell turned the tables later in the year in the general election, when the electorate was substantially enlarged as a result of the 1867 Reform Act, which provided for household suffrage.

No sooner elected, Campbell set himself the task of healing the divisions within the local Liberal Party, which he accomplished within a very short time. "Praises of his tact, his geniality, his readiness to serve the humblest of his constituents, were soon in all mouths", Spender reports (1923, p. 30), and he represented the constituency for an unbroken period of 40 years, an unusual achievement at a time when even the longest-serving and most distinguished parliamentarians had frequently to change their seats. It was these same qualities, together with his evident disinterestedness and his strength of character, which quickly commended him to his parliamentary colleagues so that, without being regarded as in any way outstanding, he was soon accepted as a 'good House of Commons man', popular both in his own party and with his political opponents. Elected as a Radical, he moved imperceptibly within a few years to a position which could be described as slightly to the left of centre of his party, and remained there for the rest of his life. In personal terms, his loyalty was commanded, almost unquestioningly, by Gladstone.

Henry Campbell was excused his very light duties in the family firm, from which, however, he received a sufficient income to enable him to devote himself full-time to his new vocation and to live in considerable comfort. His elder brother, James Alexander Campbell, eventually took over the business, and much later became a Tory MP for Glasgow and Aberdeen universities. It was at James's wedding, in 1860, where she was a bridesmaid, that he met his own wife, Charlotte Bruce, the daughter of a Scottish general. Three years older than him, it was, in Spender's words, "a case of love at first sight' (1923, p. 22), and they were married within a few months.

Thus began a partnership which was to endure until her death nearly 46 years later. It was a childless marriage, but one characterised by an unusual degree of mutual devotion. Shy, lacking in self-confidence, physically unattractive and later to become excessively fat and a semi-permanent invalid (probably due to diabetes, then an untreatable condition), she was hardly a social asset to her husband. Yet he depended on her judgement to a considerable extent, and her advice was almost invariably shrewd and to the point.

Campbell was in no hurry to make his maiden speech in Parliament, and indeed spoke rarely, but, Wilson notes, "when he did speak – largely but not always on Scottish questions – he took trouble and was brief and effective, with the cheerful iconoclasm of a reformer" (1973, p. 45). At this early stage he seems to have made no impact on Gladstone, then at the height of his power during his first ministry, but he did come to the notice of Edward Cardwell. Cardwell was Secretary for War, and in 1871 requested his appointment to the new post of Financial Secretary to the War Office. In the same year, Campbell inherited the estate at Hunton, near Maidstone, from his uncle, Henry Bannerman, and to his distaste, and even more that of his wife, was forced to hyphenate his name. As this was something of a mouthful, he encouraged his colleagues to refer to him as C.B., and the sobriquet stuck.

Edward Cardwell was a reforming War Secretary, the most notable of the 19th century. His principal reform – carried through against the unrelenting opposition of a large proportion of the officer corps and the great majority of serving and retired generals – was the abolition of the ancient practice of selling commissions and promotions, clearing the way to promotion on merit. Equally significantly, he established the principle of civilian control over the military by ensuring that the Commander-in-Chief (an office held for 39 years by Queen Victoria's cousin, the Duke of Cambridge) should be subordinate to the Secretary of State. He also instituted the system of short-term service for the infantry, thus enabling an adequate reserve of trained men to be built up, and established the linked-battalion system whereby one battalion of a regiment remained at home, while the other went abroad, while a regular interchange between the officers and men of both was provided for. He succeeded in providing Britain with a relatively small and economical professional army, and avoiding mass conscription, to which the continental powers were increasingly committed.

C.B.'s role as Financial Secretary was to prepare the estimates and supervise the funds of the War Office, which he succeeded in doing with a minimum of fuss and bother, releasing his superior to concentrate on weightier issues. Cardwell, with whom his personal relations were extremely cordial, was more than satisfied with his performance, while C.B.'s appreciation of Cardwell's achievements knew no bounds, and he became a role-model for C.B. of how a reforming minister should be. As Wilson puts it, "C.B. learnt from Cardwell that courage and determination and the will to do what seems right and to stand up to vilification and abuse are the qualities needed by statesmen whose work is to last. It was an experience he was never to forget" (Wilson, 1973, p. 54).

Disraeli's victory in the 1874 general election brought C.B.'s ministerial career to a temporary halt. The succeeding six years in opposition were relatively uneventful for him, and, as before, he took life easily, with long periods spent travelling in Europe and remaining in Scotland for several months of the year. Yet his weight in the House of Commons significantly grew, partly because, with Cardwell elevated to the Lords, he was the Liberal Party's chief spokesman on military affairs. He also gradually acquired the reputation of being the most influential MP from north of the border and his voice on Scottish affairs was always listened to with great respect.

When Gladstone formed his second government, in 1880, C.B. might reasonably have expected to be promoted, but he made no protest at being asked to resume his former post of Financial Secretary to the War Office. The evidence suggests that he had a very limited estimate of his own abilities, and did not, at that time at least, consider that he was fitted for anything more than junior office. C.B. remained for two years at the War Office, before transferring to an equivalent post at the Admiralty.

In 1884 it fell to C.B., in the absence in Egypt of the First Lord of the Admiralty, to advise the Cabinet on their response to a newspaper scare that the fleet was being starved of funds and risked being overtaken by that of France. C.B. advocated a modest supplementary estimate which he argued was necessary more for political than naval reasons. The Cabinet responded by approving an increase three times greater than he had suggested. This succeeded in neutralising their opponents.

This was almost C.B.'s last action at the Admiralty. In October 1884 he left for a month-long holiday in Scotland with his wife, only to be summoned by telegram to meet Lord Spencer, the Viceroy of Ireland, in Edinburgh. He was taken aback to be told that Gladstone wanted to appoint him as Chief Secretary for Ireland, undoubtedly the toughest and most unpleasant job in the government. C.B. declined to accept, but being pressed, asked for a further day to consider. Within three hours, however, he had written to Spencer, stating categorically: "I do not wish to undertake duties which I have reason to fear I should insufficiently discharge" (Spender, 1923, p. 59).

In the evening, however, he consulted his wife, and then proceeded to write a further letter setting out his reasons for refusal. What then transpired he recounted many years later to Augustine Birrell:

> I found a difficulty amounting almost to impossibility to get these excellent reasons into a letter. Then arose my domestic adviser and said 'See you not why you cannot write the letter. Your conscience is always telling you, as you write, that you ought to accept'. After a grand conseil de nuit, therefore, I telegraphed the next morning recanting my refusal. And this little manoeuvre remained a mystery to Spencer, and to a greater than he, Mr G. Thus is a woman ever a man's superior in intuition, and in self-sacrifice.
>
> *(Wilson, 1973, p. 76)*

C.B. remained as Irish Secretary for less than eight months. He was not a member of the Cabinet and was clearly subordinate, in practice if not in theory, to Lord Spencer, an old-fashioned Whig who was evidently uncomfortable – though less so than C.B. – with the coercive policies he was expected to carry out. C.B. himself continued very much in the same way as he had as a junior minister – fulfilling his duties with quiet efficiency, showing unremitting loyalty to his superior, but offering a flow of common-sense suggestions to meet the almost daily crises which arose. In the Commons he was a distinct success, largely deflating the spiked anger of Parnell's formidable Irish Party by his firm, unflustered but genial replies. At least one of the Irish Members – T.P. O'Connor – became a committed fan of C.B.'s, publishing a eulogistic biography soon after his death. Neither Spencer nor C.B. had started out as supporters of Irish Home Rule. Yet both independently slowly became convinced of its necessity during their terms of office. When, in 1886, the majority of both Whigs and Radicals abandoned Gladstone, when he introduced the first Home Rule Bill, both stayed firmly in the Liberal camp.

C.B.'s Irish appointment came to an end in June 1885, when the Irish Members joined with the Tories to defeat the Gladstone government on a vote on the budget. The Salisbury government which followed did not last long, resigning soon after its disappointing result in the November 1885 general election. In the new government formed by Gladstone the following February, C.B. at last became – at the age of 49 – a member of the Cabinet. He became Secretary for War, which might seem to have been an obvious appointment following his two periods as Financial Secretary in the same department. Yet C.B. did not owe his promotion to Gladstone's appreciation of his earlier services. It was due rather to royal favour. Queen Victoria firmly resisted Gladstone's first choice of Hugh Childers, who was antipathetic to her cousin, the Commander-in-Chief. She indicated to Gladstone that C.B. would be a more acceptable alternative, and Gladstone reluctantly conceded. The Queen noted in her journal, "Mr Campbell-Bannerman, a good honest Scotchman, to the War Office" (Wilson, 1973, p. 162). As for Gladstone, he warmly greeted C.B. at his first Cabinet meeting, waving his hand towards his colleagues, he said, "You will get on all right with them. You will be canny and you will be couthy." C.B later wrote, "That he should address me in the patois of my own village put me at once at my ease, and enhanced my sense of his general omniscience." J.A. Spender, in quoting this passage from C.B.'s papers, commented that "'Couthy', as Campbell-Bannerman used to explain, was something more than the opposite of uncouth. It connoted affability, amiability, accessibility, and much more" (Spender, 1923, p. 100).

C.B. remained at the War Office for the whole of the 1892–95 Liberal government, continuing under Lord Rosebery when Gladstone retired in March 1894. He was not a great innovator, being mostly concerned to preserve the reforms introduced by Cardwell 20 years earlier. He once again impressed, however, by his steadiness, his good judgement and his ability to get on well with practically all his associates. Not all his Cabinet colleagues, however, were impressed by the amount of time he spent away from London. Within two days of his appointment, he was off to Marienbad, where he went every year with his wife to take the waters, and he continued to insist on spending two months of the year abroad and at least three months in Scotland. Sir William Harcourt, who combined being Chancellor of the Exchequer with leading the House of Commons, where the government's majority was always precarious, bombarded him with sarcastic notes, including one in December 1894, saying "I really hope you will awake to the fact that there is an institution called H.M.'s Government, that there are such things as estimates, and that one day there will be a House of Commons" (Spender, 1923, p. 174).

His most notable achievement as War Secretary was, perhaps, finally to dislodge the Duke of Cambridge from the post of Commander-in-Chief. The latter, despite his 76 years, was most reluctant to go, having taken literally the pretence that his appointment was for life. It took six weeks, and the expenditure of a great deal of tact and resourcefulness, for C.B. to bring this about, using the good offices of the Queen herself to ease her relative out of his post. It was ironic that on the very day that the old buffer agreed to go, C.B. himself was the victim of a parliamentary ambush, the House of Commons voting by 132 votes to 125 to reduce his ministerial salary. The occasion for the vote was the so-called 'Cordite scandal', an alleged shortage of ammunition which later turned out to be a complete fabrication. C.B., however, insisted on standing down, and this led to the resignation of the whole Rosebery government, its chief having lost all stomach for continuing to govern without a secure majority.

Just a few months earlier C.B. had wanted to withdraw when a vacancy occurred for the Speakership of the House of Commons. The modest War Secretary, who had never thrust himself forward for any ministerial post, made a spirited bid for the position, for which he was eminently qualified as an experienced parliamentarian, liked and respected on all sides of the House. The fact that his ministerial career would be ended, after barely three years in the Cabinet, appeared of no consequence to him. "He was to his bones a House of Commons man, and a House of Commons man could, in his view, have no higher ambition" (Spender, 1923, p. 173). The opposition would gladly have supported him, and he was deeply disappointed when Rosebery and his colleagues decided that he could not be spared from the government. Neither they nor he had the faintest idea they were thereby preserving him for a greater fate.

When the Rosebery government fell in 1895, Lord Salisbury formed his third administration and lost no time in calling an election, which produced a large majority for the Tories and their Liberal Unionist allies, who were now included in the government. C.B., who had been knighted on Rosebery's recommendation, was now recognised as one of the senior figures in the Liberal Party, which, however, seemed weak, divided and thoroughly demoralised. Its two leading personalities – Lord Rosebery and Sir William Harcourt – found it almost impossible to work with each other. After each of them had successively flounced out of the leadership within three years, it must have come as a relief to many Liberals to serve under a leader who had no inflated idea of his own importance, who was genial, steady and imperturbable and had no enemies within his own party and precious few outside.

Yet although C.B.'s elevation was unanimously approved at a meeting of Liberal MPs in February 1899, his position was not strong. He was already 62, had only limited experience as a Cabinet minister and was almost universally seen as a transitional figure. Moreover, he was chosen specifically as leader of the Liberal Party in the Commons (as Harcourt had previously been) rather than leader of the party as a whole, and it was by no means a foregone conclusion that he would have become Prime Minister had the Liberals won the subsequent election. Nevertheless, he made a solid start, shrewdly choosing Herbert Gladstone (the youngest son of the Grand Old Man) as his Chief Whip, and quickly smoothing over many of the differences between his colleagues. By the summer of 1899 a string of Liberal by-election victories had made the prospect of a triumph in the general election seem possible, or even probable. Then the Salisbury government, and more especially the Colonial Secretary, Joseph Chamberlain, blundered into the Boer War, which effectively removed this possibility. Instead,

C.B. was placed in an almost impossible position, with his party split three ways, and personal antagonisms rising to new heights.

C.B.'s view was that the war could and should have been avoided, and he blamed Chamberlain for playing a dangerous game of bluff with President Kruger, dispatching sufficient extra troops to South Africa to provoke the Boers but not sufficient to ensure victory in the event of hostilities. Once the war broke out, he was in favour of prosecuting it to a successful conclusion, but not in a vindictive manner, and of holding out to the Boers the prospect of reconciliation and an early return to self-government for the two Boer republics. On one flank of his party were the so-called Liberal Imperialists, notably Sir Edward Grey, H.H. Asquith and R.B. Haldane (with Lord Rosebery hovering in the background), who expressed wholehearted support for the government. They felt particularly committed to Lord Milner, the High Commissioner in South Africa (and a former Radical) who was the leading advocate of a fight to the finish with the Boers, with an insistence on unconditional surrender.

On the left wing of the Liberal Party were the so-called pro-Boers. These included Harcourt and Morley, and especially the young David Lloyd George, who braved severe public hostility and press vilification for their opposition to the war. Although C.B.'s own position was supported by the more thoughtful of his senior colleagues, and almost certainly by the bulk of Liberal activists, most of the more prominent and colourful figures had allied themselves with the two more extremist wings. He therefore appeared at times as a lonely and isolated figure, and few thought he would survive long as leader. The nadir seemed to have been reached when, on 25 July 1900, he recommended the party to abstain on a critical amendment to a government motion tabled by the pro-Boers. Only 35 Liberal MPs followed the leadership's advice, while 40 voted for the government and 31 supported the amendment. By this time, the early military setbacks had been reversed, and the war seemed to have been effectively won. Chamberlain seized the opportunity to press for a 'khaki' election, two years before the parliamentary term was up, and while the full force of jingoism in the country could be tapped. In the contest which followed, in October 1900, Tory candidates blatantly ran under the slogan "A Vote for the Liberals is a Vote for the Boers". The Liberal Imperialists fared no better than their pro-Boer or centrist counterparts, and though the Liberal Party was not routed, it failed to regain any of the ground it had lost in 1895.

Although their main centres had been over-run, the Boers stubbornly refused to surrender and their guerrilla operations continued for almost another two years, until May 1902. This provoked an increasingly ruthless response from the British forces, including the widespread burning of farms and the herding of thousands of women and children into 'concentration camps', where the death rate from disease was appallingly high. C.B. campaigned unceasingly against the government's demands for unconditional surrender and in favour of promising the Boers an early return to self-government. He was shocked to the core when a charity worker who had visited the camps, Miss Emily Hobhouse, gave him a first-hand account. In a forthright speech, in July 1901, he denounced the "methods of barbarism" by which the war was being conducted. This speech caused outrage, and he was excoriated in the popular press and, notably, in *The Times*, and for some time there was concern about his personal safety. Among the torrent of abusive letters he received was one from a clergyman who wrote: "You are a cad, a coward and a murderer, and I hope you will meet a traitor's or a murderer's doom" (Spender, 1923, Vol. II, pp. 9–10).

C.B. was apparently unfazed by this avalanche of abuse, kept steadily to his course and, while striving manfully to keep his deeply divided party together, made no attempt to trim his views which were now evidently closer to those of the pro-Boer wing of the party. He resented the activities of the Liberal Imperialists, who formed an internal party pressure group, the Liberal League, which made strenuous efforts to obtain parliamentary candidatures for their own supporters. Wisely, however, he made no attempt to expel them, and even cautiously attempted to reintegrate Lord Rosebery back into the party, while firmly resisting the condition which he set of repudiating Irish Home Rule. Rosebery, however, was determined to "plough my furrow alone", as he put it in a speech in July 1901, and his once glittering political career sputtered out in increasing irrelevance.

By the time peace was finally negotiated, in May 1902, the wave of jingoism had largely abated. More and more people concluded that if C.B.'s views had prevailed, the war could probably have been satisfactorily concluded a couple of years earlier. By this time it was evident that the great majority of Liberals outside Parliament had rallied to his side. His strength of character had won them over, and it was now evident that – far from being a stopgap – he was the only conceivable leader to take them into the next election. This still, however, seemed several years ahead, and in the meantime his parliamentary colleagues were concerned at his limited debating skills in the House of Commons, where he was regularly worsted by Balfour, who, in August 1902, succeeded his uncle as Prime Minister.

Yet, despite his parliamentary agility, Balfour proved an inept Prime Minister, and rapidly dissipated the large fund of goodwill he had built up as Salisbury's chief lieutenant. Moreover, the early actions of his government could almost have been designed to reunite the deeply divided Liberal Party. The introduction of a tax on corn was interpreted as a frontal attack on the free trade principles sacred to all Liberals, while the Education Bill, seen as forcing Nonconformist ratepayers to subsidise Church of England schools without these being submitted to public control, provoked the opposition of a large and influential section of the population, rekindling its traditional support for the Liberals. These two measures immediately brought C.B. and Asquith back together, greatly reinforcing Liberal firepower in the Commons, where Asquith was a formidable performer.

Moreover, the attempt by Joseph Chamberlain to follow up the corn tax with a fully fledged programme of protectionism fatally split his own party, leading to a series of ministerial resignations, including his own, and the defection to the Liberals of a number of prominent Unionists, notably the young Winston Churchill. Furthermore, it provided the Liberal Party with a potent electoral rallying cry in defence of Cheap Food.

With C.B.'s warm support, Herbert Gladstone negotiated an electoral pact with the nascent Labour Party, under which Labour candidates were given a free run in 31 constituencies in exchange for not opposing Liberals in many other sensitive seats. This act of opportunism probably damaged the Liberals in the long run as it enabled Labour to obtain a sizeable parliamentary bridgehead in 1906 thereby increasing its prospects of eventually supplanting its temporary allies. Yet there is little doubt that C.B., unlike some of his colleagues, was genuinely well disposed to Labour and positively welcomed the prospect of their increased representation at Westminster.

Despite C.B.'s reconciliation with the Liberal Imperialists, they still distrusted him and, as hopes for a Liberal government rose, they made a determined bid to circumscribe his influence should he become Prime Minister. In September 1905 a plot was hatched between Sir

24 Henry Campbell-Bannerman

Edward Grey, Asquith and Haldane during a fishing holiday at Relugas in north-east Scotland. There, in Haldane's words,

> we agreed … that if Campbell-Bannerman became Prime Minister he should take a peerage, and that Asquith should lead in the Commons as Chancellor of the Exchequer. Unless our scheme were in substance carried out we resolved that we could not join Campbell-Bannerman's Government. What we thus resolved on we used afterwards … to speak of among ourselves as 'the Relugas Compact'.
>
> *(Wilson, 1973, p. 427)*

The three conspirators even, quite improperly, involved King Edward VII in their plot, persuading him personally to urge C.B. to go to the Lords on the grounds of his age and uncertain health.

It did not need a general election to put the Relugas Compact to the test. Balfour unwisely resigned in December 1905 rather than asking for a dissolution of Parliament. King Edward duly invited C.B. to form a government, coupling this with a plea to him to go to the House of Lords, which he firmly resisted. Within a few days the Compact had crumbled. Asquith, after unsuccessfully attempting to persuade C.B. to become a peer, succumbed to the offer of the chancellorship and leadership of the House of Commons, which would make him the undoubted heir apparent. Haldane and Grey were more adamant, but in the end they too gave way – Haldane accepting the War Office and Grey becoming Foreign Secretary. This was a fateful decision, which may well have led to British involvement in the First World War. The probable alternative to Grey was John Morley, who became instead Secretary for India and who would have been highly unlikely to embark on the secret agreements which Grey made with the French which effectively committed Britain to ally itself with France in the event of war with Germany.

Campbell-Bannerman was the first person to be officially appointed as Prime Minister, all his predecessors being merely designated as First Lord of the Treasury. The government he formed contained the whole gamut of Liberal opinion, from Grey on the right to Lloyd George (who became President of the Board of Trade) on the left. This enabled the Liberal Party to go into the election, in January 1906, as a united force, whereas the Tories were bitterly divided. The result was the most dramatic turnaround since the 1832 Reform Act, the Liberals returning 379 MPs against only 157 for the Tories and their Unionist allies. In addition, there were 83 Irish Nationalists and 51 Labour members (21 of them 'Lib-Labs'), all of whom would, on most occasions, vote with the government.

The reasons for the Liberal landslide and Tory debacle were enumerated by Balfour's secretary, J.S. Sanders, in a letter written shortly afterwards (Mackay 1985, pp. 226–7). In his view they were, as cited in the preceding chapter on Balfour: the swing of the pendulum, accentuated by the large Tory gains in 1900, the scandal over the importation of Chinese 'slave labour' into South Africa, the organisation of Labour and the Socialist vote, and the Nonconformist campaigning against the 1902 Education Act. In fact, the Tory gains dated more from the 1895 election, and in retrospect, one would probably somewhat downgrade the importance of the Chinese labour issue and emphasise the effect of the Tory disunity which Sanders was loath to admit.

The Liberal victory led to a dramatic transformation in C.B.'s standing in the House of Commons. Previously, he had been a hesitant and inconsistent performer, now he succeeded in imposing himself on the House with great authority. On a notable occasion, he worsted Balfour in a parliamentary debate held shortly after the latter's return in a by-election in February 1906, having lost his former seat in the general election. With the cutting phrase "enough of this foolishness", he succeeded in deflating the leader of the opposition who had made a clever-clever speech which totally failed to catch the mood of the new House.

In Cabinet, C.B. was equally dominant, though he allowed his ministers a very free rein, rarely intervening in their departmental concerns. His short period as Prime Minister did not, however, lead to a large volume of reforming legislation, although the King's Speech in 1906 foreshadowed a near record number of Bills. This was, undoubtedly, due in part to his own lack of energy. Already 69 years old and in indifferent health when he became Premier, he exhausted himself in nursing his wife day and night for several months before her death in August 1906, which left him devastated. In June 1907 he suffered the second of several heart attacks, and though this did not prevent him making an effective speech the following day proposing that the House of Lords' powers should be trimmed, he was clearly weakened, and from then onwards Asquith increasingly assumed the day-to-day direction of government business.

The second reason was Balfour's cynical decision, taken early in the Parliament, to use the House of Lords ("Mr Balfour's Poodle", in Lloyd George's words) to frustrate the will of the Commons. This tactic was first used, to devastating effect, to destroy the 1906 Education Bill, which sought to modify some of the provisions of the 1902 Bill which had so outraged Nonconformist voters. C.B. wondered later if he ought not to have used the occasion to provoke an immediate Peers vs. People election, but the showdown did not come until after his death, when Lloyd George's People's Budget was thrown out. Until then the constant threat from the Lords undoubtedly inhibited the government's reforming zeal.

It could not, however, prevent Campbell-Bannerman's greatest achievement – reconciliation with the Boers in South Africa. Consistent with the position he had taken ever since the beginning of the Boer War, he insisted on granting immediate self-government to the Transvaal and Orange River colonies, overturning not only a provisional constitution introduced under Balfour, which gave only limited representational rights, but also a proposal from a committee of his own Cabinet which went only a little further. In what several of those present, notably Lloyd George, described as a masterly performance, he almost single-handedly persuaded the Cabinet to drop the proposals and to send out a commission to South Africa to prepare the way for full self-government. Asquith, who was also present, later questioned whether the Prime Minister's role had been all that great (Wilson 1973, p. 482), but the weight of evidence points to his intervention being decisive. This was certainly the view taken by the Boer leaders, Generals Botha and Smuts, who became totally reconciled and who brought South Africa into both the World Wars on the British side. Unfortunately, the settlement did not lead to the enfranchisement of non-European voters, which the government was advised was precluded by the terms of the Peace Treaty signed at Vereeniging four years earlier, and provisions written into the new constitution to prevent racial discrimination were subsequently violated by successive South African governments both before and increasingly after the Nationalist Party came to power in 1948. This casts a serious retrospective shadow over C.B.'s achievement, but it remained an outstanding act of magnanimity.

On several occasions, C.B. revealed himself to have more radical sympathies than most of his ministerial colleagues, and he showed particular sympathy with the new group of Labour MPs elected in 1906. This twice led him, on the floor of the House, to scrap government

26 Henry Campbell-Bannerman

proposals, approved by the Cabinet, in favour of more radical measures proposed by Labour members. The first occasion – which caused great offence to Asquith and the government law officers – concerned the 1906 Trade Disputes Bill, which sought to restore trade union rights rescinded by the Taff Vale judgment of 1900. Then, in December 1906, having heard persuasive speeches from Keir Hardie and others, he accepted on the spot a Labour amendment to include domestic workers in the Workmen's Compensation Bill, after the Cabinet had resolved on their exclusion. Had C.B. lived a few years longer, it is quite conceivable that the fatal split between Liberals and Labour – which led to the Conservatives becoming the dominant governing party for most of the century – might have been averted, and that a broad left-centre party would have evolved. Such a possibility was effectively excluded by the attitude of Asquith, who did not share C.B.'s warm sympathy with working-class aspirations.

It is also possible that women's suffrage would have come sooner if C.B. had survived. As Prime Minister, he spoke – at the height of the Suffragette agitation – in favour of a Private Member's Bill to give women the vote, greatly to the irritation of King Edward. Another sign of his radical sympathies came when he addressed a conference of the Inter-Parliamentary Union, when news came in that the Tsar had dissolved the Russian Duma. C.B., who was speaking in French, added the words "La Douma est morte – Vive la Douma" to his speech, to the evident embarrassment of his Foreign Office advisers.

C.B.'s health began to deteriorate rapidly in November 1907, and by early April it was clear that he was a dying man. Bedridden at 10 Downing Street, he tendered his resignation on 5 April, and died 17 days later, still in Downing Street – the last Prime Minister to die 'on the premises'. He held the premiership for a mere two years and 122 days, and the balance-sheet of his government's achievements – apart from the South African reconciliation – may appear slender. Yet his overall achievement was remarkable.

By holding together his fissiparous party, during the dark days of the Boer War, while continuing to give a principled lead to his party and his country, he, and almost he alone, made possible the great election victory of 1906, which paved the way for the foundations of the welfare state to be laid by his successors, Asquith and Lloyd George. He himself devised the strategy which led to the eventual curbing of the powers of the House of Lords by the Parliament Act of 1913. Not a bad legacy for a man who had been affectionately but patronisingly dismissed by a backbench colleague (Sir Alfred Pease), writing in his diary in 1886, as "a jolly, lazy sort of man with a good dose of sense" (Wilson, 1973, p. 67).

Works consulted

Ruddock F. Mackay, 1985, *Balfour: Intellectual Statesman*, Oxford, Oxford University Press.
J.A. Spender, 1923, *The Life of Sir Henry Campbell-Bannerman, GCB*, 2 vols, London, Hodder & Stoughton.
John Wilson, 1973, *CB: A Life of Sir Henry Campbell-Bannerman*, London, Constable.

3

H.H. ASQUITH

Not quite in the Gladstone mould

Gladstone without the passion, and without the religiosity. That would be an inadequate, but not altogether misleading description of the last person to head a Liberal government. A complex personality, he himself attempted a somewhat tongue-in-cheek assessment of his own qualities in an idle moment at 10 Downing Street during a critical period of World War I, in March 1915:

> You were … almost a classical example of *Luck*. You were endowed at birth with brains above the average. You had, further, some qualities of temperament which are exceptionally useful for mundane success – energy under the guise of lethargy; a faculty for working quickly, which is more effective in the long run than plodding perseverance; patience (which is one of the rarest of human qualities); a temperate but persistent ambition; a clear mind, a certain quality and lucidity of speech; intellectual but not moral irritability; a natural tendency to understand & appreciate the opponent's point of view; and, as time went on, & your nature matured, a growing sense of proportion, which had its effect both upon friends and foes, and which, coupled with detachment from any temptation to intrigue, and, in regard to material interests & profits, an unaffected indifference, secured for you the substantial advantage of personality and authority. The really great men of the world are the geniuses & the saints. You belonged to neither category. Your intellectual equipment (well cultivated and trained) still left you far short of the one; your spiritual limitations, and your endowment of the "Old Adam", left you still shorter of the other.
>
> *(Jenkins, 1978, pp. 334–5)*

Though more than a little smug, this reveals a considerable degree of self-knowledge and it illuminates the reasons both for his many successes and his ultimate failure. Herbert Henry Asquith was a man uncertain of his own identity. This was superficially reflected in his inability to settle upon his own nomenclature. Publicly known as H.H. Asquith, which is how he signed his name, for the first 40 or so years of his life he was known to his family and his

DOI: 10.4324/9781003031963-4

few intimate friends as Herbert. After his second marriage, to the fashionable Miss Margot Tennant, in 1894, and following her lead, Henry was substituted.

Born 12 September 1852, his family background was more modest than that of any earlier Prime Minister. His father, Joseph Dixon Asquith, was a weaver working in the woollen trade in the Yorkshire town of Morley. A cultivated man, he lacked ambition and, in the words of his son, was "of a retiring and unadventurous disposition". He was, however, a keen and active member of the Congregationalist church, as was his wife, Emily Willans, and Asquith's earliest years were strictly bounded by the activities of the Rehoboth Chapel in Morley.

Tragedy struck when Asquith was 8 years old. His father died suddenly, at the age of 34, leaving a widow, two sons (of whom Herbert was the younger) and two daughters, one of them a month-old baby who died within five years. Emily, a semi-invalid who seldom rose from her couch, was nevertheless a strong character who had a considerable influence on her son's development. Her devotion to the Congregational Church was as strong as her husband's, but her puritanism was less rigid, and Asquith was eventually permitted to add card-playing to the voracious reading which had previously been the only permitted diversion in the household.

Emily's family, who were well entrenched in local Liberal politics and the Nonconformist churches, were more affluent than the Asquiths, and her father, William Willans, took responsibility for the education of the two young brothers. They were enrolled as day-scholars at Huddersfield College, but were subsequently transferred to a Moravian boarding school in Leeds. Willans, however, died within a couple of years, which led to a further family upheaval. Emily moved south with her two daughters to St Leonards-on-Sea, and the two boys were sent to live with their Uncle John in London, where they were enrolled (at his expense, though Asquith later insisted on reimbursing him) in the City of London School. Even this arrangement did not last long: John Willans returned to Yorkshire within a year, and the brothers were boarded out successively to families in Pimlico and Islington.

His arrival at the City of London School set Asquith firmly on the road to fame and fortune. The school did not then have much of a reputation, but it had dedicated teachers, in particular the new headmaster, Edwin Abbott. He quickly recognised great potential in Herbert Asquith and gave him every encouragement to develop his strengths, which lay particularly in English and the Classics. The young Asquith spent much of his leisure time listening to sermons by Nonconformist divines and to trials in the Law Courts, as well as – a possibility denied him when he lived in the family home – theatre-going.

His interest in the sermons seems to have lain more in their rhetorical qualities than in the Christian message which they sought to convey. Asquith was quick to learn, becoming a star performer in the school debating society and declaiming a notable oration – far in advance of his years – in honour of the original founder of the school. Abbott himself disclaimed the credit for Asquith's brilliant progress at the school, which was crowned by his winning a classical scholarship to Balliol College, Oxford, one of only two awarded for the whole country. All he had done, he said, was "to place before him the opportunities of self-education and self-improvement … simply to put the ladder before him, and up he went" (Jenkins, 1978, p. 17).

At Balliol, between 1870 and 1874, Asquith continued his ascent, achieving a double first in Classics, and becoming President of the Union, where his outstanding debating achievements were remembered for many years after. He also acquired, to a marked degree, that aura of effortless superiority which was supposed to characterise a Balliol man. In 1874 he was elected to a fellowship, but he saw his future not in academic life but in the law, which however he regarded chiefly as a stepping stone to a political career. He obtained a pupillage in Lincoln's Inn, and was called to the bar in 1876.

His legal practice, however, was slow to develop. Briefs were few and far between, and he had to supplement his meagre income by lecturing, correcting examination papers and contributing to *The Spectator* and *The Economist*. This did not inhibit Asquith from getting married the following year, at the age of 26, to Helen Melland, the daughter of a Manchester doctor, whom he had known since he was 18 and she 15. She came from a higher social stratum and brought with her a small private income of a few hundred pounds a year. Yet it was undeniably a love match, and Asquith settled down to a calm family life in Hampstead, where five children were born over the following dozen years. Writing of this period, Roy Jenkins remarked on "a surprising but strong steak of recklessness" in his character.

> It made him go to the bar instead of seeking a safer occupation. It made him marry before he had an assured income. It was later to make him enter Parliament before he had an established practice. And it made him, in the early 'eighties, when his briefs were still rare, spend nearly £300 (equivalent to at least £2,000 today) on a diamond necklace for his wife.
>
> *(Jenkins, 1978, p. 39)*

Asquith became active in Liberal politics, becoming in particular a member of the Eighty Club (so named to celebrate Gladstone's victory in the 1880 general election), a dining club and debating society which supplied speakers to Liberal branches throughout the country. The secretary was R.B. Haldane, a Scottish barrister four years younger than Asquith who became his most intimate friend. In 1883 Asquith's prospects at the bar suddenly improved when R.S. Wright, a fellow Balliol man, became Junior Counsel to the Treasury and invited Asquith to 'devil' for him. This work included preparing a detailed memorandum for the Attorney-General, Sir Henry James, on the Parliamentary Oath, which was at the centre of the prolonged and vexatious dispute concerning the right of Charles Bradlaugh, the Radical and atheist MP for Northampton, to take his seat in the Commons. This memorandum was sent on to Gladstone, who warmly commended it, and Asquith subsequently helped to draft the Corrupt Practices Act of 1883, and also wrote a guide to the Act which was distributed to Liberal election agents.

His friend Haldane, who belonged to a landowning family in East Lothian, was elected to Parliament for that constituency in December 1885. Six months later another general election followed the defeat of Gladstone's first Home Rule Bill. The Liberal MP for the neighbouring seat of East Fife had voted against the Bill and was disowned by his local association. Haldane used his influence to secure the nomination for Asquith with only one week to go until polling day. The Tories withdrew in favour of the renegade Liberal, and Asquith squeezed home with a majority of 374. He was to hold the seat for the next 32 years.

Unlike most of his predecessors as Prime Minister, Asquith made an immediate impact in the House of Commons, and was soon marked out as a rising star. As J.A. Spender noted in his entry on Asquith in *The Dictionary of National Biography (DNB)*, "His speeches were brief, pointed, trenchant and admirably timed; it was said that from the beginning he spoke with the authority of a leader and not as a backbencher" (*DNB 1922–30*, p. 29). He concentrated, initially, on the Irish question, becoming a vehement critic of Balfour's coercive policies as Chief Secretary.

Yet it was outside the House that Asquith first achieved fame and fortune. The occasion was the Statutory Commission set up in 1888 by the Salisbury government to investigate the case against Charles Stewart Parnell, the leader of the Irish Party, who, according to letters allegedly written by him and published in *The Times*, had approved the 1882 Phoenix Park murders of Lord Frederick Cavendish, the Irish Chief Secretary, and Frederick Bourke, the Permanent Under-Secretary of the Dublin administration. The Commission was established in 1886, and Parnell, who was being defended by Sir Charles Russell, one of the most brilliant lawyers of the day, chose Asquith as his junior counsel. In two days of relentless cross-examination, Russell totally destroyed Richard Pigott, who had forged the letters and who promptly decamped to Madrid, where he shot himself in a hotel.

There remained the responsibility of *The Times*, which had published the letters without taking the most elementary steps to verify their authenticity. Russell was due to cross-examine C.J. MacDonald, the newspaper's manager, but at the last minute he turned to Asquith and said "I am tired: you must take charge of this fellow" (Koss, 1976, p. 29). Totally unprepared, Asquith rose to the occasion, and in the course of two hours completely demolished the witness. This single event transformed Asquith's previously lacklustre legal career. He was soon overwhelmed by the number of briefs pouring in, decided to take silk, and within a year was admitted as a Queen's Counsel at the age of 37. He was soon enjoying an income of £5,000 a year, not much less than the top barristers of the day.

Nor did this success do him any political harm. On the contrary, his role in the vindication of Parnell, and the discomforting of the Conservative government which had sought to blacken his reputation, greatly increased Asquith's popularity within Liberal ranks.

Asquith suffered a tragic loss in September 1891, when his gentle, unambitious, home-loving wife Helen died of typhoid fever, while they were on holiday together on the Isle of Arran. He was left with five young children (four sons and a daughter), who had to wait a mere two and a half years before the arrival of a stepmother, in the form of Margot Tennant. By all accounts, she performed her duties in this regard admirably, though she was a very different character from Asquith's first wife. A brilliant society figure, known equally for her wit and her indiscretion, she was the younger daughter of a wealthy Scottish baronet, Sir Charles Tennant. Asquith was devoted to her, though their marriage undoubtedly had a negative effect on his political career. Her extravagant lifestyle (she once said: "I hope to leave nothing but debts") meant that he had to maximise his earnings at the bar and this precluded him from seeking the leadership of the Liberal Party in 1898 – ten years before he eventually took over. She was also, in part at least, responsible for Asquith succumbing to the 'aristocratic embrace', which alienated him from some of his Nonconformist supporters and blunted his radical instincts.

By the time of his second marriage Asquith was already Home Secretary. When the Liberals won the 1892 general election, the 83-year-old Gladstone departed from his normal rule of appointing to his Cabinet only those who had previously served as junior ministers, and gave Asquith, at 39, one of the plum jobs in his administration, though one which has all too frequently proved an elephant trap for its holders. The government, as a whole, left few achievements to its credit. The centrepiece of its legislative programme – the second Home Rule Bill – was overwhelmingly rejected by the House of Lords in September 1893, and a disconsolate Gladstone finally retired six months later. His successor, Lord Rosebery, who had been a forceful Foreign Secretary, proved a languid and remote head of government and conducted a permanent feud with his Chancellor of the Exchequer and Leader of the House of Commons, Sir William Harcourt. The government's unhappy life was perhaps mercifully concluded by a parliamentary ambush over the 'Cordite affair' (see page 21), after which it resigned and lost the ensuing general election of 1895.

Asquith was one of few ministers to emerge with his reputation significantly enhanced. He was held to have handled a number of tricky Home Office issues, such as the demand for the release of convicted Irish terrorists and the right to hold meetings in Trafalgar Square, with firmness and good sense, and had established himself as a master of parliamentary debate. Less to his credit was his dispatch of troops to the Featherstone colliery in Yorkshire, where striking miners were rioting, and two of them were shot dead. This incident did some lasting damage to Asquith's standing with the working class. Many years later someone shouted at him at a meeting: "Why did you murder the miners at Featherstone in '92?" Jenkins relates that his "characteristic reply" was "It was not '92, it was '93" (Jenkins, 1978, p. 69). Asquith had also been responsible for introducing two complex and important Bills – the Employers' Liability Bill, which came to grief in the House of Lords, and the Factory Bill, which greatly extended protection for the workforce. As Spender noted, "When Parliament was dissolved in 1895, he was generally seen as a future prime minister" (*DNB 1922–30*, p. 30). He was also recorded as being "the only man in the cabinet who had not quarrelled with anyone" (Iremonger, 1970, p. 228).

Thrust into opposition, Asquith promptly broke a long-standing convention which prevented ex-Cabinet ministers from practising at the bar. For him it was a matter of economic necessity. There were no parliamentary salaries in those days (they were eventually introduced under his own premiership in 1911), and – unlike most prominent politicians of the day – he did not enjoy substantial private means. His wife Margot received an income of £5,000 a year from her father, but this was by no means sufficient to maintain the Asquiths' lifestyle. Their home in Mayfair's fashionable Cavendish Square, for example, had a domestic staff of 14, plus a coachman and stable boy.

His professional labours, and the social whirl into which he was led, by no means reluctantly, by Margot, left him relatively little time for politics and he was often absent from the House of Commons. When Sir William Harcourt resigned the Liberal leadership in the Commons in 1898, only two years after the departure of Lord Rosebery, Asquith would probably have been the overwhelming choice as successor if he had not become virtually a part-time politician. In the event, he was not disposed to challenge the nomination of Sir Henry Campbell-Bannerman (see page ??), partly it seems because he regarded him as a mere *locum tenens* and doubted whether he would in fact become Prime Minister if the Liberals were returned to power.

In any case, Asquith felt a peculiar personal loyalty to Rosebery and he was among those who clung most tenaciously to the hope that he might be lured back to the Liberal leadership. When, in the following year, the Boer War broke out, he – like Rosebery – strongly supported the Tory government and, together with his close allies, R.B. Haldane and Sir Edward Grey, became a leading figure in the Liberal Imperialist faction, on the right wing of the party. They were fratricidally opposed by the pro-Boers, led by Harcourt and the young Lloyd George, and Campbell-Bannerman – unhappily poised between the two camps – had the greatest difficulty in holding the party together. Had Asquith become the leader in 1898 it is highly probable that the party would have been split in two by the war.

Within the Liberal Imperialist camp, Asquith was one of the more moderate leaders and he quietly discouraged the schismatic activities of his more rabid followers. Nevertheless, his personal relations with Campbell-Bannerman became distinctly strained, especially after he had publicly criticised his leader for his use of the phrase "methods of barbarism" to characterise the farm-burning activities of British troops in South Africa.

The coming of peace, and the provocative actions of the new Balfour government, restored harmony to the Liberal Party much sooner than anyone expected. The 1902 Education Act, which horrified Liberal Nonconformists, and Joe Chamberlain's passionate advocacy of protectionism, quickly put an end to Liberal divisions, with only Rosebery remaining disaffected. Asquith threw himself wholeheartedly into opposing the Tory initiatives, and rapidly emerged as Campbell-Bannerman's most effective lieutenant, both in the country and Parliament.

On the surface, at least, his relations with C.B. were excellent, but Asquith's doubts about his chief's capacity, coupled no doubt with his own ambition, led him to plot with Haldane and Grey to deprive C.B. of the premiership, or at least to relegate him to the House of Lords, in the event of a Liberal election victory. The 'Relugas Compact', as recounted on page 24 above, quickly collapsed in the face of C.B.'s firm resistance, but it was Asquith who proved the weak link in the conspiracy and who shied away from a trial of strength. It is clear that C.B. could fairly easily have formed a government without either Grey or Haldane: if Asquith had held out it would have been difficult, if not impossible.

Instead, he settled for the role of C.B.'s heir apparent, as Chancellor of the Exchequer and the dominant debating force on the government benches, and Haldane and Grey fell in line behind him. From that moment on, there was no real doubt that he would be C.B.'s successor, and he increasingly took over the load from his boss during the final year when C.B.'s health was visibly declining.

In the meantime, his record as Chancellor of the Exchequer had done nothing to diminish his claims to the succession. He was, in J.A. Spender's words, "orthodox, thrifty and progressive" – reducing food taxes, overhauling local government finance, establishing a differential between earned and unearned incomes for income tax and, in his final budget, making the first provisions for old age pensions.

When C.B. finally resigned, 17 days before his death on 22 April 1908, there was so little doubt about who should succeed him that King Edward VII, holidaying in Biarritz, did not even return to London for consultations. Instead, he summoned Asquith to Biarritz to 'kiss hands' on 6 April. He returned the next day with his list of Cabinet ministers already approved.

Asquith revealed himself as shrewd and decisive in his choice of colleagues. He inherited a strong team from Campbell-Bannerman, but took immediate steps to shed its weaker members and was not afraid to promote his most able colleagues to the most influential posts where their talents could shine most brightly. He was, nonetheless, careful to achieve a good political balance in his Cabinet, making it clear that he intended to run it from the centre rather than from either wing of the party. This effectively meant that space had to be found for the more radical elements to offset what otherwise might have been seen as a government dominated by the former Liberal Imperialists. This was most spectacularly achieved by the promotion of Lloyd George to be Chancellor of the Exchequer, with Winston Churchill becoming, at the age of 33, President of the Board of Trade, and Reginald McKenna First Lord of the Admiralty.

Three ineffective peers – Lords Elgin, Tweedmouth and Portsmouth – were either ejected or demoted, without a word of warning or explanation. Elgin, who was replaced as Colonial Secretary by Lord Crewe, a close associate of Asquith, bitterly complained about his treatment in a letter to Lord Tweedmouth. "I venture to think", he wrote, "that even a Prime Minister may have some regard for the usages common among gentlemen … I feel that even a housemaid gets a better warning" (Hazelhurst, 1977, p. 81).

Asquith's brutal treatment of these former Cabinet colleagues contrasted strongly with his subsequent dealings with his own ministers, whom he treated almost invariably with the utmost courtesy and consideration and to whom he showed great loyalty when they got into difficulty. Nevertheless, it accorded with Asquith's public reputation as a 'cold fish', lacking in human feelings and showing none of the spontaneous warmth of C.B. Asquith was widely admired for his intellectual qualities and his political judgement, but he was never regarded with great affection, even in his own party.

Like Campbell-Bannerman, Asquith left his ministers a pretty free run in their own departments, seldom interfering with their decisions. Neither did he play a dominant role in the Cabinet, preferring to act as a "mediator rather than initiator" (Hazelhurst, 1977, p. 82). He seldom steered the course of discussion at Cabinet meetings, preferring to sum up after others had had their say. On most issues he seemed more concerned to reach decisions which would cause the least dissension rather than those which accorded most closely with his own preferences (Cassar, 1994, p. 32).

Where Asquith did show his leadership qualities was in the House of Commons, where he retained his eminence as a debater, with his Chancellor, Lloyd George, whose style was very different, his only serious rival. Asquith presented and defended government policies with polished skill, depending on his prodigious memory, his forensic training as a barrister and his ability to master the details of a brief with seemingly little effort to carry him triumphantly through many a dangerous encounter.

Outside the Commons, Asquith's routine as Prime Minister must appear astonishingly relaxed to modern readers, though perhaps no more so than that of most of his predecessors. A voracious reader of novels, and what Jenkins describes as a "highly heterogeneous collection of books" (Jenkins, 1978, p. 262), he and Margot gave several luncheon parties each week, more often than not attended primarily by non-political personalities or Society figures from Margot's own circle. The evenings were devoted to bridge, the theatre and smaller dinner parties often in the company of two or three of the more favoured of his younger ministers, notably Edwin Montagu and Winston Churchill. The guests usually included attractive and clever young women, with whom Asquith loved to gossip and chaff. The weekends were spent either at the Wharf, the Asquiths' country house near Abingdon, or at country house parties given mostly by Margot's aristocratic friends. In the midst of this social whirl, Asquith became rather too well acquainted with the demon drink, and he acquired the nickname of 'Squiffy' in political circles, though this was unknown to the general public. This occasionally led to embarrassment in the Commons where, during the Committee Stage of the Parliament Bill in 1912, he was "so drunk that he was barely able to speak and only the traditional discretion of the House averted a scandal" (Cassar, 1994, p. 34).

Although he was probably never unfaithful to Margot, Asquith acquired a reputation for enjoying the company of young women, with one of whom, Venetia Stanley, he became completely infatuated. The beautiful daughter of the Liberal peer, Lord Sheffield, she was less than half his age and was a close friend of his daughter Violet. Because of this her frequent visits to 10 Downing Street caused little comment. Asquith got into the habit of taking long drives in the country with her on Friday afternoons, and over several years wrote to her virtually every day.

Too buttoned up to confide to any extent with his male friends, Asquith undoubtedly found it a relief to be able to express himself candidly to a whole series of women correspondents, who subsequently included Venetia's elder sister, Lady Henley. Yet from around March 1914 his

34 H.H. Asquith

attachment to Venetia became something of a mania, and he increased the flow of his letters to two or even three a day, often writing during the course of Cabinet meetings. A large number of these letters were published in 1982, and according to the editors, "Although Asquith knew that the letters were being kept, he filled them with personal, political and military secrets of every kind; and they include constant appeals for Venetia's counsel. They constitute the most remarkable self-revelation ever given by a British Prime Minister" (Brock and Brock 1982, p. 13).

Asquith was Prime Minister for 8 years and 244 days, the longest consecutive period in this office since Lord Liverpool's 15-year stretch from 1812 to 1827, and only since surpassed by Margaret Thatcher's 11-year reign. The conventional verdict on Asquith was that as a peacetime premier he showed great sureness of touch, but that as a wartime leader he was seriously out of his depth. The reality was rather more complex.

The dominant events during Asquith's peacetime premiership were the laying of the first foundations of the welfare state, the struggle over House of Lords reform and the final unsuccessful attempt to implement the Gladstonian policy of Home Rule for Ireland. The main impetus for the welfare state reforms – which included old age pensions, National Insurance for unemployment and invalidity, wages boards and labour exchanges and the beginnings of town and country planning – came not from Asquith himself, but from ministerial colleagues, notably Lloyd George and Churchill. Yet Asquith strongly backed their initiatives, and the partnership which he formed with Lloyd George provided the essential equilibrium of his peacetime government, just as their mutual loss of confidence undermined his wartime administration.

The determining pre-war event was Lloyd George's so-called 'People's Budget' of 1909. This had been necessitated by the Cabinet's decision greatly to expand naval expenditure in the face of Germany's large ship-building programme, at the same time as it was committed to a major programme of social reforms. Lloyd George's response was to propose an extra £14 million in taxation, including new taxes on land which enraged the property-owning classes. Although it had been accepted for at least 250 years that the power of the purse belonged to the House of Commons, the House of Lords rejected the budget, immediately creating a constitutional crisis of the first order.

It was clear to Asquith that an immediate general election must be held to achieve a popular mandate to override the peers' decision. He also realised that his party's patience with the Upper House was at an end and a mandate should equally be sought to curb or remove the veto which the Lords had repeatedly applied to other Liberal measures. He therefore approached King Edward VII for an assurance that, should the election produce a majority in favour of the government, he would be prepared, if necessary, to create sufficient new peers to override the Tory majority if it refused to pass the necessary legislation. The king refused, saying that he would not "feel justified in creating new peers until after a second general election" in which the veto would be the sole issue. (See Roy Jenkins, *Mr Balfour's Poodle*, London, 1964, which remains the definitive account of the struggle to reform the Lords.)

Asquith supinely accepted the King's decision, recoiling from the prospect of a People vs. Monarch election. It is, however, arguable that he had the constitutional right as Prime Minister formally to advise the King to create the necessary number of peers, and he undoubtedly treated the King with greater deference than had been shown by his Tory predecessor, Arthur Balfour, some years previously, when he had resolutely refused to let the monarch see confidential Cabinet documents. The Prime Minister also blandly ignored the views of other senior ministers, including Grey, that a more thorough-going reform of the membership and powers of the upper chamber should be attempted.

The election which followed, in January 1910, produced a parliamentary majority of 124 in favour of overriding the Lords' veto. The Liberals, however, lost their overall majority and henceforth were dependent on the support of the Labour and Irish Nationalist parties to remain in power. This had far-reaching and largely unforeseen consequences.

After the election, the Lords let the budget through without opposition, but adamantly refused to contemplate any trimming of their powers. The sudden death of Edward VII in May 1910 again led Asquith to hesitate and rather than hold the new king, George V, to his father's undertaking concerning a second election he attempted to arrive at a compromise through a conference of the leaders of both main parties. It was only after this proved abortive that he finally cornered George V, who reluctantly conceded in November 1910 that he would create sufficient peers if the situation arose, but did not wish this to become public unless it proved necessary to give effect to it in a new Parliament. Asquith immediately sought a new dissolution and a further general election was held in December 1910, which produced an almost identical result to the previous January.

The Lords did not give way even then, and it was only after the King's undertaking was revealed that a dissident group of Tory peers, led by Lord Curzon, decided to abstain, which just allowed the Parliament Act of 1911 to pass the Lords with a bare majority without the creation of additional peers. Asquith's role in this dispute was at best equivocal. While exerting himself sufficiently to ensure the passage of the budget and the removal of the Lords' absolute veto, he missed the opportunity of more far-reaching reform and wasted the better part of two years, while putting the electoral survival of his government at unnecessary risk, by acquiescing in the King's insistence on the holding of two elections.

During the course of the conflict over the Lords, Asquith had on several occasions appeared on the verge of exhaustion, and there is little doubt that the wear and tear of his long period in office was beginning to tell. While still capable of decisive action on occasion, his premiership was increasingly characterised by long periods of indecision, exemplified by the reply "Wait and See", which he repeatedly gave when questioned about the government's intentions.

This was even more evident in his handling of the Irish Home Rule issue which dominated the last two years of peace. Never a passionate believer in the cause, Asquith had successfully avoided any action to give effect to the long-standing Liberal commitment until after the January 1910 election, which left him in hock to the Irish Nationalists for his parliamentary majority. The passage of the Parliament Act in 1911 removed the possibility of a permanent Lords veto, and in April 1912 the government duly introduced a Bill to transfer power over Irish affairs to an elected parliament in Dublin. This was duly rejected by the Lords in 1912 and 1913, and was due to be passed for the third and final time by the Commons in the summer of 1914. Well before then it had become apparent that the Protestant majority in Northern Ireland was adamantly opposed to being governed from Dublin. Whipped up by the lawyer and Tory politician Sir Edward Carson (with the tacit approval of the Tory leader, Andrew Bonar Law), armed groups prepared to resist the transfer of power.

As the situation deteriorated, it became increasingly clear that only two alternatives were open to the government: firm action against those advocating and organising violent resistance or amending the Home Rule Bill to exclude, either permanently or temporarily, Protestant majority areas from the aegis of the projected Dublin Parliament. Yet Asquith temporised for month after month until March 1914 when, on the eve of the Third Reading of the Bill, he introduced an amendment which would allow the Ulster counties to opt out of Home Rule for a period of six years. This failed to appease the Protestants and was seen as too great a concession by the Nationalists. At the same time, Asquith decided on a show of force against the illegal arming of Protestant militias, only to be confronted by the so-called Curragh mutiny, when 60 British army officers at a barracks near Dublin declared that they would resign their commissions rather than act against Protestant loyalists.

In the face of incipient civil war in Northern Ireland, Asquith initiated a series of inter-party discussions, culminating in a formal conference at Buckingham Palace. It opened on 21 July, but broke up three days later without any agreement. Asquith was at the end of his tether, and was only rescued from his dilemma by the greater crisis precipitated by the assassination in Sarajevo of the Austrian Arch-Duke Franz-Ferdinand. Writing to Venetia Stanley in March 1915, he admitted that "the sudden outbreak of the Great War" had been the greatest stroke of luck in his political career (Brock and Brock 1982, p. 111).

Asquith bore little direct responsibility for the outbreak of the war, though he was certainly instrumental in ensuring British entry. This was not a development which he welcomed, and his correspondence with Venetia suggested that he would have been happy for Britain to remain a neutral spectator (Brock and Brock, 1982, p. 123). His hand was forced, however, partly no doubt by the speedy build-up of jingoistic sentiment after the German ultimatum to Belgium, but more directly by pressure within his own Cabinet. This was, effectively, split three ways. A 'war party', led by Grey and Churchill, was adamant that Britain should enter the war on the French side. Grey, in particular, felt that this was the only honourable course, no doubt influenced by the strength and consistency of the undertakings (albeit only implicit) which he had given to the French leadership over the years, and which he and Asquith had long conspired to keep secret from the bulk of their Cabinet colleagues (Coogan and Coogan 1985). On the other side was the 'peace party', led by John Morley and John Simon, who declared themselves opposed to British involvement "in any circumstances". Only a few months earlier they had rallied half the Cabinet, including Lloyd George, to resist Admiralty proposals for increased naval expenditure, and they probably represented a majority of Liberal MPs.

In the middle was a solid group of non-committed ministers, including Lord Crewe, Reginald McKenna and Herbert Samuel, who were ready to rally to any lead given by Asquith. He, however, was in no hurry to commit himself and, as usual, played a waiting game, carefully assessing the number and weight of potential resignations on either side before making a move. His overriding impulsion seemed to be to keep his Cabinet as united as possible. The intentions of two senior ministers, in particular, weighed heavily with him. One was Grey, to whom he felt a personal link of complicity; the other was Lloyd George, his only conceivable rival for the premiership. Grey had made it quite clear that he would leave the government if Britain remained neutral, but Lloyd George was desperately anxious not to resign and was furtively seeking a 'respectable' pretext to detach himself from the peace party. He seized on the German threat to Belgium, and as soon as it was clear that Lloyd George would not resign, Asquith came down decisively on Grey's side. While four Cabinet ministers proffered their resignations, Asquith persuaded two (Simon and Lord Beauchamp) to change their minds, so only Morley and John Burns, the Lib-Lab President of the Board of Local Government, actually quit the government.

The British entry into the war went smoothly enough: the Expeditionary Force of six divisions was rapidly dispatched to France, and under the enthusiastic eye of Winston Churchill, the First Lord of the Admiralty, the fleet assumed its battle stations. The appointment by

Asquith of Lord Kitchener as War Secretary was a masterful stroke of public relations; it was only later that his military shortcomings became painfully evident. The immediate consequence was that Asquith's popularity soared and he was spoken of as a great war leader in the tradition of the Elder Pitt. This impression quickly faded. The deadlock on the Western Front, and the failure of the Dardanelles campaign in the spring of 1915, led to growing disillusionment, which Asquith did little to dispel.

It should have been evident to him that, lacking a parliamentary majority, it was not practicable to conduct the war effort on the basis of a single-party government. Instead of actively seeking to form an all-party coalition – in which the Tories, with virtually the same number of MPs as the Liberals, would certainly play a major role – he firmly resisted the idea, and it was only after the Dardanelles disaster, in May 1915, that he was forced to accept the inevitable. Unfortunately, this came at the very moment when his judgement was clouded by a crisis in his personal life. To his utter consternation, Venetia Stanley announced her engagement to one of Asquith's favourite younger Cabinet ministers, Edwin Montagu, and that she was converting to Judaism in anticipation of the marriage. He took the news very hard, and broke off all communication with her.

What effect this blow had on his handling of the coalition negotiations can only be speculated, but it is undeniable that he conducted them in a stubborn, ungracious and ultimately self-defeating manner. His crucial error lay in his determination to deny the Tory leader, Andrew Bonar Law, one of the principal ministerial posts. Instead, he was fobbed off with the Colonial Secretaryship, one of a series of snubs he received at Asquith's hands. It seemed as if the Prime Minister was refusing to accept the fact that Law was the leader of his party, and that he was perversely determined to treat Balfour (who became First Lord of the Admiralty) as if he was still in command. It has been suggested that this arose from Asquith's intellectual snobbery (Hazelhurst 1977, pp. 93–4). Bonar Law was a businessman, and not an intellectual or a member of the professional classes. Asquith had already shown a marked reluctance to include many of the large number of Liberal MPs with a business background in his peacetime government, which was made up almost exclusively of professional men together with a fair sprinkling of aristocrats. Whatever his motives, Asquith's disdainful treatment of Bonar Law cost him dear. As the American historian George Cassar shrewdly commented: "in the long run ... Asquith's best chance of remaining Prime Minister would have been to turn the Unionist leader into a specially-trusted lieutenant and to have headed a genuine national ministry" (Cassar 1994, p. 109). Instead, the Tory leader became deeply disgruntled and needed little encouragement to throw in his lot with Lloyd George in the crisis in December 1916, which led to his replacing Asquith as Prime Minister.

During the 18 months of the Asquith-led coalition, his reputation steadily declined. The progress of the war went from bad to worse, and the ill-fated Somme offensive, where the British casualties totalled 420,000, including Asquith's brilliant elder son, Raymond, killed off any lingering illusions of a cheap and easy victory. Yet it was not the military reverses or the terrible carnage which destroyed Asquith's standing as a war leader. It was the growing conviction that his heart was not in it. From the beginning he had given the impression that the conduct of the struggle should impinge as little as possible on the familiar routines of peacetime life, and he was far too rational and civilised a man to indulge in the hyperbole of war. His apparent lethargy was altogether too sharp a contrast with Lloyd George, whose dynamic energy as Minister for Munitions made him the inevitable candidate for War Secretary when Kitchener was drowned in June 1916. If Asquith was temperamentally incapable of waging war wholeheartedly, he showed very little inclination to work for a peace settlement. He consistently cold-shouldered mediation attempts by President Woodrow Wilson, and when his (Tory) Minister without Portfolio, Lord Lansdowne, circulated a Cabinet memorandum, in November 1916, urging the case for a negotiated peace Asquith offered him no support.

The precise circumstances of Asquith's fall, in December 1916, have been the subject of great controversy, and need not concern us here, though they are discussed in broad outline in the next chapter, on Lloyd George. (For long the most authoritative account was believed to be that of Lord Beaverbrook, who was virtually a participant, being an intimate confidant of both Bonar Law and Carson. This appeared in the second volume of his *Politicians and the War*, published in 1932. It is challenged on several points by Jenkins (1978, pp. 422–61). The most judicious summing up is probably that of Cassar (1994, pp. 210–32).)

The situation was brought to a head by a memorandum compiled by Lloyd George and the former Tory Attorney-General, Sir Edward Carson, with the backing of Bonar Law. It did not seek Asquith's replacement as Prime Minister, but argued that the executive conduct of the war should effectively be removed from the Cabinet and entrusted to a small War Council of three or four, with Lloyd George as chairman. Asquith was not unsympathetic to this proposal, but was adamant that he himself should chair the new body, believing that otherwise he would be reduced to a mere figurehead. He met with Lloyd George and reached a partial compromise, which fell through, amid mutual recriminations, after a biased account had been leaked to *The Times*, probably by Carson. Lloyd George then raised the stakes by submitting his resignation, and the Tory ministers pulled the rug from under Asquith's feet by insisting that they would not remain in the government in the absence of Lloyd George. Asquith saw no alternative to submitting his own resignation, perhaps hoping against hope that neither Bonar Law nor Lloyd George could form an alternative government and that he would then be summoned back. In the event, the King first summoned Bonar Law, who declined, and then turned to Lloyd George, who had no difficulty in forming a government within 24 hours, despite the refusal of almost all the former Liberal ministers, as well as Asquith himself, to serve under him.

Asquith believed that he was the victim of a sordid intrigue between Lloyd George and the Tory ministers, and of an unscrupulous campaign by the Tory press, with Lord Northcliffe's papers, including *The Times*, to the fore. The reality was that his days were numbered, and it is hard to disagree with Cassar's verdict: "It was Asquith's perceived inadequacies that ended his premiership. Simply put, he no longer possessed the requisite confidence of the nation and parliament to beat back a major challenge to his leadership."

Asquith's pride was deeply hurt, though he characteristically made no public attempt to justify his wartime record. He became a sulky leader of the opposition, offering lukewarm support to the new government's conduct of the war, only challenging them on one ill-fated occasion. This was the so-called Maurice debate, in May 1918, when Asquith – to the fury of Lloyd George and Bonar Law – proposed a select committee to enquire into the preparedness of the British army to meet the German spring offensive. In the ensuing vote he was supported by 100 Liberal MPs, while 71 voted with the government. The following November, when, immediately after the Armistice, a general election was called, Lloyd George wreaked his vengeance by refusing a coalition 'ticket' to virtually all the Liberals who had voted with Asquith in the Maurice debate.

The election result was a shattering defeat for the Liberals, from which they never fully recovered. Asquith himself lost his seat, and only 26 of his followers were elected, against 59 for the Labour Party (which became the official opposition) and 474 for the coalition (338 Tories and 136 coalition Liberals).

Asquith continued as leader of the Liberal Party until 1926, including a period in which Lloyd George uneasily served under him, following the eventual reunion of the two wings of the party. There were ups and downs during these years – Asquith got back into the Commons through a by-election at Paisley in 1920, only to lose the seat again in 1924, after which he accepted an earldom. In the interim, he had, as leader of the third party in the Commons, backed the appointment of a minority Labour government, under Ramsay Macdonald, in January 1924 – only to withdraw support eight months later, precipitating the 1924 election which effectively reduced the Liberals to minor party status.

Asquith died four years later, leaving a mixed legacy to his country. On the one hand, he has been remembered as a pioneer, whose achievements have reverberated down the years, paving the way for the welfare state legislation of the Attlee government in 1945–51, as well as Blair's constitutional reforms (especially concerning the House of Lords) after 1997. But he is also remembered as the last of the 19th-century Liberals, and certainly bears some responsibility for the eclipse of the once mighty Liberal Party. It is arguable, though far from certain, that it would have been replaced, in any event, by the nascent Labour Party. What is undeniable is that this process was greatly hastened by the vendetta between Asquith and Lloyd George, and their respective followers. The opportunistic Lloyd George may have been the more culpable, but this gifted, fastidious, proud yet ultimately indecisive man must also bear his share of the blame.

Works consulted

Michael Brock and Eleanor Brock (eds), 1982, *H.H. Asquith: Letters to Venetia Stanley*, Oxford, Oxford University Press.

George H. Cassar, 1994, *Asquith as War Leader*, London, Hambledon Press.

John W. Coogan and Peter F. Coogan, 1985, 'The British Cabinet and the Anglo-French Staff Talks, 1905–1914: Who Knew What and When Did He Know It', *Journal of British Studies, 24*.

Cameron Hazelhurst, 1977, 'Herbert Henry Asquith', in John P. Mackintosh (ed.), *British Prime Ministers in the Twentieth Century*, Vol. I, London, Weidenfeld & Nicolson.

Lucille Iremonger, 1970, *The Fiery Chariot*, London, Secker & Warburg.

Roy Jenkins, 1978, *Asquith* (revised edition), London, Collins.

Stephen Koss, 1976, *Asquith*, London, Allen Lane.

J.A. Spender, article on Asquith in *Dictionary of National Biography 1922–1930*.

4

DAVID LLOYD GEORGE

"A dynamic force"

The child is father to the man, and in no case was this more true than with David Lloyd George – or Dafydd George, as he was first known. Brought up by an adoring uncle – Richard Lloyd – who persuaded him from an early age that he was an exceptional person, with no limits to what he could achieve, he unquestioningly accepted his destiny, and lived his whole life as if normal rules did not apply to himself, and that anything – or any person – that he desired was within his grasp.

Lloyd George was born in a dismal terrace house in Chorlton-upon-Medlock, Manchester, on 17 January 1863. His father, William George, was a dreamy, unsuccessful schoolmaster, who shortly afterwards resigned his post and returned to his native Pembrokeshire to rent a smallholding, but, when Dafydd was only 18 months old, caught pneumonia and died, aged 44. As well as Dafydd, he left a daughter, Mary Ellen, who was not yet 3, while his widow, Elizabeth Lloyd, was expecting a second son, William, who was born seven months after his father's death.

Left penniless, and with no one else to depend on, Elizabeth sought help from her brother Richard, a village cobbler and unpaid Baptist pastor, who was living in Llanystumdwy, near Criccieth in North Wales. Without a moment's hesitation, Richard took his sister and her children into his household and devoted himself to their upbringing. All three children were bright and intelligent, but it was soon evident that he was absolutely enchanted by Dafydd, whose charm, amiability, vitality and vivid imagination knew no bounds. The others were relatively, if not absolutely, neglected. William, who lived to be 102, and when he was 92 published a memoir entitled *My Brother and I*, recalled somewhat caustically:

> He was the apple of Uncle Lloyd's eye, the king of the castle, and like the other king, could do no wrong … Whether this unrestrained admiration was wholly good for the lad upon whom it was lavished, and indeed for the man who evolved out of him, is a matter upon which opinions may differ.
>
> *(William George, 1958, p. 33)*

DOI: 10.4324/9781003031963-5

The extraordinary extent to which William was discriminated against was personified by the fact that only Dafydd was permitted by his uncle to add 'Lloyd' to his name. When the two brothers qualified as solicitors and set up their own firm, it was known as Lloyd George & George. It was William who devoted himself to the running of the firm, working long hours while Dafydd was freed to pursue his political career, which was heavily subsidised by his brother's toil.

That – coming from a modest but not impoverished background – they were able to become lawyers at all was due to the determination of Uncle Lloyd, as he became known. A self-educated Welsh moralist, he taught Dafydd everything he knew and made sure that he made the most out of the best education then available in rural Wales. When Dafydd left school at 13, he was articled to a local firm of solicitors in Portmadoc. William, who largely made his own way in Dafydd's slipstream, actually proved the more apt pupil, gaining First Class Honours in his law examination, while his brother only achieved Third Class.

The North Wales in which Lloyd George grew up had a distinctive political culture. An overwhelmingly agricultural society, it was deeply polarised. The upper and middle classes were dominated by English landowners, the Anglican church and the Tory Party. Ranged against them were the rural poor, farm workers and small tenant farmers, predominantly Welsh-speaking, ardent chapel-goers and – at least since the Ballot Act of 1872, which protected them from the prying eyes of their Tory landlords – predisposed to vote Liberal. A further cause of dissension was the high level of drunkenness, which pitched a strong popular temperance movement against Tory publicans and brewers.

The main grievances of the mass of the population concerned the misdeeds of landowners and the privileges of the Church of England and especially its right to levy a tithe on Nonconformists. Lloyd George needed no special prompting from his uncle to determine whose side he was on, and already in his teens was taking an active part in the Portmadoc debating society and in local Liberal politics. Yet it was as a radical lawyer that he first made his name, as 'the People's David', by winning a series of local court cases, where his forensic brilliance won the day against the more pedestrian and often blundering advocates representing the establishment side. The most famous of these was the Llanfrothen burial case in 1885, when Lloyd George, having lost in a lower court, overturned the verdict on appeal and established the right of Nonconformists to be buried in parish churchyards.

Some years before this Lloyd George had already set his sights on a parliamentary career, recording in his diary following his first visit to the House of Commons, aged 17: "I will not say but that I eyed the assembly in a spirit similar to that in which William the Conqueror eyed England on his visit to Edward the Confessor, as the region of his future domain. Oh, vanity!"

Lloyd George was brought up as a strict Baptist, though he lost his religious faith at the age of 12. Outwardly, however, he conformed to the prevailing Nonconformist culture, and he retained his enthusiasm for hymn-singing and Welsh preachers for the whole of his life. His uncle hoped that he would marry one or other of the girls from the Baptist community, but Lloyd George set his sights on Margaret Owen, the daughter of a prosperous Methodist farmer, who regarded the radical young lawyer as a far from appropriate suitor.

It was a long and difficult courtship, which was hardly helped by the brutal frankness with which he made it clear that their relationship would have to take second place to his political ambitions. "I am prepared to thrust even love itself under the wheels of my Juggernaut", he wrote to her, adding "I must not forget that I have a purpose in life. And however painful the sacrifice I may have to make to attain this ambition I must not flinch."

42 David Lloyd George

Yet whatever her misgivings, which were certainly augmented by early indications that he would not be the most faithful of husbands, Maggie Owen – like nearly every one else – succumbed to his charm and they were duly married in January 1888, when he was 25 and she 21. By the end of the same year, Lloyd George was selected as prospective Liberal candidate for the local constituency of Caernarvon Boroughs, which had been a Tory gain in 1886. Two months later he became an alderman on the Caernarvonshire County Council.

He did not have to wait long before getting into Parliament. In March 1890 the Conservative MP died, and in April, in a desperately close contest, he defeated the local squire, Ellis Nanney, by a mere 18 votes. He was 27, but had come within a hair's breadth of disaster a few weeks earlier when some leading Liberal supporters discovered that he had fathered a child on a widow in Caernarvon. Given the moral climate of the time – just before the Parnell divorce case – this could well have aborted his parliamentary career once and for all. Wealthy backers, however, succeeded in hushing up the affair, by settling an annuity on the widow on condition that not a word was to be revealed. So successful was the cover-up that nothing was ever known about it until many years later when Lloyd George's elder son Richard, already middle-aged, stumbled upon the truth through a chance meeting with a Caernarvon resident in South America (Richard Lloyd George, 1960, pp. 41–4).

This was the first of a long series of extra-marital scrapes in which Lloyd George, described by his son as "probably the greatest natural Don Juan in the history of British politics", became involved, yet despite the incredible risks that he ran he never actually came a cropper. Although his predatory attitude to women later became notorious in political circles, where he was known as 'the Goat', the naturally discreet press of the time, coerced by draconian libel laws, seldom permitted itself more than the most oblique reference to his amatory activities. Nor did his 30-year-long relationship with his secretary, Frances Stevenson, which began in 1913 and eventually led to their marriage in 1943, following Margaret's death, ever make the public prints. In 1927, she bore him a daughter, Jennifer, who was successfully passed off as her adopted child.

LG's waywardness as a husband was not entirely due to his uncontrolled libido. Some at least of the blame should be attributed to his wife who, despite repeating urging, refused to come with their children to live with him in London, but chose to remain in Criccieth running the family home. The effect that this had on him can be inferred from a poignant letter which he wrote to her in August 1897:

> I have scores of times come home in the dead of night to a cold, dark and comfortless flat without a soul to greet me, when you were surrounded by your pets [i.e. children] … You have been a good mother. You have not – and I say this now not in anger – not always been a good wife.
>
> *(Grigg, 1973, pp. 241–3)*

Lloyd George's election for Caernarvon Boroughs began an unbroken term of nearly 54 years in the House of Commons. Re-elected in both the 1892 and 1895 elections, his parliamentary activities prior to 1899 were almost exclusively confined to Welsh issues. These included, notably, the campaign for disestablishment of the Church in Wales, demands for land reform, temperance legislation and opposition to subsidies for Church schools. These were subsumed in a general aspiration for Welsh Home Rule.

In pursuing these issues, Lloyd George showed scant respect for Liberal Party discipline, at one time putting the precarious Rosebery government at risk by threatening to withdraw support if priority was not given to a Disestablishment Bill. Lloyd George's aim was to achieve an autonomous existence for Welsh Liberal MPs comparable to that enjoyed by the Irish Party, an ambition which was largely frustrated by the divergent interests of North and South Wales. After ten years in the House, while he had undoubtedly established himself as the best known of the Welsh MPs, he was by no means universally accepted as their leader.

It was the Boer War, starting in 1899, which turned Lloyd George from a purely Welsh politician into a national figure. Without hesitation, he condemned it from the outset as an unjust war against a poor, brave, rural and God-fearing community, with which, as a Welshman, he instinctively empathised. Moreover, he did not flinch from accusing Joseph Chamberlain, the Colonial Secretary and chief architect of the war, of making personal profits through War Office contracts with a firm with which he had family connections He was the most prominent and most daring of the small group of Liberal MPs who took a 'pro-Boer' stance, and was the object of vitriolic attacks by the jingoistic press. He was physically assaulted on more than one occasion and barely escaped with his life when a mob broke up a meeting that he was addressing in Birmingham Town Hall. His popularity in Wales and even in his own constituency slumped, as did his standing in the Liberal Party, where the Liberal Imperialists, led by Rosebery, Asquith and Haldane, enthusiastically backed the Salisbury government, while the party leader, Campbell-Bannerman, struggled with great difficulty to maintain a middle position.

It was only after the war was over, and tempers had cooled, that Lloyd George was accorded respect for the courage he had shown and came increasingly to be recognised as the effective leader of the radical wing of the party. His attitude to the war, however, was widely misunderstood. It was not based on pacifism, nor on opposition to the maintenance, or even the expansion, of the British Empire. His essential objection was to the bullying of small nations by larger ones, and his attitude to the German invasion of Belgium in 1914 could therefore be seen as consistent with his position in 1899 rather than in conflict with it, as it has appeared to many.

In the years following the war, Lloyd George's parliamentary reputation grew steadily. He proved a resourceful opponent of Balfour's 1902 Education Act and – together with Asquith – led the Liberal attack against Chamberlain's Tariff Reform proposals which were the prime cause of the disintegration of the Balfour government. It was therefore no surprise that Campbell-Bannerman chose him as a member of his Cabinet when a Liberal government was formed in December 1905. Most of the senior posts went to Liberal Imperialists, and C.B. sought to balance this by appointing Lloyd George, then aged 43, as President of the Board of Trade.

LG took to ministerial life like a duck to water. Within his department he proved a firm and decisive administrator, he carried a shoal of Bills through Parliament at a time when other ministers had precious little to show for their labours, and he revealed remarkable powers as a conciliator in a series of industrial disputes, notably succeeding in averting a national rail strike in October 1907. He was clearly one of the success stories in C.B.'s government, and when Asquith succeeded to the premiership in April 1908 it was inevitable that he should follow him at the Treasury.

With this appointment, LG came to occupy the second place in the government. The partnership between him and Asquith – two fundamentally different but complementary talents – was to dominate British politics for most of the next decade. Given their subsequent hostility, it is remarkable how harmonious their relationship remained, and the depth of loyalty they showed to each other. Only the strains of war were to set them asunder.

The first big challenge facing LG as Chancellor was to prepare the 1909 budget. He was confronted with the prospect of the – for the time – enormous deficit of £16 million. This was caused by the necessity to finance a large naval rearmament programme (which LG had opposed in Cabinet) and the first old age pensions, of 5 shillings a week, which had been promised by the previous budget, introduced by Asquith. Lloyd George was determined to show that he could close the gap without resorting to the Tariff Reform measures advocated by the opposition and that the main burden would fall on the shoulders of the Tory land-owners, who were using their domination of the House of Lords to frustrate the government's legislative programme.

Lloyd George was the outstanding parliamentary orator of his time – perhaps of all time – but by common consent his delivery of the speech presenting his 'People's Budget' on 29 April 1909 was the worst of his long career. Yet the impact of this speech surpassed all others. It provoked Balfour – the leader of the opposition – into denouncing it as "vindictive, inequit-able, based on no principles and injurious to the productive capacity of the country", and led to the most serious constitutional crisis in modern British history.

The actual budget proposals must appear surprisingly mild to the modern reader. They involved increases in death duties (rising to 25 per cent for fortunes of over £1 million) and of income tax (6 per cent on unearned incomes) and the introduction of surtax, at 2.5 per cent, on incomes over £5,000. What really stuck in the craw of the Tories, however, was three new land taxes, of which the most prominent was a 20 per cent levy on the "unearned increment" on development land. (By a strange irony, these taxes raised very little by way of revenue, and two of them were actually repealed, on these grounds, when LG was Prime Minister in 1921.)

Opinions differ as to whether LG had deliberately set out to ensure that the House of Lords – which had not challenged a financial measure since 1678 – would fall into the trap of voting down his budget, but, if so, his plans could not have worked out better. The Lords rose to the bait with extraordinary insouciance, thus ensuring that the main political battle-line over the next few years would be 'Peers vs. People'. In this atmosphere nobody revelled more than Lloyd George who, in a series of ferocious speeches, notably at Limehouse and Newcastle, tore into the dukes "who cost as much to keep up as two Dreadnoughts – and they are just as great a terror", and damningly characterised the House of Lords as "five hundred men, ordinary men chosen accidentally from among the unemployed".

These attacks horrified Edward VII, who vainly attempted to persuade Asquith to rein in his over-bellicose Chancellor, but they made Lloyd George a popular hero and the darling of the Liberal rank-and-file. They also made it impossible for the Liberal leadership to settle for any compromise which did not ensure the predominance of the Commons over the unelected upper chamber.

Strangely enough, however, it was Lloyd George who, when in June 1910 the new king, George V, proposed an inter-party conference to try to settle the dispute over the Lords, was prepared to go further than any other politician in seeking all-party agreement. The formal conference, consisting of four Liberals led by Asquith and Lloyd George and four Conservatives led by Balfour and Lord Lansdowne, got nowhere despite meeting over a dozen times. Lloyd George then composed a remarkable memorandum proposing the formation of a coalition government which would seek national consensus and, where it could not agree, would submit issues such as free trade, Irish Home Rule, Lords reform and Welsh Disestablishment to non-partisan commissions. LG first showed the memorandum to his closest ministerial colleague and political friend, Winston Churchill, who responded enthusiastically and then approached opposition figures including F.E. Smith (later Lord Birkenhead) and Tory leader Balfour, both of whom expressed initial interest, before subsequently backing off. Asquith was amused by the proposal which he did not think would get any Liberal backing, and was then disconcerted when both Foreign Secretary Edward Gray and Lord Crewe, the Lord Privy Seal, were favourably impressed. Writing in his *Memoirs*, 20 years later, LG claimed that several senior Tories, including Lansdowne, Curzon, Walter Long and Austen Chamberlain, were also in favour. That nothing came of the proposal, which was not public knowledge at the time, was largely due to the fact that neither Asquith nor Balfour – no doubt with their own personal interests firmly in view – were prepared to take it any further. Its basic interest lies in showing that, not for the first time, LG attached relatively little weight to party political considerations.

So the Lords dispute followed its course, culminating in the passage of the Parliament Act in 1911, after two general elections and the reluctant agreement of George V to create sufficient new Liberal peers to carry the Bill through the Lords if this proved necessary – as recounted in the previous chapter on Asquith. (The full story is most entertainingly told in Roy Jenkins's *Mr Balfour's Poodle*, first published in 1964.)

Despite its momentous aftermath, the 'People's Budget' was not central to Lloyd George's role as a social reformer. This owed much more to the National Insurance Act of 1911. It was the eventual fruit of the early discussions he had had with Churchill, shortly after the formation of the Asquith government, when they jointly agreed that, within the government, they should spearhead a great crusade against poverty and deprivation. In the summer of 1908 LG went on a visit to Germany where he was immensely impressed by the social security schemes and labour exchanges introduced by Bismarck two decades earlier. He resolved to introduce contributory insurance schemes against both sickness and unemployment as soon as the parliamentary timetable allowed.

In framing his legislation, Lloyd George had to overcome determined resistance from vested interests – the big insurance companies, the medical profession, and – in the first stages at least – the friendly societies and trade unions. Using the same mixture of coercion and charm which his fellow Welshman, Aneurin Bevan, was to employ 40 years later in introducing the National Health Service, LG managed to carry the day, though not without compromising on some of his original objectives. The most eye-catching feature of his Bill was that lower-paid workers should pay 4d a week for sickness benefit, which would be augmented by further payments of 3d by the employer and 2d by the state. This was successfully presented to the public with the slogan "Ninepence for fourpence", and popular support was so strong that the Bill passed through all its parliamentary stages with virtually no opposition. The structures which it produced provided a firm basis for the much more comprehensive 'welfare state' provisions of the Attlee government of 1945–51. The passage of the Bill, which came fully into effect in January 1913, marked the high-water mark of Lloyd George's pre-war reputation.

This suffered a heavy setback with the Marconi scandal of 1912–13 which, if it had not been for the firm support of Asquith, could well have ended his political career. In April 1912, at the suggestion of his friend and colleague, Sir Rufus Isaacs, the Attorney-General, who had himself made a larger investment, he bought shares on very favourable conditions in the American Marconi Company, in the hope of making a quick profit. This was at a time when the English Marconi Company was negotiating a profitable contract with the

Postmaster-General Sir Herbert Samuel. Suggestions in the press, by among others the xenophobic *Daily Mail*, which described them as "the Welsh solicitor and the Jew barrister", that they had used private knowledge of the impending deal to enrich themselves, were met by a disingenuous denial by Rufus, who said that neither he nor Lloyd George had any prior knowledge of the English Marconi Company deal, and that neither of them had had "one single transaction in the shares of the company", making no mention at all of their investment in the associated American company.

After threats of libel action, the affair was referred to a select committee of the House of Commons, which revealed the whole story and from whose enquiries neither Isaacs nor Lloyd George emerged with much credit. The committee, however, split along party lines in drawing up its report, and the majority finding, supported only by the Liberal members of the committee, whitewashed the two ministers. Lloyd George felt constrained to offer his resignation to Asquith, who refused to accept it, and the majority report was adopted by the House of Commons in June 1913 after a tense two-day debate. Lloyd George's career was saved, but the distinct impression remained that, while he had not broken the law, he had been none too scrupulous in his business affairs. For those associated with him in his earlier unsuccessful and little publicised attempts to 'get rich quick', notably a gold-mining venture in Patagonia in the 1890s, this could hardly have come as a surprise

When war loomed in July–August 1914 LG probably believed until late in the day that Britain would, and should, keep out of the struggle. Yet he made no attempt to line up with the anti-war faction in the Cabinet, although he was assumed to be sympathetic to them, given his consistent opposition to naval rearmament and the construction of more and more Dreadnoughts, over which he had threatened to resign as recently as 1913. If LG had chosen to lead the 'peace party' – and *only* if he had done so – they might well have succeeded in keeping Britain neutral. Yet, given the rising jingoistic mood in the country, and to a lesser extent in Parliament, their stand could instead have led to the fall of the government, and its replacement by a Conservative-dominated coalition bent on war.

This was not something that LG was prepared to risk, nor it seems did he relish the prospect of resuming his lonely Boer War role as an anti-war militant. In fact, he was desperately anxious to avoid resignation and, in the words of one biographer, "throwing away, in twenty-five seconds, a position which it had taken him twenty-five years to reach – perhaps surrendering it to Churchill" (Rowland, 1976, p. 282). Frances Stevenson, who some 18 months earlier had become both his secretary and mistress, gave the game away when she wrote in her memoirs 40 years later: "the invasion of Belgium was, to be cynical, a heaven-sent excuse for supporting a declaration of war" (Frances Lloyd George, 1967, pp. 73–4).

This was seized on by Lloyd George, and indeed by the majority of Asquith's Cabinet, as reason enough to stay on board, and the number of anti-war resignations was kept down to two – John Burns and John Morley. Lloyd George was nevertheless seen as a reluctant convert to British participation, and few could have foreseen the enthusiasm with which he would embrace the struggle.

His initial contribution was to take firm steps to steady the money markets and prevent the onset of a short-term financial crisis. His actions met general approbation, not least in the City of London which had previously entertained distinctly mixed feelings about the radical Chancellor. Yet nothing prepared them, either Lloyd George's previous admirers or his critics, for the tremendous impact of the first major speech which he made after the outbreak of the war.

This was at a recruiting meeting at Queen's Hall, in London, on 19 September 1914, when LG pulled out all the stops in an emotional appeal to British youth to give their all in defence of national honour, freedom and the defence of small nations. The speech, of which 2.5 million copies were subsequently printed and distributed at government expense, was a mixture of deeply moving passages and of others of the sheerest demagogy appealing to the very jingoistic spirit which he had earlier opposed. Its reception changed LG's persona overnight. Previously seen as a highly controversial and partisan figure, he now emerged as the voice of a united national determination to see the war through to its end, whatever the cost. Recruitment soared, and Lloyd George received an avalanche of admiring letters, many from previous Conservative opponents.

John Grigg neatly summed up the transformation in Lloyd George's standing: "After the Queen's Hall meeting ... Lloyd George was Britain's war premier in waiting ... Unfortunately for the country, he had more than two years to wait" (Grigg, 1985, p. 174). During this time LG combined two roles: he was one of the government's leading actors, and its principal critic.

One persistent theme of LG's criticism – expressed through a constant stream of memoranda addressed to his ministerial colleagues – was what he regarded as the over-concentration by the allies on the Western Front, in France and Flanders, where they were bogged down in a seemingly endless but bloody stalemate. He was repeatedly urging action on what most of his colleagues regarded as 'side-shows' against Germany's allies, Austria-Hungary and Turkey. He enthusiastically supported the ill-fated Dardanelles (Gallipoli) campaign launched in February 1915, though it was Churchill, as First Lord of the Admiralty, who initiated the venture and who took the blame for its failure. Lloyd George was also a vocal critic of the failure to mobilise the production and procurement of war materiel, which led to an allegedly serious shortage of shells for the British Expeditionary Force.

It was this, no doubt, that prompted Asquith to offer Lloyd George the post of Minister of Munitions, when the disappointing conduct of the war led to the formation of the first coalition government, in May 1915. He was reluctant to give up the chancellorship, which went, not to one of the new Tory ministers, but to Reginald McKenna, his most bitter rival in the Liberal ranks. He was, however, promised sweeping powers, retained the use of 11 Downing Street, and relished the opportunity to make a direct contribution to the war effort.

It was his dynamic conduct of his new ministry, combined with the growing dissatisfaction at Asquith's apparent lethargy and ineffectiveness as a war leader, which paved the way for his assumption of the premiership 18 months later. The extent of his achievement is summed up in two sentences in Rowland's biography: "The monthly output of shells ... increased from 70,000 in May to 120,000 in September and 238,000 in January 1916. By July 1916, when the time came for Lloyd George to leave the Ministry it had reached 1,125,660" (Rowland, 1976, p. 320).

Lloyd George left the Ministry of Munitions to become Secretary of State for War, when the impressive-looking but disastrously ineffective Lord Kitchener drowned, when the ship on which he was sailing to Russia hit a mine off the Orkneys. His five months at the War Office were too brief for him to have a noticeable effect on the conduct of British military operations. Yet all the time his impatience was growing at the impasse which had been reached, as was his conviction that he alone had the vision and demoniac energy to carry the war through to a victorious conclusion. Despite this conviction, however, he did not at this time aspire to replace Asquith as Prime Minister. His objective was to replace the unwieldy

48 David Lloyd George

War Council – made up of a large, fluctuating and quarrelsome group of ministers and officials which, under the meandering chairmanship of Asquith had become a byword for indecision – with a small executive group of top ministers, shorn of departmental responsibilities, who would direct the war on a day-to-day basis, subject only to the right of the Prime Minister, at his own discretion, to refer particular decisions to the Cabinet as a whole. In LG's view, he himself should be the chairman and chief executive of this committee.

LG's dissatisfaction was shared by Bonar Law and by other leading Tories, notably Sir Edward Carson, who had become the leader of the Tory backbenchers. Together with Max Aitken (later Lord Beaverbrook), the Canadian newspaper owner and Tory MP for Ashton-under-Lyne, they joined with him in drafting a memorandum, which was sent to Asquith on 1 December 1916, proposing a reorganisation along the lines desired by Lloyd George. Asquith was not averse to the proposed arrangement, but insisted that he should not just have the right to attend the committee, but should preside over it, sensing that otherwise he would be reduced to a mere figurehead. Within two days, however, under strong pressure from Bonar Law, he climbed down and accepted a revised proposal of a supreme war committee of three men, but then again changed his mind when press leaks convinced him – wrongly it appears – that the whole scheme resulted from a plot between Lloyd George and the newspaper proprietor Lord Northcliffe, owner of *The Times* and the *Daily Mail*.

Lloyd George then threw down a direct challenge by resigning and Bonar Law followed suit. Asquith, finding himself abandoned also by the other Conservative ministers, submitted the resignation of the whole government on 5 December, perhaps still hoping that his refusal to serve under a successor would prevent an alternative government from being formed.

In fact, the Conservative leaders, notably lacking in self-confidence, were far from eager to seize the reins of office for themselves, and neither Bonar Law nor Balfour – a possible compromise choice – was prepared to govern without Asquith's support. George V, having first approached Bonar Law, then invited Lloyd George, on 7 December, to form a government, which he succeeded in doing within 48 hours, despite the refusal of all of Asquith's Liberal ministers to serve under him. In practice, the coalition government which he formed consisted of the leading figures in the Conservative Party (with the exception of Lord Lansdowne), two Labour Party ministers and a 'second eleven' of Liberals, who commanded the support of fewer than half of their fellow Liberal MPs.

Asquith remained leader of the party. In the event, his downfall had been due, not to intrigues by Lloyd George, as his supporters and family continued to claim for many years, but to his own indecision and miscalculation. His greatest mistake had been to lose the confidence of Bonar Law, who played the decisive role in making LG Prime Minister, just as he was to be the key figure in his downfall six years later. Already, in February 1916, he had written a warning letter to Asquith, saying "In war it is necessary not only to be active, but to seem active" (Packer, 1998, p. 48). His personal regard for LG had had to struggle against the deepest suspicions of his motivations. He had told the newspaper proprietor, Sir George (later Lord) Riddell, in 1911: "I like Lloyd George. He is a nice man, but the most dangerous little man that ever lived" (Rowland, 1976, p. 249).

What tipped the balance decisively for him was that he had become convinced that only LG could win the war, a conviction which was shared by Balfour, previously a friend and admirer of Asquith, who regarded it as an act of personal betrayal when he accepted the Foreign Office from Lloyd George. "As you can imagine", his niece reported him as saying, "I have no prejudice in favour of Lloyd George. I have opposed every political principle he holds – but I think he is the only one who can at the moment break down that wall of military red tape and see that the brains of the country are made use of" (Dugdale, 1936, p. 128).

LG's accession to the premiership, at the age of 54, ensured his objective of creating a small executive body, with himself at the head, to prosecute the war effort. A War Cabinet of five, which met daily, was established, consisting of himself, Bonar Law – who became Chancellor of the Exchequer and effectively Deputy Premier – and three ministers without portfolio, Lords Curzon and Milner and Arthur Henderson, the leader of the Labour Party. A Cabinet secretariat, headed by Lord Hankey, was set up, which for the first time ensured that minutes were kept and a note made of whose responsibility it was to carry out particular decisions.

The new arrangements certainly created the impression of a much more focused and effective concentration on the task in hand and Lloyd George himself continued to impress by his energy and passionate commitment, but one expert at least (George Cassar, author of *Asquith as War Leader*) doubts whether the change of leader made much difference to the actual conduct of operations. These remained largely in the hands of the generals – Sir Douglas Haig, the Commander-in-Chief in France, and Sir William Robertson, the Chief of the Imperial General Staff. LG's wartime premiership was dominated by an increasingly bitter and frustrating struggle between the Prime Minister and the two leading commanders. He was unable to replace them, because of the support they received from the King and from the Tory leaders, while they successfully blocked his efforts to divert men and resources from France to other theatres of operations – variously in Serbia, Greece, Italy, Romania, Russia and the Near East – where he was continually seeking, in vain, the 'knock-out blow' which he believed would bring Germany and her allies to their knees.

Lloyd George had been determined to avoid a repeat of the appalling blood-letting of the 1916 Somme offensive, but, with deep reluctance, agreed to Haig's confident proposal for a heavy offensive in July 1917 whose purpose was to over-run the German U-boat bases on the Channel coast. This attack, which developed into the third battle of Ypres, ended at Paaschendaele in November 1917. In the words of his private secretary, Thomas Jones, it "entailed terrible casualties, having gained no strategic advantage" (*DNB 1941–50*, p. 521).

The Western Front then degenerated into a war of attrition with no likelihood of any resolution until the slow build-up of American forces (which followed the US entry into the war in April 1917) gave the allies a decisive numerical advantage. Before this could happen, however, the collapse of Russia, and the acceptance of humiliating peace terms by the Bolshevik government, gave the Germans the opportunity – which they took to only a limited extent – of a massive reinforcement of their own forces. The result was Ludendorff's last fling offensive of March 1918, which only narrowly failed to achieve a decisive breakthrough. He could not capture Paris, but he almost brought down Lloyd George.

By April 1918, LG had at last succeeded in curbing the authority of Robertson and Haig. The former had been outmanoeuvred into resigning as Chief of the Imperial General Staff, and was replaced by the more amenable Sir Henry Wilson, while the latter was subordinated to the French Marshal, Ferdinand Foch, who became Commander-in-Chief of all the allied forces in France.

Yet LG now faced charges that he had deliberately starved Haig of reinforcements after Paaschendaele, and that this had increased the danger from Ludendorff's attack, leading to heavy British casualties. A parliamentary challenge – led by Asquith – was mounted on the basis of accusations made in the press by General Sir Frederick Maurice, former head of Military Intelligence. Lloyd George dominated the debate with a rumbustious speech in

50 David Lloyd George

which, with the aid of a barrage of statistics (which were later shown to be dubious, though it is uncertain whether LG was aware of this), he comprehensively refuted Maurice's accusations and swept the floor with the opposition. Asquith, however, unwisely maintained his demand for a select committee and divided the House. In the division, which the government won by 293 votes to 106, 98 Liberals voted against the government, while only 71 supported Lloyd George. This was to have dire consequences for the future of the Liberal Party.

The war ended six months later, and LG came to be known, with no show of reluctance on his part, as 'the Man Who Won the War'. It would, perhaps, be more accurate to describe him as the man who ensured that there would be no negotiated peace – either before or after America's entry into the war. It was his determination to go on to the bitter end – whatever the cost – that carried the greater part of the nation with him. As we have seen, he was unable to have much direct influence on the conduct of military operations. His main contribution was in mobilising the economy to meet the demands of total war, and it is certainly arguable that he had, in fact, already achieved this during his period as Minister for Munitions, and that this feat actually exceeded anything he did as Prime Minister.

During the last summer of the war, LG was much exercised about how he could continue his premiership into peacetime, and ensure victory at the general election which could not be long delayed. One possibility was to re-unite the Liberal Party and resume his partnership with Asquith, though with himself in the senior position. This plan was stymied by Asquith's firm refusal to go to the Upper House as Lord Chancellor. After toying with the idea, to which he was to return some years later, of creating his own 'centre party', LG concluded that his best bet would be to do a deal with Bonar Law under which the Conservatives and his own Liberal coalition supporters would fight the election together. Under an agreement negotiated by his Chief Whip, the Tories agreed to give a free run to 150 coalition Liberals, as well as a few Labour dissidents, in exchange for an endorsement from Lloyd George for their candidates in the remaining seats. The problem for LG was how to select the 150 individuals to whom the coalition 'coupon' would be sent, and he resolved this by denying the coupon to all the Liberals, including Asquith, who had voted against the government in the Maurice debate.

The plan worked out well – much too well for LG's long-term interest. In the December 1918 election the government won 478 seats out of an effective House of 634 (73 Sinn Fein MPs declining to take their seats). Yet of the 478, only 133 were Liberals, and 10 coalition Labour. The rest were all Tories, who by themselves commanded an absolute majority in the Commons, and to whom Lloyd George was now effectively a prisoner. It was, in reality, only a matter of time for the Tories to gain the self-confidence to ditch him and seize undiluted power for themselves.

Privately, LG realised that he had overdone it, and was distressed when the results showed that the independent Liberals were decimated, holding on to a mere 28 seats, with Asquith himself among the list of prominent losers. The Labour Party, with 63 seats, became the official opposition for the first time. "This is not what I intended at all", he said to Frances Stevenson (Frances Lloyd George, 1967). Publicly, however, he gloried in the sweeping electoral victory, and his national prestige was at its apex as he left for the Versailles Peace Conference.

Here he was part of the dominant trio made up of himself, Woodrow Wilson and Georges Clemenceau, and his approach was pitched midway between the high-minded idealism of the former and the chauvinistic vindictiveness of the latter. While determined to secure what he regarded as British interests, such as the acquisition of former German colonies in Africa and mandates for Palestine and Transjordan, he attempted, with little success, to moderate the harsh conditions imposed on the defeated Germans. He must share the responsibility for the terms finally agreed, including the quite unrealistic demands for punitive reparations which left Germany humiliated and bitterly resentful, undoubtedly playing a part in paving the way for Hitler's rise to power. LG himself was uneasily aware of what he had done, and felt chastened by the accusations made by J.M. Keynes, who resigned from the British delegation and subsequently wrote the Cassandra-like tirade, *The Economic Consequences of the Peace.*

If, at Versailles, he too often allowed his good intentions to be overridden by Clemenceau, a similar pattern soon appeared in domestic affairs, where he had to give more and more ground to the dominant Tory element in his coalition. This was seen most evidently in industrial policy, where his formerly good relations with the trade union movement were subjected to constant erosion, as the government consistently sided with the employers in a rash of disputes, while unemployment steadily mounted. Nor did the government live up to the high hopes raised by Lloyd George's election speech at Wolverhampton in November 1918 when he promised "to make Britain a fit country for heroes to live in". Its legislative programme did contain a number of important social measures, notably Christopher Addison's Housing Act of 1919. This enabled local councils to build good quality housing at low, controlled rents, the government making up the shortfall with subsidies. In the long term, this was a highly beneficial measure, leading to a substantial improvement, on a very large scale, of working-class housing standards, but Lloyd George took fright when the cost of the measure looked like getting out of hand, and – in the face of insistent Tory demands – forced Addison's resignation. Like many other left-wing Liberals at the time, the latter soon found a new home in the Labour Party. The housing programme, as well as other social reform measures, including notably the projected raising of the school-leaving age, was a casualty of the swingeing cuts in public expenditure, known as "the Geddes axe", which were implemented in 1922. Perhaps not entirely fairly, LG's peacetime government has been widely judged as among the most reactionary of the 20th century. What was undeniable was that the Prime Minister, who pre-war had been the great hope of the left, was now regarded as being on the right.

The one big achievement of Lloyd George as a peacetime Prime Minister was the (partial and temporary) solution of the Irish problem, resulting in partition and the creation of the Irish Free State. This was the outcome of a masterly negotiation which LG concluded with the Sinn Fein leaders, Michael Collins and Arthur Griffiths, when, against all expectation, he cajoled them into accepting self-rule for only a part of their country. It was a bold move, but it brought little credit to Lloyd George. Most of his Tory ministers, and even more of their MPs, were highly reluctant to see independence ceded to southern Ireland, while he had already disgusted most Labour and Liberal opinion by his earlier repressive policies in Ireland and his tolerance of 'Black and Tan' atrocities.

In late 1919, LG returned to his earlier project of creating a new 'centre party' which he hoped would embrace all but the extreme left and the reactionary right. He found few serious takers, and instead proposed a fusion between the two coalition partners. With great reluctance, Bonar Law and his colleagues agreed to a merger with the coalition Liberals, who then – with a rare show of independence and to LG's surprise and chagrin – turned the proposal down in March 1920. They were unwilling to surrender their principles on free trade and wanted to leave the door open for an eventual reunion with the Asquithians. Only Churchill, who was in any event to defect to the Tories within a couple of years, showed any enthusiasm for the proposed merger.

52 David Lloyd George

Lloyd George's position was now more vulnerable than ever, and it was further undermined, in March 1921, when Bonar Law resigned through ill health. His successor as Tory leader, Austen Chamberlain, was at least equally in awe of Lloyd George and loyal to him, but he had a far weaker control over his own party, which was becoming increasingly restless. LG, however, comforted himself with the thought that he still held one trump card. This was the Lloyd George Fund, a treasure chest of perhaps as much as £3 million, built up through the sale of honours. Such methods had been used by both Tory and Liberal governments in the past to augment their party funds, and they continued subsequently at least until the Thatcher–Major era. Where Lloyd George differed was in the scale of the operation and the brazen way in which it was conducted, and because the money did not go directly to a political party but to a private fund entirely controlled by himself.

In the end the fund did him no good. It was the source of constant innuendo, and when – after 1923 – the Liberal reunion did in fact take place, it was a major source of dissension. LG refused to transfer the fund to the Liberal Party, only doling out occasional contributions for projects which he personally approved and refusing to release a substantial amount for the 1924 election campaign, which would have enabled the Liberals to put up many more candidates. At the same time, the party was inhibited from making strenuous fund-raising efforts on its own account by the widespread knowledge that its most famous figure was sitting on so large a nest-egg.

Despite his growing isolation, Lloyd George made little effort to ingratiate himself with his Cabinet colleagues. He became more and more dictatorial, seldom consulting the full Cabinet about important decisions and being gratuitously rude to such senior figures as Churchill, Curzon and Milner. The extraordinary charm, which had become a byword, was now in distinctly short supply. Below Cabinet level, his credit with the Tories was now dangerously low, and it only required a *casus belli* and an alternative leader, to trigger a revolt.

This eventually came, not over a domestic issue, but foreign affairs, which had remained LG's main preoccupation long after the Versailles Treaty had been concluded. Both of his fellow triumvirs – Wilson and Clemenceau – had fallen from power, and Lloyd George was able to monopolise the international limelight. He was feted wherever he went – perhaps blinding him to his loss of popularity in his own country. Much of his time was spent preparing and participating in a series of international gatherings, some of which were intended – though with little success – to undo the worst consequences of Versailles.

LG was especially interested in the welfare of Greece, another small nation which attracted his instinctive sympathy. He unwisely skewed British foreign policy in favour of the Greeks in their post-war dispute with Turkey, encouraging their army to invade the Turkish mainland in the hope of seizing as much territory as possible in the wake of the disintegration of the Ottoman Empire. All went well for them initially, but in August 1922 Mustafa Kemal (later known as Atatürk) rallied the Turkish troops, who broke through the Greek lines, captured and sacked Smyrna and drove the Greek remnant into the sea. There was now nothing to stop the Turks from advancing on Constantinople, apart from a tiny British garrison guarding the Dardanelles, at Chanak. Lloyd George – backed by an ever-belligerent Churchill – telegraphed the British commander, General Harington, to deliver an ultimatum to the Turks to withdraw their forces or his own troops would attack. At the same time he appealed to France and Italy, and the British Dominions, for military support, an appeal which met with no response.

A military disaster was averted by Harington, who ignored LG's telegram and quietly negotiated a ceasefire with the Turks. Lloyd George's rash action was unanimously condemned by the press, and ominously for him, *The Times* published a letter from Bonar Law, now apparently restored to full health, adding his own weighty criticism. This was widely interpreted as a signal that he was ready and willing to take over the premiership if the opportunity arose.

He did not have to wait long. On 17 September, at a meeting at Chequers, the leading members of the government had agreed that a general election should be held, which the coalition parties would fight in tandem. There were immediate ructions within the Conservative Party, led by the party chairman, Sir George Younger, who wanted the Tories to conduct their own campaign. In an attempt to squash this challenge to his own authority, the Tory leader, Austen Chamberlain, summoned a meeting of all Tory MPs at the Carlton Club on 19 October.

At this meeting, despite the fact that most of the leading Conservative ministers – apart from Curzon, whose patience in the face of LG's repeated snubs had finally cracked – wanted the coalition to continue, it was decided by 187 votes to 87 that the Conservative Party should fight the election with its own leaders and its own programme. In the debate, the most dramatic intervention had come from the previously little known Stanley Baldwin, who had recently been promoted to President of the Board of Trade. "He is a dynamic force", he said of LG,

> and it is from this very fact that our troubles, in our opinion, arose … It is owing to that dynamic force and that remarkable personality, that the Liberal Party, to which he formerly belonged, has been smashed to pieces; and it is my firm conviction that, in time, the same thing will happen to our own party.
>
> *(Middlemas and Barnes, 1969, p. 123)*

Yet it was Bonar Law's speech, hesitant and fumbling as it was, which swayed the greater number of votes, as he eventually made it clear that he believed that the coalition should come to an end.

Within hours the Conservative ministers had resigned, and at five o'clock LG drove to Buckingham Palace to tender his own resignation to George V, who immediately summoned Bonar Law to take his place. LG and his Liberal and Conservative supporters were not unduly downcast, being confident that Bonar Law would be unable to win an independent Conservative majority at the general election, and that they themselves would soon be back in office – an outcome which Bonar Law himself half anticipated. In the event, it was not to be – the general election on 15 November 1922 produced a Tory majority of 75. Lloyd George's supporters, known as National Liberals, were reduced to 62 seats, the Asquithians won 54, while the Labour Party shot up to 142, and was now clearly the second party in the land.

At the age of 59 – still at the height of his powers – LG's political career was effectively over, though a sad coda was to continue for another two decades, during which he repeatedly attempted, with much ingenuity but little consistency, to lever himself back into power. That he failed was mainly due to his lack of a firm party base, for which he himself was primarily responsible, but also because he had lost that essential basis of trust upon which all successful politicians must depend.

Lloyd George was probably the most gifted of all the Prime Ministers of the 20th century, and he perhaps had a greater influence on people's lives than any other politician. His introduction of old age pensions and of National Insurance paved the way for the more comprehensive welfare state measures of the Attlee government, his 'People's Budget' led to the curbing of the powers of the House of Lords, while his institution of a Cabinet secretariat brought order to government decision-making. His determination in the First World War to seek victory at whatever cost had incalculable consequences not only for his own country but for the whole world. With the benefit of hindsight, one may assert with confidence that it would have been far better if he had applied his energy and ingenuity to seeking a negotiated peace, as was urged by President Wilson and by Lord Lansdowne in the stalemate which had been reached in 1916–17, instead of pursuing the struggle to the bitter end. Had he done so he would have been more worthy of the gratitude of succeeding generations, though he would not have achieved the enormous – if short-lived – popularity that he enjoyed as 'the Man Who Won the War'.

Great as were LG's achievements, the abiding impression which one gains from a study of his life is the potential which remained unfulfilled. For he was brought down – or perhaps self-destroyed – at the height of his powers. This could be attributed to his crass under-estimate of the importance of retaining a sound base of party support, but over and above this was the accumulated effect which his opportunism, demagogy, duplicity and cutting of corners – his failure to follow the rules – had on colleagues whose support he needed. In the end – as his brother William hinted – the inflated self-confidence which he imbibed from 'Uncle Lloyd' proved to be the source of his own destruction.

Works consulted

G.H. Cassar, 1994, *Asquith as War Leader*, London, Hambledon Press.
Blanche Dugdale, 1936, *Arthur James Balfour, First Earl of Balfour*, 2 vols, London, Hutchinson.
William George, 1958, *My Brother and I*, London, Eyre & Spottiswoode.
John Grigg, 1973, *The Young Lloyd George*, London, Methuen.
John Grigg, 1978, *Lloyd George: The People's Champion, 1902–1911*, London, Methuen.
John Grigg, 1985, *Lloyd George: From Peace to War, 1912–1916*, London, Methuen.
Cameron Hazelhurst, *Politicians at War, July 1914 to May 1915*, London, Jonathan Cape, 1971.
Thomas Jones, article in *Dictionary of National Biography, 1941–1950 Supplement*.
Frances Lloyd George, 1967, *The Years That Are Past*, London, Hutchinson.
Richard Lloyd George, 1960, Lloyd George, London, Muller.
Keith Middlemas and John Barnes, 1969, *Baldwin: A Biography*, London, Weidenfeld & Nicolson.
Ian Packer, 1998, *Lloyd George*, London, Palgrave Macmillan.
Peter Rowland, 1976, *Lloyd George*, London, Barrie & Jenkins.
Chris Wrigley, 1992, *Lloyd George*, Oxford, Blackwell.

5

ANDREW BONAR LAW

Tory puritan

Andrew Bonar Law has had the misfortune to be remembered – if at all – as "the Unknown Prime Minister". This was partly due to the brevity of his premiership – a mere 209 days – the shortest in modern times, but rather more to a *bon mot* attributed to Asquith, who attended his funeral in Westminster Abbey. The former Liberal Prime Minister, who had treated Law with disdain throughout his lifetime, was heard to remark how fitting it was "that we should have buried the Unknown Prime Minister by the side of the Unknown Soldier". This misfortune was compounded by Lord Blake, who chose it as the title of his highly praised biography (Robert Blake, *The Unknown Prime Minister*, 1955).

Law was a much more considerable figure than this epithet would suggest, leading the Conservative Party for ten years, playing a major role in World War I and being responsible, as we saw in the previous chapter, for both the rise and fall of Lloyd George's premiership. He might, just as appropriately, be recalled as the only Prime Minister to have been born abroad, as the first Presbyterian to hold the office, the first businessman, or even, as Roy Jenkins has suggested, the first "ordinary man".

Bonar Law was born on 16 September 1858 in Kingston, New Brunswick, a small town later renamed Rexton. His father, the Rev. James Law, was a Northern Irish Presbyterian minister, who spent 32 years ministering to his small, mainly Scottish immigrant, flock in what his son seems to have regarded in retrospect as a benighted Canadian backwater, before retiring to spend his last five years back in his native Ulster. The Rev. Law was a loving father, but a manic depressive given to long periods of gloomy introspection punctuated by bursts of religious mania, and his household could hardly have been more austere. This was compounded by the death, at the age of 36, of his wife, Elizabeth Kidston, leaving five small children, of whom the youngest, Andrew, was only 2. It was she who had chosen Bonar as his second name, it having been the surname of another Presbyterian minister who had written a book about an eminent divine whom she much admired.

Throughout his life he was known as Bonar Law, and his family and few intimates addressed him as Bonar, but unlike Lloyd George he made no attempt to turn this into a hybrid surname for his family, and all his children were called plain Law. On the death of his mother, her spinster sister, Janet Kidston, came out to Canada from Glasgow, to keep house

DOI: 10.4324/9781003031963-6

for her brother-in-law and help bring up the children, four boys and a girl. This arrangement lasted for nine years, but – following the remarriage of the Rev. Law and his starting a new family – Janet returned to Scotland, taking the now 12-year-old with her to live near her wealthy cousins in Helensburgh, a prosperous town on the Clyde, 20 miles from Glasgow. James Law appears to have concluded that his youngest son would have better prospects in life in Scotland, and agreed to let him go.

The milieu that Bonar entered in Helensburgh resembled his father's in several respects, notably strict Presbyterian beliefs and austere personal habits and tastes. Yet it differed in one important detail, that it was underpinned by very substantial wealth, which must have been an eye-opener to a penurious pastor's son. Bonar lived in his Aunt Janet's house, but nearby were two much grander mansions where four of his cousins – all well into middle age – lived. There were three brothers – Charles, Richard and William Kidston – who were partners in a firm of merchant bankers, and their sister Catherine. Only Charles was married, and he had no children, and it was not long before Bonar came to be seen as the heir that none of them had been able, or had bothered, to produce. Apart from material prosperity, Bonar owed another legacy to his cousins. Unlike the majority of the Scottish upper middle class at that time, they were staunch supporters of the Conservative and Unionist cause.

The Kidstons were kind to Bonar, but this was an inadequate substitute for the loving relationship with parents and siblings which he had been denied. He early learnt to be self-sufficient, and somewhat introverted, and appeared to have inherited a certain melancholy streak from his father. He got very little joy out of the normal pleasures of life, either then or later. A lifetime teetotaller, he had no interest in food, no appreciation of landscape or physical beauty, nor of music or the theatre, and a horror of social entertaining. He became, however, a voracious smoker, especially of cigars, a life-destroying habit which almost certainly contributed to his death from cancer at the age of 65. His enjoyment came mainly from indoor games – chess, at which he became a strong amateur player, bridge and billiards – and from tennis and golf which he played throughout his adult life.

He was sent to a boarding school at Hamilton, but at 14 was enrolled at Glasgow High School, where Campbell-Bannerman had been educated a generation earlier. He was a good, but not outstanding pupil, who was chiefly remembered for his extraordinarily good memory. No thought seems to have been given to his receiving a university education, though this could easily have been afforded, and at the age of 16 Bonar left school to join the family firm, travelling every day by commuter train from Helensburgh to Glasgow.

The Kidstons' merchant bank was mainly concerned with providing finance for the iron and steel industry. Joining the firm as a clerk, Law's work did little to expand his intellectual horizons, but he applied himself with assiduity, working long hours and quickly mastering all the details of his trade. After a few years, however, the work became less demanding, leaving him more leisure time in which to develop his own interests. He attended extra-mural lectures at Glasgow University, but most significantly became an extremely active member of the Glasgow Parliamentary Association, which ran a 'mock parliament' on a very elaborate scale. The experience, which continued for several years, was invaluable to Law, in teaching him the elements of public speaking, as well as the essentials of parliamentary procedure. Law was far from being an eloquent speaker, either then or later, but he impressed by his mastery of detail, and by the fact that his prodigious memory, and careful preparation, allowed him to speak without notes. This gave an enormous boost to his self-confidence, and implanted in him an ambition which was nevertheless to lie dormant for a great number of years.

This was because Law, extremely cautious by nature, was determined not to embark upon a political career until such time that he had established a firm, and independent, financial base. He continued to work for the Kidstons for 11 years, to their complete satisfaction, and in the normal course of events could have looked forward to eventually succeeding them in the direction of the bank. By 1885, however, their energies were waning fast, and they responded favourably to an approach from the much larger Clydeside Bank, proposing a merger. This might well have blocked Law's progress in the firm, but a lucky chance gave him an autonomous opportunity to advance in the business world.

During the 50-minute train journeys between Helensburgh and Glasgow, Law almost invariably passed the time by playing chess with fellow passengers, one of whom was a Helensburgh neighbour, Williams Jacks, a Glasgow iron trader who was anxious to cut down his business commitments upon his election as Liberal MP for Leith. He offered Law a junior partnership in his firm, for which he would have to contribute a capital sum of £7,500, perhaps equivalent to £400,000 today. Very tentatively, he approached his cousins to enquire whether they would be willing to advance the money, which they were more than happy to do.

Law then effectively took over the management of William Jacks and Co., and became a leading trader on the Glasgow Royal Exchange, participating "in two hectic daily sessions of two hours each which witnessed the exchange of millions of pounds weekly" (Adams, 1999, p. 13). With his quick reactions, mathematical abilities and cool judgement, Law became one of the most effective operators on the Exchange, while simultaneously acquiring a reputation for straight dealing. The firm's profits, and his own income, soared, and he was offered a clutch of non-executive directorships of other firms, including eventually the Clydeside Bank.

By the age of 30, Law felt able to establish his own bachelor household, inviting his unmarried sister Mary to keep house for him. Three years later, in March 1891, he married Annie Pitcairn Robley, aged 25, the daughter of a prosperous Glasgow merchant. It was undoubtedly a love match, and they went on to have six children over the next 14 years, four sons and two daughters.

Law subsequently received two legacies, worth in total £60,000 (over £3 million in current values), from the Kidston family, but it was not until he was 42 that he finally embarked on his political career. He was elected as Conservative MP for Glasgow, Blackfriars and Hutchesontown in the 1900 general election. It had been a Liberal seat, and when he was adopted as the prospective candidate two years earlier it had not seemed a likely prospect, but a split in the Liberal vote, following the sitting Member's rejection of Home Rule, together with the jingoistic sentiments unleashed by the Boer War, combined to give the seat to Bonar Law.

Law's first appearance in Parliament failed to cause a great stir. His maiden speech was totally overshadowed by that of Winston Churchill, made on the same day. Yet before very long he had secured a niche for himself as one of the very few Tory MPs with a practical knowledge of business and economics, at a time when the great majority of his colleagues were country squires or professional men. He was regarded as a pedestrian but knowledgeable speaker, who was able to discuss business affairs in a common-sense fashion, backed up with a wealth of detail. He did not have to wait long for his first appointment. Eighteen months after his election, in July 1902, Lord Salisbury resigned as Prime Minister to be succeeded by his nephew, Arthur Balfour, who immediately offered Law the post of Parliamentary Secretary to the Board of Trade.

Law proved to be an extremely competent if unflashy junior minister and, in particular, impressed the Colonial Secretary, Joe Chamberlain, who, following him in a debate, described his contribution as "one of the most admirable speeches, short though it was, to which I have ever listened in the House of Commons". This must have been especially encouraging to Law, who regarded Chamberlain as his political hero. When Chamberlain launched his campaign for Tariff Reform a year later, Law was among his most outspoken supporters, though unlike him he remained in the government, as did Chamberlain's own son Austen, with his father's approval.

Law continued as Parliamentary Secretary until the resignation of the Balfour government in November 1905, but both before and after this date became much in demand as a speaker in the country on Tariff Reform, the advantages of Imperial Preference and the fallacies of free trade. Indeed, following Chamberlain's debilitating stroke in July 1906, which terminated his active political career, Law was seen, together with Austen, as the number one advocate of Tariff Reform.

Before then Law had suffered a setback, through the loss of his seat – together with those of Balfour and 175 other Tory MPs – in the general election of January 1906. He did not, however, have to wait long to get back into the House. A vacancy was created for him, at Dulwich, and he was duly returned in a by-election in May 1906.

In May 1909 calamity struck Bonar Law, with the death of his wife, aged 43, following a gall-bladder operation. Law was devastated, and a large part of the little joy that he had allowed to enter into his life was extinguished, never to return. Subsequently, there was no record of Law showing any interest whatever in any other woman, and he certainly never contemplated remarriage. Instead, in an echo of his Aunt Janet taking over his father's household in the aftermath of his mother's early death, his elder sister, Mary, moved in, taking charge of his six children and becoming his closest confidante and adviser.

The void in his life was partly filled by an extraordinary friendship which he formed with a young Canadian businessman and self-made millionaire, Maxwell Aitken. He had first presented himself to Law, as a fellow migrant from New Brunswick and the son of a Presbyterian minister, with an investment proposition, from which Law was able to profit, but the relationship soon took on a far broader dimension. Twenty years his junior, Aitken (later the press magnate, Lord Beaverbrook) was everything which Bonar Law was not: brash, indiscreet, self-indulgent, mischief-making, witty and full of vitality. In a very short period of time, he became Law's principal counsellor, cheerleader and companion, a development not to the liking of Mary Law, who, confronting her brother, declared: "I don't like the growing influence of Max Aitken here". The lonely Bonar Law plaintively replied: "Do let me like him", which melted her Calvinist heart and stilled for ever the resentment she felt against the threatened intruder (Beaverbrook, 1928, 1932, Vol. I, p. 59).

Aitken soon benefited from the relationship, as Bonar Law used his influence to secure him a Tory seat in the December 1910 election, but he more than repaid the debt by the generous and consistent support which he unceasingly gave to Law throughout the rest of his life. The December 1910 election proved to be a hiccup in Bonar Law's own career as, responding to an appeal from Tariff Reform supporters in Lancashire, he abandoned his Dulwich seat to contest the marginal Liberal constituency of North-West Manchester. He was unsuccessful, but this did him no harm, as he was compensated with the then safe Tory seat of Bootle, for which he was returned in a by-election in March 1911.

Eight months later, Balfour, exhausted by the prolonged struggle over the House of Lords and discouraged by the severe criticism to which he had been subjected by die-hard Tory peers and MPs over his eventual acquiescence in the passage of the Parliament Act, resigned as party leader. The Tories, for the first time ever, were faced with an open contest for the succession, which, moreover, threatened to be a bloody one. The two leading candidates – Austen Chamberlain, a former Chancellor of the Exchequer, and Walter Long, former Irish Secretary – appealed to different sections of the party. Chamberlain, son and heir to the famous Joseph, represented the more urban and liberal elements, was a strong tariff reformer and, perhaps surprisingly, was a die-hard over Lords reform. Long, a country squire *par excellence*, was a more traditional Tory, of limited intelligence but regarded as a great character, and was lukewarm on Tariff Reform and an opponent of the die-hards. The personal relations between the two men were far from good, and those between their supporters positively hostile.

Nevertheless, it was believed that getting on for 90 per cent of Tory MPs were committed to one or other of them, and the prospects for a third candidate appeared bleak. This did not deter Aitken, who vigorously began canvassing on behalf of Law, who only finally decided to stand five days before the expected ballot. He had no great expectation of success, and his motivation appeared to be to put a marker down for the future.

He reckoned without the characters of Chamberlain and Long, neither of whom possessed the single-minded ambition which is often necessary to get to the top of what Disraeli described as "the greasy pole". In reality, each was more determined to deprive his rival of the crown rather than to claim it for himself, and when Chamberlain, fearing defeat, offered to withdraw in favour of Law if his opponent would do the same, Long, who harboured personal doubts as to his fitness for the leadership, readily agreed. So it was that when the scheduled meeting took place at the Carlton Club on 13 November 1911, Walter Long duly proposed Bonar Law's candidature, which was seconded by Austen Chamberlain. He was unanimously elected, and was astonished at the warmth and extent of the applause, so relieved were the mass of Tory MPs to have avoided a divisive contest.

Law had no illusions, however, that – with his relative lack of seniority and experience – he would not face severe difficulties in leading his party, and he felt genuine diffidence about the challenge which lay ahead. When Aitken sought to boost him by saying: "You are a great man now. You must talk like a great man, behave like a great man", his response was, "If I am a great man, then a good many great men must have been frauds." He resolved to consolidate his leadership by giving his parliamentary supporters what they most wanted: bitter and unrelenting opposition to the Asquith government and all its works. He was as good as his word, and by most standards the opposition which he led over the next three years was as partisan and uncompromising as at any period in British parliamentary history.

Law gave due notice to Asquith of what to expect. Walking back with him to the Commons after listening to the King's Speech in the Lords, opening the 1911–12 session, he said: "I'm afraid I shall have to show myself very vicious this session, Mr Asquith, I hope you will understand." To a large extent, Bonar Law's excessive partisanship was out of character. A man of little imagination, his approach to most issues was careful, calculating and commonsensical and he seldom allowed himself to get hot under the collar. Much later he told Austen Chamberlain that the only issues he cared intensely about were "Tariff reform and Ulster; all the rest was only part of the game" (Blake, 1955, p. 96).

Unfortunately, it was Ulster which became the most hotly contested political issue in the three years leading up to the outbreak of war. The Asquith government, at the behest of its Irish nationalist allies to whom it now owed its parliamentary majority, introduced the third Home Rule Bill, and was determined to force it through under the Parliament Act over the opposition of Tory peers. Bonar Law was less hostile in principle to Home Rule than many other Tories, notably Lord Lansdowne, the Tory leader in the Lords, who owned extensive estates in southern Ireland. On Ulster, however, he was adamant: it must be excluded from "the imposition of a tyranny", i.e. rule by a Dublin Parliament.

His feeling towards the Protestants of Northern Ireland can only be described as 'tribal'. He had never lived there, but knew the province well, as he had travelled there from Scotland almost every weekend for the last five years of his father's life, to visit him in his retirement. He identified completely with the Ulster cause, and went well beyond the constitutional duty of a leader of the opposition in encouraging armed resistance by the Ulster Volunteer Force organised by Sir Edward Carson. In July 1913, he sent a message to an Orange demonstration saying, "Whatever steps they might feel compelled to take, whether they were constitutional, or whether in the long run they were unconstitutional, they had the whole of the Unionist Party under his leadership behind them." He seriously contemplated using the Tory majority in the Lords to reject the annual Army Act and thus, in Roy Jenkins's words, "deprive the government (and the state) for two years of the use of any military power" (Jenkins, 1998, p. 218). Dining with George V at Buckingham Palace, he tried to persuade the King to refuse the royal assent to the Home Rule Bill if it was passed under the Parliament Act, and thus attempt to apply a royal veto for the first time in 200 years. "I think I have given the King the worst five minutes that he has had for a long time", he told Austen Chamberlain afterwards.

As the crisis deepened, Bonar Law somewhat reluctantly met with Asquith to seek a compromise solution, but he refused to contemplate the only formula which had a real prospect of being accepted by the Liberals, and more crucially, the Irish National Party. This was the so-called 'Home Rule within Home Rule' scenario, under which Ulster would have its own Parliament, which would, however, be subordinate to that in Dublin. Law was adamant that the total exclusion of Ulster – or at least the predominantly Protestant counties – was the only outcome that he would accept. By July 1914 total deadlock was reached, with the imminent threat of civil war. Both Asquith and Bonar Law were saved from the immediate consequences of their intransigence by the onset of a much wider war following the assassination in Sarajevo.

The outbreak of the war transformed Law from being a narrowly partisan leader to a statesman who put what he perceived to be the national interest before anything else. In a trice, his Ulster particularism was transmuted into a larger patriotism embracing the whole country and indeed the entire British Empire. Convinced that Britain should intervene on the French side, even before the German invasion of Belgium, he at once offered unconditional support to the Asquith government, and over the next nine months soft-pedalled any parliamentary opposition, despite growing Conservative concern at the conduct of the war effort. When the first wartime coalition government was formed in May 1915, he meekly acquiesced in his appointment as Colonial Secretary, even though he could and should have demanded a more major post, such as Chancellor of the Exchequer.

It is possible that his modesty on this occasion was affected by his acute embarrassment at the projected prosecution of his old firm, William Jacks & Co., for trading with the enemy. He had severed any executive connection with the firm when he was first elected to the House of Commons, but his brother John was still a partner, and Bonar Law resolved to withdraw altogether from public life if his brother was convicted. In the event, John Law was not implicated in the case – which was concerned with the failure of the firm to take sufficiently energetic steps to prevent a shipment of iron ore, already in transit from Canada to Amsterdam in early August 1914, from reaching its final destination in Germany. Two of the other partners in the firm were charged for what was, in reality, only a technical offence, and received short terms of imprisonment.

Although largely marginalised as Colonial Secretary, Law gradually emerged as one of the most influential members of the Cabinet. He was slow to make up his mind, and – initially at least – diffident in expressing his opinions, but once he had convinced himself about a particular issue he was able to argue his case forcefully and consistently. This was most clearly seen over the endless discussions on whether, and when, to bring the costly and abortive Dardanelles expedition to an end. Law eventually forced the issue by threatening to resign if the troops were not withdrawn – an operation which was then carried out without a hitch and with hardly any casualties, despite the harrowing predictions of his senior Tory colleague, Lord Curzon. A comment made at the time by a Liberal minister helps to explain the respect in which he was held by his Cabinet colleagues: "Lloyd George is always threatening to resign and we don't believe him. Bonar Law said he would resign and we knew he would" (Beaverbrook, 1928, 1932, Vol. I, p. 171).

One colleague who did not share this respect was Asquith, whose Balliol-bred snobbery prevented him from assessing this relatively poorly educated Glasgow iron trader at his true worth. He repeatedly snubbed him, and once complained to Lloyd George, "He has not the brains of a Glasgow baillie". By contrast, Law had perhaps exaggerated respect for Asquith, whom he regarded with awe. He had no greater desire than to serve him loyally, and his eventual disillusionment came only slowly and reluctantly. One turning point came in June 1916, when Law needed to see Asquith to discuss a matter of the highest urgency, and learning that he intended to extend his customary weekend in the country into Monday or beyond, motored down the 50 miles from London to Berkshire early on the Monday morning. He was shocked to find the Prime Minister playing a game of bridge with three ladies, and in no hurry to break off to discuss matters of state. (The veracity of this story, which appeared in Blake's biography in 1955, was challenged by Asquith's loyal daughter, Lady Violet Bonham Carter, in an angry letter to *The Times*. Blake's source, however, was Lord Beaverbrook, who said to his secretary, "You can tell Blake that Bonar Law told me, and he always told the truth" (Adams, 1999, p. 214).)

Despite such episodes, it was no part of Bonar Law's plan to dislodge Asquith from the premiership during the government crisis of December 1916, described in the preceding chapter. Indeed, he regarded Asquith's continuation as essential, and he only submitted his resignation when Asquith had gone back on his earlier agreement to appoint a small war committee under Lloyd George's chairmanship. Law certainly erred by failing to hand over to Asquith a document which made clear that the other Conservative Cabinet ministers were also intending to resign unless Asquith yielded. It is possible that had he done so, Asquith would have again reconsidered his position, but Bonar Law, who was invariably straightforward in his dealings, can be acquitted of any Machiavellian intent. It was sheer inadvertence that during an unpleasant and tense interview, he forgot to produce the document from his suit pocket.

Bonar Law was invited by the King to form a new government, but he declined to do so unless Asquith was prepared to serve under him, which the Liberal leader refused to do. Lloyd George then took over the relay, and it was clear from the outset that he regarded Law as the key member of his new team. Law became Chancellor of the Exchequer, Leader of the House of Commons (the first time ever that this post had been held by anybody but the Prime Minister, except when the Premier was in the Lords), and the only departmental minister included in the small War Cabinet. As Conservative leader, he was consulted on all appointments, and effectively acted as party manager on behalf of the government. Nor was Lloyd George's deference to him purely on account of his party position. He evidently valued his counsel on a personal basis, and virtually every day the Prime Minister started his working day by going through the interconnecting door into 11 Downing Street and embarking on a wide-ranging discussion with his deputy on virtually every issue on the pending agenda (a practice he continued during his peacetime coalition after 1918).

This strange partnership between two very dissimilar personalities was the bedrock on which the Lloyd George premiership rested. Bonar Law was the workhorse of the government, devoting himself without stint to his manifold tasks, a devotion which even increased following the death in action of his two eldest sons in April and September 1917. As with the loss of his wife, eight years earlier, Bonar Law was inconsolable, and his only recourse was to bury himself deeper and deeper in his work. Religion was no help to him, indeed he seems to have got the worst possible bargain from his Presbyterian upbringing. It had deprived him of most normal sources of enjoyment, but failed to bring him any consolation. Law did not believe in the after-life, and after the death of his sons, succumbed to a bleak pessimism, which almost totally extinguished the flame of his once burning ambition.

Bonar Law readily agreed with Lloyd George that the wartime coalition should be continued after the Armistice, and the 'coupon' election of December 1918 delivered an overwhelming majority, of which the Conservatives formed by far the larger part. Bonar Law relinquished the chancellorship, but retained the leadership of the House, and was effectively Deputy Prime Minister, substituting for much of the time for Lloyd George, who was abroad for long periods, both during the Versailles negotiations and afterwards. He continued to be a bulwark of strength for Lloyd George until March 1921, when his health collapsed under the strain, and he resigned from office, seeking rest in the south of France.

In retrospect, this can be seen as the beginning of the end for Lloyd George, as Law's successor, Austen Chamberlain, though equally loyal to the Prime Minister, had far less control over Conservative MPs, whose frustration was reaching a dangerous level. Law's health improved and he returned from France in the autumn in time to give his backing to the Irish treaty negotiated by Lloyd George.

It looked as though Law's career was over, but in October 1922 when Tory MPs rebelled against their leadership's decision to fight another general election under Lloyd George's leadership, they looked to Bonar Law as an alternative party leader. He reluctantly made himself available, having convinced himself that the Tories would be fatally split if they continued their alliance with the Lloyd George Liberals. This event was described in the previous chapter, and the sequel does not require lengthy retelling.

The government which Law formed on 23 October 1922 was singularly devoid of talent. Apart from Curzon and Baldwin, hardly any of the former Cabinet were willing to serve, and he had to make do with an evident second eleven, including an abnormally high number of peers. Nevertheless, on a programme of "tranquillity and stability", he succeeded in obtaining a very comfortable majority of 75 in the election of November 1922. Subsequently, this government was distinguished by only one event, and that was a stinging humiliation for the Prime Minister. Baldwin, who became Chancellor of the Exchequer, was sent to Washington to negotiate on British war debts, and finding a much more hostile reception than he had anticipated, came back with far less generous terms than Britain had been seeking, but nevertheless recommending acceptance on the grounds that this was the best settlement obtainable.

When the Cabinet met, Bonar Law made it clear that he would resign if the terms were accepted, but only one of his colleagues supported his view. The meeting was hastily adjourned overnight, and on the following morning a letter, over the pseudonym 'Colonial', appeared in *The Times*, setting out the same arguments that Law had used in the Cabinet meeting – it subsequently emerged that Law himself had written the letter. Later in the day, in the face of entreaties from all his closest associates, Law climbed down, and at a five-minute meeting of the Cabinet withdrew both his opposition and his resignation threat.

It was, however, virtually the end of his brief premiership. Feeling utterly weary, and suffering from recurrent throat pains, he left on 1 May for a cruise to the Mediterranean and "a complete rest". The cruise did not last long: he left the ship at Genoa, and – joined by Beaverbrook – proceeded to Paris, where he was examined by an eminent doctor, Sir Thomas Horder. Diagnosing cancer of the throat, without actually telling the Prime Minister, Horder advised immediate resignation. Beaverbrook concurred, and later recalled that Law "was almost light-hearted in his relief at the idea of laying down a burden which had been crushing his failing vitality". Bonar Law resigned on 20 May, dying five months later on 30 October 1923. He declined to advise the King on who should be his successor, believing that it would be Lord Curzon, though he probably had a slight preference for Stanley Baldwin (see page 69, below).

Bonar Law was a man of considerable, if narrow, abilities. At the end of his rather sad life, he could certainly claim, with Othello, to "have done the state some service", though rather more to the Conservative Party, whose fortunes he did much to restore.

Works consulted

R.J.Q. Adams, 1999, *Bonar Law*, London, John Murray.
Lord Beaverbrook, 1928, 1932, *Politicians and the War* (2 vols), London, Hutchinson.
Robert Blake, 1955, *The Unknown Prime Minister*, London, Eyre & Spottiswoode.
Lucille Iremonger, 1970, *The Fiery Chariot*, London, Secker & Warburg.
Roy Jenkins, 1998, *The Chancellors*, London, Macmillan.
Thomas Jones, article in *Dictionary of National Biography, 1922–1930*.

6

STANLEY BALDWIN

"A man of the utmost insignificance"?

In June 1883 a Harrow schoolboy was flogged by his headmaster, and his adored father was summoned to the school to be warned of his son's moral wickedness. His offence? He had composed a piece of juvenile pornography and, apparently far worse, had injured the school's reputation by posting a copy to his cousin at Eton.

Fortunately, Stanley Baldwin's father, Alfred, took an indulgent view of his son's peccadillo, despite his own fervent High Church views. The effect on Stanley, however, was unfortunate. Previously, he had stood out as one of the school's brightest pupils, winning a string of prizes, but from that moment on he became demotivated, ceased to strive for academic excellence, and cruised through the remainder of his school career – and much of his subsequent three years at Cambridge – without bothering to exert himself unduly.

He emerged with a Third Class degree, occasioning the uncharacteristically sharp remark from Alfred: "I hope you won't get a third in life". In fact, the young Stanley's failure to live up to his earlier promise had a determining effect on his subsequent career, effectively forcing him to seek to follow in the footsteps of his remarkable father, a businessman and politician, rather than those of his more artistic mother, Louisa, which would have been more in tune with his own inclinations.

Alfred Baldwin came from a long line of Shropshire yeomen who gravitated to the iron trade in the mid-eighteenth century, later setting up a foundry at Stourport-on Severn. Alfred was the youngest of 12 children of George Baldwin, who died eight months before he was born in 1841. It was George who had raised the family fortunes to a high level of affluence, but this was largely dissipated by Alfred's elder brothers who, by 1864, had brought the firm, then known as E.P. and W. Baldwin, to the brink of bankruptcy. In this year, Alfred asserted himself, took over control of the business and within six years succeeded in paying off all the debts and buying out his brothers' interest.

He moved into the ironmaster's house at Wilden, a mile away from Stourport and next door to the company's forge, and gained a reputation as a model employer who treated his workforce effectively as members of an extended family, Stanley, born on 3 August 1867, being his only child. His interests extended well beyond the family firm, and in 1892 he was elected as Conservative MP for the Worcestershire constituency of Bewdley. He became a

DOI: 10.4324/9781003031963-7

highly respected if largely silent backbencher. He also became chairman of the Great Western Railway, one of the four large railway companies before nationalisation.

Alfred Baldwin, high-minded and a largely self-taught scholar as well as practical man of business, was to marry Louisa, one of the five gifted and artistic daughters of a Methodist minister, the Rev. George Browne MacDonald. Three of her sisters were to marry painters – Edward Burne-Jones, Edward Poynter and Lockwood Kipling. The undoubted highlights of Stanley Baldwin's childhood and youth were the times he was able to spend in the company of his lively young cousins on his mother's side, notably the poet, Rudyard Kipling. Louisa herself enjoyed some success as a novelist, ghost-story writer and poet, but for 15 years of her life was confined to a couch suffering from a possibly psychosomatic illness which dated from the time of Stanley's birth.

Alfred and Louisa were affectionate parents, but with a busy father and a semi-invalid mother, the young Stanley was often left to his own devices. His was not, however, an unhappy childhood. A bookish boy, he immersed himself in the novels of Scott, in Malory's *Morte d'Arthur* and *The Pilgrim's Progress*, and he early fell in love with the Worcestershire countryside, taking long walks, the memory of which left a warm glow feeding the over-romantic view of England as a pastoral paradise which characterised many of his later speeches and writings.

Stanley's dreamy, artistic leanings might have led him into a very different career from the one he followed. While at Cambridge, he seriously considered going into the Church, and he had visions of becoming a writer and academic. Yet his poor examination results precluded this, leaving him with no practical alternative to following his father in the family business. Already when leaving Harrow, he had told his headmaster: "I am going first into the family business and then to the House of Commons" (Middlemas and Barnes, 1969, p. 16). And so it was to be – after a long apprenticeship.

An imposing patriarchal figure with a long black beard, Alfred was nevertheless of a highly nervous disposition. A God-fearing man, whose conscience never gave him an easy time, he had a pronounced facial tic. He was worshipped by his son, who remained in awe of him, constantly measuring himself against his father and constantly finding himself wanting.

At the time he left Cambridge, in 1888, his personality remained largely unformed. Outwardly, he appeared relaxed and indolent, universally liked, but not regarded by his fellows as a man of any great consequence. In reality, he was a far more complex and sensitive young man than was apparent on the surface. With no enthusiasm, but with no great show of reluctance, he entered the family business, and set himself conscientiously to master the secrets of the trade. Over the course of the next 20 years, he established himself as a thoroughly reliable but far from dynamic number two to his father, who undoubtedly derived great pleasure from their association. Meanwhile the firm steadily expanded, largely through amalgamations with other steel firms, eventually becoming part of the giant enterprise, Richard Thomas & Baldwins.

For the first four years, Baldwin stayed in the family home, but in 1892, on his marriage at the age of 25 to Lucy Ridsdale, he rented a Georgian house two miles away and cycled each day to the forge. Some years later he moved to a much grander house, Astley Hall, near Stourport, where he lived for the rest of his life. Baldwin had met his wife while staying with his Burne-Jones cousins. The daughter of the Deputy Master of the Royal Mint, she was an extrovert girl, fond of playing games, particularly cricket, of which she was a notable exponent. She proved a loyal and supportive wife, though sharing none of his aesthetic or intellectual tastes nor his love of country walks. Yet she provided companionship and good advice, and bore him four daughters and two sons, the elder of whom later became a rather eccentric Labour MP.

During the 20 years that he worked alongside his father, Baldwin gradually extended his interests, becoming a Justice of the Peace and securing election successively to the parish, rural district and county councils. He early established the custom of taking long holidays, one month each year on winter sports in Switzerland and at least another month touring the continent in the summer. With his growing family, he appeared a thoroughly contented pater-familias, taking part in country pursuits and basking in his reputation as a benevolent employer, more approachable because less formidable in appearance than his equally benevolent father.

If Baldwin was ever dissatisfied at having to play second fiddle to Alfred, he never showed it, and their relations remained excellent, though still somewhat hindered by shyness on both sides. When Baldwin contemplated heavy expenditure on Astley Hall, which he could ill afford, Alfred readily agreed to bear the cost, and then promptly forgot about it, and Stanley was too inhibited to remind him of it. In 1904 Alfred was delighted when Stanley became the prospective Conservative candidate for the neighbouring constituency of Kidderminster, regarded as being a totally safe Tory seat. Yet he was not fated to join his father in the Commons. In the 1906 general election, he was swept away by the Liberal landslide, though his father held on at Bewdley.

Baldwin had not much enjoyed the election campaign, but eagerly accepted an approach from Joseph Chamberlain, who was looking for a replacement for the Tory candidate who had been unseated at the City of Worcester because of corrupt practices. "I thought I was certain to be chosen at once", he later wrote, "and I went before the selection committee holding my head high. And they chose an Irishman who I then thought, and still think, to be vastly my inferior. So I was turned down in my own county town in favour of a stranger and bang went all my hopes" (Middlemas and Barnes, 1969, p. 40).

It seemed unlikely that Baldwin, after these two rebuffs, would ever stir himself again to seek a candidature, but within two years his father died very suddenly, which proved, in his biographers' words, to be "the greatest turning point in Baldwin's life" (Middlemas and Barnes, 1969, p. 41). Two days after the funeral, Baldwin was unanimously selected to replace his father and, as the Liberals decided not to contest the by-election, he was returned unopposed as MP for Bewdley on 29 February 1908, only 16 days after Alfred's death.

Baldwin was now 40 and for the next half dozen years was content to remain an obscure and largely silent backbencher, speaking only five times in his first six years in the House. He was a wealthy man, Vice-chairman of Baldwins Ltd and a director, like his father before him, of the GWR, and seemed entirely to lack political ambition. He was popular with his fellow MPs, was thoroughly 'clubbable' and was regarded as a 'good House of Commons man', content to spend many hours relaxing in the chamber, listening to the speeches of other Members.

His attitude changed perceptibly at the beginning of World War I. Thoroughly patriotic, he was too old to fight, but was acutely conscious that his almost entirely passive parliamentary service was making no contribution whatever to the war effort. He stirred himself to serve on several government committees of inquiry, and joined a ginger group of backbenchers critical of the Asquith government's conduct of the war. Yet by 1916 he was seriously thinking of relinquishing his parliamentary seat and concentrating on his local government responsibilities in Worcestershire. His wife, Lucy, dissuaded him, saying "give it another two years" (Williams, 1965, p. 5).

It was in December 1916 that the second decisive turning point occurred in Baldwin's political life, when Andrew Bonar Law, newly appointed as Chancellor of the Exchequer in the Lloyd George government, invited him to become his Parliamentary Private Secretary (PPS). Perhaps he ought not to have felt flattered; he had apparently been recommended to Law as somebody who, in the opinion of the Conservative Chief Whip, Lord Edmund Talbot, was "discreet enough to be safe and stupid enough not to intrigue" (Williams, 1965, p. 13).

Baldwin then had an extraordinary stroke of luck. A PPS is normally a silent, confidential adviser and general bag-carrier to his minister, but in this case it led to Baldwin's almost immediate translation to the front bench. The number two minister at the Treasury, Sir Hardman Lever, was unable initially to secure a parliamentary seat and was absent for long periods in the United States. With nobody else available to speak as his deputy in the Commons, Law asked Baldwin to substitute and for six months from February 1917 he regularly spoke from the front bench, creating a very good impression on MPs by his courtesy and the assiduity with which he replied to their questions. By July his position was regularised and he was appointed a junior minister with the title of Joint Financial Secretary.

In the December 1918 general election, Baldwin was returned unopposed, and was reappointed as Financial Secretary to the Treasury, now under Austen Chamberlain who took over from Bonar Law as Chancellor. Both of them regarded him as an adequate and agreeable colleague, without any great expectation that he would progress any higher in the ministerial hierarchy. He was, in fact, sounded out about becoming Governor-General, first of South Africa and then of Australia – basically consolation prizes for well regarded politicians not expected to rise to the top – but he declined to be considered, and a suggestion that he might become Speaker of the House of Commons was not followed up.

In June 1919 a remarkable letter appeared in *The Times*, signed F.S.T., though the significance of these initials was not recognised at the time. The writer appealed to the wealthy classes to tax themselves voluntarily to help reduce the burden of the war debts. "I have made as accurate an estimate as I am able of the value of my own estate", he wrote, "and I have arrived at a total of about £580,000. I have decided to realise 20% of that amount or say £120,000 which will purchase £150,000 of the new War Loan, and present it to the Government for cancellation."

Baldwin's self-esteem presumably benefited from his generous gesture, but its effect on the public finances was minimal. His hope that it would lead to a mass of similar donations by, amongst others, "the hard-faced men who looked as though they had done very well out of the war" (his own description of the new Tory MPs elected in 1918) was to be sorely disappointed. Only about £0.5 million, including his own gift, was received by the Treasury (Jenkins, 1987, pp. 44–5).

In April 1921 Bonar Law resigned from the government due to ill health, and in the consequent reshuffle Baldwin was promoted to the Cabinet, on Law's recommendation, as President of the Board of Trade. He held this post for 19 months during which he continued to prove himself a competent administrator, but took few initiatives and seldom intervened in Cabinet discussions. Yet behind his silence lurked a growing sense of unease concerning Lloyd George's premiership. He viewed "the Goat", as he habitually referred to him, with increasing distaste, feeling that he was continually undercutting the authority of his fellow ministers, was having a corrupting effect on public life and destroying the morale of Tory MPs, more and more of whom feared the consequences of fighting another general election under his leadership.

68 Stanley Baldwin

In September 1922, as the Chanak crisis was building up, Baldwin and his wife left for their customary long holiday at Aix-les-Bains. It was here, while his wife took the waters, that during the course of several long and solitary hill walks, he came to the conclusion that it was his God-given duty to sacrifice his own political career to end that of the 'Welsh wizard'. He was summoned back by telegram to attend a Cabinet meeting on 1 October, and eight days later Chamberlain convened a meeting of all the Conservative Cabinet ministers to endorse his view that they should fight the forthcoming general election in alliance with the coalition Liberals and under the leadership of Lloyd George. Baldwin alone (though he was later supported by the Agriculture Minister, Sir Arthur Griffith-Boscowen) stood out, saying that he could not and would not fight the election as a coalitionist, would not serve again under Lloyd George and would shortly resign as a minister. When his wife returned from holiday a few days later, he met her at Victoria station and told her, as she reported in a letter to her mother:

> I have done something dreadful without consulting you. I have been fearfully worried, but I felt that it had to come. I am resigning from the Cabinet. I shall never get a job again. I do hope you won't mind fearfully, but I've said I cannot continue to serve under the G ['Goat'] any longer.
>
> *(Middlemas and Barnes, 1969, pp. 115–16)*

So Baldwin prepared to go into the wilderness, but he was by no means as isolated as he feared. Both the Chairman of the Conservative Party, Sir George Younger, and the Chief Whip, Sir Leslie Wilson, wanted the Tories to fight the election as an independent force, a view that was fast gathering strength among Tory backbenchers and junior ministers, though all the Cabinet ministers except Baldwin and Boscowen continued to back Chamberlain (Lord Curzon was to defect at the last minute). Chamberlain summoned a meeting of all Tory MPs and ministers in the House of Lords at the Carlton Club on 19 October, and was supremely confident that he would crush any opposition.

Baldwin took the view that Chamberlain could only be defeated if an alternative candidate for the party leadership could be found. Ruling himself out as too junior and lacking in authority, he concluded that Bonar Law was the only feasible person to play this role. Together with Lord Beaverbrook (Law's most trusted and closest political friend), he began to apply pressure on the former party leader to attend the Carlton Club meeting and to make himself available. Law, worried about his health and feeling that he owed some loyalty to Chamberlain, was highly reluctant, but eventually persuaded himself (partly at the urging of his sister, Mary) that the future welfare of the Conservative Party depended on its being unhitched from the coalition.

This effectively sealed Chamberlain and Lloyd George's fate. As described in the earlier chapter on Lloyd George, the meeting voted by 187 votes to 87 to fight the election independently of Lloyd George, after a devastating eight-minute speech by Baldwin referring to Lloyd George as "a dynamic force [which is] a very terrible thing; it may crush you but is not necessarily right", and a more lumbering effort by Law, which nevertheless clinched the argument. Within hours, Chamberlain and the other Tory ministers resigned, followed by Lloyd George, and George V summoned Bonar Law to the Palace.

It was only after he had been formally elected as Tory leader that Law agreed to form a government, and his first act was to offer Baldwin the Chancellorship of the Exchequer. This was the one post which Baldwin coveted – he had been mildly disappointed not to have been appointed 19 months earlier – but now he declined, not wishing to seem to have profited from his part in unhorsing Lloyd George. He proposed instead that Law should appoint Reginald McKenna, who had been Chancellor under Asquith and was now a respected banker. Law duly approached McKenna, who was tempted, but foresaw difficulties as he was not then an MP. After three days mulling it over, he turned down the offer. Law again approached Baldwin who, having satisfied his conscience, gladly accepted and, as recounted by Roy Jenkins, "went upstairs to his wife and said: 'Treat me with respect; I am Chancellor of the Exchequer'" (Jenkins, 1987, p. 54).

The most notable event in Baldwin's brief chancellorship was his handling of the American debt settlement. The British position, firmly held by Bonar Law and most of his Cabinet, was that all inter-allied debts should be cancelled, but that in any event Britain should not be required to repay its debt to America until comparable arrangements were in place for the repayment of its own loans to its European allies, notably France and Italy, and the achievement of a realistic deal on German reparations. The Republican-dominated US Congress was, however, demanding cash on the nail, and on 27 December 1922 Baldwin left for Washington, accompanied by Montagu Norman, the Governor of the Bank of England, with a firm mandate not to agree a settlement involving payments in excess of £25 million a year.

The best that Baldwin could achieve was a funding agreement providing for annual payments of £34 million for the first ten years, increasing to £40 million for the remaining 52 years of the agreement. This was unanimously rejected by the British Cabinet in his absence, and on 27 January 1923 Baldwin returned, ostensibly to seek a new mandate from his colleagues. On his arrival at Southampton, he gave a series of interviews to American journalists, in which he revealed the details of the American offer, made it clear that he thought that they were the best available and should be accepted, and made disparaging remarks about the small-mindedness of the American senators who would have to approve the deal.

Baldwin's remarks were widely considered to be ill-judged and naïve, and were attributed to his inexperience. This view was magisterially refuted by Harold Wilson in his book on British Prime Ministers. Wilson argued that Baldwin knew exactly what he was doing, and that his purpose was to cut the ground from under Bonar Law's opposition to the projected deal. It was in connection with this episode that Wilson recalled Winston Churchill's judgement in his Memorial Address in 1947 that "He was the most formidable politician I have ever known in public life" (Wilson, 1977, p. 9).

In any event, as recounted in the preceding chapter, Baldwin succeeded in undermining Law's opposition, and the consequence was not only a weakening of the Prime Minister's authority but an increase in that of his Chancellor, particularly among his Cabinet colleagues. This may have been a factor, though probably not the decisive one, influencing the choice of Baldwin, rather than the Foreign Secretary, Lord Curzon, as Bonar Law's successor four months later, in May 1923.

The general expectation, shared by Law, was that the choice would fall on Curzon. Law stubbornly refused to advise the King, but probably had a marginal preference for Baldwin. This was greatly magnified in a memorandum drawn up by his PPS, John Davidson, which was surreptitiously passed to Lord Stamfordham, the King's private secretary, by Ronald Waterhouse, an official in Law's office, with the evident implication that it faithfully represented the retiring Prime Minister's views. (This extraordinary episode is described in detail in Blake, 1955, pp. 516–27.) In the absence of direct advice from Law, the King chose to consult Balfour, as the only living former Conservative Prime Minister, which was bad luck for Curzon, whom Balfour keenly distrusted.

Balfour came down decisively against Curzon, whom the King had earlier favoured. Of the two contenders, Curzon had by far the longer experience of high office, and was regarded as much the more distinguished figure, but suffered, probably decisively, from his membership of the House of Lords, and from his reputation for arrogance and being a difficult colleague. It is hard not to believe that Baldwin was chosen less on his own merits than on his rival's defects.

It was a cruel disappointment for Curzon, who had received a telegram summoning him for a meeting with Stamfordham, which he not unreasonably assumed would be the preamble to an audience with the King. In fact, the intention was to break the news gently to him before the King saw Baldwin. Curzon was mortified, describing his successful rival as "a man of the utmost insignificance". Nevertheless, to Baldwin's relieved surprise, he swallowed his pride sufficiently to accept his invitation to continue as Foreign Secretary, and even to propose his rival as party leader at a meeting of all Conservative MPs and peers.

Baldwin was to remain leader of the Conservative Party for 14 years, during most of which time he was the dominant figure in British politics, serving three times as Prime Minister for a total length of seven years and 82 days. This was a sufficient length of time for all of Baldwin's qualities as well as his defects to be amply displayed. The first thing that should be said about Baldwin was that he was a thoroughly decent man, probably the nicest – apart from Campbell-Bannerman – of the 20 leaders discussed in this book. He genuinely wanted to do good, was considerate to his colleagues and modest in his assessment of his own abilities except that – like Gladstone, otherwise a very different character – he was convinced that he had been chosen by God for a special purpose.

He had a simple Christian faith in God, and after God he believed in England, and the English character and the essential goodness of Englishmen of all classes. After England, he believed in the Conservative Party, which he held to be the repository of national virtue, not the representative of any class interest. A natural conciliator, he hated violence and conflict, and wished for nothing better than that the world, and industrial relations in particular, should be run on the same benevolent lines as his father's steel firm. Baldwin was often seen as a lazy man, which is not quite true. He had infinite patience, never seemed in a hurry and knew the value of waiting on events. He was capable of decisive action during a crisis, but it took a lot out of him, and he would then lapse into a period of passivity while he recovered his natural equilibrium. He took a close interest in the character and foibles of his colleagues, spending long hours in the Commons conversing with a surprisingly wide range of Members, leading Attlee to remark: "He always seemed more at home with our people, particularly the older trade union people, than his own lot" (Williams, 1965, p. 31).

He was not without guile in his dealings with other politicians, knowing how to exploit their vanity and ambitions in order to win their support. Because of his near universal benevolence, his disinterestedness and his apparent lack of ambition, Baldwin was liked and trusted by nearly everybody he met, and the aura of reassurance he conveyed became a potent electoral asset for the Conservatives.

Yet Baldwin himself was living in a dream world which bore little resemblance to reality, and this bred a dangerous complacency which in the end was to be his undoing and that of many who put their trust in him. The England in which he believed, and which he evoked so warmly in his speeches and writings, no longer existed, if in fact it ever had. A famous, but not untypical, example was the following:

The sounds of England, the tinkle of the hammer on the anvil in the country smithy, the corn-crake on a dewy morning, the sound of the scythe against the whetstone, and the sight of a plough team coming over the brow of a hill, the sight that has been seen in England since England was a land and may be seen in England long after the Empire has perished and every works in England has ceased to function, for centuries the one eternal sight of England.

(Cited in Williams, 1965, p. 46)

Few of the mine-owners and employers with whom he had to deal during the industrial troubles leading up to the General Strike shared the qualities of Baldwin's much admired father nor was the Conservative Party quite the body of philanthropists that Baldwin believed it to be. Yet the biggest difference between reality and Baldwin's perception lay in foreign affairs, a field in which he took little interest, never flying in a plane, only once as Prime Minister meeting a foreign leader (French Premier Raymond Poincaré in 1923) and virtually confining his foreign visits to Aix-les-Bains. As late as 1936, when the barbaric nature of the Nazi regime in Germany was already abundantly evident, he was able to say in a speech that he had never come across a really 'malevolent' government – "most governments seem to me to be not much better or worse than the people they govern". So long as the dichotomy between Baldwin's beliefs and the real world remained unrevealed, he commanded a remarkable degree of trust and popularity. All this turned to dust at the very end of his career when he became the object of unparalleled loathing and contempt.

All this was far into the future when he became Premier for the first time. His first term was extremely brief – a mere eight months – from 22 May 1923 to 22 January 1924. He was entirely responsible for bringing it to an end, in an ill-considered decision to call a premature general election. If the Conservative Party had not still been deeply divided, and unable to agree on an alternative leader, this could well have been the end of Baldwin's political career. But luck, and his previously unsuspected survival skills, dictated otherwise.

On becoming Prime Minister, Baldwin became deeply worried by the high level of unemployment, which at 1.5 million amounted to more than 10 per cent of the insured working population. He saw no hope of reducing this figure except by adopting the Chamberlainite policy of tariff protection, which had split the Conservative Party 20 years earlier, but had since almost become party orthodoxy. Unfortunately, he was inhibited by a pledge which Bonar Law had given a year earlier that there would be no major change in fiscal policy in advance of a further general election.

Baldwin felt it would be dishonourable to disregard this pledge, but –as he explained some years later to his private secretary, Thomas Jones, he had an additional reason to act fast. He received reports, probably erroneous, that Lloyd George, currently on a lecture tour in the US, was about to declare for protection, and he feared that if he did so, he would scoop up the Tory coalitionists into a new centre party, and that, said Baldwin, "would have been an end to the Tory Party as we know it" (Middlemas and Barnes, 1969, p. 212).

In the short run, Baldwin's electoral gamble proved a disaster. He threw away a comfortable Tory majority of 74, and finished up with a deficit of 50. The new House of Commons was split three ways, with the Conservatives on 258 seats, Labour 191 and the Liberals (newly reunited under Asquith, with Lloyd George as his deputy) with 158. The formation of a minority Labour government, under Ramsay MacDonald, with passive Liberal support (see next chapter), was the optimum outcome for Baldwin of a distinctively messy situation.

The alternatives of a government led by another Tory (Stamfordham suggested Austen Chamberlain), or the inclusion of the Liberals in either a Tory- or Labour-led coalition, would have been far less acceptable to him. A Labour government in office, but not in effective power, would, he believed, help to 'house-train' Labour without any risk of extreme Socialist policies being implemented. In the longer term, he much preferred the prospect of Labour being the main rivals of the Tories to any revival of the Liberal Party.

In the remaining nine months of the 1924 Parliament, Baldwin was, in Roy Jenkins's words, "a gentle opponent to a weak government" (Jenkins, 1987, p. 80). He played little part in its downfall, which was occasioned by the withdrawal of Liberal support in a confidence motion in October 1924 on the Campbell affair (see next chapter). This was a hara-kiri operation by the Liberals, who, in the subsequent general election on 29 October 1924, were virtually destroyed as a major political force. The result was: Conservatives 412 seats, Labour 151, Liberals 40, others 12. The total Labour vote actually increased, but the collapse in Liberal support was almost entirely to the Tories' benefit.

Baldwin waged an effective campaign, the highlight of which was that, for the first time, the party leaders were invited to make election broadcasts on the BBC. MacDonald, a powerful platform orator, chose to broadcast live from a mass meeting in Glasgow. The quality of reception was very poor, and he came over as an inconsequential tub-thumper. Baldwin settled himself comfortably into a chair in the BBC Director-General's office, and spoke softly and reassuringly, immediately establishing a rapport with his listeners. It was the beginning of the extraordinary reputation which he acquired as 'Honest Stan', the man who understood and was deeply involved in the concerns of the man in the street. Baldwin was a natural broadcaster, and used the new medium more effectively than any other democratic politician in the 1920s and 1930s, with the probable exception of Franklin Roosevelt.

His striking election victory put Baldwin in an exceptionally strong position. It enabled him to restore unity to the Conservative Party by bringing the main Conservative coalitionists back into the fold. Austen Chamberlain became Foreign Secretary, shattering the expectations of an almost choleric Curzon, who nevertheless agreed to become Lord President of the Council, while Birkenhead (F.E. Smith) went to the India Office. Curzon was to die within a year, and Baldwin then completed the work of reconciliation by bringing Balfour into the government in his place. A surprise appointment was that of Winston Churchill, who had only just rejoined the Conservative Party 20 years after his defection to the Liberals, as Chancellor of the Exchequer.

Despite his many gifts, Churchill was out of his depth as Chancellor. One of his first decisions was to bring Britain back on to the gold standard, which by greatly strengthening the pound had a disastrous effect on exports, and especially on the already deeply troubled coal industry. This was, in effect, the beginning of the countdown to the General Strike of 1926, the dominating event of Baldwin's second premiership.

He emerged with his reputation greatly enhanced, the general impression being that he had done everything possible to prevent the strike from happening, while taking prudent steps to ensure that if it nevertheless occurred it would be unsuccessful, that he acted firmly during the nine days that it lasted and then exerted himself to ensure that it would not leave a heritage of bitterness and recrimination. The truth was somewhat more complicated and less flattering. During the year before the strike the government had failed to take any decisive initiatives to secure a reorganisation of the notoriously inefficient industry, and while Baldwin had certainly exerted himself to try to secure a compromise acceptable to the Trades Union Congress

(TUC) in the final days before the strike, and actually negotiated an agreement with them, he failed to carry a majority of the Cabinet with him. The government then seized on the unofficial action of *Daily Mail* printers who refused to set a provocative article criticising the strikers, as a pretext for going back on the agreement, even though this action was condemned by the TUC and by the printers' own union.

The strike then went ahead, despite the deep reluctance of the TUC leadership. During the strike itself, Baldwin, suffering from nervous exhaustion, played little part, and subsequently his genuine attempts at reconciliation were largely frustrated by harder men in his own Cabinet, who forced through the vindictive Trade Disputes Act of 1927, and stood by imperviously while the miners were starved into submission at the end of their own strike which continued for a further seven months.

Baldwin, who campaigned on a platform of 'Safety First', confidently expected to win the 1929 general election, despite the continuing economic difficulties and the high level of unemployment. His government could claim a number of achievements, most of them due to Neville Chamberlain, Austen's younger half-brother, who had surprisingly been chosen to be Health Secretary rather than Chancellor of the Exchequer and had proved the major success story of the administration.

Like that of 1923, the election produced an indeterminate result, but this time Labour was the largest party (Labour 287, Conservatives 260, Liberals 59), and there was no serious doubt that MacDonald would again become Prime Minister of a minority government. Baldwin's party took the result very hard, and there was a determined attempt during the following two years to drive him out of the leadership. For many Tories his moderate views on social policy and on India were anathema, as was his kid-glove treatment of the Labour government and his refusal to revive the Tariff Reform issue after his earlier rebuff by the electors in 1923.

Leading the campaign against Baldwin were the press lords, Rothermere and Beaverbrook, who not only used their newspapers constantly to snipe against him, but put up by-election candidates, under the label Empire Free Trade, against the official Tory standard-bearers. They had thought that the meek and mild Baldwin would be easy quarry, but like others before them they under-estimated their man. *Cet animal est très méchant; il se défend*, and in March 1931 Baldwin struck back at his persecutors in a memorable phrase, drafted by his cousin, Rudyard Kipling. "What the proprietorship of these newspapers is aiming at is power, and power without responsibility – the prerogative of the harlot throughout the ages", he said of Rothermere and Beaverbrook, and went on to rub salt into their wounds by comprehensively routing their candidate in a by-election in the ultra-smart Westminster St. George's constituency, which they had generally been expected to win. This marked the end of the campaign against Baldwin, and of efforts to replace him by the seemingly more dynamic Neville Chamberlain.

By then the Labour government was in deep trouble, with no idea of how to tackle the steeply rising unemployment, and suffering serious defeats in by-elections. It seemed only a matter of a few months before it would be forced out of office, leading to Baldwin's inevitable appointment as Prime Minister, followed by a general election which would produce a large Conservative majority. That this did not happen, and that he had to wait another six years before regaining Downing Street, was largely Baldwin's own fault.

In July Baldwin was informed of an indirect approach from MacDonald to discuss the formation of a National government, but turned down the suggestion out of hand. Having destroyed one coalition government under Lloyd George, he had no desire to help in the formation of another one. His colleague, and effective number two, Neville Chamberlain was, however, clearly attracted by the idea. Baldwin then made the decisive mistake of hurrying off to his customary lengthy holiday in Aix-les-Bains, leaving Chamberlain to deputise in his absence.

Though twice summoned back for urgent consultations, Baldwin played little part in the ongoing discussions provoked by the Labour government's inability to agree on the cuts necessary to achieve a loan sufficient to ride out the mounting financial crisis (see next chapter). The idea of a coalition, encouraged by Chamberlain, gained ground, particularly with George V, and when the King saw Baldwin on his second return to London and asked him outright if he would be prepared to serve under MacDonald in a National government, he had little choice but to agree. The probability must be that, had he not insisted on going to Aix-les-Bains, the idea would have been nipped in the bud.

The National government was meant to last just a few weeks to see out the crisis, but – after a snap election in November 1931 which saw the Labour Party almost wiped out – it continued under MacDonald's premiership for nearly another four years until June 1935, when Baldwin finally replaced him in 10 Downing Street.

Until then, he held the post of Lord President of the Council, leading the House of Commons. In the eyes of the Labour Party, and of many other observers, MacDonald was a mere puppet and front-man, with Baldwin pulling the strings. Yet it is questionable whether Baldwin was the dominant influence in the government. Neville Chamberlain, who became Chancellor of the Exchequer after the 1931 election, arguably carried greater weight and was perhaps unlucky not to succeed MacDonald as Premier. According to Roy Jenkins, he would have been the majority choice of the Cabinet and of Tory MPs, but George V took it upon himself to appoint Baldwin without consulting them.

It might have been better if he had. Baldwin's third and last premiership did little good either to himself or his country. It was dominated by the defence issue, with which Baldwin had already been intimately concerned, as it came within his responsibilities as Lord President of the Council. The most deadly critic of Baldwin's premiership was Winston Churchill, who included the famous entry in the index of his World War II memoirs: 'BALDWIN, Rt. Hon. Stanley … confesses putting party before country'. The reference was to Baldwin's conviction that – though he had become convinced by 1934 that a major rearmament programme was necessary to combat the Nazi threat – it would be impolitic to mention this in advance of the 1935 general election, in view of the strong pacifist sentiments which he attributed to a large number of his fellow countrymen. Baldwin later admitted, in what he himself described as "a speech of appalling frankness":

> Supposing I had gone to the country and said that Germany was rearming and we must rearm, does anybody think that this pacific democracy would have rallied to that cry at that moment? I cannot think of anything that would have made the loss of the election from my point of view more certain.
>
> *(Hansard, vol. 317, col. 1144, 12 November 1936)*

Baldwin has since had his defenders, who argue that he did indeed initiate a rearmament programme, though he hardly pursued it with great energy. The most discreditable episode of Baldwin's last premiership was, without doubt, the Hoare-Laval Pact. It occurred only a month after the 1935 general election, in which he had proclaimed that "The League of

Nations is the keystone of British foreign policy", and that sanctions would be continued against Italy for her aggression against Abyssinia (Ethiopia). The Foreign Secretary, Sir Samuel Hoare, visited Paris for discussions with Pierre Laval, who was then doubling up as France's Prime and Foreign Minister. Without having any mandate to negotiate, Hoare agreed a plan to partition Abyssinia, permitting Mussolini to annex half the country. Baldwin, who had been quite unaware of Hoare's initiative, strongly defended it in the House of Commons, only to abandon both his minister and the pact within a week, in the face of a storm of public and parliamentary protest. Hoare was forced to resign, and his place was taken by his junior minister, Anthony Eden.

Baldwin's reputation was badly damaged, but both it and his popularity were redeemed by the mixture of decisiveness and discretion with which he handled the Abdication crisis in 1937. He retired shortly afterwards, amid the plaudits of the nation, collecting an earldom and the Garter on the way.

His retirement to Worcestershire was not the happy epilogue to his career that he had imagined. As the clouds darkened, and the early disasters of the war developed, he became the almost universal scapegoat for the country's unpreparedness, receiving masses of hate mail and suffering the indignity of having the beautiful wrought-iron gates of Astley Hall forcibly removed as scrap metal for the war effort.

For a man who had bathed for long years in the warm glow of popular acclaim this was almost too much to bear, and he became more and more of a recluse. He survived the war, and died a largely forgotten man in December 1947. A public appeal to raise a simple roadside memorial to him near his home raised a pathetic amount, and was only saved by a large donation from Churchill. I do not know what epitaph it bears. "Good intentions are not enough" might be the most appropriate.

Works consulted

Robert Blake, 1955, *The Unknown Prime* Minister, London, Eyre & Spottiswoode.
Roy Jenkins, 1987, *Baldwin*, London, Collins.
Keith Middlemas and John Barnes, 1969, *Baldwin: A Biography*, London, Weidenfeld & Nicolson.
Francis Williams, 1965, *A Pattern of Rulers*, London, Longman.
Harold Wilson, 1977, *A Prime Minister on Prime Ministers*, London, Weidenfeld & Nicolson.

7

RAMSAY MACDONALD

An 'aristocrat' among plain men?

No person ever did more to help build up a new political party than James Ramsay MacDonald. Few subsequently did more to damage their own creation. That was the essential tragedy of his life.

It began in the most obscure and discouraging of circumstances. He was born on 12 October 1866, the illegitimate son of a young servant girl, Annie Ramsay. She had been working on a farm near the fishing village of Lossiemouth on the Moray Firth. His father, John MacDonald, was a ploughman on the farm, who soon afterwards disappeared from the area and from all subsequent trace, though not before he and Annie had together confessed their sin before the local kirk and been granted absolution. They had been engaged to be married, and it is probable that it was Annie herself who broke off the engagement, though whether this was of her own volition or because her formidable mother, Bella Ramsay, regarded him as an unworthy suitor is far from clear and will presumably never be known.

MacDonald grew up to be an exceptionally handsome and attractive man, which led to a great deal of speculation – particularly among the aristocratic women who took him up after he became Prime Minister – that his 'real' father must have been a Highland laird, or even, it was suggested, the Duke of Argyll. There was never the slightest justification for such a belief.

He was raised in a tiny cottage in Lossiemouth, by his mother and grandmother, both of whom scratched a living as seamstresses. The centre of their lives was young Jamie, who was lavished with care and attention, neither woman doubting for one moment that he was a superior being destined for higher things. Apart from them, the greatest influence on his young life was James MacDonald (no relation), the remarkable teacher, or dominie, of Drainie village school, four miles' walk from his home.

During the ten years that he attended the school, whose 70 pupils shared a single teacher, assisted by a student teacher and a sewing mistress, Jamie acquired a remarkably wide education. He became adept at Latin and Greek, devoured the works of Scott, Carlyle, Ruskin and Hazlitt and acquired a passion for science, which he fostered by reading university textbooks which he picked up at a second-hand bookshop. At 15 he left to work in the fields, but was rescued from manual labour, after a month or two, by the dominie, who eagerly recruited his prize student to replace the pupil teacher who had left for Edinburgh.

DOI: 10.4324/9781003031963-8

He brought to his new duties a lively intelligence, a soaring imagination and a burning ambition to succeed. He had a commanding physical presence and an appealing personality, though this concealed a darker side – he was suspicious, secretive and quick to take offence, a sensitivity perhaps related to his illegitimacy. As a child the only time he had been in any trouble was when he seriously injured a fellow pupil who had referred to him as a "bastard", and as an adult he took pains to conceal his origins. When during the First World War he was viciously attacked as a "traitor" and "coward" by the right-wing jingoist Horatio Bottomley, he appeared unconcerned. Yet when Bottomley followed this up by publishing a facsimile of his birth certificate in the magazine *John Bull*, he was devastated, saying repeatedly "Thank God my mother is dead for this would have killed her" (Williams, 1965, p. 62).

MacDonald remained at the school for a further four years, deepening his own education and playing a full part in the social and intellectual life of the local community. Yet the wider world beckoned, and at 18 he began to scour the situations vacant columns of *The Scotsman*, and to apply for posts all over Britain. Eventually, he was successful, and he left in the summer of 1885 to take up a position in Bristol, assisting a clergyman to set up a Boys' and Young Men's Guild. Within six months, he was back in Lossiemouth, though it is unclear whether he had left the job of his own accord or had been found wanting by his employer. While at Bristol, however, he had become a Socialist, joining the Marxist Social Democratic Federation (SDF) and playing a very active part in its local branch.

After a few frustrating months, he left Lossiemouth again, this time for good. He headed for London, after hearing from a Bristol friend of a suitable post that might be available. On arrival he found that it had been filled only the day before, and he embarked on a dispiriting and increasingly desperate search for work, living in cheap lodgings in Kentish Town and surviving on a diet of oatmeal and hot water. Eventually, he found a temporary job addressing envelopes for the National Cyclists' Union, at 10 shillings a week, and subsequently a more permanent post in the City as an invoice clerk, starting at 12s. 6d a week.

His spare time was divided between Socialist activities – he abandoned the SDF in favour of the Socialist Union, a short-lived movement which adopted a much more moderate approach – and serious scientific studies at the Birkbeck Institute. These he hoped would lead to a scholarship at the South Kensington Museum. But his health broke down through over-work, before he was able to take the examination, and he abandoned his hopes of a scientific career. Instead, in 1888, he was fortunate to obtain a post as private secretary to Thomas Lough, a tea merchant and aspiring radical Liberal politician, who was to be elected as MP for West Islington in 1892.

This appointment substantially changed MacDonald's life. His income rose sharply, to £75 a year rising to £100, and the work was much more congenial, bringing him into contact with a wide range of radical Liberal circles, and introducing him into prosperous middle-class society. He joined the Fabian Society, the East London Ethical Society and even the Fellowship of the New Life, a Utopian Socialist group, from which the more down-to-earth Fabians had split off some years before. If the Fabians appealed to his practical sense, the Fellowship gave full rein to the high moral aspirations which were to characterise his speeches and writings throughout most of his political career. He became active in the Fabians, spending some time in 1892 as a paid lecturer touring the provinces on their behalf. By then he had resigned his post with Thomas Lough and was eking out a precarious existence as a freelance journalist.

Through his Liberal contacts, he had come into touch with the Labour Electoral Association, a body devoted to securing the election to Parliament of working men. Its favoured tactic was to obtain their selection by local Liberal associations as Lib-Lab candidates, particularly in two-member constituencies where they could balance the ticket by running in harness with more traditional middle-class candidates. Had the Liberals been more open to such arrangements it is possible that the movement towards founding an independent Labour Party might never have got off the ground. Yet time and time again, aspirant Lib-Lab candidates were turned down, and this was MacDonald's fate in 1894, when he responded to an invitation to offer himself as the second Liberal candidate in Southampton, then represented by one Liberal and one Conservative MP. He was rejected, and this prompted him to join the Independent Labour Party (ILP), which had been founded the previous year by Keir Hardie and others. He fought the 1895 general election in Southampton as an ILP candidate, coming bottom of the poll by a wide margin. His intervention, however, almost certainly led to the defeat of the sitting Liberal MP, the Tories capturing both seats.

His candidature had a momentous consequence for MacDonald. He received a cheque for £1 towards his election fund from an unknown sympathiser, signed "M.E. Gladstone". This turned out to be a 25-year-old social worker, Margaret Gladstone, who came from a distinguished and prosperous academic family. She had fallen at least half in love with MacDonald before she had even met him, and their courtship proceeded rapidly. They became engaged on the steps of the British Museum in July 1896, and married the following November.

It was an ideal partnership – Margaret, while sharing his basic values and commitment, was a much more outgoing personality, which did a lot to mitigate the aloofness which tended to surround her brooding Scottish husband. As well as bearing him six children, one of whom died in infancy from diphtheria, she threw herself wholeheartedly into all his activities, and their apartment in Lincoln's Inn, as well as their Buckinghamshire cottage, became an ever welcoming meeting place for his growing number of political associates.

As well as her personal qualities, Margaret brought, for the first time, financial security to MacDonald. Though not conspicuously wealthy, she had a sufficiently large private income to enable him to devote himself full-time to his political work. They were also in a position to undertake a series of lengthy overseas tours – to the United States, Canada, India, Australia and New Zealand, which stimulated MacDonald's interest and left him far better informed on foreign affairs than any of his Labour colleagues. Among European Socialist leaders whom he met and befriended was the notable German 'revisionist' Eduard Bernstein. MacDonald had a sure touch for international relations, and it is significant that when – in 1924 – he chose to combine the Foreign Secretaryship with being Prime Minister he was widely adjudged as a notable success in the former post, though hardly in the latter.

More immediately – and crucially for MacDonald's nascent political career – when, in February 1900, the Labour Representation Committee (LRC, later the Labour Party) was set up by the trade unions, in conjunction with a number of Socialist organisations, principally the ILP and the Fabian Society, it was able to turn to MacDonald as its secretary. Not only was he in a position to accept the post without a salary (at least for the first few years), but until 1904 the offices of the LRC and practically all its meetings were located in the back room of the MacDonalds' flat.

Together with Keir Hardie, MacDonald had been one of the prime movers in creating the LRC. During the later 1890s, he had become increasingly prominent in the ranks of both the ILP and the Fabians. Paradoxically, in the ILP, of which by 1900 he had become one of the four leading figures, he was valued for his Fabian quality of being a first-class committeeman.

In the Fabians, by contrast, where he fell foul of the Webbs, he was widely regarded as a woolly idealist, and was one of the minority of members who fiercely opposed the Boer War, which later led him to resign from the Society.

The green light for the creation of the LRC was a resolution from the Railway Servants' Union at the 1899 TUC calling for the convening of a "conference of all the co-operative, socialistic and other working organisations ... to devise ways and means for securing the return of an increased number of labour members to the next Parliament". It was only narrowly carried on a card vote, and it is improbable that it would have led to any permanent result had it not been for the skill of Hardie and MacDonald, both of whom were ILP delegates to the conference which took place in London at the Memorial Hall in Farringdon Street in February 1900. It was they who drafted the main resolutions to be put to the conference, which traced a careful middle way between the views of cautious trade unionists, most of whom were not Socialists, and the class war objectives of the SDF. The outcome of the conference was the creation of a federal-style party, which harnessed the weight of numbers and the financial resources of the trade unions (or at least the most advanced of them) to the campaigning vigour and idealism of the ILP and the pragmatic programme-making of the Fabians. The object of the party was defined as the establishment of "a distinct Labour group in Parliament, who shall have their own Whips and agree upon their own policy".

The new party put up 15 candidates in the 1900 general election, two of whom were elected – Hardie at Merthyr Tydfil and Richard Bell at Derby. MacDonald stood at Leicester – a two-member seat – where he substantially improved on his 1895 vote at Southampton, but again probably cost the Liberals the second seat, which was narrowly held by the Conservatives.

MacDonald was to continue as Secretary of the LRC, and subsequently of the Labour Party, until 1912, and then served a dozen years as Treasurer until he became Prime Minister for the first time in 1924. Even more than Keir Hardie, he could claim to be the dominant force in the rise of the new party. The first six years were the most crucial. In Marquand's words, "Between 1900 and 1906 most of MacDonald's energies were absorbed by the wearing, repetitive and time-consuming tasks of party management." He had to deal with a series of awkward and argumentative colleagues, soothing the inevitable differences between trade unionists and Socialists (particularly the wilder spirits of the ILP), and to keep every one united behind limited but practical objectives without dimming their messianic hopes for the future.

He also had his own private agenda. While he was determined that the Labour Party should remain independent of the Liberals, his own electoral experiences in Southampton and Leicester had convinced him that only through an agreement that would prevent Liberals standing in Labour's most promising constituencies could the infant party hope to gain a significant foothold in the House of Commons. This was the reasoning behind the secret Lib–Lab pact, which he negotiated with Herbert Gladstone, the Liberal Chief Whip, in 1903, behind the backs of the LRC's executive committee, though he took Hardie into his confidence.

The result was that the Liberal Party agreed to give Labour a free run in a significant number of seats. In the event, of 27 LRC candidates chosen to fight single-member constituencies, 17 had no Liberal opponents, and of 11 chosen in two-member constituencies only one faced two Liberal candidates. In return, MacDonald gave no specific guarantees, but used his influence to prevent Labour candidates being chosen in seats where they had no realistic prospect of success. The short-term results of the agreement were a brilliant success. In the rout of the Tories in the 1906 election, Labour representation went up to 30, only five of whom had faced Liberal opposition. As the Liberals themselves won 400 seats, they too felt they had done well out of the deal. In the long run, however, they may have sown the seeds of their own destruction in helping to put a new and thrustful rival on its feet.

One of the new Labour MPs was MacDonald, who again contested Leicester, for which the Liberals nominated only one candidate. In the new parliamentary Labour Party (PLP), MacDonald stood out as much the most impressive figure. By this time, he had evolved a most impressive speaking style, with a marvellously mellifluous voice, and he soon developed a mastery of parliamentary tactics. Hardie was chosen as the first Chairman of the PLP, but – though highly respected for his personal qualities and his pioneering role – he soon proved himself to be an unsatisfactory choice. He often neglected his parliamentary duties and tended to follow his own political interests rather than those of the party as a whole. MacDonald preferred to concentrate on his role as party secretary, and did not contest the chairmanship when Hardie resigned in 1908, to be succeeded, first by Arthur Henderson and then by George Barnes. Only in 1911 did MacDonald take over, but after that it became clear for the first time that the Labour Party had effectively elected a leader, rather than a mere chairman of the party meeting.

By then, MacDonald through his writings had attempted to provide the Labour Party with its own ideology which, while respectful of Karl Marx, fundamentally rejected his conclusions. In three books – *Socialism and Society* (1905), *Socialism and Government* (1909) and *The Socialist Movement* (1911) – he set out a programme which, while collectivist in its approach, was essentially moderate in tone and rejected any belief in the class war. In place of Marx, he chose Darwin as his lodestar. As summarised by Marquand, he argued that

> Marx, in spite of his great achievements, had not absorbed the full implications of Darwinian biology; trapped as he was in Hegel's dialectic, he failed to realise that social evolution, like biological evolution, resulted from the slow emergence of higher forms of life out of lower forms, not from the clash of opposing forces … In the 1840s, when Marx began his economic studies, it looked as though Britain was on the verge of revolution. No revolution had come, and 'The Marxian today still wonders why England fell from grace. England did not fall from grace. Neither Marx nor Engels saw deep enough to discover the possibilities of peaceful advance which lay hidden beneath the surface.'
>
> *(Marquand, 1977, p. 89)*

Six months after he was elected leader, MacDonald suffered a devastating blow, one from which he never really recovered. His wife, Margaret, still grieving from the death of their 6-year-old son David, fell ill with blood poisoning and died on 8 September 1911. MacDonald was inconsolable, burying himself in his work, but appearing to derive little pleasure from it. He poured his sense of loss into an intensely moving memoir, which was first published privately, and then as a full-length book, *Margaret Ethel MacDonald*, in 1912. In later years, MacDonald turned to a number of women friends for emotional support at different times, one of whom – Mary Agnes Hamilton, later a Labour MP – his children thought he might marry, though nothing came of the relationship. Of close male friends, he had none – and his relations with his political and ministerial colleagues were notoriously distant.

In the two general elections of 1910, the Liberals lost their overall majority, and henceforth were dependent on the Irish Nationalists and on Labour to maintain themselves in power. MacDonald was convinced that the Labour Party should offer consistent support to the Liberal government, which as a *quid pro quo* pushed through a series of reforms – including the payment of MPs and the legalisation of trade union political funds – to which Labour was strongly committed. These tactics cost MacDonald much of his popularity with the ILP, many of whose members wanted him to show equal hostility to 'both capitalist parties', while his fellow Labour MPs resented what they regarded as his standoffish attitude. Marquand quotes a letter from W.C. Anderson, one of his strongest supporters, warning him that his followers found him "too stern and intellectually cold", and urging him to "rope some of your men nearer to you by a kind word and, when possible, by a confidential chat about their difficulties and misunderstandings" (Marquand, 1977, p. 151).

In government circles, MacDonald was by now held in the highest esteem and was twice sounded out – once by Lloyd George and once by the Liberal Chief Whip – on the possibility of joining the Cabinet in a senior post. MacDonald was evidently tempted, but felt that it would be difficult to persuade his own party, and replied that the time was not yet ripe. Despite his internal critics, there was by August 1914 a virtually universal acceptance that MacDonald, who towered over his parliamentary colleagues, was the only possible leader.

There was therefore general consternation within the party when, on 5 August 1914, he submitted his resignation. The cause was, of course, the British declaration of war on Germany, the previous day. MacDonald, who thought that Britain should have remained neutral, did not accept that German militarism was exclusively to blame for the outbreak of war. The real cause he believed was the policy of balance of power through the creation of two hostile alliances, and part of the responsibility lay with the secretive diplomacy of Foreign Secretary Sir Edward Grey, who had encouraged the French and Russian governments to believe that Britain was committed to intervene on their side, even though there was no formal agreement to this effect.

The majority of Labour MPs, carried away by public fervour for the war, resolved to support the government's request for war credits, and, when MacDonald refused to reconsider his position, Henderson reluctantly took over as leader. Together with a group of radical Liberals, MacDonald set up a new organisation – the Union for Democratic Control (UDC) – which campaigned for a negotiated peace, with no annexations by either side, an international body to prevent future wars, general disarmament, and democratic control, through the British Parliament, of foreign policy. As the war progressed, the gap between MacDonald and the Labour leadership, which joined the coalition governments formed in April 1915 and December 1916, grew steadily wider. By contrast, he strengthened his links with the ILP, many of whose branches were militantly pacifist and who (especially after Hardie's death in 1915) increasingly looked to him for inspiration.

MacDonald unflinchingly maintained his position throughout the war, despite an avalanche of denigration from government supporters and the popular press. He maintained a correspondence with Bernstein, and placed his hopes on securing peace by contacts between the Socialist movements in the belligerent countries. This seemed a realistic possibility after the February 1917 Russian revolution, when the Dutch Socialist Party proposed to convene a conference of the Socialist International in the neutral venue of Stockholm, a proposal strongly supported by Kerensky and the Petrograd Soviet. This effected a reconciliation between MacDonald and Henderson, and the two men travelled together to Paris, where they reached agreement with the French Socialist Party on attendance at Stockholm, which Henderson later successfully recommended to a special Labour Party conference. Stockholm was abruptly aborted, however, by the British government, which refused to issue passports to any British delegates, precipitating the resignation of Henderson from the War Cabinet.

So the war continued its bloody course until November 1918, when Lloyd George finally achieved his long-sought 'knock-out blow', and went on to his overwhelming victory in the 'coupon' election the following month. This all but wiped out the Liberal Party as an independent force, and Labour, whose representation went up to 63 MPs, became the largest opposition party, though the result fell far short of its hopes. Every one of its 'anti-War' MPs was defeated, including MacDonald who was resoundingly beaten at Leicester, and even Arthur Henderson lost his seat, leaving the parliamentary Labour Party with no effective leader.

MacDonald made little effort to conceal his contempt for the feeble performance of Labour MPs during the 1918–22 Parliament, and devoted most of his energies to trying to restore the Socialist International and, in particular, to preventing the ILP from drifting off into the rival 'Third International' launched by the Russian Bolsheviks. He unsuccessfully fought a by-election at Woolwich East in March 1921, but did not get back into the Commons until November 1922, when he was returned for Aberavon in the general election won by Bonar Law's newly formed Conservative government.

Labour representation shot up to 142, including a large contingent of ILP Members from what became known as the 'Red Clyde', the Glasgow region of Scotland. Wrongly assuming from his anti-war record that MacDonald shared their left-wing views, the Clydesiders, led by Emanuel Shinwell, enthusiastically pushed his claim to the leadership, against J.R. Clynes, a somewhat colourless trade unionist and former minister in the Lloyd George coalition, who had been elected Chairman of the PLP the previous year.

In a closely fought contest, MacDonald prevailed by 61 votes to 56. Shinwell later wrote that only two men in the room were aware of the implications of the choice that was being made – himself and MacDonald. "I was confident that we were not only electing the leader of one section of the Opposition for the duration of the new Parliament but also a future Prime Minister" (Shinwell, 1973, p. 25). What neither Shinwell nor MacDonald could have foreseen was that this distant prospect would become a reality in little over a year, thanks to Baldwin's folly in calling a further general election in December 1923, resulting in a three-way split in the new Parliament (see previous chapter). The Conservatives won 258 seats, Labour 191, the Liberals 159.

In the post-electoral manoeuvring, the decisive element was the decision of the Liberal Party, briefly reunited under Asquith and Lloyd George, to put Labour into office, but without any guarantee of future support in the division lobbies. So on 22 January 1924, at the age of 57, MacDonald became the only Prime Minister of modern times to be appointed without any previous ministerial experience (until Tony Blair, 73 years later, in very different circumstances). He rose to the challenge with very little self-doubt, though he was only too aware of the paucity of talent from which to choose his ministerial team. He took the Foreign Ministry himself, Philip Snowden became an ultra-orthodox Chancellor of the Exchequer, and Arthur Henderson, who had lost his seat in the election and had to be found another in an early by-election, was somewhat grudgingly made Home Secretary, after having turned down other less senior posts. Most of the other important portfolios went to ex-Liberals or even ex-Tories, such as Lord Parmoor (the father of Stafford Cripps), who became Leader of the Lords and, effectively, deputy Foreign Secretary. This caused some resentment in the Labour Party, and particularly in the ILP, which was, however, thrown a sop by the appointment of the Clydesider John Wheatley as Health Minister and, incidentally, one of the few undoubted successes of the government.

Initially at least, MacDonald's reputation soared, both in Parliament and in the country, to which he appeared to offer commanding leadership. To his colleagues, however, he appeared less satisfactory. Most of them found him remote and uncommunicative; only with the affable but ineffectual railwaymen's leader J.H. Thomas, who became Colonial Secretary, did he enjoy anything approaching normal friendly relations. Nor did he attempt to ingratiate himself with the Liberal leaders, on whom he was dependent to remain in office. He greatly resented the patronising tone adopted by Asquith, and deeply distrusted | Lloyd George. So far from viewing them as allies, he saw them as deadly rivals for the support of progressive voters, a perception which clearly also influenced their attitude to him.

MacDonald's most important work was undoubtedly done as Foreign Secretary, where he enjoyed a rare triumph at the London conference which he convened and chaired in August 1924. Successfully reconciling bitter French and German divisions over the punitive reparations clauses of the Versailles Treaty, he paved the way for the withdrawal of the French occupation of the Ruhr. He followed this up with a visit to the League of Nations in Geneva, where – together with the new French Prime Minister Edouard Herriot – he secured the adoption amidst great enthusiasm of the so-called Geneva Protocol, providing for international arbitration of disputes and general disarmament, which unfortunately was never ratified.

Despite his continuing anti-Communism, MacDonald also opened diplomatic relations with the Bolshevik government, and began negotiations with them on two treaties concerning trade and compensation for British holders of Russian bonds, together with a possible loan agreement. Not only the Tories, but also Asquith and his fellow Liberals were opposed to the loan, and both opposition parties determined to defeat the government if the treaties were offered for ratification, but before the opportunity arose the government fell because of the Campbell affair.

John Campbell had published an article in the Communist Party's *Workers' Weekly* calling on British soldiers not to turn their guns on their "fellow workers". The Attorney-General, Sir Patrick Hastings, initiated charges against Campbell for sedition, but these were later withdrawn when it was discovered that Campbell had an excellent war record and had been severely wounded.

Both the Tories and the Liberals put down motions challenging MacDonald's handling of the affair and alleging that he had over-ruled Hastings for political reasons. MacDonald declared that if either of them was passed he would call for a general election. In the event, the Tories rejected their own motion, but voted for the Liberal amendment, and the die was cast.

The election campaign was notable for the extensive and exhausting speaking tour undertaken by MacDonald, who was hailed as "The Gladstone of Labour", where he addressed vast and adoring crowds. The Tory campaign largely consisted of depicting MacDonald and his party as front men for the Communists, in which endeavour they were assisted by the notorious Zinoviev letter. This purported to come from Grigori Zinoviev, the President of the Communist International, and called for the "revolutionising" of the British proletariat. The letter, later shown to be a crude forgery, concocted by Russian *émigrés*, but circulated with assistance from Conservative Central Office and blazoned across the columns of the *Daily Mail*, totally dominated the closing stages of the campaign. Whether or not it caused the government's defeat, it certainly provided MacDonald with an excellent alibi, and saved him from any serious recriminations in Labour's ranks. (See Lewis Chester, Stephen Fay and Hugo Young, *The Zinoviev Letter*, 1967.)

Apart from its foreign successes, the 1924 Labour government had little to show for its nine months in office. Yet it was an important milestone in Labour's onward march. It established it as the alternative party of government to the Tories, and – by its essential moderation (which even extended to its ministers, including MacDonald, donning court dress for their meetings with King George V, a subject for much mockery amidst the party's own ranks) – it went a long way to remove the irrational fears of many middle-class voters that it was unfit to govern. In fact, Labour substantially increased its vote at the 1924 election, though its parliamentary representation fell to 151 seats. The real losers were the Liberals, who returned only 40 members and were never again able to offer an effective challenge to Labour. The decline in Liberal votes disproportionately helped the Tories who, with 419 seats, dominated the new House of Commons.

As leader of the opposition for the next five years, MacDonald had a difficult time. No salary was attached to the post, and he incurred substantial expenses in carrying out his duties as party leader. The declining income from the Margaret Gladstone trust fund was barely sufficient to support his large family, and he was forced to undertake a great deal of hack journalism to make ends meet. He passed his 60th birthday in 1926, and the constant wear and tear began to tell. He was still an impressive speaker, but he had passed his prime, and no longer had the energy, or perhaps even the commitment, of earlier years. A severe illness in 1927 put him out of action for five months, and the strain on him was increased by constant struggles with the ILP, which became increasingly critical of his moderate stance.

The 1929 election again produced an indecisive result, though Labour emerged as the largest party, with 288 seats, against 260 for the Tories, with the Liberals on 59. This time, there was no question that MacDonald would become Prime Minister, though he again encountered difficulties in selecting his ministerial team. "Indeed, I should rather fight half a dozen elections than make one cabinet", he confided to his diary. He havered between choosing J.H. Thomas as Foreign Secretary and again appointing himself, but finally yielded to an ultimatum from Arthur Henderson that he would not join the government unless he could have this post. This episode did not improve the already poor relations between the two men, and their mutual suspicion and rivalry steadily increased during the ensuing two years. Philip Snowden again became Chancellor, but there was no post for John Wheatley, despite his success in 1924. Wheatley, who was to die of a cerebral haemorrhage in May 1930, had been a consistent and virulent critic of MacDonald, and his place as the 'statutory left-winger' in the Cabinet went instead to George Lansbury.

Despite having ceded the Foreign Secretaryship to Henderson, much of MacDonald's energies were again expended in international relations. He made a highly successful visit to the United States in October 1929 – the first by a serving British Prime Minister – where he managed with difficulty to bridge Anglo-American differences over naval disarmament, paving the way for the five-nation London conference, over which he presided in January– April 1930. This produced only partial agreement, with Britain, Japan and the US agreeing parities for reduced naval strength over the following six years, but France and Italy refused to comply.

In domestic policy, MacDonald was again handicapped by his lack of a parliamentary majority, and the necessity of getting Liberal support – which did not come cheaply – for any legislative proposals. From the outset, the dominating issue was unemployment, which, following the Wall Street crash in October 1929, rose inexorably, from 1.53 million in January 1930 to 2.73 million in June 1931. Few of MacDonald's ministers had any grasp of economics, and they had no idea of how to cope with the 'economic blizzard' (MacDonald's term) which had struck them. The government's response was to increase rates of unemployment benefit (which stored up trouble for them later on) and to appoint a Cabinet committee led by J.H. Thomas to consider solutions.

One of the members of the Thomas committee was the Chancellor of the Duchy of Lancaster, Sir Oswald Mosley. In January 1930 he sent a memorandum to MacDonald, advocating a major public works programme, along the lines suggested by Keynes and by Lloyd George. MacDonald referred the Mosley memorandum to another committee headed by his ultra-orthodox Chancellor, Philip Snowden. Snowden's hostility ensured that Mosley's proposals disappeared without trace, and with them any hope of Labour finding a solution to the unemployment problem. Mosley resigned in disgust, and though his stand was backed by some left-wing MPs, he was already so distrusted that he was unable to muster much support. Soon he had left the Labour Party altogether, and had plunged into gutter politics, which culminated in his creation of the British Union of Fascists. A reluctant admirer of Mosley, at that time, was Beatrice Webb, who in her diaries compared him favourably to MacDonald, who, she wrote, owed his "pre-eminence largely to the fact that he is the only artist, the only aristocrat by temperament and talent in a party of plebeians and plain men" (Cole, 1956, p. 243).

The final crisis which destroyed the Labour government was sparked by the failure of the famous Austrian bank, the Kreditanstalt, in May 1931. This immediately led to a run on German banks, and by July the pressure moved to Britain, where the Bank of England suffered heavy losses in defending sterling. At this time, MacDonald received a report from a committee of 'experts', the May Committee, predicting a budget deficit of £120 million (Snowden thought it would be £170 million), and insisting on heavy expenditure cuts, including £66 million on unemployment benefit, in order to balance the budget. MacDonald showed the report to Keynes, who advocated going off the gold standard, with an effective devaluation of 25 per cent. But neither MacDonald nor any of his Cabinet was prepared to contemplate going off gold, which Snowden told them would result in a "ruinous fall" in the standard of living of the workers. Instead there followed a long series of tortured Cabinet meetings at which they attempted to balance the budget through a mixture of tax increases and spending cuts, in which unemployment benefits (which had sharply escalated as a proportion of total government expenditure) figured largely.

In the end, they were advised that bankers in New York and Paris would be prepared to bail them out if total economies of £76 million, including a 10 per cent cut in unemployment pay, were implemented, and if the two opposition parties backed the deal. By this time nearly half the Cabinet, including Henderson (who was much influenced by the opposition of the TUC), were threatening to resign if the cuts were agreed. Finally, on 23 August, the Cabinet voted in favour by a bare majority of 11 to 9, but it was immediately clear that the government could not continue on that basis. The Cabinet agreed that MacDonald should see the King and inform him that all its members had placed their resignations in his hands. Their assumption, which MacDonald shared, was that the King would probably ask Baldwin to form an alternative government. Instead, George V asked Baldwin and Herbert Samuel, the acting Liberal leader in the absence of Lloyd George who was ill, whether they would be prepared to serve in a National government under MacDonald, and then put heavy pressure on him to continue, saying that "he was the only man to lead the country through the crisis". MacDonald was taken aback, and there is little doubt that his first instinct was to decline, but to support what he was convinced were necessary if deeply painful cuts from the opposition benches. He met Baldwin, Samuel and Neville Chamberlain, the deputy Tory leader, the following day to discuss the situation, and, according to Chamberlain's diary, told them that he would help them "to get these proposals through, though it meant his death warrant, but it would be no use for him to join a Government. He would be a ridiculous figure unable to command support and would bring odium on us as well as himself."

It would have been far better for MacDonald's posthumous reputation, and for his own subsequent peace of mind, if he had kept to this resolve, but –flattered by the King's confidence in him and following what he persuaded himself was his patriotic duty – he allowed himself to be convinced. He formed a new government, which included only three other former Labour Cabinet ministers – Snowden, Thomas and Lord Sankey, the Lord Chancellor – and attracted the support of a mere 13 Labour MPs. The new Cabinet also contained two Liberals and four Conservatives, though the Tories dominated the ranks of the junior ministers.

The government proceeded to implement the cuts which the Labour government had baulked at, but this did not prevent a further run on the pound within a few weeks, which led to the hurried decision – taken at an emergency Cabinet meeting held on Sunday 20 September – to go off the gold standard, an event which passed without any of the disastrous consequences against which the Labour government had been warned. "Nobody told us we could do this", complained an aggrieved Sidney Webb, one of the nine Labour Cabinet ministers who had stood out against the cuts in unemployment benefit only a month earlier.

Within a few days of the formation of the National government, MacDonald and his associates were unceremoniously expelled from the Labour Party, which elected Arthur Henderson as its leader. MacDonald had initially regarded the National government as purely a temporary affair to see out the immediate financial crisis, and had assumed that normal party alignments would then be reconstituted, much as he and other anti-War MPs had been reunited with the Labour mainstream after 1918. He was, however, unable to resist overwhelming pressure from his new Tory allies to seek a popular mandate for the measures that the new government had taken, and the general election held on 27 October 1931 ensured that his break with Labour would be permanent.

During the course of the campaign he was bitterly attacked by the Labour leadership, and he and the sharp-tongued Philip Snowden retaliated in kind, which made any subsequent reconciliation impossible. On the Labour side the myth grew up – and was almost universally believed – that MacDonald had plotted from almost the outset of the 1929 government to betray his colleagues and link up with the Tories. It was spelled out with great conviction by his former Parliamentary Private Secretary, L. Macneill Weir, in *The Tragedy of Ramsay MacDonald*, and, in fictional form, by Howard Spring in his novel *Fame Is the Spur*. Only the publication, in 1977, of David Marquand's biography, with its very careful examination of the sources, notably MacDonald's own extensive diaries, showed this belief to have been erroneous.

MacDonald himself also believed in betrayal – but felt that the culprits were his former Labour colleagues. They had abandoned their Socialist principles, in his view, by becoming spokesmen for a sectional interest, that of the TUC. He fought the election hard, and held his north-eastern mining constituency of Seaham against a vigorous challenge from his former agent. What he had not anticipated – and did not at all welcome – was the staggering defeat inflicted on the Labour Party as a whole. It was reduced to 52 seats, against 554 for the National government (including 473 Tories). Only one former Cabinet minister – George Lansbury – managed to hold his seat, and he subsequently took over the leadership from Henderson.

The new government was overwhelmingly Tory in its complexion, and MacDonald was increasingly seen as being a mere fig leaf, particularly after September 1932, when Snowden and the free trade Liberals resigned from the government. As during his previous governments, he played an active international role, heading the British delegation to the Geneva disarmament talks, and presiding over the Lausanne conference on phasing out German reparation payments. At least until early 1933, he remained the major influence on British foreign policy, though subsequently Baldwin, whose responsibilities as Lord President of the Council included defence, became more prominent. The Foreign Secretary, Sir John Simon, was little more than a bag-carrier.

On domestic policy, it was a different story. The leading Conservatives almost invariably got their way, and MacDonald found himself taken for granted. He bitterly resented this, and endlessly complained about his Tory colleagues in his diary, hinting in the entry for 27 December 1932 that he felt he had made a mistake in forming the National government: "Was I wise? Perhaps not, but it seemed as though anything else was impossible."

Meanwhile, his physical and mental powers began an embarrassing decline. He suffered from glaucoma, necessitating debilitating eye operations, and his lapses in concentration became more and more frequent, which had a disastrous effect on his speeches, both inside and outside the Commons. Churchill woundingly said that his speeches "compressed the largest number of words into the smallest amount of thought", while Francis Williams commented that "he retreated into incoherency because incoherency had become less painful than lucidity" (Williams, 1965, p. 130). By 1933 MacDonald had become a standing embarrassment to the government, and there can be no doubt that if he had been a Conservative he would have been pushed into resignation. Instead, in order to maintain the fiction that it was still a National rather than a Tory government, he was pressed to stay on for at least two years after he had ceased to play an effective role.

It was only in June 1935 that, with a general election approaching, Baldwin at last took over the reins, though MacDonald lingered on, taking over Baldwin's post as Lord President of the Council. There were more humiliations to come. In the general election, which the government won with a large if inevitably reduced majority (Conservatives 432 seats, Labour 154, Liberals 21), MacDonald was heavily defeated at Seaham by his old sponsor for the Labour leadership, Emanuel Shinwell. There followed a desperate search to find him another seat in a by-election, and he was eventually returned for the Scottish Universities, despite his having been a passionate opponent of university representation. He continued to sit in the Cabinet – devoid of any influence – until Baldwin himself made way for Neville Chamberlain in May 1937. In November of the same year he died at sea, aged 71, during a voyage to South America which he had hoped would restore his health.

By any reckoning, MacDonald was a major historical figure, though he hardly rates as one of the more successful Prime Ministers. His essential achievement was in creating a new political party and leading it with exceptional skill and judgement so that, from small beginnings, it became one of the two great contending parties of state. This judgement failed him in 1931, and his character flaws – his vanity and inability to take others into his confidence – no doubt contributed to that failure.

The hard knocks he then inflicted on the Labour Party might, some feared, have proved mortal, but the construct he had built proved strong enough to survive. As Marquand suggested, at the end of his biography, the Labour Party which triumphed in 1945 and transformed the face of British society was his true "monument", though few Labour MPs at the time "would have acknowledged a debt to MacDonald" (Marquand, 1977, p. 794).

Works consulted

Margaret Cole (ed.), 1956, *Beatrice Webb's Diaries 1924–1932*, London, Longmans.
Jane Cox (ed.), 1988, *A Singular Marriage: Ramsay and Margaret MacDonald*, London, Harrap.
Lord Elton, *Dictionary of National Biography, 1931–1940*, pp. 562–570.
Kevin Jeffreys (ed.), 1999, *Leading Labour: From Keir Hardie to Tony Blair,* London, Tauris.
J. Ramsay MacDonald, 1912, *Margaret Ethel MacDonald*, London, Hodder & Stoughton.
David Marquand, 1977, *Ramsay MacDonald*, London, Jonathan Cape.
Kenneth O. Morgan, 1992, *Labour People: Hardie to Kinnock*, London, Oxford.
Emanuel Shinwell, 1973, *I've Lived Through It All*, London, Gollancz.
Howard Spring, 1940, *Fame Is the Spur*, London.
L. MacNeill Weir, 1938, *The Tragedy of Ramsay MacDonald*, London, Secker & Warburg.
Francis Williams, 1965, *A Pattern of Rulers*, London, Longmans.

8

NEVILLE CHAMBERLAIN

A family affair

Many leading politicians come from political families which largely shape the course of their own political careers. Yet few have been so dominated, first by the presence, and then by the memory of his remarkable father, as Neville Chamberlain.

Joe Chamberlain was an epic figure. Sent from London at the age of 18 to run his family's screw manufacturing business in Birmingham, he became within a very few years one of the rapidly growing city's leading businessmen, and then the dominant force on the City Council, serving as Lord Mayor in 1873–75, and building up a formidable Liberal political machine in the city. Elected an MP in 1876, he entered Gladstone's second Cabinet four years later as President of the Board of Trade and effective leader of the Radical faction of the party, but broke with Gladstone over Irish Home Rule in 1886, leading his 'Liberal Unionists' into a close alliance with Lord Salisbury's Conservatives, and subsequently serving as Colonial Secretary in two Conservative Cabinets. Having split the Liberal Party in 1886, he repeated the trick with the Conservatives in 1903, when his resignation from Balfour's Cabinet, over Tariff Reform, led to its premature demise.

Joe's marital career was no less remarkable than his political progression. Brought up a Unitarian, he married (twice) into one of Birmingham's main Unitarian families – the Kenricks. In 1861, aged 25, he married Harriet Kenrick, who gave birth to a daughter, Beatrice, the following year, but died in 1863 giving birth to his elder son, Austen. Five years later, he married her cousin, Florence Kenrick, and Neville was born the following year, followed by three younger sisters until, in 1875, Florence, too, died in childbirth. In 1888, after unsuccessfully wooing the young Beatrice Potter (later Webb), who was unwilling to accept his views on male dominance, Joe wed for the third time, a young American woman, Mary Endicott, who was actually a year younger than Austen and only five years older than Neville.

The young Neville grew up in the two successive houses which Joe acquired in the Birmingham suburbs – first at Edgbaston, and then, further out, towards Moseley. Here he built a rather grand but frightfully ugly house which he called Highbury, recalling his own youth in Islington. Neville's mother died when he was 6, and the household was then presided over, in turn, by two of Joe's sisters, Caroline and Clara. Neville found his Aunt Clara cold

DOI: 10.4324/9781003031963-9

90 Neville Chamberlain

and unresponsive, and was delighted that, when he was 16, her role was taken over by Austen's elder sister Beatrice, then aged 22. She herself gave way to Joe's third wife, Mary, three years later, who proved a devoted stepmother to Neville and, in particular, to his three younger sisters.

Joe frequently entertained at Highbury, where there was a constant flow of guests, many of them visiting politicians and important national figures, as well as local Birmingham dignitaries. Yet for long periods he was away in London, and never really got on intimate terms with his younger son. As Neville recalled much later in a letter to one of his sisters, "For a good many years I respected and feared him more than I loved him … the piercing eye … few could face it with comfort." Nor was he close to his half-brother – "a certain deference", he wrote, entered into his relationship with Austen.

Nevertheless, Neville was supremely happy in the bosom of his family. He was devoted to his three younger sisters, Ida, Hilda and Ethel. The first two never married, and he unfailingly wrote to them, alternately, long, detailed letters almost every week from 1916, when he left Birmingham for London, until his death in 1940. These letters formed the principal source for his official biography, written by Keith Feiling. In addition to his sisters, he had large numbers of mostly female cousins living nearby, who were always in and out of the house, and they became a close and loving family clan, of which Neville became the natural leader. Outside the clan, however, he was shy and withdrawn, and was bitterly unhappy at Rugby, despite being an above-average pupil. It was during the school holidays that he came into his own, romping with his younger kin in the spacious grounds of Highbury, and cultivating his passions for music, bird-watching and botany, which in later life were supplemented by an equal devotion to fly-fishing.

Austen had preceded Neville at Rugby, where he had achieved every distinction, but thereafter their paths were to diverge. The elder son was destined by his father for a political career; he was educated at Cambridge, Berlin and Paris, and was elected to the House of Commons, as a Liberal Unionist, before his 30th birthday. Neville, his father decided, should go into business and the question of a university education did not arise. Instead, he was sent as a day student to Mason College, Birmingham, where for two years he studied mathematics, engineering and metallurgy, and was subsequently apprenticed to a Birmingham firm of Chartered Accountants.

Joe Chamberlain had disposed of his interest in the firm of Nettlefold & Chamberlain in 1874, but was on the lookout for investment opportunities and in 1891, when Neville was 22, he bought part of the island of Andros, in the Bahamas, and sent his younger son out to establish a sisal plantation with a view to producing fibre for rope-making. It was a singularly ill-considered venture. The soil on the island was poor and the local strain of the plant proved incapable of producing a commercial yield. Nevertheless, the young Neville threw himself into the enterprise with a fierce determination to succeed, not least to impress his father and his gilded half-brother.

He was desperately lonely, with only a white overseer, whom he did not consider his social or intellectual equal, and some 800 natives to supervise. He drugged himself with unceasing toil, and within four years had cleared 6,000 acres of bush, planted it, built roads, houses, stores and shop and a wharf, imported machinery from Cuba and began to lay a railway line to transport the fibre to the wharf. It was all in vain; the quality of the finished fibre was so poor it was impossible to find any customers to buy it. Yet Neville refused to face the facts, persevering long after there was any realistic hope of turning the venture round, and it was only after six years – in 1897 – that he returned to Birmingham and confessed that the operation was a total failure. By then, it had cost Joe more than a third of his fortune.

"It is not difficult to find in the young man on the island of Andros some of the virtues and defects that were later to be seen in the Prime Minister" was the perceptive comment of Francis Williams.

> The virtues of tenacity and courage, the defects of obstinacy and refusal to recognise any fact that did not fit in with his own hopes … [his] increasingly exasperated contempt for the general incompetence of humanity, so incapable of appreciating what was good for it, so unwilling to do what it was told … [he] was forced by the conditions of his life into a habit of inordinate dependence upon his own solitary judgment.
>
> *(Williams, 1965, p. 139)*

Yet Chamberlain blamed himself, perhaps unduly, for the Andros debacle, and determined to redeem himself, above all in the eyes of his father, by plunging into a business career in Birmingham. Family connections helped him secure controlling directorships in two medium-sized metal-making firms, but it was his clear if unimaginative mind, exceptional diligence and careful – even excessive – attention to detail which contributed to his success. He kept his head down, and after 14 years of steady if unspectacular growth by the two firms he had established himself as one of the city's leading businessmen and earned a sufficient competence to be able to consider wider horizons.

In 1911 he was 42 years old, and that year he took two decisive steps which were to determine the future pattern of his life. On 5 January, he got married to Anne de Vere Cole, the daughter of an army officer and country landowner. The marriage was to bring him great happiness, and the birth within three years of both a daughter, Dorothy, and a son, Frank. It did little to alter the public persona of a stiff, pernickety, obstinate character, whom many of his associates had regarded as an inveterate bachelor. In November, he was elected to the City Council of Birmingham, which that year was greatly expanded by the absorption of many of its suburbs within the city boundaries.

Neville was already heavily involved in civic activities in Birmingham, becoming chairman of the General Hospital and a leading campaigner for the creation of a new university, which would absorb George Mason College. He had shown little public interest in politics, though he was a fully committed supporter of the Conservative opposition to the Liberal government and of his father's Tariff Reform policies. By this time, Joe, who had suffered a devastating stroke in 1906, was totally incapacitated, though he remained an MP until his death in 1914. Austen had fulfilled his early promise, rising to Chancellor of the Exchequer under Arthur Balfour, and was currently the favourite to succeed him as Tory leader, though – as described in Chapter 6 – he eventually stood down in favour of Bonar Law. Neville still appeared to be the ugly duckling of the family, and there were few indications that he would rise to a higher position in the state than his illustrious father and brother.

Joining the Birmingham City Council was the making of Neville. He quickly revealed outstanding skills as a municipal administrator, and showed that he had inherited the radical instincts – at least as far as local government was concerned – of his father, who had first made his reputation as a reforming Lord Mayor four decades earlier. As chairman of the town planning committee, he pioneered the first comprehensive town planning schemes ever to be adopted in Britain, and – against strong opposition from banking interests – he established the first and only municipal savings bank in the country, which proved a lasting success. After only four years on the council, he became Lord Mayor in 1915 – amazingly the 11th member of his family to hold the post, but the only one – apart from Joe – to leave a distinctive mark. The condescending description of him, often attributed to Churchill but actually by Lord Hugh Cecil, as "a good Lord Mayor of Birmingham – in a lean year", was a considerable under-evaluation.

If it was not for his half-brother, Neville would probably have been content to continue serving his native city for many years, finally retiring amidst much honour as the great Panjandrum of British local government. But Austen, having joined Lloyd George's coalition government as Secretary of State for India, was asked by the Prime Minister if he could recommend a good administrator to take over the new post of Director-General of National Service, and had no qualms in suggesting his younger sibling.

Thinking it was his wartime duty to serve the government in whatever capacity was proposed, Neville immediately resigned as Lord Mayor and travelled to London to assume his appointment in March 1917, without any discussion of the extent of his responsibilities or even whether he would receive a salary.

Seven months later he resigned, feeling that the fiasco of Andros had been repeated, but this time he did not blame himself. He complained to his sisters of his "d----d well-meaning brother", but his real ire was directed at Lloyd George, whom he believed had utterly failed to give him the necessary backing to make a success of his assignment. This had been to organise voluntary recruitment both for military service, but above all for civilian work in war industries.

In fact, Neville was all at sea in Whitehall, whose ways were very different from those of Birmingham Town Hall. Not possessing a seat in the Cabinet, or even in the House of Commons, he was unable to defend himself from political attack, and was regularly outmanoeuvred by the War Office and the Ministry of Labour, which were in no mood to cede any of their responsibilities to the new department. Neville and his civil servants were subjected to a malicious campaign by Lord Northcliffe's newspapers (including *The Times*), which were anxious to abandon the voluntary principle in favour of compulsion. Stubborn as ever, Neville held on to his post for several months after it was clear that his position was hopeless, and finally threw in the towel in August 1917.

Neville drew two conclusions from this episode. One was that Lloyd George was fundamentally untrustworthy, and he resolved never again to have any dealings with him. The other was that he must get elected to the House of Commons if he was ever again to serve in a national post. Back in Birmingham, he tried – without success – to induce one or other of the sitting Tory MPs to resign in his favour, but he had to wait until the general election of December 1918, when he fought the newly created constituency of Birmingham Ladywood, to begin his parliamentary career, at the age of 49. This was far older than any other 20th-century Prime Minister, but once elected, Neville lost little time in making up for his late start.

His maiden speech, on the Rent Restriction Bill – in which he argued for more arduous conditions to be met by landlords before they would be permitted to raise rents – led to an immediate reversal of government policy. A rare achievement by a backbencher, which he followed up a few weeks later by successfully carrying an amendment against the government on the Electricity Supply Bill. These and other early parliamentary speeches were delivered with great clarity and authority, reflecting their author's formidable command of detail and the experience he had gained in local government. He introduced a Private Member's Bill to give protection to the children of unmarried mothers and was appointed to a number of influential committees, several of them as chairman. Little over a year after his election, he was offered a post in the government as Under-Secretary for Health. After some hesitation, he declined, not being able to bring himself to serve under Lloyd George.

At this time, Austen was Chancellor of the Exchequer, and in 1921 succeeded Bonar Law as leader of the Conservative Party. Though relations between the two brothers were generally good, they disagreed sharply in their views on the Prime Minister. It was therefore fortunate that Neville, who was returning from a holiday in Canada, was absent from the famous Carlton Club meeting on 19 October 1922, when Austen vigorously defended Lloyd George at a meeting of Tory MPs, and saw his own leadership swept aside as they voted by 187 votes to 87 to withdraw from the coalition government. Bonar Law consequently became Prime Minister of a purely Conservative government, and on his return to Britain, Neville received a message offering to appoint him as Postmaster-General. He hastened to consult Austen, who, he reported to his sister Hilda, "took the idea very badly, feeling that if I accepted it would be the last drop of bitterness in the cup" (Macleod, 1961, p. 87). Neville then declared that he would give up the post, and with it his political career, because "I cared more for our personal relations than for politics". Austen, shamed or, perhaps, deeply moved, immediately withdrew his opposition.

Bonar Law, and his successor, Stanley Baldwin, were both immensely impressed by Chamberlain's judgement and administrative gifts, and his ministerial career took off like a rocket. Within little over a year, he had worked his way through three successive posts, including Minister of Health (where he passed an important Housing Bill). In August 1923 Baldwin wrote to him on holiday offering him the post of Chancellor of the Exchequer, which he promptly declined, writing to his sister Ida,

> I should be a fish out of water. I know nothing of finance; I like spending money much better than saving it; I hate blocking other people's schemes and – I only thought of this after I had written – I shall have to live in Downing St. instead of Eaton Square.

But Baldwin would not take no for an answer, and after a long interview in Downing Street Chamberlain reluctantly agreed to take the post, which Baldwin himself had been occupying on a temporary basis. Not that Chamberlain had any time to show his mettle. Barely three months after his appointment, Baldwin and his government went down to defeat in the 1923 election, before he was able to produce a single budget. He could have resumed the chancellorship less than a year later, when the Labour government went down to defeat in the October 1924 election, but doggedly refused. "I am likely to be a great Minister of Health", he wrote, "but am not likely to be more than a second rate Chancellor". In choosing the lesser office, he was (consciously?) following in the footsteps of his father, who preferred being Colonial Secretary to Chancellor, under both Salisbury and Balfour.

Whether or not he was influenced by Joe's example, he was showing a clear-headed awareness of his own abilities and limitations which was not always typical of him. As Minister of Health he was the undoubted star of Baldwin's second government and clearly established himself as the number two in the Conservative hierarchy. His determination and self-confidence were remarkable. Within a week of taking office, he had circulated to his bemused Cabinet colleagues a list of 25 Bills which he intended to carry over the next four years. In the event, 21 of them reached the Statute Book, along with several others, which he had not originally foreseen.

They included a major reform of the rating system, and a comprehensive reform of local government, which also involved the abolition of the Poor Law Guardians. The general tenor of his reforms was in a socially progressive direction, which might have led to him being characterised as being well on the left wing of the Conservative Party, many of whose members resented his proposals. He averted this tag thanks to his cold public personality, which prevented him from showing any sympathy for the plight of the unemployed, and his studied contempt for the Labour leadership. Baldwin was to rebuke him for this, in June 1927 when, he wrote to one of his sisters, "Stanley begged me to remember that I was addressing a meeting of gentlemen. I always gave him the impression, he said, when I spoke in the House of Commons, that I looked on the Labour Party as dirt."

In the 1929 general election, Chamberlain shrewdly moved from the inner city constituency of Ladywood, which turned out to be a Labour gain, to the plusher seat of Edgbaston, which he represented for the remainder of his life. In opposition, Baldwin appointed him as party chairman, and he instituted the Conservative Research department and commissioned a study on the introduction of tariffs. When, in February 1931, rumbles of discontent about Baldwin's leadership reached him, he made no attempt to play them down, and passed on to his leader a savagely critical report from the Chief Agent, which implied that he should stand down in Chamberlain's favour. A shaken Baldwin agreed to go, but then changed his mind overnight and decided to fight back, excoriating the press lords, Beaverbrook and Rothermere, who had been campaigning against him, and routing the candidate whom they had put up against the official Tory in a crucial by-election in Westminster St. George's. Chamberlain was now 61, only two years younger than Baldwin, and it looked as though he had blown his best chance of succeeding him.

Yet he continued to be the party's work-horse, and his assiduity was widely contrasted with Baldwin's apparent laziness. This stood him in good stead in August 1931, when he remained in London during the death throes of Ramsay MacDonald's Labour government, while Baldwin returned to Aix-les-Bains to conclude his holiday. Chamberlain favoured the formation of a coalition government, to which Baldwin was greatly averse, but when he finally got back to London for a meeting with George V on 23 August, he found that – with the Liberals already on board – it was almost a *fait accompli*. He did not have the temerity to refuse the King's request to serve under MacDonald and "save the country". As Roy Jenkins comments, had he returned to London earlier, "he might have been asked a less direct question and been able to divert the pressure" (Jenkins, 1998, p. 344). For Baldwin, this meant that his return to the premiership was postponed for another four years; for Chamberlain it was confirmation of his still increasing authority within the Tory Party.

Chamberlain became Minister of Health in the new National government, but after the election in October 1931, when it was returned with a huge (and predominantly Conservative) majority, he replaced Philip Snowden as Chancellor of the Exchequer. This time he had no hesitation in accepting the post, as he saw that the conjunction of the economic crisis and the massive Tory majority would give him the ideal opportunity to implement the protectionist doctrines he had inherited from his father, thus bringing an end to 90 years of free trade. It mattered little to him that, in so doing, he would drive Snowden and the free trade Liberal ministers to resignation. He announced the new policy – which included a general revenue tariff of 10 per cent, variable upwards to 100 per cent for industries, such as steel, needing special safeguards, and downwards to nil for reasons of Commonwealth preference – on 4

February 1932, which he described in a letter as "the great day of my life". He ended his speech with the following words:

> There can have been few occasions in all our long political history when the son of a man who counted for something in his day and generation has been vouchsafed the privilege of setting the seal on the work which his father began but was forced to leave unfinished … I believe he would have found consolation for his disappointment if he could have foreseen that these proposals, which are the direct and legitimate descendants of his own conception would be laid before the House of Commons, which he loved, in the presence of one and by the lips of the other of the two immediate successors to his name and blood.

He was, of course referring to Austen, whom he had long ago superseded as his father's principal political heir, and who was now languishing on the back benches, from which he descended to give his brother a warm handshake. It was no accident that Neville, the late starter, had forged ahead in the political race. The elder brother was both the more pompous and the more soft-centred of the two; Neville had more iron determination in his character than Austen, who was the subject of a famous quip by F.E. Smith (Lord Birkenhead): "Poor old Austen. He always played the game, and he always lost it."

Neville was less lucky with the second half of his operation, which was to persuade the governments of the Dominions to offer reciprocal preferences to British exporters. The Ottawa conference on Commonwealth trade, which he attended with six other British Cabinet ministers in July 1932, was only a very partial success. According to Roy Jenkins, "enough discrimination was achieved to give the Americans a running grievance, but not enough to produce any great stimulus of Empire trade" (Jenkins, 1998, p. 348).

Chamberlain proved an extremely efficient Chancellor, who probably achieved the best results possible from highly inappropriate policies. His budgets, all very restrictive, succeeded in balancing the books, and by 1935 he had rescinded the last of the savage cuts imposed in 1931, and a partial economic recovery had taken place. Yet Chamberlain steadfastly refused to contemplate any Keynesian measures, and he was contemptuous of the public works programmes introduced by President Franklin Roosevelt as part of his New Deal.

Chamberlain retained the chancellorship when Baldwin succeeded MacDonald in 1935, and he held the office for nearly six years until May 1937, when he himself became Prime Minister, at the advanced age of 68, and two months after the death of Austen. Neither MacDonald nor Baldwin had shown the slightest inclination to interfere with his stewardship, and he was the undisputed master of Britain's economic policies throughout his tenure. As Prime Minister, he early showed that he had no intention of treating his own ministers with such a light hand, and – in particular – that he was determined to ensure that he was in complete command of foreign policy. His interest had been aroused in 1934, when there had been an attempt to make him Foreign Secretary to replace the ineffective Sir John Simon. Chamberlain successfully resisted the move, but he subsequently paid much closer attention to international affairs. He was more alarmed than Baldwin by the rise of Nazi military power, and less unnerved than him by the 1935 Peace Ballot which had inhibited Baldwin from embracing a full-hearted rearmament programme. It was Chamberlain who took the initiative by proposing a substantial increase in the air estimates in his 1934 budget. This may well have proved the decisive factor in the Battle of Britain six years later.

Chamberlain, too, was at first strongly in favour of backing League of Nations sanctions against Italy, following Mussolini's invasion of Abyssinia, and it was only when these appeared to have failed, having been only partially applied, that he changed his tack. There was no point, he asserted, in continuing with ineffective sanctions, and he henceforth put his faith in appeasing, first Mussolini, and then Hitler, whom he assumed were rational men, prepared to act reasonably if their legitimate grievances were met. The first obstacle to carrying out Chamberlain's intentions was his Foreign Secretary Anthony Eden – young, glamorous and vain – whom he had inherited from Baldwin.

Eden doubted the wisdom of Chamberlain's attempt to woo Mussolini by offering to legitimise his conquest of Abyssinia, and his nose was put out of joint by what he believed to be the Prime Minister's use of his sister-in-law Ivy Chamberlain, Austen's widow, who was visiting Rome, to negotiate behind his back. He was also shocked by Chamberlain's abrupt dismissal of a proposal by President Roosevelt to summon a peace and security conference in Washington. Eden resigned on 20 February 1938, and was replaced by the more compliant Lord Halifax, leaving the still very junior R.A. Butler to answer Foreign Office questions in the House of Commons, though in the event Chamberlain himself took the major questions. Shortly before, he had shifted Sir Robert Vansittart, who was known to be anti-German and anti-appeasement, from his post as Permanent Under-Secretary of the Foreign Office. He then increasingly used his personal adviser, Sir Horace Wilson, an industrial relations expert who had no experience whatever of foreign affairs, as his chief diplomatic 'fixer'.

Chamberlain's commitment to appeasement (which was not then a 'dirty' word) was by no means an unworthy one. He hated the prospect of war, having been deeply scarred by the experiences of 1914–18, when, although he was too old for military service, he had been greatly affected by the death in action of his younger cousin, Norman Chamberlain, his closest ally on the Birmingham City Council, about whom this very unemotional man had published a moving memoir. He also shared the view, more widely held on the left, that the Treaty of Versailles had been unduly harsh on Germany, and that some restitution should be made. The tragedy was that what was withheld from a democratic Germany in the 1920s was willingly yielded, with interest, to the brutal Nazi dictatorship ten years later.

Chamberlain's error, and it was an egregious one, was in persisting with the policy long after it was apparent that, so far from placating the aggressive intent of the dictators, it was merely feeding their appetites for more and more outrageous demands. The refusal to confront Hitler's illegal military occupation of the Rhineland in 1936, or to react against the German and Italian intervention on Franco's side in the Spanish Civil War, led directly to his invasion of Austria in March 1938, to which Chamberlain made no serious protest and, indeed, replied to an urgent Russian request for Anglo-French-Soviet talks on joint resistance to any future aggression, that they would be "inappropriate".

Having swallowed up Austria, the Nazi dictator switched his attention to Czechoslovakia, where the large German minority in the Sudetenland had experienced a certain degree of discrimination, which fell far short of outright oppression. Czechoslovakia had a defensive pact with France, to which Britain was morally if not legally committed. The Soviet government was also pledged to come to the aid of the Czechs. Their government expressed its willingness to grant internal self-government to the Sudetens, but the Sudeten leader Konrad Henlein – egged on by Hitler – promptly upped his demands to the outright annexation by Germany of the whole region. On 12 September 1938, in a violent speech in Nuremberg,

Hitler threatened imminent military action if the Czech government refused to cede the territory.

Edouard Daladier, the French Prime Minister, seemed ready to go to war in defence of the Czechs, provided Britain did the same, though his Cabinet was far from resolute. Chamberlain, who had earlier sent the British banker and former Liberal politician Lord Runciman to Prague, in an attempt to mediate, now sent a message to Hitler suggesting an immediate meeting to discuss a peaceful settlement. On 15 September he flew to Berchtesgaden – his first-ever flight.

At Berchtesgaden, Chamberlain did little more than listen to a long rant by the Führer, who talked of the necessity of racial unity, boasted of his success in "incorporating" the Austrian people into the Reich and stated that the three million Sudeten Germans must be similarly incorporated, and that Czechoslovakia must end its "threatening military alliance" with Soviet Russia. Chamberlain made no attempt to counter Hitler's claims, saying merely that he would have to consult his Cabinet colleagues before giving a response. In the meantime, Hitler agreed to make no precipitate move. Chamberlain was not unduly impressed by the personality of Hitler, whom he later described to his Cabinet as "the commonest little dog", and wrote to Ida "You would take him for the house painter he once was". Nevertheless, he concluded, "I got the impression that here was a man who could be relied upon when he had given his word."

He returned to London in a complacent mood, confident that if the Czechs could be dragooned into accepting Hitler's demands all would be well. After assuring a somewhat restless Cabinet of his conviction that if Hitler was allowed to annex the Sudetenland that would mark the end of his ambitions, he met Daladier and his foreign minister, Georges Bonnet, who had travelled to London. It was a difficult encounter, lasting from before lunch until late in the evening, but finally the French duo were persuaded that they, too, should leave the Czechs in the lurch, despite their treaty commitments. At two o'clock the following morning the Czech President, Edvard Beneš, was summoned from his bed by the British and French ambassadors and was told that unless his government immediately agreed to Hitler's demands Czechoslovakia would be abandoned to its fate. Faced with such overwhelming pressure, the Czechs felt they had no alternative but to give way.

Chamberlain returned for a second visit to Hitler, at Bad Godesberg on 22 September, confident of a warm reception, given that he was in a position to report acceptance of what he believed to be the Führer's demands. Not only the British, but the French and Czech governments were now agreeable, he said, to a peaceful and orderly transfer, under international supervision, of the territories with a German-speaking majority. He was appalled by Hitler's response, delivered in a tone of high hysteria. This was that there could be no question of international supervision: within a week German troops would enter an area marked on the map by Hitler himself (which would include 800,000 Czechs), and everything within the area must be handed over by the Czechs – not even a single cow might be removed. It was evident that Hitler was at least as much interested in a military triumph as in the acquisition of German-speaking territories. Chamberlain was shaken by Hitler's outburst, but undertook to transmit the terms to the Czech government, without recommending them. He returned to London to report back to the Cabinet.

Here he faced a rebellion, surprisingly led by the hitherto arch-appeaser Lord Halifax. The Foreign Secretary sharply contradicted Chamberlain's view that the Czechs should still be pressed to submit. He felt, he said, that Hitler "was dictating terms as though he had won a

98 Neville Chamberlain

war but without having to fight". Halifax's arguments swung over a majority of the Cabinet, which was also influenced by mounting evidence that public opinion was swinging in favour of standing up to the German threats. The Cabinet reached no formal conclusions, but when it adjourned the general feeling was that if German troops were to enter Czechoslovakia Britain would have to join France in declaring war on Germany.

A naval mobilisation was ordered, and civil preparations for war proceeded apace, yet Chamberlain revealed just how little prepared he was to adopt the role of war leader by the hand-wringing broadcast he made on 27 September, when he said:

> How horrible, fantastic, incredible it is that we should be digging trenches and trying on gas masks here because of a quarrel in a far away country between people of whom we know nothing.

Yet, even then, he did not give up trying. He dispatched Horace Wilson to Berlin to make a last despairing appeal to Hitler, and followed this up with a request to Mussolini to use his influence on his fellow dictator. In the midst of a fraught Cabinet meeting on 28 September a relatively conciliatory message from Hitler was handed to Chamberlain, in which he insisted that German troops would march into the areas already conceded by the Czechs after the Berchtesgaden meeting, but that plebiscites should be held in the remaining areas. This was similar to a compromise plan already drawn up by Halifax, and it was agreed that Chamberlain should seek a further meeting with Hitler to clarify his intentions. Chamberlain then left for the Commons to address a House which fully expected that Britain would be at war within a few hours. In the midst of his speech, a further note arrived from Hitler announcing that he was convening a meeting in Munich the following day with Mussolini, and inviting Daladier and Chamberlain to attend. Chamberlain announced on the spot that he would accept the invitation, and the House responded with a great outpouring of relief and exaltation.

Early the following morning, Chamberlain, a tall incongruous figure, dressed in Edwardian clothing and clutching a rolled umbrella, boarded an aircraft at Heston aerodrome, to the west of London, accompanied by Horace Wilson, a clutch of officials and his Parliamentary Private Secretary, Lord Dunglass MP (subsequently rather better known as the Earl of Home or Sir Alec Douglas-Home). The conference, from which the Czechs were rigorously excluded, started at 12.30 p.m. and continued, with lunch and dinner breaks, for about 14 hours. On paper, the agreement which was eventually reached by the four leaders and signed in the early hours of 30 September was less brutal than the terms laid down by Hitler at Bad Godesberg. The German occupation was staggered over ten days, instead of being effected on 1 October, and an international commission was to be set up to supervise the transfer of territories and to organise plebiscites in the disputed areas. In practice, it was to make little difference, as Hitler systematically flouted all the conditional elements in the agreement, which he tore up the following March, when his troops occupied Prague and the rest of Czechoslovakia. The sole purpose of the agreement seems to have been to provide a fig leaf for Daladier's and Chamberlain's sacrifice of Central Europe's only democratic state.

Chamberlain stayed on for a further meeting with Hitler, where he induced him to sign a vacuous declaration, which stated that "We regard the Agreement signed last night … as symbolic of the desire of our two countries never to go to war with one another again". This was the famous scrap of paper which he waved in the air on his arrival back in Heston, where he was greeted by a hysterical crowd, rejoicing that there would be no war.

Munich cost Chamberlain the resignation of the First Lord of the Admiralty, Duff Cooper, who joined the small band of anti-appeasement rebels led by Winston Churchill, but won him vast – if short-lived – popularity in the country. Munich subsequently became a dirty word in the English language, though Chamberlain continues to have his defenders, who argue that the agreement gave Britain a year's grace, and that it was in a better position to wage war one year later than it had been in 1938. This was no doubt true, but it is even more evident that the improvement in Germany's military might was far greater. The evidence is authoritatively examined by the historian Graham Stewart in *Burying Caesar: Churchill, Chamberlain and the Battle for the Tory Party*. His conclusion was that "the justification for Munich seems threadbare" (Stewart, 1999, pp. 310–18).

The halo surrounding Chamberlain after Munich did not long survive. After the Kristallnacht pogrom in November 1938 it appeared quite tattered, and it was totally destroyed by the Nazi occupation of Prague four months later. The desperate and unrealistic guarantees that Chamberlain then gave to Poland and Romania were almost immediately negated by the failure to back them up with an agreement with the Soviet Union, whose signature of the Nazi-Soviet pact on 23 August 1939 sounded the death knell for Poland, which was invaded by German troops nine days later. With evident reluctance, Chamberlain then declared war on Germany, after giving Hitler 48 hours to reconsider and withdraw his troops. He sought to enlarge his government by bringing in the opposition Labour and Liberal parties, but they refused to serve under him. The inclusion of Winston Churchill, as First Lord of the Admiralty, and of Anthony Eden, as Dominions secretary, was evidently intended as an assurance that the war would be conducted vigorously.

This was hardly the case; the period of 'phoney war' began, leading Chamberlain to make the unfortunate observation in April 1940 that Hitler had "missed the bus". Just over a month later, Chamberlain himself was forced to resign after a dramatic debate on a Labour censure motion. The government's majority fell from 240 to 81, with 41 Tories voting with the opposition, and 60 others abstaining. Chamberlain made a final attempt to form a coalition government, but neither Labour nor the Liberals were prepared to serve, and he submitted his resignation, in the hope that Halifax would replace him (see next chapter). The censure debate had followed the disastrous Norwegian campaign, for which, ironically, Churchill bore the responsibility as First Lord. Chamberlain, however, attracted all the blame because of his utter failure to present himself as a convincing war leader.

He joined Churchill's government as Lord President, and proved a loyal and co-operative colleague, notably – though after some hesitation – joining Churchill and his two Labour colleagues in the five-man War Cabinet in rejecting Halifax's proposal to explore peace negotiations with Hitler. By then, cancer was creeping up on him and, after an unsuccessful operation in August, he resigned on 30 September. He died on 9 November, without any regrets, saying in one of his last letters, to Baldwin, "Never for one instant have I doubted the rightness of what I did at Munich."

It was as well for his peace of mind that he retained this certitude in his own judgement. For the appeasement policy was almost entirely his own project, pursued against the advice of top Foreign Office officials and without heed to occasional dissentient voices within his own Cabinet. Not that he was in the habit of seeking advice from his ministers, whom he regarded "not as joint architects of policy but as executive officers called together from time to time to report what they were doing and to receive their instructions" (Williams, 1965, p. 161). Chamberlain was a true loner, who according to his biographer, Keith Feiling, never had a single friend in whom he was able to confide. "His family always excepted", Feiling concluded, "he did not depend on other human beings" (Feiling, 1946). Right up to the end, Chamberlain remained a man who communed only with his wife, his two adoring spinster sisters and the spirits of his dead father and brother.

Works consulted

John Charmley, 1989, *Chamberlain and the Lost Peace*, London, Hodder & Stoughton.
Peter Clarke, 1991, *A Question of Leadership*, Harmondsworth, Penguin.
Keith Feiling, 1946, *The Life of Neville Chamberlain*, London, Macmillan.
Lucille Iremonger, 1970, *The Fiery Chariot*, London, Secker & Warburg.
Roy Jenkins, 1998, *The Chancellors*, London, Macmillan.
Iain Macleod, 1961, *Neville Chamberlain*, London, Muller.
Graham Stewart, 1999, *Burying Caesar: Churchill, Chamberlain and the Battle for the Tory Party*, London, Weidenfeld & Nicolson.
Francis Williams, 1965, *A Pattern of Rulers*, London, Longmans.

9

WINSTON CHURCHILL

His finest hour

In all the other chapters of this book, the attempt has been made to deal, however briefly, with the main political events in the entire career of the personality discussed. In the case of Winston Leonard Spencer Churchill (1874–1965) this has proved impracticable – so long and varied was his career, and so many and great its vicissitudes, that such an approach would have been unrealistic within the tight space constraints of this volume. It has, accordingly, been decided to concentrate almost wholly on his wartime premiership, from 1940 to 1945, and in particular on his contribution during the fateful year of 1940.

It is, however, necessary to consider the early circumstances of Churchill's life to understand the character of the man who became Prime Minister on 10 May 1940, at the age of 65. His father, Lord Randolph Churchill, a younger son of the seventh Duke of Marlborough, was a highly unstable figure and a demagogic politician, who became a youthful Chancellor of the Exchequer, only to resign from the post in a fit of pique after five months, in December 1886, dying nine years later at the age of 45 from syphilis. Lord Randolph was married to Jennie Jerome, the beautiful daughter of an American millionaire, whose fortune, sadly, proved to be insecurely based. A woman of easy virtue, who was to run through three husbands and a reputed 200 lovers, she was a glamorous but necessarily remote figure in the life of the young Winston, who was grievously neglected by both his parents.

This did not prevent him from idolising them. He doted on his mother from afar, and – as a young man – wrote a highly readable but unjustifiably laudatory biography of Lord Randolph. From his parents he inherited extravagant tastes, but not the financial means to support them – a gap he was largely able to fill by his amazing productivity as a journalist and author. An under-educated man, who was an indifferent pupil at his public school (Harrow), he nevertheless emerged with a deep love and knowledge of the English language, modelling his own style on the great rolling passages of the works of the historians Gibbon and Macaulay.

He also learnt early on that if he was to fan the flickering interest of his absent parents he must seize every opportunity to attract attention to himself. He grew up to be an exceptionally brash young man – a show-off, but one who was prepared to work diligently to obtain his objectives. He also became oblivious to personal danger, rushing around the world from one

DOI: 10.4324/9781003031963-10

trouble spot to another in his search for glory and renown as a soldier and part-time journalist. This took him from Cuba to Sudan, the North-West Frontier and South Africa (where he escaped after being captured by the Boers) in the five years from 1895 to 1900, when he was elected for the first time as Tory MP for Oldham, at the age of 25.

The young Churchill had a pugnacious nature, but also a deeply romantic temperament. An ardent patriot, strongly committed to the British Empire, then straddling a quarter of the globe, he looked for inspiration to his warrior ancestor, John Churchill, the first Duke of Marlborough, of whom he was much later to write a four-volume biography, the success of which did much to ease the strain on his finances during the 1930s. Despite his traditional loyalties, he was by no means fixated on the past: he had an open, questing mind, which was ever seeking radical solutions to the problems of his own day. Intensely ambitious, he alienated many by his apparent self-absorption, though others were attracted by his vitality and zest for life. Among these was the 19-year-old Violet Asquith, whom he met at a dinner party in 1906, and who retained a vivid memory of their conversation nearly 60 years later, recalling that his final words were: "We are all worms. But I do believe that I am a glow-worm" (Bonham Carter, 1995, p. 16). Beneath this braggadocio, however, lay a strong melancholy streak, which manifested itself in moods of dark depression, which he referred to as his "black dog".

Violet's father was also highly impressed by Churchill, bringing him into his Cabinet at the young age of 31, and promoting him to such senior offices as Home Secretary and First Lord of the Admiralty. Personally very fond of Winston, he was less uncritically admiring than his daughter and gradually lost his faith in his reliability, concluding in a letter to Lady Venetia Stanley in 1916, "He will never get to the top in English politics, with all his wonderful gifts; to speak with the tongue of men and angels, and to spend laborious days and nights in administration, is no good if a man does not inspire trust."

Asquith's verdict in 1916 would surely have been repeated, in spades, by a large majority of politicians in the 1930s, particularly among his fellow Conservative MPs. A man who had changed his party affiliation twice, who was still widely if unjustly blamed for the Gallipoli disaster during World War I, whose five-year term as Chancellor of the Exchequer between 1924 and 1929 had been devoid of any lasting achievement, who had then wasted another five years of his life campaigning, in an unbridled way and alongside the most reactionary figures in his own party, against modest proposals to extend self-government in India, who had attacked his own party leaders with great ferocity, and had attempted a last-ditch stand in defence of King Edward VIII during the Abdication crisis, was regarded as 'unsound' if not completely off his head by all but a tiny group of admirers. Few observers would demur from the judgement of a later Tory MP and distinguished biographer, Robert Rhodes James, who entitled his book about his career up to 1939, *Churchill: A Study in Failure.*

And yet, one virtue of Churchill's was to weigh more in the scales than all his many failings – his clear-eyed view of the Nazi threat, which pre-dated Hitler's rise to power in 1933, and which he tirelessly hammered home over the following six years to the great discomfort of his party leaders. This, despite the fact that he dearly wanted to resume his ministerial career, interrupted since 1929. Baldwin regretfully, but Chamberlain emphatically, refused to include him in their governments, even though the post of Minister of Supply, almost tailor-made for a man of his qualities, was created specifically to facilitate the rearmament programme.

When war broke out in September 1939, Chamberlain felt he had no choice but to broaden his government by bringing in Churchill, particularly as both the Labour and Liberal parties had refused to serve under him. Churchill became First Lord of the Admiralty, the post he had filled at the outset of World War I, and a signal went out to all the ships of the fleet that "Winston is back". Chamberlain was pleasantly surprised to find him a co-operative and completely loyal colleague, who held himself aloof from any intrigue. It was, however, impossible to disguise the fact that he stood out as much the most combative member of the government, and his frequent and forceful broadcasts did much to rally national morale, while his personal popularity soared among the public at large, if not among Tory MPs.

He was virtually the only minister who pressed ideas for carrying the war forward aggressively against the enemy. As early as September 1939 he argued in favour of breaching Norwegian and Swedish neutrality by occupying or destroying the iron-ore fields in northern Sweden and cutting off vital supplies for the Germans through the Norwegian port of Narvik. His wider plans were not accepted, but the navy was eventually authorised to lay mines in Norwegian territorial waters, an action which was pre-empted by the German invasion in early April. Churchill then presided over a poorly planned and badly executed naval and military campaign to seize Narvik and other Norwegian ports. It was, ironically, the failure of this campaign which led to his replacing Chamberlain as Prime Minister.

Chamberlain's first reaction to the collapse of his majority in the censure debate on 7–8 May was to renew his invitation to the Labour and Liberal leaders to join a reconstructed government. Both again refused, but indicated that they would be prepared to serve under either Churchill or the Foreign Secretary, Lord Halifax. Halifax was a long-time opponent of Churchill, both as an appeaser and as an advocate of political reforms in India during his period as Viceroy, under the name of Lord Irwin, in 1926–31. He had overwhelming backing among Tory MPs and was the preferred choice of Chamberlain and of George VI. The fact that he was a member of the House of Lords was an inconvenience, but was not regarded as a serious obstacle, even by the Labour Party. It was, however, seized on by Halifax as the ostensible reason for declining the post. His real motivation was different – recalling the way in which the indecisive Asquith had been overshadowed and undermined by the more dynamic Lloyd George in World War I, he feared that he would suffer the same fate if Churchill were to serve under him as Defence Minister, in fact if not in name. There is also some evidence that he thought that Churchill's tenure as Prime Minister would be short and unsuccessful, and that he would then be called upon to clear up the mess. For whatever reason, he bowed out when the premiership was his for the having, despite passionate entreaties from, among others, R.A. Butler, his Under-Secretary at the Foreign Office, and Lord Dunglass (Alec Douglas-Home), Chamberlain's PPS, both of whom had been arch-appeasers.

Unlike Halifax, Churchill desperately wanted the premiership, and left a rather fanciful account in his War Memoirs about how he had deliberately remained silent, when Chamberlain had asked him, during a quadripartite meeting with Halifax and the Tory Chief Whip, whether he saw any difficulty about the Prime Minister being in the House of Lords. Only when Halifax had definitely ruled himself out did Chamberlain decide that he should recommend Churchill to the King. This was on the evening of 9 May; on the following morning Hitler invaded Holland and Belgium, and Chamberlain tried to go back on his intended resignation – a move which was firmly squashed by senior ministers, notably the Air Minister, Sir Kingsley Wood, who was soon to be rewarded by Churchill with the post of Chancellor of the Exchequer.

At 6 p.m. on 10 May, Churchill was summoned to Buckingham Palace, and accepted the commission to form a government. He returned to Whitehall, and worked, closeted with Attlee, until the early hours on the shape of his War Cabinet and other ministerial appointments. At

3 a.m., he at last went to bed, conscious, as he recalled in his Memoirs, "of a profound sense of relief" that he had obtained "authority to give directions over the whole scene. I felt as if I were walking with destiny, and that all my life had been but a preparation for this hour and this trial."

Lloyd George had said of Churchill: "The two great qualities for a Prime Minister are patience and courage. Winston will be defective in patience." It seemed a reasonable prediction, but was triumphantly refuted by Churchill's conduct during the first, difficult days of his premiership. In no respect was this clearer than in his handling of his dispossessed predecessor. Aware of the extreme weakness of his own position in the Conservative Party, Churchill set out to make a shield out of his former rival, and was determined to have him as a central figure in his small War Cabinet. Even in personal terms, he treated Chamberlain with great consideration, allowing him to continue to live in 10 Downing Street for a month while finding other accommodation. His first intention had been to make him both Chancellor of the Exchequer and Leader of the House of Commons, but this was vetoed by the Labour Party. In the end, Chamberlain settled for the most senior of the three sinecure offices – the Lord Presidency of the Council – in which capacity he was to chair important Cabinet committees and act as Churchill's deputy. Clement Attlee became Lord Privy Seal, and the deputy Labour leader, Arthur Greenwood, Minister without Portfolio. Halifax, who retained the Foreign Office, was the fifth member of this exclusive team.

Outside the Cabinet, senior posts were found for prominent Labour figures, such as Ernest Bevin, Herbert Morrison and Hugh Dalton, while A. V. Alexander succeeded Churchill as First Lord of the Admiralty. Most of the former Chamberlainite ministers were retained, though the least popular of them – Sir Samuel Hoare – was sacked and Sir John Simon was pushed up to the House of Lords as Lord Chancellor. The Liberal leader, Sir Archibald Sinclair – a long-term associate of Churchill's – became Air Minister.

Churchill's first appearance in the House of Commons as Prime Minister underlined his lack of Conservative support. He was loudly cheered by Labour and Liberal members, but the Tories – who had a few minutes earlier given a hero's welcome to Chamberlain when he entered the chamber – remained silent. They could not fail, however, to be impressed by the note of total defiance which he struck in the short statement he then made from the front bench – words which were to reverberate down the years:

> I would say to the House, as I said to those who have joined this government, that I have nothing to offer but blood, toil, tears and sweat. We have before us an ordeal of the most grievous kind ... You ask, what is our policy? I will say: it is to wage war, by sea, land and air, with all our might and with all the strength that God can give us: to wage war against a monstrous tyranny, never surpassed in the dark, lamentable catalogue of human crime. That is our policy. You ask, what is our aim? I can answer in one word: It is victory, victory at all costs, victory in spite of all terror, victory, however long and hard the road may be, for without victory, there is no survival.

The first fortnight of Churchill's premiership was filled with the most devastating news from the battlefronts in Belgium and France. The German army, superbly led, outflanked the Maginot line and decisively broke through the French defences at Sedan, while its panzer units raged through Belgium, reaching the Channel coast west of Dunkirk, cutting off the bulk of the British Expeditionary Force and the French First Army. Then, on 24 May, Hitler – apparently unaccountably – halted General Guderian's forces which were rapidly advancing on Dunkirk. This fatal error probably cost him total victory in the war. Churchill and his government did not then believe that it would be possible to evacuate more than a tiny proportion of the troops who had been cut off, and thought that the bulk of the British Expeditionary Force would be carted off to prisoner of war camps.

At this moment – totally unknown to the British public – Churchill faced the greatest challenge to his leadership, as the War Cabinet debated – in nine meetings over three days (26–28 May) – whether, in effect, to seek a compromise peace with Germany. The initiative was taken by Halifax, who had had a lengthy interview with the Italian Ambassador, Giuseppe Bastianini. The ostensible purpose of the discussion was to determine what price, if any, Mussolini would demand to stay out of the war, instead of coming in on the German side, as was imminently expected. Yet behind this was a wider purpose – to seek to enlist the Italian dictator as a mediator with Hitler, with a view to a general settlement, which would enable Britain, as well as France, to withdraw from the conflict. Halifax proposed that a direct approach should now be made to Mussolini to assume this role.

Churchill was totally against making such a *démarche*, but – unsure of the balance of forces within the War Cabinet – made no attempt at the outset to squash Halifax's proposal, and allowed it to be argued out at length. It soon transpired that the two Labour men – Greenwood more volubly than Attlee – were on his side, whereas Chamberlain hovered on the fence, initially appearing to tend more towards Halifax. Churchill realised that a three-to-two division in his favour would not be sufficient, as in any open split Halifax and Chamberlain would be certain to carry with them the bulk of Conservative MPs, who themselves constituted a sizeable majority in the Commons, leaving Churchill's position untenable. He gradually won Chamberlain round, and attempted to reinforce his stand by co-opting the Liberal leader, Archibald Sinclair, to join the discussions in the War Cabinet. When the Cabinet adjourned after the second of its three meetings on 27 May (the day the Belgians surrendered), the issue was still very much in doubt, with Halifax threatening to resign if he did not get his way. Churchill then took Halifax for a walk in the garden of 10 Downing Street, and used all his charm in a bid to keep his Foreign Secretary on board.

Churchill's crucial – and perhaps unpremeditated – move was his address to a meeting the following day of the most senior ministers outside the Cabinet. He recounted what happened in his War Memoirs, reporting that, after he had said, "Of course whatever happens at Dunkirk, we shall fight on":

> There occurred a demonstration which, considering the character of the gathering – twenty-five experienced politicians and Parliament men, who represented all the different points of view, whether right or wrong, before the war – surprised me. Quite a number seemed to jump up from the table and come running to my chair, shouting and patting me on the back.

This enthusiastic reception was fully confirmed in the published diaries of two of the participants of the meeting – Hugh Dalton (Labour) and Leo Amery (Conservative) – and word of it soon filtered back to the Cabinet room, which led Halifax to throw in the towel at the ensuing meeting – the last of the nine – which lasted a bare 20 minutes. Churchill made no reference to Halifax's peace initiative in his War Memoirs, in which he made the extraordinary claim that:

> Future generations may deem it noteworthy that the supreme question of whether we should fight on alone never found a place upon the War Cabinet agenda. It was taken for granted and as a matter of course by these men of all parties of the State, and we were much too busy to waste time on such unreal, academic issues.
>
> *(Second World War, II, p. 157)*

Roy Jenkins described this as "the most breathtakingly bland piece of misinformation to appear in all those six volumes" (Jenkins, 2001, p. 610), and the truth only emerged many years later with the opening of the War Cabinet minutes under the Thirty-Year Rule. The full story was finally told, in riveting detail, by the American historian, John Lukacs, in a brilliant short book, *Five Days in London, May 1940*, published in 1999. Churchill's motive in concealing it may well have been a chivalrous desire to protect the reputation of Halifax, whom he prudently replaced as Foreign Secretary with Anthony Eden in December 1940, dispatching him to Washington as Ambassador, where he proved a loyal interpreter of Churchill's policies for the remainder of the war.

Yet this episode was by far the most important in Churchill's entire premiership. It strongly suggests that if Halifax had accepted the premiership there would have been a negotiated peace with Hitler, with devastating consequences for the freedom of the world. And despite Chamberlain rallying, in the end, to Churchill's support, he also might well have sought peace if he had managed to carry on as Prime Minister (he had, already on 10 May, told the American Ambassador Joseph Kennedy that he did not see how Britain would be able to carry on if France dropped out of the war).

Less than a week after these anguished discussions, Churchill's position was immeasurably strengthened by the successful conclusion of the Dunkirk evacuation, with more than 338,000 British and allied troops brought back, although all their heavy equipment was left behind. This was the occasion for one of Churchill's major parliamentary triumphs. "Wars are not won by evacuations", he told the Commons on 4 June, but went on to evoke with matchless eloquence the newly evolving determination of the British people not to submit to Hitler's will. His closing words have etched themselves on the collective memory of succeeding generations:

> We shall not flag or fail. We shall go on to the end. We shall fight in France, we shall fight on the seas and the oceans, we shall fight with growing confidence and growing strength in the air, we shall defend our island, whatever the cost may be. We shall fight on the beaches, we shall fight on the landing grounds, we shall fight in the fields and in the streets, we shall fight in the hills, we shall never surrender, and even if, which I do not for a moment believe, this island or a large part of it were subjugated and starving, then our Empire beyond the seas, armed and guarded by the British Fleet, would carry on the struggle, until, in God's good time, the new world with all its power and might, steps forth to the liberation of the old.

Churchill strove mightily during the next fortnight to keep France in the war, despite the fall of Paris on 14 June. His last desperate throw was the proposal, emanating from Jean Monnet, and approved in a few minutes by the War Cabinet at a Sunday afternoon meeting on 16 June, to amalgamate the British and French states in an "indissoluble union". De Gaulle flew to Bordeaux to take the written proposal to the French government (having already telephoned the contents to Prime Minister Paul Reynaud). Reynaud failed to carry it through his Cabinet the same evening, and promptly resigned, leaving Pétain to seek an armistice with the Germans. Churchill's response was to make another of his magnificent orations to the House of Commons, full of echoes of Henry V's speech before Agincourt:

> The battle of France is over. I expect that the battle of Britain is about to begin. Upon this battle depends the survival of Christian civilisation. Upon it depends our own British life and the long continuity of our institutions and our Empire … Let us therefore brace ourselves to our duty and so bear ourselves that if the British Commonwealth and Empire last for a thousand years, men will still say, 'This was their finest hour'.

Yet Churchill had not finished with France. The peace agreement which Pétain negotiated did not contain cast-iron guarantees that the powerful French fleet would not fall into German or Italian hands. Churchill regarded this as a life-or-death matter, and ordered British naval commanders to present ultimata to the French squadrons in Alexandria (Egypt) and Oran (Algeria) to submit or face attack. The French admiral in Alexandria complied, but not his colleague in Oran, whose force was then largely destroyed, with the loss of 1,300 lives.

This ruthless decision, which understandably caused lasting resentment in France, had the unforeseen effect of firing the enthusiasm of Tory MPs. Previously the bulk of them had reacted lukewarmly to his parliamentary speeches, but on this occasion the whole House responded in what Churchill later described as "solemn, stentorian accord". From then on – having demonstrated that he was an iron man of action and not just a purveyor of brave words – he no longer had to contend with the sullen resentment of his own party. A dwindling group of irreconcilables remained, but the great majority now counted themselves among his supporters.

For several more months, the nation remained in daily fear of a German invasion, but by the end of October, with the daytime Battle of Britain giving way to the nocturnal Blitz, the threat was effectively over. The Battle of Britain (which was the occasion of yet another Churchillian flourish – "Never in the field of human conflict was so much owed by so many to so few") may in Roy Jenkins's words have been a "draw" – in terms of actual aircraft losses – rather than the stunning victory it appeared at the time. Yet its outcome meant that there was no question of Germany gaining aerial supremacy which, given its naval weakness, was an essential condition for a successful invasion. Other dangers remained – notably the U-boat onslaught on the Atlantic shipping routes – but by then it was reasonably certain that Churchill's gamble had come off. If Britain, on its own, could not hope to inflict defeat on the Germans, it now seemed unlikely that the enemy would be able to conquer Britain.

That it had been a gamble is incontrovertible. In the dark days of May and June a more rational man would have accepted that the war was lost, and that the only sensible course was to get the best terms possible out of Hitler. This was the judgement that King Leopold and Marshal Pétain made, and both of them were applauded – at least in the short term – by the bulk of their fellow countrymen. Nor had Churchill any solid basis for his belief that things were likely to improve. Halifax was pretty sure that they would not, and fumed in his private diary about Churchill "talking the most frightful rot". His biographer, Andrew Roberts, accurately interpreted his view by choosing "Churchill as Micawber" as a chapter heading

108 Winston Churchill

in his book, *The Holy Fox*. The only "something that will turn up" in Churchill's rosy-tinted vision at that time was American intervention on Britain's side, which, despite Churchill's friendly correspondence with President Franklin Roosevelt, was a distinctly remote prospect, particularly at a time when Roosevelt was seeking an unprecedented third term and declaring at an election meeting that "Your boys are not going to be sent into any foreign wars".

In truth, the only 'secret weapons' which Churchill had to deploy in 1940 were the force of his personality and the eloquence of his tongue. The first was evidenced by the way he galvanised his ministers, the armed forces and the Civil Service by his constant insistence on the urgency of the task. Every day a mass of memoranda flowed from Churchill's hand, many of them headed by the imperious instruction: 'ACTION THIS DAY'. As for his speeches, overblown and baroque as they now often seem, and already sounding rather old-fashioned at the time, they struck a curious resonance with people of all classes. Their immediate impact in the House of Commons was amplified many times when they were repeated in BBC broadcasts. On his 80th birthday, Churchill modestly disclaimed the suggestion that he had inspired the nation in 1940, saying: "It was the nation and the races dwelling all around the globe that had the lion heart. I had the luck to be called upon to give the roar." That was to understate his role, and he knew it. Without Churchill, it must be doubted whether the British would have summoned up the determination to resist after the disasters of May and June.

A serious argument could be made that Churchill's unique contribution was completed by the end of 1940, and that if he had then died, or been replaced by a more run-of-the-mill leader, it would have made no more than a marginal difference to the outcome of the war. For it was not won by Churchill's leadership, nor primarily by feats of British arms, but by Hitler's megalomania and grievous errors of judgement which brought both Russia and America into the war against him, ultimately ensuring his defeat.

Essential or not, Churchill continued to play a prominent role, not quite until the end of the war, but up to and beyond the final defeat of Germany in May 1945. For him, it was an all-absorbing task, to which he untiringly devoted himself – as if in a trance – at any hour of the day or night, to the continual exasperation of his hard-pressed staff. Lord Alanbrooke, for example, the Chief of the Imperial General Staff, described him in his War Diaries as "the most difficult man to work for I have ever struck ... lives for the impulse and for the present". He concluded, however, "I would not have missed the chance of working for him for anything on Earth". Churchill was forever pressing ideas on the general staff – many of them half-baked if not fantastical – for new initiatives and campaigns – and they often had the greatest difficulty in restraining his enthusiasm. He had no inhibitions in abruptly replacing unsuccessful field commanders, but though he argued fiercely with his general staff, he was never known – in contrast to Hitler – to over-rule them. He assumed the title of Minister of Defence, and, after the first few months, the War Cabinet, the size of which was considerably expanded, had little influence on the political direction of the war. For all intents and purposes, Churchill was the man in charge.

In domestic affairs it was a different matter. Churchill took very little interest in day-to-day decisions, and, for the most part, it was the Labour members of his Cabinet that made the running, particularly Ernest Bevin, the Minister for Labour, and Home Secretary Herbert Morrison. Overall co-ordination was left to his highly efficient Deputy Premier, Clement Attlee, who presided over the Cabinet during his frequent absences abroad. Ellen Wilkinson, a Labour Party minister, left a graphic description of their contrasting styles:

When Mr Attlee is presiding over the Cabinet in the absence of the Prime Minister the Cabinet meets on time, goes systematically through its agenda, makes the necessary decisions, and goes home after three or four hours' work. When Mr Churchill presides we never reach the agenda and we decide nothing. But we go home to bed at midnight, conscious of having been present at an historic occasion.

(Cited in Kingsley Martin, Harold Laski)

Throughout his premiership, Churchill attached exceptional importance to fostering his relationship with Roosevelt. He later told his private secretary, Jock Colville, "No lover ever studied every whim of his mistress, as I did those of President Roosevelt." His attempts to lure him to enter the war prior to the Japanese attack on Pearl Harbour, in December 1941, proved fruitless, but Roosevelt did approve the deal, in September 1940, to send Britain 50 old destroyers in exchange for base facilities in the West Indies, and after his re-election as President a steady stream of military supplies were sent across the Atlantic. Their first meeting, at sea in August 1941, led to the signing of the Atlantic Charter, a joint declaration of 'war aims', despite the continuing neutrality of the US. After December 1941 their correspondence became an almost daily affair; they met a further eight times, and spent a total of 120 days in each other's company. Jointly they planned the strategy for the war in the West, and it was only after D-Day, in June 1944, that it became clear that Britain was the junior partner, as the American military contribution was so much greater. Churchill's influence on the American President then declined as the latter began to give more weight to Stalin's views.

Churchill himself made strenuous efforts to establish the same rapport with the Soviet leader that he enjoyed with the US President – with only limited success. He flew to Moscow in October 1944, and reached an agreement with him on 'spheres of influence' in Eastern Europe and the Balkans. Under this agreement, Greece fell within the British sphere, and not a word of protest was received from Stalin when British forces suppressed a Communist-led uprising in Athens, in December 1944. In exchange, Stalin expected a free hand in Eastern Europe, despite giving undertakings that the right to free elections would be respected, notably in Poland, the borders of which were drastically withdrawn, in Russia's favour, at the Yalta conference in February 1945. By then, Churchill was seriously alarmed at the prospect of Soviet dominance, and tried – without success – to persuade the allied commander, General Eisenhower, to abandon his plans for a broad advance and to make a dash for Berlin to seize the city in advance of the Soviet troops.

Great war leader though he was, Churchill was no master strategist, and the historian A.J.P. Taylor identified three major strategic errors in his conduct of the war. First was the decision to concentrate on heavy bombing of German towns and cities, which he was convinced would bring German war production to a halt. It had no such effect, despite the killing of over half a million Germans. The cost to the allied cause was, Taylor argued, even greater, with production being diverted to the construction of heavy bombers, and the substantial losses of aircraft and aircrew. Mistake number two was what he described as Churchill's "obsession with the Mediterranean and the Middle East". Essentially a side-show, he argued, "it postponed any landing in northern France for two years and so helped to prolong the war". His third major error was grossly to under-estimate the risk of an attack by the Japanese, and to neglect to strengthen the defences of Singapore.

Churchill had his critics at the time, but there is no doubt that the vast majority of the British public heartily approved his conduct of the war, and an opinion poll in April 1945 showed 91 per cent support. Yet three months later, at the general election of 5 July, he was heavily defeated in a general election, and his party suffered its biggest setback since 1906. This was only very partially due to his maladroit election campaign, in which, during a broadcast, he caused widespread indignation by accusing the Labour leaders, who had loyally served with him throughout his premiership, of planning to introduce a "Gestapo" if they were elected. What brought Churchill down was his association with the Conservative Party, which had become deeply unpopular and was blamed not only for the failed appeasement policy, but also for the unemployment and economic failures of the 1930s. It could also be argued that the British electorate showed rare discrimination in deciding that, though his leadership in war had been indispensable, he was not the best person to lead the country in post-war reconstruction.

Clementine Churchill, who normally gave her husband good advice, wanted him to retire at this point, but he insisted on carrying on as leader of the opposition, though he attended to his duties very spasmodically, preferring to devote his energies to writing his six volumes of War Memoirs, and giving a series of set speeches to international audiences, in which he spelled out the danger of Soviet expansionism and preached the gospel of European unity. He became Prime Minister for a second time, at the age of 76, having narrowly won the 1951 general election. Little remained of his wartime dynamism, and he settled for a quiet life, making no attempt to reverse the widespread reforms introduced by the 1945 Labour government, even though they had – for the most part – been strenuously opposed by Tory MPs. His health was bad, and he might well have given up after a year or so, but the death of Stalin, in March 1953, persuaded him that the opportunity existed to assure world peace through a three-way summit between himself, President Eisenhower and Stalin's successor, and that only he could bring this about. It was an illusion, but Churchill carried on until April 1955, despite having had in July 1953 a severe stroke, which had been carefully hidden from the public. He then, clearly reluctantly, made way for Anthony Eden, to whom he had originally promised the succession as long ago as June 1940.

He remained an MP until October 1964, dying, full of honours, three months later. By this time, this once highly controversial figure had long since been almost universally recognised as "the greatest living Englishman", if not of all time. Nor has this view been greatly modified in the third of a century since his death, despite the appearance in 1993 of a hostile 'revisionist' biography by the historian John Charmley. Churchill may have been a man of monumental faults, but without him it is open to doubt whether hundreds of millions of Britons and other Europeans would be living in liberty today.

Principal works consulted

Paul Addison, 1978, 'Winston Churchill', in John P. Mackintosh (ed.), *British Prime Ministers of the Twentieth Century*, Vol. II, London, Weidenfeld & Nicolson.
Violet Bonham Carter, 1995, *Winston Churchill as I Knew Him*, London, Weidenfeld & Nicolson.
John Charmley, 1993, *Churchill: The End of Glory*, London, Hodder & Stoughton.
Peter Clarke, 1991, *A Question of Leadership*, London, Penguin Books.
Martin Gilbert, 1984, *Winston S. Churchill 1939–1941*, Vol. VI, London, Heinemann.
Martin Gilbert, 1986, *Winston S. Churchill 1941–1945*, Vol. VII, London, Heinemann.
Roy Jenkins, 2001, *Churchill*, London, Macmillan.
John Lukacs, 1999, *Five Days in London, May 1940*, New Haven and London, Yale University Press.

John Pearson, 1991, *The Private Lives of Winston Churchill*, New York, Simon & Schuster.
Andrew Roberts, 1994, *Eminent Churchillians, London*, Weidenfeld & Nicolson.
Graham Stewart, 1999, *Burying Caesar: Churchill, Chamberlain and the Battle for the Tory Party*, London, Weidenfeld & Nicolson.
A.J.P. Taylor, 2000, *British Prime Ministers and Other Essays*, Harmondsworth, Penguin.

10

CLEMENT ATTLEE

Quiet revolutionary

Clement Richard Attlee was born nine years later than Winston Churchill, in 1883, and came from rather lower down the social scale. Instead of Blenheim Palace, he was born in a solid middle-class house near Putney Hill. Yet he had a better start in life than the man he was to succeed as Prime Minister 62 years later. He was raised in a loving and stable family, which had no financial worries, as his father, Henry Attlee, was a prosperous City solicitor. A God-fearing man, who took family prayers each morning before breakfast, he was a Gladstonian Liberal of advanced views, who was a 'pro-Boer' during the South African War. Clement's mother, Ellen, was a cultured and educated woman, who apparently found complete fulfilment in looking after her husband, and their family of five boys and three girls. Unlike her husband, she was Conservative, with both a large and a small 'c'.

Clem, as he became known, was the second youngest child. He was under-sized (as he was to remain as an adult), and was regarded as too fragile to go to school until the age of 9, being educated at home by his mother and a series of governesses. One of these, Miss Hutchinson, had, by an astonishing coincidence, earlier had charge of the young Winston. It soon became clear that Clem was a clever boy, who immersed himself in books and developed a great love for poetry, dreaming of one day becoming a poet himself. He was, in fact, to write quite a lot of poetry, none of it above the 'good amateur' level, but mostly leavened with a mordant wit. He early developed a passionate interest in cricket, which he was to retain throughout his life, though he was an indifferent player, and the only 'sport' in which he ever gained any proficiency was billiards.

Clem was always particularly close to his brother Tom, who was two years his senior. Both were sent to a public school, Haileybury, then notorious for its bullying, which made a misery of Tom's life. Clem, however, despite his puny stature, seems to have remained unscathed, and formed a lifelong affection for his old school. He was to follow Tom to Oxford, where he studied modern history, specialising in the Italian Renaissance, and narrowly missed getting a First Class degree. He attended some debates in the Oxford Union, but, in his own words, "was much too shy to try to speak there". If he had, it would have been as a Tory, and to all appearances he was a thoroughly conventional young man.

DOI: 10.4324/9781003031963-11

Attlee came down from Oxford in 1904, after what he described as "three exceedingly happy years". He began to read for the bar, while living at his parents' home in Putney, and, having passed his exams without difficulty, joined the chambers of Sir Henry Dickens, the son of the novelist. Like other young barristers, he found that few briefs came his way, and he passed his time, pleasantly enough, by learning to ride, practising billiards and taking part in a literary society founded by his brother Tom. "This then", he recalled in his autobiography, "was the pattern of my days when in October 1905, an event occurred which was destined to alter the whole course of my life" (Attlee, 1954, p. 18).

This was his discovery of the East End of London, then mired in the most abject poverty and misery. He went to work for one evening a week at Haileybury House, a centre in the Limehouse area of Stepney, maintained by his old school, which ran a boys' club and cadet corps for youngsters in one of the most deprived districts. The painfully shy Clem found that he could unwind in the face of the warm reception which he received from the boys and his fellow voluntary workers. Soon he was going there on two evenings a week, then three and then four, and it became the main focus of his life. In 1907 the club manager resigned, and Attlee was invited to take his place, which involved living on the premises. He accepted, and, he recalled, "Thus began fourteen years' residence in East London".

His brother Tom, an architect, was similarly involved in helping out at a hostel in nearby Hoxton, and the two brothers – influenced by reading the works of writers such as John Ruskin and William Morris – became declared Socialists. Attlee always claimed, however, that the reason why he became a Socialist was the conditions of life in Limehouse. He recalled an occasion when he passed a little barefoot girl in the street, who asked him: "Where are you going, Mr Attlee?" He replied: "I'm going home for tea", and she responded: "Oh, I'm going home to see if there is any tea" (Attlee, 1954, p. 31).

Clem and Tom hastened to seek membership of the Fabian Society, and attended a meeting addressed by Bernard Shaw, Sidney Webb and other famous luminaries, including H.G. Wells, whom he found "very unimpressive". The others, however, "all seemed pretty impressive", and Attlee was rather over-awed. More to his taste was the local Stepney branch of the Independent Labour Party, to which he was taken by an East End wharf-keeper called Tommy Williams. What Attlee liked about the ILP – apart from their warm comradeship – was the essentially ethical appeal of the Socialism they preached. It was, he recalled, "a way of life rather than an economic dogma".

They were only about a dozen strong – all working men – but were highly active and organised three or four open-air meetings a week at street corners. Attlee, who was soon elected as branch secretary, threw himself into their work, performing all the most menial duties, including carrying round the tiny platform on which the street orators spoke.

He dreaded the day when he himself would be asked to perform, but when it came – on a dark night in March 1908 in Barnes Street, just off the Commercial Road – he finally overcame his shyness and got up to speak before an audience of five – all fellow members of the ILP. He was not very good, his voice carried badly, but finally about a dozen people turned up and asked questions, to which he was able to give well-informed and evidently sincere replies. He was soon much in demand, speaking at 53 indoor and outdoor meetings in 1909, and 88 in the following year.

During the daytime, he continued to go to his chambers, but he became progressively more bored with the law and hankered after doing more socially useful work. He quit the chambers in 1908, when his father died, leaving him a private income of £400 a year. He worked for some time as an organiser for Beatrice Webb's National Committee for the Break-Up of the Poor Law, and then as an 'official explainer' for the new National Insurance law introduced by the Liberal government. Then, in 1912, what he regarded as the ideal job became available, when he was appointed a lecturer in Social Policy at the newly established London School of Economics. His unsuccessful rival for the post was Hugh Dalton, whom he was to appoint as Chancellor of the Exchequer 33 years later. Attlee found the work intellectually satisfying, and it left him full freedom to carry on his work at Haileybury House and his political activities with the ILP. At this stage, he had no notion of a political career – his highest aspiration was to be elected to the Stepney Borough Council or the Limehouse Board of Guardians, for each of which he was twice an unsuccessful candidate.

In August 1914 he was on holiday in Devon with Tom and his wife. When war was declared both men decided unhesitatingly what they should do. Tom, who was a Christian Socialist, resolved to be a conscientious objector and served two harsh prison sentences during the war. Clem, an atheist though never a militant one, decided to volunteer at the earliest possible moment. Within a month, despite his age (31) and his slight stature, he was commissioned with the South Lancashire Regiment. He served throughout the war – in Gallipoli, from which he was evacuated with severe dysentery, but insisted on returning and commanded the rearguard which covered the final retreat, being the last person but one to leave the peninsula; in Mesopotamia, where he was seriously wounded by 'friendly fire'; and finally on the Western Front.

Major C.R. Attlee was demobilised in January 1919, and within two days was back in Stepney discussing the political situation with a local Jewish chemist, Oscar Tobin, who had emerged as the *de facto* Labour leader in the borough. Much had changed in Attlee's absence, with the establishment of a strong Stepney Labour Party and Trades Council, to which the local ILP branch was now affiliated. Tobin, aware that Attlee's war record would make him electorally popular, while his independent status would make him equally acceptable to the rival Irish and Jewish factions within the local Labour Party, strongly urged him to run in the forthcoming election for the London County Council. Attlee fought the Limehouse seat and was narrowly defeated, but when, in the following November, the Labour Party swept to victory in the Stepney Borough Council elections, he was nominated as Mayor, and subsequently became an alderman. Fifteen other Labour mayors were elected in London, and Attlee was chosen as their chairman and spokesman, his fame beginning to spread more widely in the Labour movement. His mayoral year – in which he provided strong intellectual and political leadership to the Council in all its activities – was regarded as an unequivocal success. In the meantime, he was adopted as Labour's prospective candidate for the parliamentary constituency of Limehouse, then a Tory-held seat.

The general election did not come until November 1922, following Bonar Law's replacement of Lloyd George as Prime Minister. By that time, Attlee was able to face the voters as a married man. In the summer of 1921 he had planned a holiday in Italy, with an old Oxford friend of Tom's, Edric Miller, who asked if his mother and younger sister Violet could come as well. Within six months Clem and Vi were married. He was 39, she 26. It was a happy and successful union, though Vi had virtually no interest in politics. She nevertheless invariably acted as a 'teller' for Clem at his election counts, and much later acquired some notoriety as his chauffeur during his nationwide election tours.

Attlee was elected with a comfortable majority, and was one of 142 Labour MPs who were recognised as the official opposition for the first time. Their initial task was to elect a new leader. Together with all the other ILP MPs, Attlee backed Ramsay MacDonald against the previous leader, J.R. Clynes, a choice they were later to regret. As leader, MacDonald chose two Parliamentary Private Secretaries, one of whom was Major Attlee, as he continued to be known for some time. A year later, after the 1923 election, in which he more than doubled his majority, he was appointed as Under-Secretary of State for War in the minority Labour government. This survived for less than a year, but long enough for him to acquire a reputation as one of its more effective junior ministers.

In opposition for the next five years, he was appointed as one of two Labour members of the commission led by Sir John Simon, set up to consider constitutional development in India, which involved two lengthy visits to the sub-continent. Before accepting, he sought and received an assurance from MacDonald that this would not preclude his inclusion in a future Labour government, and he was bitterly disappointed when MacDonald reneged on this promise when he formed his second administration in June 1929. Attlee had only just returned from India in time to fight the election, and for several months afterwards he was involved in writing the voluminous report of the commission, of which he had been much the most active member, apart from the chairman. It proposed substantial advances towards self-government at the provincial level, but fell short of recommending full Dominion status. Attlee's membership of the commission greatly stimulated his interest in both India and Burma and undoubtedly contributed to the decisiveness he showed in pressing forward with their independence in 1947.

In May 1930, Attlee finally entered the government, replacing Sir Oswald Mosley, who had resigned as Chancellor of the Duchy of Lancaster in protest against the government's lack of energy in tackling unemployment. In this sinecure office, Attlee's duties included organising the 1930 Imperial Conference, which produced the Statute of Westminster, formally recognising the independence of the Dominions, as well as piloting an Agriculture Bill through the Commons. In March 1931, he was appointed Postmaster-General, and amazed his colleagues by taking a crash course in management, the better to be able to administer his new department.

When, in the following August, the Labour government resigned and was replaced by a National government, under MacDonald's premiership, Attlee was emphatically not one of the handful of Labour MPs who were tempted to follow their former leader. Indeed, he characterised MacDonald's action as "the greatest betrayal in the political history of this country" (Attlee, 1954, p. 74). In the general election which followed, two months later, the Labour Party was all but destroyed, going down from 287 to 46 MPs. The new Labour leader, Arthur Henderson, was defeated, as was every other former Cabinet minister except the 72-year-old George Lansbury. Attlee just held on to his seat at Limehouse, in contrast to near contemporaries such as Herbert Morrison, Arthur Greenwood and Hugh Dalton, all of whom were senior to him in the party or ministerial hierarchy. The consequence was that, when the sadly diminished group of Labour MPs gathered together after the election, they unanimously chose Lansbury and Attlee as leader and deputy leader respectively.

During the next four years, Attlee carried a very considerable load. He often had to deputise for the ailing Lansbury, and their small flock was mostly elderly and undistinguished. Only Sir Stafford Cripps, the former Solicitor-General, and the youthful Aneurin Bevan were major forces in debate. Attlee had to acquire a total mastery of parliamentary procedure, and be prepared to speak on a large range of subjects with which he had previously been unfamiliar. "In 1932", he recalled, "I filled more columns of Hansard than any other Member and, as I am generally considered to be rather a laconic speaker, it can be judged that my interventions in Debate were numerous" (Attlee, 1954, p. 77). Then, in October 1935, shortly before the general election, Lansbury, who as a pacifist was unable to back the party's policy of armed sanctions in support of the League of Nations, resigned, and Attlee was elected in his place. He was not expected to serve as leader for more than a few months: he stayed for 20 years.

The general election, held on 14 November, saw only a partial Labour recovery, but 154 Labour MPs were returned, including many leading figures defeated in 1931. It was generally expected that one of these would take Attlee's place. Two were nominated – Arthur Greenwood, who had been Health Minister in the 1929 government, and Herbert Morrison, the ex-Transport Minister, who had recently won greater renown as the energetic leader of the London County Council. The results of the two ballots were as follows:

Attlee	58	88
Morrison	44	48
Greenwood	33	–

It was generally supposed that Attlee won primarily because the survivors of the 1931 Parliament voted almost *en bloc* in his favour. Another explanation was given to me many years ago by John Parker, who was elected in 1935 as a 27-year-old new MP. Morrison, he recounted, was asked at the party meeting if he would give up the leadership of the LCC if he was chosen, and declined to do so. This went down badly, and in his opinion cost Morrison the leadership. Whatever the reason, Morrison subsequently nursed a lasting grievance against Attlee, which surfaced in 1945 when he attempted, without success, to deprive him of the premiership.

The 1935 leadership election was significant for sowing the seeds of a future alliance between Attlee and Ernest Bevin. Bevin, the most powerful trade union leader at the time, had treated Attlee somewhat patronisingly, referring to him as "the little man", but he regarded Morrison with monumental distrust. When Greenwood, who had been backed primarily by trade union MPs, dropped out of the race, his supporters, many of them influenced by Bevin, nearly all switched their votes to Attlee.

Attlee was an assiduous leader of the opposition, but made little mark in the country. He firmly opposed Chamberlain's appeasement policy, but his position was undermined because of Labour's reluctance to support the government's rearmament programme. The party rebuffed Chamberlain's invitation to join his government in September 1939 and again in May 1940, but then indicated its willingness to serve under another Prime Minister, which provoked Chamberlain's resignation. Attlee joined the War Cabinet as Lord Privy Seal, and after Chamberlain withdrew from the government in September became Churchill's deputy, and chief co-ordinator of domestic policy throughout the remainder of the war until May 1945.

It was not an easy role to play, and Attlee was constantly caught between the fears of the more right-wing Tory ministers that he was using his position to foist socialistic policies on the government, and those of outside Labour critics, notably Aneurin Bevan, who thought he was not doing nearly enough in this direction. Insiders soon concluded that his was a rare voice of calm and common sense in a highly volatile team, and that he was an indispensable ally and support of Churchill in his prosecution of the war. He was, however, essentially a behind-the-scenes figure, and was far less in the limelight than other Labour ministers, such as Bevin, Morrison and Stafford Cripps.

In May 1945, when the coalition was dissolved after the German surrender, there were those – particularly among Morrison's supporters – who pressed the case for a more high-profile leader to take Labour into the general election campaign. They included Ellen Wilkinson (widely believed to be Morrison's mistress), who was the retiring chairwoman of Labour's National Executive Committee, and Harold Laski, who succeeded her in that position at the party conference held later in the month. Laski, a left-wing political science professor at the London School of Economics, promptly wrote a long letter to Attlee asking him to stand down "for the good of the party". This provoked one of his famous staccato replies: "Dear Laski, Thank you for your letter, contents of which have been noted. C.R. Attlee".

In the election campaign, while Churchill embarked on a triumphal procession with a vast train of followers, Attlee's sole entourage was his wife Vi, who drove him on a nation-wide tour in the family Hillman saloon. Everywhere he went, he received a thunderous reception, but – like nearly all other senior Labour figures apart from Aneurin Bevan – Attlee never believed he had a chance of defeating the mighty Winston. This despite the fact that a little-noticed Gallup Poll, published in the *News Chronicle*, was predicting a Labour landslide. Even the *News Chronicle* itself ignored the poll, suggesting that the result would be "a near stalemate".

In direct exchanges with Churchill during the campaign, Attlee was generally judged to have come out best. In a wild election broadcast, Churchill had gone over the top, predicting that a Labour government would adopt 'Gestapo' methods. Attlee's quiet, dignified but highly effective reply won him many plaudits. When the votes were finally counted on 26 July (three weeks after polling day in order to allow votes to come in from servicemen overseas), they produced a stunning Labour victory and the worst defeat for the Conservatives since 1906. The new House of Commons comprised:

Labour	393
Conservative	213
Liberal	12
Others	<u>22</u>
Total	640

According to election expert David Butler:

> Labour had won not because of the campaign but because the visible success of planning and 'fair shares' during the war, together with the proven competence of Labour ministers during five years of coalition government, had already made Labour seem more appealing than the Conservatives. Many in the intellectual and middle classes were disillusioned with a party that was associated with unemployment and appeasement as well as the other real and supposed failures of the inter-war period.
>
> *(Butler, 1989, p. 9)*

Attlee and Churchill had been attending the Potsdam summit with Stalin and Harry Truman, which was adjourned to allow them to return to Britain for the election results.

118 Clement Attlee

Prompted by Bevin, the Labour leader ignored a last-ditch attempt by Morrison to force a new leadership election by Labour MPs before going to Buckingham Palace to meet George VI, following Churchill's resignation. The King asked him if he had yet decided on his main ministerial choices. He replied that he had not, but was thinking of Dalton for the Foreign Office and Bevin for the Exchequer. The King, who, unknown to Attlee, had a deep personal prejudice against Dalton, suggested that he was not the best man for the job proposed. Attlee subsequently denied that he had been influenced by the King, but, nevertheless, reversed his initial intention. Morrison, who had threatened not to serve, accepted the Leadership of the House of Commons, with responsibility for controlling the enormous legislative programme foreshadowed by the Labour election manifesto, *Let Us Face the Future*. Stafford Cripps was appointed President of the Board of Trade. Rather to their surprise, Attlee also included in the Cabinet two of his most persistent critics, Bevan becoming Minister of Health and Ellen Wilkinson, Minister of Education.

The government formed by Attlee faced bigger, and more extensive challenges than any other peacetime administration, before or since. They were, essentially, five in number: (1) Post-war reconstruction, (2) Building the welfare state, (3) Extending public ownership, (4) Confronting the Soviet threat, (5) Decolonisation. Mistakes, sometimes serious ones, were made, under all five headings, perhaps most seriously over Palestine, but the verdict of history seems to be that they succeeded beyond all reasonable expectations, and the general consensus (apart from a few far right commentators, such as John Charmley and Corelli Barnett) is that this was one of, if not the most, successful peacetime governments of the 20th century. Many of the changes made were highly controversial at the time, and were fiercely opposed by the Conservative Party. But, when it returned to power, in 1951, it made no serious attempt to reverse them, and the pattern established by the Attlee government, of a mixed economy with universal welfare entitlements, remained essentially untouched until the Thatcher and Major years, more than a generation later.

The stereotypical view of Attlee as an insignificant figure who presided over a Cabinet of powerful personalities, his own personal contribution being confined to keeping them on speaking terms with each other, is a caricature. It is true that he allowed Bevin enormous latitude in his conduct of foreign affairs, that – conscious of his own ignorance in this field – he took a back seat to Dalton, Cripps and, later, Hugh Gaitskell in guiding economic policy, and that Morrison was the undisputed manager of the legislative programme. Yet he kept a tight grip over the Cabinet, making sure that decisions were taken in good time and in proper order, and proved a ruthless 'butcher' of ministers who failed to match up to his exacting standards (as Dalton discovered when he was forced to resign over a trivial and completely harmless budget leak). When he decided to intervene personally, he did so with great decisiveness. It was his decision to press ahead speedily with Burmese and Indian independence, and – less wisely – to build an 'independent' British atomic bomb when the US government went back on its wartime undertaking to share its nuclear secrets with Britain. He and Bevin forced the decision through, amidst great secrecy, and despite the formidable opposition of both Dalton and Cripps. When, at a critical juncture in the Korean War – in December 1950 – there was widespread apprehension that the US would resort to nuclear weapons or invade Chinese territory, he decided at short notice to fly to Washington (Bevin being too ill to fly) to try to exercise a restraining influence on President Truman. He received a warm welcome, and his wise counsel possibly played a part in emboldening the President to dismiss his insubordinate commander, General Douglas MacArthur, a few months later.

In the House of Commons it was widely anticipated that he would be no match for Churchill, but more often than not he got the better of their exchanges – his dry, authoritative, clipped responses regularly puncturing the overblown rhetoric of a master platform performer whose style was ill-adapted to the mundanities of parliamentary debate. Attlee was also valued for the strong and consistent support which he gave his ministers when they got into conflict with vested interests in implementing Labour policies. This was notably the case with Aneurin Bevan in his prolonged struggle with the British Medical Association over the introduction of the National Health Service. Attlee also showed good nerves, and sharp tactical skills, in seeing off plots, on two occasions in 1947, to replace him as Prime Minister by Ernest Bevin. Dalton and Cripps, with backing from George Brown on the back benches, were the chief conspirators. Morrison remained aloof: he would no doubt have welcomed a change at the top, but only if he were to be the beneficiary. If Bevin had been a willing participant, the plots might have succeeded, but he angrily repulsed his would-be sponsors, saying: "What's Clem ever done to me? Who do you think I am? Lloyd George?"

Attlee's overriding preoccupation throughout his premiership was to ensure that every last proposal in Labour's 1945 election manifesto should be carried through. In the past, governing parties had almost invariably ignored most of the specific promises they had made, regarding their manifestos more as 'mood music' rather than as blueprints for action. Attlee regarded this as a betrayal of the voters' trust, and he was determined to set a new and higher standard for the future – an objective which he triumphantly achieved, even at the cost of a certain desirable flexibility.

A fat slab of the Labour programme derived from the famous Beveridge Report, of 1942, which set out a prospectus for slaying what the author described as the five giants of Want, Disease, Ignorance, Squalor and Idleness. Three essential ingredients, Beveridge argued, were a free national health service, child allowances and full employment. The report was welcomed by all three parties in the wartime coalition. It must be doubted, however, in the light of the obstruction which Tory MPs mounted against many of the Labour proposals, whether Beveridge would have been implemented by a Conservative government if Churchill had won the 1945 election. Certainly, it is improbable that they would have carried it through with such enthusiasm, and in such amplitude, as was shown by Labour ministers, particularly in the four great pieces of legislation which came into force in July 1948 – the National Insurance Act, the Industrial Injuries Act, the National Assistance Act and the NHS Act.

Labour's welfare state legislation, together with its educational and taxation policies, were credited with going a long way to wiping out poverty and to fostering a peaceful social revolution which transformed the lives of the bulk of the British population. At the time, it established a level of public welfare clearly superior to that of other economically advanced societies, with the possible exceptions of Sweden and New Zealand. Unfortunately, subsequent governments failed to develop and refine the system, so that 50 years later it was still substantially unchanged, but was creaking along, grievously under-financed and providing levels of service markedly worse than in most of Britain's partners within the European Union. It was also the subject of a biting attack by Corelli Barnett, who argued in his book, *The Lost Victory*, that Britain in the post-war era simply could not afford to create a welfare state. The obvious retort is that it could not afford *not* to do so, and that – given the high hopes raised during the war, and the promises made – it was a political imperative to move forward. The financial cost was, of course, considerable, but it was met by substantially retaining, for most of the 1945–51 period, the high levels of taxation introduced during the war.

The other large element in Labour's domestic policy was the extensive nationalisation, which brought into public ownership the Bank of England, the railways, road transport, airlines, gas, electricity and the iron and steel industry. Here, again, the government had little choice but to act, given the run-down state and appalling labour relations in the coal and transport industries, the need to develop and integrate the public utilities which were natural monopolies, and the evident need for a change of direction at the Bank of England. The case for nationalising steel and road transport was much weaker, and these were in fact the only industries which the Tories chose to denationalise when they returned to power in 1951. Otherwise, the mixed economy established by Labour remained in place for well over 30 years until the advent of Margaret Thatcher. The record of the nationalised industries was a mixed one, but there was no doubt that they became highly unpopular and that their association with the Labour Party became an albatross around the party's neck and was an important factor in the subsequent sapping of its electoral appeal. Nor was this counterbalanced by any significant contribution to the core values of Labour. As Anthony Crosland argued persuasively in his monumental work of 1956, *The Future of Socialism*, the ownership of industry had little direct bearing on the distribution of wealth, the ability of governments to control economic policy, the status of the worker or, even, the level of efficiency of the undertaking. It would be wrong to conclude from this that the Attlee government was mistaken in all its individual acts of nationalisation, but it was misguided to make them such a central part of its strategy, while subsequent Labour proposals to extend the public sector were highly counter-productive.

What was not foreshadowed in Labour's election manifesto was the desperate struggle which would face the new government in rebuilding the economy and greatly expanding exports in the face of severe wartime losses and the abrupt end of American Lend-Lease aid immediately after the end of the war with Japan in August 1945. Yet this was not the least of the achievements of the Attlee government. Thanks to a sustained austerity programme, led by Cripps who replaced Dalton as Chancellor in November 1947, the maintenance of rationing and many wartime controls for several post-war years, and the agreement of the trade unions to accept a large measure of wage restraint – together with the resumption of American aid under the Marshall Plan in 1947 – the situation had been restored by 1950. In that year there was a surplus of £300 million in the balance of payments, an extraordinary turnaround from the £443 million deficit recorded in 1947.

The single-minded pursuit of austerity provoked a wave of discontent which was sedulously fostered by the opposition and the Conservative-dominated press. Nevertheless, the government enjoyed unprecedented success in defending its large parliamentary majority in the 35 by-elections held in Labour seats during the 1945 Parliament. Not a single one of these was lost. It was, therefore, with considerable confidence that Attlee and his colleagues faced the general election of February 1950. They were to receive a nasty shock. The result of the election, with a record turnout of 84 per cent, was:

Labour	315
Conservative	298
Liberal	9
Others	3
Labour majority	5

This result reflected a relatively small swing of 2.7 per cent from Labour to Conservative, but the Labour losses were greatly swollen by constituency boundary changes which came into effect at the general election. These were intended to reflect population movements, but had the unintended effect of building a strong Conservative bias into the electoral system (which was eventually reversed in the 1990s). Without this effect, Labour would have been re-elected in 1950 with a comfortable majority: in the event few thought that it would be able to survive for more than a few months with a single-digit majority.

The government, in fact, survived for much longer than expected, but February 1950 nevertheless represented a watershed in its fortunes. Its great achievements were in the past; thereafter things began to go badly wrong. If Attlee can fairly claim much of the credit for the earlier period, he was equally to blame – at least in part – for much of what was to follow. He was, of course, not responsible for the two great disasters which afflicted his government. The retirement and death of its two great bulwarks – Bevin and Cripps – and the sudden outbreak of the Korean War. Yet his reaction to these events certainly contributed to the eventual defeat of his government and to Labour's subsequent lengthy spell in opposition. Indeed, it could be argued that Attlee squandered an excellent opportunity for Labour to build on its successes and establish itself as the quasi-permanent party of government, comparable to the Swedish Social Democrats.

He made three serious errors of judgement. The first was in his choice of successors to Cripps and Bevin, and in particular his handling of Aneurin Bevan. Bevan, the architect of the National Health Service, was one of the great stars of the government and had won a large following in the Labour Party, which at that time extended well beyond its left wing. He justifiably felt that he had earned promotion to one of the more senior posts in government, but Attlee twice passed him over within a few months, when he appointed Hugh Gaitskell to succeed Cripps and Herbert Morrison in place of Bevin. All he was offered – and reluctantly accepted – was a sideways move to the Ministry of Labour. Both of Attlee's choices could readily be justified. Gaitskell had been an able number two to Cripps and had good qualifications as an economist, but he was a newcomer to the Cabinet and vastly junior to Bevan in his standing in the party. Morrison was Deputy Prime Minister and had been highly successful both as a wartime Home Secretary and more recently as Leader of the House of Commons. Attlee was later to characterise his appointment as Foreign Secretary as "the worst I ever made", but his failure was not predictable, and at that stage nobody realised that this highly able man was getting 'past it'. Attlee does not seem to have seriously considered Bevan for either post, which makes it all the more remarkable that he subsequently said, in a television interview with Francis Williams, that he had always expected 'Nye' to succeed him, and indeed had wanted him to. If that was true, he hardly went out of his way to bring this about.

Attlee's second grave error – for which he shared the responsibility with his Chancellor, Hugh Gaitskell, and the majority of the Cabinet, with the exception of Bevan and Harold Wilson, the President of the Board of Trade – was to accept, under strong US pressure, an unsustainable commitment to step up Britain's rearmament programme as part of its contribution to the Korean War. This involved increasing defence expenditure from 7.5 to 14 per cent of national income (a figure which was never reached and was quietly abandoned by the newly elected Churchill government the following year). To help foot the bill, Gaitskell proposed to levy charges on the National Health Service for the supply

122 Clement Attlee

of false teeth and spectacles, which immediately provoked a resignation threat from Bevan. Gaitskell insisted, and Bevan carried out his threat, being joined by Wilson and by John Freeman, a junior minister. Attlee was in hospital, being treated for a duodenal ulcer, at the time of the resignations, and always blamed Morrison, who was deputising for him at the time, "for losing three of my ministers". Yet he had been kept in touch with what was going on, and indicated that, if the choice was between Bevan's and Gaitskell's resignations, then it was Bevan who had to go.

The consequent split in the Labour Party gravely damaged its standing, while developments in the Korean War spurred inflation and put the balance of payments back into the red. Yet public support for the government remained strong, and it might still have had serious chances of increasing its parliamentary majority if Attlee had timed the next election more judiciously. This would have involved hanging on through the next winter, and probably going to the polls in the spring of 1952, when the economic situation was expected to improve (it did). Instead of this, Attlee effectively sacrificed the interest of his own party to the convenience of King George VI. The King was due to embark on an extensive tour of the Commonwealth in the New Year, and by September was already nagging Attlee to get the election out of the way before his departure. He consequently set the election date for 25 October 1951, which was just about the least optimum time for Labour.

Despite this disadvantage, the election was desperately close, and Labour would still have won had it not been for the bias in the electoral system. It gained over 200,000 more votes than the Tories, but the result, in terms of seats, was:

Conservative	321
Labour	295
Liberal	6
Others	3
Conservative majority	*21*

Attlee was then 68, and worn out by ten continuous years of high office. The time had surely come to bow out, but he lingered on in the party leadership for four more years, including the 1955 general election, in the pious hope of mending the deep split in his party. It was also widely suspected that part of his motivation was to hang on until Morrison, only five years his junior, would be seen as too old to succeed him. If so, he succeeded in his objective, as his unfortunate deputy polled only 40 votes, to 157 for Gaitskell and 70 for Bevan, when he finally stood down in December 1955.

Attlee then retired to the House of Lords, where his reputation as a wise and benign, if taciturn, elder statesman continued to increase until his death 12 years later. For the Labour Party, he remains to this day an iconic figure, though – if truth be told – he served his country rather better than his party. In his quiet way, he was every bit as much a patriot as Churchill, as the final words of his typically low key autobiography, *As It Happened*, reveal: "I have been a happy and fortunate man, in having lived so long in the greatest country in the world, in having a happy family life and in having been given the opportunity of serving in a state of life to which I never expected to be called."

A kindly, unassuming and extremely shy man, with an exceptionally well organised mind and a quiet determination to pursue the issues in which he believed, Attlee was not the person to write his own epitaph. The best he could manage was a rather smug limerick which he composed for the amusement of Tom Attlee:

> Few thought he was even a starter
> There were many who thought themselves smarter
> But he ended PM
> CH and OM
> An earl and a knight of the garter.

More apposite was the judgement of Peter Hennessy, the author of the definitive work on the Attlee government, who concluded, "that 1951 Britain … compared to *any* previous decade was a kinder, gentler and far, far better place in which to be born, to grow up, to live, love, work and even to die" (Hennessy, 1992, p. 454).

Works consulted

C.R. Attlee, 1954, *As It Happened*, London, Heinemann.
Corelli Barnett, 1995, *The Lost Victory*, London, Macmillan.
Francis Beckett, 1997, *Clem Attlee*, London, Richard Cohen Books.
John Bew, 2016, *Citizen Clem: A Biography of Atlee*, London, Riverrun.
Jerry H. Brookshire, 1995, *Clement Attlee*, Manchester, Manchester University Press
Trevor Burridge, 1985, *Clement Attlee*, London, Cape.
David Butler, 1989, *British General Elections since 1945*, Oxford, Blackwell.
Peter Clarke, 1992, *A Question of Leadership*, London, Penguin.
Bernard Donoughue and G.W. Jones, 1973, *Herbert Morrison*, London, Weidenfeld & Nicolson.
Michael Foot, 1979, *Aneurin Bevan 1945–1960*, London, Granada.
Kenneth Harris, 1982, *Attlee*, London, Weidenfeld & Nicolson.
Peter Hennessy, 1992, *Never Again: Britain 1945–1951*, London, Cape.
Roy Jenkins, 1948, *Mr Attlee: An Interim Biography*, London, Heinemann.
Kenneth O. Morgan, 1984, *Labour in Power*, Oxford, Oxford University Press.
Kenneth O. Morgan, 1992, *Labour People: Hardie to Kinnock*, Oxford, Oxford University Press.
Lord Morrison of Lambeth, 1960, *Herbert Morrison: An Autobiography*, London, Odhams Press.

11

ANTHONY EDEN

Self-destruction of a Prince Charming

It was said of the Roman Emperor Galba that everyone thought he was capable of being a ruler until he actually became one. It was Anthony Eden's great misfortune that the same came to be said of him. Born in 1897, he grew up in what he felt to be an earthly paradise – the beautiful Windlestone Hall and estate, in County Durham – but with impossible parents. He was the presumed third son, and fourth child, of Sir William Eden, 7th Baronet, whose family had been prominent in the area since the 11th century. Sir William combined the traditional pursuits of a country gentleman with being a talented amateur painter and discerning art collector, but he was most renowned for the appalling temper which led him into frequent and uncontrollable rages over the most trivial causes.

Anthony's mother, Sybil Grey, was a kinswoman both of Earl Grey, of the Reform Bill, and of Sir Edward Grey, the Liberal Foreign Secretary from 1905 to 1916. A famous society beauty, she was a woman of great extravagance, whose unthinking generosity and self-indulgence was eventually to spell ruin to her husband's not inconsiderable financial resources. Anthony grew up to hate his mother, but he loved Sir William, despite his evident deficiencies as a parent. As he grew older his physical appearance began more and more to resemble that of George Wyndham, Arthur Balfour's secretary and later a Tory Cabinet minister – a dark, handsome dilettante, with whom Sybil Eden was known to be infatuated. According to his official biographer, Anthony was well aware of the "persistent rumours" about his parentage, and "found them both amusing and interesting. But he did not really believe them" (Rhodes James, 1986, p. 18).

Like all his family, Anthony was sent to Eton, which he disliked, and where he failed to distinguish himself. From his school reports, he emerged as a highly-strung boy, who suffered from temper tantrums, but "is a nice, bright, intelligent fellow, with much that is very likeable about him" (Rhodes James, 1986, p. 25). When war broke out, in August 1914, he was 17 years old, and thereafter he became more serious- minded and applied himself more diligently to his studies. The war's effect on his family was immediate and grave. His eldest brother, Jack, a professional soldier, was killed in France as early as October 1914; his second brother, Tim, was interned in Germany, where he had been studying; his father was slowly dying – he survived until February 1915 – and his beloved Windlestone was turned into a wartime

DOI: 10.4324/9781003031963-12

hospital. Anthony's only ambition now was to join the army, but his poor eyesight led to his being rejected on several occasions. However, late in 1915, he was welcomed into a Yeomen's regiment, commanded by Lord Feversham, who was the brother-in-law of his married elder sister, Marjorie. The medical test, Eden later reported, "was hardly more than a formality" (Rhodes James, 1986, p. 36).

In nearly three years of service on the Western Front, Eden, who was promoted to be the youngest Brigade Major in the British army, saw much grim action and the death or injury of vast numbers of his comrades in arms, while his younger brother, Nicholas, a 16-year-old midshipman, was killed in the Battle of Jutland. He himself escaped injury, and was awarded the Military Cross for rescuing his wounded sergeant under enemy fire. At the end of the war, as a 22-year-old veteran, he was at a loss what to do, but without enthusiasm decided to take up a place he had been offered at Christ Church, Oxford, in October 1919. He studied Oriental Languages (Persian and Arabic), and proved an excellent student, gaining a First Class degree. His only recorded student activity was to co-found an art appreciation society, entitled the Uffizi Society, and he started to build up a modest art collection of his own, showing an excellent eye for selecting up-and-coming artists. He followed political events with close attention, but showed no interest in joining the Union Society.

On graduation, he thought of trying for the Diplomatic Service, for which his knowledge of languages – including good French and German – made him well qualified. He decided, instead, on a political career, and fought the local Durham constituency of Spennymore, losing to Labour in the November 1922 general election. In the following year, he was selected to fight a by-election in the safe Tory seat of Warwick and Leamington. His candidature, however, was overshadowed by that of the flamboyant Labour candidate. This was none other than the Countess of Warwick (a former mistress of Edward VII, famously known to him as "My Darling Daisy"), who, to complete the embarrassment, turned out to be his sister Marjorie's mother-in-law, and a relative by marriage of Eden's fiancée. The by-election was aborted in its final stages by the unexpected dissolution of Parliament, but in the general election which ensued he was returned with a large majority, the Countess coming a poor third. He was 26, and was to represent the seat, without any difficulty, for the ensuing 33 years.<

Just before the election, he had married Beatrice, the 18-year-old daughter of Sir Gervase Beckett, a wealthy and generous Tory MP, who was also the owner of a leading regional newspaper, the *Yorkshire Post*. They made a glamorous couple, and Eden was to benefit both financially and politically from the Beckett connection, but the marriage, though it produced two sons, was not a success. Beatrice was immature, and shared none of Anthony's political, artistic or intellectual interests, and it was not long before they began to drift apart, each having numerous affairs, though they divorced only in 1950.

Eden made an inauspicious start as an MP, breaching the custom of confining his maiden speech to uncontroversial matters, and it was some time before he found his feet in the Commons. He confined his occasional interventions to foreign policy issues, but eventually became Parliamentary Private Secretary to a junior minister at the Home Office. Then, in July 1926, he had a great stroke of luck. Austen Chamberlain was now Foreign Secretary, and his own PPS left on a six-month trip to Australia, and recommended Eden, whom Chamberlain hardly knew, to replace him.

He remained with Chamberlain until the Tory defeat in the 1929 general election, and they soon became immersed in mutual admiration. Eden strongly approved Chamberlain's policies, which notably included the negotiation of the Locarno treaties of December 1925,

126 Anthony Eden

reintegrating Germany into the mainstream of European diplomacy, while Chamberlain found him a highly proficient and well-informed assistant. This somewhat stiff and remote man developed warm feelings for Eden, who also became something of a favourite of the Prime Minister, Stanley Baldwin, who openly talked to him about his future as a Cabinet minister. He intended to bring him into the government, as Under-Secretary at the Foreign Office, had he won the election.

In opposition, Eden frequently spoke on foreign affairs from the front bench, and helped to restore his shaky finances (as the younger son of an estate almost bankrupted by his mother's fecklessness), by joining a stockbroking firm. A fervent supporter of Baldwin against his many Conservative critics, he joined a dining club of left-wing Tory MPs, whose leader, Noel Skelton, coined the phrase 'a property-owning democracy', which Eden was later to make his own hallmark.

The formation of Ramsay MacDonald's National government in August 1931 marked the beginning of his ministerial career. MacDonald had flirted with the idea of appointing his own talented son, Malcolm, as Under-Secretary for Foreign Affairs, but was persuaded by Baldwin to choose Eden instead. The Foreign Secretary was a Liberal, the Marquis of Reading, an arrangement which suited Eden very well, as it meant that he alone would speak for the Foreign Office in the Commons. It lasted for only two months: after the October 1931 election, Reading was replaced by another Liberal, who was well on the way to becoming a right-wing Tory, Sir John Simon. Eden found him to be a most uncongenial boss – irresolute, cantankerous and openly jealous of his much younger deputy.

Largely excluded from the policy-making loop, Eden was dispatched for long periods to Geneva for meetings of the League of Nations, where he was extremely active in the abortive disarmament conference which dragged on from 1932 to early in 1934. Nothing of value was achieved, but it did wonders for Eden's public image. As his official biographer put it:

> In a somewhat drab scene, populated by so many older and duller men, and with shadows looming everywhere, he stood out as an exciting exception. At the beginning of 1933 he was almost unknown; by the end of the year he was being hailed as a rising star, better known through photographs, films and press reports than most members of the Cabinet. Few such opportunities have occurred to a young politician.
>
> *(Rhodes James, 1986, p. 123)*

At the League, Eden established a reputation as a highly accomplished diplomat, and was particularly noted for two of his initiatives. One was his proposal that an international force, including British troops, should supervise the plebiscite in the Saarland, which led to the return of the territory to Germany after 16 years of French occupation. The second was his contribution as a mediator between Yugoslavia and Hungary, after the latter's government was suspected of complicity in the assassination of the Yugoslav King Alexander in October 1934. In reality, Eden's commitment to the League and to the concept of collective security was by no means unequivocal, but in the public eye he became their very personification, and this was the essential basis for his extraordinary popularity in the 1930s, which did not, however, extend very far within the Conservative Party.

Although he was promoted to Lord Privy Seal, still outside the Cabinet, in December 1933, he continued to chafe under Simon's overlordship. When Baldwin finally took over as Prime Minister, in June 1935, he had high hopes that he himself would become Foreign

Secretary. Instead, Sir Samuel Hoare, whom he found only a marginal improvement, was appointed. His tenure, however, lasted a mere six months. He was forced to resign in the aftermath of the Hoare-Laval pact (see Chapter 6 on Baldwin), and, at the young age of 38, Eden's hour had come.

Under Baldwin, he was given a pretty free hand, and had very little to show for his handling of the three major crises which occurred during his watch – Abyssinia (Ethiopia), the Rhineland and the outbreak of the Spanish Civil War. A careful examination of the evidence (Carlton, 1981, pp. 71–99) reveals little of the determination to resist, which he subsequently claimed in his memoir of the period, *Facing the Dictators*. Against Mussolini, he was in no hurry to lift the partial and ineffective sanctions applied by the League of Nations, but – in the face of French indifference – made no attempt to press the case for oil sanctions which he had previously supported. Nor did he pursue the one course which he himself had identified as likely to halt the Italian aggression in its tracks – the closure of the Suez Canal. On Hitler's occupation of the Rhineland, which was a breach of the Locarno agreements as well as the Versailles Treaty, he confined himself to verbal protests, even though there was some indication that the French would have supported a more muscular joint response.

Over Spain, Eden fully supported the principle of non-intervention, which effectively deprived the legal government of access to arms supplies, while hardly impeding the considerable German and Italian support for Franco, nor the more limited help which the Soviet Union sent to the Republican side. It is not true, however, that Eden took the lead in forcing the same policy on the new French 'Popular Front' government, nor is there any evidence that he shared the sympathies of a probable majority of his Cabinet colleagues with the Francoist uprising. He, in fact, tried to make the arms embargo more even-handed by proposing a naval blockade of the eastern Spanish coast. This initiative, however, was voted down in the Cabinet – Baldwin for once taking a keen interest in the issue and coming down heavily on the side of Eden's opponents.

Baldwin's retirement, in May 1937, brought an end to Eden's relative contentment as Foreign Secretary. Neville Chamberlain was far less willing than his predecessor to leave a free hand to his Foreign Secretary and – while outward courtesies were usually maintained – the tension between them gradually built up during the succeeding seven months. Eden, despite his subsequent, and largely successful, efforts to suggest the contrary, was not at all opposed to Chamberlain's early attempts to appease Hitler. He sought to draw the line, however, so far as Mussolini was concerned, whom he appeared to regard as a more serious menace than his fellow dictator. Chamberlain's considered view was that, though he was determined to pacify Hitler, he would prove an extremely dangerous enemy of Britain if his efforts failed. He consequently sought to detach Italy from its German alliance, so that Britain would not have to face two powerful foes at the same time. He was, accordingly, anxious to arrange bilateral talks in order to settle outstanding Italian grievances. These included, notably, the British refusal to give *de jure* recognition to the annexation of Abyssinia.

Eden's view was that such recognition should not be given before Italy made significant gestures of its own – such as the withdrawal of Italian 'volunteers' from Spain and a reduction in the large Italian garrison in Libya, which constituted a potential threat to Egypt. He consequently embarked on a surreptitious 'go-slow' campaign, doing everything he could to delay or frustrate the opening of talks with the Italians, while, on the surface, agreeing to carry out Chamberlain's intentions. Chamberlain soon became aware of what was going on, and fumed against Eden in his private letters to his sisters, while attempting – behind Eden's back – to use his sister-in-law, Ivy Chamberlain (Austen's widow), who was living in Rome, as a supplementary channel of communication with Mussolini's circle. The climax came in December 1937 at a joint meeting which was held – at Chamberlain's insistence – with the Italian Ambassador, Count Dino Grandi, at which Chamberlain made clear that he wished to expedite Anglo-Italian talks. An astonished Grandi sent a dispatch to Rome, containing the revealing passage:

> Chamberlain and Eden were not a Prime Minister and a Foreign Secretary discussing with the Ambassador of a foreign power a delicate situation of an international character. They were – and revealed themselves as such to me in defiance of all established convention – two enemies confronting each other, like two cocks in true fighting posture.
>
> *(Carlton, 1981, pp. 127–8)*

It was at this point that Eden decided to resign, and Chamberlain made no strenuous efforts to dissuade him. At the time – and later – many people were puzzled at Eden's resignation, and thought that the issues involved were hardly weighty enough to justify so extreme a step. (Eden did not make public his disagreement with Chamberlain's abrupt dismissal of Roosevelt's tentative peace-making initiative – see Chapter 9.) Certainly, no other Cabinet minister was tempted to follow suit. One theory is that Eden grossly over-estimated his own standing and thought that Chamberlain would not be able to continue in office without his support. Others believed that he was playing a long game, in the belief that Chamberlain would eventually become discredited and that it was better to detach himself from him in good time. Some thought he had acted purely out of pique, comparing him to Lord Randolph Churchill, whose resignation as Chancellor of the Exchequer in 1886 wrecked his political career.

One explanation was not considered at the time, but was apparently advanced by Eden himself, in conversation with his colleague and close friend, Malcolm MacDonald, then Dominions Secretary, who tried to dissuade him from resigning. According to a letter which he wrote over 40 years later, to one of Eden's biographers (Carlton, 1981, pp. 129–30), Eden told him that "he could not continue working as a Minister because he did not feel fit to do so; he felt physically unwell and mentally exhausted". MacDonald continued: "When he made that remark I decided that it would in fact be better if he did resign." He told the Prime Minister the following morning, who, he recalled, "smiled and said that he had 'slept on the matter' and had come to the same conclusion".

Whatever moved Eden to quit, and – as in the case of most major resignations – there were probably several different factors involved, the long-term effect was certainly to burnish his reputation as an anti-appeaser to a far greater extent than was justified by his actual record. Nor did he now play a very active role in opposing Chamberlain's policies, holding himself aloof from the small group surrounding Winston Churchill. Churchill, however, professed the greatest admiration for Eden, describing him in his memoirs as "one strong young figure standing up against long, dismal, drawling tides of drift and surrender". Despite his many admirers in the country, Eden had only a tiny following among Tory MPs, who were disparagingly referred to as "the Glamour Boys". Within the party, he was regarded essentially as a lightweight figure, and it is revealing that, in May 1940, when both Halifax and Churchill were widely regarded as unsuitable candidates for the premiership, there was absolutely no move to push Eden's claims. He had rejoined the government, as Dominions Secretary, in September 1939, and he was disappointed that Churchill excluded him from the War Cabinet, when he became Prime Minister, switching him instead to the War Office. It was only in December 1940, when Halifax was packed off to the United States as Ambassador, that he was able to reclaim his place as Foreign Secretary.

During the remainder of the war, he had a number of differences with Churchill, but for the most part acted as a skilful and hard-working deputy, whom Churchill recommended to George VI as his successor if he should die or be incapacitated. Nevertheless it was Clem Attlee whom he appointed as Deputy Premier, compensating Eden in 1942 with the leadership of the House of Commons. The double burden of combining this post with being Foreign Secretary undoubtedly contributed to the breakdown of his health, and by June 1945 he was seriously ill with a duodenal ulcer and consequently played virtually no part in the general election campaign. In the same month, he suffered the terrible blow of the death in action of his elder son, Simon, in Burma.

On more than one occasion, Churchill had promised Eden that he would retire in his favour at the end of the war, and he was much put out when he lingered on in the party leadership after the election rout. Even so, his medium-term prospects looked good. He was immensely popular in the country, and had no credible rival for the Tory succession. Yet beneath that suave and glamorous exterior, he was a bundle of uncertainties and insecurities. In public, he was renowned for his affability and perfect manners – yet his junior ministers and civil servants were only too aware of his violent temper, vanity and recurring obsessions. He was also a man with a guilty conscience. The world may have acquitted him of appeasement, but he brooded on his own culpability in failing to respond to the German occupation of the Rhineland in 1936, especially as captured German documents later revealed that Hitler would have backed down if Britain and France had threatened a military response. Twenty years later he was to tell his private secretary, Sir Pierson Dixon, that if Britain had resisted in 1936 the Second World War might have been avoided and "Millions of lives would have been saved" (Dixon, 1968).

In October 1951, when the Tories were finally re-elected, Eden became Foreign Secretary for the third time, at the age of 54. It was a fruitful period for his diplomacy. An armistice was concluded in Korea, and a ceasefire negotiated between France and the Vietnamese Communists, while disputes with Persia and Egypt were settled, at least temporarily. In all of these events, Eden was credited with a major role. In August 1952, moreover, he embarked on his second marriage – to Churchill's niece, Clarissa Churchill – a union which turned out to be a great deal happier than that with Beatrice Beckett. Only eight months later, however, disaster struck. He had two gallstone operations which went badly wrong, and his life was only saved by a third operation in Boston, which was successful, though he was out of action until the following October. In June 1953, Churchill had a serious stroke, which was kept secret, though if Eden had been fully fit he would most probably have taken over the premiership. R.A. Butler, the Chancellor of the Exchequer, was in charge of the government, but lacked the boldness to seize the top post for himself. So Churchill held on, and gave way to his 'crown prince', apparently restored to health, only in April 1955.

When Eden succeeded to the premiership, his reputation was at its peak. He was regarded as a master diplomat and – though his interventions in domestic politics had been minimal – he was seen as the very model of a progressive Tory, in whose hands the recently built welfare state would be totally safe. He immediately called a general election, and had no difficulty in defeating an ageing Attlee still at the head of a deeply divided Labour Party. He tripled the narrow majority which Churchill had won in 1951, giving the Tories a lead of 58 seats over all other parties.

It was a time of hope, but not for some of those who knew Eden well, who were full of foreboding. These, apparently, included Churchill himself, as well as Lord Swinton, a veteran Tory Cabinet minister who was asked by Churchill early in 1955 if he thought that R.A. Butler would do better as Prime Minister than Eden. Swinton replied that "anybody would be better than Anthony [who] would make the worst Prime Minister since Lord North. But you can't think like that now – it's too late. You announced him as your successor more than ten years ago." Churchill replied, "I think it was a great mistake" (Ramsden, 1996, p. 274).

In retrospect, it might appear that the Suez affair was solely responsible for wrecking Eden's government and ending his political career. It did not look like that at the time. Within months of his taking over, loud voices of discontent were being heard, particularly within his own party, and there was widespread speculation that he would not long survive as Prime Minister. The feeling grew that he was just not up to the job – he proved at the same time chronically indecisive, but ever ready to interfere in the minutest details of the departmental work of his colleagues, particularly, but by no means exclusively, in the Foreign Office. He also showed himself to be exceptionally thin-skinned and upset by the slightest criticism. The most painful shaft for Eden came from the normally ultra-loyal *Daily Telegraph* in an article which mocked his speaking style. To emphasise his points, Eden had the habit, it said, of punching his fist into the palm of his other hand, but stopping short of an audible impact. "Most Conservatives", the paper opined, "are waiting to feel the smack of firm government". Eden reacted by issuing a quite unnecessary and highly counter-productive denial that he was going to resign, which only increased the speculation that he would not last for long. Early in 1956 a leading political journalist, Ian Waller, made a prescient prediction in a syndicated article: "If the year goes on as it has begun it will not be Sir Anthony Eden but Harold Macmillan who reigns in Downing Street in 1957."

Despite these misgivings, Eden might well have survived and served a successful term as Prime Minister, but he was driven by an obsession. This was that the Egyptian leader, Colonel Nasser, was becoming as great a menace as Hitler and Mussolini had been in the 1930s, and must on no account be appeased. Eden saw him as a lethal threat to the British position in the Middle East and as a pawn of the Soviet Union. Several months before the Suez crisis began – in March 1956 – Eden gave an early indication to his Under-Secretary, Anthony Nutting, of his irrational attitude. King Hussein of Jordan had just dismissed the British General John Glubb as the commander of his army. Convinced that Nasser was behind this move, Eden screamed down the telephone to Nutting: "what is all this poppycock you've sent me about isolating Nasser and neutralising Nasser? Why can't you get it into your head that I want the man destroyed?" This conversation was later related by Nutting to the author Peter Hennessy, who linked it with indications that Eden might even have tried to use the Secret Service in an attempt to assassinate the Egyptian President (Hennessy, 2000, p. 61).

Suez proper began on 19 July 1956, when the US and Britain announced the withdrawal of their earlier offer to partially finance the Aswan dam in southern Egypt. Nasser's response – one week later – was to order the immediate nationalisation of the Suez Canal Company, indicating that he would use the income from canal dues to pay for the construction of the dam. Eden was by no means alone in being horrified by Nasser's action, which was strongly condemned by Hugh Gaitskell, the Labour leader, in the House of Commons. Gaitskell however made clear, and repeated this more emphatically in private letters to Eden, that he did not support the use of force against Egypt. Nor would this have been justified in terms of international law – Nasser offered full compensation on the basis of the market value of the shares, the majority of which were held by the British government, and the bulk of the remainder by private French interests.

Nevertheless, from day one Eden was determined on the use of force if Nasser refused to back down – ostensibly to achieve international control of the canal, but in reality to ensure Nasser's overthrow. The French government, led by the Socialist Guy Mollet, was equally willing to use military force. Its main motivation was to punish Nasser for his support of the rebels fighting against France in Algeria. Unfortunately for the British and French leaders, their military staffs advised them that it was not possible to launch an immediate strike, as an airborne assault was seen as too risky. A seaborne invasion, from a base in Malta, would take at least a month to prepare, they insisted.

Eden was therefore forced to try diplomatic means to resolve the dispute, while secretly liaising with the French to launch an attack on Egypt on or after 8 September. The secrecy was necessary because President Eisenhower, and his Secretary of State, John Foster Dulles, had made it crystal clear to Eden that the US would not support military action. With US backing, a conference of the leading maritime powers was held on 16–23 August, which deputed a five-man committee, led by Australian Prime Minister Robert Menzies, to visit Nasser and try to persuade him to accept an international board of control for the canal. He turned them down flat, and the British and French resolved to take their case against Nasser to the UN Security Council, in the expectation that Russia would veto any resolution requiring Egyptian compliance. They would then feel free to launch their attack, having failed to secure satisfaction from the UN.

This plan was thwarted by Dulles, who insisted on further negotiations, coming up with the idea of establishing a Suez Canal Users' Association (SCUA), made up of signatories to the 1888 Convention which guaranteed international access to the canal. The proposal was that the SCUA would be responsible for hiring pilots and collecting dues. The inaugural meeting of the SCUA was held on 19–22 September, Nasser skilfully avoided committing himself either for or against this plan, and negotiations at the UN continued in a desultory way, with the prospect of Anglo-French military action seeming to diminish with every day that passed. During this period, Eden remained in a high state of excitement. There is some evidence that he was suffering from recurrent bouts of fever, perhaps related to delayed effects of his operations in 1953. On 5 October, while visiting his wife in hospital, he had a serious attack, with his temperature rising to 105°F (40.6°C). His press officer, William Clark, who later resigned in protest against the Suez operation, wrote in his memoirs that Eden was "mad, literally mad and that he went so on the day that his temperature rose to 105°" (Clark, 1986, p. 209). Eden himself admitted to Sir Gladwyn Jebb (British Ambassador in Paris) that he had been "practically living on Benzedrine". There can be little doubt that his judgement was seriously affected at this time, though his health did not break down until later and "several contemporaries noted that in the later stages of the drama Eden displayed a calm serenity, in marked contrast to his usually excited and nervous demeanour" (Dutton, 1997, pp. 422–3).

By mid-October it seemed that the threat of war over Suez was all but over, but on 14 October two emissaries from the French government arrived at Chequers with a hare-brained scheme to involve Israel in a clandestine plot to provide a pretext for an Anglo-French attack on Egypt. It is difficult not to believe that, had Eden's judgement not been affected, he would have rejected the proposal out of hand. As it was, he travelled with Foreign Secretary Selwyn Lloyd to Paris two days later for secret talks with Mollet and his Foreign Minister, Christian Pineau, from which all officials were excluded. A week later a confidential agreement was signed in a villa at Sèvres that Israel would launch an attack towards the Suez Canal on 29 October, and that Britain and France would then issue an ultimatum to both combatants to cease fire and withdraw their forces from the canal area or the two powers would intervene to separate the two armies and secure the safety of the canal.

Eden persuaded his Cabinet – many of whose members were not informed of the details of the collusion with Israel – to back the plan, which they did with varying degrees of enthusiasm, with only one member (Sir Walter Monckton) registering disagreement, though he did not resign (he had been switched a few days earlier from his post as Defence Minister, to Paymaster-General, because of his lukewarm attitude to military intervention). Although Eden bore the main responsibility for the folly about to be committed, his two leading Cabinet colleagues were also greatly to blame. Either of them could effectively have vetoed the project if they had come out strongly against. Instead, Harold Macmillan, the Chancellor of the Exchequer, backed it with great enthusiasm, and reversed his position (in the face of a run on the pound) only after the Anglo-French forces had landed in Port Said on 5 November. R.A. Butler, the unofficial Deputy Premier, was convinced of the madness of the scheme, and told everyone so afterwards, but kept his mouth shut during the Cabinet discussions.

The Israeli attack duly took place, and the Anglo-French ultimatum was delivered. The Egyptians turned it down, and Anglo-French air attacks were launched against Egyptian air bases, in preparation for the landing by the amphibious force which had already steamed out of Malta two days before the Israeli attack. President Eisenhower, aghast at the deception employed against him by Eden and Mollet, immediately instructed the US delegate to the United Nations Security Council to table a motion demanding that Israel should withdraw from Egyptian soil and calling on all UN members to refrain from force or the threat of force. Britain and France vetoed the resolution, the first time that Western powers had ever had recourse to the veto. When a similar motion was submitted to the UN General Assembly, it was passed by 64 votes to five, only Australia and New Zealand backing the three states waging an undeclared war against Egypt.

If Eden's actions provoked near unanimous condemnation at the UN, they succeeded in splitting British public opinion right down the middle. The House of Commons erupted in uproar when Eden announced the Anglo-French ultimatum and the Speaker was forced to suspend the sitting. The Labour and Liberal parties, the churches, the bulk of the intellectual community and the *bien-pensant* press reacted in horror, while Eden enjoyed ecstatic support from most Conservatives and – according to the opinion polls – a large number of working-class voters. The dozen or so Tory MPs who opposed Eden got short shrift from their supporters, most of them being deselected as parliamentary candidates. Two junior ministers – Nutting and Sir Edward Boyle – resigned from the government, and Eden also lost his press officer, William Clark, for the same reason.

There was sullen resentment from senior ministers and officials who had been kept totally in the dark about the government's intentions. These included the British Ambassador to Cairo, Sir Humphrey Trevelyan, the First Lord of the Admiralty, Lord Hailsham, who later wrote "I was told nothing of the contingency plans, and when ships were actually beginning to move I was misled as to their true purpose", and Sir Charles Keightley, the commander of the British troops about to go into action, who was given no forewarning of the intended Israeli attack (Dutton, 1997, p. 28). The plan was misconceived in any case, but that it descended into total fiasco was at least partly due to the failure to consult, or even inform, so many key figures.

It took over a week for the allied troops to make it from Malta to Port Said, where they landed on 5 November, and began to advance southwards along the canal. But by then the pressure of the United States on the British and French governments had become irresistible. The US 5th fleet made threatening movements against allied ships, while the American Treasury blankly refused to support the pound sterling which was under pressure in the exchange markets. This was the pretext – if not perhaps the cause – of Macmillan's abrupt change of stance, which forced Eden to declare a halt of military operations on 6 November. By Christmas, the British and French troops were forced to withdraw in humiliating circumstances, with Nasser acclaimed a hero throughout the Arab world and beyond.

Those who had lauded Eden now turned against him. The more jingoistic Tories roundly condemned him for halting the operation when it was (at least in terms of securing the physical control of the canal) in sight of success. "Worse than a crime, a blunder", was the standard Tory verdict on Suez, echoing the famous judgement on Napoleon's execution of the Duc d'Enghien. It nevertheless was a crime – not least because it provided a cover for the brutal and simultaneous Soviet suppression of the Hungarian revolution.

Eden's premiership did not long survive the failure of his enterprise. His health broken, he announced on 21 November that he was flying to Jamaica to recuperate, staying at the house of the James Bond author, Ian Fleming, and leaving Butler in charge of the government. He returned on 14 December, and six days later told a direct lie to the House of Commons when he denied any foreknowledge of the Israeli attack on Egypt. He resigned, on medical advice, on 9 January 1957, to be succeeded not by Butler, as he and most other observers had expected, but by Macmillan, who was the choice of the overwhelming majority of his Cabinet. He was to live for another 20 years, as the Earl of Avon, and set out a lengthy justification in three volumes of memoirs. Yet he could never bring himself to admit the collusion with Israel. The conspirators at Sèvres had pledged themselves to eternal secrecy, but Eden's French and Israeli partners proved a great deal less discreet than his own tight circle of collaborators. Within a few months, two French journalists, Serge and Merry Bromberger, had already revealed the essential details in their book *Les Secrets de l'Expédition d'Egypte*, which were later confirmed both by Pineau and by General Moshe Dayan, the Israeli Chief of Staff.

One good thing did come out of Suez – the realisation in both Britain and France that they were no longer world powers – and could not hope, even acting together, to embark on major military operations without at least the acquiescence of their American ally. This lesson was learned more quickly in France, which within a few months signed the Treaty of Rome and committed itself to European integration. It took much longer for the British, who were to find that when they wished to follow suit they were blocked by their former partner, and were only able to join the European Community 15 years after it was established.

What should one think of Eden? For most of his life, he had appeared the soul of honour, yet he was responsible for perhaps the most dishonourable episode in British history in the 20th century – arguably even worse than Munich, which was a sin of omission, while this was one of commission. In truth, Eden was a tragic figure, who had too lightly chosen the wrong career path after World War I. Behind his elegant exterior, he lacked too many of the qualities necessary for effective political leadership at the highest level. He proved himself incapable of taking big decisions on a rational basis, his temperament was too brittle and he was too thin-skinned to cope with criticism, while his character contained more than a dash of naivety. It was a great pity that he did not follow his initial inclination to try for the Diplomatic Service – he would have cut a glittering figure presiding over the Embassy in Paris or Washington, faithfully carrying out the policies determined by his political masters, without suffering the agony of having to decide on them himself.

Works consulted

David Carlton, 1981, *Anthony Eden*, London, Allen Lane.
William Clark, 1986, *From Three Worlds*, London, Sidgwick & Jackson.
Dictionary of National Biography, 1970–1979 Supplement.
Piers Dixon, 1968, *Double Dilemma: The Life of Sir Pierson Dixon, Don and Diplomat*, London, Hutchinson.
David Dutton, 1997, *Anthony Eden: A Life and Reputation*, London, Hodder Arnold.
Peter Hennessy, 2000, *The Prime Minister: The Office and Its Holders since 1945*, London, Allen Lane.
Keith Kyle, 1991, *Suez*, London.
Anthony Nutting, 1967, *No End of a Lesson*, London, Constable.
John Ramsden, 1996, *The Age of Churchill and Eden, 1940–1957*, London, Longman.
Robert Rhodes James, 1986, *Anthony Eden*, London, Weidenfeld & Nicolson.

12

HAROLD MACMILLAN

Idealist into manipulator

Macmillan used to boast that his grandfather was a Scottish crofter, which was being somewhat economical with the truth. The last crofter in his family had been his great-grandfather, as he well knew. Grandfather Daniel Macmillan had come south to become a booksellers' apprentice in Cambridge, where – with his brother – he founded what was to become the great Macmillan publishing empire. By the time that Harold Macmillan was born, in 1894, the family, already immensely wealthy, had long been established in one of the most fashionable quarters of London, and any Scottish connections were but a distant memory.

His father, Maurice, was Daniel's second son, a cultured, diffident man, who was totally in thrall to his American wife Nellie, a talented musician, but a bit of a harridan, with no inhibitions in expressing her strong views and prejudices, which included a large dose of Mid-Western Protestantism. Macmillan was the youngest of three brothers, but was soon selected by his ambitious mother as the one most likely to make his mark in the world, and she lost no opportunity to push him forward. In later life, Harold was to write: "I can truthfully say that I owe everything all through my life to my mother's devotion and support." As Prime Minister, he was to tell a friend: "I admired her but never really liked her … she dominated me and she still dominates me".

A solitary and withdrawn child, who got more affection from his nanny than his parents, he was unhappy at Eton, from where he was removed at the age of 15 on the grounds of ill health. This was probably the actual reason, though his official biographer, Alistair Horne, refers coyly to "inevitable rumours" that he left for the "usual reasons" for boys to be expelled from public schools. He was highly inhibited and, according to Lord Blake, who knew him well, found it hard in later life "to relate at all easily to his contemporaries, to his children and to women" (*DNB*, p. 276). After Eton, he was educated at home by tutors, with one of whom – Ronnie Knox – he was to form a close and affectionate relationship. Knox, who much later was to gain renown as a leading Roman Catholic theologian, was then a young Anglo-Catholic priest, who had been at Oxford with Harold's eldest brother, Daniel. Still trembling on the brink of conversion to Rome, he was to be unceremoniously ejected from the household by a furious Nellie Macmillan, who had no intention of seeing her son being corrupted by Popish

DOI: 10.4324/9781003031963-13

doctrines, and who also feared the growing attraction between her 17-year-old son and his 22-year-old tutor.

Despite the loss of his formidable tutor, Macmillan was able to win an Exhibition to Balliol College, Oxford, where he spent a gloriously happy two years between 1912 and 1914, gaining First Class Honours in the first part of his Classics degree, which he was never to complete. At Oxford, he renewed his friendship with Knox, who was now a chaplain at Trinity College, and – together with another close friend – strongly urged him to take the final plunge and convert to Rome. To Knox's consternation, however, Macmillan himself – fearful of his mother's reaction – decided to remain an Anglican, even if a High Church one, which he was to remain for the rest of his life. Macmillan played an active role in the Union, becoming successively Secretary and Treasurer, with a good chance of succeeding to the Presidency if the war had not intervened. He espoused radical causes, but seemed very unsure of his party affiliation – or perhaps was hedging his bets – as he became a member simultaneously of the Canning (Tory) and Russell (Liberal) clubs, as well as the Fabian Society (Labour). He supported a motion "That this House approves the main principles of Socialism", and in his maiden speech attacked the 'public school' system.

Like most of his Oxford contemporaries, Macmillan, aged 20, hastened to join up in the early days of the war, and was commissioned as a second lieutenant in the King's Royal Rifle Corps. His mother then used influence to get him transferred to the much smarter Grenadier Guards, and in the summer of 1915, Macmillan went to France, where he was to remain for most of the rest of the war, acquiring a reputation for gallantry (but no decoration) and being seriously wounded three times. He emerged from the war, feeling a great sympathy with the largely working-class soldiers that he had commanded, and only just alive. He was rotting in a poorly equipped military hospital, but the determined and energetic Nellie got him transferred to a private hospital in Belgrave Square, just round the corner from his family home, an action which Macmillan thought saved his life.

Now aged 24, Macmillan could not bear the thought of returning to Oxford, so many of his contemporaries having perished in the war. He retained his army rank of captain, and in 1919 went to Ottawa as aide-de-camp to the Governor-General of Canada, the ninth Duke of Devonshire. This post was secured for him by his ever scheming and social-climbing mother, who may perhaps have been partly influenced by the fact that the Duke had several daughters of marriageable age. If so, her foresight was rewarded, for Harold fell deeply in love with the youngest of them, the 19-year-old Lady Dorothy Cavendish. The wedding at St Margaret's, Westminster, on 21 April 1920, was the social event of the year. The bride's party was packed with the cream of the aristocracy, including the future King George VI, and the bridegroom's with the pride of Macmillan authors, including Henry James and Thomas Hardy.

By this time, Harold himself was already working as a senior editor in the family firm, then headed by his uncle Frederick, who was flanked as co-directors by Harold's father Maurice, and his cousin George. Alongside Harold, in the second layer, was his eldest brother Daniel and another cousin, Will. He found he had a natural aptitude for the work, and greatly enjoyed his contacts with such eminent authors as Hardy, Kipling, Yeats and Sean O'Casey, and younger writers, including the economists John Maynard Keynes, G.D.H. Cole, Colin Clark and Lionel Robbins. Still very buttoned up, however, he did not, on his own admittance, succeed in making friends with any of them, except O'Casey, a self-proclaimed Communist and atheist.

Despite his contentment at being a publisher, Macmillan – again influenced by his mother – now began to contemplate a political career. Still harbouring radical views, and fervently admiring Lloyd George, his logical political home would have been one of the two branches of the Liberal Party, but opportunism gained the upper hand, and sensing that the Liberals were a busted flush, he approached Conservative Central Office, offering his services to fight a "tough seat". A wealthy, rather cerebral young publisher, with a fine war record, the Tories lost no time in dispatching him to Stockton-on-Tees, a predominantly working-class constituency in the North-East, represented by a Liberal. What the average Stockton elector made of this earnest, rather uptight young man, with a duke's daughter at his side, may only be conjectured, but he came very close to winning the seat, a mere 73 votes behind the Liberal, with Labour a close third. The following year, aged 30 – in the 1924 election – he came out on top, 3,000 votes ahead of Labour, with the former Liberal MP in third place.

Macmillan was appalled by the high level of unemployment in Stockton, and by the hardship and poverty of many of his constituents, feeling the same sympathy for them that he had for the men he had commanded on the Western Front. Their plight was the main theme of the periodic speeches he made in his early years in the Commons. Ponderous and poorly delivered, they soon won him the reputation of being a parliamentary bore, though few doubted the sincerity and disinterestedness of his views. More influential was a short book which he wrote, with three other young MPs, entitled *Industry and the State*, setting out the case for unorthodox measures (described as "Socialistic" by more mainline Tories) to mitigate the effects of unemployment. Macmillan followed this up with a number of unsolicited memoranda which he sent to various ministers, one of which, addressed to Winston Churchill, the Chancellor of the Exchequer, was acknowledged by him to be the original source of the Derating Act of 1927, which, by relieving industrial enterprises of the burden of paying rates to local authorities, increased their profitability and thereby enhanced their prospects as employers. Macmillan and his three fellow authors became the nucleus of a Tory progressive group, mockingly referred to by fellow Conservative MPs as the YMCA. The group notably included Robert Boothby, Churchill's lively and mischievous PPS, who was to have a devastating influence on Macmillan's private life.

As an MP, Macmillan continued to work for his publishing house during the mornings, while attending the House of Commons in the afternoon and evening. Three children – a son and two daughters – were born during the first six years of his marriage, and, while Harold was for the most part busily occupied in London, they were living with their mother at Birch Grove, the family's country residence in Sussex. Already a large Victorian pile, it was substantially extended in the 1920s by Nellie Macmillan, who ruled the roost as a materfamilias, with Harold's family allocated a large wing on the first floor. Nellie had persuaded her husband that – though Harold was the third son – he should be the sole heir of Birch Grove, though she should have the right to continue to live there during her lifetime.

This situation, of living under the same roof as her dominant mother-in-law, was undoubtedly oppressive for Dorothy, who had perhaps married Harold at a young age principally to get away from her own overbearing mother. Described by Horne as being "neither clever nor intellectual, but shrewd", she soon became discontented, and increasingly bored by her worthy but unexciting husband. The arrival of the handsome, amusing and buccaneering figure of Bob Boothby in Macmillan's circle had the proverbial effect of applying a spark to dried tinder. Dorothy immediately fell head over heels in love with him, and started what proved to be a lifelong affair, which she pursued with the absolute minimum of discretion. In 1930, she gave birth to a third daughter, Sarah, of whom Boothby was undoubtedly the father. Dorothy wanted a divorce, but Macmillan refused. A proud man, deeply hurt by his wife's infidelity, he

138 Harold Macmillan

suffered a nervous breakdown, but – determined to keep up appearances – resigned himself to a lonely and bleakly unhappy existence. He retreated into his books, reading widely in history and the classics, and returning repeatedly to the novels of Trollope and Jane Austen. Dorothy never let go of Boothby, but – particularly after he became Prime Minister in 1957 – provided companionship if not conjugal love to her husband. As for Boothby, who had been seen as a much more likely political prospect than Macmillan, his career spluttered out in the early 1940s, after he was found to have used undue influence to enrich himself while a junior minister. While he remained an MP and, later, a life peer, he was to be remembered mostly for his rumbustious performances in television discussion programmes.

In the same year – 1929 – that Dorothy began her liaison with Boothby, Macmillan suffered another disaster – the loss of his Stockton seat in the general election which brought Ramsay MacDonald back to the premiership. He subsequently narrowly avoided a far worse fate – that of becoming a close associate of Sir Oswald Mosley. In May 1930 Mosley resigned as a minister in the Labour government because of its failure to tackle unemployment. Macmillan immediately fired off a letter to *The Times*, warmly supporting Mosley's action. When Mosley subsequently founded his New Party, pledged to a planned economy, this strongly appealed to Macmillan who seriously considered defecting from the Tories. He drew back at the last moment, saving himself from probable electoral humiliation at the subsequent general election and from the taint of having been a fellow traveller of Mosley in the early stages of his headlong flight into Fascism. Instead, Macmillan, having unsuccessfully flirted with the possibility of fighting a safe Tory seat in the South-East, stuck to Stockton, which he easily regained in the landslide election of October 1931.

Throughout the 1930s, Macmillan was probably the most unorthodox of all the Tory MPs, rebelling against the party line on a wide range of issues. His main concern was still unemployment, and he persistently argued for Keynesian remedies, especially in his book, *The Middle Way*, published in 1938, which also advocated the nationalisation of the mining industry. It was not surprising that his views proved more acceptable in Labour circles than within his own party. Indeed, Frank Pakenham (later Lord Longford), a Tory who had switched to Labour, attempted to persuade Macmillan to follow suit. He replied: "When I consider the prospect of associating with your wild young men of the Left, I have to remember that I am a very rich man" (Horne, 1988, I, p. 119). Nevertheless, Macmillan was far more willing than most other dissident Tories to consider joint action with Labour MPs to oppose the policies of his own government, and in a newspaper article in 1936 had floated the idea of a centre party which, he suggested, should be led by Labour's Herbert Morrison.

Apart from Churchill, he was also the most consistent and determined opponent of appeasement. In 1936 he had been one of only two Tory MPs to vote against the government in a foreign affairs debate following the fiasco of the Hoare-Laval agreement, and actually resigned the party whip for a while. He also backed A.D. Lindsay, the 'popular front' candidate in the Oxford by-election following the Munich agreement, against the official Conservative nominee, Quintin Hogg. (Another Tory who supported Lindsay was Edward Heath, who was then an undergraduate at the University.) As Horne commented, "It is difficult to see how [Macmillan] could have stood as an orthodox Conservative candidate if a general election had been held in 1939 or 1940."

Macmillan's estrangement from the Conservative leadership was only brought to an end when it was replaced in May 1940, with Churchill succeeding Chamberlain as Prime Minister. Macmillan was one of the 41 Tory MPs who had voted to ensure Chamberlain's downfall, and his immediate reward was the ministerial office which had previously eluded him during 16 years as an MP. Even then, it was far from being a grand appointment – Parliamentary Secretary to the Ministry of Supply. He was 46 and was to remain a junior minister for nearly three years, under a series of senior figures, including Herbert Morrison and the press baron, Lord Beaverbrook. He was to prove competent and highly resourceful, and in December 1942 his big opportunity arose. Following the successful US-led occupation of French North Africa, Churchill decided to appoint a Resident Minister at the headquarters of the allied commander, General Dwight Eisenhower, as a counterweight to Robert Murphy, President Roosevelt's personal representative. He was only Churchill's second choice, but he accepted with alacrity. The post was of Cabinet rank, but though he was not a member of the War Cabinet he was to report directly to Churchill.

Soon established in a luxury villa in Algiers, Macmillan visibly flowered under the warm Mediterranean sun. Eisenhower greeted his arrival with suspicion, but Macmillan played up his half-American ancestry for all its worth, and all his previous stiff formality fell away from him in the more relaxed atmosphere of a largely American military headquarters. Before long he was playing a major political role, brokering the agreement under which General de Gaulle and the former Vichy General Giraud reluctantly shared the leadership of the French Committee for National Liberation, a provisional government in embryo. He also played a significant supporting role in the Casablanca summit meeting between Churchill and Roosevelt in March 1943. The focus later moved to Italy, with the invasion of Sicily and the secret negotiations for Italy to change sides in the war, in which he played a part as a go-between with representatives of the new Italian government which had replaced Mussolini. With Eisenhower's departure for England to prepare for the Normandy landings, Macmillan was attached to the headquarters of the British General Alexander, who commanded the allied forces in Italy. In effect, he became a viceroy in charge of civil government in Italy, as the Acting President of the Allied Control Commission. The nominal President was Alexander, who was far too busy with military matters to play any part. Macmillan contrived to include Greece, from which German troops retreated in the autumn of 1944, and even Yugoslavia, within his sphere of influence. This aroused the bitter hostility of Anthony Eden, who resented his poaching on the Foreign Office's and his own competence. Eden conspired unsuccessfully to have Macmillan recalled, while – for his part – Macmillan cast envious eyes on the Foreign Office, unwisely hinting to one of Eden's senior officials that he thought he could do the job better.

Macmillan even fancied himself as a strategist, helping Alexander to devise a plan, known as Operation Armpit, for a major thrust through northern Italy and the 'Ljubljana Gap', which, he argued, would bring Anglo-American forces into Vienna and Prague well ahead of the Russians. Churchill responded with enthusiasm, but it was vetoed by the Americans who insisted on proceeding instead with the already planned Operation Anvil – the invasion of southern France. Macmillan always insisted that if his plan had gone ahead the Iron Curtain would have been 250 miles further east than it actually was, but subsequent military opinion has been sceptical about its feasibility. What is certain is that his advocacy did him no harm with Churchill, who was also mightily impressed by his handling of the situation in newly liberated Greece, in December 1944, when, with the country plunging into civil war, Macmillan's proposal to install Archbishop Damaskinos as Regent may well have thwarted a Communist takeover.

The final wartime episode involving Macmillan – in May 1945 – was the sending back to almost certain death or torture of thousands of Russian and Yugoslav combatants and civilians

140 Harold Macmillan

who had been assisting the Germans and were captured by British forces in Austria. The decision to do this had been taken, in principle, at the Yalta summit the previous February, and Macmillan's responsibility was confined to advising the army commanders on the spot to proceed accordingly. His final years were clouded by accusations made much later, notably in a book published by Count Nikolai Tolstoy, and which featured in a sensational libel action, that Macmillan was personally responsible for sending back White Russian émigrés not covered by the Yalta agreement, for deceiving his friend General Alexander and for conspiring to delude the Yugoslavs into believing that they were being evacuated to Italy. None of these accusations was ever substantiated, despite detailed investigation. Macmillan must share the general guilt of those who carried out the policy, but the specific responsibility rests with Churchill and Roosevelt who agreed it with Stalin at Yalta. The repatriation of large numbers not strictly covered by the Yalta undertaking was due to the excessive zeal, or carelessness, of individual British officers, and cannot be placed at Macmillan's door.

Before the repatriations were carried out, Macmillan had been recalled to Britain, where – on the collapse of the coalition government – Churchill invited him to join his new 'caretaker' Cabinet, offering him the post of Air Minister, which he assumed on 25 May 1945. Two months later he was out of office, having lost his seat at Stockton by a majority of nearly 9,000. Within another four months he was back in the Commons, a by-election vacancy having occurred in the safe south London suburban constituency of Bromley. The Harold Macmillan who took up his seat in November 1945 was a changed character from the Tory rebel of the 1930s. It would be an exaggeration to say that the young idealist had been transformed into a cynical middle-aged manipulator, but there is an element of truth in that. He was certainly a great deal more self-confident and extrovert, more concerned about the pursuit of power and less scrupulous about the means to be employed. He was also much less *boring*. He had become an accomplished conversationalist, and his speeches, while still tending to be over-long and over-prepared, were much better delivered and were spiced with occasional flashes of wit. He was now a force to be reckoned with, and though few foresaw his rise to the premiership nobody doubted that he would be a senior figure in any future Tory government.

During the next six years, Macmillan proved to be one of the most pugnacious critics of the Attlee government, despite the fact that many of its policies closely resembled those he himself had advocated during the 1930s. He was now extremely partisan in his approach, even, on the occasion of his daughter Catherine's marriage to Julian Amery, crossing off from the invitation list the names of several prominent Labour politicians, including Clement Attlee, who had been closely associated with Amery's father, Leo, in the wartime coalition government. Macmillan played only a limited role in the widespread reforms adopted within the Conservative Party, struggling to make itself re-electable after its landslide defeat. It was Macmillan's long-term rival, R.A. Butler, who oversaw the reshaping of Conservative policy, involving the acceptance of all the major reforms introduced by Labour, while the parallel changes to the party's organisation and electoral machine were the work of Lord Woolton, the party chairman, and of the lawyer, Sir David Maxwell-Fyfe (later Lord Kilmuir). Nevertheless, Macmillan certainly expected to be offered a major post when Churchill formed his government in October 1951, and was deeply disappointed to be made Minister of Housing and Local Government, subjects on which, in his own words, he "knew nothing".

It was this appointment, however, which was to be the real making of Macmillan. The Tories' annual conference, normally a placid affair, had got out of hand in 1950 when the delegates, against the wishes of the platform, had insisted on setting a target of building 300,000 new houses per year, a figure which the party leadership regarded as quite impracticable (the current level was not much more than 200,000). Now Churchill challenged Macmillan to achieve it. "It is a gamble", he said, "which will make or mar your political career. But every humble home will bless your name if you succeed."

On 1 December 1953, Macmillan was able to make a triumphant announcement: the target had been reached. It had been achieved through his own tireless energy – and ceaseless bullying (with Churchill's full support) of other ministers to release scarce supplies and financial resources desperately needed for other urgent purposes, such as school-building, road construction and industrial expansion. It had been achieved, in part, through the efforts of his junior minister, Ernest Marples, a professional builder, and of his remarkable Permanent Under-Secretary, Dame Evelyn Sharp. And it had been reached through a savage reduction of the minimum standards for public housing set by his predecessor, Aneurin Bevan. Never mind, the target had been reached, and Macmillan shamelessly took all the credit for it, and was rewarded with standing ovations from subsequent Tory conferences. He was the hero of the hour, and he waited impatiently for promotion to one of the senior offices of state. But this had to wait on Churchill's retirement, which would release the Foreign Office on Eden's promotion to No. 10, and Churchill was in no hurry to go. He clung on until April 1955, and in the meantime, Macmillan had to make do with the Ministry of Defence to which he was appointed in October 1954. He did not enjoy the experience, finding that Churchill, whose powers in general were rapidly waning, still retained a close interest in defence matters and was constantly interfering.

It was an immense relief to Macmillan, when he finally retired, and, as expected, Eden appointed him Foreign Secretary. The relief did not last long. The new Prime Minister wanted to conduct his own foreign policy, and was reluctant to give Macmillan his head. After only eight months, and much to Macmillan's chagrin, he replaced him by a much junior figure, John Selwyn Lloyd, who he rightly judged would be more compliant. Macmillan was made Chancellor of the Exchequer, replacing Rab Butler, who became Leader of the House of Commons. Macmillan made a mighty fuss, and tried to impose conditions, one of which, that Butler should not formally be designated as Deputy Premier, he was granted, though Butler continued to preside at Cabinet meetings in Eden's absence.

Macmillan started off with the ambition of becoming a great reforming Chancellor, but is remembered in that role for a single gimmick, the introduction of Premium Bonds, in the only budget he was to present. The truth is that, for the greater part of the year that he held the office, he neglected his duties – especially during the Suez dispute – to concentrate his attention on foreign and defence issues. Thus he failed, unlike his French opposite number, to draw on credits from the International Monetary Fund, which would have helped prevent any subsequent run on the pound.

Of all Eden's ministers, he was the most gung-ho in urging the use of military force, and even submitted a memorandum suggesting that Israel should be associated with an Anglo-French attack several weeks before the French came up with their own plan to collude with the Israelis. He also, perhaps unintentionally, seriously misled Eden into believing that Eisenhower would support British military action, after a meeting with the President in mid-September, a meeting from which the British Ambassador, Sir Roger Makins, who was present, and took detailed notes, drew precisely the opposite conclusion. Then, when the Anglo-French invasion had just started, he took fright at the fall of the pound, which he had done nothing to guard against, and demanded an immediate cessation of activities. Macmillan was dubbed as "First in, and first out" by Harold Wilson in a devastating critique of the Suez operation, but his performance did him no apparent harm, despite the presumption that his first stance would have alienated the anti-Suez Tories, and his later one the much more numerous pro-Suez element.

Two months later, when Eden resigned, the Queen failed to ask his advice as to whom to call on as his successor, though he went out of his way to express his appreciation of the way in which Butler had led the government during his absence. She did consult Churchill, but the choice was effectively made by the retiring Cabinet, who were interviewed one-by-one by their two senior colleagues in the House of Lords, Lord Salisbury and Lord Kilmuir. Salisbury (grandson of the Prime Minister) had difficulty in pronouncing his 'r's, and said to each in turn: "Well, which is it, Wab or Hawold?"

Of the members of the Cabinet, only one, Patrick Buchan Hepburn, the Minister for Works, plumped for Butler. Macmillan's appointment came as an almost total surprise to the general public, virtually all the newspapers having predicted that Butler would be chosen. Had the vacancy occurred six months earlier, there is very little doubt that he would have won the prize, but the Suez episode was a disaster for him. He was seen as weak and indecisive, and the constant talk of appeasement had cruelly revived memories of his pre-war record as a close collaborator of Neville Chamberlain. Macmillan, by contrast, was seen as strong and determined, even if his judgement left a great deal to be desired.

Macmillan's appointment looked remarkably like a poisoned chalice, and he himself told the Queen that he doubted whether he would survive for more than six weeks. Yet he took immediate steps to calm the situation, starting by subtly emphasising the contrast between his own and Eden's more febrile approach by pinning to the Cabinet office door a notice with the words "Quiet calm deliberation disentangles every knot". This was a quotation from W.S. Gilbert's *The Gondoliers*, and thus began the enduring legend of Macmillan's 'unflappability'. Nevertheless, during his first year in office, he had a distinctly rocky ride. Already in March 1957, he suffered his first Cabinet resignation, when Lord Salisbury, the Leader of the House of Lords, quit in protest against the release from captivity of the Cypriot independence leader Archbishop Makarios, who had been deported to the Seychelles a year earlier. Salisbury had a substantial following among right-wing Tories, and was later to be the focus of resistance to decolonisation in Africa, but his departure from the government had little immediate impact. More serious, in the short term, for Macmillan was a rebellion of right-wing MPs, eight of whom resigned the party whip in May, when the Cabinet, in a final acknowledgement of the futility of the Suez operation, recommended British shipowners to use the canal and pay dues to Egypt. Throughout the year, the government was dogged by appalling opinion poll figures, giving a large lead to Labour, and poor by-election results. Then, in January 1958, he lost his entire Treasury team, when Peter Thorneycroft, the Chancellor of the Exchequer, and his two junior ministers, Enoch Powell and Nigel Birch, resigned, claiming that the expansionist economic policies which Macmillan was pursuing would have disastrous inflationary consequences. Macmillan, who was about to depart on an extensive Commonwealth tour, airily dismissed the resignations as "little local difficulties", and was widely admired for his aplomb.

Almost the first, and certainly the most important, step that Macmillan had taken to put the Suez disaster behind him, was to meet with President Eisenhower in Bermuda in March 1957. The purpose was to restore the close Anglo-American relationship, which – aided by his wartime association with Eisenhower, and it must be admitted a generous helping of obsequiousness – Macmillan succeeded in doing. Also at Bermuda, Eisenhower agreed that the US would supply Britain with guided missiles, which allowed the fiction of an 'independent' British deterrent to be maintained. Soon after this the first British hydrogen bomb was exploded, conscription was abolished, defence expenditure sharply cut, and the era of excessive dependence on nuclear weapons in British defence policy began.

By the spring of 1958 the worst was past, and – though opinion polls and by-elections continued to go badly – Macmillan had succeeded in consolidating his government and binding up the wounds in his own party. Equally importantly, he had impressed his own personality on the consciousness of the voters. No grey, anonymous figure, he: what the public saw was 'a bit of a card'. Elements of Macmillan the showman had already been revealed as Housing Minister; as Prime Minster he was to undergo a substantial makeover. In Horne's words,

> Gone were the little commissar-like spectacles, the 'Colonel Blimp' moustache had been ruthlessly pruned, the disarrayed teeth fixed – which somehow transformed the toothy, half-apologetic smile; the hair had assumed a more sophisticated shapeliness. Here was a new, almost dapper figure, with instant authority; the television 'personality had arrived'. (Horne, 1989, II, p. 145)

It was not, however, a very modern persona. He still wore Edwardian clothes, went shooting on ducal grouse moors, and stuffed his government with Etonians (half the Cabinet), and other aristocrats, many of them his relations by marriage. In the short term, at least, this image did him no harm. It coincided with the last flourish of deference voting by a section of the working class. Moreover, at least until 1960–61, he was far more popular than his Labour opponent, Hugh Gaitskell, who came over to the public as too earnest and too cerebral (a little like the pre-war Macmillan, in fact). Attempts to mock Macmillan's image only rebounded on his critics. Epithets such as MacWonder and Supermac, applied to him ironically by Aneurin Bevan and the left-wing cartoonist Vicky, were taken at face value by many people and added to his growing renown. In July 1957, Macmillan made a speech at Bedford, when, drawing on an earlier slogan used by the Democrats in the 1952 US elections, he said: "Let us be frank about it: most of our people have never had it so good." He was referring to the growing prosperity, as post-war shortages had come to an end and more and more people were owning motor cars, television sets and washing machines for the first time. The general sense of well-being which this engendered disguised the fact that it was precisely at this period that Britain began to fall seriously behind its continental neighbours, with lower growth rates and higher inflation. Never mind, most people were better off than before, and the Tories claimed – and duly received – the major credit for it.

It took time, however, for this feeling to work through to their political advantage, and it was only in early 1959 that the Labour lead in the opinion polls disappeared, and confidence began to grow in the prospects of a Tory victory. Macmillan was in no hurry to put this to the test. In order to bolster his image as an international statesman, he undertook two initiatives. One was to invite himself to Moscow, where, wearing an outsize fur hat (which unknown to his Soviet hosts he had acquired in Finland in 1940, where he had gone on an abortive mission to organise Western help against the Russian invasion), he was able to achieve unprecedented media coverage, despite the relative paucity of the results of his talks with Nikita Khrushchev. Then followed his masterstroke – an invitation to the tremendously popular US President 'Ike' Eisenhower to visit him in London, where he allowed himself to be shamelessly exploited for electoral purposes by agreeing to appear in a relaxed television discussion with Macmillan, which turned out to be an exercise in mutual admiration. The Labour Party, whose leader, Hugh Gaitskell, had been refused any contact whatever with the American President, fumed, but could do nothing about it. A few months later, in October 1959, Macmillan faced the electorate, with the slogan "Life is Better with the Conservatives – Don't Let Labour Ruin it", and was returned with a sharply increased majority of 100 seats. Gaitskell, who put up a spirited fight, was widely blamed for rashly promising that a Labour government would not put up income tax. This probably was counter-productive, but even if he had fought an impeccable campaign the odds would still have been stacked against him.

The 1959 election was Macmillan's greatest triumph, but it marked a watershed in his premiership. Before then virtually everything had gone right for him; afterwards almost everything went wrong. His main political initiative during his second term concerned the European Economic Community (then usually known as the Common Market), and it cannot be denied that he made a botch of it, as he himself recognised in his memoirs. "I shall never cease to blame myself", he wrote, for not having acted earlier and more decisively to pursue British membership, first of the Coal and Steel Community (ECSC) and then of the EEC. He wasted his first term of office in promoting the European Free Trade Association (EFTA), essentially a spoiling tactic, which it rapidly became clear was in no way an adequate substitute for EEC membership. Then, he hesitated for the best part of two years, before, on 31 July 1961, announcing a rather half-hearted application. He exerted himself, with no little skill and ruthlessness, to maximise support within his own party – only 40 out of some 4,000 delegates opposed the application at the Conservative conference in October 1961 – but made no attempt at all to secure cross-party support. This undoubtedly was a factor in pushing the Labour leader, Hugh Gaitskell, who was initially believed by his friends to be mildly pro-EEC, into the hostile camp, thereby undermining the force of the British application.

Edward Heath was appointed to conduct the membership negotiations. He acquired an impressive mastery of the details of a very complex process, stubbornly holding out for the best deal obtainable in every chapter of the negotiation. In retrospect, this, too, can be seen as a mistaken tactic, as it only added to the delay in bringing the proceedings to a conclusion. (Later applicants for EEC membership – notably Greece – found that they did better to agree quickly to whatever was offered, knowing that their bargaining power would be much greater once they were *inside* the Community.) In the event, it was the accumulated delays which proved crucial in the failure of the application. It had always been suspected that de Gaulle was at best lukewarm to British entry, but French public opinion was broadly in favour, and the General was in a weak position to enforce his will. Then, in October 1962, he won a crushing majority in a referendum on the presidency, following this up with a sweeping electoral victory one month later, and his authority was transformed. Peeved by Macmillan's behaviour at his meeting with President Kennedy at Nassau, in December 1962, when he won the US leader's reluctant consent to bolstering Britain's nuclear deterrent, while not securing equivalent assistance for France, he announced the French veto on 29 January 1963, only two days after his Foreign Minister, Maurice Couve de Murville, had told Heath that "nothing can now stop these negotiations from being a success".

The normally ebullient Macmillan was shattered by this setback, confiding to his diary "All our policies at home and abroad are ruined". De Gaulle's rebuff was only one of a series of setbacks for Macmillan during his second term of office. His economic policies started to go seriously awry, and not only the Tories', but his own personal opinion poll ratings plunged, leaving him far behind Gaitskell and, after his death, Harold Wilson. There followed a series of by-election disasters, after one of which, in July 1962, Macmillan promptly sacked one-third of his Cabinet, including Selwyn Lloyd, the Chancellor of the Exchequer, and the Lord Chancellor, Lord Kilmuir. The 'night of the long knives' was widely seen as a panic reaction, the Tory Chief Whip, Martin Redmayne, remarking to Rab Butler that "For once the unflappable actually flapped". A cartoon in the pro-Conservative *Sunday Express* showed a battered Macmillan, as the captain of the ship 'Never had it so good', saying, "Members of the crew, I have driven the ship on the rocks. For such striking incompetence, you're fired."

The remaining months of his premiership were blighted by the twin scourges of satire and scandal. The satire boom, which began with the Cambridge Footlights review *Beyond the Fringe*, was followed by the BBC programme *That Was the Week That Was*, which portrayed the formerly dynamic leader as a clapped out anachronism. The damage to his image was compounded by his handling of the Vassall and Profumo affairs. He emerged badly from the Vassall spy scandal, in November 1962, when he over-hastily demanded the resignation of a junior minister who was later revealed as blameless. Then came the much more damaging Profumo affair, in which the War Minister was discovered to have shared the favours of a call girl with a Soviet agent, and in which Macmillan was revealed as being gullible and out of touch. He was severely shaken by the subsequent confidence debate, on 17 June 1963, when the normal Tory majority of 97 fell to 57 due to a spate of abstentions. The heaviest blow was a devastating speech by Nigel Birch, one of the three Treasury ministers who had resigned in 1957. He quoted Browning's poem *The Lost Leader* (originally written as an attack on Wordsworth for abandoning his youthful idealism):

> … let him never come back to us!
> There would be doubt, hesitation and pain,
> Forced praise on our part – the glimmer of twilight,
> Never glad confident morning again!

"Never glad confident morning again" undoubtedly reflected the view of the majority of Tory MPs, who now saw Macmillan as an electoral liability and – though lacking the will to push him out – earnestly hoped that he would make way for another standard-bearer to take them into the general election, now possibly only a few months away. Macmillan, now nearing 70, agonised for several months over whether to continue, deciding – only on the night of 7–8 October 1963 – that he would do so and would lead the Tories at the general election. He announced this to the Cabinet the following morning, only to be stricken by severe pains, which led him to adjourn the meeting early. He had an inflamed prostate gland, necessitating an immediate operation. Macmillan, known for his hypochondria, convinced himself that he had cancer, and decided he must resign forthwith – a decision he was to regret for the rest of his life.

He made one other decision: that, come what may, he would not be succeeded by Rab Butler, who was the obvious choice. His motives for doing down the man who had served him loyally and efficiently as a deputy for nearly seven years were complex. He no doubt despised him as a Man of Munich, but both the rival contenders whom he sought to promote were equally tarred with the same brush. Lord Hailsham (Quintin Hogg) had been the pro-Munich Tory candidate in the Oxford by-election in October 1938, while Lord Home had actually attended the Munich conference as Neville Chamberlain's PPS. Whatever drove him to it, Macmillan, who supervised the whole selection process from his sickbed, was utterly

146 Harold Macmillan

unscrupulous in his methods. He got the Chief Whip and the Lord Chancellor to conduct highly suspect soundings of Cabinet ministers and Tory MPs, and then "cooked the books", according to the then Tory Chairman, Iain Macleod, before reporting to the Queen that Lord Home had more support than any other candidate. It is arguable that had the Queen, or her advisers, been less guileless, they would have taken other soundings before sending for Lord Home, but Macmillan had really put her in an impossible situation. It is also true that if Butler, who undoubtedly would have been the majority choice if there had been a proper ballot either of the Cabinet or of Tory MPs, had had the guts to refuse to serve under Home, he could probably have forced the issue in his own favour (see next chapter). As it was, Macmillan did a serious disservice to his own party by landing it with the leader who was least well qualified to be Prime Minister and least likely to be a successful vote-winner at the subsequent general election.

Macmillan was Prime Minister for six years and 281 days – the fourth longest tenure in the century, after Thatcher, Wilson and Asquith. Technically, he was rated as one of the more effective Prime Ministers, but his long period in power was notably barren in its achievements. He pushed ahead with decolonisation, but not in the territories with a substantial settler population, though he prodded the South Africans to abandon apartheid in his "Wind of Change" speech. Not a single parliamentary Bill passed by his government has reverberated down the years as a landmark piece of legislation, unless it was the introduction of life peerages. The truth is that by the time he became Prime Minister, Macmillan had long ceased to be a reformer. He was the complacent leader of an essentially complacent country. Apart from wanting to increase British influence in the world, which led him to support both an 'independent' nuclear deterrent and British entry into the EEC, he had no deeply felt objectives. Instead, he was determined to put on a good show, and for a long time he succeeded in this, adding greatly to the gaiety of the nation. He attracted a variety of theatrical nicknames, including Mac the Knife, the Actor-Manager, and the Old Poseur. But like most old troupers, he went on rather too long, the audience got bored, and he ended up being likened to *The Entertainer*, in John Osborne's play. By 1963, it was time to leave the stage, as he subsequently conceded in his memoirs. He was to live another 23 years, refusing to take a peerage until his 90th birthday, when he became Earl of Stockton. This, apparently, was in part because he periodically harboured the (quite unrealistic) hope that he would be summoned back to lead a government of national unity. In his old age, he acquired a new reputation as a fount of wit and wisdom, and became something of a national treasure. It was rather a lonely life – his wife had died in 1966, and he lived virtually alone with his books in the cavernous house at Birch Grove, occupying himself with the affairs of his publishing firm and his duties as Chancellor of Oxford University, to which he had been elected while still in Downing Street. Consulted by Mrs Thatcher during the Falklands War, he later fell out with her when he likened her privatisation projects to "selling off the family silver". He died in 1986, and the most apt verdict on him was probably that of Lord Blake who, commenting on his lifelong admiration for Disraeli, wrote in the *DNB*: "It is arguable whether Disraeli was a great prime minister, but he was certainly a great character. The same can be said of Harold Macmillan."

Works consulted

Robert Blake, article in *Dictionary of National Biography, 1986–1990 Supplement*.
Martyn Bond, Julie Smith and William Wallace (eds), 1996, *Eminent Europeans*, London.

David Butler and Richard Rose, 1960, *The British General Election of 1959*, London, Macmillan.

Alistair Horne, 1988 (I), *Harold Macmillan 1894–1956*, London, Macmillan.

Alistair Horne, 1989 (II), *Harold Macmillan 1957–1986*, London, Macmillan.

Anthony Howard, 1987, *Rab: The Life of R.A. Butler*, London, Macmillan.

John Ramsden, 1996, *The Winds of Change: Macmillan to Heath 1957–1975*, London, Longman.

Anthony Sampson, 1968, *Macmillan: A Study in Ambiguity*, Harmondsworth, Penguin.

Hugo Young, 1998, *This Blessed Plot: Britain and Europe from Churchill to Blair*, London, Macmillan.

PLATES

1 Arthur James Balfour, first Earl of Balfour, by George Charles Beresford, © National Portrait Gallery, London

2 Sir Henry Campbell-Bannerman, by Alexander Bassano, © National Portrait Gallery, London

3 Herbert Henry Asquith, first Earl of Oxford and Asquith, by Reginald Haines, © National Portrait Gallery, London

4 David Lloyd George, by Sir William Orpen, © National Portrait Gallery, London

5 Andrew Bonar Law, by Walter Stoneman, © National Portrait Gallery, London

6 Stanley Baldwin, by Howard Coster,
© National Portrait Gallery, London

7 James Ramsay Macdonald, by Bassano Ltd,
© National Portrait Gallery, London

8 Neville Chamberlain, by Henry Lamb,
© National Portrait Gallery, London

9 Winston Churchill, by Walter Stoneman,
© National Portrait Gallery, London

10   Clement Attlee, by George Harcourt, © National Portrait Gallery, London

11   Sir Anthony Eden, first Earl of Avon, by Baron/Stringer, © Getty Images

12 Harold Macmillan, first Earl of Stockton, by Bentley Archive/Popperfoto, © Getty Images

13 Sir Alex Douglas-Home, by Rex Coleman and Baron Studios, © National Portrait Gallery, London

14 Harold Wilson, by Ruskin Spear, © National Portrait Gallery, London

15 Sir Edward Heath, by Bern Schwartz, © National Portrait Gallery, London

16 James Callaghan, by Bern Schwartz, © National Portrait Gallery, London

17 Margaret Thatcher, by Bern Schwartz, © National Portrait Gallery, London

18 Sir John Major, by David Levenson, © Getty Images

19 Tony Blair, by Eamonn McCabe/Popperfoto, © Getty Images

20 Gordon Brown, by Number 10gov from the National Archives, © Crown copyright

21 David Cameron, by Number10gov from the National Archives, © Crown copyright

22 Theresa May, by Andrew Parsons/i-Images, © Crown copyright

23 Boris Johnson, by Ben Shread/Cabinet Office, © Crown Copyright

13

ALEC DOUGLAS-HOME

Right man, wrong century?

The 14th Prime Minister of the 20th century was a 14th Earl, an improbable occurrence and one never likely to be repeated. Alexander Frederick Douglas-Home was born on 2 July 1903, the eldest of seven children of the 13th Earl of Home (pronounced Hume). He himself was to undergo several name changes, becoming successively Lord Dunglass, Earl of Home, Sir Alec Douglas-Home and, finally, Lord Home of the Hirsel. According to his official biographer, D.R. Thorpe, his "upbringing was privileged even by the standards of the upper classes of the time". He was descended from two of the most powerful and wealthy families in Scotland. The Douglases, famous robber barons, had been the scourges of the English for several centuries; the Homes had betrayed their own countrymen to collaborate with their English oppressors, and, in 1603, the first Earl came down to London with King James I, as one of his most trusted admirers. The Douglas and Home families were united by marriage in 1832, and, when Alec was born, his grandfather, the 12th Earl, owned well over 100,000 acres, with estates in Berwickshire and Lanarkshire – the latter containing valuable coal deposits – as well as several grouse moors, valuable fishing rights over a long stretch of the River Tweed, and castles at Douglas and the Hirsel, near Coldstream.

Alec's family environment was a happy one. His father – Charlie – reportedly an exceptionally nice man, was a conventional landowner, and part-time banker in Edinburgh. His mother, the former Lady Lilian Lambton, daughter of the Earl of Durham, was a more radical influence. Known teasingly in the family as "the well-known socialist", she was to vote Labour in the 1945 election, even though her son was by then a junior Conservative minister. Alec was educated at home by a governess until the age of 10, when he was dispatched to a prep school in Hertfordshire, where he stayed until 14, the school having contrived to retain him for an extra year because of his prowess on the cricket field. By then already known as Lord Dunglass (a courtesy title he assumed when his father became the 13th Earl), he arrived at Eton on the same day as a boy called Eric Blair (George Orwell), though their careers, both at school and later, were sharply to diverge. In every respect, except academically, where he was – at best – no more than average, Alec's time at Eton was an outstanding success. Elected a member of Pop, an elite society of senior boys, the literary critic, Cyril Connolly, included

DOI: 10.4324/9781003031963-14

a remarkable vignette about him in his own autobiographical essay, originally published in 1938:

> The other important Pop was Alec Dunglass, who was President and also Keeper of the Field and Captain of the Eleven. He was a votary of the esoteric Eton religion, the kind of graceful, tolerant sleepy boy who is showered with favours and crowned with all the laurels, who is liked by the masters and admired by the boys without any apparent exertion on his part, without experiencing the ill-effects of success himself or arousing the pangs of envy in others. In the eighteenth century he would have become Prime Minister before he was thirty; as it was he appeared honourably ineligible for the struggle of life. (Connolly, 1938, p. 245)

From Eton, in 1922, Dunglass proceeded to Oxford, where he enrolled in Christ Church, the most socially exclusive college, where the ambience, especially among his own group of friends, resembled that recounted by Evelyn Waugh, in *Brideshead Revisited*. It was, according to Home's biographer, "a carefree world of hunting, cricket, bridge and champagne, though racing was becoming one of Dunglass's interests at this time" (Thorpe, 1996, p. 32). He also began to take an interest in politics, and attended meetings of several political clubs, while steering clear of the Union. He studied history, obtaining only a Third Class degree, possibly, in part, because of a mysterious illness which afflicted him at the time of his finals, though, according to one of his tutors, it "did not really matter to him what sort of academic label he would bear on leaving Oxford" (Thorpe, 1996, p. 31). He came down in 1925, and made no attempt to seek employment, even as the manager of the family estates, which his father would have been pleased for him to do. Instead, he decided to 'swan around' for a couple of years, devoting his time to an endless round of cricket matches, point-to-point meetings, shooting parties, salmon fishing and country house visits. He went on a cricket tour to South America, with the MCC, and played for a variety of clubs, including the local Coldstream side, the Eton Ramblers, the Free Foresters and I Zingari. He had a natural talent for the game, had been coached by top-class professionals at Eton, and was probably good enough to play regularly for an English county side if he had had the inclination.

He had, however, more serious interests in view, one of which was to become an MP – not, his biographer insists, because of *noblesse oblige*, but through a genuine ambition to hold senior office. Because of his social background, he had no difficulty at all in getting selected as a Conservative (or Unionist, as they were known in Scotland) candidate. He just mentioned to Sir John Gilmour, the Secretary of State for Scotland, and to Noel Skelton, MP for Perth, that he would like to contest a seat at the 1929 general election, and an immediate invitation arrived to fight Coatbridge and Airdrie, a predominantly industrial seat close to the family estates at Douglas. The 25-year-old Dunglass, who had led such a cloistered life, had a rude awakening when he faced the working-class electorate of the constituency. One of them – a miner – recalled him, 44 years later in a BBC programme, as being "Probably the rawest and most immature candidate I have ever seen at any time". Another recalled him as being "pathetic on the platform, absolutely pathetic" (Thorpe, 1996, p. 44). Dunglass was easily defeated by the Labour candidate, but was not put off by the experience and in 1931 eagerly accepted an invitation to fight the Lanark constituency, formerly held by a leading Scottish Tory, Walter Elliot, which had been a narrow Labour gain in 1929. As part of the landslide victory won by

150 Alec Douglas-Home

Ramsay MacDonald's National government, Dunglass easily defeated his Labour opponent with a nearly two-to-one majority. He was 28, and his foot was on the first rung of the political ladder.

No sooner was the election over, than he reached the second, when he was invited to become PPS to Noel Skelton, who was Under-Secretary at the Scottish Office. Skelton, who was to die of cancer only four years later, was regarded as one of the most promising of younger Tory politicians and was the unofficial leader of a group of progressive MPs, including Anthony Eden. Working as Skelton's 'eyes and ears', Dunglass became familiar with the very wide range of economic and social issues for which the Scottish Office was responsible. This familiarity was extended to English and Welsh affairs, in 1935, when he transferred to become PPS to Anthony Muirhead, the Under-Secretary at the Ministry of Labour. Home impressed people equally by his great courtesy and by the conformity of his views. Very much on the 'respectable' wing of the party, he firmly rebutted overtures from such subversive characters as Winston Churchill. Nevertheless, as a PPS to junior ministers, he remained a minor player on the Westminster stage. In 1936, however, he received a notable step-up when he was asked to perform the same duties for the Chancellor of the Exchequer, Neville Chamberlain. Chamberlain liked his protectionist views, and another factor which they had in common was their love of bird-watching. The same year, at the age of 33, he had married Elizabeth Alington, six years his junior and the daughter of his former headmaster at Eton. The marriage, which was to last almost 54 years, was a happy one, and was to produce a son and three daughters. Dunglass remained with Chamberlain when he became Prime Minister, a few months later, and was a wholehearted participant in his appeasement policy.

He accompanied Chamberlain to the Munich conference with Hitler, and for ten days afterwards, Chamberlain, who was exhausted physically and mentally, went with his wife and the Dunglasses to the Hirsel to recuperate, at the invitation of the 13th Earl. Subsequently, Dunglass was heavily involved in the by-election which took place in Kinross and West Perthshire, in December 1938. The sitting MP, the Duchess of Atholl, had been de-selected by the local Conservatives because of her criticism of Chamberlain, and promptly resigned her seat to fight a by-election on an anti-Munich platform. Described by a later Tory MP, Robert Rhodes James, as "one of the dirtiest by-election campaigns of modern times, from which only the duchess emerged with any distinction", Dunglass's participation did him little credit, and he makes no reference to it in his autobiography. He, in fact, was the star speaker on behalf of the Tory candidate, who was narrowly elected, and the posters advertising his meetings read: COME AND HEAR THE TRUTH ABOUT MUNICH FROM THE MAN WHO WAS THERE WITH THE PRIME MINISTER.

An unconditional admirer of Chamberlain, Dunglass remained with him to the bitter end, even declining office as a junior Scottish Office minister in September 1939 in order to continue as his parliamentary aide. On the day war was declared – 3 September – Dunglass was involved in a bizarre incident, which does much to explain his subsequent image as a comic character out of P.G. Wodehouse. He had driven down to the South Downs, with his brother Henry, to search for a rare species of butterfly. Arrested in some woods by a suspicious Special Constable, who, when Dunglass claimed to be the Prime Minister's PPS, replied "Yes, and I'm the Queen of Sheba", it required a hurried phone call to 10 Downing Street before he was prepared to release his captives. Amazingly, he was again to be arrested, by the Oxfordshire police, in similar circumstances a year later.

Dunglass was appalled when Churchill replaced Chamberlain as Prime Minister in May 1940, and joined in a last-ditch effort to persuade Lord Halifax to take over, describing Churchill and his associates as "gangsters". A month later, he was reported as having told the wife of a Tory whip that "since W[inston] came in, the H of C had stunk in the nostrils of decent people" (Stewart, 1999, p. 426). It was unsurprising that Churchill found no place for Dunglass in his coalition government. Instead, Dunglass intended to join up, as did his four younger brothers, one of whom was killed in action. He already had a commission in the Lanarkshire Yeomanry, but his plans were thwarted by a breakdown in his health. He had tuberculosis of the spine, and in September 1940 underwent a vital operation, and was then incarcerated in a plaster cast for two years, during which he was unable to leave his home. It was only in July 1943 that he was well enough to resume his work as an MP. He made the most of his period of inactivity, which seemed to have the effect of focusing his mind on serious issues and maturing his personality. He read very extensively, notably historical and biographical works, and was the only British Prime Minister known to have read Marx's *Das Kapital* from cover to cover. The only effect this had on him was to strengthen his already fervent anti-Communism, which was further reinforced by his contact with Polish soldiers billeted at Douglas Castle. One of these, Count Starzenski, a former private secretary to the Polish foreign minister, Colonel Beck, gave him a first-hand account of the horrors of the Russian occupation of eastern Poland between 1939 and 1941.

In the spring of 1945, Dunglass emerged as one of the fiercest critics of the Yalta agreement, which effectively put Poland at Russia's mercy. He made a powerful speech in the Commons, and was one of 21 Tories to vote against the government when the House was divided on a backbench motion regretting the transfer of "the territory of an Ally" to "another Power". The former appeaser of Hitler was not prepared to bend the knee before Stalin. Churchill was probably not best pleased by Dunglass's repudiation of what he had agreed at Yalta, but nevertheless when a Conservative 'caretaker' government was formed three months later, at the end of the war in Europe, he was appointed as joint Under-Secretary at the Foreign Office. This was almost certainly due to the influence of the Tory Chief Whip, James Stuart, who effectively selected all the junior members of the government. A fellow Scottish aristocrat, and a descendant of King James V of Scotland, he was to continue to be Dunglass's mentor and protector for the best part of a decade.

Dunglass remained a minister for just two months, at the end of which he was heavily defeated in his Lanark constituency in the July 1945 general election, which swept Labour into power. He regained the seat with a narrow majority in 1950, but in July 1951 his father died, and he entered the House of Lords as the 14th Earl of Home. Three months later the Conservatives won the 1951 general election, and James Stuart was appointed Secretary of State for Scotland. He immediately asked for Alec Home to become his number two, as Minister of State. For the next four years he was the man on the spot, supervising the work of the Scottish administration from its headquarters in Edinburgh, and every now and then making a vice-regal-style tour throughout the country, almost invariably staying in the castles or country houses of various grandees, often his own relatives. Stuart, who was one of Churchill's closest associates, spent nearly all his time in London, leaving Home to operate on a very loose rein. The disadvantage for him was that he himself was very seldom in the national capital, and thus remained fairly unknown to the great majority of political actors, let alone the general public outside Scotland. This position only marginally improved in April 1955, when Eden brought him into his Cabinet as Secretary of State for Commonwealth Relations. In this

152 Alec Douglas-Home

post, he was largely invisible because of his membership of the Upper House, while he was frequently away on visits to Commonwealth countries and territories.

He was confirmed in this post, in January 1957, when Macmillan succeeded Eden, and after another couple of months combined it with the leadership of the House of Lords, when Lord Salisbury resigned over the Cyprus issue. All together, he held the Commonwealth Relations portfolio for a record period of over five years. During this time he became very close to Macmillan, who valued his traditional background and relatively right-wing views as a counterweight to the younger, more radical figures he was bringing into his Cabinet, such as Iain Macleod, Edward Heath and Reginald Maudling. Then, in May 1960, he gave Home a staggering promotion, making him Foreign Secretary in place of Selwyn Lloyd, who became Chancellor of the Exchequer. The appointment went down almost universally badly. This was not primarily because of doubts over Home's capacity, but because of a very widespread feeling that it was inappropriate, and an affront to the House of Commons, to have a Foreign Secretary in the House of Lords. The *Daily Mirror* opined that it was "the most reckless political appointment since the Roman Emperor Caligula made his favourite horse a consul", and the Labour Party put down a censure motion in the Commons. Macmillan recorded in his diary that "Gaitskell made the cleverest and most effective speech I had heard him make. My reply was not too good, but the Party rallied round." In fact, criticism within the Tory Party was almost as great as from the opposition, and it made for a difficult beginning for Home. In the event, he made an adequate, if far from outstanding Foreign Secretary, and was actually aided by not having to spend time nursing a parliamentary seat. He was also greatly helped by the appointment, as his deputy, of Edward Heath, as Lord Privy Seal, who took over complete responsibility for European issues and proved a highly effective number two.

Home became a popular figure among foreign diplomats because of his old world charm and congenial manner, and they respected him for his straight talking. Even the Soviet Foreign Minister, the dour Andrei Gromyko, was known to thaw in his presence. He was also easily the best-liked member of the Cabinet, with no known enemies, with the single exception of Iain Macleod. Macleod had become Colonial Secretary in 1959, with a brief to speed up decolonisation, and he resented what he regarded as obstructionism by his colleague at the Commonwealth Relations Office. Macleod, who had famously been attacked as "two clever by half" by Home's friend and predecessor as Leader of the Lords, Lord Salisbury, had a low opinion of Alec Home's intellectual capacity and regarded him as a reactionary of the deepest hue.

Home thoroughly enjoyed being Foreign Secretary, and no doubt regarded himself as being exceptionally fortunate to have reached what must have seemed the peak of his career at the age of 57. Yet, in November 1960 an event occurred which was eventually to give an altogether unexpected twist to his destiny. This was the death of the Labour peer, Lord Stansgate, which had the immediate effect of disqualifying his eldest surviving son, the prominent Labour MP, Tony Benn, from sitting in the House of Commons. The same fate had affected Home himself, in 1951, and he had uncomplainingly complied, as well as Quintin Hogg (Lord Hailsham), who had impotently raged against it, in 1950. Benn was made of sterner stuff, fighting a by-election in his Bristol South-East constituency, and winning it handsomely with a majority of 13,000 over his Conservative opponent, who was nevertheless awarded the seat by an election court. Public opinion was clearly on Benn's side, and the government was eventually forced to introduce a Bill enabling hereditary peers to disclaim their titles during their lifetime. Under the original draft, this would only have come into effect after the ensuing general election, but a Labour amendment was accepted in the Lords that it would apply as soon as the Bill received royal assent. Within hours of this happening, Benn disclaimed his title; Home and Hailsham did not, but the passage of the amendment, in July 1963, was to transform the outcome of the Tory leadership contest three months later.

As recounted in the preceding chapter, this was triggered by Macmillan's mistaken belief that he had cancer, and the announcement that he was to resign was made, on 10 October, to the annual Tory conference by Lord Home, in his capacity as President of the National Union of Conservative Associations. The febrile atmosphere of the conference was hardly calculated to ensure that there would be a calm and judicious assessment of the merits of the competing candidates, whom it was not then generally known would include Home. Indeed two days earlier he had privately offered his services, along with the Lord Chancellor, Lord Dilhorne, as an impartial 'collector of voices' within the Cabinet, from which his colleagues quite naturally concluded that he was not himself in the running. Earlier in the year, when it had looked as though Macmillan would be forced to resign in the wake of the Profumo affair, the hot favourite was seen to be Reginald Maudling, the youthful Chancellor of the Exchequer. Yet his star inexplicably faded during the summer, and neither he, nor two other younger potential candidates – Heath and Macleod – were now seen as likely contenders. The effective choice seemed to be between Rab Butler and Lord Hailsham, who had become eligible since the passage, on 31 July, of the Peerage Act, which gave existing peers a six-month window of opportunity to disclaim. Butler had much the stronger claim in terms of experience and ministerial achievement, and was far ahead in the opinion polls; Hailsham was known to be very popular among the Conservative rank-and-file, and was believed to be Macmillan's preferred choice. Yet Home was evidently holding himself in reserve as a compromise candidate. He had arranged to have a medical check-up to see if he was fit enough to bear the strains of the premiership, and a number of highly influential supporters, including Selwyn Lloyd, Heath and John Morrison, chairman of the 1922 Committee of Conservative backbenchers, were already canvassing on his behalf.

When he went to see Macmillan in hospital before his operation, on 9 October, he was strongly urged to make himself available. The Prime Minister was perhaps having second thoughts about Hailsham, who a day later effectively blew his chances by the theatrical way in which he announced he was disclaiming his peerage, and by parading himself around the Tory conference, with his baby daughter and her bottle in his arms. This upset the more decorous Tories, who, according to Home's biographer, believed "that the proper person to be dispensing such attention was the nanny – and in private" (Thorpe, 1996, p. 525). After this, Macmillan switched his support to Home, and set in motion a series of soundings (invariably conducted by Etonians, as Macleod later observed in a biting article in *The Spectator*, when he alleged that a "magic circle" had fixed the selection on the orders of Etonian Macmillan for the benefit of Etonian Home). There can be little doubt that the soundings (of Cabinet members, Tory MPs and peers, and constituency representatives) were deeply flawed, and that the way in which the questions were put strongly skewed the answers in favour of Home. The overall effect was to give more weight to negative opinions rather than positive expressions of support. It was only on this basis that it was possible to conclude that Home "enjoyed more support than any other candidate". There is no serious doubt that Butler would have emerged on top, at least as far as the parliamentarians were concerned, if a straightforward ballot had been arranged, while Hailsham was clearly the favourite of the constituency associations. Home may have emerged as 'the lowest common denominator', but that is hardly a way to

154 Alec Douglas-Home

choose a party leader in the approach to a difficult election, let alone a Prime Minister. Even on this basis, the poll was later shown to be wildly inaccurate. The scorecard which Lord Dilhorne kept of Cabinet members' preferences, which was published much later, showed both Macleod and Sir Edward Boyle plumping for Home (Ramsden, 1996, pp. 205–6). Both indignantly denied this, and said that their votes had been cast for Butler. Macleod's accusation that Macmillan and his henchmen had "cooked the books" was never effectively refuted.

When Macmillan received the soundings, on 17 October, he decided to recommend the appointment of Home when the Queen came to see him in hospital the following morning to receive his resignation. Word leaked out of what was intended, and the supporters of the other candidates reacted in fury. Eight Cabinet ministers were strongly opposed to Home, and at a late-night meeting held at Enoch Powell's flat, both Hailsham and Maudling agreed to back Butler for the premiership, and to refuse to serve under Home. If Butler's nerve had held, the crown was his. As Powell later graphically put it in a television interview, he and his colleagues had, in effect, given Butler a loaded pistol. He replied, according to Powell, "Will it go off with a bang?" "Well, Rab", they responded, "a gun does make rather a bang when it goes off." Butler's response, in Powell's fanciful account, was "Well, thank you very much, I don't think I will. Do you mind?" (Thompson and Barnes, 1971, p. 219). Home got to know of the opposition to him, and suggested to Macmillan that he should delay his recommendation to the Queen, only to be told, impatiently, "Go ahead. Get on with it" (Ramsden, 1996, p. 204.) So Macmillan railroaded it through, but when Home saw the Queen later in the day, he declined to 'kiss hands' on his appointment, merely saying that he would try to form a government and then report back. His first, highly tricky interview was with Butler, and he handled it with great tact, dangling before him the prospect of being Foreign Secretary, a long-standing ambition which Macmillan had twice refused him. Butler asked for some hours to consider, and then, to the despair of his supporters, meekly accepted. Maudling and Hailsham then agreed to serve under Home, only Macleod and Powell, whose weight was insufficient to make a crucial difference, deciding to boycott the government which Home was able to form on the following day. Macleod objected to Home because he thought he was utterly unsuitable, Powell for a more fastidious reason. He believed that Home had been less than straight in letting his Cabinet colleagues believe that he had no intention of becoming a candidate.

So Home became Prime Minister on 19 October 1963. His first task was to disclaim his peerage and secure election to the House of Commons. Fortuitously a vacancy existed due to the death of the Tory MP for Kinross and West Perthshire, where he had campaigned in the earlier by-election in 1938. The Tory candidate obligingly stepped down in his favour, and Home was duly elected on 7 November. Even now, he did not become plain Mr Home, which would have been more in tune with the modernising message which the Tories were planning to make the basis of their electoral appeal, but chose to be known as Sir Alec Douglas-Home (having been made a Knight of the Thistle in 1962). This was only the first of a string of tactical errors which Home was to make during the 363 days of his premiership, which was aptly described as "a twelve-month election campaign against the odds" (Ramsden, 1996, p. 214). He had the great misfortune to be pitched against Harold Wilson. Opinions differ about Wilson's record as Prime Minister, but nobody disputes that he was the outstanding leader of the opposition of the 20th century. He established a total domination over Home in the twice-weekly duels at Prime Minister's Question Time, and completely outclassed him as a television performer. Home had given a terrible hostage to fortune, when, in September 1962, in an interview with *The Observer*, he said that he doubted whether he would ever become Prime Minister because "When I have to read economic documents I have to have a box of matches and start moving them into position to simplify and illustrate the points to myself". This interview was mercilessly recalled, and Home was caricatured as the 'matchstick man' and unfavourably compared to Wilson, who had a formidable reputation as an economist and was impressing many people with his speeches invoking the "white heat of the technological revolution".

He, probably wisely, declined all invitations to debate directly with Wilson on television, but the contrast between their performances was telling. Occasionally, Home was able to score points, as when he commented that his opponent must be "the 14th Mr Wilson", but the satirical TV programme *That Was the Week That Was* got it about right when it dubbed the contest "Dumb Alec versus Smart Alec". Occasionally Wilson overdid the mockery, and viewers began to feel sorry for Home, but this was hardly a reassuring basis for building support. Home wryly accepted that he was ineffective on television, and recounted in his memoirs a conversation which he had had with a make-up girl:

Q. Can you not make me look better than I do on television?

A. No.

Q. Why not?

A Because you have a head like a skull.

Q Does not everyone have a head like a skull?

A. No.

(Home of the Hirsel, 1976, p. 203)

As Prime Minister, Home was calmness itself, and it has been suggested that he, rather than Macmillan, merited the epithet 'unflappable'. He set himself a leisured pace, and I well remember a conversation I had a few years later with Sir Derek Mitchell, his Principal Private Secretary, who went on to fulfil the same role with Harold Wilson. "Harold", he said "was the complete professional, working non-stop at the job. Alec would spend a couple of hours being Prime Minister, and would then disappear for a while to the upstairs flat to get on with his own life." He probably exaggerated the contrast, but it had the ring of truth. Home showed himself singularly devoid of ideas for political initiatives. His electoral strategy consisted basically of hanging on like Mr Micawber, waiting for something to turn up. Possible election dates, first in March and then in June, were passed up because of Labour's continuing lead in the opinion polls, and Home resolved to go on almost to the bitter end, eventually choosing 15 October as polling day (the last possible date, under the five-year rule, would have been 5 November, and Home subsequently regretted that he had not waited until then). Nor did his government have much of a legislative record during his premiership. The only significant Bill passed was the abolition of retail price maintenance, a measure insisted on by Edward Heath who, as Secretary for Trade and Industry, was determined to make his own personal mark as a radical reformer. It was fiercely resisted by Tory MPs and within the Cabinet, as a

156 Alec Douglas-Home

likely vote-loser among small traders, even though it meant lower prices for the consumer, and Home only persisted with the Bill because he feared that Heath would resign if it were withdrawn.

The decision to delay the election almost paid off, as by August the Labour opinion poll lead had evaporated. Yet it managed to pull ahead again during the actual campaign, when Home made what Thorpe described as "probably the worst mistake of his entire premiership". Questioned in a television interview about pensions, he replied that "we will give a donation to the pensioners who are over a certain age", the use of the word 'donation' appearing to confirm the Labour assertion that the Conservatives, and Home in particular, were patronising and remote from the concerns of ordinary people. In the event, Labour finished up with an overall majority of only four, the result being:

Labour	317
Conservative	303
Liberal	9
The Speaker	1

Some of Home's supporters claimed that this result justified his selection as leader, and that it had been a great achievement of his to pin back Labour to such a slender lead. The opposite view that the Tories would have done better under another leader, and especially Rab Butler, carried more conviction. It was not only Home's shortcomings, and his evident inability to personify the Tories' modernising themes, which made his task so difficult, but the whole manner of his selection, and the widespread belief that Macmillan had cheated, fatally undermined public confidence. Harold Wilson, for one, was convinced that he would have lost the election if Butler had been his opponent.

Home himself blamed Macleod and Powell for the Labour victory, and for a brief moment shed his normal gentlemanly manner, and to the amazement of his entourage let loose a flood of expletives against them when the last results trickled in on the afternoon of 16 October. Yet, for the most part, he took the defeat philosophically, assuming it meant the virtual end of his political career and that he would soon be able to resume his beloved country pursuits in Scotland. He stayed on, however, as leader of the opposition, and – accepting the view that the Tory tradition of 'evolving' a leader had been irremediably discredited – appointed a committee to produce proposals for a direct election by MPs. By February 1965, the new system was ready, and five months later it was brought into effect, when Home resigned the Tory leadership. He was not exactly pushed out, but criticism had been building up of his failure to put the new Labour government under pressure in what was expected to be a short period before another election. One damning set of opinion poll findings, which put Home well behind Wilson on every one of a long list of attributes including "sincerity", was sufficient to persuade him that the time had come to bow out, and Heath duly defeated Maudling in the subsequent poll of MPs on 27 July. Heath insisted that Home remained in his Shadow Cabinet, and, when, against expectations, he won the 1970 general election, appointed him for a further term as Foreign Secretary. This continued until the February 1974 general election, when the Tories, in turn, were unexpectedly defeated. Home remained as an MP until the following September, and re-entered the House of Lords, as a life peer with the title Lord Home of the Hirsel, in January 1975. He lived for another 20 placid years, dying, aged 92, on 9 October 1995, just a few months after Harold Wilson.

When Lord Dunglass came down from Oxford with his mediocre degree in 1925, a reasonable expectation might have been that he would one day become chairman of the Berwickshire County Council or, more likely, Lord Lieutenant of the county. Instead, he was to rise to the highest post in the state, where, sadly, he proved to be out of his depth, without however committing the egregious errors of a Neville Chamberlain or an Anthony Eden. Cyril Connolly was perhaps right to conclude that he was born in the wrong century. Two hundred years earlier, he would never have made a Walpole or a Chatham, but might well have held his own with the likes of the Earl of Wilmington and the Duke of Portland.

Works consulted

D.E. Butler and Anthony King, 1965, *The British General Election of 1964*, London, Macmillan.
Cyril Connolly, 1938, *Enemies of Promise*, London, Routledge & Kegan Paul.
John Dickie, 1964, *The Uncommon Commoner*, London, Pall Mall.
Lord Home of the Hirsel, 1976, *The Way the Wind Blows*, London, Collins.
John Ramsden, 1996, *The Winds of Change: Macmillan to Heath, 1957–1975*, London, Longman.
Graham Stewart, 1999, *Burying Caesar: Churchill, Chamberlain and the Battle for the Tory Party*, London, Weidenfeld & Nicolson.
Alan Thompson and John Barnes, 1971, *The Day before Yesterday*, London, Panther.
D.R. Thorpe, 1996, *Alec Douglas-Home*, London, Sinclair-Stevenson.
Kenneth Young, 1970, *Sir Alec Douglas-Home*, London, Dent.

14

HAROLD WILSON

Master – or victim – of the short term

Wilson was only the third person of what used to be known as 'humble origins' to become Prime Minister, and his family background was markedly more comfortable than that of Ramsay MacDonald, and also of David Lloyd George. Yet Harold Wilson could claim to have been the first 'meritocratic' Prime Minister, coming up through a public education system which enabled him to compete with, and outshine, his contemporaries from upper- and middle-class backgrounds. Like his four predecessors – Attlee, Eden, Macmillan and Home – and three of his successors – Heath, Thatcher and Blair – he was an Oxford graduate, but his academic achievements surpassed all of theirs.

According to Philip Ziegler, his 'authorised' biographer, Wilson's family were "low church, low-living, lower middle class and proud of it". He was born in Huddersfield, on 11 March 1916, seven years after his sister, Marjorie, who was later to become a headmistress, and who proved to be a notably bossy if affectionate sibling. Their parents, both active in the Congregationalist church, and the Scouts and Guides movements and with ties to the fledgling Labour Party, had migrated from Manchester some years earlier. Harold's father, Herbert Wilson (who bore a remarkable physical resemblance to the novelist C.P. Snow, who was quite unexpectedly included, as a life peer, in Wilson's 1964 government), was a skilled industrial chemist, who had missed out on a university education because of lack of means. Herbert's elder brother, Jack, had twice been election agent to Keir Hardie, the first leader of the Labour Party. A man credited with an "extraordinary memory", for which Harold was also to be famous, Herbert had to uproot himself and his family several times in search of work, and was to suffer two prolonged periods of unemployment. His wife, the former Ethel Seddon, also had a brother – Harold – who was an active Labour Party worker. He emigrated to Australia, and was to rise to the level of Speaker of the West Australian Parliament, though by then he had abandoned his Labour affiliations.

The young Harold grew up in a frugal household, and his first interests closely mirrored those of his family and its immediate circle. He became a fanatical boy scout, an activity for which he was later to be much mocked – behind his back – by his more sophisticated political associates, and a fervent supporter of Huddersfield Town football team, the Manchester United of its day. At primary school he was more noted for his memory and tenacity than for

DOI: 10.4324/9781003031963-15

his brilliance, but he won a scholarship to the local grammar school, and later – when Herbert was forced to move his family to Cheshire in search of employment – became the star pupil, and only sixth-former, in the newly established Wirral Grammar School, from which he won an Open Exhibition to Jesus College, Oxford.

Three events, in particular, were to be remembered from his childhood. At the age of 8, his father took him on a sight-seeing trip to London, where he was photographed outside the front door of 10 Downing Street. This was to be reproduced many times 40 years later when he became Prime Minister, leading to the perhaps mistaken assumption that this had been a serious childhood ambition. A more significant influence on him was probably a visit to Australia, which he made with his mother, at the age of 10, to visit her Seddon relatives. This seems greatly to have expanded his horizons. Third, at the age of 14, was his apparently miraculous cure from typhoid, which killed six of his fellow scouts on a camping trip, and from which he narrowly survived after three months in hospital, during which his weight went down to 4½ stone. His grandfather commented, "The lad is being saved for something", and his entire family was convinced that Harold was a special child and would go on to do great things.

He did not disappoint them. At Oxford, where he lived an exceptionally frugal life – not wishing to make more than the minimal demand on his family's straitened resources – he concentrated almost exclusively on his work, eschewing the social charms of the University which had largely occupied the time of his predecessor as Premier, Alec Douglas-Home. Wilson studied Politics, Philosophy and Economics, and achieved one of the highest First Class Honours ever awarded, going on to win two of the grandest essay prizes in the University – the Webb Medley prize for economics and the Gladstone history prize, an extraordinary achievement for a non-historian. He was immediately snapped up by the Master of University College, Sir William Beveridge, to assist him in his research on unemployment and the trade cycle, and was elected to a junior research fellowship at the College. During his time as a student, he had taken only a peripheral interest in politics, never speaking at the Union, and soon migrating from the Labour Club, dominated by public school Marxists, to the Liberals, becoming the club treasurer, though not showing any deep or lasting commitment to Liberalism. It was not until 1939 that, under the influence of G.D.H. Cole, an Economics Fellow at University College and the leading Oxford Socialist of his generation, he joined the Labour Party in Oxford, without playing a very active role.

At the age of 18, when still at school, Wilson had met his future wife, Gladys Mary Baldwin, the daughter of a Congregationalist minister, at a tennis club in the Wirral. Within three weeks, he announced to her, (a) that he was going to marry her, and (b) that he would become Prime Minister, the second of which assertions she did not take seriously. The marriage only took place six years later, on 1 January 1940. By this time, Harold, who had been supporting his parents during a lengthy period of unemployment for Herbert, now forced to resettle in Cornwall to find another job, felt at last in a position to establish his own household. Mary, who had been a shorthand-typist, was entranced by Oxford, and felt that there was no better fate than to become the wife of a don. She little knew what to expect from her future life, despite Harold's forecast to her in 1934.

In fact, their life together in Oxford was extremely brief. Wilson had registered for military service, but, as an economist, was instead ordered to work as a temporary civil servant. By April, he was transferred to London, where he undertook a series of demanding jobs related to the economic planning of the war effort, working under the supervision of such eminent economists as John Jewkes, Lionel Robbins and, again, William Beveridge. Wilson found Beveridge, a notably cold and self-centred man, an uncongenial boss, but professionally they were an extraordinarily good match. Inveterate workaholics, they both scorned theory and worshipped facts, the careful collection of which they saw as the starting-off point for the framing of policy. In June 1941, Beveridge, who was seen by ministers and senior officials alike as a disruptive influence, was eased out of his job as Chairman of the Manpower Committee of the War Cabinet secretariat, and asked to chair an inter-departmental inquiry into the co-ordination of social insurance. It was meant to be a backwater, but the Beveridge Report, when it appeared in 1942, was a political sensation, and became the blueprint for much of Labour's post-war social legislation. Beveridge had asked Wilson to become the secretary of this committee, but he declined because he was already fully stretched by his other responsibilities. Thus did he narrowly avoid becoming one of the founding fathers of the welfare state.

Instead, he accepted a post in the Board of Trade concerned with the mining industry, whose poor levels of production were threatening the war effort. Wilson revolutionised the collection of statistics in what was universally seen as a chaotic industry, and created a much firmer base for policy planning. Among the many officials he impressed was Hugh Gaitskell, another temporary civil servant, who was a personal assistant to Hugh Dalton, the President of the Board of Trade. Asked to assess the personnel of the Mines Department, he wrote a glowing encomium on Wilson, whom he described as "extraordinarily able. He is only twenty-six, or thereabouts, and is one of the most brilliant younger people about." Seeing how the government machine worked from the inside re-ignited Wilson's dormant political ambitions, and encouraged by Dalton, he decided to seek a parliamentary constituency. At his second attempt, in September 1944, he won the nomination at Ormskirk, a sprawling constituency on the outskirts of Liverpool, and not regarded as a good prospect for Labour. Yet, aided by a split right-wing vote, and the overwhelming national swing to Labour, he was duly elected in July 1945, at the age of 29.

On polling day, he published a book, *New Deal for Coal*, which he had written in five weeks, drawing on his experience at the Mines Department. This provided a practical blueprint for the nationalisation of the industry to which the Labour Party had long been committed, but had devoted very little thought to its implementation. Wilson's book proved a godsend to the incoming Minister of Fuel and Power, Emanuel Shinwell, and, together with the formidable reputation which Wilson had gained as a civil servant, may have been the reason why – almost alone of the newly elected Labour MPs – he was given an immediate post in the government, of which he was the youngest member. He became Parliamentary Secretary to the Minister of Works, George Tomlinson.

He served for 18 months, without making any great splash. He was regarded as forceful and effective, but lacking any sort of profile, either with the general public or within the Labour Party, while, according to his biographer, Ben Pimlott, his "ministerial speeches notoriously emptied the House", being "technical, repetitive, excessively detailed, over-prepared and lacking in humour". Nevertheless, he succeeding in attracting the favourable notice of senior members of the government, notably Sir Stafford Cripps, the President of the Board of Trade, and in March 1947 he became one of his junior ministers, as Secretary for Overseas Trade. He remained in this post for only six months, during which time he distinguished himself as a tough negotiator with Soviet ministers in two rounds of trade talks in Moscow, in which he was pitted against the formidable Armenian, Anastas Mikoyan. In late September, Cripps took overall charge of economic policy, becoming Minister for Economic Affairs, a post he soon combined with that of Chancellor of the Exchequer, when Hugh Dalton resigned in November, following a trivial budget leak. Cripps relinquished the Presidency of the Board of Trade, and Wilson was promoted to take his place on 29 September. He was 31 years old, the youngest Cabinet minister since 1806, and a good ten years younger than any of his new colleagues.

Still, like other economic ministers, under the overlordship of Cripps, he nevertheless enjoyed a fair degree of autonomy, and basked in the aura of success which the rapidly improving trade figures cast upon him. He made a big impact as the man who made a 'bonfire' of wartime controls, most of which were shed under his stewardship, starting with a large batch which were consigned to the flames on Guy Fawkes Day 1948. The choice of this date was one of many indications that the previously technocratic minister was rapidly learning the techniques of public presentation. Only one event marred Wilson's otherwise triumphal tenure of the Board of Trade, and this was totally unknown to the public. Its was his role in the 1949 devaluation of the pound.

This was forced on the government by heavy pressure on sterling, and a subsequent drain on the reserves, which built up during the first half of the year. Many economists began to believe that devaluation was a necessary corrective, and that the sooner it was applied the better. This view was strongly resisted by Treasury officials and, in particular, by the Chancellor, who felt that it was a moral imperative to maintain the value of the pound, especially because of the faith put in it by Commonwealth and other governments, who kept their foreign reserves in sterling. Meanwhile, Cripps's health was causing increasing concern, and, in July, he left to stay at a clinic in Zurich, leaving three relatively young ministers, all of them professional economists and former wartime temporary civil servants, in charge of economic policy, under the notional control of the Prime Minister, a self-confessed economic ignoramus. These were Hugh Gaitskell, Minister of Fuel and Power (though still outside the Cabinet), Douglas Jay, Economic Secretary to the Treasury, and Wilson. In the course of the next few weeks, both Jay and Gaitskell became convinced of the necessity to devalue and put the case strongly at a series of meetings with Attlee, Herbert Morrison and senior officials. Wilson was much more hesitant, appeared to change his stance erratically, and was suspected of playing politics with the issue in the hope of strengthening his position as Cripps's likeliest successor in the event of the latter's early resignation.

If this was his objective, it failed disastrously. On the contrary, he created a bad impression, both on Attlee and other senior ministers, and within the Treasury, whereas Gaitskell, who had previously not been viewed as a possible Chancellor, won high marks for his clarity and decisiveness. The devaluation was effected in September 1949, and was seen as a grave blow to the government's standing, though it went on to win the general election, the following February. Its majority, however, shrank to five seats, and it was regarded as inevitable that a further election would be held within a very few months. In fact, the government held out for another 20 months, during which it suffered a series of hammer blows. The first of these was the resignation of Cripps due to ill health in October 1950. Gaitskell, who already after the election had been made Minister of State at the Treasury, effortlessly moved up to take his place. Wilson was visibly put out, and so was another – more senior – member of the Cabinet, Aneurin Bevan, who felt that his great success in launching the National Health Service should have earned him promotion to one of the senior posts in the government. Bevan's dissatisfaction grew, five months later, when that other bulwark of the Attlee government, the dying Ernest Bevin, was replaced as Foreign Secretary by Herbert Morrison, while he himself was fobbed off with a sideways move to the Ministry of Labour.

Meanwhile, the Korean War was still raging, and under pressure from the United States the government decided, in early 1951, sharply to increase its rearmament programme. This decision brought Bevan and Wilson together, both arguing that the proposed level of expenditure was unrealistic and would gravely weaken the economy. They failed to convince their Cabinet colleagues, but in mid-March, Hugh Gaitskell, as Chancellor of the Exchequer, proposed a budget which, alongside other economies, sought to rein in expenditure on the National Health Service, including making charges for false teeth and spectacles which had previously been supplied free of charge. The amount of money to be saved was trivial in relation to the budget as a whole, but Gaitskell held his ground in the face of a threat by a furious Bevan to resign if the proposal went through.

In the event, two other ministers resigned along with Bevan – John Freeman, a promising junior minister, and – to general astonishment – Harold Wilson. Bevan's resignation was widely regretted, but understood. Many Labour MPs regarded it as quixotic, but few questioned his motives. It was seen as a principled action by a deeply emotional man who did not always calculate his moves wisely. The reaction to Wilson was quite different. His was seen as an act of pure opportunism, particularly on the right wing of the party. They saw it as an attempt to ingratiate himself with the left, with whom he had not previously been identified, and to attach his star to that of Nye Bevan, who was widely seen as a future Labour leader and Attlee's successor.

Even on the left, Wilson's motives were questioned, but he was quickly accepted as Bevan's number two in the developing rebellion which secured overwhelming support among Labour's rank-and-file, though alienating opinion in the trade unions and among a majority of Labour MPs. Bevan and Wilson were excoriated for splitting the party, and paving the way for defeat in the October 1951 general election. On the other hand, it soon became apparent that they had been right, and their colleagues wrong, in their judgement about the feasibility of the rearmament programme, which was quickly dropped by the incoming Conservative government.

In personal terms, Bevan's resignation undoubtedly damaged his career, and, together with a number of subsequent ill-judged actions, helped to destroy his previous excellent chances of succeeding to the party leadership. In Wilson's case, however, it is arguable that it proved an essential step on his way to the top. Nevertheless, it represented a considerable gamble at the time, and his subsequent path was far from smooth. One early effect of his resignation was to round him out as a politician. He received an avalanche of invitations to speak at meetings organised by constituency Labour parties. This took him to venues all around the country, and helped to familiarise him with a Labour movement previously almost unknown to him. He became a great deal more assured as a platform speaker. Always much respected for his knowledge and authority on economic issues, he broadened his canvas and began to speak in a more punchy and partisan way across the whole political spectrum. He inserted a previously unsuspected strain of wit into his speeches, and became increasingly adept at handling hecklers.

At the 1952 Labour Party conference at Morecambe, where the Bevanites made an almost complete sweep in the elections to the constituency party section of Labour's National Executive Committee, he and Richard Crossman succeeded in displacing two great stalwarts, Herbert Morrison and Hugh Dalton, who had sat on the committee since the 1920s. This gave him a valuable foothold in Labour's national organisation. He had less success in running for the Shadow Cabinet, elected by Labour MPs, gaining only 13th place in a ballot for 12 members in November 1953.

During this time, though publicly seen as Bevan's chief lieutenant ("Nye's little dog", as Dalton contemptuously put it), Wilson grew increasingly impatient with him, deploring his unpredictability and his unwillingness to consult with his allies. Temperamentally, they were very dissimilar, and Wilson's views on many current issues were, in fact, far closer to Gaitskell's than to Bevan's. He seems to have privately concluded that Bevan had blown his chances of ever becoming leader, and that Gaitskell was more likely to be Attlee's successor. He was unwilling, however, to break with Bevan, and was put in a quandary when the Welshman impetuously resigned from the Shadow Cabinet in April 1954, after a disagreement with Attlee over policy in the Far East. As runner-up in the ballot, Wilson was entitled to take the place vacated by Bevan, an action which most of the Bevanites regarded as rank disloyalty. Wilson hesitated long and hard, but eventually agreed to join the Shadow Cabinet, an action which perhaps foreshadowed his decision to vote for Gaitskell rather than Bevan or Morrison, when Attlee finally resigned the leadership in December 1955.

Wilson was still only 39, ten years younger than Gaitskell, and no doubt reckoned that he stood an excellent chance of serving as Chancellor in a future Gaitskell government, and eventually succeeding him in the leadership. He accordingly assured Gaitskell of his total loyalty, and was as good as his word in the four years up to the 1959 general election, by which time he was already Shadow Chancellor. Had Labour won the election, Wilson would almost certainly have become Chancellor and, with the death soon after of Nye Bevan, the most powerful figure in the government after Gaitskell, with every prospect of being his eventual successor. Instead – against his instincts – he found himself pitched into a struggle against his party leader which threatened to destroy all the goodwill built up during their previous four years of close co-operation.

Labour had entered the election campaign with high hopes of victory, and was shocked by the ease with which the Tories, only three years after the Suez fiasco, swept back to power with a greatly enhanced majority. The major reason for their success was undoubtedly the national sense of material well-being after the ending of wartime and post-war shortages. Gaitskell and his closest associates, however, concluded, with some justification, that a subsidiary cause was that Labour was widely seen as a doctrinaire nationalising party, even though this perception was hardly justified by the party's current policies. They fixed their attention on the Labour Party's constitution, dating from 1918, in particular on its Clause IV, which called for the public ownership of "the means of production, distribution and exchange", and decided that it must be repealed or amended to emphasise that the party was not bound by ancient shibboleths. It was an ill-considered move, which ran up against deeply held sentiments in many sections of the party, particularly in the trade union movement, and was subsequently abandoned in a humiliating about-turn. Wilson, who had not been consulted, thought it was ludicrously inappropriate, believing that not one voter in a thousand knew about Clause IV and that to make a fuss about it would only draw attention to its provisions.

His other clash with Gaitskell was much more serious. At the party conference at Scarborough, in October 1960, a resolution in favour of unilateral nuclear disarmament was carried, despite a passionate speech by Gaitskell, in which he had pledged himself "to fight, fight and fight again to save the party we love". Gaitskell refused to accept his defeat, and resolved to continue the struggle in the hope of reversing it the following year. Wilson, whose own views on defence policy were very similar to Gaitskell's, thought that the differences

164 Harold Wilson

should be papered over and a compromise document should be prepared by the National Executive Committee. He was taken aback when his former comrades from the Bevanite group decided to challenge Gaitskell's leadership at the beginning of the new parliamentary session the following month, and strongly pressed Wilson to be their candidate. He resisted their importunity, and only consented to stand when another prominent former Bevanite, Anthony Greenwood, put his hat into the ring. Wilson did not want a contest, but if there had to be one he was determined that no one else should be the left-wing candidate. In the ballot of Labour MPs, he secured the respectable, but somewhat disappointing, total of 81 votes, against 166 for Gaitskell.

Wilson's action revived all the old charges of opportunism which had been levelled at the time of his ministerial resignation, and he grievously offended the Gaitskellite wing of the party, now in the ascendant. He was regarded as thoroughly untrustworthy and feelings akin to hatred were freely expressed. Wilson feared that he would be dropped from his post as Shadow Chancellor, and exerted himself to bolster his position. For the time being, he managed to hold on, but a year later Gaitskell triumphantly succeeded in reversing the Scarborough conference decision, and was riding high. Wilson was then switched to Shadow Foreign Minister, hardly a demotion, though not a change that he welcomed. His position in the party and his rising reputation as one of the foremost debaters in the House of Commons made him an indispensable member of Gaitskell's team, but though he tried hard to ingratiate himself with the leader, the distrust remained. His attempt to become deputy leader of the party, in November 1962, by challenging the erratic George Brown, who had succeeded to the position on the death of Bevan in 1960, was unsuccessful. He was almost universally regarded as the more able man, but lost by 103 votes to 133, due to the continuing hostility of the Gaitskellites. His long-term prospects for the leadership did not look good at that point. While guaranteed senior office in the event of a Labour victory in the forthcoming election, it seemed likely that he would subsequently be overtaken by a trio of slightly younger Gaitskellites of outstanding ability, Roy Jenkins, Tony Crosland and Denis Healey.

Everything changed with the sudden death of Gaitskell in January 1963. As deputy leader, George Brown was the favourite to succeed him, but, alarmed by his unpredictability and his alcoholism, several leading Gaitskellites refused to back him. "It's a choice between a crook [Wilson] and a drunk", Crosland remarked, and together with Douglas Jay and others promoted the candidature of James Callaghan, who had succeeded Wilson as Shadow Chancellor. Brown proceeded to alienate many of his potential supporters by his bullying tactics, while Wilson projected a calm and statesmanlike air. He led on the first ballot by 115 votes to 88 for Brown and 41 for Callaghan, and easily beat Brown by 144–103 in the run-off.

Wilson continued on his statesmanlike course as leader of the opposition, confirming all his Shadow Cabinet colleagues in their posts, even though only one of them had voted for him in the leadership ballots. The former Bevanite group had, of course, been his own core supporters, and he justified his favoured treatment of the Gaitskellites to them by saying that he was forced to run "a Bolshevik revolution with a Tsarist Shadow Cabinet". In his final year, Gaitskell had not only triumphed over his enemies in the Labour Party, but had also established a commanding lead in the opinion polls, now being the preferred choice of a majority to the rapidly fading Harold Macmillan. All this would now be lost, Labour feared, but to its delighted surprise, Wilson's succession was followed by a further increase in the Labour lead. His somewhat dubious reputation in certain Labour political circles had never communicated to a wider public, and he started off with a virtual clean slate with the mass media exposure which began with his election as leader. Young (46 – 22 years younger than Macmillan), energetic, forceful yet moderate in his views, with an easy manner and a classless appeal, he seemed to many to be the British answer to John F. Kennedy, then at the height of his renown, three months after his successful handling of the Cuban missile crisis. He built assiduously on the good initial impression which he had created, making virtually no serious mistakes in the unexpectedly long period – 21 months – before the 1964 election. He was helped, of course, by the self-inflicted wounds of his Tory opponents, from Macmillan's mal-adroit handling of the Profumo affair to the questionable circumstances in which Douglas-Home acceded to the premiership. During this period, he established a greater domination, as leader of the opposition over the Prime Minister, than any of his predecessors or successors, though Tony Blair perhaps came close in 1995–97. Yet, despite Wilson's Herculean efforts, he was unable completely to dispel long-standing fears of what a Labour government might do, and in the final weeks before the election the Labour lead in the opinion polls shrank to nil. The election, after all, became a closely fought affair, and on 15 October 1964 Labour was elected with a majority of only four seats.

Nevertheless, the election of Labour after 13 years in opposition, and with Wilson, at 48, easily the youngest Prime Minister of the century so far, raised high expectations. Most of these were to be dashed by a decision taken within the next 24 hours, without proper consideration or consultation with their colleagues, by three exhausted men – Wilson, James Callaghan, who was appointed Chancellor of the Exchequer, and George Brown, First Secretary and Minister for Economic Affairs. The Tories had left the economy in a parlous state, Reginald Maudling, the Chancellor of the Exchequer, having introduced a give-away budget the previous March, in anticipation of an early election, and then failing to take any remedial action during the summer as the balance of payments position sharply deteriorated. Treasury and Bank of England officials advised the trio that immediate action was imperative, with three options available. These were devaluation of sterling, import quotas or temporary tariff surcharges.

The pound was clearly over-valued, and opprobrium for a new devaluation could easily have been shifted onto the outgoing government, but Wilson – with painful memories of his involvement in the 1947 devaluation – was determined not to go down the same route again. He had little difficulty in persuading his two less experienced colleagues to choose the third option – temporary import surcharges. It is easy, with the advantage of hindsight, to condemn the decision, as many have done. In the circumstances, however, it was an understandable choice to make, and Wilson should not be unduly blamed for his misjudgement. What is less easy to condone is his absolute refusal to reconsider the issue, which became the "great unmentionable" until the eve of the final humiliating debacle of November 1967. According to Sir Alec Cairncross, the government's economic adviser, "There was no meeting between 1964 and 1967 between ministers and officials on whether, when and how devaluation should be done" (Pimlott, 1992, p. 474).

Despite this initial mistake, Wilson's government got off to a tremendous start, impressing the country with its dynamism and wealth of ideas. Wilson himself completely dominated the political landscape, enjoying an unprecedentedly good press for a Labour leader, and maintaining his mastery in the Commons, where he continued to worst Douglas-Home in their twice-weekly confrontations at Question Time. The Tories changed leader, in August 1965, choosing Edward Heath on the assumption that he would be able to hold his own with Wilson, but it made very little difference.

166 Harold Wilson

It was a government of near beginners. Apart from Wilson himself, only the veteran James Griffiths (Welsh Secretary) and Patrick Gordon Walker (Foreign Secretary) had ever served in a Cabinet before. Gordon Walker was an early casualty. He had lost his seat in the general election, but had still been appointed by Wilson, only to lose again in a by-election vacancy created for him, in January 1965, and promptly resigned, being replaced by the able, but unexciting, Michael Stewart. Wilson's key colleagues – George Brown and James Callaghan – had served as junior ministers in the Attlee government. Wilson hoped to provoke 'creative tension' between them by installing both in economic departments – Callaghan in the Treasury and Brown in the newly created Department of Economic Affairs, with a mandate to produce a National Plan, which was intended to transform the British economy. Neither man was perfectly fitted for his job. Brown was highly intelligent and full of energy and drive, but was erratic, undisciplined and only intermittently sober. Callaghan was a much more controlled individual, with sharp political antennae, and seemed by contrast 'a safe pair of hands'. Yet he had only a limited grasp of economics, did not get firmly in control of his department and was too ready to defer to the judgement of his Prime Minister who was regarded, at least initially, as an economic as well as a political wizard.

Wilson early recognised the potential of his three slightly younger Gaitskellite rivals, giving each of them important posts. Denis Healey went straight into the Cabinet as Defence Secretary. Tony Crosland, much the most economically literate minister, became number two to George Brown, and began by having a furious row with him over his agreement with Wilson not to devalue. He soon moved on, becoming Education Secretary, in succession to Stewart, in January 1965. Roy Jenkins started off as Aviation Minister (outside the Cabinet), turned down the Education post, but became Home Secretary 11 months later.

The 1964 Labour government had its ups and downs, but its overall impact was extraordinarily positive, and Wilson got great credit for his skilful handling of his knife-edge majority. The highlight was undoubtedly the launch, in September 1965, of George Brown's National Plan, which – based largely on copying the successful French experience of indicative planning – confidently predicted that the notoriously sluggish British growth rate could be raised to the dizzy level of 3.5 per cent over nine years, enabling the social and economic life of the nation to be transformed. Wilson then cruised to an easy victory in the general election of March 1966, which increased his majority to 98 seats.

Wilson seemed at the height of his power, but it was not long before the chickens released by his refusal to devalue began to come home to roost. An ill-considered budget introduced by Callaghan in April, followed by disappointing balance of payments figures and a strike by the National Union of Seamen, which seriously disrupted the export trade, led to a run on the pound in July. Wilson was absent on a visit to Moscow, and was disconcerted to find on his return that both Brown and Callaghan had been converted by Crosland, Jenkins and other ministers to the necessity for devaluation. Wilson, who suspected a plot against his own leadership, quickly won over Callaghan, who agreed to the alternative of a major deflation, involving severe cuts in expenditure, the statutory restriction of prices and wages and the virtual abandonment of the National Plan targets. A furious Brown was determined to resign, but was bought off by the offer of the Foreign Office, the post he had always coveted. The hapless Michael Stewart was stripped of his responsibilities, and was compensated by Brown's title of First Secretary of State and the now sharply downgraded Department of Economic Affairs.

These events marked a watershed in Wilson's premiership. The almost universal esteem in which he had previously been held began to fade. The press, which hitherto had shown excessive admiration, now swung to the opposite extreme, and he became the butt of increasingly intemperate and often viciously personal attacks. Within the Labour Party, and particularly among Labour MPs, his critics began to multiply, both on the right and on the left. This became far worse a year or so later, when, in November 1967, a renewed run on sterling forced the devaluation against which he had for so long set his face. Wilson's humiliation was made even worse by his complacent – and widely mocked – television broadcast, in which he assured viewers that "the pound in your pocket" would not lose 14 per cent of its value. Callaghan insisted on resigning as Chancellor, proposing Crosland, by then President of the Board of Trade, as his successor. Wilson demurred, and instead chose Jenkins, partly because he was anxious to keep Callaghan in the government, and the easiest way to achieve this was by a straight swap of jobs with the Home Secretary. There were other reasons, too, one perhaps being that whereas Crosland was the better qualified economically, he found Jenkins a more congenial colleague. He was, however, taking a risk, as Jenkins, who had already attracted widespread support among MPs for the progressive reforms he had backed as Home Secretary and for his commanding speeches in the Commons, would be a formidable rival if his leadership came under challenge.

Initially, however, it appeared as though Jenkins had been handed a poisoned chalice. For devaluation, if inevitable, was no easy option. It had to be bolstered by an even more severe deflation than in the previous year, and four major government policies were reversed. The British military presence East of Suez was abandoned, a large order for F-111 fighter planes was cancelled, prescription charges were re-introduced into the National Health Service and the raising of the school-leaving age to 16 was postponed. Despite these radical measures, there was an exceptionally long and nerve-shattering wait until the gaping deficit in the balance of payments began to improve. In the meantime, the government became increasingly unpopular and lost a long series of by-elections, many of them in normally ultra-safe seats. Wilson himself became deeply unpopular, but respect for Jenkins continued to grow as he played a cool and steady hand and retained his parliamentary dominance over the opposition.

Wilson had come to depend, to a perhaps excessive extent, on his 'kitchen' Cabinet for moral support and political advice. Chief among them was his political secretary, Marcia Williams (later Baroness Falkender), who had served him throughout the long years of opposition and continued to do so up to and beyond his final retirement in 1976. The two were extraordinarily close, and there was much speculation about the nature of their relationship. This was probably not – and certainly not primarily – a sexual one. On the whole, she gave him good advice, but she was something of a loose cannon and – according to the published accounts of other members of the 'kitchen' Cabinet – was given to hysterical outbursts, particularly in later years. Wilson was accused of paranoia, in suspecting imaginary plots against his leadership, and his tight group of advisers was believed to be fanning his fears. Not all the plots were imaginary: the supporters of both Jenkins and Callaghan periodically schemed to supplant him, but no overt move was ever made. This was because the two men were rivals, and neither was prepared to subordinate his own claims to the other. "Willing to wound, but afraid to strike" best summed up the attitude of a fair number of Labour MPs during this period, and later again, in opposition, in 1970–74.

Much of Wilson's attention during his first premiership was focused on international affairs, three issues in particular predominating: Rhodesia, the European Community and Vietnam. There can be little argument that Wilson seriously mishandled the illegal declaration of independence by the white settler regime of Southern Rhodesia in October 1965, and was subsequently repeatedly outmanoeuvred by the settlers' leader, Ian Smith. It may not have been a crucial error to rule out in advance any resort to military force – the arguments for or against were finely balanced – but it was certainly a mistake to publicise this decision. The evidence is that the Rhodesian military was reluctant to fight British military forces and might very well have restrained Smith and his cabinet from declaring UDI if they had thought it was a possibility. Wilson subsequently grossly over-estimated the prospect of economic sanctions bringing Smith to heel, saying that it would "take weeks rather than months". In fact, it took 14 years – and a prolonged guerrilla war – before the settler regime finally backed down, and negotiated an agreement with Margaret Thatcher's government which led to majority rule and independence for Zimbabwe.

Wilson had backed Gaitskell in 1962, when he had opposed the first British application to join the European Economic Community, but five years later, in tandem with his Foreign Secretary, George Brown, he launched a further application, which the two men energetically pressed forward in visits to the capitals of the six member states. They received some encouragement from French Premier Georges Pompidou, and they were received in Paris with much courtesy by President Charles de Gaulle. A formal application was tabled in May 1967, after a positive vote of 488–62 in the House of Commons, but in the following November – before the negotiations began – de Gaulle pronounced his second veto. Wilson had announced that he "would not take no for an answer", and soon after de Gaulle resigned as President, in 1969, he resolved to have another try, though he insisted that "the terms must be right". Negotiations, the government decided, would begin soon after the forthcoming general election.

On the Vietnam War, Wilson was seriously cross-pressured. A vigorous protest movement, largely made up of Labour Party supporters, called for him to dissociate himself from the American intervention. At the same time, President Lyndon Johnson was constantly pressing him to join in the war on the US and South Vietnamese side, as Australia had done. Wilson was acutely aware of the importance of US financial help to back up sterling, and was willing to offer moral, but not material support to the US effort. He made several attempts to mediate in the dispute, once through an aborted Commonwealth mission, and another time in conjunction with the Soviet Union, but the Vietnamese Communists were not prepared to accept him as an honest broker, and nothing came of his efforts to achieve a ceasefire. The most that can be said is that he did well to avoid sending even a token military force to Vietnam, but the sum total of his endeavours had no visible effect on the outcome.

One of Wilson's boldest ventures was to attempt to reform industrial relations in Britain through legislation which would have clipped the wings of the increasingly unpopular trade union movement and forced it to behave in a more socially responsible manner. The occasion was the report, in 1969, of the Royal Commission on Trade Unions, chaired by Lord Justice Donovan. This produced a number of commonsensical but unexciting proposals for reform, but the Employment Minister, Barbara Castle, thought that something more emphatic was called for. With Wilson's strong support, she produced a White Paper, *In Place of Strife*, which proposed that ministers should be given powers to order pre-strike ballots and impose a 28-day 'conciliation pause', while a new Industrial Board would have powers to impose fines on unions and individuals who breached the new rules. Compared to the legislation later imposed by the Heath and Thatcher governments, this was pretty mild stuff, but it caused uproar among the trade unions. They exerted immense pressure on Labour MPs to oppose the Bill which Castle subsequently introduced. Resistance within the Cabinet was led by the

Home Secretary, James Callaghan, who infuriated Wilson by using his position on Labour's National Executive Committee openly to oppose the Bill.

This got bogged down during several months' struggle in the Commons, during which the government abandoned an important measure to reform the House of Lords in order to free more parliamentary time. Finally, the Chief Whip, Robert Mellish, informed the Cabinet that there was no prospect of success, and one by one the members of the Cabinet abandoned a humiliated Castle and Wilson. They had rushed into the venture without proper consultation and completely misjudged the mood of their own party. What was meant to be evidence of the government's ability to control the unions turned into a demonstration of its impotence. It would have been far better to have gone ahead with Lord Donovan's modest reforms. At this stage – mid-1969 – the government was still doing abysmally in opinion polls and by-elections, and hopes of a recovery before the next general election had been all but abandoned.

Yet during the summer of 1969 the balance of payments position dramatically improved, and by the following spring it was showing a substantial surplus, while Labour was rapidly catching up in the opinion polls. Jenkins was under some pressure to produce a pre-election give-away budget, but resisted the temptation and followed his judgement that only a mildly expansionist one was justified. Soon after, however, Labour went into the lead in the polls, and good local election results in May 1970 stampeded Wilson into calling an early general election for 18 June, rather than waiting until October, by which time the Labour advantage might well have consolidated.

Throughout the election campaign, Labour led in the polls and there was an almost universal expectation that Wilson would pull off his third consecutive victory. Unwisely, however, Labour based its claim for re-election almost exclusively on its success in restoring the balance of payments. Disaster struck three days before polling day, with the publication of the monthly trade figures for May, showing a large deficit. This was almost certainly the main reason for Edward Heath's remarkable victory, when he succeeded in turning a Labour majority of nearly 100 into a Tory one of 30. The May trade figures later turned out to be aberrant, due to the chance inclusion of a hefty bill for the order of fighter planes from the US. Had the election been a week earlier or a month later, Labour would most probably have won, but its recovery had been too recent and too shallow to withstand the shock.

Both Wilson and his party were devastated by the unexpected defeat, and embarked on nearly four unhappy years in opposition, wracked with recriminations and disputes. There was no doubting the sense of disappointment at the record of Wilson's first government, after the exceptionally high hopes entertained in 1964. The biggest let-down – inevitably linked to the refusal to devalue during the first three years in power, though it is far from certain that it would otherwise have been achieved – was the failure to transform the economy and jack up the lagging growth rate through the aborted National Plan. This central failure overshadowed the otherwise notable achievements of the government, particularly in the field of education. The years 1964–70 saw the largest ever expansion in higher education, including the establishment of the Open University, and an end to the 11-plus examination through the widespread introduction of comprehensive schools. Equally important was the rash of 'Home Office' reforms, including the abolition of capital punishment, homosexual law reform, the ending of theatre censorship, divorce reform and the decriminalisation of abortion. Each of these long-overdue measures was effected by Private Members' Bills, but none of them would have been passed without government encouragement and, crucially, the provision of parliamentary time. The minister most directly involved was Roy Jenkins, but Wilson could also justifiably claim much of the credit for making Britain a more civilised country than he had found it in 1964.

Yet Wilson had lost much of his bounce and self-confidence, and signally failed as leader of the opposition to repeat the dominance he had shown in his earlier period in this role. He also found it impossible to stand out against the left-wing tide of anti-Europeanism which swept through the party and the trade unions as the Heath government successfully negotiated membership of the EEC on terms which most of Wilson's former ministerial colleagues believed he would have found acceptable as Prime Minister. Throughout the summer of 1971, he gave more and more ground to the anti-EEC elements in the party, while assuring the pro-EEC minority that they would have the right to a free vote when the terms were put to the Commons, a promise which in the end he was unable to keep. Eventually, 69 Labour MPs (including the present author) felt compelled to vote, in defiance of a three-line whip, in order to ensure that British membership would go ahead. The episode did immense damage to Wilson's reputation, as he was widely accused of cowardice and inconsistency.

He was deeply hurt by the criticism, maintaining that his overriding duty was to prevent the Labour Party from splitting in two over the issue, and that in consequence it was necessary for him to subordinate his own feelings. On one occasion, his patience snapped, and he said to a meeting of his Shadow Cabinet: "I've been wading in shit for three months to allow others to indulge their conscience". Although he had been unwilling or unable to prevent the majority coming out against Heath's membership terms, he subsequently exerted himself to prevent an irrevocable Labour decision to withdraw from the EEC. Clutching at a proposal originally advanced by Tony Benn for a referendum to decide the issue, he managed to secure agreement that Labour would first attempt to renegotiate the terms before putting the final decision before the British people.

Few people (not including Wilson himself) seriously believed that Labour would have much chance of winning the next general election, but this was reckoning without Edward Heath. Locked in a struggle with the National Union of Mineworkers, who were in an all-out strike (see next chapter), he rashly called a general election in February 1974 on the issue of "Who governs Britain?" and then badly mishandled his campaign. The result was a 'hung Parliament' – the first since 1929 – with Labour four seats ahead of the Tories, even though it polled fewer votes. The result gave Wilson an unexpected, and many believed undeserved, chance to redeem his reputation. This he was able to achieve, at least partially. He re-entered Downing Street as a chastened man, with none of the over-confidence he had shown in 1964. Once again, he inherited a precarious economic situation, largely due to the oil shocks following the Yom Kippur War of 1973, which had released ferocious inflationary pressures. Wilson's team this time round was a much more collegiate affair, with the Prime Minister showing little disposition to interfere in his colleagues' ministerial fiefs. The key figures were Denis Healey, as Chancellor of the Exchequer, Michael Foot – the left-wing veteran and Nye Bevan's political heir, brought in to pacify the unions as Employment Secretary – and, above all, James Callaghan, as Foreign Secretary, but *de facto* Deputy Premier. Roy Jenkins, who had hoped for the Treasury or the Foreign Office, reluctantly accepted a further stint as Home Secretary, but was no longer a central figure in the government. As soon as it was formed, Wilson hastened to settle the miners' strike on give-away terms, and the following October invited the electorate to form a judgement on his new government, contrasting the calm which it had brought about with the "chaos" left by the Heath administration, with Britain working only a three-day week, because of the shortage of coal supplies. If he had hoped to repeat his triumph of 1966, he was to be disappointed, but he did manage to secure a parliamentary majority for his previously minority government, though its overall lead was only three seats.

The key event of Wilson's second premiership was the referendum in June 1975 on British membership of the EEC. Shortly after his return to office, he instructed Callaghan to begin a renegotiation of the terms obtained three years earlier by Heath. Britain's European partners, especially German Chancellor Helmut Schmidt, were sympathetic, and he managed to secure a number of concessions. Several of these were of a cosmetic nature, but in the end he managed to cobble together a deal which could be plausibly presented as an improvement on what Heath had achieved. Wilson's difficulty was that a large number of people in the Labour Party, and within his own Cabinet, remained hostile. He solved this problem by a brilliant stroke, calling upon a precedent from 1932, when the members of Ramsay MacDonald's 'National' government agreed to suspend collective Cabinet responsibility on the issue of Tariff Reform. Wilson proposed that Cabinet members should be free to support either side in the referendum campaign, even though the government would be recommending a 'yes' vote. The Cabinet split 16–7 in favour, though a special Labour Party conference came down emphatically on the 'no' side. Six months before the referendum, the antis had a strong lead in opinion polls; in the event the pros won by two-to-one. The reason was almost certainly the greater public confidence in the judgement of the leaders of the yes campaign. Wilson, Callaghan, Heath, Jenkins and the new Tory leader, Margaret Thatcher, were all vastly more popular than the leading antis – Enoch Powell, Tony Benn, Michael Foot, Barbara Castle and Ian Paisley. The real victor, however, was Wilson, who had been so much despised for his earlier tergiversations over the EEC. As the journalist Peter Jenkins put it, he had obtained his three objectives: "to keep his party in power and in one piece and Britain in Europe". Now there was nothing left for Wilson to do but retire with honour.

The following March he would be 60 years old, and Wilson had long planned to withdraw at about this time. He was an exhausted man, his wife, Mary, desperately wanted him to quit, and he was perhaps already detecting early signs of the waning of his mental powers which was to culminate some years later in Alzheimer's disease. So, secure in the belief that his elected successor would be the four years older Callaghan, with whom, despite their earlier rivalry, he had worked in close harmony throughout his second premiership, he announced his resignation on 16 March 1976. It was an impressive exit – the only voluntary resignation by a Prime Minister in the 20th century who was still relatively young, in reasonably good health and under no political pressure to stand down. Then he went and spoilt it, by producing a resignation honours list containing a number of distinctly dicey characters. This led to a vast amount of speculation that there must be some other hidden, and discreditable, reason for his departure. This had come as a complete surprise to most people, despite the fact that Wilson's lawyer and confidant, Lord Goodman, had for several months past been dropping gentle hints, which were mostly ignored, to quite a number of leading political figures. However, no skeleton has ever emerged from Wilson's cupboard, and a generation later one must conclude that he gave up for the reasons suggested above. Wilson lived for a further 19 years after his retirement. He wrote several more books, presided over a committee of inquiry into the City of London and became a life peer in 1983. Thereafter he gradually faded from public view, and his once famous memory sadly deteriorated. He died on 24 May 1995, aged 79.

Wilson was not a great Prime Minister, but he was much better than many people, including myself, were willing to concede at the time. He had strengths and weaknesses. The strengths included a very quick mind, good tactical sense, immense resourcefulness, an ability to manage a difficult and often querulous party and probably a better understanding of the gut feelings of ordinary voters than any other contemporary politician. He was a cautious man, who disdained any form of extremism, and regarded doctrinal disputes on such issues as public ownership as tedious "theology". He was accused of having no deep beliefs – a mistaken view. He was strongly committed to greater equality, the breaking down of class barriers, and the importance of planning. He abhorred racialism, and was a strong believer in sexual equality. He was a moderate believer in European integration, but was not prepared to give it priority over keeping the Labour Party together, though in the end he was instrumental in ensuring that Britain remained within the EEC.

His greatest weakness was his tendency to adopt short-term expedients, which often undermined his longer-term goals. One of his most famous sayings was "A week is a long time in politics", and he was accused of having no strategic vision. A kindly and considerate man, he was a natural conciliator who shied away from conflict, and constantly sought to avoid difficult decisions by seeking compromises where no happy mean actually existed. "A master of fudge and mudge" was David Owen's damning description. Some of his opponents in the Labour Party regarded him as being exceptionally devious, a charge which was undoubt-edly exaggerated. He was vain, ambitious and sometimes opportunistic, but probably no more so than the generality of politicians. He was the first – and only – professional econo-mist to become Prime Minister, but he had no more success in solving the problems of Britain's economic decline than any other post-war Premier. He did, at least succeed, in very trying circumstances, in keeping the Labour Party together, and winning four out of the five elections which it fought under his leadership. This was no mean achievement, and one which his immediate successors were quite unable to emulate. No sooner was he gone, than the party began to split apart, and condemned itself to 18 years in opposition.

Works consulted

D.E. Butler and Anthony King, 1965, *The British General Election of 1964*, London, Macmillan.
David Butler and Michael Pinto-Duschinsky, 1971, *The British General Election of 1970*, London, Macmillan.
Peter Clarke, 1992, *A Question of Leadership: From Gladstone to Thatcher*, Harmondsworth, Penguin.
Bernard Donoughue, 1987, *Prime Minister: The Conduct of Policy under Harold Wilson and James Callaghan*, London, Cape.
Kevin Jeffreys, 1999, *Leading Labour: From Keir Hardie to Tony Blair*, London, Tauris.
Austen Morgan, 1992, *Harold Wilson*, London, Pluto.
Kenneth O. Morgan, 1987, *Labour People: Hardie to Kinnock*, Oxford, Oxford University Press.
Ben Pimlott, 1992, *Harold Wilson*, London, HarperCollins.
Harold Wilson, 1971, *The Labour Government 1964–70*, Harmondsworth, Penguin.
Philip Ziegler, 1993, *Wilson: The Authorised Life of Lord Wilson of Rievaulx*, London, Weidenfeld & Nicolson.

15

EDWARD HEATH

Cheerleader for Europe

In 1916, within four months of each other, were born the two men who, half a century later, were to face each other for ten years as rival party leaders and contest four general elections. They came from similar social backgrounds, but different geographical regions which were strongly to mark their characters – Wilson from Yorkshire, Edward Heath from Kent, where he grew up in the seaside town of Broadstairs, from where, on a clear day, he could see the coast of France. Continental Europe was a living reality to him from his earliest days.

Heath, who was known as a child, and still as a young man, as Teddy, was born on 9 July 1916. His father, William Heath, was a carpenter, who later set himself up as a builder and decorator. His mother, the former Edith Pantony, had worked as a lady's maid. Teddy had a younger brother, John, born in 1920, but was much the brighter of the two children, and became his dominant mother's favourite, and the focus of the family's hopes. William Heath was a skilled craftsman and became a well-respected local small businessman. Fiercely anti-trade union, the mild Liberalism of his youth was to evolve into firm Conservatism. Something of a ladies' man, he was an easy-going congenial character with few intellectual interests. His influence on his elder son seems to have been limited, and Teddy grew up very much a mother's boy. The qualities and habits which she instilled in him – the exceptional importance of cleanliness and tidiness, the necessity for hard work, for taking responsibility for others, and a decent ambition to advance his own position in life – early marked him out as exceptional among his schoolfellows at the local Church of England primary school, where he always seemed old for his years. He also showed a precocious talent for music, which his parents encouraged, buying him an upright piano, which they could scarcely afford. The cost, Heath recorded in his autobiography, was £42, which they paid for in 24 monthly instalments of £2 each. Just before his 10th birthday, he sat for the scholarship examination for the local fee-paying grammar school, Chatham House School, at which he won a free place.

Heath was regarded as an ideal pupil at his school, where he won virtually every honour, except in sport, though he was felt by some to be almost unnaturally self-contained. His father wanted him to become an accountant, but Heath set his heart on going to university, though, as he was to recall, "I knew that my family would never be able to provide the money to fund me for three years" (Heath, 1998, p. 20). He sat a scholarship examination for Balliol College,

DOI: 10.4324/9781003031963-16

Oxford, but did not do sufficiently well to win an Exhibition. He was, however, offered a fee-paying place, which he was able to take up only because the Kent County Council offered a loan of £90 a year, repayable when he graduated. So he arrived in Oxford, in October 1935 – one year later than Wilson – to read Politics, Philosophy and Economics at Balliol. He was not there for long before an opportunity arose which transformed his financial situation, and gave him a prominent position in the College. The College organ scholarship, worth £100 a year, became vacant, and Heath successfully applied for it. His duties were to include playing the organ in the College chapel at eight o'clock every morning and on Sundays, while also giving him opportunities for conducting choirs and orchestras and even composing. It was to run for three years beginning the following October, which meant that he was able to spend four years in Oxford, rather than the normal three.

Heath worked selectively hard at his studies, but, in contrast to Wilson, they did not monopolise his activities. Apart from music, these were centred on the Oxford Union and on the Oxford University Conservative Association, of both of which he became President, as well as of the Federation of University Conservative Associations, and of the Junior Common Room in his own college – Balliol. Heath did not commit himself to the Tory cause without due consideration. In his autobiography, *The Course of My Life*, he admits being attracted to the Liberals, who, he said, "remained committed to an open society, and to freedom in both the social and economic spheres ... but it was already clear to me that they were a spent force in British politics" (Heath, 1998, p. 28). He wrote that he never considered joining the Labour Party, but – before going up to Oxford – attended the 1935 TUC conference at Margate, out of curiosity. He witnessed there the savage attack by Ernest Bevin, then leader of the Transport and General Workers' Union, on George Lansbury, the pacifist Labour Party leader, who shortly afterwards resigned. "I was pleased that the trade unions were finally committing themselves to tackling fascism", he wrote,

> but still considered that socialism smacked too much of state control. I concluded that a moderate form of Conservatism offered the best foundation for a free society, and that the best course for me was to campaign for that brand of thinking within the Conservative Party. But I continued to believe in fairness and deplored the snobbishness of many Conservatives.
>
> *(Heath, 1998, p. 29)*

Heath thus established himself, from the outset, as being firmly on the progressive wing of the Conservative Party, and soon became a strong opponent of Neville Chamberlain's appeasement policies, both in relation to Germany and Spain. He was one of very few Conservatives who wholeheartedly committed themselves to the Republican cause in Spain, travelling to Barcelona with a student delegation, and narrowly escaping death when the cars in which they were travelling were machine-gunned by a Francoist plane. He also visited Germany, where his conviction of the deadliness of the Nazi threat was only strengthened by his attendance as a spectator at a Nuremberg rally, and a subsequent unexpected encounter, at a cocktail party, with several Nazi leaders, including Goebbels, Goering and Himmler.

After the Munich agreement, in August 1938, Heath successfully moved a motion in the Union that "This House deplores the Government's policy of Peace without Honour". There happened to be a by-election vacancy at Oxford, and Heath proposed himself to the local Tories as their candidate, while making it clear that he was opposed to the Munich agreement.

He was turned down, and the young Tory barrister, Quintin Hogg (later Lord Hailsham), was brought in to defend the seat and also Chamberlain's appeasement policy. Heath then threw himself wholeheartedly into the campaign for the Independent candidate, running on an anti-Munich ticket, and in whose favour both the Labour and Liberal candidates had withdrawn. This was A.S. Lindsay, the Master of Balliol, whom Heath greatly admired and was much influenced by, despite his being a strong Labour supporter. Lindsay's campaign attracted enormous attention, and he succeeded in halving the Tory majority, without however preventing Hogg (later to be Lord Chancellor in Heath's Cabinet) from making his parliamentary debut at the age of 31.

Heath, who was still universally known as Teddy, was a popular figure at Oxford, and mixed easily with Labour supporters, such as Denis Healey, Roy Jenkins and Tony Crosland, who were friends and rivals in the Union. From their subsequent accounts, he appears to have been much more relaxed than the rather buttoned up character they later confronted across the floor of the House of Commons. Yet Heath apparently felt some social insecurity in a pre-war Oxford, where the vast majority of his fellow students were public schoolboys from far more affluent backgrounds. His biographer, John Campbell, suggests that this was to blame for the "curious accent" he developed, "with its tortured and artificial vowel sounds which later attracted such mockery", and was "markedly different from the soft Kentish burr of his father or – more significantly – of his brother John, who went to the same school but not to Oxford" (Campbell, 1994, p. 18).

Heath graduated in the summer of 1939, with a Second Class degree. He was disappointed not to get a First, but considering the range of his non-academic activities this was as good a result as he could reasonably have expected. He was then faced with a career choice, and hesitated between music and politics, to which he saw the law as a stepping stone. He consulted the Professor of Music, Sir Hugh Allen, who appears to have told him that, though he was a good musician, he was unlikely to reach the very top as a conductor. "On the other hand, if you go into politics, you will always have music as an amateur to enjoy for its own sake", Heath recorded him as saying (Campbell, 1994, p. 38), and – without undue disappointment – he prepared to take up a scholarship to Gray's Inn to read for the bar. Meanwhile, in August 1939, he left for a visit to Danzig and Warsaw, and was hitch-hiking home through Germany when the Nazi-Soviet pact was announced. He got out of the country only just in time, and returned to London on 1 September, the day of the German invasion of Poland.

He hastened to register for military service, but was not actually called up until the following July, after the fall of France. In the meantime, he was encouraged by the Foreign Office to depart on a lengthy student debating tour of the United States, which was regarded as a good opportunity to project the British viewpoint to American audiences. Like other young budding British politicians, Heath was greatly impressed by much of what he saw in America, without however being bowled over by the experience, nor did it, Campbell observed, "diminish the primary commitment he instinctively felt to Europe" (Campbell, 1994, p. 41). When Heath was eventually called up, he was given a commission, as a second lieutenant in the Heavy Anti-Aircraft Artillery. By the time he was demobbed, six years later, he had risen to Lieutenant Colonel.

Heath took his army duties exceptionally seriously. He saw relatively little action, but proved himself an outstanding administrator, and a firm but fair commanding officer. He was noted for the assiduity and speed which he showed in getting to the root of any problems which arose. Campbell comments that "this is characteristic at each successive stage of his

176 Edward Heath

career – and in his private pursuits too – Heath has set himself quickly and thoroughly to learn the ropes. He had always been a formidably quick learner" (Campbell, 1994, p. 48). Heath ended the war in Germany, where he had been on the eve of its outbreak, and stayed on for a year as part of the army of occupation. He travelled extensively around the country, and was deeply affected by the extent of the destruction. The moral he drew from this was that Europe must never again be torn apart by internecine conflict: "only by working together", he later wrote, "had we any hope of creating a society which would uphold the true values of European civilisation. Reconciliation and reconstruction must be our tasks. I did not realise then that it would be my preoccupation for the next thirty years" (Heath, 1998, p. 106).

Heath returned to civilian life in July 1946, and the Broadstairs home of his parents. He had lost the desire to read for the bar, but his inclination to follow a political career was as strong as ever. He was determined to find a parliamentary seat, but in the meantime had to earn his living. He took the Civil Service examination, and finished equal top, with another former Balliol man. He was assigned to the Ministry of Civil Aviation, being disappointed not to be chosen for the Treasury. As a civil servant, Heath greatly impressed his colleagues by his administrative qualities and resourcefulness, many of them believing that he would rise to the very top of the service. He was, however, only a bird of passage, resigning in October 1947, as soon as he had been selected as a prospective parliamentary candidate.

This was his fourth try; the first three times he was beaten by rivals with a traditional public school background. The Tories in Bexley, however, a Labour-held marginal seat in the Kentish suburbs, with "a large homogeneous population of the lower middle class and upwardly mobile skilled working class" (Campbell, 1994, p. 60), were specifically on the lookout for a candidate who had risen successfully from a similar background. Heath sailed through the selection meeting, and plunged himself into the work of nursing the constituency with enormous energy and careful military-style planning of all his activities. Meanwhile, he needed a job, and took the first one which was offered – news editor of the *Church Times*, a weekly Anglican newspaper. It was not a happy choice – Heath soon became bored, though he carried out his duties with his customary efficiency. After some 18 months, he took a large salary cut, and went to work for a city bank, Brown, Shipley, which undertook to teach him the banking business, while encouraging his political activities. He stayed on with them, on a part-time basis, after he became an MP.

He won the Bexley seat in the general election of February 1950, when the Labour government's previously large majority was cut to five seats. He had two strokes of luck. The sitting Labour MP, Ashley Bramall, had been an old associate of his in the Oxford Union, and happily agreed to an extensive series of debates with Heath. This was a great help to Heath in getting himself known throughout the constituency, and Bramall no doubt later regretted his magnanimity. Even more helpful to Heath was the intervention of a Communist candidate, whose votes – more than three times the size of Heath's majority of 133 – must have come almost exclusively at Bramall's expense. This enabled Heath to squeeze in, and once elected he was never to be shifted. He remained the MP for Bexley, and its successor seat, of Old Bexley and Sidcup, for 51 years, retiring at the age of just under 85 at the 2001 election.

The 1950 class of new Tory MPs was regarded as a vintage crop, including notably three young men who had already distinguished themselves in the Conservative Research department, under the aegis of Rab Butler – Iain Macleod, Reginald Maudling and Enoch Powell. The 33-year-old Heath, now known as Ted, was not seen as an equally promising figure, but made something of a mark by calling for British membership of the European Coal and

Steel Community in his maiden speech. He then briefly associated himself with the One Nation Group of socially conscious Tory MPs, before disappearing for eight years into the anonymity of the Whips' Office, first in opposition, and, after the Tory victory in the 1951 general election, as a paid government whip, the most junior form of ministerial office. The Whips' Office was traditionally a place where less bright, but diligent MPs, with little hope of further promotion, were parked. Heath lost no time in demonstrating that he was in a different category. He threw himself into the work of the office with the same enthusiasm and application that he had shown throughout his army career. He soon devised a complex card index system cataloguing every conceivable piece of information about Tory MPs, including their peccadilloes, and where they might be found at any time during the day or night. The Chief Whip, Patrick Buchan-Hepburn, a languid Scottish aristocrat, was mightily impressed and soon made Heath his deputy, devolving to him the greater part of his own responsibilities. In December 1955, eight months into Eden's premiership, he became Minister of Works, and Heath was promoted to take his place.

The following year he faced his first great challenge, with the eruption of the Suez crisis. Heath's closest friends believed that he disapproved of the Anglo-French invasion, but he kept his private views to himself, both at the time and for the rest of his life. He saw his job as being to hold his party together during a period of extreme turbulence, and he devoted himself to ensuring that party revolts, on either the pro- or anti-Suez side, were kept to minimal proportions. This he was able to achieve through Herculean efforts, and a mixture of tough and tender methods. Macmillan, who replaced Eden in January 1957, regarded it as essential to retain Heath's services during the first difficult months and years of his own premiership. During this time the relationship between the two men was extremely close. Macmillan consulted him on a very wide range of issues – going well beyond parliamentary management, the traditional activity of Chief Whips – and on the whole received excellent and wholly loyal advice from him. Under Eden, Heath had been the first Chief Whip ever to attend Cabinet meetings on a regular basis, and Macmillan continued the practice, which has continued ever since. For his part, Heath had an unprecedented opportunity to build up personal links within the party. This compensated him for the greater public exposure of his contemporaries – Macleod, Maudling and Powell – all of whom preceded him into the Cabinet, and were seen, as he at this time was not, as future contenders for the leadership.

It was only after the 1959 election that he was to enter the Cabinet, as Minister for Labour, replacing Macleod, who became Colonial Secretary. He did not stay long in the post. In July 1960, Macmillan chose the Earl of Home as Foreign Secretary, and sought to balance this by appointing a second Cabinet minister as his deputy, and to answer for the Foreign Office in the House of Commons. Heath hesitated to accept what was technically a demotion, but was reassured when he was rewarded with the office of Lord Privy Seal and given special responsibility for relations with Europe. When, a year later, the government agreed to apply to join the European Economic Community, he was the natural choice as chief negotiator, a task on which he embarked with total enthusiasm, being instantly awarded the title of 'Mr Europe' by the popular press. In the event, it ended in failure – thanks to the veto of President de Gaulle – but it was a venture from which Heath emerged with tremendous credit. During 18 arduous months, he devoted himself single-mindedly to the task in hand, showing extraordinary stamina, resourcefulness and mastery of detail, stubbornly defending what he deemed to be essential British or Commonwealth interests, but always seeking a way through to the desired objective, which he was able to present with a rare passion, belying his reputation as a

178 Edward Heath

cool pragmatist. His efforts went down particularly well in his own party, where he – perhaps more effectively than Macmillan – played a decisive role in winning round the great majority of those who had initially harboured doubts.

It also turned Heath, who previously had been strictly a behind-the-scenes operator, into an instantly recognisable public figure. This was reflected by his appearance for the first time in newspaper cartoons as one of the small group of leading Tory figures. Even so, Heath had not quite reached the point where he was seen as a credible contender for the party leadership. He recognised this himself, and when Macmillan's resignation was announced at the Tory conference in October 1963 (see Chapter 14), he quickly emerged as one of Alec Home's strongest supporters. He was no doubt influenced by his esteem for Home, under whom he had worked amicably in the Foreign Office, but it cannot have escaped his notice that there was a serious risk of Reginald Maudling, the Chancellor of the Exchequer and one year younger than himself, being chosen, and effectively blotting out his own chances in any future contest. In the event, Maudling's candidature faded, and it was Rab Butler who was pipped at the post by Macmillan's blatant manipulation, but the outcome was very much to Heath's advantage. Home appeared, from the outset, as only a stop-gap leader, and all the other actual or potential contenders had been damaged in one way or another by the contest. Butler and Hailsham were effectively out of the running for the future, Maudling was seen to have failed, while Macleod and Powell offended against the Tory code of party loyalty by their refusal to join Home's government.

Heath probably hoped to become Foreign Secretary in the new government, but that post was reserved for Rab Butler, as his non-negotiable price for agreeing to serve under Douglas-Home, as the new Premier chose to be called. Instead he was appointed to head a beefed-up Trade and Industry department, with a brief to promote economic modernisation and competition. Determined to make his mark, he promoted the only major piece of legislation to be passed in the remainder of the Parliament. This was the Bill to abolish retail price maintenance (see Chapter 14), which was introduced and forced through against the resistance of a powerful group of Tory MPs, including several senior ministers. Heath certainly made an impact as a forceful and reform-minded minister, but in the process revealed a hitherto unsuspected streak of authoritarianism and a lack of consideration for the feelings of his colleagues, including junior ministers in his own department, notably Edward Du Cann, who became a lasting enemy.

After the Tory election defeat, in October 1964, Heath was appointed Shadow Chancellor, and favourably impressed Tory MPs by the vigour, and mastery of detail, which he showed in leading the opposition to James Callaghan's first budget, in the Finance Bill proceedings in the following spring. This may have been the deciding factor in his victory over the more languid Reginald Maudling, in the first ever leadership ballot, when Douglas-Home resigned in July 1965. He polled 150 votes, to 133 for Maudling, and 15 for Enoch Powell. Tory MPs were comparing him, not only with Maudling, but also with Wilson, whose toughness and mental agility they thought he would emulate. An unspoken comparison was also with Douglas-Home; they wanted a new leader who was as little like a 14th Earl as possible, and Heath's modest background was undoubtedly seen as an advantage. What was not considered an asset was Heath's bachelor status at the age of 49, a source of endless speculation in political circles. The general consensus was that he was a repressed homosexual, which, however, does not seem to have been the case. In fact, as a young man, he had courted – though in a spasmodic way – a local doctor's daughter in Broadstairs, Kay Raven, and apparently expected to marry her, though he never got round to proposing. He refers to this cryptically in his autobiography, saying: "One day she suddenly let me know that she was marrying someone else. I was saddened by this ... maybe I had taken too much for granted." He was never known subsequently to take any sexual or romantic interest in any other woman, though he had a number of close female friends. He seems to have sublimated his feelings in music and – at a later stage – sailing, which he took up only in his fifties, with conspicuous success, winning the famous Sydney-Hobart yacht race at his first attempt. His single status may have been an electoral handicap, though there is no firm evidence of this, but it liberated him to apply himself full-time to politics; indeed he expected the same commitment from his associates and subordinates, seemingly oblivious of the conflicting claims of their wives and families. This undoubtedly proved an asset to Heath in his rise to the top: the downside was that he had nobody to unburden himself to when the going got rough.

It was not long before many Tory MPs began to regret the choice they had made. Heath proved no match for Wilson, who regularly rang rings round him in their parliamentary encounters, while on television he often appeared wooden and ill at ease. It is doubtful whether any other Tory leader would have done much better in the March 1966 general election, when Labour stormed back with a majority of 97, but it was Heath who was blamed by his party, and a whispering campaign against his leadership soon got under way, which was never completely silenced until his unexpected victory in June 1970. During most of the 1966 Parliament the government was highly unpopular, falling far behind in the opinion polls and performing abysmally in local elections and by-elections, where it lost a string of normally safe seats. This meant that Tory morale remained high, and there was no overt movement to dislodge Heath from the leadership, despite the fact that his own poll rating fell well behind that of his party. However, when the election campaign got under way in May 1970, Labour leapt into a strong lead in the polls which was maintained right up until polling day, and the almost universal expectation was that it would win. The dismayed Tories were quick to blame their own leader, and it was an open secret that a high level party delegation would wait on him immediately after the election and demand his resignation.

It is doubtful if even Heath himself believed that the Tories would win the election. During the previous four years, he had presided over a comprehensive rethink of the party's policies, and its election manifesto was far more detailed than ever before, with the emphasis on three main themes – lower taxation, trade union reform and membership of the European Economic Community. During the campaign, however, Heath concentrated on a single issue – rising prices – which he hammered home continuously, promising that the Tories would take action to cut them "at a stroke". This struck a responsive chord among voters, though the principal reason for Labour's defeat was almost certainly the release just before polling day of monthly trade figures which appeared to undermine its claim to have solved the balance of payments problem (see Chapter 14). The election result was:

Conservative	330
Labour	287
Liberal	6
Others	7
Conservative majority	30

180 Edward Heath

This unexpected triumph put Heath in a very strong position, and immediately silenced his many critics. It also had the unfortunate effect of making him surer than ever of his own judgement and even less inclined to seek advice from colleagues. Five of these would have carried sufficient weight to be able to force their views on him in other circumstances, but for one reason or another were not in a position to do so during the period of his government. Iain Macleod was appointed to the key post of Chancellor of the Exchequer, but died within a month of his appointment, a body blow to the new government. His successor, Anthony Barber, was in no sense an adequate replacement. Macleod's death cost Heath not only the shrewdist tactician in his team, but also incomparably the best performer, both in the House of Commons and on television – a particularly serious loss given Heath's own deficiencies in these departments. Reggie Maudling, the Tory Deputy Leader, became Home Secretary, but was now too laid back to make his views strongly felt, and resigned office in July 1972, when questions were asked about his unwise business associations. Enoch Powell, who had been dismissed by Heath from the Shadow Cabinet in 1968, following his notorious 'rivers of blood' speech on immigration, was left out of the government, and became a persistent critic from the back benches. Quintin Hogg was again dispatched to the Lords, as a life peer, to become Lord Chancellor, and subsequently regarded his role as strictly non-political, while Alec Douglas-Home, who became Foreign Secretary for the second time, also largely abstained from intervening in domestic affairs. So Heath was effectively on his own, and though other ministers, such as William Whitelaw, Robert Carr, Lord Carrington and James Prior, subsequently became quite close to him, none of them was able to speak to him on a basis approaching equality.

Heath was also unlucky to come to power at a time of world economic disorder, when the post-war Keynesian consensus was coming to an end, the Bretton Woods agreement on fixed exchange rates was collapsing, and strong inflationary pressures, culminating in a quadrupling of oil prices in the last months of his premiership, combined to blight his best endeavours. The consequence was that he had one historic achievement to his credit – British adhesion to the EEC – but that most of his other endeavours ended in failure. On Europe, his own personal contribution was central, and it is doubtful whether any other Prime Minister, in the circumstances of the time – and with the Labour opposition coming down heavily against him – could have pulled it off. From the outset, Heath made two crucial decisions. One was to restrict the negotiations, ably conducted by Geoffrey Rippon, to an absolute minimum number of crucial issues, of which the continued access of New Zealand farm products to the British market was perhaps the most difficult. The other was to stake everything on winning the goodwill of the French government, and its Gaullist President, Georges Pompidou, and to persuade him that Britain would be a constructive member of the Community rather than a Trojan Horse on behalf of the United States. Despite Rippon's best efforts, the talks appeared to be bogged down by May 1971, and Heath went to Paris to hammer out the differences face-to-face with Pompidou in a two-day summit. Pompidou, a tough but relatively open-minded man, who did not share the prejudices or God-given sense of mission of his predecessor, was impressed by Heath's sincerity, straightforwardness and deep European commitment, and at the concluding press conference announced that the main issues had been resolved. Within a few days, the roadblocks in the membership talks were lifted one-by-one, and by mid-June the negotiation was virtually over.

Heath then faced the daunting prospect of getting the membership terms approved by the House of Commons, where his nominal majority was over 25, but where up to 40 Tory

MPs were anti-EEC. Thanks to the positive votes or abstentions of 89 Labour Members (see Chapter 14), he achieved the surprisingly high majority of 112 in the vote on principle on 28 October 1971. Thereafter it was a hard slog to get the Bill incorporating the terms through the Commons, where the Committee stage was taken on the floor of the House. A single defeat would have killed the Bill, and the process was a protracted and precarious affair, with the bulk of the Labour rebels, having satisfied their consciences by their act of defiance to their party whips in October, now doing what they were told. All together there were 105 divisions on the Bill between February and July 1972, with the government's majority falling to as low as four, but it emerged unscathed, thanks to a small number of Labour veterans not standing for re-election who abstained on the most crucial occasions, and to a masterly performance by Francis Pym, the Tory Chief Whip.

Heath showed courage and fortitude in his handling of the rapidly deteriorating situation in Northern Ireland, where he unhesitatingly followed the policy pursued by his Labour predecessor of pressurising the Protestant-dominated Stormont government to remove discriminations against the Roman Catholic minority. When they failed to do so, and with violence increasing both from the IRA and from Loyalist paramilitaries, he acted, in March 1972, to suspend Stormont and institute direct rule from London, appointing Willie Whitelaw as Northern Ireland Secretary. This was a brave decision for a Tory Prime Minister, half of whose parliamentary majority was made up of Ulster Unionist MPs, traditionally allied to the Tories, but vehemently opposed to direct rule. The appointment of Whitelaw proved an inspired choice. In less than two years, he not only achieved a steady fall in the level of violence, but coaxed Unionists and Nationalists into participating in a power-sharing executive to rule from Belfast. Led by the Unionist Brian Faulkner, with Gerry Fitt of the Social Democratic and Labour Party as his deputy, it was created under the Sunningdale agreement reached in December 1973. Sadly, however, Faulkner did not succeed in carrying the bulk of Unionists with him, and the new agreement was fatally undermined by the February 1974 general election, when anti-Sunningdale candidates made a clean sweep of the Unionist-held seats. It collapsed three months later in the face of massed Loyalist demonstrations, which the new Labour government, and its Northern Ireland Secretary, Merlyn Rees, were unable to counter. The Sunningdale agreement was, perhaps, premature, but it paved the way for more successful power-sharing initiatives launched by the Major and Blair governments a generation later.

Yet it was by his domestic policies that he would stand or fall, and in these Heath was singularly unsuccessful. He had grown to loathe and despise Harold Wilson, and determined from the outset that his government would be as dissimilar as possible to its predecessor. He began by repudiating the statutory incomes policy of the Wilson government, and its interventionist approach to industry, saying that in future such decisions would be left to market forces. He then hastened to show that he would succeed where Labour had failed by introducing an Industrial Relations Bill which bore more than a passing resemblance to the trade union reforms which Barbara Castle had humiliatingly failed to enact a year earlier. Heath was no crude anti-union agitator, and genuinely believed that his Bill would offer new opportunities and benefits for unions which registered under its provisions. This would be a fair *quid pro quo*, he felt, for the creation of an Industrial Relations Court, which would help ensure a more rational and orderly system of settling disputes. This intention was certainly shared by his Employment Minister, Robert Carr, who was in charge of the Bill. Yet Carr made the fatal mistake of rushing its introduction, without allowing adequate time for consultation with the interests involved, which convinced even moderate trade union leaders that the government was utterly unwilling to take account of their views. They therefore mounted a concerted attack on the Bill, browbeating Labour MPs into resisting it root-and-branch at every stage of the parliamentary process. The Bill reached the Statute Book, with no serious amendment, by August 1971, but it was a Pyrrhic victory. The Industrial Relations Act soon became a dead-letter. Most unions refused to register, thus losing the privileges offered to them, while both the government and employers soon became unwilling to apply its penal clauses for fear of creating 'martyrs' among trade unionists sent to prison for 'contempt of court', against the intentions of the authors of the Act.

So the battle to get the Bill through had been in vain, and had seriously compromised the prospect of trade union co-operation in the government's anti-inflation policies. These were its number one priority, certainly during its first two years. In place of Labour's statutory approach, Heath depended on a policy of voluntary wage restraint, which initially proved surprisingly successful. The big exception was the miners' strike in February 1972, which the government firmly resisted, but which – thanks largely to the 'flying pickets' tactics employed by a new young miners' leader, Arthur Scargill – rapidly threatened to close the nation's power stations. The government was forced to back down, and acquiesce in an arbitration award of 27 per cent, far above the norm, and which threatened to open the floodgates to inflationary claims from many other unions. An even greater shock for the government was the rapid rise in unemployment, which the previous month had breached the highly symbolic one million mark, easily the highest total in post-war Britain, and representing an increase of almost 50 per cent during Heath's premiership. Henceforth reducing unemployment became his overriding priority, and he resolved on a policy of all-out growth. He accordingly performed what his critics (initially confined to Enoch Powell and his small group of supporters) lost no time in characterising as U-turns. He abandoned the market, in favour of government action to control unemployment, and substituted statutory for voluntary restriction of wage increases. The Chancellor, Anthony Barber, was instructed to aim for an annual growth of 5 per cent, and the government, which had already shocked its right-wing critics by nationalising the ailing Rolls-Royce firm, proceeded to bail out United Clyde Shipbuilders and other 'lame ducks' threatened with closure, while steeply increasing investment in the nationalised industries. In November 1972, Heath announced a three-stage statutory control of prices and incomes, beginning with a pay, price, rent and dividend freeze.

For almost a year, these measures largely attained their objectives, unemployment fell rapidly and wage inflation was contained. There were, however, adverse side-effects – interest rates soared, and property prices rocketed as a result of the 'Barber boom'. Yet, by the autumn of 1973, when the pay policy was due to move into its milder Stage Three, there seemed an excellent prospect that Heath would have a success story to tell when he faced the general election expected in late 1974 or early 1975. All this was changed by the Yom Kippur War, of October 1973, which was followed by a cut-back of oil supplies and the quadrupling of oil prices. This meant that coal, a declining industry for many years, suddenly became highly competitive with oil, and relatively under-priced. The miners seized the opportunity to put in a substantial pay claim – far greater than could be accommodated under Stage Three – and when this was refused, began an overtime ban with the evident intention of running down coal stocks to improve their bargaining position if they later moved to strike action.

Probably the only way the government could have saved Stage Three was by declaring that – because of the oil crisis – the miners were a special case, and that their pay claim, and theirs alone, would be settled outside its framework. This course was actually argued for by Enoch Powell, who in other circumstances might have been expected to oppose surrender to a blind union threat, but was turned down by Heath and his colleagues. Believing that they could not afford to give way a second time to the miners, and mistakenly believing that they were now in a stronger position to stand up to them than 18 months earlier, they stood their ground. In order to conserve both oil and coal stocks, Heath announced on 13 December that a three-day week for industry would be enforced from 31 December. The public seemed to be on the government's side, and several ministers, notably Lord Carrington, the newly appointed Energy Secretary, began urging Heath to call an immediate election on the issue "Who governs Britain?" Much evidence suggests that had Heath taken this advice, and called an election for January or early February, he would indeed have won. Yet he was highly reluctant to do so, and for another month tried desperately to seek means to persuade the miners to back down and call off their threatened strike, which was due to start on 1 February. The TUC intervened, and made the extraordinary offer that all other unions would undertake to conform to Stage Three if the miners were accepted as a special case. The government turned down the offer, the strike duly began, and Heath called an election for 28 February. A Tory landslide was predicted, and the opinion polls seemed to back this up. Yet the election campaign failed to go the government's way. Wilson fought a more skilful campaign than had been expected, and the Tories were unable to confine it to the single question of "Who governs?" To their dismay, the issue of rising prices, with which they had made so much play in 1970, with Heath's promise to cut the rise in prices "at a stroke", came back to haunt them, as inflation had, in fact, substantially increased. The most damaging event of the campaign was the publication of a report by a body called the Relativities Board, to which the government had referred the miners' claim, which appeared to show that it had got its sums wrong and that the miners were much less better off in relation to other workers than had previously been believed. A further setback to Heath was the defection of Enoch Powell, who resigned his candidature and urged voters to support Labour in order to ensure that there would be a referendum on the EEC. Another surprise factor in the campaign was a strong surge in support for the Liberals, very largely at the government's expense, though it did not win the Liberals many new seats. Despite their setbacks during the campaign, the overwhelming expectation was still that the Tories would win, and the inconclusive result, which gave them more votes but fewer seats than Labour (a reverse of the 1951 result), came as a devastating shock. The new Parliament's composition was:

Labour	301
Conservative	297
Liberal	14
Nationalists	9
Others	14

The 14 others included 11 Ulster Unionists, who normally would have been included in the Conservative total, putting them ahead of Labour, and in striking distance of an overall majority. Those elected on this occasion, however, wanted to have nothing to do with Heath, whom they blamed for the imposition of direct rule in Ulster. Nevertheless, Heath made one last desperate throw by offering a coalition to the Liberals, with its leader, Jeremy Thorpe, joining the Cabinet, probably as Home Secretary. Thorpe was tempted, but aware that his own party was unwilling, and that in any event, without the Ulster Unionists, Heath would still be several votes short of a parliamentary majority, declined. Heath's attempt to hold on to power collapsed over the weekend following the election, and was seen as a major misjudgement. It showed him up as a 'bad loser' and even worse tactician. Yet it was a true reflection of his stubborn character. In the face of defeat, he never contemplated for a moment resigning the Tory leadership or even offering himself for a vote of confidence by his party. He just hung on and, even more remarkably, attempted to do so again the following October, after a further general election defeat, when Wilson's minority government (just) succeeded in gaining an overall majority.

This time, however, he faced an open revolt. He had now lost three elections out of four, and many Tories – including, most damagingly, Edward Du Cann, now chairman of the influential 1922 Committee of Tory backbenchers – were determined that he should be challenged in a leadership ballot. There was no obvious rival, and if Heath had willingly offered himself up for re-election, he might well have succeeded, despite the discontent. As it was, he resisted for several months, which only spurred his more fervent critics to find a challenger – *any* challenger – to put up against him. Their first choice was Sir Keith Joseph, the former Social Services Secretary, who was known to have harboured doubts about Heath's policies and U-turns, though he had never considered resigning. He ruled himself out, as did Du Cann, who was facing public criticism because of his business affairs. It was only then that – in the absence of any more heavyweight alternative – the former Education Secretary, Margaret Thatcher, threw her hat into the ring (see Chapter 17).

Neither Heath nor his supporters took her candidature seriously. Nor, perhaps, indeed did the majority of those Tory MPs who voted for her, seeing her only as a stalking horse who would do Heath just enough damage to enable more senior figures, notably Willie Whitelaw, a Heath loyalist, to offer themselves in the second ballot. Hardly anybody expected her actually to poll more votes than Heath, which immediately knocked him out of the running and gave her sufficient momentum to see off Whitelaw and three other contenders in the second ballot. The tragedy for Ted Heath was that he was largely responsible for his own undoing. He had led a remarkably loyal and harmonious Cabinet, which had not suffered a single resignation on policy grounds, despite its change of direction. Yet over the years he had offended a high proportion of Tory MPs by his gruffness and insensitivity to their views. It had not always been so. As Chief Whip under Eden and Macmillan, he had been a popular figure, going out of his way to be agreeable to his charges, and being much readier to use carrots rather than sticks to ensure their compliance. He evidently regarded this as being an essential part of his job. As Prime Minister and party leader, however, he felt no such compulsion: his task now was to run the country, and he had no time for small talk with 'bit players', such as backbenchers.

If Ted Heath had been a 'bad loser' to Labour in February 1974, he was an even worse one to Thatcher, never reconciling himself to her victory during the whole 15 years that she led her party, an attitude which won him the epithet of "the longest sulk in history". She, for her part, did not make it any easier for him, systematically rubbishing his government at every turn, despite the fact that she had been a compliant member and only became a critic retrospectively. Heath, who had made his own predecessor, Alec Home, Foreign Secretary, hoped that she would offer him the same courtesy, and was not amused when she instead proffered the Washington Embassy, making it crystal clear that she saw this as an opportunity to get him out of the way. It was not surprising that he became her most trenchant critic, subjecting her monetarist policies and seemingly heartless indifference to rising unemployment to withering criticism, while saving his most savage barbs for her failure to consolidate his European achievements, and for instead pursuing the elusive path of the so-called 'special relationship' with the US. The force of his criticism was, however, blunted, by the widespread assumption that it was motivated by sour grapes.

In return, Thatcher's supporters mounted a formidable indictment against him, maintaining that his government had started out with similar intentions to hers – to destroy the post-war consensus of a mixed economy and to replace it with a resurgent capitalism. On this basis, they argued, Heath had failed, while Thatcher had triumphed. This was fundamentally to misinterpret Heath's intentions. He had never been a prophet of untrammelled capitalism, had never preached monetarism or advocated widespread privatisation. On the contrary, he wished to bolster the mixed economy by making it more efficient. When the early policies of his government failed to achieve their objective, he changed tack. "When the facts change, I change my mind, what do you do, Sir?" The words were spoken by J.M. Keynes, but they might well have come from Heath. He was a true pragmatist, whose approach to economic issues was in truth rather similar to Wilson's, though he would not have approved the comparison.

Heath can claim to have been the most intellectually honest Premier of the second half of the century, seldom hiding behind the half-truths and evasions which were the stock-in-trade of too many of his rivals. It could, equally, be said of him that he was a poor politician – with a weak tactical sense, and a limited ability to communicate his message. In many ways, he would have been more suited to a career as a senior civil servant, and it was noticeable that as Prime Minister he formed closer relationships with mandarins, such as Sir William Armstrong, the Head of the Home Civil Service, than with his political colleagues. One of his more important innovations was to form the Central Policy Review Staff, or Think Tank, to provide independent, but non party-political advice to ministers.

On one issue, Heath never changed his mind – that of the fundamental virtues of the European Union (as the EEC became). He continued to laud it throughout the 30 years or more following his negotiation of British entry. It was a great sadness to him that his view gained ever diminishing support from his own party, though paradoxically the majority of his Labour opponents subsequently swung round to his side, with varying degrees of enthusiasm.

Works consulted

David Butler and Dennis Kavanagh, 1974, *The British General Election of February 1974*, London, Macmillan.

David Butler and Michael Pinto-Duschinsky, 1971, *The British General Election of 1970*, London, Macmillan.

John Campbell, 1994, *Edward Heath: A Biography*, London, Pimlico.

Edward Heath, 1998, *The Course of My Life*, London, Hodder & Stoughton.

Douglas Hurd, 1979, *An End to Promises*, London, Collins.

John Ramsden, 1996, *The Winds of Change: Macmillan to Heath, 1957–1975*, London, Longman.

16

JAMES CALLAGHAN

Labour's conservative[1]

Born in obscurity, raised in hardship, a long hard struggle in the trade union movement ... This was the life story of a long list of leading Labour Party figures in the first half of the 20th century, the most outstanding being Ernest Bevin. The last of the line was to be James Callaghan, born in Portsmouth on 27 March 1912. His father, also James, was a Chief Petty Officer in the Royal Navy. He came from an Irish Catholic background, and had run away to sea in his teens, changing his name from Gargohan. This, together with the fact that he was half-Jewish, was quite unknown to his son until *The Sun* newspaper researched his genealogy after he became Prime Minister in 1976. Callaghan' s father married a very young widow, Charlotte Cundy, whose first husband had died in a naval accident. She was a strict Baptist, and the elder James gave up his religion to marry her. Their children were brought up in his new faith. There were to be two of them – Dorothy, born in 1904, and Leonard James, eight years later. He was always known as Leonard, or Len, only adopting his second name in his early thirties, when he entered politics.

When Leonard was 4, his father was wounded in the Battle of Jutland, and after the war he was transferred to less strenuous work as a coastguard at Brixham, in Devon. Here the family lived a relaxed and happy life, which came to an abrupt end in 1921, when the old sailor, still only 44, collapsed and died from a heart attack. Charlotte was devastated, and the family descended into near poverty, as she received only a small lump sum and no pension from the Board of Admiralty. She moved the family back to Portsmouth where they lived a life barely above subsistence level in a bleak series of furnished rooms. There was some relief in 1924, when the newly elected Labour government awarded her a pension of ten shillings a week. This was sufficient, Callaghan later recalled, to turn her into an enthusiastic Labour voter; he himself, under the influence of their Scottish landlady, was already, from the age of 11, running errands for the Labour committee rooms during general elections.

Politics, however, played little part in the family's life, which was centred on the local Baptist church, in whose varied activities the young Leonard willingly participated, becoming in due course a Sunday school teacher. A tall, bright and good-looking boy, he attended Portsmouth North Secondary School, where he was far from being a star pupil, being particularly poor at mathematics, and not taking his studies very seriously. He was, however, keenly interested

DOI: 10.4324/9781003031963-17

in English and history and became a voracious reader at the local public library. His head-master, he recalled in his autobiography, "decided I should enter the Senior Oxford Certificate, which I passed easily enough, with exemption from matriculation. I was told that this would qualify me for entrance to a university, though such a far-fetched idea had never entered my calculations." Instead, he sat an examination to become a Civil Service clerk. "This", he wrote, "was an occasion for rejoicing at home, for I had fulfilled my mother's ambition that I should secure a permanent job offering a pension at sixty. I suppose she was influenced by her own past insecurity."

So, in the autumn of 1929, aged 17, he left home to work in the tax office at Maidstone, in faraway Kent, at a salary of £52 a year, plus a cost-of-living allowance. In comparison with many of his fellow school-leavers, who faced the prospect of life on the dole, he felt himself to be exceptionally privileged. The local Baptists put him in touch with their co-religionists in Maidstone, who arranged lodgings for him. For a time, he continued to take part in church activities, notably in the Sunday school, where he very soon met his future wife, Audrey Moulton. She was the daughter of a local businessman and deacon of the Baptist church, who for Callaghan was the acme of the middle-class respectability and security that his mother had craved. He was 17, and she 16, when they met, and they subsequently embarked on a lengthy engagement, marrying only in 1938, when he had attained some financial security and she had completed her higher education, becoming a domestic science teacher. It was to be a long and happy marriage, with three children, the eldest of whom – Margaret – was, as Baroness Jay, to be a Cabinet minister and Leader of the House of Lords, under Tony Blair. Callaghan was soon to lose his Baptist faith, but he retained many of the puritanical attitudes with which he had been imbued.

It was not long before Callaghan began to get bored with his largely routine work as a tax official. He carried out his duties conscientiously, but reserved his enthusiasm for his trade union activities. He joined the Association of Tax Clerks (AOT), a small union which however succeeded in recruiting 95 per cent of its potential membership without the aid of a closed shop. He soon became branch secretary, and made a name for himself as a rebel who wanted the union leadership to adopt a far more militant stance against the employers. He was espe-cially active in campaigning for better conditions for new entrants to the profession, and in attacking its rigid class structure, under which the administrative grade was reserved for public school and university men, the executive grade was for grammar school products, while only the clerical grade (to which Callaghan belonged) was open to those who had been educated at ordinary secondary schools. He was soon marked down as a trouble-maker by the union's general secretary, Douglas Houghton (later a Cabinet colleague of Callaghan's), who, however, took a more benign view after his election, in 1932, to the union's national executive, at the early age of 20. He was to detect in Callaghan a basic moderation and pragmatism, which was often concealed by the forcefulness with which he expressed his views. Four years later, when the union – now known, after an amalgamation, as the Inland Revenue Staff Federation (IRSF) – decided to elect an assistant general secretary, Houghton backed him against 31 other candidates. Len Callaghan, as he was known, was successful, and at the age of 24 became the number two official of the union, at a salary of £350 – far more than he had been earning as a tax clerk.

Over the next three years, Callaghan developed into a highly effective union negotiator, and built up an extensive network of contacts in other unions besides his own. He also met Harold Laski, the Professor of Government at the London School of Economics and a leading

188 James Callaghan

figure on the National Executive Committee (NEC) of the Labour Party, whose book, *The Grammar of Politics*, had already greatly influenced his own political thinking. Laski, for his part, was much impressed, and wanted Callaghan to enrol as an external degree student at the LSE under his personal supervision. Callaghan could not spare the time from his union work, but Laski also encouraged him to consider a parliamentary career, recommending him to Labour headquarters as a likely candidate. When war was declared, in 1939, Callaghan attempted to join up, although his union post was held to be a reserved occupation. He was accepted for the army, but vigorously protested, saying that both his father and his maternal grandfather had been sailors, and he wanted to join the navy. The union insisted on retaining his services until March 1943, however, when he finally got his way and joined the navy as an ordinary seaman, subsequently being promoted to sub-lieutenant. He had a relatively quiet war, seeing no action except during the later stages in 1945, when the battleship in which he was serving in the Far East set off in pursuit of two Japanese cruisers which were, however, too speedy to be caught.

A year or so earlier a decisive event occurred in his life when he was selected as prospective Labour candidate for the Cardiff South constituency, for which he was nominated by contacts in the IRSF. It was a close-run thing: he won the selection by a single vote over the pacifist schoolteacher, George Thomas, who was instead chosen for the neighbouring seat of Cardiff West, and ended his career as Speaker of the House of Commons. Callaghan attributed his success to having turned up in a glamorous naval uniform, but perhaps equally helpful had been his reply to a question asking if he was a Catholic. "No, a Baptist", he replied, which enabled the many chapel-goers in the audience to vote for him in good conscience. Cardiff South was a good prospect, the defending Tory MP's majority being a mere 541 votes. Callaghan had no trouble in reversing this in the Labour landslide of July 1945, with a majority of more than 11,000. On becoming a candidate, he had dropped the name of Len, and chose henceforth to be known as James, or more usually Jim. When he reached the House of Commons, there was a further change in his nomenclature. Previously, he had always been known as '*Callagan*', with the h left silent. Tory MPs addressed him instead as '*Callahan*', with a silent g. He liked the sound of it, and this is how he has been known ever since.

Callaghan arrived at Westminster with something of a reputation as a left-winger. At the Labour Party conference, the preceding December, he had made a powerful speech supporting a resolution endorsing a large-scale programme of nationalisation, which was passed against the wishes of the party leadership. It had been moved by Ian Mikardo, later a leading light in the left-wing Tribune group, and, like Callaghan, a native of Portsmouth, though the two men were never close associates. Following the vote, Herbert Morrison, Labour's deputy leader, approached Mikardo and Callaghan and said: "Do you realise that you have just lost us the general election?" As soon as the government was formed, Callaghan was invited to become PPS to a junior minister, John Parker, the Under-Secretary for the Dominions. He resigned after a few months, when he voted – together with 22 other Labour MPs – against the terms of an American loan. For the next 22 months he was a backbencher, but one with independent views, though he was careful to keep his rebellions against the party whips to minimal proportions. He associated with the Keep Left group of Labour MPs, but declined to sign a report which they published calling for more Socialist-oriented policies. He did, however, lead a revolt in a parliamentary committee, which led to the government reducing the period of national service from 18 months to 12.

Then, in October 1947, he was appointed to his first government post, as Parliamentary Secretary for Transport, being switched to a similar position in the Admiralty, where as an ex-sailor he felt more at home, in March 1950. In both posts he made his mark as an energetic and competent minister, well able to take care of himself in the House and a good publicist outside. At the Admiralty, his senior minister, Viscount Hall, was in the House of Lords, and he made the most of his opportunity as spokesman for the department in the Commons. In March 1951, Hall left the government, and was replaced by Lord Pakenham (later Lord Longford). Callaghan had hoped to be promoted in his place, and had the temerity to write to the Prime Minister complaining that he had been overlooked. Somewhat surprisingly, Attlee, who was usually pretty short with unsolicited applicants for office, did not take it amiss and sent an emollient reply.

Seven months later, Labour was to lose the October 1951 general election and to embark on what turned out to be 13 dreary years in opposition. They were years, however, in which Callaghan's political career took a sharp upward turn. He was only one of perhaps 50 junior ministers in the Attlee government, and not the most prominent of them. Yet he took to opposition like a duck to water, was immediately elected in the annual ballot for 12 members of the Shadow Cabinet (elected by MPs), and was the only MP to be re-elected every year throughout the years of Tory power. Equally remarkable was his performance in the ballot for the constituency party section of Labour's NEC, usually dominated by left-wingers. He polled well every year he stood, and on six occasions was one of the seven MPs elected.

One key to his success was the quality of his speeches, both in the House of Commons, and at party conferences and meetings throughout the country. He was not a brilliant orator, but a highly confident and forceful speaker, with an almost unerring ability to gauge the feeling of an audience and to tell them what they wanted to hear. He was also one of the first British politicians to master the art of television, where he was a frequent performer in political discussion programmes. Equally important, however, was the assiduity with which he cultivated his fellow MPs, even the most obscure and undistinguished of them – they all had votes for the Shadow Cabinet! 1 well remember, as a young delegate to the annual Labour conference in the mid-1950s, spending an evening in his company and that of another Shadow minister, Michael Stewart. Callaghan challenged him to come up with some information about every member of the parliamentary Labour Party. Stewart, who embarked on the game with some reluctance, gave up after about 200, but Callaghan was able to provide details about all 277 of them. Popularly known as "Sunny Jim", Callaghan exuded an air of amiability, which concealed the fact that he was also on occasion capable of being a bully. He had few, if any, enemies in the party, carefully avoiding committing himself in the growing rivalry between Nye Bevan and Hugh Gaitskell, though he ended up as a supporter of the latter in the 1955 leadership election. What was important, he loudly proclaimed, was the unity of the party.

Callaghan's ascent was helped by the portfolios he was given to shadow. He started off with Transport, where his three years as a junior minister enabled him to speak with authority, but in 1956 Gaitskell switched him to the Colonies, where he was a great success over the next four years. He led a united party in its opposition to the government's attempt to force a settler-dominated federation on Southern and Northern Rhodesia and Nyasaland against the wishes of the African population. During this period he met virtually all the nationalist leaders (and future rulers) of British colonies and formed a good relationship with many of them. He was rewarded by topping the poll for the Shadow Cabinet in 1960, but in the same year failed to win the deputy leadership of the party on the death of Bevan, coming third to

190 James Callaghan

the right-winger George Brown and the left-wing Fred Lee. The following year, Callaghan received a crucial promotion, when Gaitskell, anxious to move the less than totally loyal Harold Wilson from the Shadow chancellorship, shifted him to Foreign Affairs and appointed Callaghan in his place. The party leader had some misgivings. Callaghan had proved himself an effective parliamentary performer and had achieved a prominent position in the party, but lacked economic credentials. At Tony Crosland's prompting, Nuffield College, Oxford – of which Callaghan was already an honorary fellow – assembled a distinguished cast of economists to offer him guidance. Gaitskell was not entirely satisfied, and there was much speculation that, if he formed a government, the actual job of Chancellor would go to somebody else. This might well have been Crosland, whose economic expertise was held in the highest regard by Gaitskell, or, just possibly, Douglas Houghton, Callaghan's old boss and a formidable authority on taxation matters. The unexpected death of Gaitskell in January 1963 put paid to such prospects. Callaghan himself was a candidate for the succession (see Chapter 14), achieving a respectable third place behind Wilson and George Brown, and almost certainly casting his own vote for Wilson in the second ballot. He was immediately confirmed in his position as Shadow Chancellor, though Wilson planned to reduce his potential powers as Chancellor by creating an economic diarchy between him and George Brown, who was pencilled in to take over a new and powerful department of Economic Affairs.

So it transpired, in October 1964, when Labour secured its narrow majority in the general election. Wilson's intention had been to produce a 'creative tension' between the two men, to prevent either from becoming so powerful as to constitute a challenge to his own leadership, but also to clip the wings of the Treasury, which Labour had long regarded as a baleful influence on the innovative intentions of reforming governments. It did not work out exactly as planned. There was tension, all right, but it was hardly creative and caused a maximum of frustration to both men. Callaghan was gradually to achieve the upper hand, largely due to the Treasury's control over spending and Brown's volatility and unpredictability. By the time of the July 1966 crisis, which culminated in Brown's removal to the Foreign Office and the effective collapse of his much vaunted National Plan, Callaghan's victory was almost complete. Michael Stewart, who succeeded Brown, inherited a much diminished Department of Economic Affairs. The triumph over Brown, his senior in party terms, did not mean that Callaghan was a successful Chancellor. His former occupation as an Inland Revenue official had left him with a sure touch on taxation matters, and he was responsible for introducing some successful innovations. Yet on economic policy, he was sadly out of his depth, though he nearly always put up a good show in defending his policies in parliamentary debates. He offered no resistance to Wilson's determination not to devalue in October 1964, though the pound was clearly seriously over-valued, and – more reprehensibly – acquiesced in his insistence that it should thenceforward be an unmentionable subject. He had a momentary wobble in July 1966, but thereafter was himself adamant that there should be no devaluation until the last moment, before the inevitable occurred in November 1967. He had one considerable achievement as Chancellor – the negotiation by the Group of Ten industrial countries, under his chairmanship, of Special Drawing Rights (SDRs), which greatly expanded international liquidity. Yet his own sense of failure when the devaluation was announced was almost complete, and he insisted on resigning, and prepared to leave the government. Wilson, however, was desperate that he should stay, and proposed that he should swap jobs with the Home Secretary, Roy Jenkins, to which Callaghan agreed. His own recommendation that Crosland should succeed him was ignored.

Callaghan went to the Home Office as a much chastened man, and for some time afterwards kept a low profile. Yet his spirits soon began to recover, and he established a firm control over his new department, where he proved a much less liberal figure than his predecessor. This was most clearly reflected in his introduction of the Commonwealth Immigration Act of 1968, which was rushed through Parliament in three days and was described by *The Times* as "Probably the most shameful measure that Labour members have ever been asked by their whips to support". It took away from Kenyan Asians with British passports the right to enter the United Kingdom, and went flatly against firm assurances given to them at the time of Kenyan independence by the then Colonial Secretary, Iain Macleod, who forcefully pointed this out in the parliamentary debate. Thirty-five Labour MPs voted against the Bill, but Callaghan was able to claim that most Labour MPs representing constituencies with large immigrant populations were strongly supportive of him, and that public opinion was predominantly on his side.

While at the Home Office, Callaghan was quietly consolidating his position within the Labour Party, and building up a power base for any future contest for the party leadership. In October 1967, while still Chancellor, he had contrived, through discreet lobbying of trade union leaders, to get himself elected to the treasurership of the Labour Party, defeating the left-wing candidate, Michael Foot, by more than 2-1. This post was of great symbolic significance, as it was the only position in the party chosen by all sections of the annual conference, but as the unions commanded 80 per cent of the votes their influence was predominant. From then on, they tended to think of Callaghan as *their* representative in the leadership of the party, and Callaghan increasingly saw himself as playing this role.

The crunch came, in early 1969, when the Employment Secretary, Barbara Castle, produced her proposals for trade union reform in the White Paper, *In Place of Strife*. As a former trade union official, Callaghan was horrified. Unions were voluntary bodies, who should be left to control their own affairs, he believed. This was not an appropriate matter for legislation. His view was widely supported within the parliamentary Labour Party and by the great mass of trade union activists. If Callaghan had restricted himself to arguing against Castle's proposals within the Cabinet nobody could reasonably have objected. He went much further – by breaking collective Cabinet responsibility, and casting his vote against the proposed measures in the Labour NEC, on 26 March, when a motion to reject the projected Bill was carried by 15 votes to 6. Wilson was outraged, and seriously considered dismissing Callaghan from the Cabinet, but in the end decided instead to exclude him from meetings of the so-called 'inner cabinet' of senior ministers. Callaghan's conduct made him the hero of backbench opponents of the proposed Bill, and of many trade unionists, but alienated most of his Cabinet colleagues who thought he had behaved shabbily. The ill-feeling, particularly with Wilson, persisted for some time, but Callaghan's position was largely vindicated the following June, when the government withdrew the Bill in the face of a declaration by the Chief Whip, Bob Mellish, that there was no chance of getting it through the Commons.

In August 1969, Callaghan's action, as Home Secretary, of sending troops to Northern Ireland to head off the threat of sectarian violence did a lot to restore his reputation. He was hailed by both sides of the divide as a conciliator, but unfortunately his handling of Northern Irish affairs had little beneficial effect in the long term, the province descending into large-scale terrorist violence during the succeeding year. It was left to the incoming government of Ted Heath to impose direct rule. For Callaghan, however, Ulster remained a distinct plus on his c.v., and the episode also helped to heal his relations with Harold Wilson.

192 James Callaghan

Labour's unexpected defeat in the June 1970 general election left Callaghan vying with Roy Jenkins as probable contenders for the succession if Wilson should stand down, which he quickly demonstrated was not his intention. The Labour Party was about to be plunged into violent controversy over its attitude towards the renewed British application for EEC entry, and it was this dispute which enabled Callaghan decisively to overtake Jenkins who previously had appeared the favourite. Callaghan, a confirmed Atlanticist, was lukewarm about Europe, but was far from being a doctrinaire opponent. Nevertheless, his fine political antennae soon detected that Labour and trade union opinion was shifting in an anti-EEC direction, and he decided to help it on its way in a speech of breathtaking cynicism, which he delivered in Southampton in May 1971. Seizing on an off-the-cuff remark by President Pompidou that he would like French to be the language of Europe, he expatiated on the virtues of the "language of Chaucer, Shakespeare and Milton", and concluded, in a passage drafted by his Eurosceptic son-in-law, Peter Jay: "If we are to prove our Europeanism by accepting that French is the dominant language in the Community, then the answer is quite clear, and I will say it in French to prevent any misunderstanding: *Non, merci beaucoup*."

Few observers doubted that Callaghan was offering himself as an alternative leader to Wilson if he did not oppose the membership terms being negotiated by Ted Heath, and this is certainly how Wilson himself interpreted the speech. He was determined not to be outflanked by Callaghan, and in the following weeks decisively shifted his position in an anti-EEC direction. By the autumn both men had settled on a common position, which won majority support at the TUC and Labour conferences, and within the parliamentary Labour Party. This was to oppose the Heath terms, but to seek to renegotiate them and then submit the result to a popular referendum. This prevented an immediate party split, and left the pro-European minority within the PLP with the invidious choice of voting either against their party or their convictions. As described in earlier chapters, 69 decided to vote in favour of the terms, and another 20 abstained, enabling British entry to go ahead.

After this episode, Callaghan seems to have concluded that he no longer had a realistic prospect of succeeding Wilson, who was four years his junior. Some years before, he had bought a farm in Sussex, which gave him a great deal of pleasure, and he even contemplated leaving politics altogether when Anthony Barber, the Chancellor of the Exchequer in the Heath government, proposed to nominate him as managing director of the International Monetary Fund, a proposal which was effectively stymied by Valéry Giscard D'Estaing, the French Finance Minister. Callaghan also had a serious prostate operation in early 1972, and though this was completely successful, it brought with it, in the words of his biographer, Kenneth O. Morgan, "the first intimations of mortality [and] had its psychological impact on Callaghan as for many men his age" (Morgan, 1977, p. 376). Wilson, too, probably sensed a slackening in Callaghan's ambition, and his more relaxed approach, and this enabled the two men to work together in unaccustomed harmony for the remainder of their years in opposition, and in government after the February 1974 general election.

Following the election, Callaghan went to the Foreign Office, the only person, other than R.A. Butler, to have filled all of the three senior ministerial posts of Chancellor, Home Secretary and Foreign Secretary. As in his earlier posts, his record was mixed. He was generally judged to have fallen too much under the influence of his US colleague, Henry Kissinger, and he badly mishandled the Cyprus crisis in April 1974. He failed to act decisively as the representative of one of the three countries named as guarantors of Cypriot independence, and must bear a heavy responsibility for the subsequent Turkish invasion, which led to the partition of the island. But the crucial task handed to Callaghan in his new post was to renegotiate British membership of the EEC, and on that he played a blinder. Despite his earlier opposition to British membership, he and Wilson were agreed – implicitly, if not in as many words – that the best outcome of the renegotiation was one which would enable Britain to remain within the Community. He embarked on the negotiation in the style of a trade union leader pursuing a major wage claim, banging his demands down heavily on the table, and then involving himself in prolonged haggling over the details before emerging and claiming that he had got the best bargain available – even though it bore little relation to his opening bid. It worked. Although many of the concessions which he won turned out in the long term to be merely cosmetic, the package he brought back appeared substantial enough to persuade many doubters that it was a marked improvement on the Heath terms. As recounted in Chapter 14, it enabled the government to win a sweeping 2-1 majority in the June 1975 referendum, prevented a split in the Labour Party and closed the issue of British membership, not unfortunately for all time, but at least for half a decade.

Wilson concluded that Callaghan was a safe pair of hands, and at the end of the year – through a Cabinet colleague, Harold Lever – sent him a confidential message that he intended to resign in three months' time and that Callaghan should prepare himself for the succession. He was as good as his word, and when, on 16 March 1976, he announced his decision to the Cabinet, Callaghan was the best prepared of the six contenders who emerged. Two of these – Michael Foot and Tony Benn – were from the left, and three – Roy Jenkins, Denis Healey and Tony Crosland – from the centre-right. Callaghan himself was bang in the centre, but his real strength lay in the fact that he had made very few enemies during his long political apprenticeship. His two strongest rivals were undoubtedly Foot and Jenkins, but each suffered from the weaknesses of the very qualities which had brought them to prominence. Foot had been the political heir of Nye Bevan, and much the most eloquent advocate of left-wing policies – this had brought him many admirers, but as many critics. The same was true of Jenkins, whose passionate support of the cause of European integration had been triumphantly vindicated in the 1975 referendum, but had left him in a minority within his own party, and it was only the pro-Europeans who were now ready to support him. Callaghan had never stood out strongly for any political objectives (other than his opposition to trade union reform) and so had avoided alienating any significant bloc of Labour MPs. He was to be elected *faute de mieux*, on the third ballot, by 176 votes to 137 for Foot, after Foot had led him on the first ballot by 90 votes to 84. Callaghan had succeeded in picking up a large majority of the second preference votes for the four other candidates who had withdrawn or been eliminated.

On forming his government, Callaghan made a number of personnel changes. He kept Healey on as Chancellor, but preferred Crosland to Jenkins as Foreign Secretary, which prompted the latter to accept an invitation to become President of the European Commission. Callaghan let it be known that he intended that, at a later date, Healey and Crosland would swap jobs, a plan which was thwarted by Crosland's sudden death, in February 1977, when he was succeeded by the much younger David Owen. The other key appointment was Michael Foot, as Leader of the House of Commons, who became – with Healey – Callaghan's closest collaborator. Much to her chagrin, Barbara Castle was peremptorily dropped. From the outset, Callaghan created a good impression as Prime Minister. If he had not been a conspicuous success in his earlier posts, he had at least accumulated a great deal of experience, and he presented himself as a tried and trusted servant of the state, firmer and more straightforward than Wilson, and oozing avuncular charm and reassurance.

Yet the legacy he took over from Wilson was a forbidding one: a tiny parliamentary majority and a host of economic problems. The most serious of these appeared to be inflation – down from the horrendous 26 per cent recorded the previous summer, but still a stubborn 13 per cent, and expected to rise again. Fresh pressure was also building up on the pound sterling, which the government desperately hoped to reverse. The twin policy on which it embarked was to combine wage restraint with cuts in government expenditure. In July 1976, agreement was reached with the TUC and the Confederation of British Industry (CBI) for a 5 per cent limit on pay increases, with a maximum of £4 a week. This resulted in a considerable decline in living standards, and a year later the unions were not prepared formally to agree on a limitation. The government, however, set a target of 10 per cent for wage increases, and largely imposed it within the public sector, while sanctions were imposed on private firms which breached the guidelines. On public expenditure, the government believed it had done as much as anybody could reasonably expect, when, in July 1976, Healey announced cuts of £1 billion, in addition to those he had already made in his two previous budgets. Despite the fact that both the inflation rate and the balance of payments were improving, however, international confidence remained low, and the slide in the pound continued. By September, it had fallen to $1.56, from $1.93 when Callaghan had taken over. Healey concluded that the only way to staunch the flow was to seek a massive loan from the International Monetary Fund – $3.9 billion, the largest that the IMF had ever been asked for. The IMF demanded further spending cuts of £1.4 billion, to which the Cabinet reluctantly agreed, after a long series of meetings at which Crosland, the Foreign Secretary, had cogently argued that cuts on this scale were unnecessary. He persuaded the majority of his colleagues, but Callaghan eventually came down on Healey's side, and Crosland backed down on the basis that the Prime Minister and Chancellor could not be seen to be overridden on a central issue of economic policy. In the event, less than half the loan was taken up and the balance of payments rose rapidly into surplus, which retrospectively corroborated Crosland's judgement, but by then he was already dead. By then, too, Labour had lost its parliamentary majority through by-election losses and defections, and in March 1977 faced the imminent prospect of defeat on a confidence motion tabled by Margaret Thatcher, which would have precipitated an immediate general election.

At the last minute, Callaghan, using all his skills as a trade union 'fixer', negotiated the Lib–Lab pact with Liberal leader David Steel, which guaranteed Liberal backing in key parliamentary votes in exchange for policy consultations. This was a masterstroke: the pact not only provided him with security of tenure, but increased his ability to resist left-wing demands for more Socialistic legislation. He and his government used the period of respite well, and by the summer of 1978 they had built up a strong position for themselves, with their economic policies working well, while Callaghan had established himself as an influential figure in world affairs, being treated as a respected partner by Presidents Carter and Giscard D'Estaing and by Chancellor Helmut Schmidt. It was then that Callaghan threw it all away, by what can only be described as a serious loss of nerve.

He made two crucial errors of judgement – in both cases without adequate consultation with his Cabinet or even his closest political advisers. The first concerned the continuation of the government's incomes policy, which, in the view of the authors of the 1979 Nuffield Election Study (Butler and Kavanagh, 1980, p. 22), had "worked far better than expected". The union leaders, aware that pressure from their members was building up fast after several years of restraint, were unwilling to agree a voluntary limit for wage settlements. Furthermore, both

Jack Jones, of the Transport Workers' Union, and Hugh Scanlon, of the Engineers, powerful left-wing figures who had co-operated with the government over wage restraint, had retired and had been succeeded by weaker figures less inclined, and less able, to be co-operative. Inflation was now down to 8 per cent, but there was little confidence that it would not rise again. Callaghan unilaterally insisted on a limit of 5 per cent, with another 2 per cent for "anomalies". Even his Chancellor, Denis Healey, a hawk on incomes policy, thought this too rigid and inflexible, and few Cabinet members thought that it could be sustained in the face of mammoth pay claims expected in the autumn. A 10 per cent target would have been more feasible, most felt. In terms of public relations, however, a 5 per cent limit had much to commend it, as it would suggest to the electors that a reduction of inflation to 5 per cent or less was in the offing. This would have gone down well if Callaghan had held an election in October 1978, before the wage round began; it was tempting providence to delay the poll until after it had been put to the test.

The objective case for holding the election in October was overwhelming. All the evidence was that the economic indicators had greatly improved, but were likely to deteriorate by early in 1979. Labour had regained the lead in the opinion polls, and the fact that Callaghan made no effort to persuade the Liberals to extend the Lib-Lab pact when it expired at the end of July led to the almost universal expectation that the election was imminent. This was reinforced by unofficial briefings given – in good faith – by Callaghan's political adviser, Tom McNally, that polling day would be on 5 October. The probability is that this was Callaghan's intention in early August, when he left for a short month on his Sussex farm, but he subsequently changed his mind, without however telling anybody. He did make a ritual effort to consult his Cabinet, asking them to send him by post their preferred election dates. The majority wanted an early poll, though Michael Foot, and to a lesser degree, Denis Healey, favoured delay.

Callaghan bluntly announced to the Cabinet, when it met on 7 September, that there would be no autumn election, and repeated the message to an incredulous nation in a television broadcast the same evening. It was possible, in party terms, to make a reasonable case for delay, as a Labour victory was by no means assured, though Labour would probably have entered the campaign as favourite, given Callaghan's high standing in the country and his large personal lead over Margaret Thatcher in the polls. What was highly imprudent was to dispense with the safety belt of a renewed pact, either with the Liberals, or alternatively with the Ulster Unionists or the Scottish Nationalists (both of whom might well have been open to offers), to see him through the winter and guard against the possibility of a surprise parliamentary defeat. The responsibility for taking this risk was Callaghan's alone, and it was his second major error.

The sequel was far worse than anybody predicted, and has gone down in history as "the winter of discontent". Pay restraint was voted down by large majorities at the annual TUC and Labour Party conferences, and an avalanche of pay claims greatly exceeding the 5 per cent limit were tabled. The floodgates opened, in early December, when the Ford Motor Company, after a three-week strike, settled for 17 per cent – a figure far higher than public sector employers could possibly afford. This did not prevent their unions, notably the National Union of Public Employees, from demanding parity and launching a series of highly damaging strikes by lorry drivers, oil tanker drivers, and, above all, local government and health service workers, which effectively destroyed any hopes of a Labour victory in an early election. It was not the economic effects of the strikes which hurt Labour, but the psychological impact of 'human interest' stories reported on television: stories of the dead remaining unburied and the sick being refused admission to hospitals. In a few short weeks Labour's main electoral

196 James Callaghan

asset – its ability to get on well with the trade unions – was cruelly mauled, and the Tory lead in the opinion polls shot up to a massive 20 per cent by early February.

Callaghan contributed to his own discomfiture by his response to reporters when he was interviewed at London's Heathrow airport, on his return from a summit conference on the lush French Caribbean island of Guadeloupe. Asked to comment on the "crisis", he unwisely replied that no crisis existed, and the pro-Tory newspapers were not slow to draw the contrast between the Prime Minister sunning himself on West Indian beaches and the suffering British public. The first direct evidence that the industrial strife was hurting Labour came on 1 March, when Welsh and Scottish electors voted in a referendum on whether to establish devolved parliaments in Cardiff and Edinburgh. The Welsh proposals had long been given up for lost, but the Scottish ones had enjoyed strong public support, with a consistent majority of nearly two-to-one in opinion polls. In the event, they scraped through by the tiny margin of 51.6 per cent to 48.8 per cent – not enough to enable the proposals to go through under the terms of the Scottish Devolution Act. It was immediately clear that the disappointing result was due to the deep unpopularity of the government following the January strikes. The Scottish Nationalist MPs, in their frustration, turned against the government, and suicidally decided to support a non-confidence motion tabled by Margaret Thatcher, which would precipitate them into a general election which they were ill-prepared to fight. The Liberals too – no longer beholden to the pact – prepared to vote against the government, as did the bulk of the Ulster Unionists.

The result was bound to be desperately close, but Callaghan – devastated by the conduct of the trade unions – seemed to have lost the will to fight on. He vetoed three separate initiatives proposed by his fellow ministers to stave off defeat, including concessions to the Ulster Unionists, and the offer by the wife of a dying Labour MP to bring her husband to the environs of the House in an ambulance, so that he could be 'nodded through' the division lobby by the whips, as was allowed by the Standing Orders of the House. Any one of these would almost certainly have saved the day, as the motion was lost, on 28 March, by a single vote – 311 to 310 – and Callaghan found himself to be the first British Prime Minister in more than 50 years to be trapped into fighting a general election at a time not of his own choosing. Many of his ministers privately felt that he was more concerned with his reputation than with the survival of his government. The influence of his self-effacing but strong-minded wife, Audrey, was suspected. She was determined, they felt, that her husband should be remembered as a man of principle rather than as a wheeler-dealer.

Had Labour won the vote, the government could probably have held on until the following October, when its general election chances would have been rather better, as the rawest memories of the winter of discontent began to fade. It is improbable, however, that it could have won – the damage had been too great. As it was, Callaghan fought a highly dignified campaign in April, drawing strength from his massive lead over Thatcher in public esteem, as measured by the polls. He succeeded in making up some ground during the campaign, but the Tories won a comfortable majority on 3 May, when the result was:

Conservative	339
Labour	269
Liberal	11
Others	16
Conservative majority	43

Callaghan's premiership was the end of an era. He represented the best – and some of the worst – of 'old' Labour. Fixated on the triumphs of the 1945 government, he had no vision of the future and no strong political convictions, other than to improve the lot of working men (he was not much of a feminist). Deeply conservative (with a small 'c'), he was not, despite his many qualities, the person to lead his party down fresh paths, as was desperately needed. He seems to have sensed this himself, remarking to his political adviser, Bernard Donoughue, during the 1979 campaign:

> There are times, perhaps once every thirty years, when there is a sea-change in politics. It then does not matter what you say or what you do. There is a shift in what the public wants and what it approves of. I suspect there is now such a sea-change – and it is for Mrs Thatcher.
>
> *(Morgan, 1977, p. 269)*

Callaghan would have been well advised to give up the party leadership immediately after the election, when, almost certainly, he would have been succeeded by Healey, his evident preferred choice. Instead, he hung on for a further year, fighting a forlorn rearguard action against left-wing forces for the control of the party. Healey was then narrowly beaten by Michael Foot, a distinguished parliamentarian but who was to prove an ineffectual leader, and whose election was soon followed by a party split leading to the creation of the Social Democratic Party. Callaghan himself settled comfortably into the role of elder statesman, which merged into a serene old age.

Note

1 This was the title of a profile I wrote for *The Economist*, in the last week of his premiership, in April 1979. Forty-two years later, I see no need to revise this judgement.

Works consulted

David Butler and Dennis Kavanagh, 1980, *The British General Election of 1979*, London, Macmillan.
James Callaghan, 1987, *Time and Chance*, London, Collins.
Ken Coates (ed.), 1979, *What Went Wrong*, Nottingham, Spokesman.
Peter Kellner and Christopher Hitchens, 1976, *Callaghan: The Road to Number Ten* London, Cassell.
Kenneth O. Morgan, 1997, *Callaghan: A Life*, Oxford, Oxford University Press.
Howard R. Penniman (ed.) , 1981, *Britain at the Polls, 1979*, Washington, DC, American Enterprise Institute.

17

MARGARET THATCHER

Grocer's daughter to Iron Lady

When Alfred Roberts, a Grantham grocer, and his wife, Beatrice, had their second and last child, on 13 October 1925, they apparently hoped to have a son, rather than a sister, for their 4-year-old daughter, Muriel. Beatrice, indeed, may never have got over her disappointment, and seems to have failed to develop a warm, loving relationship with the child, who was named Margaret Hilda. Alfred reacted differently, treating her exactly the same as if she were a boy, and the young Margaret grew up doing everything she could to meet her father's expectations, always declaring that he was the role-model for her life.

Alfred Roberts was a formidable figure. The son of a Northampton shoe-maker, he left school at 13, to work in the tuck shop at Oundle, the boys' 'public' school, moving on to a series of jobs in grocery shops before becoming, at the age of 21, the manager of a grocery store in the Lincolnshire market town of Grantham. After six years, he had saved enough to take out a mortgage and buy his own shop, with living accommodation upstairs, on the outskirts of the town. Working immensely hard, he and Beatrice were soon able to expand, by taking over two neighbouring shops, and opening a sub-post office, as well as a branch in another part of the town. By the time that Margaret was born, the family was already prosperous, but the household was conducted in a highly parsimonious manner, with no labour-saving devices, and all the girls' clothes being made by Beatrice, a skilled dressmaker. The frugality of their lifestyle was attributed to Alfred's strong religious principles. A Wesleyan Methodist local preacher, and strict Sabbatarian, his daughters attended church four times each Sunday, and were discouraged from participating in frivolous entertainments. Alfred also became a leading local government figure in Grantham, being elected to the town council in 1927, reaching the aldermanic bench in 1943, and serving as Mayor in 1945–46. Originally a Liberal, he was elected as an Independent, which in Grantham, as in many other small towns at that time, effectively meant Conservative.

Margaret's most thorough biographer so far, John Campbell, casts doubt on whether she was quite so devoted a daughter to Alderman Roberts as she later claimed, pointing out that, after she left Grantham for good at the age of 18, she only returned on very rare occasions to visit her parents. (Nor, according to the political scientist, Sir Bernard Crick, was the alderman quite such an estimable character as she makes out. In 1997, he recounted in *Punch* magazine

DOI: 10.4324/9781003031963-18

(21 June 1997), how he had been told by elderly Grantham residents that he had a reputation for paying low wages and groping his female shop assistants.) Nevertheless, Campbell identified in her three qualities which she clearly owed to her father's precepts and example. First, he argues, it was he "who instilled in her the habit of hard work, as something both virtuous in itself and the route to self-advancement". Second, he gave her a powerful impulse towards public service – "her restless belief in her duty to put the world to rights was only a projection on a wider stage of the same missionary impulse which took Alfred from the pulpit of Finkin Street church to the council chamber". His third, "and perhaps most important legacy" was, he argues,

> an exceptionally powerful moral sense. More than anything else in her political make-up, it was her fierce confidence that she knew right from wrong – even if what was right was not always immediately attainable – which marked Margaret Thatcher out from contemporary politicians ... This rare moral certainty and unreflective self-righteousness was her greatest political strength in the muddy world of political expediency and compromise; it was also in the end her greatest weakness.
>
> *(Campbell, 2001, pp. 30–1)*

What she did not get from her father, Campbell asserts, was her anger and aggression, the root of which he believes was an internalised revolt against the narrow provincialism in which she was brought up and to which she outwardly conformed.

Apart from her father, the greatest influence on the young Margaret Roberts was growing up during the Second World War. This made her immensely patriotic, spurred by the nationalistic poetry of Rudyard Kipling and the leadership of Winston Churchill, whom she hero-worshipped. It also helped to shape her later attitudes both to Europe and the United States. Europeans, she grew to believe, lacked backbone – they had supinely succumbed in the face of the Nazi threat. Americans, on the other hand, of whom there were many in the Grantham area, which was surrounded by US Air Force bases, had come to Britain's aid, and the two countries had then gone on together to liberate the feckless West Europeans.

Margaret Roberts attended a local grammar school, the Kesteven and Grantham Girls School, where she was noted for her diligence and serious attitude. She was usually at or near the top of the class, but was regarded as lacking in imagination and a sense of humour. She early decided to aim at university, and perhaps already in her teens dreamed of a political career. She was offered places at Nottingham University and at Bedford College, London, but – against the advice of her headmistress – decided to sit the scholarship examination for Somerville College, Oxford. She did not win a scholarship, but was offered a place, and in October 1943, just 18, she went up to Oxford to study for a degree in chemistry.

She did not fit in very well at Somerville, where the ambience – personified by the principal, Dame Janet Vaughan – was frankly left-wing and imbued with the spirit of wartime idealism and egalitarianism. Margaret Roberts not only loudly proclaimed herself a Tory, but one with stridently right-wing views, which did not go down well even with the bulk of her fellow Conservatives, who were mostly on the progressive wing of the party. This did not prevent her from becoming a keen member of the Oxford University Conservative Association, of which she eventually became President. On Sundays, she attended the Wesley Memorial Church, and she was active in student Christian groups, even to the extent of preaching – like her father – in local village churches. Yet her primary commitment was clearly to politics, and in the 1945 general election campaign, she hastened back to Grantham, where – at the age of 19 – she acted as a warm-up speaker at meetings held by the local Conservative candidate. Despite the best efforts of what the local paper described as "the very youthful Miss M.H. Roberts, daughter of Alderman A. Roberts of Grantham", the candidate unexpectedly went down to heavy defeat against the sitting Independent MP, who had snatched the seat from the Tories in a wartime by-election.

Margaret came to regret studying chemistry, which was not very relevant to a political career, but at least it would enable her to earn a living while she sought to put her feet on the lower rungs of the political ladder. She left Oxford in June 1947, with a good Second Class degree, to work as a research chemist for a plastics company in Colchester. She joined the local Young Conservatives, and the following year attended the annual Conservative conference at Llandudno, where she was introduced to the chairman of the Dartford Conservative Association, who was looking for a candidate for his constituency, a Labour stronghold in east Kent. Aged 23, she faced competition from four male opponents at the subsequent selection conference, in January 1949, but made an astonishingly favourable impression and was chosen unanimously. She also missed the last train back to London, and a local businessman in the audience gallantly offered her a lift in his car. His name was Denis Thatcher.

She was to fight two general elections at Dartford – in 1950 and 1951 – and proved an immensely popular candidate among the Tory rank-and-file, who were entranced by her enthusiasm, boundless energy and the ferocity with which she excoriated the Labour government. Two months after the second contest, she was to marry Denis Thatcher, who became, in her own words, the "rock" on which she was to build her career. A divorcé, whose first wife had also been called Margaret, he was the head of a family paint-manufacturing business, which was subsequently taken over by Burmah Oil, of which he was to become a director. An affable, sport-loving man, with strong but unsophisticated political views which chimed in well with Margaret's own, his wealth was sufficient to enable her to drop her work as a chemist and read for the bar, where she was to qualify as a tax lawyer. Her 'bachelor girl' digs were exchanged for a luxury flat in Chelsea, and when their twin children, Mark and Carol, were born two years later there was no difficulty about paying for childcare and, later, expensive school fees. It would be unjust to suggest that Margaret married Denis for his money; there was a strong basis of love and affection in the marriage, but it undoubtedly greatly reduced the pressures on her as she single-mindedly pursued her way up the 'greasy pole'.

Margaret Thatcher was now determined to land a safe Tory seat, and hoped to use the contacts which she had built up with Kent Tory MPs to help her on her way. These included Ted Heath, elected in 1950 for Bexley, a neighbouring seat to Dartford, but her highest hopes were fixed on Sir Alfred Bossom, the elderly and enormously rich MP for Maidstone, who took a fatherly interest in this attractive young woman whom he hoped would be his successor. It was not to be, and Thatcher encountered a marked resistance to selecting a woman candidate in several other seats which she sought. It was only in 1958 that she enjoyed better luck – in Finchley, a north London suburban constituency, where she was narrowly chosen, despite strenuous efforts by the retiring MP, Sir John Crowder, to prevent her selection. As at Dartford, Thatcher threw herself wholeheartedly into the task of nursing the seat, and had built up a large and enthusiastic local following by the time of the 1959 general election, when she was returned with the very comfortable majority of 16,260. She was five days short of her 34th birthday.

The 1959 election was the apogee of the Macmillan premiership, and Thatcher was one of no fewer than 365 MPs who crammed the Tory benches. Much remarked as the youngest and most glamorous of the dozen Tory women MPs, few if any observers noticed her most significant characteristic. This was that she was not – as she herself confirmed much later – a "consensus politician". This marked her out as different from the vast majority of Conservative MPs. Though, for electoral reasons, they deliberately exaggerated the differences which separated them from their Labour counterparts, in their hearts and in their private conversations, they recognised that these were, in reality, only marginal. They were fully signed up to the welfare state, enacted by their political opponents, and to the mixed economy, where the only serious difference was whether the steel industry should be in the private or the public sector. This apparent unity of approach was personified by the term "Butskellism", conflating the names of Rab Butler and Hugh Gaitskell, coined by a journalist on *The Economist*, but in wide circulation in the 1950s and 1960s. Thatcher did not go along with this – the Manichean world view she had inherited from her father led her to believe that she was engaged in an unending struggle with evil, which she interpreted as 'Socialism', making precious little distinction between the Labour Party and Soviet Communism. Nevertheless, she was intensely ambitious and was shrewd enough to recognise that if she wanted to get on she must suppress her instincts and conform to the prevailing view. At Westminster she was seen as a typical moderate Conservative; in her speeches in Finchley, however, reported only in the local press, she gave vent to much more full-blooded language, which was also reflected – though more obliquely – in her Conservative conference speeches. Looking round among her fellow Tory MPs, she recognised a few kindred spirits. One of these was Enoch Powell, but he was controversial, and she avoided getting too close to him.

She had an immediate stroke of luck in drawing third place in the ballot for Private Members' Bills, which meant that, very unusually, her maiden speech was devoted to introducing her own piece of legislation. This was a relatively minor Bill to improve the access of the press to local government committee meetings, but it was duly passed and she won widespread and highly flattering coverage in the national press. Within two years she had joined the government, the first MP elected in 1959 to be promoted and the youngest ever woman minister. She served for three years as Joint Parliamentary Secretary for Pensions and National Insurance until the Conservative election defeat in October 1964. Here she won high marks for her efficient conduct of business and her confident and highly combative parliamentary performances. On the debit side, was the widespread feeling, in her own party as well as the opposition, that she was instinctively unsympathetic to the welfare claimants who were her department's main responsibility. She was also felt to be rather too ready to upstage her minister, the aristocratic and retiring Richard Wood, later Lord Holderness.

After the general election, she became something of a workhorse for the Tory opposition, filling a succession of junior Shadow posts, and – with her tax lawyer's expertise – excelling herself by exposing a whole series of ill-thought-out measures in James Callaghan's budgets of 1966 and 1967. When Ted Heath was elected as Tory leader in 1965, he decided that he should have a token woman in his Shadow Cabinet, and James Prior, his PPS, suggested Thatcher. In his memoirs, he recounts Heath's response:

> There was a long silence. 'Yes', he said, 'Willie [Whitelaw, the Chief Whip] agrees she's much the most able, but he says that once she's there we'll never be able to get rid of her. So we both think it's got to be Mervyn Pike'.
>
> *(Prior, 1986, p. 42)*

Miss Pike, also a former junior minister, was regarded as an agreeable but unambitious colleague whom nobody seriously expected to rise much above her present level. The fact that she was preferred to Thatcher strongly suggests that the latter was regarded as altogether too pushy and opinionated. In fact, by 1967, Pike withdrew on the grounds of ill health, and there was then no alternative to appointing Thatcher, who was strongly backed by the Shadow Chancellor, Iain Macleod. She then became in rapid succession the Shadow minister for power, for transport, and, finally, for education.

After the June 1970 election, Heath duly appointed her Education Secretary, and she soon became one of his most controversial ministers, notorious for her early move to abolish free milk in primary schools. This earned her the tag "Margaret Thatcher, milk snatcher", and she was described by *The Sun* as "The most unpopular woman in Britain". In fact, her record at Education was, on balance, a creditable one. Her decision on free milk was taken in the face of enormous pressure from the Treasury for spending cuts, which she largely fended off, offering only this small token so as not to make any economies which would damage *educational* needs. In particular, she preserved the infant Open University, which the incoming Chancellor, Iain Macleod, who died soon after, had earmarked as a prize candidate for the chop. Later she was able to win additional funds for raising the school-leaving age and expanding the newly-established polytechnics. She was hardly an enthusiast for comprehensive schools, and infuriated many local authorities (including some under Tory control) by the pernickety way in which she considered their change-over plans, but more plans were approved during her period than under any other minister, Labour or Conservative. Within the department, civil servants found her excessively impatient and abrasive, and there were many rows with senior officials, usually sparked off by her attempts to exceed her statutory powers. This was, to some extent, offset by her personal concern for the welfare of her staff, and she came to be admired for the forceful way in which she stood up for the interests of the department.

Thatcher's relations with the Prime Minister were formally correct, and, indeed, somewhat fawning on her part. At no time did she emerge as a critic of his policies, even if, in retrospect, she claimed to have misgivings. It is clear, however, that he found her a somewhat tiresome colleague. He instinctively reacted against her gushing manner, and her adopted persona as a prosperous, middle-class, Home Counties lady. He thought that she talked too much in Cabinet, and took care to seat her at the far end of the table, out of his eye-line. He did not take her seriously as a contender, when she challenged him for the party leadership after his second successive general election defeat in October 1974, reportedly telling her, "You'll lose", when she, out of courtesy, informed him of her decision. Thatcher's emergence as a candidate owed much to opportunism, but also to her natural combativeness and a newly developed conviction. Although, as we have seen, she had never inwardly subscribed to the consensual approach of her colleagues, she had hitherto lacked an ideological basis for challenging it. This was now provided for her by Keith Joseph, who had been Health and Social Security Minister in the Heath government, and the only Cabinet minister known to have had serious doubts about the direction of his policies. A high-minded Jewish baronet, who was given to agonising about the effects of policies which he had agreed, he gradually became converted to the monetarist ideas previously championed by Enoch Powell and the right-wing think tank, the Institute of Economic Affairs. Strongly influenced by the Chicago economist Milton Friedman, they repudiated Keynesian ideas for running the economy, and proclaimed that the rampant threat of inflation could only be combated by strict control of the monetary supply, that is by deflating the economy. Heath's attempts to control prices and wages by a statutory policy and direct intervention in industry only made the situation worse, in their view. Joseph prepared to challenge Heath for the Tory leadership in the autumn of 1974, but effectively destroyed his chances by an 'over the top' speech in Birmingham, in which he suggested that "our human stock" was threatened by the birth of too many children to adolescent mothers "in social classes four and five". In the face of the anger and ridicule which this provoked, Joseph withdrew from the battle, and when Edward Du Cann, the leader of the Tory backbenchers, also ruled himself out, Thatcher leapt into the fray, with Joseph's blessing.

It required guts for her to do so, but perhaps she was not risking all that much. Only if she polled a derisory vote would she have been seriously damaged, and she would surely have advanced her standing in the party, and won the gratitude of the new leader, if she sufficiently undermined Heath to make him vulnerable in the second ballot, when weightier candidates, notably Willie Whitelaw, could be expected to make themselves available. Hardly anybody at that stage saw her as anything more than a 'stalking horse'. She owed her actual election to the Machiavellian tactics of her campaign manager, Airey Neave, a former Intelligence officer. He deliberately under-estimated her support, telling enquirers that she was "doing well but not well enough", so as to encourage anti-Heath MPs who wanted the chance to vote for another candidate to support her in the first ballot. Neave later admitted to having 120 firm promises, but put it about that she was sure of only 70 votes. In the event, she polled 130, against 119 for Heath, and such was her momentum that there was nothing to stop her in the second ballot (see Chapter 15).

Thatcher did not shine as leader of the opposition against either Wilson or Callaghan. The latter, in particular, patronised her to an appalling extent in their clashes in the House, and nearly always came out on top. Nor did she make a positive impact in the country: her opinion poll ratings remained poor, even though her party was ahead for most of the period between 1976 and 1978. After Callaghan had bolstered his position through the operation of the Lib-Lab pact, it began to look as though her chances of leading the Tories to an election victory were slipping away. It is, indeed, highly unlikely that she would have succeeded if Callaghan – as everyone expected – had seized the favourable opportunity of an election in October 1978. If that had happened, and she had gone down to defeat, she would most probably have been dumped in short order by the Tories, and would have rated no more than a footnote in the history books. As it was, the "winter of discontent" which followed Callaghan's miscalculation (see Chapter 16) opened the way for her to be the longest-serving Prime Minister of the century and one of those who had the greatest impact on the country's destiny.

Elected with a majority of 43 seats, on 3 May 1979, her new Cabinet appeared to be dominated by former associates of Ted Heath, few if any of whom had voted for her in the leadership election three years earlier. Thus Lord Carrington became Foreign Secretary, with Ian Gilmour as Foreign Affairs spokesman in the Commons, Willie Whitelaw, Home Secretary, James Prior, Employment Secretary, Norman St John-Stevas, Leader of the Commons, Lord Soames, Leader of the Lords, Francis Pym, Defence Secretary, Peter Walker, Agriculture Secretary, and so on. They were the most prominent figures in the party and she could not afford to leave them out, especially as she had refused to include Heath. From the outset, however, the new Prime Minister was determined to keep the main economic portfolios in the hands of people sympathetic to her recently acquired monetarist convictions, people she habitually referred to as "one of us". She would have liked to make Joseph Chancellor of the Exchequer, but regarded him as too unstable, and instead chose Sir Geoffrey Howe, the former Solicitor-General, who had been a key figure in the Heath government, but was, like her, a convert to monetarism. John Biffen, formerly a close associate of Enoch Powell and a monetarist of long standing, became Chief Secretary to the Treasury, and John Nott, a merchant banker, President of the Board of Trade. These three, together with the Energy Secretary, David Howell, formed a sort of 'inner cabinet' on economic policy, from which Prior was ostentatiously excluded.

It was the successive budgets of Geoffrey Howe, and after 1983 of his successor, Nigel Lawson, which were the main instruments of Thatcher's monetarist policies. The first of these, in June 1979, made a resounding impact. Trailed as a tax-cutting budget, it reduced the standard rate of income tax from 33 to 30 per cent, and the maximum marginal rate from 83 to 60 per cent. Projected cuts in public spending, of 3 per cent or more, by no means made up for the loss in revenue, which was made good by a near doubling of value-added tax (VAT), which was consolidated at a single rate of 15 per cent. Thatcher seemed oblivious of the fact that this would have a devastating effect on inflation, still just under 10 per cent when she was elected but soon to rise above 20 per cent, or that the public spending cuts would boost the unemployment figures. This was not, however, lost on some of her Cabinet ministers, including Prior (who privately described the budget as "a disaster"), Gilmour and Walker. Thatcher quickly dubbed colleagues who queried her policies as 'wets'. As well as these three, their numbers grew over the next year to include Stevas, Pym, Soames and Carrington, though the latter spent so much time abroad that he was seldom around to support his colleagues when their fears were expressed in Cabinet meetings. Whitelaw also broadly sympathised with the wets' approach, but he had determined from the start to be a super-loyal colleague of Thatcher, and her main buttress of support, so he usually refrained from weighing in on their side.

Howe's second budget, in March 1980, added a further sharp twist to the deflationary screw, pitching the country into a deep recession. In Hugo Young's words:

A uniquely painful experiment was being made … By the date of its second anniversary, the Government had presided over the biggest fall in total output in one year since 1931, and the biggest collapse in industrial production in one year since 1921. Unemployment, up by a million in the past twelve months, was rising towards the once unimaginable total of three million.

(Young, 1993, pp. 232–3)

Moreover, despite the deflationary policy, inflation had leapt to 20 per cent, while high interest rates and an over-valued pound were having a severe effect on exports and dealing a body blow to manufacturing industry. To all, except its most uncritical supporters, the government's policy appeared to be a ghastly failure. Thatcher was unshaken, saying, "After almost any operation, you feel worse before you convalesce. But you do not refuse the operation when you know that without it you will not survive." Nevertheless, by the autumn of 1980, the almost universal expectation was that she would soon abandon the policy, and perform a U-turn, as Heath's government had done at a similar stage, in 1972. Thatcher defiantly rejected this course in her speech to the 1980 Tory conference. In words deftly chosen by her speechwriter, the playwright, Ronald Millar, she alluded to the title of a once well known play by Christopher Fry (*The Lady's Not for Burning*), saying: "You turn if you want to. The lady's not for turning."

Howe went on to introduce yet another deflationary budget, in April 1981, but the following July, when he presented a paper to the Cabinet proposing further spending cuts of £5 billion in the following year, the Cabinet exploded in open revolt. Leader of the rebellion was the Environment Secretary, Michael Heseltine, appalled by widespread rioting in the Toxteth area of Liverpool, which he believed to have been the consequence of the mounting unemployment which Howe's policies had produced. Not only all the leading wets but even Biffen and Nott joined in the criticism, and Joseph and Leon Brittan (now Chief Secretary) were the only ministers to back Howe up. He was instructed to go away and do his sums again. This, effectively, marked the end of the extremist phase of monetarism. Henceforth it was applied in a gentler, more sensitive and attenuated form by Howe, and by his successor, Nigel Lawson. Thatcher acquiesced in the change, while refusing to admit that any alteration had occurred. She vented her anger, instead, on the leading wets, three of whom – Gilmour, Soames and Education Secretary Mark Carlisle – were purged from the government in a reshuffle two months later. Stevas had already been sacked the previous January, and henceforth she steadily filled the Cabinet ranks with her own 'placemen' to ensure that the July revolt would never be repeated. Prior, she judged to be too big a fish to be chopped: instead he was sent to be Northern Ireland Secretary – well away from her main political concerns.

As Employment Secretary, Prior had implemented the Tories' election pledge to introduce a trade union reform Bill, providing public money for union ballots on strikes and leadership changes, banning secondary picketing and making it more difficult for unions to obtain a 'closed shop'. Unlike the earlier efforts by the Wilson and Heath governments, Prior's Bill was not only legislated but was put into effect, being reluctantly accepted by the trade unions. The Tory right wing were disgusted that Prior had not introduced a more full-blooded measure, and were encouraged by Thatcher in their criticisms, though formally she supported Prior's position. Prior was succeeded by the much more right-wing Norman Tebbit, and his Bill was to be followed by two far harsher measures.

During its first three years in office, the Thatcher government's successes were few and far between. One of them was the settlement of the Southern Rhodesian conflict, which had festered on since Ian Smith's declaration of independence in 1965. The protracted effect of sanctions, pressure from neighbouring states and the continuing guerrilla war had finally brought the illegal regime to its knees, and at the Lancaster House Conference in December 1979, it agreed to transfer control back to Britain, which would conduct multi-racial elections leading to independence for Zimbabwe the following April. The success of the conference was largely due to the diplomacy of Lord Carrington, but Thatcher deserves credit for letting him go ahead, despite her own deeply held suspicion of African nationalist leaders. Less obviously successful was Thatcher's handling of the dispute over the excessive British contribution to the budget of the European Economic Community. She was totally justified in taking a firm stand, but she went about it in the wrong way. Her hysterical behaviour at the second EEC summit she attended, at Dublin Castle in December 1979, when she thumped the table and demanded "my money back", unnecessarily antagonised her fellow heads of government, notably German Chancellor Helmut Schmidt and French President Valéry Giscard D'Estaing. Despite agreements on temporary palliatives, the dispute lingered on until the Fontainebleau summit in June 1984 when, due to the initiative of a new French President, François Mitterrand, a satisfactory settlement, involving substantial rebates, was finally reached. Thatcher probably gained popular support by her over-robust tactics, but it seems probable that a comparable deal could have been reached several years earlier if she had shown more subtlety in her approach.

By the spring of 1982, after almost three years in power, it looked as though the Thatcher government was completely washed up, and few observers gave it any hope of winning re-election. Both the government, and Thatcher personally, had the worst record ever in opinion polls. The Tories were then running a poor third, behind Labour, and very far behind the alliance of Liberals and the newly created Social Democratic Party, which had established an impressive lead, and took three by-election seats from the Tories in quick succession between October 1981 and March 1982. Then the government was rescued by the folly of one man – General Leopoldo Galtieri, the Argentine dictator.

His invasion of the Falklands in 1982 could, and perhaps should, have been the final *coup de grace* for Margaret Thatcher. For she had inadvertently provoked the invasion by withdrawing, as an economy measure and against the repeated advice of the Foreign Secretary, Lord Carrington, the British naval vessel which had been patrolling Falklands waters as a deterrent against Argentine threats. Yet when the Argentines launched their almost bloodless occupation of the Falklands, on 2 April 1982, and the House of Commons erupted in anger on the following day, it was Carrington and his fellow Foreign Office ministers who resigned, while Thatcher stayed put. She then showed tremendous energy and determination in ordering the assembly of a naval task force to sail, within three days, to the South Atlantic, with the declared intention of ousting the Argentine invaders. Most observers, including the majority of her Cabinet, assumed that the real objective was to back up diplomatic pressure on Argentina to agree to a peaceful withdrawal to be followed by negotiations through the United Nations. In retrospect, it seems clear that both Thatcher, and her closest military advisers – the Chief of the Defence Staff, Sir Terence Lewin, and Admiral Sir Henry Leach – were determined on a military reconquest, despite the enormous risks involved. When the US Secretary of State, General Al Haig, embarked on a marathon round of shuttle diplomacy, between London and Buenos Aires, the British Prime Minister, over-ruling her new Foreign Secretary, Francis Pym, insisted on a considerable tightening up of what the Americans regarded as eminently reasonable conditions and the Argentine junta turned them down. The baton was then taken up by the UN Secretary-General, Javier Peres de Cuellar, and by the Peruvian President Belaunde, who produced a revised version of the Haig proposals which appeared to meet both British and Argentine demands, and which he was confident that Galtieri would accept.

This plan was effectively torpedoed by the most controversial action of the war – the sinking of the Argentine cruiser, the *General Belgrano*, with the loss of 368 lives. The ship was well outside the 'total exclusion zone' which the British had proclaimed, and was actually steaming away from it. Thatcher announced to the Commons that it was sailing towards the zone, a fiction which she endeavoured to maintain for some years afterwards, well after any possible operational reason for dissembling had passed. When the Labour MP Tam Dalyell accused her of "lying", he was suspended from the House for using 'unparliamentary language', but Thatcher, who, with her War Cabinet, personally ordered the sinking, knew very well that his stricture was justified. The sinking of the ship, and the enormous loss of life, provoked popular outrage in Buenos Aires, and Galtieri felt compelled to repudiate the Belaunde plan, despite his earlier assurances to the Peruvian President. So the undeclared war proceeded, and the British proved victorious, partly due to US assistance personally ordered by President Reagan, which was far more extensive than was realised at the time. Even so, it was a victory dearly bought – 254 British servicemen were killed and another 777 wounded. Argentine losses were at least twice as great, so the total number of casualties was undoubtedly higher than the Falklands' population of 1,800.

For the Thatcher government – and even more for herself personally – the Falklands War proved a watershed. Hitherto, all their efforts appeared to be dogged by failure, and they were mired in the deepest unpopularity. From then onwards – right up almost to the last year of her premiership, with only a few blips – it appeared to be a non-stop success story. The initial boost came from the wave of jingoism, fanned by the popular press, which was reflected in the extraordinary swings in the opinion polls recorded between April and July 1982. The Tories shot up in the Gallup Poll from 31 to 46 per cent, while the Liberal–Social Democrat bubble was well and truly burst, their support going down from 37 per cent to 24 per cent. The Prime Minister herself did everything she could to inspire a mood of national triumphalism. "We have ceased to be a nation in retreat", she boasted, "doubts and hesitation were replaced by confidence and pride that our younger generation too could write a glorious chapter in the history of liberty". Not everyone accepted the gloss which she had put on the struggle. One writer in *The Guardian*, for example, tellingly quoted Voltaire's *Candide* on the "folly" of British and French soldiers "fighting over a few acres of snow on the borders of Canada, and that they spend more money on this glorious war than the whole of Canada is worth". Yet this was very much a minority view.

As well as boosting Thatcher's popularity, the Falklands had an extraordinary effect on her self-confidence. She saw herself as walking in Churchill's footsteps, and subsequently had no hesitation in evoking the name of 'Winston' to justify her every initiative. As one Cabinet minister said to Hugo Young at the time, the victory "fortifies her conviction that she is right on every subject" (Young, 1993, p. 280). Henceforward, she acted as a virtual dictator, reducing the role of the Cabinet to that of a supporters' club. Ministers were appointed or dismissed at will, those who were not sacked were ruthlessly briefed against when they threatened to step out of line, and controversial decisions were seldom discussed in Cabinet, the Prime Minister preferring to settle them on a one-to-one basis with the minister most concerned. Peter Walker, who eventually became the only surviving 'wet' in the Cabinet, privately compared her approach to that of the Duke of Wellington, who wrote after the first meeting of his Cabinet: "An extraordinary affair! I gave them their orders and they wanted to stay and discuss them." Walker would conclude his account by saying: "I'm so glad we don't have Prime Ministers like that today." Francis Pym did not long survive his defeatism during the Falklands War, being dropped immediately after the 1983 election. Whitelaw was dispatched to the House of Lords at the same time, becoming its leader until his retirement in 1986. Until then, he remained the one minister whose views – usually expressed in private – she listened to with any regularity. Treating her with the softest of kid gloves, he largely fulfilled the role which Bagehot attributed to the monarchy – "the right to be consulted, the right to encourage and the right to warn". A wise old bird, he was credited with having saved her from many a rash venture, though there were also frequent occasions when his advice was disregarded.

The Falklands not only transformed Thatcher's standing in her own country, but also abroad. She was not universally admired for her wartime leadership – the feeling in West European countries, which had rather reluctantly agreed to apply sanctions against Argentina, was that her reaction had been somewhat 'over the top' – but all recognised that she had brought a new decisiveness and assertiveness to the direction of British foreign policy. In the US, the reservations were far fewer and her popularity soared. She was seen – and saw herself – as a natural partner for Ronald Reagan, who had described the Soviet Union as "the evil empire" and who welcomed her as a rumbustious ally in the fight to extend the frontiers of 'freedom' around the world. The prolonged 'love-in' between Margaret and Ron was somewhat incongruous – she an inveterate workaholic who devoured every official paper put in front of her and peppered it with sharp comments, he the nearest approach to a part-time

President that the US has had in modern times. Yet they shared the same ideological approach and their personal chemistry worked like a dream. As for the Soviet Union, its leaders acquired a healthy respect for the British leader, whom they christened the 'Iron Lady', a description which she took as a compliment.

It was as the Iron Lady that Thatcher presented herself in the general election of June 1983, one of the most one-sided contests of the century. On the face of it the Tories should have had little chance – unemployment had soared to 3 million, and though inflation was now down to not much more than the European average, very few of the promises they had made in 1979 were kept. Yet their opponents were in near total disarray. The Labour Party had split, with many of its more modern-minded and attractive figures defecting to the newly formed SDP, and it was saddled with unrealistic and unpopular policies. Furthermore, it had, in Michael Foot, a leader who had fought his first parliamentary election in 1935, at the age of 22, and had done very little to adapt his electioneering style in the intervening period. As for the Liberal-SDP alliance, it polled astonishingly well for a third party, but not nearly well enough to overcome the handicaps imposed by the British electoral system. It polled 25.4 per cent, against 27.6 for Labour, but it won not many more than one-tenth the number of seats. All together the Tories polled 700,000 fewer votes than in 1979, but their majority shot up from 44 to 144:

Conservative	397
Labour	209
Lib-SDP	23
Others	<u>21</u>
Conservative majority	144

Safely re-elected, Thatcher pressed forward, less cautiously than before, on her self-appointed mission to undo the post-1945 consensus. An extensive reshuffle brought Geoffrey Howe to the Foreign Office, and Nigel Lawson, a much younger and very self-confident monetarist ideologue, to the Treasury. These two ministers were to be her loyalest and most industrious supporters until 1989–90, when she fell out with both of them, with disastrous consequences for herself. The dominating event of Thatcher's second term was the miners' strike of 1984–85. Once again, she was lucky in her opponent. Arthur Scargill, the charismatic but hot-headed President of the National Union of Mineworkers, impulsively brought his members out to resist pit closures which he believed were imminent, but made the cardinal error of refusing to allow a strike ballot. This led to the loss of much of the public sympathy which the miners could normally rely on, and, crucially, provoked the defection from the union of a substantial slice of its membership, which formed the Union of Democratic Mineworkers, and carried on working. After a whole year – often marked by violent scenes between pickets and the large number of police officers mobilised to protect miners continuing to work – the strike finally collapsed, and the National Coal Board proceeded to implement a closure programme even more drastic than Scargill had predicted. Thatcher was triumphant, insensitively bracketing her victory over the miners with that over the Argentines in the Falklands. The symbolic significance was huge – after the two previous miners' strikes which had defeated the Heath government – and it graphically confirmed Thatcher's success in taming the trade union movement. This owed as much to the high unemployment as it did to the three Bills which she had pushed through to reduce their powers. The weakening of the unions was reflected in a sharp decline in their membership – over 13 million when she was elected, down to 6.7 million when Labour finally regained power in 1997.

Apart from the miners' strike, the most dramatic event of the 1983–87 Parliament was the Westland affair, in December 1985 and January 1986. This was provoked by a dispute between two Cabinet ministers, Trade and Industry Secretary Leon Brittan and Defence Secretary Michael Heseltine, over whether the American helicopter company Sikorski should be permitted to take over the smaller British firm, Westland. This was vehemently opposed by Heseltine, who actively championed a rival bid by a European consortium in order to keep control this side of the Atlantic. Thatcher backed Brittan, as did a majority of the Cabinet, but was unwilling to face a showdown with Heseltine and resorted to 'dirty tricks' to discredit him. She was caught out, and Heseltine resigned in protest, dramatically stalking out of a Cabinet meeting. The hapless Brittan was fingered as the 'fall guy', and reluctantly resigned, but Thatcher then faced a Labour motion of censure, and was seen to be extremely vulnerable, she herself warning her private secretary on the way to the debate, "This may be my last day as Prime Minister". In the event, the opposition leader, Neil Kinnock, made a hash of his speech, as he himself readily acknowledged, and let her off the hook. In the long term, however, it did her immense harm, her reputation for truthfulness was severely damaged, and the highly ambitious and vengeful Heseltine was released to the back benches from where he prepared his slow-burning campaign to replace her.

It was during Thatcher's second term that another of her more distinctive policies got into its stride. This was privatisation, hardly mentioned in the Tory election manifesto in 1979, but gradually building up to a crescendo as one by one the great state corporations were sold off, yielding an additional revenue, which grew from a mere £377 million in 1979–80 to over £7 billion in 1988–89, despite being offered at knock-down prices. The policy proved highly popular, particularly among the investors, many of whom were able to make instant capital gains by selling on their shares. Largely as a result, the number of individuals owning shares grew from 3 to 9 million in ten years, a major step towards the Tory ideal of a "property-owning democracy". Alongside this, more than a million council houses were sold to their sitting tenants – again at very favourable prices – which was an even more popular measure, appealing as it did to many working-class electors and helping to lure them away from their previous Labour sympathies. Apart from housing, all together two-thirds of the public sector was sold off during Thatcher's premiership, and the proceeds helped to move the budget into a large, though temporary surplus, enabling substantial further cuts, in both the higher and standard rates of income tax, to be made in Nigel Lawson's budgets preceding the 1987 election. This promised to be a more closely fought contest than 1983, partly because Michael Foot had been replaced by the younger and more energetic Neil Kinnock, who had persuaded his party to jettison some of its more unpopular policies and had shown great courage in facing up to the extreme left. However, he was seen as inexperienced and lacking in *gravitas*, and succeeded only in reducing the Tory majority from 144 to 102 seats, although he decisively beat off the Liberal-Social Democratic challenge for second place. Thatcher became the first Prime Minister in more than 150 years to win an overall majority in three successive elections, and her standing and reputation, not to mention her arrogance, reached unprecedented heights. Angrily dismissing suggestions that she might retire half-way through her third term, she announced her intention of "going on and on".

Thatcher and her ministers talked a lot about "taking government off people's backs" and "setting the people free", but many of their policies had a centralising effect and increased the power of the national government. This particularly applied to their health service reforms and to local government, where the abolition of the Greater London Council and the other metropolitan authorities, the removal of powers from elected education authorities and the progressively tighter control over local government finance all led to a strengthening of Whitehall at the expense of local representatives. Nor were civil liberties increased by this supposedly libertarian government. Hugo Young mounted a formidable indictment in his biography:

> Where the citizen's liberty met state power, the citizen experienced new deprivations. The Police and Criminal Evidence Act 1984 created large police powers. The reach of the security service was extended. A new Official Secrets Act rendered a bad law worse, criminalizing whistleblowers in government and editors who so much as mentioned certain secret activities of the state. The Home Secretary claimed executive power to impede normal reporting, in the name of anti-terrorism in Ireland. This was a government that incessantly interfered with individual liberties in this way.
>
> *(Young, 1993, p. 612)*

The third term did not go particularly well, with Lawson beginning to lose control of the economy, and inflation shooting up to 10 per cent, more than it had been when Thatcher was first elected. The Thatcherite claim to have produced a British 'economic miracle', comparable to West Germany's, began to appear risible. Thatcher had always been seen as an exceptionally lucky politician, but it is of the nature of luck that at some time it begins to run out. In the summer of 1989, she celebrated her tenth anniversary as Prime Minister, the longest uninterrupted premiership since Lord Liverpool's 15-year tenure in 1812–27. In retrospect, she would have been well advised to bow out at this stage, as Whitelaw and other leading Tories privately thought at the time, in which case her reputation as a successful if highly controversial Prime Minister would have been assured. As it was, she clung to power, became progressively more unpopular and steadily lost support within her own party, becoming the only Prime Minister in modern times to be ejected from office at the behest of her own party. For this to happen, however, required the interaction of three distinct factors – her stubborn pursuit of a deeply unpopular policy, her growing anti-European obsession and her appalling treatment of her Cabinet colleagues.

The unpopular policy was, of course, the poll tax, or Community Charge, as it was officially known – a highly regressive tax designed to replace the domestic rates. The rating system was far from perfect, but it had the great advantage of being easy to collect, and because it was long established it was not an active source of complaint against the government currently in power. Thatcher decided to abolish it for no better reason than that she had promised to do so more than ten years earlier, when she had been Shadow Environment Minister before the October 1974 election; though she also saw the poll tax as a means of curbing expenditure by local authorities, particularly those under Labour control. The tax was introduced in Scotland in 1989, and in England and Wales in 1990, and provoked enormous discontent, leading to riots in the streets of London and a widespread refusal to pay. More damaging to Thatcher was the plunge in support for the Conservatives, who fell over 20 points behind Labour in the opinion polls and lost a string of by-elections, both to Labour and the Liberal Democrats. Large numbers of Tory MPs were terrified that they would lose their seats if the tax was not withdrawn; a smaller number were convinced that the only way to avoid electoral disaster was to change their leader. In December 1989, they availed themselves of the (hitherto unused) provision for an annual poll on the leadership, by putting up a 'wet' backbencher, Sir Anthony Meyer, as a 'stalking horse' candidate. He polled 33 votes, against Thatcher's 314. This was not enough to undermine her, but another 27 MPs abstained, which meant that she had lost the support of more than one-sixth of the party. It was a warning shot which she did not heed.

Meanwhile, the Chancellor of the Exchequer had become convinced that the solution – both to rising inflation and to high interest rates – lay in bringing the pound sterling into the exchange rate mechanism of the European Monetary System (EMS). The official position had long been that Britain would join "when the time was right", but Thatcher had set her face against ever naming the day, even though a large majority of her ministers had long been in favour. Lawson decided that the next best thing would be to obtain exchange rate stability by 'tracking the Deutschmark', and using the resources of the Bank of England to ensure that the floating rate remained at or near three DM to the pound. It took some time for Thatcher to realise what was going on, but when she found out she ordered Lawson to desist, publicly humiliating him in the process. Lawson did not give up, and before the EU summit in Madrid, in June 1989, he and Geoffrey Howe went to see the Prime Minister and threatened to resign unless she gave a clear indication at the summit that Britain would in fact join at an early date. Thatcher was furious, but nevertheless produced a form of words to satisfy them at Madrid; but she took her revenge a month later, when she quite unexpectedly removed Howe from the Foreign Office. Howe was devastated, and seriously considered resigning, but reluctantly agreed to become Leader of the House, with the additional title of Deputy Premier, which Thatcher's spokesman, Bernard Ingham, promptly assured the press was purely honorific. Lawson did not long survive his colleague, resigning in October 1989 because of what he regarded as intolerable interference by Thatcher's part-time economic adviser, Sir Alan Walters. The new Chancellor was Thatcher's young protégé, John Major, who had already been made Foreign Secretary three months earlier, and was now replaced in this role by Douglas Hurd. These two men were now irreplaceable, and together finally persuaded Thatcher that Britain should join the EMS the following October, when, however, the crucial error was made of entering at an unrealistically high level.

A more immediately lethal error was made by Thatcher later the same month when she attended yet another EU summit, in Rome, discussing economic and monetary union, and reported back to the House of Commons with a statement laced with bitter anti-European rhetoric. This so incensed the long-suffering Geoffrey Howe that he resigned from the government, and then astonished the House with a blistering resignation speech, which was televised live. In total contrast to his normal soporific style, he dissected Thatcher's record with consummate forensic skill. Within 24 hours, Michael Heseltine, who had been waiting almost five years for an opportune moment, threw his hat into the ring and challenged Thatcher in the annual leadership ballot. It was immediately clear that she was in deadly peril – although it was her anti-Europeanism which had provoked the challenge, it was the raging discontent over the poll tax which threatened to sap her support. Under the Tory election rules, she required not only a majority of the votes cast, but a lead of 15 per cent over her nearest challenger, to win on the first round. Although she fulfilled the first requirement, she was four votes short of the second, polling 204 votes to 152 for Heseltine. She defiantly announced that she would carry on into the second ballot, but her position soon proved untenable. She conducted one-to-one interviews with her Cabinet ministers, a clear majority of whom told her that she had no chance of winning and recommended that she should withdraw. "This was treachery", she later said in a television interview, "treachery with a smile on its face". It was the end of her premiership, but not of her political activity. She intervened in the second round, personally telephoning many of the MPs still loyal to her, asking them to vote for John Major rather than Douglas Hurd or Heseltine, and then announced that she would be "a good back-seat driver" during Major's premiership. In fact, she soon became disillusioned with him and gave strong moral support to his anti-EU critics within the party (see Chapter 18), and then went on to back both William Hague and Ian Duncan Smith in subsequent leadership ballots. Increasingly embittered, she ended up as a considerable embarrassment to her successors and to the more moderate elements within her party, while retaining a fanatical following among the ageing rank-and-file.

Thatcher was – by a wide margin – the most divisive Prime Minister in the period covered by this book, and the division remains to this day. There are very few 'don't knows' when people are asked their opinion of her. To her admirers, she is the greatest Premier since Churchill, a leader who restored Britain's greatness, reversed a long-running economic decline, put the unions in their place, fostered a spirit of enterprise and fought to resurrect old and trusted values. To her critics, she was an uncaring power maniac, who deliberately fostered unemployment, decimated British industry, redistributed incomes in favour of the rich, neglected public services and left Britain dangerously isolated in Europe. What both sides might agree on is that she was *effective*, and that her apparent insensitivity probably made her more so. For good or ill, she made more difference to the country that she led for 11 years and 209 days than did the great majority of the other 54 politicians (all men bar one) who have held the office of Prime Minister.

Works consulted

John Campbell, 2001, *Margaret Thatcher: Vol. I, The Grocer's Daughter*, London, Pimlico.
John Campbell, 2003, *Margaret Thatcher: Vol. II, The Iron Lady*, London, Cape.
Alan Clark, 1994, *Diaries*, London, Phoenix.
Peter Clarke, 1992, *A Question of Leadership: From Gladstone to Thatcher*, Harmondsworth, Penguin.
Tam Dalyell, 1982, *One Man's Falklands*, London, Cecil Woolf.
Brenda Maddox, 2003, *Maggie: The First Lady*, London, Hodder & Stoughton.
James Prior, 1986, *A Balance of Power*, London, Hamish Hamilton.
Margaret Thatcher, 1993, *The Downing Street Years*, London, HarperCollins.
Margaret Thatcher, 1995, *The Path to Power*, London, HarperCollins.
Hugo Young, 1993, *One of Us* (final edition), London, Pan.
Hugo Young, 1998, *This Blessed Plot: Britain and Europe from Churchill to Blair*, London, Macmillan.

18

JOHN MAJOR

"Thatcherism with a human face"

It has become customary to think of the premiership of John Major as a mere transitional interlude between the dominant figures of Margaret Thatcher and Tony Blair. In fact, Major was one of the longer-serving Prime Ministers of the 20th century. He spent seven-and-a-half years in 10 Downing Street – longer than Attlee, Macmillan, Lloyd George or Stanley Baldwin. Often described, rather unfairly, as a 'grey man', he came from a more exotic background than any of his fellow Prime Ministers of the century. Born on 29 March 1943, his father, Tom, was already almost 64, and his mother, Gwen, 38. Tom had had a varied and adventurous life. Brought up in the United States, where he won but did not take up a scholarship to the West Point Military Academy, and played junior league baseball, he returned to Britain with his family in his late teens and worked on a London building site before embarking on a long theatrical career, including a spell as a circus trapeze artist, before opening a business as a manufacturer of garden gnomes. His original name was Abraham Thomas Ball, and he had adopted Major as a stage name, eventually hyphenating it to Major-Ball. Twice married, each time to partners in his theatrical acts, he also had many affairs, which meant that the future Prime Minister had at least two half-siblings, one of whom, a sister, he only became aware of after he became Prime Minister.

Tom Major, who had spent most of his theatrical life touring in music halls on both sides of the Atlantic, retired in 1930, aged 51. He had recently got married for the second time, and rapidly fathered three children, the eldest of whom, a boy, was stillborn, but Patricia, born in 1930, and Terry, in 1932, both survived. There was then an 11-year gap until their younger brother, John, was born in 1943. Tom and Gwen went to live in Worcester Park, a prosperous south London suburb, where they rented, and later bought a bungalow, and Tom ran his business, known as Major's Garden Ornaments, from his back garden. It was a successful enterprise; the family bought a car, sent the two children to private schools and employed domestic help. When war broke out, however, demand for his products dwindled, and Tom, who was feeling his years and whose health was declining, closed down the business. Their standard of living collapsed, but Gwen went to work in the local library, and earned just enough to keep the wolf from the door. After the war, the business was re-started, with both Gwen and Terry playing an active part, but the pre-war prosperity was never regained and life became

DOI: 10.4324/9781003031963-19

an unending struggle. John attended the local council school, passing the 11-plus examination and going on to the nearest local authority grammar school, Rutlish School, three miles away in Merton. This was a school with relatively low academic standards, but which consciously aped 'public' schools, with its own cadet force and so on. John was repelled by the school's ambience, was thoroughly demotivated, showed no signs of distinction throughout his school career, except on the cricket field, and left at 16 with very poor GCE results. Writing in his autobiography, 40 years later, he expressed bitter regret for having let his parents down, and for failing totally to take advantage of what the school had to offer. He did, however, strongly criticise them for insisting that he should be registered at the school as John Major-Ball, despite his vehement objections at the time. He evidently foresaw that he would be constantly mocked and bullied because of the 'Ball', which was confirmed by one of his classmates when he was interviewed by his biographer, Anthony Seldon, in 1996. A deeper reason for his alienation was almost certainly the final collapse of the family business in 1955, which led to the sell-off of their home and abrupt removal to rented rooms in the depressed working-class area of Brixton, in inner London, As John Major was to recall:

> It was a sad comedown, part of the top floor of a four-storey Victorian building in Coldharbour Lane. We had two rooms for the five of us ... Dad, Terry and I slept in one room, and Mum and Pat in the other. This second room was used as a dining room and lounge during the day. We shared a cooker on the landing with the other top-floor tenant, a middle-aged bachelor. The lavatory, two floors below, was used by all the tenants. There was no bathroom. We washed at the sink or in a tub.
>
> *(Major, 1999, pp. 15–16)*

Their landlord, Tom Moss, a man in his mid-fifties, was a mystery to John and his brother and sister. It was only later that they discovered that he was, in fact, their half-brother, the offspring of an affair between Tom Major and a young dancer in 1901. The removal to Brixton meant that John now had a journey of an hour and a half each way to his school, which, added to his sense of shame and the stress of having to live in such cramped circumstances with ageing and increasingly ailing parents, was another contributory factor to his turning in on himself. On leaving school, he started work as a clerk for an insurance firm, which he greatly disliked. He soon left to work as a labourer, making garden gnomes, with his brother Terry, for the small company which had taken over his father's failed business. Soon after, his father died, at the age of 82, and his mother's health being poor, he left his work to look after her for a time, and then found it impossible to get another job, being unemployed ("unemployable, I feared", as he later wrote) for six months in 1963. One job he failed to get was as a bus conductor, being turned down, he recounted, because he was too tall. He eventually landed a job with the London Electricity Board (LEB), which he found "mind-numbing", but it was a "cheerful, happy place". "So far", he was to recall, "I had not made much of my life. School – a failure; career – I had none; sport – not good enough; politics – I was only playing at it. I needed a career and qualifications" (Major, 1999, p. 30). He began to take correspondence courses to get more O levels.

It was, in fact, politics which gave the young Major the motivation which he had previously lacked. Given a ticket to attend a House of Commons debate by the local Labour MP, Marcus Lipton, when he was 13, he immediately fell in love with the place and formed the ambition to become an MP. At 16, he signed up to the Brixton Young Conservatives, perhaps influenced by his parents who were both 'gut instinct' Tories. His biographer, Anthony Seldon, remarks that "many of his embryonic views – on privilege, authority, social advance and race – put him closer to Labour", but

> he chose to see Labour as the party that denied individual expression and treated people as groups ... The Conservatives offered him the passport out of the ghetto; their emphasis on individuality and personal freedom struck a deep chord in the young man. They were also the party of prosperity, of a world he aspired to join.
>
> *(Seldon, 1997, pp. 19–20)*

The Brixton Young Conservatives soon became the main focus of the young Major's life; he joined in all their activities, in particular becoming their star soapbox speaker at meetings they held regularly outside Brixton pubs, and rose to become the branch chairman. His father died when he was 19, and shortly afterwards he began a relationship with a divorcée 13 years his senior with two young children, which caused his mother much distress. It could, however, be argued that his affair with Jean Kierans, a leading Brixton Conservative, was the making of John Major. A woman of sophisticated tastes, she smartened John up, greatly boosted his self-esteem, and gave him the stimulus to improve himself which his own family had not provided.

At the age of 21, Major stood for election to the Lambeth Council, but was heavily defeated in a strong Labour ward. The same year – 1965 – he left the LEB, and started work at a local branch of the District Bank (later taken over by NatWest). He now formed serious ambitions of becoming a banker, and studied to take the first of what proved to be a long series of banking exams. After a year, he left to take a more senior post at Standard Bank, on the understanding that he would have to serve for a lengthy period in an overseas branch of the bank. This turned out to be in Nigeria, six years after the country achieved independence in 1960. Major was posted to Jos, a small town in the northern region, where he settled in happily, though feeling acutely uncomfortable about the colonialist attitudes of many of his fellow expatriates. Major, who had freely mixed with the Black population of Brixton, had no difficulty in accepting his African colleagues as equals, and insisted on being on first name terms with them, which soon marked him out as not being a 'racialist'. In the event, his stay in Nigeria lasted barely five months: he was severely injured in a car crash, and had to be flown back to London for lengthy restorative treatment, especially to his knee-cap which had been shattered by the accident. Major was appalled by the likely consequences of the accident, saying "This has ruined everything", not least lamenting the fact that he would be unlikely ever to play cricket again, a sport which he loved and at which he had shown distinct promise. In fact, the dramatic shortening of his overseas posting made possible an early blossoming of the political career for which he hankered.

The bank treated him very decently, slotting him into a job in their investment and international division, where his working hours were 9.15 a.m. to 4.45 p.m., enabling him to get off early for the evening's political activities. In May 1968 –aged 25 – he stood for the Lambeth Council for a second time, again in what was normally regarded as a safe Labour ward. But this was the nadir of the Wilson government's unpopularity, following the forced devaluation of the previous November, and the Tories swept to an overwhelming victory, winning 57 out of the 60 seats on the council. Major immediately specialised in housing policy, becoming, in short order, Vice-Chairman and then Chairman of the Housing Committee. He was to prove himself exceptionally vigorous and innovative in this role, forging a formidable partnership

216 John Major

with the Director of Housing, Harry Simpson, who later went on to be Director of the Northern Ireland Housing Authority, and subsequently of the Greater London Council.

In the spring of 1970 an incident occurred, which showed just how strong was Major's belief in racial equality. The local Tory parliamentary candidate, James Harkess, was a right-wing lawyer, with Powellite views. In his autobiography, Major recalled the events of the annual general meeting of the Conservative Association:

> Harkess made a speech that was strongly anti-immigrant. I was appalled at his intolerance, and embarrassed, too, as we had a new West Indian member present, who must have been mortified. I replied angrily from the chair, rebutting Harkess's remarks, and the atmosphere turned sulphurous.
>
> *(Major, 1999, p. 46)*

Convinced that Harkess's views would damage race relations in Brixton, as well as the Conservative cause, Major subsequently went ahead with a motion to consider the adoption of a new candidate. This was, however, overtaken by Harold Wilson's sudden decision to hold a general election, and it was felt to be too late to consider a change. Harkess remained the candidate, being roundly defeated by the defending Labour MP.

Major's personal situation was transformed during his three years on the Lambeth Council. His mother died in September 1970, aged 65, and a few weeks later he got married to Norma Johnson, a teacher and fanatical opera-lover, whom he had met while canvassing during the GLC election, the previous April. Norma invited him to an opera performance: Major promptly fell asleep, but they got engaged ten days later. His relationship with Jean Kierans, which had lasted seven years, had gradually been winding down and Major now gently broke it off. He and Norma started their married life in a small bachelor flat he had bought in Streatham, but, in 1971, when Major lost his seat on the council, they moved to a three-bedroomed house in suburban Beckenham, where they lived more comfortably with their two children, Elizabeth, born in 1971, and James, 1975.

Meanwhile, Major had successfully completed his banking exams, and felt that the time had come to seek a parliamentary seat. He stood twice for St. Pancras North, a working-class inner-London constituency, in February and October 1974, where his experience as a Lambeth councillor stood him in good stead, and his progress was favourably noted by Conservative Central Office. It was a different matter being selected for a safe Conservative seat, where his humble birth and upbringing was not held to be a recommendation by many members of selection committees. He did his best to burnish his c.v., describing himself as an 'international banker', which did more than justice to the junior management position he had reached at the Standard Chartered Bank. After several rejections, he finally struck lucky, in 1976, at Huntingdonshire, a cast-iron Tory seat, which blended lush rural areas with an overspill population from London. He then had a three-year wait until the 1979 general election, but threw himself into nursing the constituency with enormous energy, speaking to an estimated 450 meetings, and treating the constituency as if it was a super-marginal. His efforts were to be rewarded with a majority of over 21,000, in place of the 9,000 achieved by his predecessor, one of the best Tory performances in the election which brought Margaret Thatcher to power.

When Major arrived in the Commons, he was regarded as unremarkable by most of his new colleagues. Yet he showed exceptional diligence in familiarising himself with the procedures of the House, and – while not seeming to push himself – was very ready to take on any chore, however menial. He decided, at first, to specialise in two areas where, he rightly believed, he had more experience than most – housing and local government. His work on the committee of the 1980 Housing Bill attracted favourable notice from his party whips, and Seldon records his growing popularity with his fellow Tory MPs. One described him as "Hard working, very keen and not at all bombastic. Everyone liked him", and another said:

> I'd have listed John Major among my five best friends. Probably there were ten of us who would have said the same thing! But he probably wouldn't have listed any of us as his close friends. He had that knack of making people feel you were precious to him.
>
> *(Seldon, 1997, pp. 50, 53)*

Major carefully avoided identifying himself with any particular faction in the party, but was regarded as being mildly on the left wing, largely because of the exceptional concern he showed for the effect of policies on people who were handicapped or were on low incomes. After a while, Major began to chafe on the back benches, as one by one the more prominent of the new Tory MPs elected in 1979 were appointed to junior ministerial office. He had to wait until January 1983 before the call came, and this was to be an assistant whip, in Seldon's words "the lowest form of ministerial life", but it was the first step on the ladder.

With his assiduity and his gift for getting on with his colleagues, Major took to the Whips' Office like a duck to water, but feared he had irredeemably blighted his chances of further promotion when he had a fierce argument with Margaret Thatcher, after he had, tactlessly but honestly, reported to her on backbench grievances. In the event, it did him no harm – within weeks he was appointed to his first post in a ministerial department, as Parliamentary Under-Secretary for Social Security, the same position which Thatcher herself had occupied, 25 years earlier. Within a year, he was promoted to Minister of State in the same department, and soon established a reputation as a competent, hard-working and sensitive minister, without being seen in any way as a high-flyer. Nevertheless, nine months later, he made it into the Cabinet, an unusual achievement after only eight years in the Commons. When he was summoned to see the Prime Minister, he expected and hoped that she had him in mind as Chief Whip, a post for which his personal qualities would have made him an excellent choice. Instead, he was made Chief Secretary to the Treasury, in charge of keeping public spending down. He owed his appointment to the advocacy of the Chancellor of the Exchequer, Nigel Lawson, who wanted somebody who was good at sums, and ideally would have preferred an accountant. Major was the next best thing: he looked and sounded like an accountant, and his background as a banker (though probably a more junior one than Lawson supposed) seemed an ideal qualification. He made an inauspicious start in his new post, fearing he was out of his depth, and Lawson recalled how he would "come and see me at Number 11, ashen-faced, to unburden himself of his worries and seek my advice" (Lawson, 1992, p. 719). Yet by making an enormous effort – for some time his working day extended from 6 a.m. to midnight – he mastered his brief, and proved himself a remarkably skilful negotiator in his encounters with spending ministers, many of whom were far senior to him. Generally, he got his way in sharply reducing their bids, though he was adept at sugaring the pill by making exceptions for particular pet-schemes. Thus he was able to keep expenditure pretty rigorously under control, without unnecessarily alienating his colleagues. There were two notable exceptions. One was the Health and Social Security Secretary, John Moore, seen for a time as a special favourite of Thatcher's and rumoured to be groomed by her for the succession. The other was the right-wing Environment Secretary, Nicholas Ridley. Both became sworn enemies, but Major had the last laugh. Moore soon disappointed his sponsor's hopes, and was quickly demoted and then left the government because of ill health, while Ridley was later forced to resign after expressing outrageously anti-German sentiments in an interview with the editor of *The Spectator* (Lawson's son, Dominic), which he claimed was meant to be 'off the record'.

Thatcher was well-pleased with Major's performance, and he appeared to many to have replaced Moore as her favourite. At the same time, her relations with Lawson were sharply deteriorating, and by early in 1989 she probably had marked Major down as a likely replacement for the Chancellor. She was not yet ready, however, to dispense with Lawson's services, but after the June 1989 Madrid summit of the European Union, when Foreign Secretary Geoffrey Howe had joined with Lawson in pressurising her to name a date for entry into the European Monetary System (see Chapter 17), she promptly sought revenge by unexpectedly dropping him from the Foreign Office in a reshuffle a few weeks later. The obvious replacement for Howe would have been Douglas Hurd, a foreign policy specialist who was then Home Secretary, but Thatcher did not want somebody with independent views in the Foreign Office, and instead chose Major whom she correctly surmised would offer no threat to the dominant role she sought for herself. In fact, Major – still technically the most junior figure in the Cabinet – was perplexed to be promoted to an office for which he had no relevant experience or qualification. He took it to heart, when Charles Powell, the Prime Minister's foreign policy adviser, jokingly asked him what was the capital of Ecuador. It was painfully obvious to an embarrassed Powell that he hadn't the faintest idea.

Major's tenure of the Foreign Office lasted a mere 94 days – long enough for the staff to learn to appreciate him as a thoughtful, considerate and notably unstuffy boss, but not for him to have any discernible influence on foreign policy, though an article in *The Times* did contrast his anodyne approach to European Community affairs with the "ferocious rhetoric of the Prime Minister". Only one episode excited much comment. This was his semi-public humiliation by Thatcher, when after Major had negotiated a joint statement on sanctions against South Africa with other foreign ministers at a Commonwealth conference in Malaysia, she had insisted on issuing a separate communiqué setting out a far harder British line.

Yet within a day of their return from Malaysia – on 26 October 1989 – Major was able to swap the Foreign Office for a post which attracted him a great deal more, and to which – at least on paper – he was far better suited. Goaded beyond endurance by his own treatment from the Prime Minister, Nigel Lawson handed in his resignation (see Chapter 17), and Thatcher happily turned to Major to take his place. Less happily, she felt she now had no alternative but to make Douglas Hurd Foreign Secretary. Major was now 46, and had achieved the post which, a decade earlier, he had confided to other newly elected MPs, was his ultimate ambition. He looked forward to a lengthy spell as Chancellor, but in the event stayed only for 13 months. He introduced one budget, the most notable feature of which was the introduction of 'Tessas' (Tax Exempt Special Savings Accounts), whose impact was increased by the fact that this was the first Budget Speech ever to be televised live. The budget was, however, widely criticised, notably in the City of London, for not doing enough to combat inflation, which was again moving into double figures. Major undoubtedly felt much more at home at the Treasury than he had at the Foreign Office, but did not regain the authority which he had eventually achieved as Chief Secretary. He was handicapped by his ignorance of economics, and suffered (in his own oversensitive mind, at least) by constant comparisons between his hesitant approach and the much more self-confident manner of his predecessor, Nigel Lawson. He also, for the first time, experienced the resentment and envy of Tory MPs convinced that he had been promoted beyond his merits and inclined to view him as 'Mrs Thatcher's poodle'.

The most important decision taken during his chancellorship was entry into the exchange rate mechanism (ERM) of the European Monetary System. By the time of his appointment, Thatcher was virtually in a minority of one in her Cabinet in her reluctance to take this step, which was strongly urged by the Bank of England, the City of London and overwhelmingly by the serious press. It still took nearly a year before the partnership of Major and Hurd (which replicated the earlier alliance of Lawson and Howe) was able to argue her round. Major's role was later described by the Permanent Secretary to the Treasury, Sir Peter Middleton:

> Major went out of his way to be sensitive to what the PM wanted to do, and the fact that he was sensitive meant they got on pretty well. It also meant that he got his way on most issues. He played her with all the skill of a fly fisherman after a big and suspicious salmon. He would raise the subject, then drop it when she objected, then come back to it from a different angle at their next meeting.
>
> *(Seldon, 1997, p. 112)*

The decision was long overdue, but the way in which it was implemented meant that Britain failed to obtain the benefits expected, and which the other members of the ERM had enjoyed during the previous 11 years. Despite warnings from economists, Major made no attempt to negotiate entry at a lower level than the current market rate of DM2.95, which was a serious over-valuation of the pound. This blunder came back to haunt him with a vengeance, and was the principal reason for the shipwreck of his own government.

Within weeks of this decision being taken, Thatcher was ousted from the premiership (see Chapter 17), and – on 28 November 1990 – Major became Prime Minister at the age of 47, the youngest thus far of the century. In retrospect, it may seem surprising that he was chosen, as he was clearly the least experienced and least qualified of the three contenders. Yet he enjoyed marked advantages over his rivals. Heseltine was seen as too adventurous, too disloyal and too left-wing by the majority of Tory MPs, and his large score in the first round was more a measure of Thatcher's unpopularity than of his own support. Had she contested the second round, he might well have won, but once she withdrew, his prospects sharply declined. In reality, the real contest was between Major and the Foreign Secretary, Douglas Hurd, and five factors weighed strongly in his favour. First was his genuine popularity among his fellow Members, as Nigel Lawson later observed: "He never let up on his instinctive networking; he became a near universally liked figure in the party" (Seldon, 1997, p. 83). Allied to this was his detachment from any clearly defined faction within the party. This was most notable concerning Europe – at around this time Major had candidly confessed to a sympathetic journalist that he revelled in the fact that both the pro- and anti-Europeans believed that he was on their side. Third, was what could only be described as a class factor. His modest background – which had told against him when he was seeking a safe Tory seat – was now seen as a trump card in the coming electoral campaign against Labour, much to the chagrin of the old Etonian, Douglas Hurd. Fourthly, Thatcher threw her considerable weight on his side, enabling him to scoop up practically the whole of her loyalist support. Lastly, he had a much more efficient election team, shrewdly led by Norman Lamont, the Chief Secretary to the Treasury, whom Major unwisely rewarded, by promoting him to be Chancellor of the Exchequer. The result was:

John Major	185
Michael Heseltine	131
Douglas Hurd	56

Technically, there should have been a third round, as Major had just failed to secure an absolute majority, but both the other candidates promptly withdrew.

Not wishing to be seen as a surrogate for Thatcher, who had already announced that she would be "a very good back-seat driver", Major lost no time in implicitly distancing himself from her when he told a small crowd gathered outside Downing Street, when he returned from his meeting with the Queen, "I want us to build a country which is at ease with itself". Apart from Lamont, Major's first ministerial appointments were well judged, and helped to secure an early closing of party ranks. Hurd was confirmed as Foreign Secretary, and Michael Heseltine rejoined the government as Environment Secretary, with a brief to find a replacement for the highly unpopular poll tax in double-quick time. Chris Patten, who vacated the Environment Department, was appointed Chairman of the Conservative Party, where he was to prove himself a skilled electoral tactician. Within the Cabinet, Major made a diffident start, wondering aloud at his first meeting whether he was up to the job. Yet nearly all his colleagues found him a breath of fresh air, after having suffered from Thatcher's authoritarian ways for the previous 11 years. "Major has restored Cabinet government" several of them delightedly announced, welcoming the fact that he allowed important decisions to be argued out, if necessarily at length, around the Cabinet table rather than being settled by *diktat* or by bilateral deals between the Prime Minister and the minister most directly concerned. The general public, also, seemed pleased by Major's early moves – the enormous Labour lead in the opinion polls disappearing overnight, and the Tories gaining a narrow lead which they kept for three months. Most observers, however, credited this more to the demise of Thatcher than to Major's positive impact. The inheritance that he came into was an unenviable one. He benefited from the impact of the first Gulf War, which – unlike its successor 12 years later – was generally popular, and Major was able to exploit this by getting himself photographed addressing the troops in the desert, and mixing with them informally. Otherwise, however, the outlook looked distinctly bleak, as Britain was entering the longest recession since World War II, with unemployment again approaching the 3 million mark.

By mid-March 1991, Heseltine was able to deliver on his pledge to produce a realistic, and obviously fairer, alternative to the poll tax. This was the Council Tax, effectively a revamped version of the former rating system, but less regressive, and its introduction was to be smoothed by the transfer of a great wodge of local expenditure to the national budget. The proposal was well received, but in the same month Labour again went ahead in the opinion polls, scotching any idea that Major might call a snap election to cash in on the Gulf War victory. In June, Major produced his own distinctive policy initiative, with the publication of the *Citizens' Charter*, which aimed to improve public services by providing consumers with more choice, information and opportunities to lodge complaints. Otherwise, Major's main preoccupation during his first term in office was the sorry state of Britain's relations with the European Community. He immediately set out to improve them by making an early visit to Chancellor

Helmut Kohl, in Bonn, where he was warmly received, and made an excellent impression on his hosts, giving a widely publicised speech, of which the opening words were:

> My aims for Britain in the Community can be simply stated. I want us to be where we belong – at the very heart of Europe, working with our partners in building the future. This is a challenge we take up with enthusiasm.

This speech greatly heartened the pro-Europeans in the Conservative Party, who were then still in a majority. Yet it was not long before Major began to back-pedal to appease the so-called Eurosceptics, a small but growing force, who were encouraged, privately at first but then increasingly openly, by Margaret Thatcher. So far from seeking to put Britain at the heart of Europe, he ensured at the Maastricht summit, in December 1991, that it would remain on the sidelines, by obtaining opt-outs from two of its main projects, the Social Charter and, especially, Economic and Monetary Union (EMU). Major returned triumphantly from Maastricht, saying he had won "game, set and match" in his negotiations with the other EU leaders, but all that he had done was to store up future trouble for himself (and his successor). Despite the opt-outs, the Eurosceptics reacted violently against the Maastricht agreement, which Thatcher was later to characterise as "a treaty too far".

Labour continued to lead in the polls, and there were further by-election losses to both Labour and the Liberal Democrats (though not as sweeping as in Thatcher's time), so Major was discouraged from seeking an early dissolution, and the 1987 Parliament continued until March 1992, when polling day was set for 9 April. The general expectation was that Major would lose, but not heavily. His low-key leadership style was favourably compared to that of his predecessor, and Ken Clarke's description of his approach as "Thatcherism with a human face" rang favourable bells with many electors. On the other hand, the Labour opposition was in a far healthier state than in 1987, with Neil Kinnock having succeeded in junking many of its unpopular and unrealistic policies and winning growing respect for standing up to left-wing extremists. Yet Major's personal standing in the polls was far higher than Kinnock's, and the government's main problem was its perceived failure in combating the recession. The Tory strategists, guided by Chris Patten, therefore decided that their best hope of staving off defeat was not to offer positive proposals but to stake everything on casting doubt on Labour's economic competence, coupling this with a fierce assault on its spending plans. The cost of these was grotesquely exaggerated, with horror stories of enormous tax increases being enthusiastically taken up by the tabloid press, all of which, apart from the *Daily Mirror*, was on the Tories' side. Major himself was seen to fight a plucky campaign, in the face of an almost universal expectation of defeat, which was, however, hardly justified by the very narrow Labour lead in the opinion polls. Against the advice of party professionals, he insisted on augmenting his carefully controlled programme of ticket-only meetings, with a series of impromptu open-air gatherings in marginal constituencies, which he addressed from a soap box, recalling his early days in Brixton. It was a risky venture, but it seemed to pay off.

In the event, the polls had got it wrong – the Tories led Labour by the apparently comfortable margin of 7.5 per cent, which, however, yielded them an overall majority of only 21 seats. It was a triumph for Major, but it would probably have been better for his subsequent reputation if he had narrowly lost. He would then have been credited with having led his government with some skill, and away from the electoral abyss which it appeared to be facing in the last days of Thatcher.

As it was, it was downhill almost all the way after he regained Downing Street on the morning after the election. Within five months, his government suffered a devastating and largely self-inflicted blow, on 'Black Wednesday' (16 September 1992), which demolished its own claims to economic competence, and from which it was quite unable to recover over the remaining four-and-a-half years that it stayed in office. The genesis of 'Black Wednesday' was Major's own decision, as Chancellor of the Exchequer in October 1990, to take the pound into the ERM at too high a level against the Deutschmark. In early September the pound was under enormous speculative pressure, and at a meeting of EU finance ministers in Bath, presided over by Norman Lamont, he refused to allow any discussion of an ordered realignment of currencies. Instead, he repeatedly harangued the President of the Bundesbank, Helmut Schlesinger, who was present as an observer, to reduce German interest rates in order to reduce pressure on the pound and other currencies, notably the Italian lira. Schlesinger, whose constitutional position as head of the bank precluded him from taking advice from any politicians, let alone foreign ones, angrily refused, and threatened to leave the meeting, when Lamont returned to the attack for the fourth time. Major, who fully supported Lamont's tactics, then compounded the blunder by making an ill-advised speech in Glasgow, despite warnings from two of his closest advisers, Sarah Hogg, the head of his Policy Unit, and Sir John Kerr, the UK Permanent Representative to the EU. Speaking in the most personal terms, he ridiculed any idea of devaluation or of changing the parities within the ERM. Three days later, the Italians decided to re-value and temporarily to leave the ERM, and Prime Minister Giuliano Amato telephoned Major to enquire whether Britain would follow suit. Major firmly declined, but within three days, after a harrowing few hours in which he had agreed with Lamont to raise interest rates to 15 per cent, and billions of pounds had been lost by the Bank of England in a vain effort to halt the speculative flow, he agreed with Lamont and three other senior colleagues to let the pound float and to leave the ERM (temporarily, they said, but it never rejoined).

Major, who was badly worsted by the new Labour leader, John Smith, in the subsequent parliamentary debate, felt humiliated by the disaster and seriously contemplated resignation, though he was persuaded by colleagues to stay on. Yet much of his authority was gone, and he was widely regarded thereafter as one of the 'walking wounded'. Throughout the whole remainder of his premiership, Labour was leading in the opinion polls by a margin of 20 per cent or more, the government set a new record by losing every single by-election during the Parliament, while his own poll ratings fell to unprecedentedly low levels. Black Wednesday was also the occasion of a serious falling-out between Major and Lamont, who years later were still exchanging bad-tempered recriminations about each other's conduct during the affair. Lamont half-heartedly offered his resignation, which Major refused, but eight months later he peremptorily sacked him, offering the Environment Department as a face-saver. Lamont indignantly refused, and insisted on making a highly damaging personal statement to the Commons, in which he asserted that the government gave "the impression of being in office but not in power". Thereafter, he became a consistent and bitter critic, who effectively put himself at the head of the Eurosceptic rebels on the back benches.

If Major's second administration had otherwise been seen as competent, it might have been able, with time, to overcome the disaster of 'Black Wednesday' which, objectively, was no worse than that suffered by Wilson's government at the time of the 1967 devaluation. Yet it was only one, if much the most serious, of a whole series of self-inflicted wounds that were to beset Major and his ministers. Many of these derived from their increasing divisions over

Europe, and they were exacerbated by his seeming inability to act decisively. This was most apparent over the long delays in seeking ratification of the Maastricht treaty. Formally signed in February 1992, it was finally approved by the House of Commons, in a confidence vote, only on 23 July 1993, a day after it had been defeated in a division in which 23 Tory MPs voted against the government. After Maastricht only seven Tory MPs, led by Norman Tebbit, had opposed the government on a motion approving the outcome, and the majority was 86. There would have been no difficulty at all in ratifying the treaty (including the British opt-outs) before the general election in April. But Major put if off until the summer, and then for a further year, following the first Danish referendum, which narrowly rejected the treaty in July 1992. In the meantime, the strength of the Eurosceptics, now openly backed by Thatcher and surreptitiously encouraged by Cabinet ministers such as Michael Howard, Michael Portillo, John Redwood and Peter Lilley, steadily grew. Asked by a television interviewer, Michael Brunson, whether he ought not to sack his disloyal ministers, Major replied that he did not want "three more of the bastards out there". These words were meant to be 'off-the-record', but were accidentally picked up by a BBC sound-line, and became widely known. Major's Cabinet opponents were subsequently invariably referred to as "the bastards" by the press.

The ratification of Maastricht did not end the agitation of the Eurosceptics, who were now strongly backed by most of the pro-Tory press, including the normally ultra-loyal *Daily Telegraph*, and by the mass of Tory supporters in the country. Major now set himself on a course of appeasement, but like the original payers of *Danegeld* found that every concession was met by further demands. British ministers became increasingly obstructive at EU meetings, and the nadir was reached at an EU summit in June 1994, when Major vetoed the appointment of Belgian Prime Minister Jean-Luc Dehaene as President of the European Commission, even though he was the preferred candidate of all the other member states. This was intended as a 'macho' demonstration of strength, but in fact only underlined Major's weakness. The ostensible reason for Major's veto was Dehaene's supposedly 'federalist' views, but the falsity of this excuse was exposed a month later when Major accepted the appointment of Luxembourg Prime Minister Jacques Santer, who went out of his way to explain that his views were identical to Dehaene's. The net result was that the EU finished up with a less effective President than it otherwise might have had. Nor did this irresponsible action lead to any letting up of the Eurosceptics' demands. These were now stepped up to include an assurance that Britain would "never" join the single currency or, at the very least, not during the course of the next Parliament. This demand won widespread backing throughout the party, and might well have been acceded to by Major if it had not been for the resolute opposition of senior Cabinet ministers, notably Michael Heseltine, who became Deputy Premier in July 1995, and Ken Clarke, who had replaced Norman Lamont as Chancellor of the Exchequer in May 1993. Eventually, Major did pledge that a Conservative government would not enter the single currency without securing a mandate to do so in a referendum, an undertaking which was subsequently also made by Labour.

The most ill-considered initiative undertaken by Major was his 'Back to Basics' campaign, which he launched in his speech to the Conservative conference in 1993. It was meant to emphasise the issues of law and order and education, but was given a moralistic twist by Tory spin-doctors, who linked it to the maintenance of 'family values'. To their undisguised horror, the tabloid press took this as an invitation to launch a veritable witch-hunt against ministers whose personal conduct did not match up to the highest moral standards. All together 15 ministerial resignations occurred during the 1992 Parliament, an unprecedented total, of which only three were on policy grounds. Nearly all the rest were linked to sexual or financial scandals, and Major himself was severely damaged by his apparently equivocal response, first resisting and then demanding resignations in several cases, including the high-profile case of David Mellor, a personal friend and a rising figure within the Cabinet. Major was almost certainly more embarrassed than he otherwise would have been, as he was nursing his own guilty secret. For several years he had conducted an affair, which continued after his promotion to the Cabinet, with the prominent Tory MP, Edwina Currie. She eventually revealed the details only in 2002, when she published her diaries. Major then acknowledged the affair, saying it was the thing about which he had been "most ashamed" during his entire political career.

The scandals concerning ministers and Tory MPs were linked by the press to others involving dodgy contributions to Tory funds, and the attempt to cover up ministerial responsibility for illegal arms sales to Iraq. The result was that the government acquired an unenviable reputation for 'sleaze', which was to dog it up to and throughout the 1997 election campaign. By the summer of 1995, dissatisfaction with Major had spread to all sections of the Conservative Party, and there were increasing calls in the press for his replacement by a more competent and more decisive leader. There was intense speculation that in the autumn he would be challenged by a 'stalking horse' candidate who would sufficiently undermine his position so that more heavyweight challengers could emerge. Those most favoured were Michael Portillo, the Employment Secretary and darling of the Eurosceptics, and Michael Heseltine, the Trade Secretary, who was now seen as the main hope of the party mainstream. In a rare moment of decisiveness, Major launched a pre-emptive strike, and in June suddenly resigned the party leadership, inviting his opponents to "put up or shut up". Neither Portillo nor Heseltine (who was promoted to the deputy premiership) responded to the challenge, though both reserved the right to contest a second round if one was required, but John Redwood, the Eurosceptic Welsh Secretary, resigned his post to enter the contest, hoping to cream off the support which otherwise would have gone to Portillo. Technically, Major needed only 165 votes (an overall majority and a lead of 15 per cent over the nearest challenger) to win on the first round, but privately decided that this would not be enough to restore his authority and that he would withdraw if he polled less than 215 votes (Major, 1999, pp. 608–47). In the event, he narrowly exceeded this target, polling 218 votes, to 89 for Redwood, with 20 abstentions or spoiled ballot papers. The result cleared the air to a certain extent, and ensured that there would be no further contest before the general election, but was not nearly decisive enough to put an end to the internecine strife within the party.

More difficulties lay ahead, including the privatisation of two industries which even Thatcher had left alone – coal and the railways. Both exercises were handled badly. In preparation for selling off coal, Heseltine announced a further massive programme of pit closures, which then had to be extensively modified in the face of overwhelming criticism, though most of the closures eventually went ahead, leaving only a skeletal remnant of a once mighty industry to be disposed of. Even less popular were the proposals to dismantle British Rail and lease off franchises to a wide variety of private contractors who would be ill-prepared to provide a co-ordinated service. Privatisation, which had undoubtedly been an electoral asset to the Tories throughout the 1980s, now became a liability. A final misfortune which hit the Major government, and which they were generally seen to have very badly mishandled, was the outbreak of 'mad cow disease' (BSE), which also led to a renewed dispute with the European Union.

On the positive side, however, and very much to Major's personal credit, was his patient handling of the Northern Irish question, leading to the signing, with the Irish Prime Minister Albert Reynolds, of the Downing Street Declaration in December 1993, and the declaration by the IRA of a ceasefire in August 1994, which lasted for 18 months. Hopes of turning this into a permanent peace settlement foundered, however, despite the valiant efforts of the American mediator, Senator George Mitchell. In the end, neither the IRA nor the Ulster Unionists were prepared to make the minimum concessions necessary, and later on Major did not feel in a position to apply maximum pressure on the Unionists, as he depended on their votes (or abstentions) for parliamentary survival, after by-election losses and defections to both Liberal Democrats and Labour had deprived him of a majority.

Paradoxically, after the humiliation of 'Black Wednesday', its handling of the economy should also be seen as a success story for the Major government. Under the skilful guidance of Ken Clarke, who replaced Lamont as Chancellor of the Exchequer in May 1993, economic recovery soon set in, and by 1997 nearly all the indicators were looking good, with unemployment well down and interest rates and inflation both low. Yet the government was so discredited that it got little benefit from it. John Major wryly referred in his memoirs to a maxim formulated by Chris Patten, "There is no such thing as a voteless economic recovery" (Major, 1999, p. 609). As the final date for a general election approached, the Tories still remained 20 points adrift in the opinion polls. The gap was slightly narrowed during the campaign, but the result of the election, which took place on 1 May 1997, could hardly have been more conclusive:

Labour	419
Conservative	165
Liberal Democrats	46
Others	29
Labour majority	179

It was the worst result for the Tories since the 1906 election, or possibly that of 1832. There were other reasons for the spectacular defeat, notably the transformation of the Labour Party and the extraordinary popularity of Tony Blair, who had been leading it since the death of John Smith in May 1994. But it is the considered opinion of the leading pollster, Robert Worcester, that a landslide defeat was already "inevitable" after 'Black Wednesday' and Major's mishandling of the Maastricht ratification (Worcester and Mortimore, 1999). After 18 years of Tory rule, the argument that it was time for a change was extremely strong, and any Tory leader would no doubt have had great difficulty in retaining power. Yet Major's own shortcomings must have been, at least in part, responsible for the scale of the defeat. He was not the weak nonentity that is sometimes pictured. Hard-working and intelligent, he had clear ideas of his own about the direction in which he wanted to lead his party and his country, which could be summarised as broadly following Thatcherite economic polices, though applying them with a more sensitive hand, while adopting a much more liberal approach to social issues. He emphatically did not share Thatcher's view that "there is no such thing as society" – when he sought the premiership in 1990 he declared that it was his aim to make Britain a "classless society" by the year 2000. In less stressful times, he might well have led a successful government as a Tory social reformer, in the Shaftesbury-Disraeli tradition. A born conciliator, he was ill-prepared to counter the venom and the self-destructive instincts of the Eurosceptic wing of his party. Had a more forceful leader been chosen in 1990, such as Michael Heseltine, or even Douglas Hurd, there might have been a happier outcome. But perhaps not: a death wish had entered the soul of the Tory Party, comparable to that which afflicted Labour a decade or so earlier. The closest parallel, however, was the Balfour government, riven by dissension over Tariff Reform in 1903–05, and which went down to a similar calamitous defeat in the 1906 election.

Unlike Balfour, who clung to the Tory leadership for another six years after his defeat, and then went on to serve for a further dozen years in senior Cabinet posts, Major lost no time in bowing out, which he did with considerable dignity. On the morrow of the election, he announced his resignation as party leader on the steps of Downing Street, with the words "When the curtain comes down it is time to leave the stage", and then went off to watch a cricket match at Lords. He reserved any recriminations for his autobiography, published two years later, a thoughtful and well-written volume, which is less self-serving than the great majority of political memoirs. Unfortunately, he proved to be rather better as an author than as a politician. A man of evident decent instincts, but limited abilities: as Prime Minister he pushed these abilities to the limit. It was not enough.

Works consulted

David Butler and Dennis Kavanagh, 1992, *The British General Election of 1992*, London, Macmillan.
David Butler and Dennis Kavanagh, 1997, *The British General Election of 1997*, London, Macmillan.
Alan Clark, 1994, *Diaries*, London, Phoenix.
Edwina Currie, 2002, *Diaries 1987–1992*, London, Little Brown.
Nigel Lawson, 1992, *The View from Number 11*, London, Bantam.
John Major, 1999, *The Autobiography*, London, HarperCollins.
Terry Major-Ball, 1994, *Major Major: Memories of an Older Brother*, London, Duckworth.
Anthony Seldon, 1997, *Major: A Political Life*, London, Weidenfeld & Nicolson.
Robert Worcester and Roger Mortimore, 1999, *Explaining Labour's Landslide*, London, Politico's.

19

TONY BLAIR

Fallen idol

Tony Blair enjoyed greater and longer-lasting popularity than any other British Prime Minister in modern times. He won three elections, two of them with landslide victories, and it is certainly conceivable that, had he not led Britain into the Iraq War, he might have gone "on and on", in Margaret Thatcher's words, and rivalled the longevity in office of such early giants as Walpole (nearly 21 years) and the Younger Pitt (nearly 19). As it was, he fell somewhat short of Thatcher's 20th-century record of 11½ years.

"I was not born into the Labour Party", he famously told his party conference in 1995. This simple statement goes some way to explain both the successes and the failures which he experienced in the 13 years following his election as Labour leader in 1994. What he *was* born into, on 6 May 1953, was a somewhat tangled family tree. His father, Leo, was the illegitimate son of an actor, Charles Parsons (stage name: Jimmy Lynton), and Celia (Gussie) Ridgeway, an actress, who came from a wealthy landowning family but was living a vagabond life with two early marriages and numerous affairs to her name. Three years after Leo was born, now divorced from her second husband, she and Parsons legitimised their liaison, but had already passed on the infant Leo to foster parents in Glasgow, James Blair, a shipyard worker, and his wife, Mary, a dedicated Communist. Leo, who was brought up in a council tenement block, left school at 14 to work as a clerk for the Glasgow City Corporation, and for three years was secretary of the Scottish Young Communist League. In 1942, aged 18, he joined the army as a private, but by the time he was demobilised, in 1947, he had risen to the rank of major, with a fierce determination to make his way in the world. He got a job as a junior tax inspector, whilst studying law by night at Edinburgh University, becoming a law tutor and subsequently a lecturer in administrative law at the University of Adelaide. Before departing for Australia, in 1954, however, he had established a family of his own, marrying Hazel Corscaden, the step-daughter of a Glasgow butcher, of Protestant Northern Irish origin, in 1948. They had three children, the eldest of whom, William, was born in 1950. When the second son followed, three years later, he was named Anthony Charles Lynton Blair, but was given no indication of the significance of his second and third names until 1994, when the *Daily Mail* dug up the details about his grandparents during the Labour leadership election. In the words of Blair's first biographer, Jon Sopel, "Tony Blair had known that his father had been adopted, but it

DOI: 10.4324/9781003031963-20

was something Leo did not speak about, and equally something the children didn't ask about" (Sopel, 1995, p. 6). The family was completed with the birth, in Australia, of Sarah, in 1956.

They stayed in Australia for three years, by which time Leo Blair, who had long since shed his Communist affiliations, had formed a firm ambition to become a Conservative MP, and returned to Britain with the primary intention of pursuing this aim. He successfully applied for a job as a law lecturer at Durham University, read for the English bar and began to practise as a barrister in Newcastle upon Tyne, while becoming chairman of the local Conservative Association, where he was remembered as being full of charm and intensely ambitious. The young Tony was sent, as a day-boy, to the Durham Choristers' School, where he was renowned for his ever-present smile, as well as being a very good pupil, who took part in all the school activities, playing cricket and rugby for the school teams, singing in the choir and acting in school productions. From a toddler onwards, he had shown marked extrovert tendencies, always ready to put himself on show. Meanwhile, his father, who later confessed to having nursed ambitions to be Prime Minister, was all set to take the first important step in his own political career, being the hot favourite to secure the nomination for the safe Conservative seat of Hexham, in rural Northumberland. Then, on 4 July 1964, disaster struck. He suffered a devastating stroke, from which he was not initially expected to recover, and which left him without the power of speech for three years. The 11-year-old Tony went down on his knees and prayed with his headmaster, Canon John Grove, for his father's recovery. Their prayers were answered, but it took an unconscionably long time, and it permanently put paid to his hopes for a parliamentary career.

A further misfortune was to follow: Tony's younger sister Sarah fell seriously ill with Still's disease, a form of infantile rheumatoid arthritis, which necessitated her hospitalisation for two long years, after which she emerged only partially cured. Tony's mother, Hazel, exhausted herself looking after her sick husband and daughter, and possibly neglected her second son in the process, while her own mother, who was suffering from Alzheimer's disease, came to live with them, and proved an additional burden. The family income sharply declined, the university kept open Leo's job and paid him throughout the three years that he was out of action, but his earnings at the bar fell away. Blair himself was later to recall: "Don't get me wrong, it was a happy childhood, but it also seemed as though I was spending every spare minute in Durham hospital, visiting either my father or sister … and there was a lot of worry and uncertainty attached to that" (Sopel, 1995, p. 12). Tony was yet to reject his father's chosen party, and just before leaving the Choristers' School, at the age of nearly 13, he stood as the Tory candidate in a mock election timed to coincide with the 1966 general election.

He left to go to Fettes, the 'Scottish Eton', where the majority of the pupils were the sons of wealthy Scottish businessmen, and this experience was to turn him into a rebel, though never an extreme one. Tony won a scholarship to go to the school, which was necessary as his father was no longer in a position to pay the full fees. One of the worst examples of an unreconstructed Victorian-age 'public' school, it had a culture of bullying and a host of petti-fogging restrictions, including firm rules about exactly how many buttons of the boys' blazers must be kept done up at all times. Blair particularly objected to the custom of fagging, and the fact that senior boys were entitled to cane the younger ones, almost at will. Blair was thrashed many times, ran away on one occasion and on another narrowly escaped expulsion. His rebellion did not appear to have any political overtones, but was manifested by a consistent flouting of authority. As earlier, he was noted at Fettes for his ever-present smile, and often devastating charm, so that he remained popular even with those to whom he caused offence.

Blair's greatest distinction at Fettes was as an actor: he got rave notices in the school magazine for his role as Mark Antony in *Julius Caesar*, and for playing the lead part in the R.C. Sherriff play, *Journey's End*.

After a gap year, spent in London, where, with other 'public' school types, he scratched a living as an impresario for rock bands, he went to St John's College, Oxford, to study law. Unlike most other future politicians of his generation, who found themselves at Oxford or Cambridge, Blair had nothing to do with either the Union or student political clubs. Initially, at least, he devoted himself to having a 'good time', his main interests being rock music, and girls, for whom, as a good-looking young man, over six feet tall and with an open, friendly manner, he had a ready attraction. He became the lead singer for a group called The Ugly Rumours, modelling himself very much on Mick Jagger, and being much remarked for the androgynous nature of his performances. There was, however, a more serious side to his three years at Oxford. He fell in with a group of high-minded, quasi-Marxist students, mostly from Commonwealth countries, led by an Australian priest and Christian Socialist, Peter Thomson. Blair maintains that Thomson converted him to both Christianity and Socialism. He was already a nominal believer, despite the atheism of his father, while from his mother, who was to die of cancer at the age of 52, shortly after his graduation, he had acquired much of her social conscience but little of her Presbyterianism. Under Thomson's influence, Blair was confirmed into the Church of England, and for some time considered taking Holy Orders. Thomson introduced him to an elderly, and once quite well-known, Scottish theologian, John Macmurray. Macmurray was the prophet of a 'communitarian' form of Christianity, whose effect, according to Blair's second biographer, John Rentoul, "was to invert Adam Smith's dictum 'Social and self-love are the same'. Smith said that if we follow our self-interest, we benefit the whole community. Macmurray said that by pursuing the community's interests we benefit the individuals within it, including ourselves" (Rentoul, 2001, pp. 41–2). Blair was bowled over by Macmurray's teaching, and proclaimed that it had become the basis of both his religious and political beliefs.

Blair graduated in June 1975, with an Upper Second Class degree, and, moving to London, where he shared a flat in Earl's Court with an Oxford friend, signed on for a one-year bar course at Lincoln's Inn. He also joined the Labour Party, becoming secretary of his local ward branch at the first meeting he attended. He then applied for a pupillage at the chambers of Derry Irvine, a QC with strong Labour Party connections. Irvine had already selected another young prospect, called Cherie Booth, who had graduated with First Class Honours in Law at the London School of Economics, and had come top of the year in the bar exams, well ahead of Blair. Irvine had intended to take on only one pupil, but was so impressed by Blair's enthusiasm that he accepted him as well. Irvine found Blair a quick and willing worker, and assigned him to handle a sheaf of trade union cases, which put him in touch with leading figures in the trade union movement. He also got to know John Smith, who was to be his predecessor as leader of the Labour Party, and who was a close personal friend of Irvine's. He and Cherie were initially wary of each other, being rivals for promotion within the chambers – Blair eventually won out, and Cherie left to join another firm. By then, however, the personal chemistry between them was well developed, Cherie subsequently saying, "Once you succumb to Tony's charm, you never really get over it." On 29 March 1980, they were married at his college chapel in Oxford. Like Tony, Cherie had had a difficult childhood, and her family situation somewhat mirrored that of Tony's father, Leo. Her father was the well-known actor Tony Booth, an Irish Catholic and strong Labour Party supporter, who claimed to be related to the actor John Wilkes Booth, who assassinated President Lincoln. For Cherie, however, he had been very much an absentee father, abandoning his first wife Gale, and leaving her to bring up Cherie and her younger sister Lyndsey alone, earning a living in the Lancashire town of Crosby by working in a fish and chip shop and other menial jobs. Booth then went on to have another five marriages or serious liaisons, which produced five half-sisters for Lyndsey and Cherie. Unlike Blair, Cherie had deep roots in the Labour movement, joining the party at the age of 16.

In May 1982, Blair put himself forward to be the Labour candidate for a by-election in Beaconsfield, a normally solidly Tory Home Counties seat, but which it was thought that the SDP might well win, in the light of its three successive by-election victories in Croydon, Crosby (where Cherie had unsuccessfully tried for the Labour candidature) and Glasgow Hillhead. The Falklands war intervened, puncturing the SDP challenge, and the Tories held on comfortably enough, Blair coming in a poor third, and losing his deposit. He then embarked on a long search to find a safe Labour seat to contest at the forthcoming general election, and when the election was declared he had still not found one. Yet, there was one remaining seat which had not made its selection – Sedgefield in County Durham. Blair headed off for the constituency with only a vague hope of picking up a nomination, and more by luck than judgement succeeded. He was duly selected on the fifth ballot by the constituency Labour Party. The election itself was a virtual formality: he had a majority of over 8,000 over his Tory opponent, with the SDP/Alliance candidate coming in third.

The overall election result was a disaster for Labour, which polled its lowest percentage vote since 1918, and saw Thatcher's majority rise from 44 to 144. Blair, aged 30, was the youngest of the 209 Labour members elected. Soon after he was asked to share a room in the Commons, with the new MP for Dunfermline East – Gordon Brown. Two years older, Brown had vastly more political experience than his new room-mate. A former chairman of the Scottish Labour Party, he had contested the 1979 general election for Edinburgh South, and already had behind him a distinguished academic career, as well as having worked as a television editor and reporter. Brown took Blair under his wing, and, on Blair's own account, taught him all the basic political and communication skills which he previously lacked – how to draft a press release, the importance of bullet points and sound-bites, and the difference between a punchy political speech and a reasoned appeal to judges sitting in the High Court. Blair regarded Brown with something approaching awe, and shared the common view (certainly held by Brown himself) that he was a future leader of the party. The two men, who grew extraordinarily close, agreed on the fundamental necessity of modernising the Labour Party, stripping it of all its unelectable policies and undemocratic structures so that it could present a much more appealing face to the voters. This aim was shared by the new party leader, Neil Kinnock, who within a few months of their election promoted both of them to be junior frontbench spokesmen. At Kinnock's prompting, Peter Mandelson, the Labour Party's new communications director, used his considerable manipulative skills to ensure that the two men achieved maximum exposure on radio and television programmes, estimating that they would make a far more favourable impression than most of their rivals on the opposition benches.

Over the next dozen years, with Brown always one step ahead, they worked their way steadily up the Labour Party's hierarchy, achieving election to the Shadow Cabinet and filling successively more senior Shadow portfolios. In July 1992, following Labour's disappointing election defeat, John Smith succeeded Kinnock as leader, appointing Brown as Shadow Chancellor and Blair as Shadow Home Secretary. This was an enormous challenge for Blair, and he took it with both hands. Identifying the popular belief that the Tories were the 'law and order' party, and that Labour was 'soft on crime', he set out to change this public perception and to turn a vote-losing into a vote-winning issue. Few people would have given him much chance of success, but the opinion polls recorded a remarkable turnaround. In 1992, according to the Gallup Poll, the Tories enjoyed a 21-point advantage over Labour on the issue. Two years later, Labour had established a five-point lead. Nobody doubted that Blair was responsible. He had shifted Labour's focus from explaining away the sociological causes of crime to a deep concern for the plight of victims, and had conspicuously refrained from opposing the ever more draconian measures introduced by the new Tory Home Secretary, Michael Howard. Above all, however, he had pulled off the trick by utilising a brilliant sound-bite, which in less than a dozen words succeeded in encapsulating both the traditional Tory and traditional Labour approaches: "Tough on crime, and tough on the causes of crime." This, he endlessly repeated in television debates, and neither Howard nor any other Tory spokesman was able to find an effective riposte.

By this time, and largely unremarked by most of his colleagues, including Brown, Blair had emerged as by far the most persuasive political performer on television. His over-ready smile may have put off a small minority of viewers, but most responded positively to his youth, charm, conviction and well-presented arguments. By contrast, Brown came over as formidably well-informed, but dour and more obviously repetitive. This was the underlying reason why it was Blair and not Brown who was chosen to succeed John Smith, after his sudden death on 12 May 1994. The immediate reaction of some observers was that Brown, who had proved a highly effective Shadow Chancellor, would be a 'shoo-in', but within a few hours it became clear that Blair had overtaken him in terms of support among Labour MPs, and was determined to put himself forward. Even worse for Brown was the publication within three days of opinion polls showing that Blair was far ahead of any potential rivals so far as public opinion was concerned. The MORI poll, for example, showed Blair with 32 per cent, John Prescott with 19 per cent, Margaret Beckett 14 per cent, Brown 9 per cent and Robin Cook 5 per cent. This was immediately sufficient to put Cook, Labour's best debater (who would have been a formidable challenger if the choice had been restricted to Labour MPs instead of an electoral college made up of parliamentarians, trade unionists and Labour Party members), out of the running. After 15 years in opposition, the party was desperately anxious to choose the person best placed to win a general election, and the opinion polls gave an enormous boost to Blair's chances. Although Brown was widely regarded as a more heavyweight figure and more intellectually distinguished than Blair, he seemed less well placed to win back voters in the south of England, which was the key to Labour's electoral success. That he was a Scotsman and, unlike Blair, not a family man, were probably seen as additional handicaps. Two years earlier, at the time of John Smith's election, the two men had agreed that they would not oppose each other in the event of a future contest, in order not to split the modernisers' vote. At that time, it had been clear that Brown would be the stronger candidate, and he regarded this agreement as a guarantee that Blair would not run against him. He was irate that Blair was now intent on supplanting him and was putting enormous pressure on him not to declare his own candidature. What probably made it all the more galling for Brown was that it was he who had suggested the famous "tough on crime" sound-bite which had been so effective in furthering Blair's dizzy ascent. Eventually, he concluded that he couldn't win, and agreed to meet Blair at an Islington restaurant, the Granita, to strike a bargain. Blair agreed that Brown would become Chancellor if Labour won the election, with much more sweeping powers over both economic and social policy than any previous Chancellor had enjoyed. He also suggested that if Labour were to win two successive elections, he would make way for Brown some time during the second term. Brown took this as a firm promise, yet it is doubtful whether Blair intended it as such. Brown then participated in a photo-opportunity with Blair, and declared his support for his campaign. Blair went on to win the contest convincingly, with majorities in all three sections of the electoral college. The overall result, in percentages, was:

Blair	57.0
Prescott	24.1
Beckett	18.9

Although they continued to co-operate closely, and the government formed after the 1997 election was almost a diarchy, this episode marked the end of the intimate friendship between Blair and Brown. The latter was badly bruised and continued to harbour resentment, which he was scarcely able to conceal. It would probably have been better to have cleared the air, and for both to have contested the leadership election. Blair would almost certainly have won, and – as it was an exhaustive ballot – there was no serious risk of letting in a more 'traditionalist' candidate, such as Prescott.

The new party leader set himself single-mindedly to achieve one objective – to make Labour electable. He was able to build on the steps already taken by Neil Kinnock and John Smith, but he was to reveal a ruthlessness and determination which went far beyond anything they had shown. The fact that he had come to the party as an 'outsider' was a positive advantage, as he had no scruples or inhibitions about sweeping aside policies, attitudes and institutions which had become part of the mindset of most of those who were more rooted in the party. This was quickly evidenced by his assault on Clause Four, the famous article in the Labour Party constitution which called for the "common ownership of the means of production, distribution and exchange". This nearly 80-year-old provision was at odds with the actual practice of Labour governments, but it allowed their Tory opponents to picture the party as doctrinaire nationalisers. Hugh Gaitskell had come a cropper when he tried to delete the clause after the 1959 general election defeat, and at least four of his five successors had been embarrassed by its provisions but had felt powerless to do anything about it. Blair used his first speech as party leader to announce to the 1994 party conference that he would be proposing a replacement clause, which would be submitted for approval to a special party conference in March 1995. Many thought he was heading for a humiliating rebuff, but he threw himself into the campaign, addressing Labour Party meetings throughout the country in shirtsleeves, and when the vote was taken at the special party conference, Blair's innocuous re-wording, which excised any mention of 'public ownership', or even 'equality', from the party's aims, was approved by a 2-1 majority. It was a triumph, and Blair drove home the message even further by effectively re-naming the party New Labour, even though there was no official change of name. The Tories were nonplussed, as John Major acknowledged in his autobiography, "They pronounced themselves 'new' Labour, and with that single word denied their past ... Effective it certainly was. It did us untold damage" (Major, 1999, p. 694).

Blair, clearly influenced by Bill Clinton's success in winning election in 1992 by driving the Democratic Party sharply to the right, consolidated his New Labour makeover by redrawing "its policies on tax, inflation, the minimum wage, exam league tables, opted-out schools, Northern Ireland, regional government and the House of Lords ... in each case, policy change moved Labour closer to the Conservatives" (Rentoul, 2001, p. 264). He even, daringly, spoke admiringly of Mrs Thatcher, and clearly regarded her as some sort of role-model, in her methods, if not her objectives. Blair's greatest coup was to help rid Labour of its reputation as a 'tax and spend' party. In agreement with Gordon Brown, he made a firm commitment not to increase either the standard rate, or – more controversially – the maximum rate of income tax, which had been reduced by the Tories to 40 per cent, lower than in most other Western countries, where 50 or 60 per cent was the norm. Brown followed this up by pledging not to increase expenditure during the first two years of a Labour government beyond the levels currently planned by the Tory Chancellor, Kenneth Clarke. These moves pre-empted any attempt by the Tories to repeat their scare tactics of the 1992 election, when Labour was accused of planning massive tax increases; they were already inhibited by the fact – well publicised by Labour – that they themselves had introduced no fewer than 22 tax increases, despite their pledges at the previous election.

Blair also revolutionised Labour's presentation and handling of the media, under the tutelage of Peter Mandelson, and the political consultant Philip Gould, whose 'focus groups' became an essential tool in trying out new initiatives. Alastair Campbell, a talented tabloid journalist, was recruited as Blair's press adviser, and initiated a much more focused and pro-active approach to the media. This even extended to pro-Tory newspapers, which no previous Labour leader had contemplated wooing, regarding their hostility as a badge of their own rectitude. Particular attention was paid to Rupert Murdoch's newspapers, one of which, *The Sun*, had vilified Kinnock during the 1992 election and had – not implausibly – claimed to have been the crucial factor in ensuring Major's victory – "It Was The Sun Wot Won It" declared its post-election headline. Campbell's efforts certainly paid dividends. *The Sun* endorsed Labour at the outset of the 1997 election campaign, while both Lord Rothermere's *Daily Mail* and Conrad Black's *Daily Telegraph* notably softened their approach.

Consciously or otherwise, Blair was running not so much against the Tories, but against 'old Labour', abandoning if not always attacking most of the policies with which it had recently been associated. Indeed, it was much clearer what Blair was against than what he favoured; he tended to speak in vague generalities, evoking mood music rather than setting out detailed policy proposals, thus denying his opponents concrete targets to attack, and earning himself the nickname 'Tony Blur'. What Blair was offering the country, however, was not so much new policies as a new man – himself. Largely through his television appearances and his platform speeches – less so his performances in the House of Commons, where he usually but not invariably came out on top in his encounters with John Major – he had created an astonishingly favourable impression, which was reflected in a massive lead in the opinion polls. He came over as fresh, youthful, energetic and eloquent – a beacon of hope and optimism, very much as John F. Kennedy had done in his presidential campaign three decades earlier. He also evoked more contemporary comparisons with Bill Clinton, though as one Tory minister wryly remarked, he was even more effective "because he kept his trousers zipped up".

It was not only Blair's popularity, however, which set the stage for the sweeping Labour victory on 1 May 1997. At least equally responsible was the bitterly divided state of the Tory Party, which must make it highly probable that Labour would have won, even if John Smith had not died three years earlier. Smith lacked Blair's charisma, and would not have gone nearly so far in reforming the Labour Party, but he was a highly respected figure who had already opened up a wide lead in the polls before his death. Had he survived, the Tories might well have done rather better, but it is improbable that, with 'Black Wednesday' (see Chapter 18) never lived down, they would have been able to escape defeat. As it was, Labour under Blair's leadership won a majority of 179 seats, eclipsing even their famous victory of 1945, when Clement Attlee led by 146.

Blair, who had established close behind-the-scenes relations with the Liberal Democrat leader, Paddy Ashdown, had secretly intended to form a coalition government, with Ashdown joining the Cabinet as Home or Foreign Secretary. This would have effectively recreated the broad progressive alliance which had existed prior to World War I, the collapse of which led – in the view of Roy Jenkins, with whom Blair was also in close contact – to the Tory dominance throughout the greater part of the 20th century. Yet so overwhelming was Labour's victory, that any thoughts of coalition soon evaporated, Blair realising that even he would not be able to persuade his own party to give up part of the fruits of victory, when there was no pressing need to do so. The Cabinet he formed was one of beginners – after 18 years of Tory rule neither he nor any of his colleagues had ever served in a Cabinet before, and only three of them had experience of junior ministerial office. Nevertheless, none of them appeared lacking in self-confidence, and the general level of competence was high, though there were few obvious heavyweights, apart from Brown, the new Chancellor, and to a lesser extent, Robin Cook, the Foreign Secretary. The other major offices were filled by John Prescott, who became Deputy Premier and headed an unwieldy department combining Environment and Transport, Jack Straw, Home Secretary, and Lord Irvine, Blair's legal mentor, as Lord Chancellor. David Blunkett, universally admired for overcoming the handicap of blindness, was to prove an energetic and resourceful Education Secretary.

Yet the government was dominated, from first to last, by two men, Blair and Brown, who made a formidable combination, though not always a harmonious one. Blair certainly consulted with Brown on all important matters, but hardly at all the Cabinet as a whole. The long, detailed discussions which characterised Major's Cabinets rapidly became a thing of the past, and Blair quickly reverted to the Thatcher model of short and relatively infrequent meetings, with most decisions taken at *ad hoc* meetings with individual ministers or in small groups. More influential than any Cabinet minister, other than Brown, were Blair's three closest advisers. Peter Mandelson was appointed, initially, as Minister without Portfolio, outside the Cabinet, but was constantly at the Prime Minister's beck and call. Jonathan Powell, a former Foreign Office official who had resigned to run Blair's office while in opposition, became his Chief of Staff, taking over many of the normal responsibilities of the Principal Private Secretary, though he was denied the actual title after Civil Service protests. A younger brother of Charles Powell, who had been one of Thatcher's closest advisers, he was entrusted by Blair with many delicate tasks, including overseeing the Northern Ireland Office, much to the chagrin of the Secretary of State, Mo Mowlem. The third, and most influential of the triumvirs was Alastair Campbell, appointed to head the government's information services, but so close to Blair that he was popularly known as 'the real deputy Prime Minister'.

The new government was fortunate in having been bequeathed a healthy economic situation by its predecessors, thanks largely to the stewardship of Ken Clarke as the last Tory Chancellor. All previous Labour governments had entered office in less favourable circumstances, and had had to contend with almost immediate financial crises. This time it was different, and Blair's team lost no time in consolidating and, indeed, improving on the hand which it had been dealt. Within days of taking office, Brown took the bold step of handing over to the Bank of England the regulation of interest rates, within the limits of an inflation target set by the government. This meant that interest rate policy was no longer subject to crude political manipulation, and the change was warmly welcomed by most economic commentators. Brown kept to his promise of keeping spending down over the first two years to the limits set by the Tories, despite pressure from his own backbenchers. "Prudence with a purpose" was his motto, holding out the prospect for considerable expansion at a later date, when much of the debt accumulated by the previous government would have been paid off. He was then able to announce very substantial increases in the money available for schools and the National Health Service. In the meantime, he embarked on a sustained 'welfare to work' programme, designed to take large numbers off the unemployment register and to provide them with productive jobs or training opportunities. The programme was largely financed by a 'windfall tax' levied on privatised firms which had been sold off cheaply by the previous government, and were making excessive profits. The government kept its promise not to raise income tax, but succeeded in increasing its revenues by a series of 'stealth taxes', which had no visible effect on the incomes of most taxpayers. The most controversial of these was the abolition of tax relief on the investment income of company pension schemes. Brown used the yield from these taxes to increase benefits skewed towards people on low incomes, and the redistributive effect was probably as great as it would have been if he had been in a position to raise the maximum income tax rate. Although he was criticised for attempting too much 'fine tuning' in his budgets and welfare policy changes, few would question that Gordon Brown was one of, if not the most successful of post-war Chancellors of the Exchequer. His record was summarised in the following terms by the authors of the 2001 Nuffield election survey, normally regarded as impartial observers:

> Inflation stayed below 3 per cent, GDP grew annually by about 2.5 per cent over the next four years. Opposition prophecies of doom were refuted regularly by the monthly economic statistics. Unemployment fell from 1.9 million in 1997 to under 1 million in 2001. Gordon Brown was able to boast of his achievement in paying off a sizeable proportion of the national debt, helped by buoyant tax revenues and by £22bn from the sale of digital channels in 2000. £34bn of government borrowing was paid off and debt servicing fell from 44 per cent to 32 per cent of government expenditure.
>
> *(Butler and Kavanagh, 2002), p. 2)*

In addition, and for the first time ever, Britain's economic performance, as measured by the usual indicators, was better than that of the European Union as a whole.

If economic and social policy had largely been sub-contracted to Brown, Blair himself certainly kept close control over the various constitutional changes which figured prominently in his first term. Devolution to Scotland and Wales was quickly legislated, and was approved by a large majority in a referendum in Scotland, but by only a slender one in Wales. In the subsequent elections, conducted under proportional representation, Labour emerged as much the largest party, but without an overall majority, and Lab-Lib coalitions were formed in both countries. Labour also legislated to set up a Greater London Authority, with its own elected mayor, and this too was approved in a referendum by London voters. Blair, however, who was already being accused of 'control freakery' because of the tight discipline he sought to exercise over the Labour Party, seemed unwilling to accept the logic of these reforms and to leave the choice of leadership to the local populations. He manipulated trade union block votes (which he had previously sought to curb) in order to impose less popular candidates to lead the new assemblies in Wales and London, instead of Rhodri Morgan and Ken Livingstone respectively.

He just pulled it off, but in each case it ended in tears. In London, Livingstone refused to accept what he dubbed a "rigged vote", stood for Mayor as an Independent and was very easily elected, with the unfortunate Labour candidate, Frank Dobson, who had resigned as Health Secretary to contest the election, reduced to a poor third place. The outcome in Wales was only marginally better: Blair's choice, Alun Michael, was only able to secure a mediocre victory in the election, and was soon forced out by the Assembly members to make way for Morgan.

A notable achievement of the Blair government was to incorporate the European Convention of Human Rights directly into British law, which was effected by the Human Rights Act of 1998. Less praiseworthy was the Freedom of Information Act, which was a pale shadow of the measure which Labour had trailed while in opposition, and which was regarded as a betrayal by many supporters of open government, both inside and outside the Labour Party. Blair himself, however, felt he had gone much too far, and later described himself as a "a naive, foolish, irresponsible nincompoop" for introducing the measure (Blair, 2010, p. 516). He also disappointed his party over House of Lords reform. A Bill to replace the great majority of hereditary peers was duly passed, after a compromise was struck with Lord Cranborne, the Tory leader in the Upper House. Cranborne had failed to consult William Hague, who promptly sacked him, though the deal went through. It allowed some 92 'hereditaries' to remain in the House pending a more thorough-going reform. No progress was made on this, however, Blair wishing to proceed to an entirely nominated Upper House, while a majority of Labour, Liberal and even Conservative MPs wanted at least a partially elected chamber.

Labour had had discussions, before and after the 1997 election, with the Liberals on the question of electoral reform, and had promised in its election manifesto to hold a referendum on whether to change over to proportional representation (PR) for elections to the House of Commons. Although an independent commission was appointed, presided over by Roy Jenkins, which produced a report in favour of a hybrid system with a strong proportional element, no referendum was in fact held, a rare example of a specific manifesto commitment by Labour not being honoured. Blair, in fact – unlike his predecessor Neil Kinnock – had never been convinced that PR would be desirable, and the promise had been made as an inducement to the Liberal Democrats, when he expected to be in need of their support. When this transpired not to be the case, he soon lost interest. For their part, the Liberal Democrats, though naturally disappointed, failed to kick up any sort of fuss about the broken promise. PR was adopted for the European elections, as well as in those for the devolved assemblies.

In Northern Ireland, Blair followed up Major's earlier initiative, with rather greater success, partly because of his superior negotiating skills, but also because he was not dependent on Unionist support to maintain his parliamentary majority. The climax came, in April 1998, when – with much assistance from the US mediator George Mitchell, and with President Clinton helpfully available at the other end of a phone – he and Irish Premier Bertie Ahern were able to conclude the Good Friday Agreement with the main Northern Irish political parties (except for Ian Paisley's Democratic Unionists). Under this agreement, the Nationalist parties (including Sinn Fein) agreed that Northern Ireland should continue to be part of the United Kingdom as long as this was the wish of the majority of the population, while the Irish Republic agreed to amend its constitution renouncing its claim on the six Northern counties. In exchange the Unionists agreed to form a power-sharing executive with the Nationalist parties. Provisions were made for the release of convicted Republican and Loyalist prisoners provided that their organisations maintained a permanent ceasefire, and for the 'de-commissioning' of arms held by paramilitary groups on both sides. The agreement was to be underpinned by referenda on both sides of the Irish border, which took place a month later, producing a positive majority of 94 per cent in the Irish Republic, but only 71 per cent (including a bare majority of Unionists) in the North. Other people besides Blair and Ahern were responsible for the success of the negotiation, including the Northern Irish Secretary, Mo Mowlem, and Jonathan Powell, but few people would deny that Blair's contribution, which involved three long days of hard bargaining and the trading of subtle compromises, during which he showed enormous patience, intellectual agility and stamina, was crucial. An exhausted Blair told the concluding press conference that the negotiators had felt "the hand of history" on their shoulders as they reached the end of their transactions. This was not the end of the rocky road in Northern Ireland, and the process continued to have its ups and downs, including one particularly bloody outrage in Omagh, in August 1998, in which 29 civilians were killed by Republican extremists, but since then there has been relative peace and security in the North, and hope has replaced despair. A power-sharing executive was sworn in, led initially by Ian Paisley, with Sinn Fein's Martin McGuinness as his deputy, which proceeded to govern with surprising harmony, though there have been occasional blips.

If Blair achieved more than most people expected in Northern Ireland, his record concerning the European Union was a frank disappointment, at least to Europhiles. Proclaimed as the most pro-European Premier since Ted Heath, he made a good start by adopting a co-operative attitude during the Amsterdam summit, in June 1997, ending the growing isolation in which Britain had found itself during at least the latter half of the Major premiership. He did not, however, succeed in his aim of breaking into the tight Franco-German alliance, which had long been the driving force behind European integration. He did hold an important bilateral summit with President Jacques Chirac, at Saint-Malo in 1998, when they agreed a measure of Anglo-French defence co-operation which helped to launch the beginnings of a European Defence and Security Policy (EDSP). On other issues, though, the French President and his German Socialist partner, Gerhard Schröder, kept him at arm's length. Blair responded by attempting to organise a rival power bloc within the EU by cosying up to the centre-right leaders of the other two large member states, Spain's Jose-Maria Aznar and Italy's Silvio Berlusconi.

Yet Blair's hopes of providing constructive British leadership for the EU were blighted, largely because of his own hesitancy and irresolution. He had formed the view that it was essential for Britain to join the single currency, due to be established in 1999, but had reluctantly agreed, in 1996, to promise a referendum on the issue, when Major had conceded this to his Eurosceptic critics. Boldness would have counselled holding an immediate poll after his election in May 1997, when the honeymoon period was in full swing and his own enormous popularity would most likely have produced a favourable result, despite the fact that the opinion polls were showing a majority in favour of keeping the pound. He passed up the opportunity, and later allowed himself to be consistently outmanoeuvred by Gordon Brown, a relative sceptic on the issue. Brown bounced him into agreeing an announcement, in October 1997, that Britain was unlikely to be one of the founding members of EMU in 1999, and that a decision to join was improbable during the course of the current Parliament. He also acquiesced in linking the ultimate decision to five largely subjective 'tests' on the effect on the British economy, which the Treasury, under Brown's direction, would be responsible for carrying out. The long delay involved in making these assessments, which continued until March 2003 –when only one of the five was judged to have been met – made it impossible to

238 Tony Blair

launch a wholehearted campaign to convince public opinion. In the meantime, the opposition in the polls, stirred up by a great deal of mendacious reporting in the Murdoch, Black and Rothermere press, grew greater and greater, so that the prospects of winning a referendum, even if the tests were judged to have been passed, grew increasingly bleak. Sadly, Blair's own words, spoken in 2001, could well be applied to himself: "The history of our engagement with Europe is one of opportunities missed in the name of illusions – and Britain suffering as a result" (Stephens, 2004, p. 207).

Blair's hesitancy over Europe was not reflected in his broader approach to foreign affairs, where, fortified by his Christian faith, he hastened to give a marked moralistic twist to British policy. There was no doubt that Blair took his religious beliefs seriously. He was the first British Premier since Gladstone known to be a regular Bible-reader, but his approach is somewhat eclectic, as he has also read the Qur'an three times, and described Islam, in an interview with *Muslim News*, in March 2000, as "a deeply reflective, peaceful, very beautiful religious faith" (Rentoul, 2001, p. 351). Although ostensibly an Anglican, he regularly attended Roman Catholic services with his wife and children, who were educated in Catholic schools. (In 2008, after he had left the premiership, he was himself received into the Catholic faith.) The medley of religious influences to which he had exposed himself convinced him that Britain has a moral duty, where circumstances permit, to use its influence, and where necessary its armed strength, to intervene in defence of justice and democracy throughout the world. This put him in the direct line of succession to the mid-19th-century Premier, Lord Palmerston, who did not share his Christian faith, but who proclaimed a Pax Britannica, and used gunboat diplomacy to promote it. Britain's military strength was insufficient to give Blair the same scope for international intervention, but, as a book published in early 2003 pointed out, it was "some feat to go to war five times in six years" (Kampfner, 2003, p. ix). Three of these, the air strikes against Saddam Hussein, in 1998, the Kosovo war a year later, and the dispatch of British troops to Sierra Leone in 2000, occurred during his first term of office. Although there was some vocal opposition, especially to the Kosovo operation, he also attracted much admiration and support, and had little difficulty in carrying public opinion along with him. This perhaps added dangerously to his self-confidence, leading him into a much rasher, and infinitely less popular venture in 2003.

Blair was fully aware of how damaging the repeated accusations of 'sleaze' had been against his Tory predecessors, and was determined that his own administration should not be tarred with the same brush. "We must be whiter than white", he told his MPs on the morrow of their election victory. It was hardly to be – though the number and the seriousness of the scandals which arose were far less, his government was unable entirely to escape criticism on this score. The most serious incident concerned a Labour promise to ban advertising and sponsorship by tobacco firms. Six months after the election, Blair received a visit at Downing Street from Bernie Ecclestone, the head of Formula One motor racing, who argued persuasively that the sport would suffer grievous harm if tobacco sponsorship was brought to a sudden end. Blair listened sympathetically to his case, and then sent a memo to the Health Secretary asking him to look for a way "to protect the position of sports in general and Formula I in particular". It then transpired that Ecclestone had earlier given a £1 million donation to Labour, and – in the face of press criticism – the party referred the matter to the incoming chairman of the Committee on Standards in Public Life, who advised that the donation be returned, which it was. Blair angrily denied in a television interview that his decision on sponsorship had been affected in any way by knowledge of Ecclestone's gift, saying: "I think most people who have dealt with me think I'm a pretty straight sort of guy". His public standing was still very high, and most people seemed prepared to give him the benefit of the doubt. There were to be three Cabinet resignations during Blair's first term, including two by Peter Mandelson, the first of which reflected on his personal judgement and the second on the Prime Minister's, but – on the whole – Labour escaped being bracketed with the Tories over 'sleaze'. It was another monosyllable – 'spin' – which came to be seen as its Achilles' heel.

The high priest of spin was seen to be Alastair Campbell, who had wrought wonders for Labour in opposition, and continued to render signal service to Blair for several years subsequently. His most notable coup was to compose Blair's 'spontaneous' reaction to the death of Princess Diana, whom he described as "the People's Princess", striking a chord with the British public and adding enormously to Blair's own, already high, reputation. Yet eventually the law of diminishing returns began to set in. Campbell repeatedly made excessive claims on behalf of the government, for example by double-counting the amount of money being spent on successive education and health service initiatives. His own relations with the media also began to deteriorate, as he upset more and more journalists by his bullying manner, and by his frequent and often unjustified complaints to radio and television producers and executives about their political coverage.

The first Blair government was able to deliver on the great majority of its specific promises, but as the end of the 20th century loomed, there was no doubting the widespread sense of disappointment about its performance. Yet Labour continued to enjoy a massive opinion poll lead over the Tories, with no sign of a mid-term revolt, and only one very temporary blip, in September 2000, at the time of the fuel tax protests. One reason for this was the almost total failure of the Tories to regain public confidence, which in turn was partly due to their choice of William Hague as leader in 1997 in preference to the vastly more experienced and more popular Kenneth Clarke. Although Hague was a good performer in the House of Commons, and often had Blair in difficulty at Question Time, his political judgement was poor, and he never established a rapport with the general public. His choice of "defending the pound" as his major campaign theme was a crucial error: although a majority of voters remained sceptical of changing to the Euro, this was never a salient issue for more than a minority. When the voters returned to the ballot boxes in June 2001, their verdict was almost identical to that of 1997, with Labour gaining an overall majority of 165, and the Tories winning precisely one more seat than four years earlier. There was, however, one significant difference, the turnout was down by over 12 per cent, and at 59.4 per cent was the lowest since 1918. A contributory factor was clearly the widespread perception that Labour was certain to win, but it was widely seen as a measure of the disillusionment with the whole political process, which had set in during Blair's premiership, and a stark warning for the future.

The re-elected government lost no time in indicating that its top priority would be to match the large additional spending on public services with reform measures which would make a qualitative difference and ensure that the money would not be dissipated on inessentials or spent in pursuit of producer interests. Unfortunately, however, Blair and his ministers failed to consult widely within the Labour Party before launching their reforms, which led to two major rebellions by Labour MPs, on foundation hospitals and top-up fees for universities, which could well have toppled Blair if they had been supported by just a few extra dissidents. Greater consultation was promised for the future after the 'top-up' debate in February 2004, but many remained sceptical, feeling that the government had got into the habit of taking adequate backbench support for granted.

240 Tony Blair

For Blair, however, these were mere sidelines to his main preoccupations during his second term, which were concentrated on international affairs and, in particular, on his relationship with President George W. Bush. He demoted his independent-minded Foreign Secretary, Robin Cook, to be Leader of the Commons, appointing the more pliable Jack Straw in his place. Straw had been a notably illiberal Home Secretary, sometimes even being compared unfavourably with his Tory predecessor, Michael Howard. There was no reason to doubt, however, that he was faithfully following Blair's intentions, and his own successor, David Blunkett, was an equal disappointment to penal reformers and human rights campaigners. Blair's fixation on Bush began on the day of the latter's election, in November 2000, when he put out immediate feelers to ensure that he would be the first foreign leader invited to the White House after the inauguration in January 2001.

Blair's immediate bonding with Bush seemed odd, after his apparently warm relationship with Bill Clinton, a fellow Oxford graduate who shared many of his political views and with whom he had launched the so-called Third Way initiative to unite centre-left leaders across the world. But Blair had a sharp eye for power, and a singular lack of sentiment, in choosing his associates, and seems to have concluded that the overriding priority for Britain was to forge a close link with the US President, whoever he might be. Despite his vaunted pro-Europeanism, it soon became clear that this meant more to him than keeping in step with other EU leaders. His burgeoning relationship with Bush was cemented by the outrage of 11 September 2001, when Blair hastened once again to Washington to pledge unconditional support in the war against terrorism. On 20 September, seated next to Laura Bush in the visitors' gallery, he listened to Bush's speech to both houses of Congress. Gesturing towards him, Bush said that America had "no truer friend than Great Britain", and Blair was given a standing ovation.

Britain was the major ally of the US in the war against the Taliban, and despite some anti-war opposition, Blair had little difficulty in carrying his country, and his party, with him, notably in a barnstorming speech to his party conference in October. The speech went well beyond justifying the war in Afghanistan, pleading for a new world order which would come to the aid of victims of oppression wherever they were – "The starving, the wretched, the dispossessed, the ignorant, those living in want and squalor from the deserts of northern Africa to the slums of Gaza, to the mountain ranges of Afghanistan: they too are our cause." The quick and relatively cost-free victory in Afghanistan, despite the failure to capture or kill Osama Bin Laden, helped to convince Blair of the realism as well as the moral justification of his cause, and he began to lend a sympathetic ear to US plans for regime change in Iraq. He was anxious, however, that any action should be under UN auspices. He set out to persuade Bush to follow this path, despite the contrary advice he was getting from Vice-President Dick Cheney and Defence Secretary Donald Rumsfeld, who favoured unilateral US action. Blair's view reinforced that of Secretary of State Colin Powell, and Bush agreed to take the problem of Iraq's non-compliance with the UN disarmament resolutions to the Security Council. Blair may well, however, have unwisely left Bush with the firm impression that, if the UN route failed, Britain would still support a war. What was to prove even more damaging was that he was to base his case for going to war almost entirely on the "imminent threat" of Iraq's weapons of mass destruction (WMD) rather than the evil nature of Saddam's regime, which it appears was what really motivated him. The sequel does not need to be recapitulated in detail here – how the UN agreed to send inspectors back into Iraq on an "intrusive" basis, how the inspectors found no such weapons even though they had been guided to hundreds of sites by the "best intelligence" the US and Britain were able to provide, how on US insistence the inspections were cut short even though the chief UN inspector, Hans Blix, and his team thought that the job could be properly completed within another two to three months, how no UN resolution permitting an invasion was even put to the vote, how the invasion went ahead with only US, British and Australian forces involved, with striking military success, at least in the short run, and how after a further year's search by a US-led team no WMD were discovered.

From first to last, Blair remained convinced of the rightness, indeed the righteousness, of his decisions, though even his powers of persuasion were insufficient to convince a majority of his fellow citizens. A massive revolt, of 139 Labour MPs, occurred in the Commons, and, on the eve of the war, the biggest ever protest demonstration was held in London and other towns and cities. Though the opinion polls showed majority support while British forces were directly involved in action, this soon slumped when the large-scale fighting concluded. Allegations, broadcast on the BBC by the journalist Andrew Gilligan, that Blair and his entourage had deliberately exaggerated the threat of WMD, led to a bitter dispute between the government and the Corporation, and the suicide of Dr David Kelly, the arms inspector who had been the source of Gilligan's story. Blair then did himself no favours by appointing an ultra-Establishment judge, Lord Justice Hutton, to conduct a one-man inquiry into the events leading up to Kelly's death, with very narrow terms of reference. Hutton's report came down so heavily on the government's side, and was so critical of the BBC, that the public saw it as a 'whitewash'. A large majority in the opinion polls concluded that Blair had lied and had deliberately deceived the nation over the WMD threat. From that time onward, Blair was dogged by demonstrators carrying placards captioned "B.Liar". Several other inquiries, notably one presided over by former Cabinet Secretary (Lord) Robin Butler, probed Blair's role in the lead-up to the Iraq War, and criticised his decision-making practices, without however condemning his actions or questioning his integrity. A much wider public inquiry into Britain's role in the Iraq War, chaired by Sir John Chilcot, and ordered by Gordon Brown after he became Prime Minister, began work in July 2009 and completed its hearings in February 2011, but the report was not published until 2016.

What Blair lost through the Iraq War was the instinctive feeling of trust which he had built up with the British public, who had seemed to regard him as more than a cut above 'ordinary' politicians. This led to a catastrophic fall in his opinion poll ratings, though much less so in those of his party. Pressure then began to build up within the party for Blair to stand down in Brown's favour before the next general election. Blair became acutely depressed, and – distracted and worried by family problems – accepted an invitation from Deputy Prime Minister John Prescott to a private dinner with Brown. Prescott then withdrew to allow them to talk frankly together, and when he returned, Blair, according to his own account, said to him:

> I have made it clear I won't serve a full term and will go before an election, but I need Gordon's full and unconditional support. John said he thought that was sensible. We parted.
>
> (Blair, 2010, p. 497)

But no sooner had he made this promise than he relented, and – pressed by his wife and several Cabinet ministers – he decided to stay on, justifying the decision to himself by Brown's failure to co-operate fully in the new range of New Labour policies he was now pursuing. These included, notably, the provision of new 'academy' schools, outside local government control, and the creation of 'foundation' hospitals within the NHS, with increased possibilities to co-operate with the private sector. He did not communicate his change of mind to his Chancellor, who was understandably devastated when, several months later – on 30 September 2004 – he made a dramatic announcement, while Brown was abroad attending an IMF meeting. This was to the effect that he would fight the next general election, with the intention of serving another full term if Labour won, but would not then contest a fourth election. When Brown returned, they had a stormy meeting, at which Brown allegedly declared that he would never again believe anything Blair said to him. Brown contemplated resignation, but clenched his teeth and chose to stay on, deciding, in effect, that his pathway to No. 10 would now be determined by intrigue rather than an open challenge. For his part, Blair was pressed strongly by many of his advisers to sack, or attempt to re-shuffle, his Chancellor, but decided that this would be too risky a venture.

The election was held on 5 May 2005, with the following result:

Labour	355
Conservative	198
LibDems	62
Others	31

Labour secured an overall majority of 67 seats, which ordinarily would have been regarded as a highly satisfactory result. Yet this compared to a majority of 165 in the previous election, so it was seen as a marked setback. Polls taken during the campaign revealed that the Iraq War and the consequent unpopularity of Blair were the principal reasons for the fall in Labour support. They also suggested that the much greater popularity of Gordon Brown – who against Blair's original intention had been brought in to front the campaign in a 'double act' with the Prime Minister – had possibly saved Labour from defeat, or at least, from a much smaller majority. So Blair emerged much weakened, with few people now believing that he would be able to serve out another full term. In fact, he was able to survive for another two years before Brown finally succeeded in winkling him out of No. 10. In the meantime, Blair made ineffective attempts to find a plausible candidate to run against Brown for the party leadership, his hopes resting mainly on David Miliband, then the Environment Secretary. But Miliband took the view that Brown was unbeatable, and declined to stand, as did all other likely contenders (see Chapter 20). So, when Blair finally announced his forthcoming resignation, on 2 May 2007, he coupled it with a recommendation to elect Brown as his successor. Brown was duly elected unopposed at a special Labour Party conference on 24 June, and Blair's premiership ended three days later. He had served for ten years and 56 days.

Blair was still only 54 years old, and full of energy, when he left Downing Street, anxious to continue to play an important public role. He would have liked to have been chosen as the first President of the EU's Council of Ministers, and Brown duly nominated him. But the other EU leaders were unenthusiastic, partly because of his role in the Iraq War, but – evidently – also because they did not want to be overshadowed by someone who was already a major international figure, so the post went to Belgian Premier Herman Van Rompuy. President George W. Bush was instrumental in securing him the role of Middle East Peace Envoy of the 'Quartet' group (the UN, US, EU and Russia), and he energetically pursued this role, but with little success, largely due to inadequate support from Bush, lack of co-operation from Israeli Prime Minister Binyamin Netanyahu, and the intransigence of Hamas. In fact, he has never been seen by the Arabs as an 'honest broker', due to his previous unswerving support for Israel.

He published a memoir, *A Journey*, in 2010, including a well-argued defence of his Iraq policy, which – unlike the majority of his Cabinet – he still felt was justified. He made a lot of money advising companies and foreign governments on international issues, and devoted himself to a range of 'good causes' including climate change, development work in Africa, and establishing a Faith Foundation to encourage collaboration between people from different religions. So, lots of activity, but he still exuded the air of an unfulfilled man.

How will he be viewed by history? He should be credited with modernising both the Labour Party and the country through a serious of (incomplete) constitutional reforms, presiding over a period of steady economic growth and the improvement of public services, especially health and education. His government made good progress on reducing child poverty, but did not reach its ambitious targets, and its record on transport and on housing left much to be desired. Overall, the balance of his record on domestic policy is likely to be a favourable one, but as a force for change in British society, he will be seen as a distant third to Clement Attlee and Margaret Thatcher among post-World War II Premiers. In international affairs, he reached 'superstar' status, and arguably increased British influence in the process. But his reputation was punctured by Iraq, and he seems doomed to be remembered more as a 'fallen idol'.

Works consulted

Leo Abse, 2003, *Tony Blair: The Man Who Lost His Smile*, London, Robson Books.

Tony Blair, 2010, *A Journey,* London, Hutchinson.

Hans Blix, 2004, *Disarming Iraq*, London, Bloomsbury.

Vernon Bogdanor, 2010, *From New Jerusalem to New Labour: British Prime Ministers from Attlee to Blair*, London, Palgrave Macmillan.

David Butler and Dennis Kavanagh, 1997, *The British General Election of 1997*, Basingstoke, Macmillan.

David Butler and Dennis Kavanagh, 2002, *The British General Election of 2001*, Basingstoke, Macmillan.

Nick Cohen, 2003, *Pretty Straight Guys*, London, Faber.

Philip Gould, 1998, *The Unfinished Revolution*, London, Little Brown.

John Kampfner, 2003, *Blair's Wars*, London, Free Press.

Dennis Kavanagh and David Butler, 2005, *The British General Election of 2005*, London, Palgrave Macmillan.

John Major, 1999, *The Autobiography*, London, HarperCollins.

James Naughtie, 2001, *The Rivals*, London, Fourth Estate.

Andrew Rawnsley, 2000, *Servants of the People*, London, Hamish Hamilton.

John Rentoul, 2001, *Tony Blair: Prime Minister*, London, Little Brown.

Steve Richards, 2010, *Whatever It Takes: The Real Story of Gordon Brown and New Labour*, London, Fourth Estate.

Anthony Seldon, 2004, *Blair*, London, Free Press.

Anthony Seldon, 2007, *Blair Unbound*, London, Simon & Schuster.

John Sopel, 1995, *Tony Blair: The Moderniser*, London, Michael Joseph.

Philip Stephens, 2004, *Tony Blair: The Making of a World Leader*, New York and London, Viking.

Jack Straw, 2012, *Last Man Standing,* London, Macmillan.

20

GORDON BROWN

Dominant Chancellor, uncertain Premier

Gordon Brown was the fourth Scotsman to become Prime Minister of the United Kingdom, after the third Earl of Bute, Sir Henry Campbell-Bannerman and Sir Alec Douglas-Home. Some would argue that he was the fifth, advancing the claims for inclusion in the list of Harold Macmillan. Yet Macmillan was, at best, only a 'notional' Scot: apart from being half-American, he was part of the second generation of his family to be born and raised in England, as members of the anglicised 'ruling class'. Brown, however, is very much the real thing. Born in Govan, a working-class suburb of Glasgow, on 20 February 1951, his father, the Rev. John Ebenezer Brown, was descended from a long line of shepherds and tenant farmers from Fifeshire, while his mother, the former Jessie Elizabeth Souter, was the daughter of a builder and ironmonger from west Aberdeenshire. Named James Gordon Brown, he was the middle of three sons, the eldest, John Souter Brown being born in 1948, and the youngest, Andrew, in 1959. Three years after he was born, the family moved to the Fife seaside (and mining) town of Kirkcaldy, where the Rev. Brown was minister of St Brycedale church, or kirk, as it is known in the Church of Scotland.

The Rev. Brown's parishioners were predominantly miners and factory workers and their families, lowly paid, and often living under the threat of unemployment. Yet – largely due to legacies which Gordon's mother had received – the Brown family was able to maintain a middle-class standard of living, though their lifestyle was austere. They lived in a commodious house, the doors of which were always open to those in need, and the message which the minister preached each Sunday was very much a social gospel. As Gordon was to recall in an interview many years later, in 1993:

> I was very much impressed with my father. First, for speaking without notes in front of so many people in that vast church. But, mostly I have learned a great deal from what my father was able to do for other people. He taught me to treat everyone equally, and that is something I have never forgotten.
>
> *(Routledge, 1998, p. 25)*

DOI: 10.4324/9781003031963-21

At 4, a year younger than all his classmates, Gordon was enrolled at the local primary school, Kirkcaldy West, and was soon outstripping all his competitors, being particularly quick at sums. He excelled at all subjects, and was also outstanding at sports, particularly football, forming an early ambition to become a professional footballer, becoming, alongside his father, an avid supporter of Raith Rovers, in the Scottish Football League. At 10, he left – again a year early – to proceed to Kirkcaldy High School. Here he was one of the 'guinea pigs' selected for a remarkable experiment, designed to fast-forward the most intelligent boys and girls through the school. Some 11 boys (including his closest school friend from Kirkcaldy West, Murray Elder) and 25 girls were chosen for an 'E-Stream', which was subjected to a pressure-cooker regime designed to ensure that they would achieve outstanding examination results at an earlier than usual age. For Gordon, it appeared to be a complete success: he took his O levels, in eight or nine subjects, at the age of 14, and his 'highers' (the Scottish equivalent of A levels) at 15. He sat five subjects, and achieved an A in all of them. Gordon, however, considered that the whole E-Stream experiment had been a cruel failure. Aged 16, he wrote in an essay:

> I watched as each year one or two of my friends would fail under the strain. I saw one girl who every now and then would disappear for a while with a nervous breakdown. I stood by as a friend of mine, who I knew was intelligent enough, left school in despair after five years of strain with no university or higher qualifications. I thought continually of how it could have been for these young guinea pigs, how the strain of the work, the ignominy and rejection of failure could have been avoided. All this, I thought I saw better than any educationalist in his ivory tower.
>
> *(Routledge, 1998, p. 12)*

Even for himself, the outcome had been less than satisfactory. He felt he had no alternative to starting university at the age of 16, two years younger than his fellow students. There was no point in staying at school for a further year, as there was nothing more for him to learn there, the only prospect was that of becoming Head Boy. Nor had the concept of a 'gap year' yet caught on, at least in towns like Kirkcaldy. So, in the autumn of 1967, he reluctantly joined his elder brother John, at Edinburgh University, where he was to read history. Six months earlier, during a rugby match between his school and its 'Old Boys', he had been injured in a scrum, and emerged from the match with impaired vision. Assuming it would soon rectify itself, he never bothered to consult a doctor, but during his first weeks at university he headed a ball during a football match and his sight worsened. This time he did see a doctor, who discovered detached retinas in both eyes. Despite four operations at the Edinburgh Royal Infirmary, and being ordered to lie immobile for six months in a darkened hospital ward, he lost the sight of his left eye, and for a time it was feared that he would go completely blind. The right eye was eventually saved, and he was discharged with orders not to play contact sports. Gone was his aspiration to become a professional footballer, but, more significant were the lasting physical and psychological effects. The former included a certain rigidity in muscles on the left side of his face, which made it difficult for him to smile and contributed to the dour reputation which he was later to acquire. The latter greatly reinforced his existing determination to push himself, to work harder than anyone else, and to prove that it was not only in the country of the blind that the one-eyed man is king. As a student at Edinburgh this ambition was to be more than amply fulfilled. Professor Henry Drucker, at that time a junior politics lecturer at Edinburgh, described Brown as: "an important figure, even as an undergraduate. He was hugely popular, a natural politician: totally self-assured. He was good to everybody, and everyone wanted to know Gordon Brown. He was a bit like a Bill Clinton figure" (Routledge, 1998, p. 43).

It was a time of great unrest and agitation in universities throughout Europe and North America, and Gordon Brown emerged as the most effective, but far from the most extreme, student leader in any British university. Not for him the excitement of leading 'sit-ins' and mass street demonstrations. His method was the careful accumulation, and presentation, of facts calculated to embarrass the university authorities and to bolster the legitimate, and sometimes not so legitimate, claims of the student body. Brown soon became chairman of the University Labour Club, but his main forum, initially, was his editorship of the student newspaper, through which he launched a series of campaigns which infuriated the ultra-conservative Principal (or Vice-Chancellor), Sir Michael Swann. Swann was an office-holder in the Anti-Apartheid Movement, and assured the University Court that none of the university's investments were in companies known to be active in support of apartheid. Brown obtained a copy of a secret stockbroker's report which revealed extensive financial involvement in such companies, and he rushed out a special issue of the paper demanding that the university should dispose of its holdings. He launched a petition to this effect, signed by 2,500 students and 300 staff, and Swann was forced to change stockbrokers and liquidate the shares. Brown's next target was the rectorship of the university, which had become a largely honorific post, though the Rector was legally entitled to chair meetings of the governing body, the Court. Elected by the students for a three-year term, in earlier times the Rectors had been leading politicians, including Gladstone, Disraeli, Churchill, Lloyd George and Baldwin. More recently, however, the candidates had usually been figures from the media or show business, who did not take the job very seriously. As Paul Routledge comments: "This absentee-rector situation suited the authorities admirably. The Principal presided over a group of establishment yes-men, who simply rubber stamped his wishes" (Routledge, 1998, p. 48).

In 1971, Brown, then aged 20, put himself at the head of a campaign to elect a student as Rector, who would go on to chair the meetings of the University Court, and ensure that issues of concern to the student body were properly considered. Brown proposed that Jonathan Wills, his flatmate and close collaborator, then a postgraduate student, should be the students' candidate. He went on to defeat the satirist Willie Rushton, and – to the horror of Swann – proceeded to take the chair at meetings of the Court, but after only one year, anxious to pursue his own career, resigned his post. Brown was the overwhelming choice of the student body to succeed him, but the university authorities sought a heavyweight figure to oppose him, and came up with Sir Fred Catherwood, a leading industrialist, who had acted as an adviser to Harold Wilson's Labour government and chaired the National Economic Development Council (or 'Neddy'), a forum for consultation between the government, industrialists and trade union leaders. Brown emerged as victor, with more than 60 per cent of the votes, and proved to be a much more active and resourceful Rector than his predecessor, pressing a series of far-reaching reforms on a reluctant university administration. When the Principal high-handedly dismissed an assessor appointed by Brown, and forbade his attendance at the Court, Brown took him to a court of law, which ruled in Brown's favour, and the assessor was restored to office and all business transacted in his absence was declared void. Swann and his colleagues next tried to take away the right of the Rector to chair the Court's meetings, and appealed to the university's Chancellor, the Duke of Edinburgh, who previously had played only a ceremonial role. They were astonished when he turned them down, unaware that Brown's then girlfriend, Princess Margarita of Romania, who was studying sociology and politics, was the Duke's god-daughter, and had presumably lobbied him on Brown's behalf. This was the last straw for Swann, who shortly afterwards left Edinburgh to become Chairman of the Governors of the BBC.

Brown graduated in 1972, reputedly having scored the highest marks ever recorded in his final examinations, and embarked on a Ph.D., his chosen subject being the development of the Labour Party in Scotland between 1918 and 1929. He had hoped to secure a full-time academic post in the university, but he had made so many enemies in the administration through his activities as Rector, that this proved impossible, and he was fobbed off with a small amount of part-time teaching. In 1976 he moved to Glasgow to take up a lectureship in politics at the city's College of Technology, and also became a tutor for the Workers' Educational Association. After four years he resigned to become a producer and investigative journalist for Scottish TV. His spare time, however, was taken up almost completely by Labour Party activities, his overriding objective being to secure election as an MP. He had narrowly missed selection as Labour candidate for Edinburgh South, a Tory-held marginal, in the October 1974 general election, when he was 23, but was adopted as its prospective candidate two years later.

Brown was living in a large but chaotically organised apartment – with about six flatmates – the scene of many a raucous student party, of which Brown was the life and soul. Yet as a beer rather than a spirits drinker, he was never seen to be the worse for wear, and, as a 'son of the manse', kept well clear of drug-taking, not even succumbing to the occasional whiff of 'pot'. In almost permanent attendance was his glamorous girlfriend, Princess Margarita of Romania, a great-great-granddaughter of Queen Victoria, and 53rd in succession to the British throne. As a matter of form, she kept her own flat, and, when Brown was visited by his strait-laced mother, care was taken to ensure that the intimacy of their relationship was concealed from her. It lasted for five years, and most of Gordon's friends assumed that they would get married, but it was not to be. Margarita often felt neglected because of the avidity of Gordon's political activities, while he might perhaps have feared that his reputation as a campaigner for the poor and dispossessed might have been compromised by marriage to a princess. Eventually, Margarita's patience snapped, and she up-sticked and began an affair with a handsome fireman – also a Labour activist but less single-mindedly so than Brown – which was to last for six years. Much later, she said in an interview: "It was a very solid and romantic story. I never stopped loving him, but one day it didn't seem right any more. It was politics, politics, politics, and I needed nurturing" (*Harpers & Queen* magazine, August 1992). Brown was devastated, and confessed after a long drinking session with his tutor, Owen Dudley Edwards: "It's the greatest mistake of my life. I should have married Margarita." He was then in his mid-twenties, and though he went on to have several other serious relationships, he did not marry until he was 49, in 2000. Margarita also appears subsequently to have found it difficult to commit herself – she only married (to a Romanian actor, Radu Duda) in 1996, at the age of 47.

Meanwhile, Brown's commitment to the Labour Party took up more and more of his time. Alongside his Ph.D. thesis, he wrote and published a highly regarded biography of James Maxton (1885–1946), a famous Clydeside Labour MP, and leader of the left-wing Independent Labour Party (ILP). In 1975, aged 24, he also edited *The Red Paper on Scotland*, a 368-page collection of essays by the youngest and brightest left-wing figures in Scotland. This set out an agenda to modernise and radicalise the country and its institutions, including notably the Scottish Labour Party. He became a member of its Executive Committee, and later its chairman, and was responsible for organising its campaign in favour of devolution in the 1978 referendum called by the Callaghan government. Earlier that year he had been strongly urged

248 Gordon Brown

to run in a by-election in the safe Labour seat in Hamilton. It would have been a tremendous opportunity for him, but he hesitated, and finally declined to put his name forward, on the grounds that he felt committed to stick to Edinburgh South, a far less promising seat, where he was the prospective candidate. This was not the full story, however; the 'frontrunner' for the nomination was George Robertson, who was backed by the powerful Municipal and General Workers' Union, of which he was a senior official. The cautious Brown was unwilling to risk defeat, and in the process make influential enemies (Robertson went on to become Defence Secretary in the Blair government, and Secretary-General of NATO). This episode prefigured his refusal to fight against Tony Blair for the Labour leadership in 1994. Less understandable was that Brown went on to turn down the candidature for another good constituency – Leith – where he would not have faced a powerful rival. So he stayed with Edinburgh South, where – in the 1979 general election – he trimmed the Tory majority, but still lost by 2,460 votes. He had to wait to get into Parliament until the 1983 general election, when, aged 32, he was returned with a majority of over 11,000 votes. for Dunfermline East, the neighbouring constituency to Kirkcaldy, where he had grown up.

Brown made an immediate impact in the Commons, making a highly praised maiden speech, highlighting the unemployment figures in his constituency, and generally throughout Scotland. He became a close friend and collaborator of another new Member, Tony Blair, two years his junior and vastly less experienced in Labour Party politics, with whom he shared a small office. Within two years, Brown was appointed a frontbench spokesman on trade and industry, and in 1987 he was elected as the youngest member of the Shadow Cabinet, with the task of 'shadowing' John Major, then the Chief Secretary to the Treasury. Blair also became a Shadow spokesman, for energy, and both of them benefited enormously from the activities of Peter Mandelson, who, in 1985, was appointed as Labour's Director of Communications. An important part of his job was to recommend to the BBC and other broadcasting organisations suitable persons to present the Labour viewpoint in television and radio broadcasts. With Kinnock's encouragement, he repeatedly called on the services of Blair and Brown, whom he saw as the most personable and persuasive of the younger generation of Labour politicians. In the process, he became a close friend and collaborator of the two men, particularly Brown. In the many discussions between the trio at this time, many of the ideas which went into the later launch of New Labour were thrashed out.

Brown's big moment came in October 1988, when the Shadow Chancellor, John Smith, had a serious heart attack and was ordered to take at least three months' complete rest from politics. The Labour leader, Neil Kinnock, asked Brown to deputise for Smith during his absence, and his first great test came on 1 November, when the Chancellor, Nigel Lawson, presented his autumn statement, presenting a rosy picture, which hardly coincided with the underlying economic situation. In Paul Routledge's words, "Brown fell upon Lawson like a wolf on the fold" (Routledge, 1998, p. 148), and with a wealth of statistics cast serious doubt upon virtually all the assumptions on which the Chancellor had based his statement. Lawson was seriously discomfited, and the Labour benches erupted with delight. Later the same month, when Labour MPs held their annual vote to choose the Shadow Cabinet, he topped the poll, rising from 11th place the previous year. Somewhat to his embarrassment, he even eclipsed Smith, who was pushed down into second place. From that moment on, he began to be seen, and talked about, as a future leader of the Labour Party. However, when a vacancy in that post occurred four years later, with Neil Kinnock's resignation after Labour's defeat in the 1992 general election, he was not among the candidates who opposed the favourite, John Smith, whom he strongly backed. He would have liked to contest the deputy leadership, but thought that the party would not accept two Scotsmen in its most senior posts. Blair himself considered running; though born in Edinburgh he was clearly of English stock. He decided against, partly through fear of losing, but also not to upset Brown, who would not have enjoyed seeing his 'junior partner' leapfrog him in the party hierarchy. Smith, however, lost no time in appointing Brown as Shadow Chancellor, which gave him a dominant position in the new leadership team. His friend, Tony Blair, who was still seen at the time as being much junior to him, was also given a big promotion, becoming Shadow Home Secretary.

The general expectation, backed by most opinion polls, had been that Labour would win the 1992 election, or at least emerge as the largest party. In the event, the Tories, led by John Major, were returned with an overall majority of 21. Their victory was universally attributed primarily to their success in painting Labour as a 'tax and spend' party, with fearsome predictions of massive tax increases if Labour won. The new Shadow Chancellor determined that this should never happen again, and that under his aegis Labour's economic policies should always be marked by fiscal prudence. In particular, he determined that Labour should be in a position to give cast-iron assurances before the next election that there would be no increase in the basic rate of income tax. In pursuit of this objective, he ruthlessly vetoed virtually every policy proposal by his fellow Shadow ministers, which would involve additional expenditure. This made him highly unpopular with many of his colleagues, including notably, David Blunkett, the blind Shadow Education Minister, who was bristling with ideas for expensive educational reforms.

The sudden death of John Smith on 12 May 1994 was a devastating event for Brown. He undoubtedly saw himself as the heir apparent, but genuinely grieved at the loss of his friend, and thinking it unseemly to begin campaigning before the burial of the Labour leader, he devoted himself to writing heartfelt tributes to him. He was appalled to discover that Blair had immediately thrown his hat into the ring, and was pressuring him not to split the modernising vote by standing against him. He felt he had been betrayed by Blair, whom he believed was committed to supporting him by an agreement they had made two years earlier. He was even more upset by Peter Mandelson who was privately backing Blair's bid, and giving television interviews in which, without naming names, he implied that Blair would be a better prospect as a vote-winner. This view appeared to be corroborated by opinion polls, which showed Blair with a commanding lead, and Brown coming only fourth among five projected candidates. Blair undoubtedly owed his large lead to his skill as a performer on television, and the assiduous efforts he had made to court the press, which Brown had failed to do. Brown also suffered from his rough treatment of his fellow Labour MPs, among whom his support was now far from overwhelming. Nevertheless, his two brothers strongly urged him to run, as did his band of close parliamentary supporters, led by his namesake, Nick Brown, an influential trade unionist MP. They were convinced that if he launched a vigorous campaign he would rally sufficient support to overhaul Blair. Brown was sceptical, believing that his only hope of beating Blair was to run a ruthless and highly demagogic campaign, branding Blair as a toff and a closet Tory, appealing to the serried ranks of leftists and backward-looking trade unionists in the party. This would have destroyed his own reputation as a moderniser, and Brown reluctantly concluded that he had no alternative but to seek a deal with Blair which would maximise his own power and influence in the party, in exchange for his endorsement.

So after covert negotiations with Blair and his entourage, Brown met his rival on 31 May at an Islington restaurant, the Granita, and agreed a deal, subsequently confirmed in writing, that he would become Chancellor with effective control over not only the economy but virtually the whole range of domestic policy, and be consulted on all important appointments. Not included in the written agreement was a promise by Blair to relinquish the prime ministership in Brown's favour during the course of a second term, if any, of a Labour government. Blair appeared to have a guilty conscience about his treatment of his former close friend, and offered this as a sop to Brown's feelings, probably not taking his own words very seriously. Brown, however, took them at face value, and clearly regarded them as a firm commitment.

Despite his severe disappointment, Brown buckled down and worked closely and constructively with Blair to build up New Labour in the three years leading up to the 1997 election. He successfully concealed the bitter sense of betrayal which he felt against Blair, and focused it instead on Peter Mandelson, with whom he broke off all personal relations for more than a dozen years. Yet he was a changed man, as Robert Peston, then the political editor of the *Financial Times*, observed:

> The change that came over him in that period, compared with his personality before he decided not to challenge Tony Blair for the leadership of the Labour Party in June 1994, was startling. He became manifestly less relaxed. Every thought and deed was controlled. He retreated into himself and became much duller.
>
> *(Peston, 2005, pp. 21–2)*

As Shadow Chancellor, Brown built up his own little 'court' of advisers and core supporters. His main adviser, whom he recruited from the *Financial Times*, was the economist Ed Balls, whom Brown relied on very heavily, not only for economic advice but as a general sounding board for all his ideas and projects. He was later joined by Ed Miliband, son of a leading Marxist academic and the younger brother of David Miliband, who was advising Blair, and by Charlie Whelan, his press adviser. He was also assisted by Geoffrey Robinson, a millionaire Labour MP, who permanently rented a suite of rooms at the Grosvenor House Hotel, overlooking Hyde Park. Here he lived, when staying in London, and it was here that Brown met almost daily with his close collaborators to plot his every move and to plan his future chancellorship, when Robinson was scheduled to join him as a senior Treasury minister. They agreed on three major policy commitments, which would be announced in advance of the 1997 general election, in order to secure public confidence that a 'New Labour' government would be fiscally prudent. The first was to promise that Labour would keep to the very tight spending plans already announced by the Conservative Chancellor, Ken Clarke, for the first two years of government. The second was a commitment not to raise either the standard rate of income tax – then at 23 pence in the pound – or even the higher rate of 40 pence. Brown had considered this too low compared to other countries and wanted to raise it to 50 pence, but this had been vetoed by the even more cautious Blair. Thirdly, Brown sought that rare commodity – a popular tax – in order to raise sufficient revenue to finance his ambitious plans to reduce unemployment ("Welfare to Work"). He hit upon a one-off 'windfall' tax on the public utilities, which had been privatised by the Thatcher and Major governments. They had been sold off far too cheaply, and they then used their quasi-monopoly status to make enormous profits and pay very high salaries to their top managers. Robinson, a former chief executive of Jaguar Cars, was set to work on a draft Bill that would be legally watertight. He consulted the accountancy firm of Arthur Anderson, and did such a good job that the public utility bosses eventually withdrew their loud threats to challenge the legal validity of the ensuing legislation.

Brown's pledges undoubtedly contributed to the massive Labour landslide in the general election of 1 May 1997. On 2 May, he was duly installed as Chancellor of the Exchequer, and – unlike all his other Cabinet colleagues – with the right to nominate his entire team of junior ministers. These included Alistair Darling as Chief Secretary to the Treasury and Geoffrey Robinson as Paymaster-General. Both Ed Balls and Ed Miliband joined them in the Treasury as special advisers, and Charlie Whelan as press spokesman. Brown hit the ground running. His first action, when he entered the Treasury for the first time on the afternoon of 2 May, was to present the deeply surprised Permanent Secretary, Sir Terence Burns, with a letter addressed to Eddie George, the Governor of the Bank of England. The letter announced that henceforward it would be responsible for setting interest rates, thus depriving governments of the possibility of manipulating them for political purposes. When the news was announced it was very widely welcomed, and was greeted by the press as restoring the independence of the Bank of England. The Bank, however, lost its role of supervising and regulating commercial banks. Brown announced the creation of a new regulating body, the Financial Services Agency. This also was widely welcomed, but not by George, who was initially inclined to offer his resignation in protest. He resented not having been consulted in advance, but swallowed his pride and agreed to stay in his post.

Despite enormous pressure from within his own party, Brown kept to his pledge to adhere to Tory spending limits during his first two years in office. He defended this policy as "prudence with a purpose", and made it clear that once financial security and a healthy budget surplus had been achieved, more ambitious policies could be anticipated. What was the "purpose" he had in mind? In a very perceptive book (Richards, 2010, *Whatever It Takes*), the journalist Steve Richards seeks to unravel Brown's intentions, and the difficulties he faced in carrying them out. His overriding passion, Richards argues, was to fight against poverty, both in Britain and in the developing world, and to achieve a more equal society. Brown, however, was convinced, by Labour's experience during the 1992 general election campaign, that the British electorate was viscerally opposed to tax increases, and that he would have to proceed with the greatest circumspection. He determined, therefore, to 'do good by stealth' by raising additional revenues by apparently 'painless' measures. By and large, he was successful in this endeavour, and by the end of his chancellorship, in 2008, he was a popular figure, widely seen as the most successful Chancellor in modern times. He was also seen as a tax-cutter rather than increaser, cutting the standard rate of income tax from 23 per cent to 20 per cent, and corporation tax from 33 per cent to 28 per cent. The only 'visible' tax increase during his chancellorship was in his 2002 budget, when National Insurance contributions were raised to pay for a major expansion in public spending in health and education. Other than this, and a range of 'stealth' taxes, Brown relied on a steady growth in tax revenues arising from economic growth, which averaged 2.7 per cent a year, compared to 2.1 per cent in the Eurozone. A great admirer of Anthony Crosland, the author of the highly influential *The Future of Socialism* and a senior minister in the Wilson and Callaghan governments, Brown was thus able to carry out Crosland's preferred policy of financing redistribution through the proceeds of growth. He also benefited from another 'windfall' wheeze, netting £22.5 billion through the auction in 2000 of telecoms spectrum licences. Brown made only one obvious error in his tax strategy, but it was an egregious one. In his 1999 budget, he announced a new, low starting rate of income tax, of 10 pence in the pound, replacing the basic rate of 23 per cent for the first £2,230 of taxable income. Commending it, the Chancellor said:

> The 10p rate is very important because it is a signal about the importance of getting people into work and it's of most importance to the low paid. This is not about gimmicks. This is about tax reform that encourages work and families.

The move proved very popular, and Brown received much praise, but in his last budget, in 2008, he insensitively abolished the rate, to help him achieve a 'masterstroke' of reducing the basic rate from 22 pence to 20 pence, the lowest level since 1930. The change was not due to come into effect until 2009 when Brown was no longer Chancellor, but when it did it provoked massive protests, not least within the Labour Party, which gravely damaged the standing of the government which he had formed only a few months previously (see below). Despite this, his overall record as Chancellor was highly successful, though it led him, hubristically, to claim to have finally banished the cycle of 'boom and bust', which had long afflicted the British economy. This claim came back to haunt him during his later premiership.

From 1997 to 2007, Brown was not just Chancellor, but also effectively co-leader of the government with Tony Blair. This could have been a source of enormous strength if their dissimilar qualities had been able to combine in a symbiotic relationship. Instead, their mutual distrust and resentment led to constant disharmony, which undermined, though it did not destroy, the effectiveness of the government. It had many achievements to its credit, but fewer than it might have had if their previous close friendship had not degenerated into almost open enmity. This was kept relatively under control during the first parliamentary term which ended with the 2001 general election. There were, however, constant rows over 'turf wars', as Brown tried to muscle in on more and more of his Cabinet colleagues' responsibilities, and concealed from Blair, until the very last minute, major policy initiatives, including the contents of his budgets. Blair retaliated in his first Cabinet reshuffle, in July 1998, when he purged several of Brown's leading supporters from ministerial posts, demoting Nick Brown from Chief Whip to Minister for Agriculture. He also installed his own close ally, Stephen Byers, as Chief Secretary to the Treasury in place of Alistair Darling, who was promoted to Social Security Secretary. Brown greatly resented this, regarding Byers as a 'spy' installed at the very centre of his own Treasury. Both Blair and Brown's 'spin doctors' thought nothing of anonymously briefing the press about their respective masters' faults, most notoriously when Brown was described as having 'psychological flaws'. It was widely assumed at the time that Alastair Campbell had been responsible for this, though he indignantly denied it. It was later suspected that Blair himself was the author of these incriminating words (Peston, 2005, p. 15).

Despite the serious disharmony between the two men, which was largely concealed from the general public, there was only one serious policy difference between them during the first parliamentary term. This was over British entry to the Eurozone, of which Blair was a strong advocate. He was little inhibited by an electoral commitment to hold a referendum on the issue, being convinced that the high popularity of the government would ensure a successful outcome, despite opinion poll evidence that a majority (though at that time not a large one) were opposed. Brown, greatly influenced by Ed Balls and by cautious Treasury officials, was much less optimistic, and outmanoeuvred Blair over the issue, ensuring that entry would not be sought in advance of the following general election, and that the Treasury would be the arbiter of when, if ever, entry should be sought (see Chapter 19, above). For better or for worse, it was Brown who decided that Britain should not adopt the Euro, at least for the foreseeable future.

On 3 August 2000, the long bachelorhood of Gordon Brown finally came to an end. Aged 49, he married the 36-year-old Sarah Macaulay at a small ceremony in the living room of his Fife home, conducted by the Rev. Sheila Munro, a Church of Scotland minister. They had been together for around five years, but their courtship had been conducted with great discretion. They had first met in 1994, when Sarah, who had founded her own small public relations firm, Hobsbawm-Macaulay, with Julia Hobsbawm, daughter of the Marxist historian Eric Hobsbawm, was undertaking a project on behalf of the Labour Party. It was clearly a love match, and Gordon's friends noted that he became notably more relaxed and outgoing after the marriage. Then, in January 2002, they suffered the tragedy of losing their prematurely born baby, Jennifer Jane, when she was only 10 days old. Their sorrow turned to joy, with the birth of a healthy son, John, in October 2003, followed by his younger brother, Fraser, in July 2006. The parents were again devastated some months later, when Fraser was diagnosed with cystic fibrosis, and the news was insensitively splashed on the front page of the Murdoch newspaper, *The Sun*. Unlike some other leading politicians, Gordon Brown and his wife have taken exceptional care to protect their children from public exposure.

With scarcely a blip in its high popularity levels, the Blair government successfully concluded its first parliamentary term with a second landslide majority in the general election of June 2001. Any illusion that Blair might have held that his Chancellor was satisfied with his current lot was rudely shattered on the Monday after the election when Brown abruptly demanded that Blair should give him a date when he would resign as Prime Minister (Richards, 2010, p. 184). Blair temporised, but Brown continued to confront him with the issue at regular intervals during the second parliamentary term. It did him little good: Blair had no intention of making an early withdrawal, and instead started to think of alternative leadership candidates, fixing initially on David Blunkett, the blind Home Secretary, and Alan Milburn, Health Secretary. At one stage, in December 2001 during a dinner at Downing Street, Blair allegedly offered Brown a deal: he would stand down in his favour if Brown fully backed Euro entry (Seldon, 2007, p. 206). Brown declined, and two months later explained to a Cabinet colleague, Clare Short, that he "could not conceive of recommending that Britain join the Euro to advance his own prospects at the expense of the economic interests of the country" (Seldon, 2007, p. 207).

If Blair's offer had been sincere, he soon regretted it, and it seems likely that around this time he privately decided that he would not keep to his promise to stand down during the course of the second term. Yet his position was greatly weakened by the disastrous consequences of the Iraq War (see Chapter 19), and in December 2003 he made a conditional promise to Brown that he would stand down by the time of the Labour Party conference in September 2004. He backtracked on this, to Brown's evident fury, and was able to survive to fight a third general election, in May 2005, when his parliamentary majority was more than halved. Thereafter he was clearly a 'lame duck' Prime Minister, with poll ratings inferior to Brown's, yet it took another two years for the latter, "willing to wound", in Alexander Pope's words, "and yet afraid to strike", to eject him from Downing Street. In his last few months as leader, Blair's strongest supporters desperately sought to find a candidate who could contest the leadership against Brown. The most plausible was the Environment Secretary, David Miliband, but, concluding he could not win, he refused what he considered to be a poisoned chalice. Several other less likely people were approached, including even Jack Straw, then the Leader of the

254 Gordon Brown

Commons, who claims he was approached at least twice by Blair himself, saying "You could do it, you know, Jack" (Straw, 2012, p. 490).

None could be found to contest the ballot, and on 24 June 2007, Brown was elected unopposed as Labour leader at a special conference in Manchester, having been nominated by 313 out of 356 Labour MPs. A left-wing Labour MP, John McDonnell, had hoped to run against him, but failed to win the requisite number of nominations. Harriet Harman, who had fought off four rivals, narrowly beat the favourite, Alan Johnson, for the deputy leadership. Three days later, on 27 June, Brown succeeded Blair as Prime Minister. His new government was carefully balanced between leading 'Blairites' and his own long-standing supporters. The most senior appointments were Alistair Darling as Chancellor of the Exchequer, David Miliband as Foreign Secretary, Jacqui Smith, the former Chief Whip, as Home Secretary, and Jack Straw as Justice Secretary. Ed Balls was sent to head the new Department for Children, Schools and Families, with a private understanding with Brown that after he had gained experience of running a large department he would be promoted to Chancellor (an understanding not communicated to Darling). Ed Miliband became Cabinet Office Minister, and was later promoted to Energy Secretary, while Douglas Alexander became Secretary of State for International Development, and was named as Labour's election co-ordinator. Sue Nye, who had been an adviser to Brown since 1992, was made Director of Government Relations, while Damian McBride, an abrasive civil servant, became his press secretary. Six former Cabinet ministers – John Prescott, John Reid, Margaret Beckett, Patricia Hewitt, Lord Falconer and Hilary Armstrong – left the government, not all of them voluntarily. Brown, who wished to be seen as a national rather than a mere party leader, made strenuous efforts to create a 'government of all the talents'. His most daring move was to invite the former Liberal Democrat leader, Paddy Ashdown, to join the Cabinet as Secretary of State for Northern Ireland. Ashdown was keen to accept, but felt constrained to ask permission from his party leader, Menzies Campbell, who promptly vetoed the idea. So Brown had to content himself with appointing a number of junior ministers from outside the ranks of the Labour Party, though all but one of them subsequently joined the party. Appointed life peers, they included the distinguished surgeon, Professor Ara Darzi, Admiral West, a former First Sea Lord, and Mark Malloch Brown, formerly Deputy Secretary-General of the United Nations. The most curious appointment was that of Digby Jones, a former Director-General of the CBI, who had high Tory and Eurosceptic views. He became Minister of State for Trade and Industry, but resigned in high dudgeon after only 15 months, saying that being a junior minister was "one of the most dehumanising and depersonalising experiences" any one could have (*The Guardian*, 15 January 2009).

Some of Tony Blair's closest associates had expressed privately, and sometimes publicly, the view that Brown would not be up to the premiership. In his first few months in office, he appeared to have triumphantly refuted these fears, and his opinion poll ratings, and those of the Labour Party, soared upwards – too much, in fact, for his own good. In just a few weeks a Conservative lead of 4–6 per cent had been turned into a Labour one of 6–9 per cent. Moreover, Brown was receiving an excellent press – including notably from the normally Tory-supporting *Daily Telegraph*, *Daily Mail* and *Spectator* – for the calm and effective way in which he dealt with three crises which arose in quick succession. These were a terrorist attack at Glasgow airport, widespread flooding in England and Wales and an outbreak of foot and mouth disease. It had been no part of Brown's plans to hold a general election so soon after his arrival at No. 10. Indeed, he had pencilled in the late spring or early summer of 2008, by which time he hoped to have achieved a record of solid achievement.

Yet newspaper speculation soon built up that he would capitalise on his spiralling popularity and opt for an autumn poll. In late August, one of Brown's advisers, Spencer Livermore, sent him a memo setting out the case for an immediate general election. Brown showed little interest, and left the memo lying on his desk for three weeks. Then in September, the crash of the Northern Rock bank caused widespread panic, which led to a further rise in Brown's poll ratings. Although his immediate response was hesitant, he was seen as a safe pair of hands to deal with the crisis, due to the high reputation for economic competence which he had built up as Chancellor. By the end of the month, when the Labour lead in the polls had reached 10 per cent, most of Brown's closest associates and advisers had become convinced of the case for holding an early election, as had many Labour MPs representing marginal seats. Older (and wiser?) hands in the party were more sceptical. On the Friday before the annual Labour conference, Brown lunched at Chequers with Livermore, Douglas Alexander, Ed Balls, Ed Miliband, Damian McBride, and an American polling expert and speechwriter, Bob Shrum. With varying degrees of enthusiasm, they all urged him to fire the starting gun. Brown remained reluctant, but agreed to commission a poll in marginal constituencies to make a more informed assessment of Labour's prospects. The news of the poll soon leaked out, along with a series of steps taken by the Labour Party to prepare for a campaign, and the speculation in the media broke all bounds. The atmosphere at the Labour conference in Bournemouth was euphoric, as enthusiasm built up day by day. At the end of the week, the normally down-to-earth Cabinet minister, John Denham, summed up the general feeling by saying: "We could turn a majority of 60 with two and a half years to run into a majority of 100 with five years to run" (Rawnsley, 2010, p. 504).

Brown ended the week in high good humour. He had not firmly decided on an election, but was excited by evidence that the Tories were panic-stricken at the prospect of a crushing defeat, and concluded that he should 'stir the pot' in the hope of provoking widespread recriminations at their own conference the following week in Blackpool. He also resolved to steal the thunder of the first day of their conference by a lightning visit – his first – to the British troops serving in Iraq.

It was a major miscalculation. The threat of annihilation at the polls united the Tories rather than exacerbating their differences. David Cameron kept his head and rose to the occasion, showing a confidence which he did not feel, and delivering a defiant address, without notes or autocue, and ending with the words: "So, Mr. Brown, what's it to be? … Let the people decide … call that election. We will fight. Britain will win" (Elliott and Hanning, 2012, pp. 340–1). Speaking earlier in the week, the Shadow Chancellor, George Osborne, dropped a bombshell, when he brought forward a proposal which the Tories had intended to announce during the actual election campaign. This was to abolish inheritance tax on all estates of less than £1 million, which effectively excluded most middle-class families from paying the tax. His announcement was greeted with thunderous applause throughout the hall, and an overwhelmingly positive response in the press. It chimed in with public fears that the apparently never-ending rise in house prices was bringing more and more people over the existing tax threshold. Brown's visit to Iraq also went awry: he was roundly condemned at the conference and in the media for involving British soldiers in what appeared to be an election stunt. By the end of the conference, three opinion polls revealed a sharp fall in the Labour lead. One poll showed a drop from 11 per cent to 4 per cent, another from 10 per cent to 3 per cent. The third poll showed that the Tories had closed an eight-point gap and were now at level pegging (Rawnsley, 2010, p. 507).

On the Friday – 5 October – Brown met his closest advisers in 10 Downing Street to discuss the findings of their own poll in 150 marginal seats. These were presented by the Labour Party's American pollster, Stan Greenberg. The message was not very optimistic. "The balance of risk", Greenberg said, "was a small win", perhaps a 20-seat majority. But, he added, "I can't guarantee what your majority will be". Some of Brown's team felt that they had gone so far it was impossible to pull back, Livermore arguing strongly that, "If we don't do it, the only people who will be celebrating are Tory Central Office" (Rawnsley, 2010, p. 508). Others, including Brown himself, were disheartened. Later in the day Brown called a further meeting, and

> asked each of them in turn – Alexander, Balls, Livermore, [Ed] Miliband, McBride and Nye – what they thought. No-one expressed a clear view. No-one wanted responsibility for the decision. "So we are not going to do it then?" asked Brown morosely. Everyone avoided his gaze.
>
> *(Rawnsley, 2010, p. 508)*

Brown had only his own hesitation to blame. He should have made a firm decision, one way or the other, at least a week earlier. If he had decided on an election, he should have announced it at the Labour conference, which would have given him an excellent launching pad. If not, he should have put an end to the speculation before it became uncontrollable, by stating firmly that there would be no election in 2007. Either way, he would have remained in control of the political agenda.

It is impossible to be certain what the result would have been had he decided on an election. Most likely, it would have yielded a small Labour majority, but it is understandable that – having waited so long to attain the premiership – Brown was unwilling to put it at risk after barely four months. Had he lost he would have been the second shortest-serving Prime Minister in British history, after only Canning, who died in office after 119 days. Brown added to his humiliation by the cack-handed way in which he explained his decision. Asked at a press conference whether he had been deterred by adverse poll figures, he vigorously denied it, even saying that he would have called the election off even if the polls had predicted a majority of 100 seats. This exposed him to the devastating rebuke by David Cameron, at Prime Minister's Questions two days later, that: "He's the first prime minister in British history to flunk an election cos he thought he was going to win it."

Brown's reputation was severely damaged by the whole episode. The Tory claim that he had "bottled the election" was very widely accepted, and he was henceforward seen, and was repeatedly described in the press, as a "bottler" or a "ditherer". The verdict of his very sympathetic biographer, Steve Richards, was:

> The three weeks of election fever, followed by an announcement that there would be no election, destroyed Brown's premiership … He was now doomed to stumble on without a personal mandate and without a strategy for dealing with the long and precarious journey that lay ahead before an election could be called.
>
> *(Richards, 2010, pp. 285 and 303)*

It was "long and precarious" because the Tories established an immediate lead in the polls, which they maintained, with fluctuations, almost continuously throughout the following three years. There was not a moment during this period when Brown could have called an election with any realistic hope of winning. Another serious consequence was a breakdown in the mutual confidence of Brown and his entourage. There were recriminations and resignations, and the spirit of *camaraderie* which had previously held them together was gravely weakened. This only exacerbated the chaotic state of the internal organisation of 10 Downing Street under Brown. Used to the tidy and smooth-running organisation of the Treasury, Brown seemed incapable of imposing an effective structure on the Prime Minister's Department. He failed to appoint a chief-of-staff to succeed the enterprising and highly efficient Jonathan Powell, who had acted for Tony Blair, nor did he find a press spokesman of the calibre of Alastair Campbell, or Bernard Ingham, who had served, respectively, Blair and Thatcher. There was no clear hierarchy among his staff, and Brown's organisation of his own time was far from optimal. As ever, he worked fanatically hard, and for very long hours, but he was a poor delegator, and his 'people management', both of his staff and his ministers, left very much to be desired.

'The election that never happened' was followed by another self-imposed disaster four months later, in the run up to Alistair Darling's first budget. The abolition of the 10 pence tax rate, announced the previous year in Brown's last budget, was due to come into force, and Darling warned Brown that as many as one-fifth of voters would be adversely affected by the change, though the remaining four-fifths would benefit by the reduction of the standard rate from 22 to 20 per cent. Brown flatly denied that anybody would be worse off, saying that the introduction of working tax credits and other budget changes would more than cancel out the losses. Brown was wrong, as a growing number of Labour MPs, alerted by anxious constituents, soon suspected, and he was confronted at an angry meeting of the parliamentary Labour Party. Brown stubbornly insisted he was right, and invited MPs who thought otherwise to send him their evidence. The anti-poverty campaigner and former junior minister, Frank Field, then tabled an early day motion demanding that the 10 pence rate be maintained until a compensation package was worked out for those who would be net losers. Forty Labour MPs promptly signed up, enough to defeat the government if they voted against the budget proposals. At the last moment, Brown gave way, and instructed Darling to introduce compensatory measures, costing the Exchequer £3.5 billion, whereupon Field withdrew his motion. It was too little and too late, and disaffected Labour voters took their revenge in the May 2008 local elections, one week later. They were Labour's worst results in 40 years, the party came in third place nationally, and in the London mayoral election the inexperienced and buffoonish Tory candidate, Boris Johnson, defeated the Labour incumbent, Ken Livingstone. In the same month, the Tories won the Crewe and Nantwich by-election from Labour with a swing of 17.6 per cent, the first Tory by-election win from Labour in 26 years.

These dire results sparked off the first of three attempts to overthrow Brown as party leader, and displace him from the premiership. The leader of the first, in the autumn of 2008, was the former Home Secretary, Charles Clarke, who had been sacked by Blair in May 2006 after a scandal about the failure to deport foreign prisoners who had served sentences for serious crimes. Clarke, despite being a long-time critic of Brown's, had been severely disappointed when he made no move to bring him back into the government when he succeeded Blair. In September 2008 Clarke publicly called on the party to repudiate Brown, who, he claimed, was leading the party to "utter destruction". Meanwhile, David Miliband wrote an article in *The Guardian*, which was widely interpreted as a disguised leadership bid, and a number of Labour MPs promptly called for Brown's resignation, in the hope of provoking a revolt in the Cabinet.

This did not materialise, but a group of three ministers, Justice Minister Jack Straw, Chief Whip Geoff Hoon and Work and Pensions Secretary James Purnell, started to meet periodically to monitor the developing situation. Of the three, Straw was the most influential, and if he had chosen to lead a Cabinet coup against Brown it would have had a high probability of succeeding. But Straw, who clearly aspired to the leadership himself, knew that he was only, at best, the third favourite – after Alan Johnson and David Miliband – and sat tight. Meanwhile, Brown took steps to bolster his own position. He made an effective speech at the Labour conference in late September, and his implied rebuke – to both Cameron and Miliband – that "this was no time for a novice" to take over, went down well. He then proceeded to a masterly Cabinet reshuffle, in which he surprised the world by bringing back his old friend-turned-enemy, Peter Mandelson, from Brussels to become Business Secretary and unofficial Deputy Premier. Henceforward, Mandelson became Brown's closest associate in government, and one of the few to whom he would listen if they proffered critical advice.

Nevertheless, Brown continued to receive a bad press, with repeated stories of 'dithering' and of his bad temper and disloyalty towards colleagues. He was particularly damaged by reports that his former press adviser, Damien McBride, was implicated in a failed attempt to set up a website devoted to spreading scurrilous stories about leading Tory politicians. Brown denied any knowledge of the affair, and promptly dismissed McBride, but this did him little good. Then, in May 2009, a veritable tsunami hit the government in the form of the 'exposure' by the *Daily Telegraph* of details of MPs' expenses claims over the previous five years. Brown himself had nothing to hide, though the paper focused on a trivial sum which he had claimed for his share in cleaning expenses for a flat he had jointly occupied with his brother. It was entirely legitimate, and the *Telegraph* was later forced to withdraw its innuendoes and publish an apology. Yet the damage to the government was considerable: although Labour MPs had collectively been no more avaricious than Tories, the paper featured them more prominently, and two ministers, Home Secretary Jacqui Smith and Communities Secretary Hazel Blears, resigned from the Cabinet in the wake of the allegations, though claiming loudly that they had done nothing wrong. Their departure coincided with the June 2009 European elections, in which Labour was badly mauled, coming in third place with less than 16 per cent. On polling day itself, Purnell, despairing of any hope for the government while Brown remained as leader, submitted his own resignation and wrote to the Prime Minister suggesting that he should do the same. It was a moment of maximum danger for Brown, and for once the alleged 'ditherer' acted decisively to shore up his position. In a lightning reshuffle, he promoted his main putative rival, Alan Johnson, to be Home Secretary, while Mandelson's responsibilities were greatly expanded and he was given the title of First Secretary of State. The first thing that Mandelson did, in the middle of the night, was to phone David Miliband and other Cabinet ministers to persuade them not to follow Purnell into resignation. If they had done so, it would undoubtedly have been the end of the Brown government. Purnell, a hopeless conspirator, had made no attempt to co-ordinate his resignation with any prospective allies, and neither Straw nor Hoon made any move to support him. Yet Brown was frustrated in his intention to replace Alistair Darling with Ed Balls, as Chancellor of the Exchequer, which he had long planned to do. Darling refused point-blank to take any other post in the government, and Brown did not feel strong enough to sack him, and face his criticisms from the back benches.

Even Brown's strongest supporters were bitterly disappointed at his performance as Prime Minister, which was now widely seen as a total failure. Yet his reputation was boosted by the onset of the world financial crisis in 2008–09, when, in the words of the leading economic journalist William Keegan, he proved to be "the right man, in the right place, at the right time" (Keegan, 2012, p. 47). In September 2007, when there was a run on the Northern Rock bank, he had been slow to acknowledge that temporary nationalisation was the inevitable prerequisite to its rescue, but a year later he was well ahead of the game. When three of the largest banks – the Royal Bank of Scotland, Lloyds and Halifax Bank of Scotland (HBOS) – were on the brink of collapse, and their bosses had no idea where to turn, Brown (advised by former investment banker and junior minister, Baroness Shriti Vadera) immediately stepped in. The solution, he insisted, was two-fold: emergency measures to increase liquidity, combined with a massive recapitalisation of the banks, which only the government could provide. In return, the government would take an equity stake in the banks, which would eventually be sold off, hopefully making a profit for the taxpayer. During a hectic weekend, the Chancellor Alistair Darling wrestled with the, largely, uncomprehending bank bosses, finally convincing them that unless they accepted the government's offer their game was up. Meanwhile, Brown had been desperately trying to convince French President Nicolas Sarkozy and German Chancellor Angela Merkel that they too should recapitalise their banks if the whole international banking system was not to seize up. Sarkozy, at least, was persuaded, and invited Brown to attend a meeting of the 15 heads of state of the Eurozone, where he delivered an extraordinary address, which convinced almost all his auditors. "My friend Gordon has the right plan, we must do it in Europe", Sarkozy said, and recapitalisation of the French and German banks followed almost immediately. In America too, the newly elected President Obama and his incoming Democratic administration were highly impressed, and worked closely with Brown in preparation for the G20 summit of world leaders, which Brown was due to chair in London in April 2009. Brown totally dominated this meeting, the result of which was

> nothing less than an agreement on what Brown dubbed "a $1 trillion rescue plan for the world's economy", via a huge boost in the resources of the IMF (principally) and the World Bank, aimed at stabilising the system after the biggest decline in GDP, industrial production and world trade since the Great Depression of 1929–32.
>
> *(Keegan, 2012, p. 74)*

In addition, Brown later claimed, some $3 trillion was injected into the budgets of national economies in anti-recessionary measures. Brown was rewarded with international acclaim for his efforts. Nobel Prize winner for Economics, Paul Klugman, suggested in the *New York Times* that he may have "saved the world financial system", a *Time* magazine headline ran "Gordon Brown goes from zero to hero" and a leading American peace foundation proclaimed him World Statesman of the Year. In Britain, there was also a positive reaction, with the Labour deficit in the polls narrowing from 16 to 7 per cent, but the improvement was not sustained.

The Tories were undecided whether to react by attacking Brown's moves as irresponsibly increasing British debts, or to rally round as a patriotic gesture. In fact they simultaneously tried both approaches, with Osborne taking one tack, and Cameron the other. Finally, they settled on the former, attacking Brown for reckless profligacy, and demanding severe expenditure cuts to reduce the fiscal deficit. Brown wanted to follow a Keynsian course of massive investment to lift Britain out of the recession, going into the next election offering the alternative of Tory cuts or Labour investment. He was restrained by Darling and the Treasury, who insisted on the necessity of having a plan to pay off the debt in a finite period. So Labour entered the election campaign with a commitment to pay off half the debt within five years, but not to implement cuts until economic recovery was well under way. In retrospect, this appears quite a reasonable approach, but it cut little ice during the election campaign which terminated on 6 May 2010. A still unpopular Brown, who seemed to have lost all the *élan* and presentational skills of his earlier days, abandoned by most of the press, and heavily outspent by his opponents, went down to defeat, in an election which produced a 'hung' | Parliament. The result was:

Conservative	306
Labour	258
Liberal Democrats	57
Others	29

As recounted in Chapter 21, the Liberal Democrats chose to go into coalition with the Conservatives, despite a bid by Brown (who offered to give up his prime ministership in the process) to form a "progressive alliance" with them, with support from some of the smaller parties.

So, Brown's premiership came to end after two years and 321 days. Brown retained his parliamentary seat, but retired to the back benches, and virtually disappeared from Parliament. When Dominique Strauss-Kahn resigned as Director-General of the International Monetary Fund, in May 2011, he would have been a strong candidate for the succession, but the new Cameron government rushed to nominate France's Christine Lagarde instead, with Cameron making mean remarks about Brown being a 'deficit denier'. Instead, Brown has devoted much of his time to charitable work, particularly concerning overseas development.

Despite his great abilities, and his stellar performance over the banking crisis, Gordon Brown's premiership was undoubtedly a disappointment. Some, particularly his Blairite critics, have argued that he was temperamentally unsuited for the role. Yes, he was a good strategist, they concede, and able to rise to the big occasion, but he was ill-prepared to meet the daily challenge of a constant stream of unexpected events. There is something in this, but the more likely explanation is that the opportunity came to him much too late. If he, rather than Blair, had succeeded John Smith back in 1994, he might well have made a better fist of the top job. As it was, he had to wait 13 long years, full of raised hopes and crushing disappointments, before he was able to take over the helm. For understandable reasons, he was burned up with resentment, and became increasingly paranoid and distrustful of his colleagues, and profoundly risk-averse. So it was a badly bruised and hesitant figure who took over the premiership in 2007, in contrast to the supreme self-confidence which he had shown on becoming Chancellor. Moreover, the years of grindingly hard work had taken their toll, and at 56 he appeared no longer capable of communicating effectively either with his colleagues or with the electorate as a whole. He fought a dogged election campaign in 2010, but compared not only to Clegg, but also to Cameron, he appeared a rather lumbering figure, somewhat slow on the uptake. It was a sad end to a career that had begun full of promise.

Works consulted

Francis Beckett, 2007, *Gordon Brown: Past, Present and Future*, London, Haus Books.
Gordon Brown, 2010, *Beyond the Crash: Overcoming the First Crisis of Globalisation*, London, Simon & Schuster.

Alistair Darling, 2011, *Back from the Brink*, London, Atlantic Books.
Francis Elliott and James Hanning, 2012, *Cameron: Practically a Conservative*, London, Fourth Estate.
Dennis Kavanagh and Philip Cowley, 2010, *The British General Election of 2010*, London, Palgrave Macmillan.
William Keegan, 2004, *The Prudence of Mr. Gordon Brown*, London, Wiley.
William Keegan, 2012, *"Saving the World"? Gordon Brown Reconsidered*, London, Searching Finance.
Peter Mandelson, 2010, *The Third Man: Life at the Heart of New Labour*, London, Harper Press.
James Naughtie, 2001, *The Rivals: The Intimate Story of a Political Marriage*, London, Fourth Estate.
Robert Peston, 2005, *Brown's Britain*, London, Short Books.
Giles Radice, 2010, *Trio: Inside the Blair, Brown, Mandelson Project*, London, I.B. Tauris.
Andrew Rawnsley, 2000, *Servants of the People: The Inside Story of New Labour*, London, Hamish Hamilton.
Andrew Rawnsley, 2010, *The End of the Party: The Rise and Fall of New Labour*, London, Viking.
Steve Richards, 2010, *Whatever It Takes: The Real Story of Gordon Brown and New Labour*, London, Fourth Estate.
Paul Routledge, 1998, *Gordon Brown, The Biography*, London, Simon & Schuster.
Anthony Seldon, 2007, *Blair Unbound*, London, Simon & Schuster.
Anthony Seldon and Guy Lodge, 2010, *Brown at 10*, London, Biteback.
Jack Straw, 2012, *Last Man Standing*, London, Macmillan.

21

DAVID CAMERON

The accidental architect of Brexit

When David Cameron was a schoolboy at Eton, he was surrounded by the busts of many of the 18 Etonians who had been British Prime Ministers (more than a third of the total) and perhaps wondered whether there would ever be another one. Twenty-five or so years later, he resolved any doubts by becoming, at the age of 43, the youngest Premier since Lord Liverpool, in 1812.

There are some (perhaps even including himself) who believe that he was born to rule. He is the great-great-great-great-great-grandson, through an illegitimate line, of King William IV, which makes him a distant cousin of Queen Elizabeth II. Through both his parents, he is descended from several generations of Etonians: on his father's side, mostly wealthy stockbrokers, and on his mother's, baronets and Tory MPs. Born on 9 October 1966, he had an elder brother, Alexander, and sister, Rachel, and was to have a younger sister, Clare, five years his junior. His father was Ian Cameron (1932–2010), a senior partner, like his father and grandfather before him, of the stockbroking firm, Panmure Gordon. Ian had been born with deformed legs, which were eventually amputated, and he was widely admired, not least by his younger son, for his fortitude and determination not to allow his disability to prevent his leading an active and constructive life. Cameron's mother, the former Mary Fleur Mount (born 1934), had several distinguished relatives, including Alfred Duff Cooper, a leading Tory Cabinet minister and close associate of Winston Churchill. Her cousin, Ferdinand Mount (a baronet though he does not use his title), is a well-known author and served as head of the Downing Street Policy Unit under Margaret Thatcher. 'Ferdy' Mount, himself a somewhat unconventional character, described his family in the following terms:

> The Mounts are very old fashioned, slightly stiff, you might say … They had a very comfortable upbringing. They were churchgoing, I don't think any of them have ever been divorced. They are straitlaced and full of a sense of duty.
>
> (Elliott and Hanning, 2012, p. 8)

Mary Cameron may be less forbidding than this suggests, but certainly inherited the sense of duty. She served as a Justice of the Peace in Berkshire for many years, as did her mother and grandmother before her.

DOI: 10.4324/9781003031963-22

When David was born, the family were living in Phillimore Place, Kensington, but three years later they moved to the idyllic village of Peasemore, six miles north of Newbury, Berkshire. Their new home was a spacious Queen Anne mansion, the Old Rectory, with its own swimming pool and tennis court. There was also a live-in nanny, a family retainer of the Mounts, who had helped to bring up Mary a generation earlier. At the age of 7, David was dispatched to Heatherdown, near Ascot, perhaps the most exclusive preparatory school for boys in the whole country. Determinedly old-fashioned in its methods, pupils were required to learn by rote the names and dates of all the Kings and Queens of England, as well as the names and order of the books in the Old and New Testaments. David Cameron's capacity to learn speeches by heart, so that he could deliver them without notes, which served him so well on at least two crucial occasions much later in life, perhaps owed something to his 'prep school' experiences. These were not uniformly happy. Corporal punishment was freely administered by the headmaster, and the young David was thrashed several times for such offences as talking in chapel and stealing strawberries from the headmaster's garden. On the whole, David settled down well at the school. He is remembered by contemporaries as being very well adapted, "always smiling, very social and chatty" and "with a good ability to get on with people".

Although his family was wealthy, David apparently came from near the lower end of the social scale represented at the school. His biographers record that among the 80 or so sets of parents of his contemporaries were: "eight honourables, four sirs, two captains, two doctors, two majors, one brigadier, one commodore, two princesses, two marchionesses, one viscount, one lord (unspecified) and one queen (*the* Queen)" (Elliott and Hanning, 2012, p. 20).

David did not particularly excel academically at Heatherdown, where his results were no better than average. Nevertheless, he did well enough at the end of his time there to win admission to Eton, which was the ultimate objective of sending him to the school. He was to be one of its last pupils. It closed its doors in 1982, the super-rich having apparently concluded that it was no longer the fashionable thing to send their children away from home at such a tender age.

At Eton, Cameron initially acquired the same reputation he had enjoyed at Heatherdown, of being bright, amiable, but of no more than average ability. Then, at the age of 16, he had a nasty shock, coming within an ace of being expelled from the school. In a scandal, which reached the national newspapers, a number of his fellow pupils were thrown out of the school for smoking, and dealing in, cannabis. Cameron had not done any dealing, and was let off with being fined, 'gated' and having to copy out 500 lines of Latin verse. Much later, on the eve of the 2010 general election, he recalled in a newspaper interview the effect this had had on him:

> When I was 16 I was definitely going off the track a bit, losing interest in school and study and doing things wrong … I remember thinking, "Hold on a minute, if you carry on like this you're not going to get any decent grades, you're not going to make much of your life".
>
> *(Daily Mail, 10 April 2010)*

So, he buckled down, paid much more attention to his classes, broadened his interests, and, when he took his A levels, in 1984, scored three As – in History of Art, History, and Economics with Politics. He then sat the entrance exam for Oxford University, and was awarded an Exhibition at Brasenose College.

Cameron's time at Eton coincided with the early years of Margaret Thatcher's premiership, and she became a heroine to the vast majority of Eton schoolboys, all but a tiny proportion of whom came from Conservative family backgrounds. Cameron was no exception, and became a strong admirer of the 'Iron Lady', though the Conservatism which he came to embrace was of a more compassionate and moderate brand than hers. There was one exception: his Euroscepticism. Like his hero, he often railed against the authorities in Brussels, and like her his time as Prime Minister would come to a sticky end because of Europe.

His biographers interviewed several of his close associates at the school, who recalled that "his real passion was reserved for railing against the iniquities of the 'Common Market'" (Elliott and Hanning, 2012, p. 40). While at Eton, Cameron, who expressed the preference to be known as 'Dave', was generally regarded as being very friendly and approachable. Some of his contemporaries, however, regarded him as arrogant, and thought the charm was only put on for people he wanted to impress, while treating others with disdain. Several of them claimed to have detected an inner determination and ruthlessness behind the surface charm. For whatever reason, Cameron failed to be elected to the elite Eton Society, 'Pop', which was evidently a disappointment for him. Opinions differ as to whether Cameron had already decided on a political career while still at school. Elliott and Hanning noted that, though he attended meetings of the school's prestigious Political Society, he made no attempt to be elected to its committee, which would have entitled him to meet the speakers, who included senior Cabinet ministers, more informally over dinner. "Unlike", they add, "Boris Johnson, a year his senior" (Elliott and Hanning, 2012, p. 41).

Nevertheless, for the first three months of his gap year before Oxford, he worked in the House of Commons as an intern with Tim Rathbone, the very 'liberal' Conservative MP for Lewes, who was his godfather. He then left for Hong Kong to work for another three months for the Jardine Matheson shipping agency, whose Chairman, Henry Keswick, was a close associate of his father. Cameron arrived in Oxford in October 1985 to read Politics, Philosophy and Economics. He was later described by his tutor, Professor Vernon Bogdanor, as "one of the ablest students he had taught" (BBC News programme, 6 December 2005). His contemporaries remember him as someone who was extremely well organised, dividing his time very efficiently, and presenting his views, both in writing and in discussion, extremely clearly and with great good humour. He mixed in well with his fellow PPE students, but his social life revolved mostly around Old Etonians, and he joined the exclusive Bullingdon Club of wealthy young men, renowned for their heavy drinking and loutish behaviour. Also prominent in 'the Buller', as it was known by its members, was Boris Johnson, who by all accounts joined more enthusiastically in their destructive orgies than the more self-disciplined Cameron. Nevertheless, Cameron was once summoned by his college authorities to explain why the furniture in his rooms had been systematically vandalised. He declined to name the culprits, and footed the bill for the damage. Cameron had strings of girlfriends, while at Oxford, and at least one serious relationship, with a diplomat's half-German daughter, Francesca Ferguson. It lasted for 18 months, and she took him to Kenya for a safari, and to visit her parents, her mother remarking to her: "That chap is going to be Prime Minister one day". Soon after returning to Oxford, however, Cameron 'dumped' her rather abruptly, apparently more keen on working hard to secure a First in his degree than to spend his time courting (Elliott and Hanning, 2012, pp. 64–5).

While at Oxford, Cameron played no part in the Union, and did not join the Conservative Association. There was no doubt, however, that he was a convinced Tory, and Vernon Bogdanor remembered him as having "moderate and sensible Conservative political views" (*Sunday Times*, 25 March 2007). In the summer of 1988, Cameron sat his finals, and – as predicted by Bogdanor – duly obtained a First. This virtually assured him a smooth entry into whatever career he chose. At the time, he was still divided in his mind between business and politics. He had already applied for a number of management consulting and banking jobs, and also to *The Economist*, but nothing had come of them. He now decided to apply for a post at the Conservative Central Office, and was invited for an interview. Waiting to interview him was the deputy director of the party's research department, Alistair Cooke (later Lord Lexden). He was surprised to receive a telephone call from a man who announced, in a 'grand' voice, that he was calling from Buckingham Palace. He said:

> I understand that you are to see David Cameron. I've tried everything I can to dissuade him from wasting his time on politics, but I have failed. I am ringing to tell you that you are about to meet a truly remarkable young man.
>
> *(Elliott and Hanning, 2012, p. 73)*

According to Cooke, this "unsolicited testimonial" had no effect, either way, on the decision to offer Cameron an appointment. He was "clearly outstanding", he reported years later when the story emerged in the press. Cameron himself was puzzled, believing that the caller was probably Sir Alastair Aird, then the Comptroller of the Queen Mother's Household, and the husband of Cameron's godmother. But Aird vehemently denied it, as did Sir Brian McGrath, Secretary to Prince Philip, a family friend and neighbour of the Camerons. Perhaps, after all, it was an anonymous hoaxer.

Cameron started work at the Conservative Research Department (CRD) on 26 September 1988. He was to remain there, or on secondment to a series of Cabinet ministers, for six years. He soon established a reputation as a keen, quick and highly efficient worker, and by 1990 had been promoted to Head of the Political Section, under the overall direction of Andrew Lansley, who 20 years later was to serve under him as Secretary of State for Health, and later as Leader of the Commons. Among his colleagues at the CRD were several young researchers who later became his close associates as leader of the opposition and Prime Minister. These included Steve Hilton, whom he appointed as Director of Strategy at 10 Downing Street, and who was reputed to be his most influential adviser. Others, including George Osborne, became important politicians in their own right. Also working at the CRD was Laura Adshead, whom Cameron had known at Oxford, and with whom he now started a passionate affair, which lasted a year and apparently ended badly. Cameron resolved never again to date anyone in politics, and Adshead asked for "compassionate leave" from her work, and subsequently, in a complete change in her lifestyle, became a nun.

Soon after John Major succeeded Margaret Thatcher as Prime Minister, he asked the CRD for help in preparing for the very testing, and then twice-weekly, sessions of Prime Minister's Questions. Cameron was selected for this role, and every Tuesday and Thursday he had to get up very early in the morning to report to 10 Downing Street, where he was set to go through with a toothcomb all the daily newspapers in preparation for briefing the Prime Minister on any tricky issues which were likely to come up, and to suggest suitable lines of response. He met with Major at 9 a.m., and then again over lunch, where the Prime Minister rehearsed his lines and took away a more detailed brief which Cameron had prepared during the morning. He performed his task well. The *Sunday Times* reported, on 30 June 1991, "John Major's

266 David Cameron

performances have become sharper of late", and attributed the improvement by name to the previously unknown 24-year-old researcher. In the 1992 general election, which the Tories were expected to lose, Cameron was given the crucial task of briefing Major every morning before his daily press conference. This involved him getting into Conservative Central Office by 4.30 each morning, having seldom gone to bed before midnight, and working all day scouring the papers and television programmes for negative points to use against Labour. The entire Tory campaign was linked round two themes – to paint Labour as an irresponsible 'tax and spend' party and to undermine public trust in the Labour leader, Neil Kinnock. Cameron provided much of the 'ammunition' needed for these purposes, and, together with his side-kick, Steve Hilton, he got much of the credit within the party for Major's surprise success. Not all senior Tories, however, were enamoured with Cameron. Lord McAlpine, for example, a former Tory Treasurer and close friend of Lady Thatcher, excoriated him in a press article, referring to his "obvious arrogance" (Elliott and Hanning, 2012, p. 111). Some younger Tories also were clearly envious of his success, and fearful that he would leapfrog over them in his ascent up the party hierarchy.

At the election, Major's political adviser, Judith Chaplin, was elected Tory MP for Newbury, and Cameron was greatly disappointed that Major did not choose him as her successor. Instead, he was chosen by Norman Lamont, the Chancellor of the Exchequer, as the more junior of his two policy advisers. Cameron reluctantly agreed, complaining that the salary offered was below his expectations. Within a few months he probably regretted taking the job. He was pictured in all the newspapers, lurking embarrassedly behind the Chancellor on 'Black Wednesday', 16 September 1992, when Lamont announced Britain's humiliating withdrawal from the European exchange rate mechanism (ERM). Worse was to come a few months later, when Lamont was abruptly sacked as Chancellor and refused to accept demotion to a more junior Cabinet post. Meanwhile, Judith Chaplin had suddenly died, and Cameron briefly contemplated offering himself as candidate for her Newbury constituency, which included his family home at Peasemore. Fortunately for him, he thought better of it: in the ensuing by-election the Tory majority of over 12,000 votes was converted to a Liberal Democrat one of the same dimensions. At about this time, however, he took steps to ensure that he was included in the Conservative list of recommended candidates.

The incoming Chancellor, Kenneth Clarke, did not retain Cameron's services. He was instead chosen to assist the new Home Secretary, Michael Howard, to counter the challenge from his Labour 'opposite number', Tony Blair, To the chagrin of the Tories, he had succeeded in appropriating their mantle as the 'law and order party' with his 'tough on crime, tough on the causes of crime' message, and Howard was determined to win it back. Cameron himself became fascinated by Blair, whom he met in the course of his duties, and struck up a friendship with his adviser, Tim Allan, arranging occasional dinners with him at which they discussed the merits and faults of their respective bosses. This did not deter Cameron from helping Howard devise a series of ferociously tough measures, which he unveiled at his famous 'Prison works' speech at the 1993 annual Conservative conference. One of Howard's junior ministers, Sir Peter Lloyd, whose own views were distinctly 'liberal', doubts whether Cameron fully shared "the determinedly right wing views of his boss". "I remember thinking in ministerial meetings", he recalled, "he is a bright chap – does he really believe all this nonsense?" (Elliott and Hanning, 2012, pp. 158–9).

While working for Lamont, Cameron had started a new relationship. This was with Samantha Sheffield, who had been a school friend of his younger sister, Clare. Clare had invited her to join in a Cameron family holiday in Tuscany, and the pair were instantly attracted. Five years younger than her new admirer, Samantha was a rather wild art student in Bristol, frequenting 'rave' parties, and hanging out with a very Bohemian crowd at her local pub, described by one of her friends, the hip-hop star, Tricky (Adrian Thaws), as a place where: "bikers mixed with drug dealers, hippies, students and guys from the ghetto. It was a cool pub but … there were always fights" (Elliott and Hanning, 2012, p. 137). But she came from a very grand family: her father, Sir Reginald Sheffield, 8th Baronet, had large estates in both Yorkshire and Lincolnshire, and her mother, Annabel, who had divorced from 'Reggie' when Samantha was still a small child, was now Viscountess Astor. She could also eclipse Cameron's royal connections, as a descendant of Charles II and Nell Gwynn, and was a distant cousin of Princess Diana. Less intellectual than his previous girlfriends, she enchanted David, who soon proposed marriage. But she thought she was much too young, at 22, and – perhaps recalling that her mother's early marriage had collapsed after barely five years – decided that they must wait, so they became only 'secretly engaged'.

By 1994, however, Cameron, now very keen indeed to become an MP, thought it would be advantageous to get some experience in business, and also to earn more money, as his income as a party 'apparatchik' had fallen far behind those of most of his Etonian and Oxford friends, who were virtually all engaged in commerce or the more high-paying professions. His future mother-in-law came to his aid. Annabel Astor, herself a highly successful business-woman, was a close friend of Michael Green, the Chairman of Carlton Communications, which had extensive interests in advertising and in television, including the London weekday franchise on ITV. Green hired him at almost double his salary as an aide to Michael Howard, and he eventually became the company's director of communications, essentially a PR and lobbying job. Cameron made it clear at the outset that his overriding priority was to become a Tory MP in the shortest possible time, and Green, anxious to curry favour with the Conservatives, acquiesced. Cameron started working for Carlton in September 1994, and his search for a safe Tory constituency began in earnest. He had unsuccessful forays at Ashford, Epsom and Reading, but in January 1996 he was selected at Stafford, a newly redistributed constituency, which was projected to have a Tory majority of around 8,000. Six months later, on 1 June 1996, he and Samantha, now working as creative director at Smythson's, the upmarket stationers in New Bond Street, were married at St Augustine's church, East Hendred, Oxfordshire. All seemed set fair, but John Major's government was deeply unpopular, and 'New Labour', under Tony Blair's dynamic leadership, was soaring in the polls. When the general election took place on 1 May 1997, there was a swing to Labour in the Stafford constituency of 10.8 per cent, slightly larger than the national average. Cameron lost by over 4,000 votes, and returned disconsolately to resume his job at Carlton. He was now, effectively, chief press officer of the group, and pursued his role in a notably aggressive manner. He was highly effective, but according to his biographers, succeeded in alienating a number of senior financial journalists, who accused him of dissembling and not being above playing 'dirty tricks' (Elliott and Hanning, 2012, p. 187).

His search for a parliamentary seat continued. He narrowly missed out on the selection for the West Sussex seat of Wealden, but had a stroke of luck a year later, in 2000, when Shaun Woodward, the Tory MP for Witney, the Cotswolds constituency adjacent to Newbury and where his mother-in-law, Annabel Astor, had her country home, defected to the Labour Party. Cameron seemed a natural for the seat, and was duly selected. He went on to be elected, in this very safe Conservative seat, in the 2001 election with a majority over Labour of just under

268 David Cameron

8,000. The first decision he had to take on election was whom to back as the party leader, William Hague having resigned following the heavy Tory election defeat. He decided to vote for Michael Portillo, who – despite his earlier record as a fervent right-winger – presented himself as the modernising candidate, and was seen as the favourite. He led on the first two ballots by MPs, but was squeezed by a single vote into third place in the third ballot, as other candidates were eliminated. Had he made it into the run-off between the two top candidates, he would almost certainly have been elected as he was by far the most popular among the wider party membership, to whom the decision was now referred. What probably cost him the chance was his admission during the campaign that he had "experimented" with homosexual relations when he was a student. So the final choice was between the former Chancellor of the Exchequer, Kenneth Clarke, and the almost unknown Iain Duncan Smith, an ardent Thatcherite. Clarke lost by a 3-2 margin, undoubtedly because of his pro-European views. Cameron gave his final vote to Duncan Smith, despite being far closer in his views to Clarke on everything except Europe.

Cameron was fortunate as a newly elected MP to be invited to serve on the Home Affairs Select Committee. At its first meeting, he successfully proposed that it should launch an investigation into heroin addiction and "options for changing the law towards cannabis". He rapidly revealed himself as one of the most 'liberal' members of the committee, advocating the decriminalisation of cannabis and the downgrading of Ecstasy from a Class A to a Class B drug. He also soon formed a close association with George Osborne, the newly elected MP for Tatton, whose background was not dissimilar to his own. Nearly five years younger, the heir to a baronetcy, he was not an Etonian but was educated at St Paul's school, and studied at Oxford, where he was a member of the Bullingdon Club, and subsequently worked at the Conservative Research Department, as a ministerial aide, and as speechwriter to William Hague as leader of the opposition. A much earlier committed 'moderniser' than Cameron, their views gradually merged, with Osborne generally leading the way. They were neighbours in the Notting Hill area of west London, and soon got into the habit of driving together daily between their homes and the House of Commons. Gathering round them was a smallish group of mostly young and newly elected members, nearly all of them wealthy and public-school-educated, and committed modernisers. They frequently dined together, and were generically known as the 'Notting Hill set'.

On 8 April 2002, the birth of their first son, Ivan, gave great joy to David and Samantha, but a week or so later they learnt the devastating news that he was severely disabled, and would be unlikely ever to walk or talk. He was diagnosed with Ohtahara syndrome, an extreme form of epilepsy. He lived for nearly seven years during which he required constant round-the-clock care, was often in great pain and was in and out of hospital. His parents' lives were greatly disrupted, but they lavished love and affection on him, and were heartbroken when he died, following a series of uncontrollable seizures at St Mary's Hospital, Paddington early in the morning of 25 February 2009. They had been told that there might be a one in four chance that any subsequent children would suffer from the same condition, but were brave enough to take the risk, and had three further children, all completely healthy – Nancy, born in January 2004, Arthur Elwen, in February 2006, and Florence, born after Cameron had become Prime Minister, in August 2010. The experience of having Ivan had a marked effect on Cameron. He was so deeply impressed by the care and devotion that his son received from the National Health Service throughout his short life that he became a passionate advocate on its behalf. This undoubtedly helped to improve the Tory Party's image, as it had long lagged behind

Labour in the public's estimate of the two parties' support for the NHS. More personally, his friends noticed that he became much more patient and sympathetic about other people's misfortunes, and shed some of the blandness and self-satisfaction which he had previously radiated.

The newly elected party leader, Iain Duncan Smith, was finding it extremely difficult to match Tony Blair at Prime Minister's Questions, and before long, both Cameron and Osborne, together with Boris Johnson, the newly elected MP for Henley, were drafted in to help prepare for the, now weekly, encounter, every Wednesday. Despite their help, Duncan Smith showed little improvement, and the party became more and more dissatisfied with his parliamentary performances. In July 2003, Cameron was given his first frontbench job – as 'deputy Shadow Leader of the House' – and made a conspicuous debut, with several newspapers identifying him as a possible future party leader. Duncan Smith's own leadership had not much further to run. In October, the requisite number of Tory MPs – 25 – formally demanded a vote on whether there should be a leadership ballot. Friends of Duncan Smith pressed him to stand down, fearing that he would suffer a humiliating defeat, but he insisted on holding his ground. In the event, he was defeated, but by a narrower margin than had been expected – 90 votes to 75.

A contest for the leadership was then expected, with the likely candidates being Michael Howard, who had established himself as the most effective debater on the Conservative side of the House, and David Davis, who was regarded as having done an excellent job as Chairman of the all-party Public Accounts Committee, and who was widely seen as the carrier of the Thatcherite flame. Yet Davis was leaned on not to run, and probably calculated that if, as seemed highly likely, the Tories lost the next general election, he would then be chosen to pick up the pieces. So Howard was elected unopposed, without the necessity of holding a ballot of party members. He performed much better as opposition leader than his predecessor, but did no more than dent Labour's majority at the general election, held on 5 May 2005. The Tories made 35 gains, winning 198 seats, against 355 for Labour and 62 for the Liberal Democrats.

Howard announced his intended resignation on the morrow of the election, but agreed to carry on until the party conference in October. In the meantime, he reshuffled his Shadow Cabinet to give much greater prominence to younger MPs. He offered the Shadow chancellorship to Cameron, who declined, perhaps because he was leery of facing the formidable Gordon Brown across the dispatch box. Instead, he chose the Education portfolio, and Howard appointed Osborne as Shadow Chancellor, at the same time encouraging him to run for the party leadership. Osborne accepted the post, but after reflection concluded that he was too young, at 33, to be a viable leadership contender. Cameron, however, quickly decided, with strong support from his wife, that he would like to run, and in early June summoned a secret meeting of the Notting Hill group of MPs, of whom 14 attended, including Osborne, Boris Johnson, and Michael Gove, a former journalist on *The Times*, who had only just been elected to the House. Most agreed to back his candidature, though some wished he had rather more fire in his belly, and others feared that he would be seen as 'too posh'. Cameron's campaign did not take off, and by early September the number of his supporters had shrunk to nine. Meanwhile, it was generally assumed that the contest would effectively be between David Davis and Ken Clarke, though the thrusting young right-winger, Liam Fox, and former Foreign Secretary, Malcolm Rifkind, also entered the lists. As the party conference approached, Cameron took two vital steps to revive his flagging fortunes. He spent £20,000 on promotional activities, including an American-style launch meeting at the Royal United Services Institute in an auditorium specially jazzed up for the occasion. This was very favourably received by the assembled journalists, who contrasted it with a similar event held by David Davis the same day "in the fusty oak-panelled surroundings of the Institute of Civil Engineers" (Elliott and Hanning, 2012, p. 293). The speech which Cameron made was reported as inspiring, while Davis's was dismissed as "disappointing", so the young challenger received an excellent press. He also sought to ingratiate himself with the growing anti-European section of the party by matching Liam Fox's promise to take the Conservative Group out of the European People's Party, to which most of the main centre-right parties in the EU belonged. He thereby risked marginalising the British Conservatives in the European Parliament, but felt the step was necessary to avert the threat of Fox overhauling him in the race for votes. This concession to the Eurosceptic fringe of his party was a harbinger of his willingness to put party management over the national interest, a tendency that would eventually have tragic consequences for him as well as the country in the Brexit referendum of 2016.

The party conference opened in Blackpool, and all the five candidates were given a specific day on which they could address the conference (and, through the television coverage, the party membership). First off was Rifkind, whose speech kindled little enthusiasm, and he shortly afterwards withdrew from the contest, in favour of Clarke. It was his turn the following day, and though he made a lively and witty speech it was received with little warmth. On Wednesday, 4 October, Cameron's moment arrived, and he took the conference by storm. Speaking without any notes and wandering freely round the platform with microphone in hand, he made a passionate appeal to change and modernise the party, saying he wanted people to "feel good about being Conservatives again". Approaching his peroration, he continued:

> There is a new generation of people taking on the world, creating the wealth and opportunity for our future. We can lead that generation … Changing our party to change our country. It will be an incredible journey. I want you to come with me.

It was the speech of a lifetime, and the conference responded with great enthusiasm. In 20 minutes, Cameron had moved from being a rank outsider to a leading contender. He was half-way home, and his success was virtually assured on the following day, when Davis made a dull and uninspiring speech which shattered the hopes of his previously large band of supporters. Then Cameron was thrown out of his stride by press speculation, particularly in the *Daily Mail*, about his alleged drug-taking while at Oxford. He refused to give a direct answer, but said that he led 'a normal student life', and was profoundly relieved when after a few days the story died a natural death. Two weeks later, when Parliament resumed, the 198 Tory MPs proceeded to an exhaustive ballot to reduce the four candidates to two, with the following result:

	1st ballot	2nd ballot
Davis	62	57
Cameron	56	90
Fox	42	51
Clarke	38	–

Although Davis led on the first ballot, the margin was much narrower than expected, and when Clarke was eliminated Cameron won almost all his votes, while Davis's score actually fell. The two leading candidates were then submitted to a postal ballot of the party membership, with Cameron winning by a margin of more than 2-1:

Cameron	134,446 votes
Davis	64,398 votes

On 6 December 2005, he was declared elected as party leader, and, consequently, leader of the opposition. It was an amazing achievement after less than five years as a Member of Parliament. It was a great gamble for the party to turn to somebody so young and inexperienced, and it was a reflection of how desperate they had become after losing three elections in a row under three different leaders.

As leader, Cameron had no doubt as to what his mission should be. It was to 'detoxify' the image of the Conservative Party, which was now widely seen, in the words of his colleague, Theresa May, as "the nasty party". During the leadership campaign, he had – perhaps unwisely – proclaimed himself to be the "heir to Blair". Now, he and his entourage, largely made up of youngish former employees of the Conservative Research Department, consciously modelled themselves on the Labour leader and his 'New Labour' colleagues. They pored over the book written by Blair's strategy adviser, Philip Gould, *The Unfinished Revolution* (1999). This painstakingly spelled out every inch of the journey which the Labour Party had taken from the depths of 1983, when it was seen as a backward-looking, ideologically obsessed party, tied to outdated doctrines of nationalisation and punitive levels of taxation, to the all-conquering 'New Labour' which had swept to power in 1997. Andrew Cooper, who was to become Cameron's Director of Strategy in 10 Downing Street, handsomely acknowledged the debt the Tories owed to Gould in a memorial volume published after his premature death in 2011 (Kavanagh, 2012, pp. 132–51). His chapter is entitled "How Philip Gould Helped to Save the Conservative Party". It was not just that the Tories under Cameron adopted the *methods*, particularly the extensive use of focus groups, employed by Gould, but they also adapted the *tone* of their message, particularly in the speeches and television appearances of their leader. These were consistently moderate, reasonably argued, open-minded and optimistic – or 'schmoozing the public', as less friendly observers might put it.

By no means all the Tories welcomed Cameron's new approach, and there was much resistance within the party to many of his initiatives. These included his attempts to ensure that the party in Parliament – overwhelmingly made up of white, public-school-educated males – was broadened by the adoption as candidates of many more women, ethnic minority and state-educated candidates. His efforts in this direction had some effect, despite the sullen opposition, but even after the 2010 general election the party's representation was still heavily weighted towards the privileged classes. Cameron also went out of his way to bury Conservative hostility to the gay community, announcing himself in favour of civil partnerships, and under his leadership – for the first time – a number of Tory MPs 'outed' themselves as homosexual. Cameron also placed great emphasis on environmental issues and the threat of global warming, travelling to northern Norway, and being photographed sledging with husky dogs to dramatise his concern about the issue. He was also widely pictured cycling each day from his home to the House of Commons, but the effect of this was somewhat undermined when it was revealed that he was followed on his route by his official car carrying his shoes and papers. This did not prevent him from using the slogan 'Vote Blue Go Green' in the 2006 local elections.

In the House of Commons, he was able to at least hold his own in his weekly confrontations with Tony Blair, now a somewhat diminished figure in the aftermath of the Iraq War and with rumblings of discontent within his own party.

The public response to Cameron's leadership was generally favourable, and by the summer of 2006 the Tories overtook Labour in the polls for almost the first time in over a decade and steadily increased their lead until mid-2007, when Brown replaced Blair as Prime Minister. There was then a sharp reversal during the new Prime Minister's honeymoon period, and by October 2007 the Tories appeared to be facing a heavy defeat in the general election which now appeared imminent. Yet Cameron kept his nerve (see Chapter 20), and defiantly rallied his party in a speech – again without notes – at the Conservative Party conference. This, together with a desperate pledge by George Osborne to raise the inheritance tax threshold to £1 million, led to a sharp narrowing of Labour's poll lead, and Brown, humiliatingly, called off the election which he was about to announce. In retrospect, this appears to have been the decisive event in Cameron's rise to power, and thereafter it seemed highly probable that he would overhaul Labour at the next election, the main uncertainty being whether he would obtain an overall majority. The Tories immediately went into a lead in the polls, which they maintained, with fluctuations, right up until polling day in 2010.

The remaining two-and-a-half years of Brown's premiership were something of an anti-climax, except for his deft handling of the banking crisis, which resulted in some improvement in his polling position, which was not, however, sustained. He became deeply unpopular, not least because of the scandal over MPs' expenses, which hit all parties, but Labour as the government party was the more damaged. This was partly because the *Daily Telegraph*, which broke the story, gave the greatest prominence to Labour 'delinquents', and also because Cameron proved more adroit in handling the issue and acted more promptly in seeking to discipline his MPs. The big irony is that Cameron's own reputation would be severely damaged after he left office by a lobbying scandal when his attempts to influence his former parliamentary colleagues on behalf of Greensill Capital were exposed by the media.

Even when he was still in office, Cameron's continuing efforts to 'decontaminate' his party achieved only partial success. Although his own standing with the public became increasingly positive, he never rivalled Blair's earlier charisma, and deep reservations about the Conservative Party persisted among many uncommitted voters. Nevertheless, the Tories entered the 2010 general election campaign with high hopes of success. The Labour Party appeared in disarray, it had lost almost all its support in the press, with the sole exception of the Mirror group (even *The Guardian* had abandoned ship), and it was heavily outspent by the Tories, whose normally ample funds were augmented by massive donations from Lord Ashcroft, the controversial billionaire and former Vice-Chairman of the party. Yet the Conservative campaign was blown off course by the apparent surge of support for the Liberal Democrats, following the first of three television debates in which Nick Clegg comprehensively outperformed his two rivals. Consequently the Tories turned all their fire on the LibDems, in particular by launching a sustained attack on their proposal of a partial amnesty for illegal immigrants. They also, in great secrecy, held a top level meeting at which they discussed in detail the terms of a coalition agreement which might be offered in the event of a 'hung' Parliament. It was a prudent step. Although the Tories emerged from the election as the largest party, they were 20 seats short of a parliamentary majority. The overall result of the election of 6 May 2010 was:

Conservative	306
Labour	258
Liberal Democrats	57
Others	29

No party was in a position to form a majority. There would either have to be a minority government or a coalition. The salient fact about the figures was that, whereas Conservatives plus Liberal Democrats could produce a majority, Labour plus Liberal Democrats could not. Any left-centre coalition would have to seek additional support from among the minority parties – Scottish and Welsh Nationalists, Northern Irish Members and one Green.

The election result was a bitter disappointment to Cameron, and threatened to put his leadership in question, but he acted with great speed and determination to extract the maximum advantage from the situation. In the early afternoon of 7 May, he called a press conference, at which he made a "big, open and comprehensive offer to the Liberal Democrats" to form a coalition. Some of his colleagues had argued instead that he should form a minority government, asking the Liberal Democrats to reach a 'confidence and supply agreement' enabling him to get urgent legislation through, but with no guarantee of support for other government policies. Yet Cameron decided to go for what he considered the 'jackpot'. It seemed a long shot. The LibDems presented themselves as a left-of-centre party, and during the election campaign they had sided with Labour on the crucial issue of whether to begin with expenditure cuts before the fragile economic recovery had been consolidated. Yet Cameron was fortunate that Nick Clegg, unlike all previous leaders of his party, was right-of-centre, and moreover had developed a very marked aversion to Gordon Brown. So he responded with alacrity to Cameron's offer, and the first meeting between negotiating teams of the two parties was held on the same day. Brown responded by ringing Clegg and proposing a "progressive alliance", with a pledge of immediate legislation on electoral reform, and promising, at the very least, a referendum on the Alternative Vote (AV). Clegg held him at arm's length, though he later agreed to parallel talks with a Labour team. These never really took off, and were effectively used by the Liberal Democrats to improve their bargaining position with the Tories. Several Cabinet ministers were less than enthusiastic about a deal with the LibDems, but Brown was very determined and, when it appeared that his own leadership would be an obstacle, offered to stand down within a few months of a government being formed. His gesture came too late, the LibDem talks with the Tories went very well, and when Cameron reluctantly agreed, as a "final offer", to a referendum on AV, which the Tories would be free to campaign against, it was clear that an agreement would soon be reached. Brown threw in his hand, and drove to the Palace to resign on the afternoon of 11 May, and within an hour Cameron had kissed hands on his appointment.

On the following afternoon, he and Clegg gave a joint press conference in the rose garden of 10 Downing Street to present their government and the coalition agreement which underpinned it. There was much comment about the evident good feeling between the two men. They had much in common: the same age (43), the same wealthy background, 'public' school and Oxford education. Cameron had used all his ample charm on his LibDem partner during the previous days, and had been generous in his offer of ministerial positions. Clegg was offered, and accepted, the post of Deputy Premier, and four others of his colleagues were included in the Cabinet, rather more than they were mathematically entitled to, given their representation in Parliament. Fourteen other Liberal Democrats became junior ministers,

For Cameron, the coalition agreement was undoubtedly a good deal. He had preserved all the policy options which were important to him, and the only substantial concession he had been forced to make was over the AV referendum. It also enabled him to shed policy commitments which, while popular among Tory backbenchers, were embarrassing and/or unrealistic, such as the massive raising of the threshold for inheritance tax and attempting to repatriate powers from the European Union. For the Liberal Democrats it was to prove a great deal less satisfactory. They were forced to reverse their policy on expenditure cuts, and had made a major error in not making any attempt to secure concessions over the raising of student tuition fees, which they had very loudly campaigned against, all their candidates publicly signing a pledge to vote against any increase. One part of the agreement was equally satisfactory to both parties. This was the institution of a fixed parliamentary term, which virtually guaranteed the continuation of the government for a full five years. Provided the two parties stuck together, the next election would not be held until Thursday, 7 May 2015.

The Cabinet which Cameron formed had 23 members. The Tory appointments included George Osborne as Chancellor of the Exchequer, William Hague as Foreign Secretary, Theresa May as Home Secretary, Andrew Lansley as Health Secretary and Michael Gove as Education Secretary. David Davis was not included. The Liberal Democrat appointees included Vince Cable as Business Secretary, Chris Huhne as Energy Secretary and David Laws in the key post of Chief Secretary to the Treasury. He was forced to resign after less than three weeks because of serious irregularities in his expenses claims, and was replaced by Danny Alexander. At the rose garden press conference, Cameron had hailed not just a new government, but a "new politics", with two parties giving up their distinctive preoccupations in the national interest. It was, indeed, a dramatic change over recent practice, effectively the first peacetime coalition government since Lloyd George's administration in 1918–22. (The so-called 'National government', formed in 1931, was to all intents and purposes a Tory administration, with the ageing and ineffective Ramsay MacDonald merely a figurehead Prime Minister.)

Cameron's government had at least one thing in common with Tony Blair's. It was dominated by the relationship between the two most powerful ministers. Yet whereas Blair and Brown were suspicious and resentful of each other, relations between Cameron and Osborne appeared to be harmonious. This may be because the relatively laid-back Prime Minister was happy to allow his hyper-active and hyper-political Chancellor to dominate the government's agenda. He readily deferred to his judgement, and Osborne was both the government's strategist and chief tactician. He had already assumed these roles in opposition, when he had, with considerable success, sought to blame the recession not on the greed and imprudence of bankers but on the alleged profligacy of Gordon Brown. He had committed the Tories to an immediate programme of expenditure cuts in a bold attempt to pay off the accumulated debts within the course of a single Parliament. This became the centrepiece of the new government's programme, and its success or otherwise came to be seen as its lodestar. Osborne began his austerity blitz with an emergency budget in June 2010, imposing immediate expenditure cuts of £6.2 billion, together with a steep rise in VAT. He followed this up, in October, with a spending review which fixed very tight spending limits for each government department up to 2014–15, with only Health, Education and International Development ring-fenced to protect them from real expenditure cuts. Other measures included wage freezes for the public sector, deep cuts in benefit payments, the tripling of university tuition fees and a purge of 'quangos', with 192 to be abolished and another 118 merged. The screw was progressively tightened in subsequent budgets, and though Osborne repeatedly claimed that "we are all in this together", the brunt of the burden was clearly being felt by the less well off. Virtually the only sacrifice demanded of the wealthy was the withdrawal of child benefit from those whose incomes exceeded £40,000 (later amended to £60,000, with a partial reduction for those earning more than £50,000). Initial reactions were largely favourable, with international economic organisations praising Osborne's policy, the press being broadly supportive, and opinion poll findings reassuring.

Meanwhile the Labour Party had made rather a meal of its choice of a leader to succeed Gordon Brown. This process involved five candidates, and lasted over four months before the result was declared at the Labour Party conference on 25 September 2010. During this period, arguably, the Labour Party virtually threw away its chances of winning the next election, not due for another five years. Government ministers, both Tory and LibDem, following the lead of George Osborne, continuously emphasised in all their speeches that they had inherited a "mess" of epic proportions from the Labour government, often adding that it was as bad as – or even worse than – in Greece and that they were in the process of clearing it up. "They crashed the car last time. Do you want to give them the car-keys again?" became the doorstep canvassing version of their refrain. The Labour leadership candidates, with Ed Miliband to the fore, were so anxious to distinguish themselves from New Labour that they made no attempt to defend the record of the Brown government. By the time the leadership contest was over, the Tory narrative was already widely accepted as accurate, and Labour attempts to discredit it were largely unsuccessful. The flat denials of any Labour responsibility fell on disbelieving ears: it would have been far better to admit, with the benefit of hindsight, that there had been a degree of over-spending in the years before 2008, but that this was only a relatively minor cause of what was a world-wide recession, whose origins were in the United States. The leadership election itself was deeply embarrassing for Labour. Ed Miliband's decision to run against his elder brother, David, who was the frontrunner, was portrayed in the press as an act of fratricide, and the fact that his narrow victory was secured by the votes of trade unionists, while a majority both of MPs and party members backed David, was seen as undermining his legitimacy. This was a golden opportunity for Cameron, who had an easy time in Parliament, repeatedly scoring points off the new Labour leader, Ed Miliband, who started off very much on the back foot.

In May 2011, the Conservatives actually won additional seats in the local elections, which normally result in opposition gains. The Liberal Democrats, however, suffered severely for their about-turn on tuition fees and for flouting the wishes of large numbers of their former voters who did not approve of their siding with the Tories. They lost 747 seats, their worst performance in 30 years. In the opinion polls Cameron had established a large personal lead over Miliband, while Clegg's support had crumbled. In one year he had dropped from being the most to the least popular of all the main political figures. This proved to be the high-water mark of Cameron's popularity in his first term. Soon after, things began to go wrong for him on a number of fronts. These included relations with his Liberal Democrat allies, who were seriously put out – not only by the 2-1 margin by which they lost the AV referendum (which took place on the same day as the local elections), but by the way the Tories had conducted themselves during the campaign. Cameron reneged on his promise not to get personally involved, and the Liberals were appalled by the fact that the official literature of the 'no' campaign, paid for by Tory donors, contained a large photograph of Nick Clegg and accused him of breaking his election promises. This did not shatter the coalition, but thereafter there was a steady worsening of relations between the two partners, and none of the complicity which had marked the early days. Within the Conservative Party, and particularly in the Tory press, which had never liked the coalition, there was growing hostility towards the LibDems. This was especially evident among backbench MPs, fuelled by the frustration of a large number who thought, not necessarily correctly, that they would themselves have become ministers had a coalition not been formed. They blamed the LibDems for the government's failure to carry out 'real' Tory policies. Their constant pressure had its effect on Cameron, who was pushed notably to the right, both in the appointments he made in a number of small government reshuffles and in his policy choices, which undermined to some extent his earlier efforts to 'detoxify' his party. A later contretemps with the LibDems came in 2012, when Cameron announced the dropping of a Bill to reform the membership of the House of Lords, following a rebellion by right-wing MPs. Clegg took the opportunity to withdraw support for another Bill redistributing seats and reducing the size of the House of Commons. The LibDems had foolishly committed themselves to this Bill, only to discover later that it would have a devastating effect on their own representation. The Tories had expected to make a net gain of at least 20 seats from the same measure and saw its now inevitable defeat as a heavy setback to their objective of obtaining a majority in the 2015 poll.

Perhaps the most damaging development for Cameron was the introduction, in January 2011, of the Health and Social Care Bill by Andrew Lansley. This provided for a comprehensive structural reorganisation of the NHS, with greatly increased opportunities for private sector interests to be involved. It had not been foreshadowed in the Conservative election manifesto nor in the coalition agreement, and it ran into a storm of criticism, with all the leading medical associations in violent opposition. The passage of the Bill had undone all his previous efforts to present the Conservatives as friends of the NHS, and Labour's traditionally large lead on health issues had been fully restored.

Almost as damaging was the long-running 'phone-hacking' saga, which principally involved the Murdoch press. Cameron had already been heavily criticised for hiring the former editor of the *News of the World*, Andy Coulson, as the government's Director of Communications. In 2007, Coulson had quit his newspaper job following an earlier phone-hacking scandal. He denied knowing anything about 'hacking' under his editorship, but successive exposés in *The Guardian* undermined his credibility, and he resigned his Downing Street post in January 2011, much to the embarrassment of Cameron. Coulson was subsequently charged with corruption, hacking, perverting the course of justice and perjury. Rebekah Brooks, the chief executive of News International, was also arrested on various charges, as were a large number of Murdoch journalists, and, much later, a couple from the Mirror group. Within a few months the scandal went nuclear with the revelation that the *News of the World* had hacked the phone of child murder victim Milly Dowler. This led to the abandonment of News Corporation's bid to take over BSkyB, just as the Culture Secretary Jeremy Hunt was on the brink of approving it. Cameron felt constrained to set up a public inquiry, led by Lord Justice Leveson, into the culture, practices and ethics of the British press. The inquiry examined no less than 337 witnesses, including Cameron and three preceding Prime Ministers. Highly embarrassing revelations emerged about the closeness of Cameron to Murdoch and his chief lieutenants, notably Brooks, whose home was in Cameron's constituency, and with whom he and Samantha socialised a great deal. Cameron promised in advance to accept whatever Leveson recommended "unless it is bonkers", but when the judge produced his voluminous report, in November 2012, he started to backtrack. Cameron accepted the proposal for a new authority, but baulked at the suggestion of statutory regulation, saying that it was a 'Rubicon' he would not cross. He was taken aback when not only Ed Miliband, but also Nick Clegg insisted that the Leveson recommendations should be accepted in full. Cameron dispatched his Cabinet Office Minister to negotiate a compromise with the other party leaders and with representatives of the hacking victims.

Like other Tory Prime Ministers before him, Cameron faced difficulties over Europe, largely of his own making. He kept his promise to withdraw British MEPs from the European People's Party, but faced much derision when he aligned them instead with a collection of extreme right-wing and oddball parties, some tainted by homophobia and anti-semitism. He then pushed through the European Union Bill, which required a referendum to be called before any additional powers whatsoever could be transferred to the EU. In December 2011, in what his biographers describe as "a bungled too-clever-by-half diplomatic manoeuvre" (Elliott and Hanning, 2012, p. 485), he vetoed a proposed new EU treaty designed to help Eurozone countries co-ordinate their response to the recession. Twenty-five of the then 27 member states promptly signed their own treaty and won the right to use EU institutions for implementing it, but leaving Britain without a voice in their deliberations. Finally, after much hesitation, Cameron made a long-delayed speech, in January 2013, saying that if the Conservatives won the 2015 election they would seek to renegotiate the terms of Britain's relationship with the EU, and then hold an 'in/out' referendum. All of these actions owed something to Cameron's own Eurosceptic views, but much more to his desire to placate the right wing of his own party, and to head off the growing electoral threat from the United Kingdom Independence Party (UKIP). They appeared to have precisely the opposite effect – the more UKIP was appeased, the greater the demands it made, and the more support it got from the voters. The biggest shock to the Tories came in the Eastleigh by-election, in February 2013, caused by the resignation and imprisonment of the former Liberal Democrat minister, Chris Huhne. The Tories had expected to capture the seat, but were devastated when the UKIP candidate came from nowhere and pushed them down into third place, narrowly failing to win the seat, which the LibDems retained with a reduced majority. However, all of these setbacks on Europe pale into insignificance when set beside his decision to hold an unnecessary referendum on Britain's EU membership in 2016, as we will see below.

Cameron took a largely successful gamble in March 2011 when, together with French President Nicolas Sarkozy, he led the way in seeking a UN mandate for a no-fly zone over Libya in the face of a threatened massacre of the inhabitants of rebel-held Benghazi. Other nations, including a reluctant US, joined in, but after the first few days, in which the American input was crucial, it was the British and French who led the operation and made the largest contributions to the allied efforts. These enabled the rebel forces to triumph, with the final overthrow and death of Colonel Gaddafi some seven months later. The exercise, which involved no British casualties, was widely acclaimed, and brought much credit to Cameron, whose role was compared highly favourably to that of Blair over Iraq. Later, when Libya descended into chaos, and effectively became a 'failed state', he himself was subjected to widespread criticism for his failure to provide effective aid to the democratically-elected Libyan government. When, in August 2013, President Obama projected air strikes against the Syrian government's use of chemical weapons against its insurgent population, Cameron proposed British participation, and was mortified when this failed to be approved by Parliament, when the Labour Party was joined by 30 Tory MPs and nine Liberal Democrats to vote it down. After that, Cameron appeared to take a conscious decision not to involve himself in international diplomatic initiatives. His absence was widely remarked, in February 2015, when

278 David Cameron

Angela Merkel and François Hollande encountered Presidents Putin and Poroshenko in Minsk, to agree a strengthened ceasefire agreement in eastern Ukraine. Two months later, in spite of persistent British attempts to persuade other NATO states to increase their spending on defence to at least 2 per cent of their GNP, Osborne declined to 'ring-fence' military expenditure in his long-term budgetary proposals, which meant that Britain would be unable to meet this target in two to three years' time.

Yet it was on his and Osborne's economic policy that Cameron's first term as Premier would largely be judged, and this did not go well, at least for the first three years. As predicted by their critics, the earlier expenditure cuts blocked off the incipient recovery, with large job losses in the public sector not being compensated by a more modest growth of private employment. There was little if any economic growth, with a double-dip recession being recorded in early 2012, and a triple-dip only narrowly averted a year later (these figures were later revised to show only one year in actual recession, with the economy thereafter 'flat-lining'). At the beginning of 2012 Britain registered the largest trade deficit since 1955, and the highest unemployment – at 8.4 per cent – for 17 years. Osborne conceded that there was now no prospect of paying off the debts by 2015, and revised his target to 2017–18. Leaders of the world's main economic bodies, the IMF, the World Bank, the World Trade Organization and the Organisation for Economic Co-operation and Development (OECD), who had originally welcomed the government's strategy, now called for a halt to austerity and for economic policies which would foster growth. There were widespread calls for a 'Plan B', but ministers ploughed stubbornly on, repeating Thatcher's mantra of the mid-1980s, "There is No Alternative". Then, in March 2012, Osborne committed a major political error, with what became known in the press as "the omnishambles budget". As well as a series of petty taxes which raised little money, but caused great upset respectively to charity donors, grandmothers, hot pastry eaters and caravan owners, the budget reduced the marginal tax rate for incomes over £150,000 from 50 to 45 per cent. This was immediately seized on by the Labour Party, which claimed that Osborne was effectively sending a cheque averaging £100,000 to each of 13,000 millionaires, at the same time that he was cracking down on the poorest elements of society. It appeared to make nonsense of Osborne's claim of "all being in it together". The public seem to have agreed: in the local elections two months later, the Tories lost 328 council seats in England alone, and the already seriously depleted LibDems another 190. In Parliament, Cameron had by now lost his easy mastery over Miliband, whose performances had greatly improved, and who frequently put the Prime Minister in difficulties. By the beginning of 2013 the position looked even worse, with Britain losing its AAA rating with Moody's credit agency, which Osborne had repeatedly claimed as the justification of his austerity policy.

Osborne's strategy was now widely condemned as a comprehensive failure, and the polls showed that even most Tory voters expected their party to lose the next general election. Moreover, the prospects of the Liberal Democrats agreeing to continue the coalition in the event of another 'hung' Parliament seemed increasingly bleak, and the UKIP threat of stealing Tory votes appeared greater than ever. Yet all was not lost: Cameron still had a healthy lead over Miliband in his personal ratings, many voters still blamed Labour rather than the Tories for Britain's economic difficulties, and the Labour poll lead, at 10–12 per cent, was not any greater than the 'normal' opposition lead in mid-Parliament. Moreover, renewed cuts in welfare benefits, which came into force in April 2013, seemed to go down well with many voters, who responded to Osborne's scarcely disguised attempt to paint the beneficiaries as work-shy layabouts. During 2013 there was a gradual improvement in the economic situation with unemployment steadily falling and a large number of new jobs being created, though many of these were low-paid or on zero-hours contracts. The improvement continued through 2014, and by the end of that year, with sharply falling oil and gas prices and inflation coming down to nearly zero, the average level of incomes finally reached, and began to exceed, the 2010 level. The Labour criticism of the coalition shifted from denial that there had been any recovery to asserting that the benefits had accrued only to a wealthy minority and that the living standards of the many had shown no improvement. This criticism had much resonance, and the Tories expressed dismay at what appeared to be "a voteless recovery". Their poll rating remained stuck at around 30 per cent, though the Labour lead over them declined to around 5 per cent in early 2014, the extra votes going not to them but to UKIP and, to a lesser extent, the Greens. UKIP's support soared, enabling them to win the largest number of seats in the European Parliament election in June 2014, pushing the Tories into third place behind Labour, while the Liberal Democrats were reduced to a single seat.

In September, the long awaited referendum on Scottish independence took place. The opinion polls had fairly consistently predicted an easy victory for the "no" side, with a likely margin of 60–40 per cent. But as the campaign moved to its closing stages, the gap dramatically narrowed, and a week before voting, a YouGov poll put the "yes" side two points ahead. General panic broke out, but was calmed by a timely intervention by former Labour Prime Minister Gordon Brown, who retained his standing and popularity in Scotland, despite having lost it in other parts of the UK. He persuaded the three main parties to agree a promise of 'maximum devolution' to Scotland if it voted to remain in the Union. This did the trick, and on 15 September the Scots voted "no", by 55.3 per cent to 44.7 per cent. Ominously for Labour, four of its strongholds, Dundee, Glasgow, North Lanarkshire and West Dunbartonshire, voted for independence. Cameron issued a statement welcoming the result, and pledging to redeem the pledge of 'devomax', but said at the same time that legislation would be introduced to prevent Scottish MPs voting on English issues. The Scottish National Party (SNP) expressed shock that Scottish MPs were to be treated as 'second class' members, and protested loudly. Disheartened by their referendum defeat, this new grievance acted as a shot in the arm, and they began campaigning again with great vigour, recruiting a large number of new members. Within a few weeks, an independent committee, under the chairmanship of Lord Smith of Kelvin, a crossbench peer, produced a report listing a series of new powers, including proposals on taxation, which should be transferred to the Scottish Parliament. The report was generally welcomed, except by the new Scottish First Minister, Nicola Sturgeon, who said she was disappointed, and wanted further talks with the British government.

Later in the year, two sitting Tory MPs, Douglas Carswell and Mark Reckless, defected to UKIP, and retained their seats in subsequent by-elections, despite Herculean efforts by the Tories to defeat them. This led to near panic among the Tories as the general election approached less than six months away. Their election strategy had long been agreed, and was openly based on that of the 1992 election, in which Cameron had been intimately involved (see page 266 above). That had two elements – depicting Labour as the party of soaring taxation, and its leader, Neil Kinnock, as not being up to the job of Prime Minister. This time Labour was stigmatised for "creating the mess" in 2010, which the Tories claimed to have successfully cleared up by their "long-term economic plan", while Miliband was vilified not only for his alleged incapacity but also for his supposedly extreme views, being dubbed as 'Red Ed' by most of the Tory-supporting press. The Tories had much earlier appointed the

Australian election organiser, Lynton Crosby, to direct their election campaign, which he did with ruthless efficiency, insisting that all his candidates, even senior Cabinet ministers, follow his instructions to the letter. Armed with a treasure chest, mostly subscribed by hedge funds and other business donors, at least three times as large as Labour's, and with the support of at least 85 per cent of the press, measured in terms of their circulations, the Tories had two principal fears. One was that the UKIP surge would continue, principally at their expense, and enable Labour to scrape an election victory with 35 per cent, or so, of the total vote. The other was a fear that Miliband would come off best in election debates with Cameron, and this would enable him to overcome his negative image. When the broadcasting authorities came up with plans to largely repeat the formula used in 2010, when Clegg had outshone his rivals, the Tories refused to participate, and the broadcasters eventually agreed to a 'compromise' arrangement for a couple of multi-party encounters, excluding a one-on-one debate between Cameron and Miliband. This exposed Cameron to accusations of cowardice, but he evidently calculated that this would be a lesser risk than that of being outshone by the Labour leader. Miliband in fact had an excellent campaign, and his poll ratings shot up, though still remaining worse than Cameron's. He made only one serious mistake, but that was an egregious one. A week before polling day, in a widely watched BBC *Question Time* programme, he, Clegg and Cameron were separately quizzed by a studio audience made up of equal numbers of party supporters and undecided voters. Asked if he now regretted Labour's over-spend before the 2010 election, and whether he would now apologise for it, he defiantly answered "no", and went on to boast of the benefits which this spending had produced. An audible murmur of disbelief then spread across almost all the audience, and at that moment – if not long before – Labour's defeat was assured.

The campaign had been dominated by the opinion polls, conducted by no fewer than 11 organisations. There were marginal differences in their findings, but they all told essentially the same story. This was that the Labour lead had almost evaporated by Christmas, and thereafter a virtual dead heat between Labour and the Conservatives was indicated, right up until polling day. The Scottish polls indicated that the SNP would make enormous gains, perhaps even wiping out Labour, which was defending 41 of the country's 59 seats. In compensation, it looked as though Labour would win perhaps 40–55 seats in England and Wales. Almost every single poll, and the great majority of political commentators, concluded that another 'hung Parliament' would result, quite likely with the SNP holding the balance of power. Few doubted that they would decide to prop up a Labour government, even if the Tories finished up with the largest number of seats. Panic now gripped the Conservatives, who had been assured all along by Lynton Crosby that there would by then have been a large swing back of votes to them from Labour. They therefore suddenly produced a flurry of promises of tax cuts and spending proposals, all of them unfunded, which threatened to undermine their reputation for fiscal responsibility. They even, through the mouth of Defence Minister Michael Fallon, launched a vicious personal attack on Ed Miliband, saying he had stabbed his own brother in the back, and would be willing "to stab his country in the back" by scrapping the Trident missile system in order to secure the backing of the SNP. This was seen to be hitting below the belt and backfired on the Tories. But their message during the final days of the campaign, that a minority Labour government propped up by the SNP would lead to their being "blackmailed" or "held to ransom", was widely disseminated, notably by former Prime Minister Sir John Major. It may well have had a significant effect on still undecided voters.

On polling day, 7 May 2015, the reputation of the polls was rudely punctured by an exit poll, commissioned by the BBC and other broadcasting organisations, and released promptly at 10 p.m., as the polling booths closed. It showed the Tories very far ahead of Labour, the Liberal Democrats almost eliminated, the Scottish Nationalists taking every seat bar one, and UKIP with few if any seats. Widely suspected to be an aberrant poll, as the night wore on it was seen to have been extremely accurate, except that it under-estimated the Conservative performance, which was good enough for them to have won an overall majority of 12 seats. The final result, in terms of seats, was as follows:

Conservative	331
Labour	232
SNP	56
Liberal Democrats	8
UKIP	1
Greens	1
Others	21
Total	650
Con. majority	12

The Conservatives had won a famous victory, proclaimed by Cameron the following day as "the sweetest victory of all", made all the sweeter by the fact that his three rival party leaders – Miliband, Clegg and Farage – all stood down on the morrow of the poll, though Farage later withdrew his resignation. In reality, the Tories had not won the election, Labour had lost it, and the real victor had been the SNP, and its dynamic new leader, Nicola Sturgeon. She had destroyed the Labour Party in Scotland, and fatally undermined its position in England, where it had confidently expected to win a large number of Tory and LibDem marginal seats, but fell short in many of them, probably due to fears of a minority Labour government depending on SNP support to keep them in power.

Cameron lost no time in appointing a new government, the first Conservative-only Cabinet since 1997. He did not change any of the occupants of the great offices of state – Chancellor, Foreign Secretary, Home Secretary and Defence Secretary – but set about replacing the former Liberal Democrat Cabinet ministers with Conservatives such as Sajid Javid, Amber Rudd, Greg Hands and David Mundell. But in spite of the fact that he had secured a parliamentary majority which many thought was beyond his reach, Cameron's second government proved to be more precarious than the first.

For one, once he had got rid of the Liberal Democrats, the government's majority of 12 seats was distinctly less comfortable than the 76 enjoyed by the coalition. But the biggest challenge for the Prime Minister came from his own promises on Europe. In 2013 he had promised to hold an in/out referendum on Europe, but even many of his own Eurosceptic backbenchers did not expect him ever to deliver on it, as they doubted he would win an outright majority. The LibDems would surely block such a vote as the price for supporting a new government. But now that the Liberal Democrats were excluded from the government, Cameron found himself hoisted on his own petard. After having promised in his bid for the leadership to stop 'banging on about Europe', he opened the door for the issue to dominate politics like never before.

Cameron's plan was to follow the lead of Harold Wilson who in 1975 had renegotiated the terms of membership of the European Community before securing a two-thirds majority for continued membership in a referendum. Rather than defending the old, unpopular European status quo, he would sell a new and improved version to the British public. In his Bloomberg speech of 2013 he mentioned various aspects that should be at the heart of a new settlement such as economic reforms, the idea of reversing the progress towards European integration, and protecting the rights of non-Eurozone members. But the issue against which his renegotiation would ultimately be judged was not even mentioned: immigration. The right of European citizens to live and work in other countries had led large numbers of Eastern Europeans to move to the UK, filling many of the skills shortages which had long blighted Britain's companies, farms and welfare state. Although they made a net contribution to the economy the government made no attempt to plan their integration or to give extra resources to local authorities to create extra school places or fund more GPs in the places where they settled. The rise of net migration to the UK – from 177,000 in 2012 to 209,000 in 2013 and 318,000 in 2014 – was helping UKIP surge in the polls. And so, as David Cameron began his process of renegotiation with the EU, he pledged to work to tackle the question of immigration. In the event the renegotiation process was a damp squib, and Cameron abandoned hopes of securing an 'emergency brake' on immigration, settling instead for a scheme to stop paying benefits to EU nationals. Other EU member states ended up making greater concessions than many had expected but when the referendum was called, it became clear that the renegotiations would not take the Remain campaign over the line. Cameron would have to make his case based on the benefits of the EU as a whole rather than his new settlement.

One of the first casualties of the campaign was the unity of the 'Notting Hill set'. Both George Osborne and Michael Gove had opposed the idea of holding a referendum when Cameron had first suggested it in 2012, but once it was called they found themselves on different sides. David Cameron was shocked and disappointed by Gove's 'betrayal' in supporting the 'Leave campaign', while his successful campaign to persuade Boris Johnson to join him provided 'Vote Leave' with a formidable front-man.

Throughout the campaign, and even after the count, the opinion polls suggested that the Remain side would win. An exit poll on the night of 23 June declared that Remain had won by a margin of 52 to 48 per cent. But when the votes were counted, the result would be exactly the other way around. The vote divided the country between old and young; graduates against manual workers; cities against towns; Scotland, Northern Ireland and London and the university towns against non-metropolitan England and Wales. The 'Leave' victory now has a feeling of inevitability about it, but if just 600,000 voters had behaved differently, Cameron's bet would have paid off. What went wrong?

The truth is that it was a mix of bad luck, bad judgement and bad faith. In the first category, you could include the state of the Labour Party and the refugee crisis. When David Cameron first called for an in/out referendum in 2013 he assumed that the Labour Party would be led by a committed Remainer who would put the full weight of their party's machine behind staying in the EU. Nobody could have predicted that Jeremy Corbyn, one of a tiny handful of Labour Eurosceptics, would lead the party, and his failure to mobilise his supporters meant that the Remain campaign's leading lights were Conservatives. Another piece of bad luck was the way that the refugee crisis erupted in 2015 in the wake of the Syrian conflict, thrusting questions of migration centre-stage and leading to a sense that the EU was in crisis. What is more, the referendum was called at precisely the moment when global politics was moving from a division between left and right to one between insiders and outsiders, with anti-establishment forces capturing the agenda across Europe and America.

This bad luck was compounded by Cameron's (and Osborne's) bad judgement. The 'Stronger In' campaign did not have a compelling slogan, a clear set of arguments or an emotional appeal to the voters. By contrast, the Leave campaign had a powerful slogan ('Vote Leave, Take Back Control') and a clear set of arguments around the cost of EU membership, the need to control immigration and the need to repatriate sovereignty. What is more, while the Leave campaign took no prisoners, Cameron refused to attack Johnson and Gove because he thought that 'blue on blue' attacks would damage the Conservative Party's longer-term electability.

Vote Leave suffered from no such qualms. "We were up against a campaign", said Cameron's chief of communications, Craig Oliver, "that was prepared to mislead on an industrial scale". The most powerful symbol of this was the false claim on the side of the Vote Leave bus that "we send the EU £350 million a week" (when the reality is that the UK's net contribution was more like £136 million). Other false claims included the idea that Turkey would join the EU and send millions of people to the UK and the idea that Britain could stay in the single market without following EU rules.

Right until midnight on 23 June, Cameron thought that he would win the referendum. He even went so far as to write a victory speech. "We are on a long walk to a Greater Britain", he wrote, "thanks to the British people, we have taken what I believe is an important step forwards". In the event he was not able to deliver this victory speech but instead made another one conceding defeat and announcing his resignation as Prime Minister. Within three weeks he would be replaced by Theresa May and it was already clear that Cameron's legacy would likely be a smaller rather than a 'Greater Britain', with Brexit raising questions about secession not just in Scotland but in Northern Ireland too.

When a box of chocolates is handed round, the most popular choice is often the one with the smoothest surface, but the hardest centre. So it often is with politicians. The trouble with Cameron was that, though he was the smoothest by far, his innards were as soft as marshmallow. Just why can be deduced from his memoirs, in which he talks frankly of his privileged upbringing by upper middle-class parents in the idyllic Berkshire village of Peasemore.

Cameron was keen to use office as an attempt to detoxify the Conservative Party. To an extent, he succeeded in this, broadening the base of the party by increasing the number of women, state-educated and BAME candidates, and introducing a number of reforms, such as same-sex marriages. But his administration was marked mostly by two factors – austerity and his progressive surrender to the demands of UKIP, whom he had initially characterised as "fruitcakes, loonies and closet racists". He finished up by agreeing to an in/out referendum on the EU, for which there had been previously very little public demand. His failure to stand up to them was the ultimate cause of his downfall, and of the sad fate which awaits our country.

Works consulted

Tim Bale, 2015, *Five Year Mission: The Labour Party under Ed Miliband*, Oxford, Oxford University Press.
Vernon Bogdanor, 2011, *The Coalition and the Constitution*, Oxford, Hart Publishing.
David Cameron, 2020, *For the Record,* London, William Collins.
David Cameron and Dylan Jones, 2008, *Cameron on Cameron: Conversations with Dylan Jones*, London, Fourth Estate.
Matthew d'Ancona, 2013, *In It Together: The Inside Story of the Coalition Government*, London, Viking.
Francis Elliott and James Hanning, 2102, *Cameron: Practically a Conservative*, London, Fourth Estate.
Philip Gould, 1998, *The Unfinished Revolution*, London, Little Brown.

Mehdi Hasan and James Macintyre, 2011, *Ed: The Milibands and the Making of a Labour Leader*, London, Biteback Publishing.

Dennis Kavanagh, 2012, *Philip Gould: An Unfinished Life*, London, Palgrave Macmillan.

Dennis Kavanagh and Philip Cowley, 2010, *The British General Election of 2010*, London, Palgrave Macmillan.

Simon Lee and Matt Beech, 2011, *The Cameron-Clegg Government: Coalition Government in an Age of Austerity*, London, Palgrave Macmillan.

Tim Shipman, 2016, *All Out War*, London, William Collins.

Ryan Shorthouse and Guy Stagg (eds), 2013, *Tory Modernisation 2.0: The Future of the Conservative Party*, London, Bright Blue Publishing.

22

THERESA MAY

"A bloody difficult woman"?

With the possible exception of Edward Heath (see Chapter 15), Theresa May came from a more humble background than any other Tory Prime Minister. Both of her grandmothers were in domestic service, one of her grandfathers was a sergeant-major and the other a porter. Her father, Hubert Brasier, assisted his climb out of the working class by winning a place at a grammar school, and subsequently at Leeds University, where he gained First Class Honours in Theology before studying to become a priest at the College of the Resurrection, at Mirfield, West Yorkshire. He then became a chaplain at a hospital in Eastbourne before becoming vicar of two successive churches in prosperous parishes in south Oxfordshire. The young Theresa grew up as a classic Home Counties Tory, with party membership vying with the church and the local cricket club as the focal points of her life. It was a world away from the aristocratic or upper middle-class ambience in which David Cameron, George Osborne and others of her contemporaries grew up, and this may well have contributed to the chip which some critics have discerned on her shoulder.

Theresa Mary Brasier was born, in Eastbourne, on 1 October 1956. Her father, a highly committed Anglo-Catholic, was a hard-working parson, who eschewed party politics as he had a burning desire to preach the Gospel to all of his parishioners, irrespective of their political views. Relatively little is known of Theresa's mother, the former Zaidee Barnes, though as she was named after the wife of Abraham, it may be assumed that she was brought up by deeply religious parents. She happily accepted all the duties expected of a vicar's wife, but was also an active member of the Conservative Party. She was a talented amateur musician, and, according to her daughter, who talked about her in a *Desert Island Discs* interview in 2014, an excellent cook. Theresa's education began at a state primary school in the Oxfordshire village of Heythrop, but at the age of 11 she transferred to a fee-paying Roman Catholic school, St Juliana's Convent School for Girls. After two years, she was moved back into the state system, winning a place at the local Holton Park Girls' Grammar School, which – during her time at the school – was transformed into Wheatley Park Comprehensive School, a change she regretted, though as she was already in the sixth form it probably made little difference to her education. By her own account, "I was probably Goody Two Shoes at school" (Jackson, 2018, p. 478). In an interview with *The Sun*, in 2016, one of her cousins recalled that "Theresa was a

DOI: 10.4324/9781003031963-23

very pleasant and polite girl. As the daughter of the village's vicar, she had a lot to live up to" (Prince, 2017, p. 18). It is clear that the Rev. Brasier had immense influence on his daughter, and she seems to have inherited many of his characteristics – serious-minded, hard-working, diligent and respectful of authority, with, perhaps, a somewhat limited imagination. From her mother, she imbibed her political views, but it was from her father that, while still in her early teens, she asked permission to join the Conservative Party (Prince, 2017, p. 22). He agreed, but asked her to be discreet. Already, aged 12, she had announced her ambition to become a Tory MP, and several years later she was reported by fellow students to have expressed disappointment that Margaret Thatcher had become the first woman Prime Minister, an honour to which she had herself aspired.

In February 1974, aged 17, she was the Tory candidate in a mock election at her school to coincide with the general election. She was routed by the Liberal candidate, with Labour coming a poor third. Her victor, the school's head girl, Rosalind Burton (later Hicks-Greene), recalled many years later the speech which Theresa made on this occasion:

> I can recall thinking to myself that it was a very typical, safe Conservative speech, very much grounded in safe Conservative policies as they were at the time … I'm afraid she was very quiet, very studious, she was not a charismatic person, but you felt that you could absolutely believe what she was saying and you could trust her.
>
> *(Prince, 2017, p. 29)*

From her father, Theresa had acquired a great love of cricket, and they spent many hours together in the vicarage following Test matches on television or radio. One player, in particular, whom she came to idolise, was Geoffrey Boycott, a surprising choice for many, as he was one of the most boring players in the game, grinding out runs at an abysmally slow rate with the apparent object of maintaining a high batting average, come what may. May remained a great admirer of Boycott, and insisted on awarding him a knighthood in her resignation honours list in September 2019, despite his earlier conviction for domestic violence in a French court. Some time before, she told an interviewer that she had been "a Geoffrey Boycott fan all her life. It was just that he kind of solidly got on with what he was doing" (Prince, 2017, p. 24). By her teens, she had already acquired a taste for fashionable – and sometimes expensive – clothes with which to adorn her tall but somewhat gangly figure. As an 'only child', she kept very much to herself, but was respected by most of her classmates as a studious, hard-working if somewhat prim fellow pupil. Her academic results at the school were excellent. She obtained 11 O levels, and four A levels, one at scholarship grade. Nobody was surprised that she won a place at Oxford, going up to St Hugh's, one of the four women's colleges at that time, to study geography – perhaps a surprising choice, as it had little relevance to her already firm career plans, but it was a subject in which both her secondary schools had specialised. She was not yet 18 years old.

At Oxford, her chief interest was the University Conservative Association, and it was at one of their discos that she met her future husband, Philip May, 11 months her junior and two years behind her at the university. The introduction was made by one of the Association's most glamorous members, Benazir Bhutto, whose father was President of Pakistan at the time. The son of a shoe salesman from near Liverpool, Philip was a quiet, charming, rather shy man, with a dry, northern sense of humour, whose main interests, including politics and cricket, coincided almost exactly with those of Theresa. It was not long before they became an 'item', but nearly three years before they announced their engagement. Theresa also made friends at Oxford with several fellow students who later became Tory MPs and ministers, notably Damian Green and Alan Duncan. She graduated in 1977 with a Second Class degree, and joined the Bank of England as a graduate trainee. Philip, who studied history, graduated two years later, and followed Theresa into 'the City', joining the stockbroking firm of Zoete and Bevan, which later merged with Barclay's Investment Bank. Finally, in September 1981, the couple tied the knot, and were married at St Mary's church, in Wheatley, by Theresa's father, the Rev. Hubert Brasier.

Within a year, Theresa's father was dead, killed in a motor accident on his way to conducting an evensong service in another local church. Soon afterwards, her mother, who suffered from multiple sclerosis, also died, leaving Theresa with no close family. She had no siblings, and it later transpired that the couple were unable to bear any children, a matter of great sensitivity to them. Theresa was thus unusually dependent on her husband, whom she has repeatedly described as her "rock". The couple bought a modest house in Wimbledon, but later moved to more extensive premises in the poshest part of the town. They immediately joined the local Conservative Association, and greatly impressed their fellow members by the enthusiasm with which they participated in all its activities. This was particularly so during the annual local elections, when they addressed thousands of envelopes and spent many long hours canvassing. It was not long before Philip was elected president of the constituency association and Theresa won a seat in the Durnsford ward of Merton. The council was finely balanced with a small Labour majority, and she quickly emerged as one of the most active and partisan of the Tory councillors. She soon became deputy leader of the Tory group, and when it gained control of the council in the 1988 elections she was chosen as chairwoman of the prestigious education committee. At Oxford, where he became President of the Union Society, and initially in Wimbledon, Philip had appeared the more likely of the pair to make his name in national politics, but he seemed content to play second fiddle to his wife, and to concentrate on his increasingly prosperous career in banking. Theresa too was no slouch in the City, distinguishing herself as a researcher at the Bank of England, and, in 1994, switching to a senior post at the Association for Payment Clearing Services (APACS), where she remained until 1997.

In 1989, Theresa, aged 32, made her first attempt to be selected as a parliamentary candidate, in the London constituency of Holborn and St Pancras, a safe Labour seat. It was a near miss: she lost by a single vote. According to her first biographer, Rosa Prince, she wore a short leather skirt at the selection conference. The men "loved it", she wrote, "It was too much for women, however, and they voted against her" (Prince, 2017, p. 66). This was the beginning of a long and arduous search to find a safe parliamentary berth, which was crowned with success only eight years later. After several more failures, she was desperate to find a seat – *any* seat – which she could contest at the next general election. She hit upon North West Durham, a safe Labour seat centred on the steel town of Consett. It was 270 miles from her home in Wimbledon, but she nursed the seat assiduously for over two years, even going so far as to buy a house in one of its more genteel villages. Yet, in the 1992 general election, she lost to Labour by almost 14,000 votes. In third place came Tim Farron, the future leader of the Liberal Democrats, who was then the 22-year-old president of the students' union at Newcastle University.

Two years later, she suffered an even heavier defeat, when she stood in a by-election in yet another safe Labour seat, Barking, in east London, where she came a very poor third. There then began a long and dispiriting trek through a series of selection conferences in safe

288 Theresa May

Conservative seats, in every one of which she lost out to a male contender. As the 1997 general election loomed, with the prospect of a sweeping victory for Labour under Tony Blair, only one decent prospect remained. This was Maidenhead, a new constituency carved out by the boundary commissioners in the redistribution of 1993. There was every indication that this would be a 'dead cert' for the Tories, and the competition for the seat was intense, including several sitting MPs looking to contest a safer seat. The contenders also included the future Chancellor of the Exchequer, Philip Hammond, and a young employee of the Conservative Research Department by the name of David Cameron.

May's best hope was that Conservative Central Office might use whatever influence it had on her behalf. Largely through the widespread use of all-women shortlists, a very large number of women had been adopted as Labour candidates, and the Tory leadership was nervous that its own small contingent of women MPs would be swamped. It was desperate that at least one new Tory woman Member would emerge from the general election. Whether or not she received help from 'on high', Theresa swept through the opposition and emerged as a surprise winner. It was later suggested that the local party had been unimpressed by her more glamorous rivals, and had been looking for a committed party activist with a strong record in local government. That was what they got.

On 1 May 1977, now aged 40, Theresa May finally made it to the House of Commons. The result in Maidenhead was:

May, Mrs T.M. (Con)	25,344
Ketteringham, A.T. (Lib Dem)	13,363
Robson, Ms D. (Lab)	9,205
4 others	3,033
Majority	11,981

It was goodbye to Wimbledon for Theresa and Philip. They immediately sold their house, and moved to a highly desirable residence in the idyllic village of Sonning, just outside Maidenhead, and within the boundaries of Theresa's new constituency. As expected, the overall result of the election was a sweeping victory for Labour, which won 418 seats, against 165 for the Tories, 46 for the LibDems and six for the SNP. Labour finished up with the then record number of 101 women MPs, against 13 for the Tories, three for the LibDems, two for the SNP, and the Speaker, Betty Boothroyd.

May was the only Tory newly elected woman Member, and she stood out as one of the most competent and confident of the women on the Tory benches. The new leader, William Hague, soon brought her on to his front bench, initially as a junior spokesperson on Education. Within two years she was a full member of the Shadow Cabinet where she remained for 11 years until 2010, when the Tories entered government, in coalition with the LibDems. But she was constantly shuffled around between different portfolios, in each of which she performed adequately without becoming any sort of parliamentary star. In 2002, Iain Duncan Smith, who had unexpectedly succeeded Hague as leader, following the disastrous result of the 2001 general election, gave her a leg-up by appointing her as Chairwoman of the Conservative Party, the first woman to hold that post. May was delighted by the opportunity to get around the country meeting with party activists in every different type of constituency. Yet she was appalled at the state of the organisation and by the attitudes of many party officials. She was determined to help modernise the party and make it more acceptable to the mass of voters.

She decided that shock treatment was necessary, and that she would apply it during her speech to the annual Tory conference in September 2002. "You know what people call us?" she asked, "the nasty party". She went on:

> In recent years a number of politicians have behaved disgracefully and then compounded their offences by trying to evade responsibility. We all know who they are. Let's face it, some of them have stood on this platform ... they have tried to make political capital out of demonising minorities ... and indulged themselves in petty feuding or sniping instead of getting behind a leader who is doing an enormous amount to change a party which has suffered two landslide defeats ... At the last general election 38 new Tory MPs were elected. Of that total only one was a woman and none was from an ethnic minority. Is that fair? Is one half of the population entitled to only one place out of 38?

Before this speech May was a virtually unknown politician. Now she dominated the headlines of virtually every newspaper and TV and radio news bulletin. This, and the high-heeled leopard-skin shoes which she wore for the occasion, imposed her firmly on the public consciousness. The speech was deeply embarrassing for the Tory activists, and many of them reacted violently to it, though the more thoughtful of them concluded that there was more than a germ of truth in what she said. On balance, the 'nasty party' speech damaged her short-term prospects within the party, but in the longer term it enhanced her reputation.

One person who was most offended by the 'nasty party' speech was Michael Howard, a right-wing figure, who was Shadow Chancellor of the Exchequer at the time. He was unanimously chosen as Tory leader in October 2003, when Duncan Smith lost a confidence vote of Tory MPs. Howard was chosen not so much because of his views, but for his skills as a parliamentary debater. He was virtually the only Tory MP who regularly got the better of Tony Blair and his ministers in Commons debates. One of his first actions was to dismiss May from the party chairmanship, though she remained in the Shadow Cabinet. This was a bitter disappointment for May, and an undoubted setback, though the episode had greatly increased her public recognition, and she was now seen as a leading figure in the party. Under Howard's leadership, the Tories improved their position in the 2005 general election, but came nowhere near winning. Howard immediately resigned as leader, and no fewer than five candidates contested the succession (see Chapter 21). May would have liked to be one of them, but when she sounded out fellow MPs she found that she had virtually no support. She cast her vote for David Cameron, whom she saw as a fellow moderniser. For some time she had been using her influence to ensure that more women and minority ethnic candidates were chosen as parliamentary candidates, particularly in winnable seats. Early in 2005, together with Baroness Jenkin, the wife of Bernard Jenkin MP, she founded a pressure group, Women2Win, to encourage more women to come forward and to offer them mentoring and, in some cases, financial assistance. May was never in favour of all-women shortlists, but advocated the creation of a 'Gold List' of promising women and BAME (black and minority ethnic) candidates, which would be circulated by the party leadership to every constituency association. The idea was taken up by Cameron after his election, but was called the 'A List'. It had a considerable effect, and at the next election, in 2010, the number of Tory women MPs shot up from 17 to 49 while BAME Tory MPs went up from two to eight. May has often been compared by fellow Tories to Margaret Thatcher, usually to her disadvantage. As an advocate of sexual equality, however, she scores more highly. Thatcher did nothing to promote the interests of women, and when she formed her Cabinet in 1979, she was the only female member. By contrast, there were seven women in May's Cabinet in 2017.

When Cameron became Prime Minister in 2010, and formed a coalition government with the LibDems, he was anxious to have at least one woman in a major post, and chose May as his Home Secretary, the second woman ever to hold this post after Labour's Jacqui Smith, who served under Gordon Brown. This was a great surprise to many, including May, who had never shadowed Home Affairs, and whose career seemed to have peaked after her sacking as party chairwoman. This was a great opportunity for her, but many saw it as a poisoned chalice, given the propensity of Home Secretaries to stumble into one of the many 'elephant traps' associated with the portfolio. She made a shaky start, and subsequently had her ups and downs, but when her term of office ended, a near record six years and two months later, her balance was clearly on the credit side. She was now, in the eyes of many Tory MPs, a credible candidate for the prime ministership.

May was also appointed as Minister for Women and Equality, and throughout her term of office her attention was mostly focused on security, police issues, human rights and immigration. In her early months in the post, she was mainly concerned with modifying or reversing measures adopted by her Labour predecessors. These included scrapping plans to introduce compulsory identity cards, and the abolition of 'ASBOs' – Antisocial Behaviour Orders – introduced under Tony Blair as long ago as 1998. Her voting record on gender issues in opposition had been widely criticised as 'reactionary', but May delighted her critics by openly repudiating her earlier views. She announced that she was now in favour of gay adoption and strongly backed an initiative by her Liberal Democrat under-secretary, Lynne Featherstone, to legalise gay marriage. She pushed this through the Cabinet, and the Bill was passed by the Commons, on a free vote, in July 2013, by 400 votes to 175. A majority of Tory MPs voted against the Bill, but it received almost unanimous support from Labour and LibDem Members.

But if May shifted to a more 'liberal' position on sexual and social issues, she maintained her hard-line stance on immigration. She took seriously Cameron's pledge to reduce the net migration figure from several hundred thousand to "tens of thousands". There was, she believed, little she could do to stem the flow from EU member states, but she set out consciously to create a 'hostile environment' for incomers from other countries whom she felt had no legal right to remain. This led to official harassment of substantial numbers of long-term residents, including members of the 'Windrush generation', who were in the country quite legally, but who lacked the documentation to prove it. At least 83 persons were illegally deported and thousands more were detained, lost their jobs or were denied benefits or medical care to which they were entitled. It was only in 2017, when May had become Prime Minister, that a public scandal erupted, and May's successor as Home Secretary, Amber Rudd, was forced to resign. She was not blameless for the way in which the scandal was handled, but few doubted that the major ministerial responsibility lay with May.

In a number of individual cases, May's attempts to deport foreign residents were frustrated by courts of law, including the European Court of Human Rights. The most notable case involved Abu Qatada, a Muslim preacher of Jordanian nationality, who had repeatedly been arrested and imprisoned on terrorism charges but had never been brought to trial in the UK, though he had twice been tried in his absence in Jordan and found guilty. The Home Office had several times attempted to deport him to Jordan, but was thwarted first by the (British) Special Immigration Appeals Commission (SIAC), and then by the European Court of Human Rights, on the grounds that his convictions in Jordan may have been obtained by the torture of witnesses. A furious May flew to Jordan to seek assurances from the Jordanian authorities that in any retrial such evidence would not be admitted. Eventually, she succeeded in securing a new treaty between Britain and Jordan conceding this point, and Qatada was duly deported on 7 July 2013, 11 years after his first arrest. May, who had previously been mocked for her stubborn persistence in what appeared to be a lost cause, became something of a national heroine in the popular press. The fact that he was subsequently acquitted of all charges in two subsequent trials in Jordan, and finally released from prison in September 2014, was not much reported in the British press, and did little to reduce May's *réclame*.

Throughout her period as Home Secretary, May was highly critical of the police, and, in particular, of the Police Federation, the bobbies' 'trade union'. No sooner had she been appointed than she received an ultimatum from the Chief Secretary to the Treasury, David Laws, to agree a substantial cut in her department's budget, as part of the £6 billion retrenchment agreed by the newly formed coalition. She was the last Cabinet minister to agree a settlement, having demanded a face-to-face meeting with Laws at which she vigorously argued her corner. In the end, she very reluctantly gave way, and promptly unloaded the major part of the cuts imposed onto the police budget, leading to a 20,000 cut in police numbers over the following six years.

She followed this up by imposing sharp reductions in overtime payments to police officers, which brought her into prolonged conflict with the Police Federation, who gave her a very hard time when she addressed their annual conference in 2011. May was furious at her hostile reception, but was not at all intimidated. She pressed ahead with her policies, cut off any official funding of the Federation, and threatened to introduce legislation to restrict its powers if it did not adopt a list of 35 reforms on which she insisted. The Federation reluctantly gave way, and three years later she returned to their conference and gave a triumphalist speech to a chastened audience. One reform which she herself initiated was not seen as a resounding success. This was the election of police and crime commissioners for each of the policing areas in England and Wales, apart from the Metropolitan Police Force. When the first such elections were held in November 2012, there was a miserable turnout of between 10 and 20 per cent,

From the moment she entered the Home Office, May determined that this would be her fortress, and that she would brook no opposition. She resented the need to bring major decisions to Cabinet for approval, and was unforgiving towards any colleagues who ventured to question her judgements. Within her department she came to depend very heavily on two young 'Spads' (Special Advisers), whom she consulted on virtually every issue, Nick Timothy and Fiona Hill. These two soon acquired a reputation for throwing their weight around, and for bullying civil servants and junior ministers. Both of them held relatively liberal views on many social issues, but Timothy, in particular, was a hard-line advocate of Brexit. Their loyalty to May was absolute and they yearned for the time when she might become Tory leader, and Prime Minister, while recognising that she had many personal defects which might stand in the way to her promotion. They resolved to do everything in their power to alleviate these defects. May, for her own part, was extremely tight-lipped about her ambitions. But in September 2010, at a private dinner party, at the Skylon restaurant, near the Royal Festival Hall, attended only by Philip May and one other ministerial aide, Hill openly asked her "Would you like to be Prime Minster?" May replied with the one word, "Yes", but later made it clear to the pair that there must be no plotting or intrigue to undermine David

Cameron (Seldon, 2019, pp. 19–21). It must have seemed a very long shot to the two would-be conspirators. May was ten years older than Cameron, who gave no indication of being ready to stand aside, and was under no immediate threat within the party. Moreover, the Chancellor of the Exchequer, George Osborne, seemed to be building up an impregnable position from which to make a leadership bid if a vacancy was to occur. Then there was the seemingly improbable possibility that Boris Johnson, then lounging on the back benches, might make a successful bid.

Her biographer, Rosa Prince, commented that:

> In the six years she served as Home Secretary, May became embroiled in feuds with a staggering number of fellow ministers, MPs, officials, organisations and individuals who crossed her path. She would almost always emerge triumphant. [These included] her Conservative colleagues, Cameron, Osborne, Gove and Kenneth Clarke – who memorably described her as 'a bloody difficult woman' during the 2016 leadership campaign – as well as the Liberal Democrats, Nick Clegg, Vince Cable and Chris Huhne. She also clashed publicly with one of the three Liberal Democrat ministers assigned to her department, Norman Baker, and a Conservative, Baroness Neville-Jones. Brodie Clark, the head of the UK Border Force and the entire senior management of the Police Federation were also put to the sword.
>
> *(Prince, 2017, pp. 220–1)*

The highly distinguished Permanent Under-Secretary of the Home Office, Dame Helen Ghosh, apparently found May so difficult to work with that she resigned her post after less than two years, and departed to head the National Trust. May did not, however, always come out on top, and, to her great chagrin, lost both of her top advisers in the process. In a dispute with Michael Gove, in June 2014, about alleged mismanagement of Muslim faith schools in Birmingham, Cameron removed Gove from his post as Education Secretary, but insisted on the sacking of Fiona Hill for her ill-advised role in the dispute. Then, in November 2014, when Nick Timothy defied an order for Spads to help the Conservative candidate in a by-election in Rochester and Strood, where the Tory MP, Mark Reckless, had defected to UKIP, he was peremptorily removed from the list of potential Tory candidates for the safe seat of Aldridge-Brownhills. Timothy resigned soon after, and left to take up a post with the New Schools Network, a body advocating the launching of more 'free' schools.

Meanwhile, the coalition was becoming increasingly unpopular, largely because of the effects of its austerity policies and, in particular for the Liberal Democrats, their broken promises on student fees. The Labour Party had overtaken the Tories in the opinion polls as early as November 2010, and remained in front, with varying margins, for the next four years. There was a growing belief (and fear among Tory MPs) that Ed Miliband would become Prime Minister after the next general election, either leading a majority government or a minority one backed by the Scottish Nationalists. Sensing the likelihood of a Tory defeat, and the subsequent resignation of Cameron, Timothy and Hill judged that it was time for May to raise her profile and advertise her availability as a potential leader. In November 2014, she conducted what the *Daily Mail* called a '3-day blitz' during which she made three appearances – an interview on the BBC *Desert Island Discs* programme, a reception where she was presented with a 'Politician of the Year' award by the Political Studies Association, and a public speech in which she ranged well beyond the limits of her 'Shadow' responsibilities and laid out her vision of how Britain should go forward. Each of the three was interpreted as a bid for the party leadership, though May was diplomatic enough to say during her 'Desert Island' interview that: "David Cameron is a first class party leader and Prime Minister, and I hope he will continue to lead the party for a very long time." The sincerity of May's apparent disclaimer was immediately put in doubt by a profile in *The Spectator*, which quoted an anonymous 'friend' (presumed to be Nick Timothy) as saying:

> She doesn't rate Cameron any more. She did, but not any more. There was a time early on when she would want to please David, but slowly she has seen just how incompetent that operation is. She's given up on him.
>
> *(Prince, 2017, p. 306)*

Six months later, the surprise result of the 2015 general election put paid to May's hopes that there would be an early opportunity to contest the Tory leadership. The Scottish Nationalists, under their popular new leader, Nicola Sturgeon, all but wiped out the hitherto dominant position of the Labour Party in Scotland, while in England and Wales the fear of their dominating a weak minority Labour government greatly boosted the Tory vote. Additionally, the Liberal Democrats lost 49 of their 57 seats, predominantly to the Tories, who – against all expectations – finished up with an overall majority of 12 seats. It looked as though Cameron was guaranteed a further four or five years in power, though he had acknowledged during the campaign that he would not fight a further election, naming Osborne, May and Johnson as potential successors.

Apart from replacing the LibDem ministers, Cameron made few changes to his government, and, in particular, kept his three most senior colleagues in their previous departments, Osborne as Chancellor, Philip Hammond as Foreign Secretary and May as Home Secretary. There had been speculation that Osborne, after five gruelling years at the Treasury, might be switched to the Foreign Office, but he preferred to remain in place, confident that this was the best launching pad for the premiership when Cameron stood down. May might have feared being demoted following the sharp deterioration of her relations with the Prime Minister, but Cameron felt the necessity of having a woman in one of the senior posts, and there was no plausible alternative to May in sight. Cameron had not expected to win an overall majority, and probably believed he would have been able to junk his commitment to a referendum on EU membership, as the LibDems would have demanded this as their price for continuing the coalition. Now he had no option but to proceed, as the pledge had been given top billing in the Tory election manifesto.

His attempt to negotiate changes with the EU which would have enabled the government to recommend continued membership was only partially successful, in particular because he failed to circumscribe the freedom of movement for workers. He nevertheless felt that the undertakings that he in fact received were sufficient to secure majority backing from the British electorate. It was clear that the Cabinet was not united behind his view, and it was agreed that Cabinet collective responsibility should be suspended to permit individual members to campaign on either side. Six ministers decide to support 'Leave' and 24 'Remain'. May was among the most cross-pressured, but decided to back Remain, without great enthusiasm. She hedged her bets by demanding British withdrawal from the jurisdiction of the European Court of Human Rights, not actually an EU institution, though it was widely believed to be. Cynical observers believed she was doing this to advertise to Leave voters that she was *really* on their side. It may, however, have been a sign of her frustration that the Court had long obstructed her determined and ultimately successful attempt to deport Abu Qatada. Whatever her motivation, it outraged Cameron and his team. On 13 separate occasions during the referendum campaign, according to Cameron's press adviser, Craig Oliver, he asked May to take a higher profile during the campaign, and 13 times she declined, becoming known in the Remain camp as 'Submarine May' (Prince, 2017, p. 326). Her timidity did her no apparent harm.

David Cameron's resignation, announced on the doorstep of 10 Downing Street within hours of the unexpected referendum result, precipitated the leadership contest she had eagerly awaited. The previous favourite, George Osborne, immediately bowed out, his appeal having evaporated, following his maladroit budget of March 2016, and his aggressive conduct of the Remain campaign, including providing Treasury estimates of the cost of Brexit to the British economy which were so precise (down to the last pound) that they were just not believed. The bulk of Osborne's supporters now lined up behind May, who, in launching her campaign, attempted to make a virtue of how much she differed from her rivals. Speaking at a press conference in a London club, she said:

> I know some politicians seek high office because they're driven by ideological fervour. And I know others seek it for reasons of ambition or glory. But my reasons are much simpler … Public service has been a part of who I am for as long as I can remember. I know I'm not a showy politician. I don't tour the television studios. I don't gossip about people over lunch. I don't go drinking in Parliament's bars. I don't often wear my heart on my sleeve. I just get on with the job in front of me.
>
> *(Prince, 2017, p. 339)*

Two other contenders entered the lists – Pensions Secretary Stephen Crabb, and former Defence Secretary Liam Fox – but it looked inevitable that the final choice would lie between her and Boris Johnson, widely seen as the favourite. It did not work out that way (see Chapter 23) The last-minute decision by Michael Gove, Johnson's leading supporter, to abandon him and put forward his own candidature, threw the contest wide open. Johnson immediately withdrew, and Gove's apparent 'treachery' led to the transfer of the bulk of his support to the previously unfancied middle-range minister, Andrea Leadsom, who qualified to contest the leadership with May in a postal ballot of party members.

Tory leadership election, July 2016, MPs' ballots

First round		Second round	
Theresa May	165	Theresa May	199
Andrea Leadsom	66	Andrea Leadsom	84
M. Gove	48	M. Gove	46
S. Crabb	34		
L. Fox	16		

May and Leadsom were expected to embark upon a strenuous programme of nationwide debates before the choice was made in September 2016. Leadsom then blew her chances in an interview with *The Times*, in which she insensitively suggested that as a mother she was better qualified to be Prime Minister than the childless Theresa May. This caused so much revulsion that she felt compelled to withdraw from the contest, and May was duly proclaimed as the winner, and 'kissed hands' with the Queen a few days later on 13 July 2016.

On her return from Buckingham Palace, May gave a short speech, written by Nick Timothy, with a much more left-wing flavour than usually expected from Tory Prime Ministers. She promised to fight against "burning injustice" that:

> If you're born poor, you will die on average 9 years earlier than others.
>
> If you're black, you're treated more harshly by the criminal justice system than if you're white.
>
> If you're a white, working-class boy, you're less likely than anybody else in Britain to go to university.
>
> If you're at a state school, you're less likely to reach the top professions than if you're educated privately.
>
> If you're a woman, you will earn less than a man. If you suffer from mental health problems, there's not enough help to hand.
>
> If you're young, you'll find it harder than ever before to own your own home.
>
> But the mission to make Britain a country that works for everyone means more than fighting these injustices. If you're from an ordinary working class family, life is much harder than many people in Westminster realise. You have a job but you don't always have job security. You have your own home, but you worry about paying a mortgage. You can just about manage but you worry about the cost of living and getting your kids into a good school. If you're one of those families, if you're just managing, I want to address you directly.

There is little doubt that these words genuinely reflected May's intentions, and her words were much analysed in the media. In fact, however, they bore no resemblance to the policies she actually put forward in the three years and 11 days of her premiership. These were almost completely dominated by her lengthy, and ultimately unsuccessful, attempts to take Britain out of the European Union.

Within minutes of entering 10 Downing Street, May sat down at her desk, and with undisguised relish began the task of forming her new government, which was strikingly different from its predecessor – only 13 of the 22 members of Cameron's Cabinet were retained, and only four in their previous jobs. The first person to be dispatched was the previous number two, the Chancellor of the Exchequer, George Osborne. Summoned to an interview, of barely ten minutes, he had already worked out in his mind the offers he expected to receive. His preference was the Foreign Office, but if this was not on offer he would be content to retain his previous post. Failing that, there was a very short list of senior posts that he might consider. He was flabbergasted when May revealed that she had nothing to offer. According to his own account, he took this rebuff on the chin, said "Thank you, Prime Minister", and withdrew. Unofficial leaks, however, suggested that May had subjected him to a severe dressing down (Prince, 2017, pp. 356–7).

The next victim of May's wrath was Michael Gove. Unlike Osborne, he was not surprised to be left out of May's team, assuming this to have been the consequence of their past differences and his 'treachery' to Johnson. The latter had been May's second interviewee, after Osborne, and was surprised by the welcome reception that he received. Not only did she enthusiastically offer him the Foreign Secretaryship, but she said he would be flanked by two leading 'Leave' supporters – David Davis as Brexit Secretary and Liam Fox as International Trade Secretary – who would be jointly responsible for negotiating British withdrawal from the EU. May proceeded to balance these appointments by giving the other two top jobs – the Chancellor of the Exchequer and Home Secretary – to two leading 'Remainers', Philip Hammond and Amber Rudd. Six other Cabinet ministers from the Cameron era – John Whittingdale, Oliver Letwin, Nicky Morgan, Stephen Crabb, Ed Vaizey and Theresa Villiers – were dropped, two of them having been offered, and declined, demotion to more junior posts. A key appointment, that of government Chief Whip, went to Gavin Williamson, who had organised her leadership campaign, with enormous efficiency. Together with Nick Timothy and Fiona Hill, who immediately returned to duty as joint chiefs of staff, he was to wield more influence than most members of the Cabinet.

Having been known as a lukewarm supporter of Remain, May hastened to indicate that she accepted the result of the referendum, but was in no hurry to commit herself to details. On Timothy's advice, she uttered the Delphic phrase, "Brexit means Brexit", and it was several weeks before her intentions became at all clear. Given the narrowness of the referendum result, the blatant lies told by the 'Leave' campaign (most notoriously notably on the side of Boris Johnson's campaign bus), the balance of opinion in the House of Commons, the government's small majority of 16 seats (soon reduced to 14 by a by-election loss), and the chaos within the Labour Party, the most obvious choice would have been to seek to achieve the widest possible consensus within Parliament. This would most likely have resulted in a 'soft' Brexit, retaining close relations with the EU, including remaining in the Customs Union and perhaps even the Single Market. Instead of which, May made no effort to reach out and, indeed, tried to exclude Parliament from playing any role at all in the exit procedure. She proposed that an application to withdraw, under Article 50 of the Treaty of Lisbon, should be made to the EU, without being first submitted to the House of Commons. The government were stopped in their tracks by a private citizen (an investment manager, Gina Miller), who unexpectedly obtained a ruling in the High Court that parliamentary consent would be necessary before the Article 50 application could be made. The government appealed the ruling, but it was upheld in the Supreme Court, by a majority of eight votes to three. Unabashed, the government continued the march towards Brexit and duly introduced the European Union (Notification of Withdrawal) Bill, which passed by 498 votes to 114, including 47 Labour MPs who defied a three-line whip unwisely imposed by Jeremy Corbyn.

May declined to consult MPs from any other party in framing the terms on which she hoped to negotiate Britain's departure from the EU, but paid particular attention to the European Research Group, made up of around 80 Tory MPs (including seven ex-Cabinet ministers), all of whom were pledged to secure the hardest of Brexits. Led by Steve Baker, a former junior minister, and Jacob Rees-Mogg, dismissing all talk of aiming at more moderate solutions, such as those negotiated by Norway or Switzerland, as BRINO (Brexit in Name Only), they insisted on complete withdrawal from both the Single Market and the Customs Union, and, in particular, no role for the European Court of Justice. Within a month or two it gradually became clear that these had become the government's own demands, not through conviction, but because of May's fears that she might otherwise be driven out of the party leadership by a coup aimed at replacing her by Davis, Johnson or Gove.

Meanwhile, pressure began to build up for a snap general election, to take advantage of the parlous state of the Labour Party, which had fallen more than 20 per cent behind the Tories in the polls. This would give May an overwhelming majority in the Commons, it was argued, enabling her to force through whatever form of Brexit she desired. This course was repeatedly argued in the Tory-supporting press, and was backed by influential figures, such as William Hague, and privately by the two chiefs of staff, Timothy and Hill, and several senior Cabinet ministers, including David Davis and Philip Hammond. May consistently rejected this advice, and vehemently denied that an election would be called. Then, during the Easter recess, in 2017, she departed with her husband for a walking holiday in North Wales, ruminated on the problem, and changed her mind. On her return, she sounded out only a few senior figures, and finding only Johnson strongly arguing against, summoned a Cabinet meeting, and announced that an election would be held on 8 June. This was unanimously approved by the Cabinet, with no opposition from Johnson, whose facial expression, according to Fiona Hill, revealed that "he knew he was fucked" (Shipman, 2018, p. 195). May then emerged into Downing Street to announce the news to a battery of microphones, saying that the election would be: "a choice between strong and stable leadership in the national interest, with me as your prime minister, or weak and unstable coalition government, led by Jeremy Corbyn" (ibid.).

The Tories went into the election with a larger lead over their opponents than in any previous contest, and confident that they would emerge with a three-figure parliamentary majority. In the event, their majority was completely wiped out, and they were able to stay in office only through a humiliating confidence and supply agreement with the Democratic Unionist Party (DUP), whose ten MPs just tipped the balance, giving the government a total of 328 seats, against 314 for the combined opposition (seven Sinn Fein MPs declined to take their seats). To win the support of the DUP, the government was forced to pledge £1 billion in additional investment in Northern Ireland, characterised by the opposition as 'bribes' of £100 million per DUP MP.

What had gone wrong? Virtually everything, beginning with May's pledge, repeatedly given, not to hold a snap general election. This was taken seriously by large numbers of electors, and many of these – marginal Tory voters – reacted strongly and either abstained or switched their votes to another party. May then revealed herself to be a very poor campaigner – her speeches, mostly delivered to carefully controlled ticket-only meetings, were criticised as poorly delivered and repetitive, while she found great difficulty in handling the questions thrown at her. Her speaking style was widely seen as "robotic", and she was dubbed "the Maybot" by a sketch-writer in *The Guardian*, which was taken up by many other papers. Her repeated self-description as "strong and stable" was widely mocked, and "weak and wobbly" was substituted in thousands of websites. Meanwhile, Jeremy Corbyn conspicuously failed to live up to his billing as a bogeyman. He conducted himself with dignity, and aroused great enthusiasm at a series of rallies held in cities and major towns throughout the land. The Labour organisation was chaotic, but its manifesto, *For the Many, Not the Few*, was highly popular, decisively rejecting the 'austerity' policies of the Tories, and featuring the abolition of student fees and a phased renationalisation programme for the railways. During the campaign, Corbyn's poll ratings steadily improved, while May's sank.

If Labour's manifesto was seen as a relative success, that of the Tories, drafted by Nick Timothy and Ben Gummer (the Paymaster-General), and seen in advance by very few Cabinet ministers or senior Tory officials, came to be regarded as a near total disaster. Entitled *Forward, Together*, it was a broad-ranging document, designed to present the party as less ideological and more open-minded, but without specifically rejecting or modifying its Thatcherite legacy. Ninety-nine per cent of its contents were completely ignored by the media and by the mass of voters, but attention was focused on the paragraph on social care.

For years there had been concern that elderly people living in care homes, and unable to pay the fees, had, in many cases, been forced to sell their family homes in order to meet the costs. Successive governments had conceded that this was a problem, but none had proposed any action to resolve it. The Tories now proposed that nobody owning less than £100,000 would be required to pay for social care, and that if they were forced to sell their homes they would be allowed to continue living there until their death when their heirs would be required to settle up. The proposal did not, however, set any 'cap' on the amount that they would be expected to pay. This was immediately seized on by the press, which dubbed the proposal a 'Dementia Tax', payable by the afflicted, while the healthy were exempt. Tory canvassers reported a dreadful reaction on the doorsteps, and when May was asked by a voter on a television programme, "how he could be sure that he would not be bankrupted to pay for his social care ... she did not seem able to explain the policy" (Cowley and Kavanagh, 2018, p. 191). There was an immediate sharp drop in the Tories' poll lead, and within a couple of days, speaking in Wrexham, May announced, after all, that there would be a cap, and that the details would be given in a government Green Paper. Pressed by journalists to admit that she had committed a U-turn, she claimed hysterically that: "Nothing has changed. Nothing has changed." Her campaign fell apart, and 'strong and steady' was never heard again, except in tones of derision. The Conservatives squandered a 21-point lead over Labour at the start of the campaign and ended by out-polling Corbyn's Labour Party by just 2 per cent on polling day. As a result, the Conservative Party lost 13 seats in the House of Commons, in the process losing its majority.

Thanks to support from the DUP, May was able to cling to office, but her authority was sharply diminished. She had intended to remove Philip Hammond from the Treasury and trim other ministers who were lukewarm about Brexit, but she dared not tamper with the most senior Cabinet ministers, and indeed felt compelled to restore Michael Gove to office, who was surprised and happy to be appointed Environment Secretary. The most senior figure to be sacked was the Education Secretary, Nicky Morgan, who was replaced by Justine Greening. The most significant promotion was that of Damian Green, former Work and Pensions Secretary, to First Secretary of State, and effectively number two in the government. Green, formerly a leading Remainer who had shifted his position, was a close personal friend of May, whom he had known since their Oxford days.

Negotiations resumed with the EU, in which the latter was at a clear advantage. It was represented by Michel Barnier, a skilful and highly experienced negotiator, who had a clear mandate from the Commission and the Council of Ministers, whereas his opposite number, David Davis, had little clear idea what he was aiming at. He made short, and infrequent, visits to Brussels, where he gave breezy press conferences, where he had little of consequence to say. When he reported back to the Commons, he found it very difficult to cope with the forensic questioning of his Labour counterpart, Keir Starmer. May clearly had little confidence in his abilities, recruiting the Permanent Secretary of his ministry, Ollie Robbins, as her personal adviser on the EU, and using him, behind Davis's back, for serious negotiations with Barnier and his staff. The negotiations were divided into two parts – the withdrawal agreement, including, crucially, the financial and policy obligations of both sides, and the future relationship between the UK and the EU. The EU negotiators refused to proceed to the second phase until the first had been completely agreed.

This primarily involved three issues – the financial settlement which Britain should make to redeem all the liabilities of its 40-odd years of membership, mutual citizenship rights for British residents in the EU, and EU residents in Britain, and the need to ensure that there would be no hard border between Northern Ireland and the Irish Republic after Brexit. The first issue was expected to be the most difficult, with estimates varying between £50 billion and £100 billion floated as the likely cost to the British. After much hard bargaining, it was finally agreed that the cost would be much more modest – between £36 and 39 billion. The citizens' rights issue was also eventually settled to mutual satisfaction, but the Irish border proved more difficult, as the Irish government (with strong backing from the other EU member states) refused to allow the negotiations to continue without an iron-clad assurance that there would be no hard border. Eventually, the British agreed a 'backstop' guarantee that, unless an agreement was reached that the entire UK would remain in a customs union with the EU, Northern Ireland would do so, on its own. This was agreed in December 2017, enabling the second phase of negotiations – on Britain's future relationship with the EU – to commence.

Meanwhile, the shape of May's government had changed considerably, thanks to a wave of resignations, several of which had been prompted by the #Me Too movement, following the charges of rape and other sexual harassment offences against the film producer, Harvey Weinstein. The first senior casualty was Defence Secretary Sir Michael Fallon, who resigned on 1 February 2017, saying that his behaviour had "fallen below" the standards expected of him. He was controversially replaced by the Chief Whip, Gavin Williamson, who was widely believed to have proposed himself for the job. He did not last long: on 1 May 2019, he was peremptorily sacked by May for leaking details of a meeting of the National Security Council. Another Cabinet minister who was sacked was the International Development Secretary, Priti Patel, who had embarked on political discussions with Israeli ministers and officials, without any authorisation. But the most painful loss for May was that of her number two, Damian Green. He was accused by a woman journalist and Tory activist Kate Maltby, writing in *The Times*, of having, indirectly, propositioned her. He would probably have survived, but a Cabinet Office inquiry picked up an incident dating back to the Blair years when he was suspected of revealing official secrets. He was never charged with an offence, but his parliamentary office was raided by the police, who confiscated his parliamentary computers. They found no incriminating evidence, but discovered vast amounts of pornography stored on one of them. This had not been publicised at the time, but in December 2017 a Scotland Yard detective told the BBC that he had been "shocked" by the amount of pornography that he had found. Green was then questioned about this by the Cabinet Office's head of propriety and ethics, and gave what they judged as evasive and dishonest replies, which they considered was a breach of the Ministerial Code. When this was reported to May, she thought she had no alternative but to ask Green for his resignation. Some of May's government's resignations were for trivial reasons, and at a time of high political controversy some resignations were perhaps inevitable, but May's government set an all-time record for the number of dismissals and resignations – 35 – over a term of three years and 11 days.

Things remained difficult in the negotiations with the EU. David Davis pointed to the Free Trade Agreement, patiently negotiated over a nine-year period with Canada, and said that the

UK should aim to achieve "Canada plus, plus".Yet the EU declined to offer the terms agreed with Canada to a competitor country on its own doorstep, and insisted that there should be a 'level playing field', with regard to services, workers' rights and other provisions. In effect, what it was offering was 'Canada, minus, minus'. It also insisted on the backstop being included in the agreement.When a draft agreement was reached with the EU negotiators in July 2018, May summoned the Cabinet to a conclave at Chequers to approve the terms before submitting them to Parliament for a 'meaningful vote'. There was a tense debate, at which every Cabinet minister was asked to give his or her own views. At the end of the discussion, the motion was put to the meeting, with the clear indication that anybody voting against would be regarded as resigning from their post. Not a single member did so, and May heaved a sigh of relief, sensing that she was out of the woods. The relief did not last long.Two days later David Davis decided that he must resign and asked for a meeting with May. He was immediately summoned to a meeting with the Chief Whip, Julian Smith, who tried to buy him off with the offer of the Foreign Secretaryship, even though Johnson had not yet resigned (Seldon, 2019, p. 441). Davis declined, and released his letter of resignation. This provoked Johnson, fearful of being outflanked by Davis in any future leadership election, to follow suit. He was succeeded as Foreign Secretary by Jeremy Hunt, the Health Secretary. Three other ministers also resigned, Brexit Secretary Dominic Raab, Esther McVey, the Work and Pensions Secretary, and the Brexit Under-Secretary, Steve Baker, who again became Chairman of the European Research Group and henceforth May's chief tormentor.

May now faced a hard struggle to get her withdrawal agreement through the House of Commons. Her chances appeared slim, as both the DUP and the European Research Group pledged not to support it, and May postponed the vote, which was due in December 2018. It was then announced by Sir Graham Brady, Chairman of the 1922 Committee of Tory backbenchers, that more than the requisite number of Tory MPs (48) had demanded a vote of no confidence in her leadership.The vote was held on 12 December, and she won by 200 votes to 117.This, in theory, meant she was safe until December 2019, as Tory rules stated that no further confidence votes could be held in the following 12 months, but the fact that as many as 117 were against her was an ominous sign, given the overall parliamentary arithmetic.

At this point May announced that she would not lead the Tories at the next general election. This did not save her from an overwhelming defeat a month later, on 15 January 2019, when the 'MPV' ('meaningful parliamentary vote') on the withdrawal agreement was eventually held. The government went down by a majority of 230 votes – 432 to 202 – the largest majority ever in parliamentary history against a sitting government. Soon after, three pro-EU Tory MPs, led by former minister, Anna Soubry, defected from the party to join eight Labour Members, led by Chukka Umunna, to form the Independent Group for Change, later renamed Change UK. Another new party emerged around the same time. Nigel Farage, having fallen out with his former supporters in UKIP, announced in March 2019 that he was going to form a new party, the Brexit Party, which would fight every seat in the European Parliament elections in May 2019, which Britain would be required to hold if it did not leave the European Union on 29 March. Some commentators predicted a re-alignment of British politics around Brexit divisions, with the Eurosceptic Brexit Party and the pro-European Change UK and Liberal Democrats challenging the dominant position of the divided Conservative and Labour parties. The Brexit Party was spectacularly successful, at least in the short run. It easily mopped up the vast bulk of UKIP supporters, as well as making deep inroads into the Tory vote. It finished up at the top of the poll, with 30.5 per cent of the vote, while the Tories came fifth, with 14.3 per cent, their worst result in three centuries.The Labour Party also suffered from its confused positioning on Brexit and picked up just 10 out of the 77 British seats, behind the LibDems on 16. But, in spite of the spectacular results, the two main parties managed to regain their control of British politics, while the new pro-European party, Change UK, failed to win a single seat.

The Skripal poisoning affair in March 2018 went some way to restoring May's standing as Prime Minister. Her firm and proportional response helped bolster her reputation, both domestically and internationally. Conversely, Corbyn's questioning of the overwhelming evidence of Russian guilt largely damaged his own fast diminishing credibility. This possibly assisted May to do rather better on the second 'meaningful vote' on the withdrawal treaty, on 12 March 2019, when she lost by 149 votes (391 to 242). May concluded from this that she had no hope of reversing this vote without the support of the opposition, something that wiser heads had long been telling her. Corbyn, himself a covert supporter of Leave, would probably have welcomed an agreement, but Keir Starmer, who led Labour's negotiating team, insisted that the party as a whole would not accept any agreement unless it was subjected to a referendum.

This in fact was now the only way in which she might have got her proposals through, but she vehemently refused to consider it, despite the fact that opinion polls showed a consistent majority in favour, and that very large street demonstrations – of more than a million people – backed a 'People's Vote'. With the aid of the Speaker, John Bercow, who made a series of controversial procedural rulings which permitted the House as a whole to decide the matter, there was then a short period in which it could decide between alternative proposals for resolving the Brexit impasse. None of these, however, achieved a majority. So, on 29 March, May made a third and final attempt to get her proposals through, and lost by 344 votes to 286. Thirty-four Tory MPs voted against, as well as all the DUP Members. Anthony Seldon commented, "For all the Herculean effort, only five Labour MPs voted for the motion" (Seldon, 2019, p. 595).

It was now the end of the road for Theresa May and, after consulting Sir Graham Brady and very few others, she appeared on the steps of 10 Downing Street on 25 May to say:

> I am today announcing that I will resign the leadership of the Conservative and Unionist Party on Friday 7 June so that a successor may be chosen … I will shortly leave the job that it has been the honour of my life to hold, the second female Prime Minister but certainly not the last. I do so with no ill will, but with enormous and enduring gratitude to have had the opportunity to serve the country I love.

She stumbled over the last few words, visibly revealing a tear, but succeeded in bringing a dignified end to what had been a spectacularly unsuccessful government. It need not have happened. May was a woman of some ability and integrity, whose judgement was often at fault. She almost invariably under-estimated the strength of opposition to what she proposed. It was only in her final days at Number 10 that she gave any indication that she recognised the concessions she would need to make to get parliamentary approval for a deal. However, by that stage, it was too late to convince either the opposition or her own side that she was sincere. She had no option then but to quit, perhaps reflecting on the words of Omar Khayyam, the medieval Persian poet and mathematician, who wrote:

> The moving finger writes; and, having writ, moves on:
> Nor all thy piety nor wit shall lure it back to cancel half a line,
> Nor all thy tears wash out a word of it.
> (Edward Fitzgerald, translator, 1868,
> *The Rubaiyat of Omar Khayyam*)

Works consulted

Virginia Blackburn, 2016, *Theresa May: The Downing Street Revolution*, London, John Blake.

Philip Cowley and Dennis Kavanagh, 2018, *The British General Election of 2017*, London, Palgrave Macmillan.

Christopher Jackson, 2018, *Theresa May: Power, Chaos and Chance*, London, Eyewear Publishing.

Rosa Prince, 2017, *Theresa May: The Enigmatic Prime Minister,* London, Biteback.

Anthony Seldon, with Raymond Newell, 2019, *May at Ten*, London, Biteback.

Tim Shipman, 2018, *Fall Out: A Year of Political Mayhem*, London, William Collins.

23

BORIS JOHNSON

Statesman or buffoon?

A Man so various that he seem'd to be
Not one, but all Mankind's Epitome,
Stiff in Opinions, always in the wrong;
Was Everything by starts and Nothing long;
But, in the course of one revolving Moon,
Was Chemist, Fiddler, Statesman and Buffoon;
Then all for Women, Painting, Rhyming, Drinking,
Besides ten thousand Freaks that died in thinking.

John Dryden was a prescient fellow. He wrote his satirical poem, *Absalom and Achitophel*, in 1681, when his target was George Villiers, the second Duke of Buckingham, whose family home, appropriately enlarged and embellished, has served as the principal royal residence since the time of George III. His description might just as well apply to Britain's 55th Prime Minister, Boris Johnson.

Alexander Boris de Pfeffel Johnson was born in New York on 19 June 1964, of very mixed ancestry. His father, Stanley Johnson, was a grandson of Ali Kemal, a Turkish journalist and politician, who was lynched by a nationalist mob in Izmir in 1922. Ali's first wife, who was half-English and half-Swiss, had separated from her husband and gone to live in Bournemouth, where she died in childbirth in 1909. Her (and Ali's) son, Osman, was brought up by his English grandmother, Margaret Johnson, and his name was changed to Wilfred Johnson, but he was always known as 'Johnny'. Johnny's wife had both French and German ancestors, notably the de Pfeffel family, which is descended, through an illegitimate line, from the dukes and kings of Würtemberg and from King George II. Consequently, Boris is a distant cousin of the Queen (Gimson, 2016, p. 10). He is also an eighth cousin of David Cameron (Purnell, 2012, p. 21). His tangled ancestry was minutely probed in a BBC television programme, *Who Do You Think You Are?*, on 20 August 2008.

DOI: 10.4324/9781003031963-24

Stanley Johnson is an amiable man – though with a bad temper (Bower, 2020, p. 10) – and tends to play everything for laughs. He has a reputation for unreliability, and has had a chequered career, with many setbacks, but has invariably succeeded in landing on his feet. Educated at a West Country 'public' school, Sherborne, and Exeter College, Oxford, where he won the Newdigate Prize for poetry, he married a fellow student at the age of 23, and won a Harkness Fellowship, which enabled him to do postgraduate work in the US. His wife was Charlotte Fawcett, who came from a distinguished academic family, one of whom had founded the Fawcett Society, renowned for its advocacy of women's rights. She deferred the final year of her degree to accompany Stanley to the States, and eventually to Mexico, where, with Charlotte heavily pregnant and the couple short of cash, they met up with a wealthy 'friend of a friend', Boris Litwin, who insisted on buying them first class air tickets to New York to save Charlotte the rigours of taking a bus. Immensely grateful, Charlotte promised to name her baby after him if it should be a boy. He never knew if she kept her word because within a few weeks he had died. When Boris was still a baby, he was found to be hard of hearing, and this contributed to his being a lonely child, cut off from much human contact, apart from his younger siblings. At the age of 8 or 9, he had operations to insert grommets into his ears. Since then his hearing has been normal. Even before then, he had shown marked evidence of precocity and fierce ambition. Asked what he wanted to be when he grew up, he replied, without hesitation: 'World King' (Rachel Johnson, 2020, p. 11).

As a boy, and still today within his family, Boris Johnson was known as Al or Alex, but while at Eton, he decided that 'Boris' was more distinctive, and he is now virtually the only political figure known solely by his forename, both nationally and, increasingly, internationally. Stanley has had great influence over Boris, who resembles him in many ways, but is more focused and more ambitious than his father. Stanley was appointed as an EU official in 1973, and subsequently, in 1979, was elected a Conservative Member of the European Parliament for Wight and East Hampshire. He served for a single five-year term, and then, in 2004, returned to his post at the European Commission. Meanwhile, Boris was joined by three younger siblings, Rachel (born in 1965), Leo (1967) and Jo[seph] (1971).

When Stanley was appointed to his Commission post, in 1973, he moved his family to Brussels, and Boris attended the European School in the Brussels suburb of Uccle. Here he made a number of friends, including Marina Wheeler, a daughter of Charles Wheeler, the distinguished BBC correspondent. In 1974, Charlotte, who was working as a portrait painter, had a nervous breakdown, and was committed to the Maudsley Hospital for depression. She was in and out of hospital for several years, and in 1980, due to the multiple infidelities of Stanley, they divorced. Charlotte had now recovered and went to live in a flat in Notting Hill, where her children went to live with her, interspersed with visits to Stanley on his rather spartan Somerset farm. She later married a leading American political scientist, Nick Wahl, and lived happily with him in New York for eight years, until his untimely death at the age of 68.

Boris was happy at the European School, but Stanley was ambitious to send his son to Eton, and was advised to transfer him to a posh 'prep' school, Ashdown House in East Grinstead, where he duly won a scholarship to Eton, to which he proceeded in 1977, aged 13. Here he started on a high note, deeply impressing his teachers by his knowledge of Latin and Greek and easy command of modern languages. The Master of the College, Martin Hammond, sent a glowing report to Stanley at the end of his first term, but each successive report shows progressive disillusionment, culminating in July 1982 when he wrote:

This has been a pretty disappointing year … He is, in fact, pretty idle about it all … Boris has something of a tendency to assume that success and honours will drop into his lap. Not so, he must work for them.

(Gimson, 2016, p. 44)

Hammond went on to question whether it would be wise to appoint Boris as Head Boy of the College during his final term, though this was done. By then, Boris was wildly popular with his fellow pupils, who elected him a member of the exclusive Eton Society, 'Pop' (made up of the school prefects, an honour which was withheld from his great rival, David Cameron, who was two years behind him at the school). So his school career ended in a blaze of glory, and in 1983 he left for a 'gap year', teaching English and Latin at Geelong Grammar School in Australia.

In 1982, he began a four-year course at Balliol College, Oxford, studying 'Greats' (Greek, Latin, Philosophy and Ancient History). Initially, at least, he tended to associate mainly with fellow Etonians, among whom he had two especially close friends – Charles Spencer, later the 9th Earl Spencer, and younger brother of Princess Diana, and Darius Guppy, the half-Iranian son of the writer and singer Shusha Guppy. One of his few non-Etonian friends was Andrew Gimson, later a journalist on the *Daily Telegraph*. Gimson was to write a biography of Johnson, first published in 2006, which later went through at least four revised editions. In the book, Gimson revealed that one of Boris's aspirations in Oxford was to find a wife of distinction, as his father had a generation earlier. He wasted little time in seeking one, scraping an acquaintance with Allegra Mostyn-Owen. She was seen as the contemporary equivalent of the protagonist of Max Beerbohm's Oxford novel, published in 1911, *Zuleika Dobson* – 'the most beautiful, cleverest and richest girl in the University', who was lusted after by all the male students. Allegra's fame spread even wider when her photograph, taken by David Bailey, appeared on the cover of *Tatler* magazine, and then of *Vogue*.

Allegra was not immediately taken by Boris, whom she found scruffy, and was put off by his Tory views, but she found him amusing and gradually warmed to him.

He became my best friend, a much better friend than any of the girls I knew at the time … He introduced me to poetry which I didn't know at all, and there were lots of good jokes, and lots of bad jokes. And in my own way I didn't really think he was making a play for me despite the fact that there was lots of curry *à deux* at the Kismet Tandoori.

(Gimson, 2016, p. 77)

But 'making a play' was exactly what Boris was about, and he pursued her with unrelenting vigour.

Apart from the conquest of Allegra, Boris had two overwhelming ambitions while at Oxford – to be elected as President of the Oxford Union, and to attain a 'First' in his final degree exams. He became one of the most active participants in Union debates, and in November 1984 launched his campaign for the presidency. But he was restricted by his almost exclusive association with Etonians and fellow Balliol men, and one day his rival candidate, Neil Sherlock, a grammar school boy and future Liberal Democrat grandee, was surprised to receive an invitation from Allegra to have tea with her in her rooms in Trinity College. When he arrived, she unleashed a paean of praise for 'my Boris', and appealed to him to relinquish his candidature in Boris's favour. Sherlock kept his head and resisted Allegra's charms, and went on to defeat Boris by 661 votes to 558. With two exceptions (Roy Jenkins and Boris's predecessor as MP for Henley, Michael Heseltine), previous defeated candidates had meekly accepted their defeat and made no second attempt on the presidency. But his defeat rankled with Boris and a year later he again raised his standard, this time conducting a more professional and cynical campaign.

The appeal of the Social Democratic Party was then at its height and swept through Oxford University. Boris did not join the new party, but on the eve of the Union election made a brilliant speech in a debate on the motion 'This House has had enough of two-party politics' – praising the new party's policies to the skies. He was duly elected by 809 votes to 466. For some, a black mark against Boris was his membership of the notorious Bullingdon Club, made up almost exclusively of very wealthy public school boys. Their meetings held in posh restaurants invariably descended into drunken orgies in which the restaurant was trashed, as were the college rooms of newly elected members. These included the future Polish Foreign Minister, Radek Sikorski, David Cameron and George Osborne, all fellow members in Boris's time. If the restaurants had complained to the police, they would undoubtedly have been charged with causing criminal damage. Instead, they contented themselves with sending hefty bills to the club, which organised whip-rounds among its members. Boris, apparently, was the most reluctant to contribute.

In August 1985, during the summer vacation, Boris wrote to Allegra from Lisbon, where he was on a working holiday with his sister, Rachel, and her boyfriend, Sebastian Shakespeare, asking her if she had yet broached the subject of marriage with her parents. They were a formidable pair. Allegra's mother, Gaia Servadio, of Jewish descent, was a glamorous Italian journalist and novelist, a member of the Italian Communist Party who made a habit of attending annual conferences of the Labour Party. Her husband, Willy Mostyn-Owen, was an immensely wealthy art historian who was Chairman of Christie's. A direct descendant of Owen Glendower, the last Welshman to be Prince of Wales (in the early 15th century), he was the owner of Woodhouse, a historic estate in Shropshire, and a castle in Scotland, so large that Gaia claimed never to have counted the number of bedrooms. Allegra took Boris to meet them, and they were not impressed. Gaia was appalled by his scruffiness, and Willy appears to have suspected him of being a fortune-hunter. Despite this, the couple announced their engagement.

Boris narrowly missed his objective of attaining a 'First', largely because of spreading his activities too thinly and his aversion to 'details'. He was affronted that David Cameron, whom he had outshone, both at Eton and Oxford, in every way, achieved this result with quiet efficiency. Bitterly disappointed, Boris, who had been widely seen at Oxford as a future Prime Minister, now temporarily lowered his sights. He had seen himself taking a top job in the media, as a stepping-stone into politics, and now accepted the offer of a highly-paid but predictably boring post in management. He lasted for one week and then submitted his resignation, but not before he had collected his signing-on fee (Gimson, 2016, p. 88). He managed to secure a position as a trainee journalist on *The Times*, who sent him for three months to train on the *Wolverhampton Express & Star*.

He and Allegra were married on 5 September 1987. It was a grand society occasion, with the reception in the grounds of Woodhouse. Here the guests were treated to a recital from the *Marriage of Figaro* and the world première of a piece by Hans Werner Henze entitled *Allegra e Boris – Duetto Concertante per Violino e Viola*. Both the bride and groom were 23 years old, and the occasion was somewhat marred by Boris's behaviour. He had hired morning dress for the wedding, but when he opened his luggage found he had left it behind. He had to borrow trousers from the local MP, John Biffen, but his shoes were too big for Boris and he had to wear his own shabby pair. To make matters much worse he lost his wedding ring somewhere in the grounds, and it was never found. Despite this, it was a happy day for Allegra, but looking back she said, "When we got married that was actually the end of the relationship instead of the beginning" (Gimson, 2016, p. 87).

After his three months in Wolverhampton, which he did not enjoy, Boris was mostly employed in writing up agency stories for the inside pages of *The Times*. One day he was given a piece about an archaeological dig of what was suspected to be a palace of Edward II. Boris improved the story by adding a fictional quote from Dr Colin Lucas of Balliol College, who happened to be his godfather. Lucas was not amused, and wrote a bitter letter of protest, believing that his own reputation among historians was now in tatters. Boris was shown the door, but was lucky enough to have invited the editor of the *Daily Telegraph*, Max Hastings, to a debate at the Oxford Union and Hastings had taken a shine to him. He invited Boris to become the newspaper's correspondent in Brussels, responsible for covering the European Union.

Among his new colleagues in the Brussels press corps was the present author, who was able to follow his career closely for the five years that he remained in the Belgian capital. Boris claimed not to understand the ways of the EU, saying in effect "all you clever chaps know what's going on but I haven't a clue". This did not prevent him writing a barrage of articles for his paper, decrying the EU and subjecting the European Commission, in particular, to satire and ridicule. Many of his pieces were highly amusing, but not all of them were true. Boris did not hesitate to make things up as he went along. Among the fictions he created was a directive banning 'bendy' bananas and a plan to dynamite the Berlaymont building, the HQ of the Commission, when it was found to be infested with asbestos.

Some journalists were annoyed to be rung by their papers demanding to know why they hadn't themselves produced 'scoops' comparable to Boris's, but on the whole he was a popular figure – he was amusing and good company and they did not take offence. Nor did they take him seriously, though the long-term effect of his articles was to turn a large number of Tory newspaper readers sharply against the EU. Among Boris's riskier ventures, during the 1992 general election campaign, was to conclude a bet for £1,000 with the correspondent of *The Guardian*, John Palmer, that the Tories would win the election. The polls showed Labour in the lead, and one morning the present author received a panicky phone call, asking plaintively what he should do. I advised him to lay off his bet with bookmakers to cover the bulk of his loss. He thanked me profusely, but if he followed my advice he would have been far worse off, as the Tories unexpectedly won.

Allegra joined Boris in Brussels, but did not enjoy it. Boris treated her like a trophy wife, and made little effort to modify his lifestyle to take account of her susceptibilities, giving her little moral support while she agonised over the breakdown of her parents' marriage after 28 years. He was out a lot chasing stories, and thought nothing of flying off to Zagreb or Istanbul without warning, so she often had to face the humiliation of phoning the paper's London office to find out where he was. She signed up for a legal course, and flew back to London to pursue it, later rejoining Boris for a final attempt at reconciliation. But he met up again with his former school friend from the European School, Marina Wheeler, the half-Indian daughter of the BBC's Charles Wheeler. A left-wing lawyer working in Brussels, she fell desperately in love with Boris, to the horror of her many friends, who could not stomach the idea of her marrying a Tory. She became pregnant, and Allegra graciously accelerated the divorce proceedings so that they could be concluded before the birth of the child. Boris and Marina immediately married, and a month later their daughter, Lara Lettice, was born. The couple settled down to a happy married life, and three further children followed over the next six years. Marina was more self-sufficient than Allegra had been, and found enough satisfaction from her legal work and growing family responsibilities to keep her content. If Boris enjoyed any illicit sexual encounters, in Brussels or during his frequent visits abroad, he kept them to himself.

As for Allegra, who remained on friendly, if distant, terms with Boris, she completed her legal studies, but did not attempt to practise. Instead, she became an artist and taught a weekly art course at an east London mosque. In 1994 the *Telegraph* recalled Boris from Brussels, and he was given a major promotion, becoming assistant editor and chief political columnist, doubling up with writing a weekly column for the *Spectator*, which was under the same ownership. He became an expert interviewer, and his weekly interviews, sometimes with eminent personalities but often with humbler folk, became a popular feature of the Saturday edition of the paper. Boris was extremely prolific, and turned out a vast number of articles of varying quality, but almost always lively and full of humour. He soon became a popular broadcaster, much in demand for chat shows and other more serious programmes.

It was around this time that when appearing on a television quiz programme, one of the other contestants suddenly produced a 1990 telephone recording of a conversation between Johnson and his Oxford contemporary, Darius Guppy. Guppy had served a prison sentence for fraud and asked Johnson to find the address of the journalist he believed had 'shopped' him to the police so that he could arrange to have him beaten up by a couple of strong men. Boris, somewhat reluctantly, agreed to this, but later thought better of it.

As the 1997 general election approached, Boris made himself available for selection as a Tory candidate. He was turned down for the London seat of Holborn and St Pancras, for which as an urbane, Oxford-educated journalist he might have seemed a good fit, but was chosen instead for the largely rural, partly Welsh-speaking and Labour-inclined constituency of Clwyd South, where he seemed a fish out of water. Yet he campaigned with great verve, and was disappointed to lose to Labour by nearly 14,000 votes. As he put it himself, "I fought Clwyd South, and Clwyd South fought back!" In the election which swept Tony Blair to power with a majority of 179 seats, this result was nothing to be ashamed of. Shortly afterwards, the new proprietor of the Telegraph group, Conrad Black, offered Boris the editorship of the *Spectator*, but on the explicit condition that he would give up his parliamentary ambitions. Boris accepted.

Within a couple of months, however, word reached Black that Boris had approached two separate safe Conservative seats seeking selection. A furious Black described him as "ineffably duplicitous" and summoned him to explain what he had done. He recalls that Boris replied that "it was outrageous and that we would be quite within our rights to sack him" (Purnell, 2012, p. 190). Yet he told Black that he wanted more than anything to become an MP, and was confident that he could do both jobs well. Despite his reputation as a hard-faced businessman, Black relented, and allowed Boris to stay on. Fearful, however, of Boris's unreliability, he insisted on the appointment of an ultra-efficient deputy editor, Stuart Reid, to be responsible for all the more tedious editorial duties, and to make sure that the paper came out on time. The arrangement proved highly satisfactory. Boris engaged lively and attractive authors to contribute to the paper, while his own myriad activities brought useful publicity, and the circulation rose by 10 per cent to 62,000 during the five years of his editorship.

In 2001 Boris was duly chosen as the Conservative candidate for the safe seat of Henley, whose MP, Michael Heseltine, was standing down on his appointment to the House of Lords. Heseltine's views on Europe were opposed to Boris's, as were those of the favourite for the succession, who finished up in second place. Boris's success was widely attributed to his anti-European views.

Boris's debut in the Commons was hardly a stunning success. His fellow Tory backbenchers were resentful that he retained his editorship, and many were envious of his fame and his large extra-parliamentary income. This was exasperated by his irregular attendance at the House and his reluctance to devote himself to the hard grind of serving on select committees. Michael Howard, however, who was elected unopposed to the Tory leadership in October 2003, after the vote of no confidence in Iain Duncan Smith, appointed Johnson as frontbench spokesman on higher education, and Boris entered into his new responsibilities with great enthusiasm, giving a series of well-thought-out speeches at a variety of universities and other educational bodies. Yet in October 2004, Boris came within an ace of being sacked from his Shadow appointment. The beheading in Iraq of the Liverpool-born aid-worker, Ken Bigley, by Islamic terrorists provoked mass demonstrations in Liverpool. *The Spectator* ran an editorial accusing the city of "mawkish sentimentality" over the death, and went on to accuse "drunken Liverpool fans" of responsibility for the death of 50 football fans at the Hillsborough disaster in 1989, when the actual number of deaths was 96 (the fans were later exonerated). Howard immediately ordered Johnson (who was not the author of the editorial) to travel to Liverpool to make an abject apology to the city. Boris complied, and avoided being sacked from the front bench.

Yet his reprieve was only temporary – thanks to the waywardness of his private life. Boris was hardly a 'matinée idol', having undistinguished features and a tendency to overweight. Yet he was almost irresistible to women thanks to his lively and humorous conversation. He embarked on a series of affairs, the most serious of which was with Petronella ('Petsy') Wyatt, the daughter of the former Labour MP Woodrow Wyatt who later, as a life peer, became a vehement Thatcherite. Petronella was already working as a journalist at *The Spectator* when Johnson became editor, and it was not long before they embarked on a passionate affair initially unknown to the rest of the staff. They got into the way of spending their lunch breaks together and meeting for longer periods in her nearby flat. It seems likely that Boris – whether intentionally or not – led Petronella to believe that he intended to leave his wife, Marina, and set up home with her. But he never got round to doing this and she made ineffective attempts to break off their affair, at one stage leaving for a period in the United States where she became engaged to somebody else, but nothing came of it. On her return she became pregnant by Boris and had an abortion.

A series of leaks in the press began to publicise the affair, sometimes obliquely as when a journalist on the *Daily Mail* wrote about Petronella having a lover with a "custard coloured mop of hair". Eventually, when Petronella had a second abortion, fuller stories began to appear which circulated widely. An alarmed Michael Howard insisted that Boris should come clean. Boris replied nonchalantly that the story was "an inverted pyramid of piffle". Convinced that he was lying, Howard peremptorily dismissed him from his Shadow ministerial post. It looked like the end of Johnson's political career, but soon after he saw new possibilities when the party sought a candidate for the London mayoralty to challenge the formidable Labour (and previously Independent) Mayor, Ken Livingstone. They decided to hold a primary election for which apparently only mediocre contenders signed up. Sensing his chance, Boris threw his hat into the ring and emerged as the victor for the Conservative candidacy by a wide margin. The Tory leadership was not happy about this as they feared he would blunder his way to defeat in the actual election.

But David Cameron, who replaced Howard as leader of the Conservative Party, exerted himself to insist Boris kept to a strict rule-book drawn up by Lynton Crosby, the tough-minded Australian political organiser who had helped the Tories in his native country win a series of elections. Boris behaved himself and emerged as a surprise winner in May 2008 when the Conservatives captured a majority on the Greater London Assembly, and he led Ken Livingstone decisively in the mayoral poll. The vote took place under fair weather conditions. Many voters used the elections to show dissatisfaction with the Labour government that had been in power for 11 years, and Johnson's personal vote for the mayoralty was not out of line with his party's strong performance in the Assembly elections. His election meant he gave up his seat as MP for Henley.

Johnson's achievements as Mayor as an effective administrator were limited, but his record at self-promotion was triumphant. Not everybody admired his insistence on replacing 'bendy buses' with a rejigged Routemaster design, or his heavily branded Boris Bikes (which had in fact been initiated by his predecessor), while several other imaginative projects – such as the construction of a new airport on an island in the Thames estuary – were widely regarded as impractical (as was his later idea of building a 'garden bridge' over the Thames). However these eye-catching schemes allowed him to maintain a high profile and to project energy and independence.

In May 2012, when Johnson came up for re-election, the national picture was very different from 2008. The Conservatives were back in power at national level in coalition with the Liberal Democrats, and many Londoners used the elections to show their opposition. However Ken Livingstone's campaign to regain the mayoralty was an abysmal failure. He undoubtedly suffered from the coverage of the *Evening Standard* – which had a monopoly on London news – now owned by a former KGB official, Alexander Lebedev, who went out of its way to blackguard Livingstone and build up Johnson. Livingstone also made a number of unforgivable mistakes in his own campaign, reigniting ideas of his anti-semitism. On election day, while the Labour Party comfortably won a majority of the seats in the London Assembly, it was Johnson who won the mayoral vote, by a substantial margin. This had the effect of greatly inflating Johnson's reputation within the Conservative Party as a vote-winner.

As so often in Johnson's life, his political dramas went hand-in-hand with marital and extra-marital ones. In 2008 Boris started a new affair with Helen Macintyre, a vivacious 35-year-old art dealer, and wooed her under the nose of her live-in boyfriend, Pierre Rollin, a Canadian financier. Some months later, when she became pregnant, Rollin took a DNA test which showed he was not the father of the child, who was christened Stephanie. Neither Johnson nor Macintyre seem to have taken the affair very seriously and there was never any question of Boris taking responsibility for the upbringing of his conspicuously blonde daughter. Boris had appointed Macintyre as an unpaid 'art adviser' without following the guidelines about registering his personal relationship with her. During the 2010 general election campaign, when Boris was returned as MP for Uxbridge, he was asked how many children he had and refused to answer. The correct answer at the time would have been six – unless he had other undeclared illegitimate offspring.

Late in 2009, 17 years after divorcing Boris, Allegra Mostyn-Owen married a second time, to a Pakistani Muslim, 22 years her junior. Her family disapproved, but she received a warm letter of congratulation from Boris, who switched the arrangements for his next mayoral tour to include a visit to the mosque where the marriage was celebrated. Allegra told the press that she was not converting to Islam, but "at my current stage in life I am unlikely to conceive children so we have agreed that so long as he chooses a good partner, then I am happy to live together in an extended family" (*The Week*, 8 January 2010).

But the affair which much later came to haunt Johnson as Prime Minister was a four-year tryst with Jennifer Arcuri, a blonde and vivacious Californian digital entrepreneur who was 21 years his junior. The tabloids feasted on stories about her pole-dancing and topless pictures, but the more troubling questions concerned the fact that she had been added to the invitation list for three trade delegations led by Johnson, as well as being given six-figure government contracts as late as 2019. Under the rules of the Mayor's office, Johnson should have declared his relationship with her, which he never did. The affair eventually petered out and Arcuri got married to a business associate.

A major element in Johnson's successful bid as Mayor to increase his following and his reputation was the 2012 Summer Olympics. It was the Labour government of Tony Blair which succeeded in winning the right to hold the Games, but it was Boris who was invited to the closing ceremony of the 2008 Games in Beijing, when he made a big splash by promising that London would be an even bigger and more spectacular occasion than the Chinese extravaganza. From then on, he seized every conceivable opportunity to associate himself with British preparations for the Games, sometimes exposing himself to ridicule as when he got stuck on a cable zip-wire while holding Union Jacks in front of a crowd of photographers. When the Games took place, Johnson was an almost permanent presence, taking credit amongst others for the highly acclaimed opening ceremony devised by the film director Danny Boyle, and for the very successful British performance which yielded a record-breaking number of awards, including 29 gold medals. David Cameron, the Prime Minister, who had also hoped to enhance his own reputation, suffered the humiliation of being constantly overshadowed by his Etonian contemporary and constant rival.

When Boris was running for his second term as Mayor he was repeatedly asked if he would seek to return to the Commons before the end of his term. He promised that he would not, but as the years went by, doubts arose over Cameron's prospects of winning the next general election, and Boris's supporters became nervous that if he failed to win a seat at the election, he would not be eligible to be a candidate for the leadership, for which he and the Chancellor of the Exchequer, George Osborne, were joint favourites.

In the summer of 2014, the MP for Uxbridge and South Ruislip, a Tory seat with a majority of more than 11,000, announced his forthcoming retirement, and Boris reported pressure from a long list of Tory MPs that he should aim to be the party's new candidate. He accepted and was easily elected by the local Tories. Boris was duly elected as the MP in 2015 when Cameron surprised everybody by winning an outright majority, which allowed him to remain as Prime Minister. Johnson served out his second term as London Mayor, which ended in May 2016, and he was then widely seen as Cameron's eventual successor. It did not work out that way.

One of the biggest ironies of Johnson's career was the ease with which he pivoted from being the ultimate embodiment of a cosmopolitan outward-looking Britain at the London Olympics in 2012, to the most visible symbol of English nationalism as the effective leader of the Vote Leave campaign in the Brexit referendum. It was not immediately obvious to either Boris or anyone else that he would play this role. He allegedly told friends he was "veering all over the place like a supermarket trolley", finding it impossible to decide which side to back. During the weekend before he made up his mind, he wrote two alternative articles for the *Daily Telegraph*, one backing 'Remain' and the other 'Leave'. He finally revealed his intentions on the morning of 21 February 2016, but from then onwards there was no doubt. Together with Michael Gove and Labour MP Gisela Stewart, he agreed to head one of the two official 'Leave' campaigns, and embarked on a widely publicised campaign tour, using a bus emblazoned with the false claim that the cost of EU membership to British taxpayers was £350 million per week (the actual sum was more like £136 million when the rebate and UK receipts of funding were factored in). In the face of repeated demands that he should withdraw this claim, he vehemently refused.

The chief strategist for the campaign was Dominic Cummings, who coined the slogan 'Vote Leave, Take Back Control' and pioneered the use of big data and social media, enlisting the help of controversial political consultants such as Cambridge Analytica, who would also be used in Donald Trump's presidential campaign a few months later. Nigel Farage led the other campaign, which put forward a more extremist case, centred around immigration, and probably widened the base to include many people who normally would not have taken part in a political campaign.

Opinion polls had suggested that the result of the referendum would be a narrow victory for Remain of about 5 per cent, whereas the actual result – the product of a higher than expected turnout – gave the Leave campaign 52 per cent while Remain got 48 per cent. David Cameron immediately resigned as Prime Minister and Boris was seen as the victor. However, Johnson failed to translate his success in the referendum into an immediate ascent to the prime ministership – partly through his own mistakes and partly through the 'treachery' of Michael Gove, who torpedoed Johnson's leadership campaign minutes before it was formally launched.

With surprising ease, Johnson bounced back from his humiliation and soon became the favourite to succeed Theresa May if she failed to deliver a Brexit acceptable to the Conservative Party. May tried to prevent Johnson from becoming leader of the Eurosceptic fringe by inviting him to become Foreign Secretary, a post which he filled with less than total distinction. European governments took a dim view of him throughout that time because they blamed him for having lied about the EU during the referendum campaign. Beyond Europe he committed a series of gaffes. On a visit to Myanmar he shocked his hosts – and the British Ambassador – by reading an imperialistic Kipling poem. When British diplomats were working behind the scenes to secure the release from prison in Iran of Nazanin Zaghari-Ratcliffe – a dual-national falsely accused of espionage – he undermined her story that she was only making a family visit in a clumsy statement to the House of Commons. Throughout his time as Foreign Secretary he refused to criticise Trump and as a consequence found himself making weird contortions on policy issues, from climate change to Iran. Johnson maintained strong links to the European Research Group of Eurosceptic rebels, who embraced him when he resigned his Cabinet post in protest at Theresa May's withdrawal agreement. While she struggled repeatedly to put together a parliamentary majority for her deal, Johnson began preparing the ground for yet another leadership campaign.

On 25 May 2019, Theresa May, having lost her third attempt to push her agreement through the House of Commons by 58 votes, finally accepted defeat, and announced that she would step down from the party leadership as soon as a successor (also to be Prime Minister) had been elected. Johnson immediately threw his hat into the ring. By 13 June, he had been joined by nine other contestants, when the first of five exhaustive ballots of Tory MPs for the party leadership was held. The last of these resulted in Johnson leading Jeremy Hunt by 160 to 77 votes, with Gove narrowly behind on 75. The contest then went to Conservative Party members in the country, who voted by 2 to 1 for Johnson.

Leadership election results

MPs' vote

Candidate	First ballot: 13 June 2019		Second ballot: 18 June 2019		Third ballot: 19 June 2019		Fourth ballot: 20 June 2019		Fifth ballot: 20 June 2019	
	Votes	%	Votes	%	Votes	%	Votes	%	Votes	%
Boris Johnson	**114**	**36.4**	**126**	**40.3**	**143**	**45.7**	**157**	**50.2**	**160**	**51.1**
Jeremy Hunt	43	13.7	46	14.7	54	17.3	59	18.8	77	24.6
Michael Gove	37	11.8	41	13.1	51	16.3	61	19.5	75	24.0
Sajid Javid	23	7.3	33	10.5	38	12.1	34	10.9	Eliminated	
Rory Stewart	19	6.1	37	11.8	27	8.6	Eliminated			
Dominic Raab	27	8.6	30	9.6	Eliminated					
Matt Hancock	20	6.4	Withdrew							
Andrea Leadsom	11	3.5	Eliminated							
Mark Harper	10	3.2	Eliminated							
Esther McVey	9	2.9	Eliminated							
Spoilt ballots	0	0.0	0	0.0	0	0.0	2	0.6	1	0.3
	313	100.0	313	100.0	313	100.0	313	100.0	313	100.0

Members' vote

Candidate	Members' vote	
	Votes	%
Boris Johnson	**92,153**	**66.4**
Jeremy Hunt	46,656	33.6
Spoilt ballots	509	0.4
Turnout	139,318	87.4

As Johnson led by a wide margin in each of the first three MPs' ballots, the main interest was in who would come second to him in the next ballot and thereby qualify to oppose him as one of the two candidates in a 'runoff ballot' of party members in the country: Jeremy Hunt in the lead, with Michael Gove close behind. In the fourth ballot, Gove crept ahead, leading

314 Boris Johnson

Hunt by two votes. This alarmed the Johnson camp, as Gove's reputation as an unconditional supporter of Brexit made him highly popular among the rank and file of the party. It was an open secret that a cluster of Johnson's most faithful supporters were tipped off to switch their votes to the less-popular Hunt in the fourth ballot. This they did, enabling Hunt to regain his narrow lead and qualify for the party members' ballot on 20 June.

On the next day Johnson's prospects were threatened by a major change in his personal life. In the weeks preceding the leadership election it became widely known that Boris, whose wife Marina had sued him for divorce, had started a new relationship with Carrie Symonds. He had known her since 2012 when he was campaigning for the mayoralty and she was seconded by Conservative Party Central Office to join the campaign (she had joined the Conservative Party staff as a press officer in 2009, rising to become Director of Communications).

At the outset of the campaign for party members their relationship led to a deeply embarrassing episode during which Johnson and Symonds were overheard having a violent shouting match at the south London flat where she lived. Neighbours complained to the police, fearing for her safety after she had screamed to him "get out of my flat!" and "get off me!", complaining that he had spilt red wine over her sofa. The police called at the flat and were reassured by the couple that nothing untoward had happened, but the story was over all the newspapers, particularly *The Guardian*, on the following morning. Johnson's spokesman attacked the neighbour, claiming that he was a Labour Party activist who was out to cause trouble. Johnson survived this unfortunate prelude to his campaign, but news of Johnson's affair dominated press reports and it was soon revealed that Symonds was pregnant and had become engaged to Johnson. In spite of the *Sturm und Drang* about Symonds, Johnson won a decisive 2-1 victory over Hunt in the party members' ballot.

On 24 July 2019, the day following his victory in the ballot, Johnson was summoned by the Queen, who invited him to form a government, which he rapidly proceeded to do, dropping no fewer than 17 members from the existing Cabinet, the largest number ever when a new Prime Minister replaced a predecessor from the same party. The major posts in the new government went to Sajid Javid as Chancellor of the Exchequer, Dominic Raab as Foreign Secretary, Priti Patel as Home Secretary, and Michael Gove as Chancellor of the Duchy of Lancaster, with responsibility for carrying out the legislation to achieve Brexit. Jeremy Hunt, the runner-up in the leadership election, had assumed that he would continue as Foreign Secretary, but angrily declined to accept demotion to the post of Defence Secretary, and retired instead to the back benches, though he was later elected as Chairman of the Select Committee on the Health Service, for which he had been responsible under both Cameron and May for almost six years. Perhaps more significant than any of the Cabinet appointments, Dominic Cummings, the chief strategist of the Leave campaign in the 1916 referendum, was installed in 10 Downing Street as chief adviser to the Prime Minister. A former adviser to Iain Duncan Smith, and for much longer to Michael Gove, Cummings had achieved great notoriety for his insistence on having his own way, and the utter disdain with which he treated supporters and rivals alike, earning himself the epithet of 'career psychopath' from David Cameron.

Virtually the only Cabinet members who enjoyed any significant degree of independence were Javid and Amber Rudd, who retained her post as Work and Pensions Secretary. Neither remained in the government for very long. On 7 September 2019 Rudd resigned from her post, and from the Conservative Party, against Johnson's action in withdrawing the party whip from 21 MPs who had voted in favour of a procedural motion brought by the opposition. These included two former Chancellors of the Exchequer and Winston

Churchill's son-in-law, Nicholas Soames. Sajid Javid resigned as Chancellor two months later, when Johnson demanded that he should sack all his economic advisers and share the services of his own team. Javid told the press that "no self-respecting minister would accept those terms", and was replaced by the Chief Secretary of the Treasury, Rishi Sunak, a man of Indian origin replacing a man of Pakistani origin. The remaining new members of the Cabinet did not include anyone of obvious distinction, and included several who had been sacked, or resigned, from previous governments, following scandals, not all of a minor nature. These included Gavin Williamson, Priti Patel, Grant Shapps and Theresa Villiers.

With the defection of former junior minister Philip Lee to the LibDems on 3 September 2019, Johnson lost his working majority in the Commons, and on the same day put himself into a much clearer minority by withdrawing the whip from 21 Tory MPs. This meant that he lost control of the parliamentary timetable, thanks also to a series of controversial rulings by the Speaker, John Bercow. Johnson's 'purge' constituted a major clear-out of the more 'liberal' Tory MPs. It was a clear sign that Johnson would tolerate no opposition from within the party to his determination to leave the EU whatever the cost. On 5 September 2019 Boris suffered a further loss, when his youngest brother, Jo Johnson, a Tory MP and middle-ranking minister, a convinced Remainer, announced his resignation, both as minister and MP, saying, "In recent weeks I have been torn between family loyalty and the national interest. It's been an unresolvable tension."

Having lost his parliamentary majority, Johnson moved quickly to forestall, or at least postpone, the prospect of further parliamentary defeats. He advised the Queen to prorogue Parliament for the unprecedented period of more than a month, instead of the normal break of just a few days between parliamentary sessions. This was immediately challenged in three court actions, which arrived before the Supreme Court on 24 September 2019. The Court ruled that, in effect, Johnson had "lied to the Queen" on the purpose of the prorogation, which it declared would have had "the effect of frustrating or preventing the constitutional role of Parliament in holding the government to account". The attempted prorogation, it ruled, was unlawful, and, therefore, void. The following day Parliament returned and amended its records to show that it had been "adjourned" and not "prorogued". Johnson received a very poor press for his actions, and suggestions were even made for his impeachment. But the general public seemed hardly bothered about the matter either way. Johnson calmly proceeded to ask the Queen for a 'normal' prorogation from 8 October until the State Opening on 14 October.

Meanwhile, on 17 October, the government unexpectedly agreed with the EU the terms of a withdrawal agreement. This followed a meeting between Johnson and the Irish Taoiseach Leo Varadkar, at which Johnson had conceded that there should be a border between Britain and Ireland running through the Irish Sea, leaving the UK province of Northern Ireland in both the EU Single Market and the UK Single Market, subject to some form of EU controls on trade with mainland Britain. Characteristically, Johnson vehemently denied that he had agreed to any such thing, but it was clear that he had, and the withdrawal agreement was submitted to Parliament on 19 October, when it was amended, against the will of the government, by 322 votes to 306, withholding approval until legislation implementing the deal was passed, and forcing a delay to Brexit until 31 January 2020. Johnson realised that the only way he could escape from his dilemma and hope to regain control of Parliament was to force an early general election. But this course seemed blocked by the Fixed Term Parliament Act, which apparently gave the opposition a veto over the choice of an earlier date for the poll.

316 Boris Johnson

Boris was rescued from this dilemma by gross errors of judgement by the leaders of two of the main opposition parties, Labour and the Liberal Democrats. Both parties were opposed to the government's policies, particularly over Brexit, and so long as Johnson was unable to call a general election were well placed to force a compromise solution through the House of Commons. This would probably have taken the form of a second referendum, for which there was much public support, and which repeated opinion polls had indicated would most likely have produced a majority for Remain. But the LibDems were avid for a general election, which they wrongly believed would secure them many gains, while Jeremy Corbyn, backed by a minority of his MPs whose constituencies were believed to be pro-Brexit, was opposed to a second referendum. Although Johnson lost his attempt to secure an election under the Fixed Term Parliament Act, he found another procedure which required only a simple majority. The opposition could easily have blocked this, but in a wanton spirit of kamikaze, the majority of opposition MPs voted for their own election failure in a Commons vote of 438 to 20.

Election day was set for 12 December 2019. There was little doubt about the result of the campaign. No fewer than 12 polling companies published predictions, nearly all of whom put the Tories approximately 11 per cent ahead of Labour, with the Liberal Democrats trailing Labour by about 12 per cent. The major issues of the campaign were whether – as the Tory election manifesto said – 'To get Brexit done', and the relative appeal of the two party leaders, Boris Johnson and Jeremy Corbyn. Both were controversial figures but Corbyn proved himself to be far more unpopular than his opponent. Whereas Johnson's personal ratings at the end of the campaign were 41 per cent approve/51 per cent disapprove, the figures for Corbyn were 21 per cent approve/71 per cent disapprove. Whereas Leave voters disproportionately supported the Tories, the same was not true of Remainers, who divided their votes between Labour, LibDem and moderate Tory candidates. It was highly significant that the Conservatives captured 48 Labour seats, almost all in the so-called 'Red Wall' of Wales, the Midlands and the North, previously thought safe Labour seats. Labour gained only one seat from the Conservatives, in Putney where the Tories had deselected former minister Justine Greening as their candidate. It is clear that Corbyn proved far more of a disadvantage to Labour than Johnson to the Tories.

Among the Red Wall constituencies that the Tories scooped up were Tony Blair's former constituency of Sedgefield and Dennis Skinner's notorious seat of Bolsover in the former Durham mining area, as well as seats in the West Midlands, including two in Wolverhampton and all three of the Stoke-on-Trent constituencies. A consequence of this was a significant shift of constituency pressure within the Conservative Party as it had acquired a new phalanx of voters in favour of redistribution of wealth, and of backbench MPs strongly pushing for what Johnson himself described as 'levelling up' policies.

The first goal that Johnson set himself was leaving the European Union, which he accomplished on 31 January 2020, 43 years after Britain first joined. The terms of the deal he negotiated were far more 'Britain outside the EU' than the compromises Theresa May had sought.

It was not surprising that having won the election and delivered on Brexit, Johnson was in a state of euphoria. Everything seemed possible to him. He became engaged to Carrie and announced that she would have their baby by the early summer. It was at this moment that the threat of COVID-19, hitherto of concern only to a small group of scientific experts, became the central issue in British politics – but it took Johnson a while to realise it. He missed the first five meetings of COBRA, the government's disaster advisory group, and it was only on 20

March 2020 that he instituted a series of daily press conferences at which he himself appeared, flanked by Chris Whitty, the chief medical officer, and Sir Patrick Vallance, the government's chief scientific adviser, as well as a revolving cast of other advisers. The conferences were broadcast live on television. Earlier press reports about strict lockdowns being imposed in Italy had provoked derisory comments, but now the government's experts were arguing that the UK itself was only a couple of weeks behind Italy in the advance of the pandemic, and that similar lockdown measures were vital in the UK.

From then on increasingly more alarming statements emerged from SAGE, the government's scientific advisory group, including an estimate that 500,000 people would die if the virus was left unchecked. But for two weeks the government dithered and refused to follow the example of other European and Asian countries by ordering a lockdown. Eventually, on 23 March, people were required to stay at home and not go to work unless it was impossible for them to carry out their duties from home. It has been estimated by the Resolution Foundation think tank that this delay could have cost as many as 27,000 lives.

On 27 March Boris Johnson revealed that he himself had tested positive and was suffering from 'mild symptoms' of Covid. The symptoms got worse and on 5 April he was taken to St Thomas' Hospital across the river from Westminster. A day later he was transferred to intensive care and serious doubts emerged that he would survive the infection. The Foreign Secretary, Dominic Raab, took over the running of the government while Johnson's life was in the balance. But on 9 April Johnson was moved back to a general ward and three days later he was released from hospital and sent to Chequers to convalesce. On 29 April, his and Carrie's son was born and he was named after Boris's grandfather, Wilfred, who was universally known as Johnny (so his actual name was not generally known). On 6 May the UK death toll was announced as being the highest in Europe and economists estimated that the economic damage to the country was the worst in the OECD. The grim statistics were attributed to delays in locking down, mistakes with testing, and sourcing of personal protective equipment for medical staff. A shaken country was relieved that Johnson had survived, but the days of euphoria had well and truly passed.

During the first lockdown daily deaths fell in May and June and stayed at low levels during the summer, which encouraged the government to ease lockdown gradually and urge people to return to pubs and restaurants to begin to limit the economic damage. In September schools were opened as normal. But during the course of that month the numbers of serious infections rose again to dangerous levels. Once again Johnson dithered, fearing backbench opposition to further lockdowns, even as the government identified a new and more deadly variant of the virus, that originated in Kent. Although the government experimented with a complicated tiering system for different areas, it was not until after Christmas that the UK was ordered into another lockdown. The second wave of infections once again threatened to overwhelm the National Health Service and the overall death toll grew to 125,000.

Dominic Cummings's role in reinforcing Johnson's determination that only the hardest form of Brexit should emerge from the final negotiations with the EU was probably decisive, not least in stiffening Boris's resolve on a number of occasions. Cummings established a virtual rule of terror in Downing Street, with eminent civil servants, Cabinet ministers and special advisers forced to give way in humiliating circumstances. His list of casualties included a Chancellor of the Exchequer, a Cabinet Secretary and the Permanent Secretaries of several of the great offices of state. Perhaps the most dramatic incident was when he fired Sonia Kahn, Sajid Javid's special adviser, over an alleged leak and asked armed police officers to escort

318 Boris Johnson

her from Downing Street. She later won substantial damages in a court action for wrongful dismissal.

Cummings's dominance came to typify the revolutionary nature and seeming hypocrisy of Johnson's Downing Street. A few days after the country went into lockdown – and people were prohibited from leaving their homes even to go to their parents' funerals – Cummings drove 260 miles across the country with his wife and infant son, although they were all suffering from Covid-style symptoms. After it was revealed by the press that Cummings had again broken lockdown rules to drive from his parents' farm in County Durham to the picturesque tourist attraction of Barnard Castle, Johnson still refused to discipline him. Cummings organised a press conference in the rose garden of 10 Downing Street in May 2020 to justify himself. Johnson's reliance on Cummings was so great that he faced down demands from many of his MPs to sack his adviser for several months. But eventually even Cummings overreached and was summarily dismissed in November 2020, just days before the hard Brexit divorce deal he had done so much to engineer came into force.

Although Johnson insisted that it was far too early to assess Britain's response to the Covid pandemic in comparison to other countries, the press lost no time in doing this, showing that not only in Asia – where apart from in China, countries such as Taiwan and South Korea were lauded as having done everything to diminish the impact of the pandemic – but even within Europe, the UK was judged to have performed badly, particularly in relation to Germany, and on the basis of the number of deaths per million people had a worse outcome than countries like Italy, Spain and France. Johnson found it difficult to defend this record in Parliament, where the forensic questioning by the new opposition leader Keir Starmer regularly caught him on the back foot. Johnson made no serious attempt to answer Starmer's questions and resorted instead to ill-tempered bluster. Nor did he make any friends with the newly departed EU. A series of petty insults were delivered, including denying the newly appointed head of the EU delegation the status of ambassador. But the adverse reactions to the government were reversed in February and March 2021 with the news of the development of a UK-based vaccine and the successful programme of rolling out vaccines to the population, which coincided with perceived shortcomings in the EU's own efforts. By April 2021, the UK had inoculated over 60 per cent of its adult population at a time when most EU member states had achieved less than 25 per cent; although by the end of the summer of 2021 many EU member states were catching up or even overtaking the UK performance. In the long run, then, the damage done to the government's reputation over its delayed handling of the Covid crisis may not stick and it is too soon to attempt to predict its impact on the result of the next general election, due at the latest in 2024.

But how about the Johnson government's reputation after all the other pitfalls of his first two years? Johnson has made himself into a commanding presence after driving leading big beasts out of the party and surrounding himself with a Cabinet and advisers of little repute. He has shown a willingness to boost a nationalist United Kingdom (with English nationalism growing hand-in-hand with sectarian instincts in other part of the Union). He is a deeply ambitious man ('world king') who has played up his personality as a buffoon, appealing to millions in the UK (and less so to the world at large) as a larger-than-life personality and funny, rumbustious performer in the House of Commons. His charisma touches voters in the Conservative shires but many more in the more conservative working class. His carefully contrived exaggeratedly-tousled blond hair, perhaps a little thinner after a period in office, his deliberately scruffy appearance, his regular marital and extra-marital affairs, all have critical appeal to people looking for a swashbuckling English hero. His deserved reputation as an incorrigible and unrepentant liar to suit his convenience, his Trumpism, his extraordinary ability to avoid any accountability for his decisions, merely seem to strengthen this appeal. By contrast, his appeal to his own Tory parliamentary party derives less from any confidence in his qualities than from his ability to win elections.

Through Brexit, Johnson has already driven, for good or ill, a major change in the UK's position in the global world. Early consequences are not favourable: indeed it is widely thought that he was dismayed when the result of the referendum was announced, with few if any plans to implement it. Was it just a bit of populist opportunism or mischief-making, like his time in Brussels for the *Daily Telegraph*, or getting his own back on his rival Cameron who beat him to the top post? As well as his conscious buffoonery, Johnson is no fool. But a statesman? Unlikely.

What will his legacy be? Leaving the European Union? The tragic failures of his initial Covid response? His ability to call upon vaccines to accelerate the UK's recovery? Or the reinvention of the Conservative Party as the party of working-class voters in the north of England? Much will depend on his and his government's performance over the next three years. But perhaps even more important may be how effective Keir Starmer proves to be in stimulating and sustaining opposition. The jury is out.

Works consulted

Tom Bower, 2020, *Boris Johnson: The Gambler*, London, W.H. Allen.
Ian Brunskill (ed.), 2015, *The Times Guide to the House of Commons 2015*, London, Times Books.
Ian Brunskill (ed.), 2017, *The Times Guide to the House of Commons 2017*, London, Times Books.
Ian Brunskill (ed.), 2020, *The Times Guide to the House of Commons 2019*, London, Times Books.
David Cameron, 2019, *For the Record*, London, William Collins.
Andrew Gimson, 2016, first published 2012, *Boris: The Making of the Prime Minister*, London, Simon & Schuster.
Boris Johnson, 2002, *Friends, Voters, Countryman*, London, HarperCollins.
Boris Johnson, 2015, *The Churchill Factor: How One Man Made History*, London, Hodder Paperbacks.
Rachel Johnson, 2020, *Rake's Progress: My Political Midlife Crisis*, London, Simon & Schuster.
Dennis Kavanagh and Philip Cowley, 2018, *The British General Election of 2017*, Basingstoke, Palgrave Macmillan.
Sonia Purnell, 2012, *Just Boris: A Tale of Blond Ambition*, London, Aurum.
Tim Shipman, 2016, *All Out War*, London, William Collins.
Tim Shipman, 2017, *Fall Out: A Year of Political Mayhem*, London, William Collins.

INDEX

Note: Page spans in **bold** indicate the main chapter for the particular Prime Minister indexed.

Abbott, Edwin 28
abdication crisis 75, 102
abortion law reform 169–70
Abyssinia 75, 96, 127
Addison, Christopher 51
Afghanistan 240
Ahern, Bertie 236, 237
Aitken, Max *see* Beaverbrook, Lord
Alanbrooke, Lord 108
Alexander, A.V. 104
Alexander, General Harold 139, 140
Alexander, King of Yugoslavia 126
Allen, Sir Hugh 175
Amato, Giuliano 222
Amery, Julian 140
Amery, Leo 105
Anderson, W.C. 81
Andros 90–2
Anglo-French Entente 13
Anglo-German alliance 14
Anglo-Japanese Treaty 13
anti-terrorism 210
appeasement 96, 97, 99, 103, 110, 110, 116, 117,
    127, 128, 129, 138, 142, 150, 151, 174, 175
Arcuri, Jennifer 311
Argyll, Duke of 76
Armstrong, Sir William 185
Ashdown, Paddy 234, 254
Asquith, Herbert Henry 1, 2, 3, 4, 13, 15, 16, 22,
    23, 24, 25, 26, **27–39**, 43–4, 45, 46, 47, 48, 49,
    50, 51, 53, 55, 59, 60, 61, 66, 69, 71, 82, 83, 102,
    103, 146
Asquith, Joseph Dixon 28
Asquith, Margot 15, 28, 30, 31, 33

Asquith, Raymond 37
Asquith, Violet 33, 61, 102
Atholl, Duchess of 150
Atlantic Charter 109
atomic bomb, British 118
Attatürk, Kemal 52
Attlee, Clement 1, 2, 3, 4, 16, 39, 45, 53–4, 70,
    103, 104, 105, 108, 109, **112–23**, 129, 140, 158,
    161–2, 163, 166, 189, 213, 234, 243
Attlee, Ellen 112
Attlee, Henry 112
Attlee, Tom 112–14, 123
austerity policies 273, 274–5, 278–9, 283, 292,
    297
Austria 96, 140
Aznar, José Maria 237

Back to Basics 223
Bagehot, Walter 207
Balance of Payments 120, 122, 165, 166, 167, 169,
    179, 194
Baldwin, Alfred 64–6, 71
Baldwin, George 64
Baldwin, Gladys Mary *see* Wilson, Mary
Baldwin, Louisa 64, 65
Baldwin, Stanley 2, 4, 14, 53, 62, 63, **64–75**, 82,
    85, 86, 87, 93, 94, 95, 96, 99, 102, 126–7, 159,
    213, 246
Balfour, Arthur James 1, 2, 4, **6–15**, 23, 24, 25, 29,
    32, 34, 37, 43, 44, 45, 48, 57, 58, 69–70, 72, 89,
    91, 93, 124, 226
Balfour, Lady Blanche 6
Balfour Declaration 14
Balfour of Burleigh, Lord 11

Balfour, James Maitland 6
Ball, Abraham Thomas *see* Major, Tom
Ballot Act (1872) 41
Balls, Ed 250, 251, 252, 254, 255, 256, 258
Bank of England 69, 85, 120, 165, 211, 219, 222, 234, 251, 287
Bannerman, Henry 18
Bannerman, Janet 16–17
Barber, Anthony 180, 182, 192
Barnes, George 80
Barnett, Correlli 118, 119
Bastianini, Giuseppe 105
Battle of Britain 95, 107
Beauchamp, Lord 36
Beaverbrook, Lord 38, 48, 58, 61, 63, 68, 73, 94, 139
Beck, Colonel 151
Beckett, Beatrice 125, 129
Beckett, Sir Gervase 125
Beckett, Margaret 231, 232, 254
Belgium 36, 43, 46, 60, 103, 104
Bell, Richard 79
Beneš, Edvard 97
Benn, Tony 152–3, 170, 171, 193
Berlin, Congress of 9
Berlusconi, Silvio 237
Bernstein, Eduard 78, 81
Bevan, Aneurin 2, 45, 115–17, 118, 119, 121–2, 141, 143–4, 161–4, 170, 189–90, 193, 287
Beveridge Report 119, 160
Beveridge, Sir William 119, 159, 160
Bevin, Ernest 2, 104, 108, 116, 117, 118–19, 121, 162, 174, 186
Biffen, John 204, 205, 307
Birch, Nigel 142, 145
Birkenhead, Lord 45, 95
Birmingham City Council 91, 96
Birrell, Augustine 17, 19
Bismarck, Otto von 45
Black, Conrad 233, 308
Black Wednesday 222, 225, 233–4, 266
Blair, James 227
Blair, Leo 227, 228, 229
Blair, Mary 227
Blair, Sarah 228
Blair, Tony 1, 2, 3, 4, 39, 82, 158, 165, 181, 187, 213, 225, **227–43**, 248, 249–50, 252, 253–4, 257, 260, 266, 267, 269, 271, 272, 274, 277, 288, 289, 290, 299, 308, 311, 316
Blair, William 227
Blake, Robert 55, 61, 135
Blix, Hans 241
Blunkett, David 234, 240, 249, 253
Boer War 10, 11, 13, 21, 25, 26, 31, 43, 46, 57, 79
Bonar Law *see* Law, Andrew Bonar
Bonham Carter, Lady Violet *see* Asquith, Violet
Bonnet, Georges 97

Booth, Cherie 229–30, 241
Booth, Gale 230
Booth, John Wilkes 230
Booth, Lyndsey 230
Booth, Tony 229–30
Boothby, Robert 137–8
Bossom, Sir Alfred 200
Botha, General 25
Bottomley, Horatio 77
Bourke, Frederick 30
Boyle, Sir Edward 132, 154
Bradlaugh, Charles 29
Bramall, Ashley 176
Brasier, Hubert 285, 286, 287
Brasier, Zaidee 285, 287
Bretton Woods agreement 180
Brexit 270, 277–8, 281–3, 291, 293–4, 296–7, 298–301, 312, 314, 315–16, 317, 318, 319
Brexit Party 300
British Union of Fascists 85
Brittan, Leon 205, 209
Bromberger, Serge and Merry 133
Brooks, Rebekah 276
Brown, Andrew 244
Brown, Fraser 253
Brown, George 119, 164, 165, 166, 167, 168, 190
Brown, Gordon 1, 2, 64, 164, 165, 166, 168, 190, 230, 231–2, 233, 234, 235, 237, 241–2, **244–61**, 269, 272, 273, 274, 275, 279, 290
Brown, Jane 253
Brown, Jessie Elizabeth 244
Brown, John 253
Brown, Rev. John Ebenezer 244, 245
Brown, John Souter 244, 245
Brown, Sarah 253
Bruce, Charlotte 18
Buchan-Hepburn, Patrick 177
Burma 115, 129
Burne-Jones, Edward 65
Burns, John 36, 46
Bush, George W. 240, 242–3
Bush, Laura 240
Butler, David 117
Butler, R.A. 2, 96, 103, 129, 130, 132, 133, 140, 141, 142, 145, 146, 153–4, 156, 176, 178, 192, 201
Butler, (Lord) Robin 241

Cairncross, Sir Alec 165
Callaghan, Charlotte 186
Callaghan, Dorothy 186
Callaghan, James 2, 4, 5, 164, 164, 165, 166, 167, 169, 170, 171, 178, **186–97**, 201, 203, 247, 251
Callaghan, James Snr (Gargohan) 186
Callaghan, Margaret *see* Jay, Baroness
Cambridge University 2, 6, 7, 8, 17, 18, 21, 64, 65, 90, 135, 145, 229

322 Index

Cambridge, Duke of 18, 21
Cameron, David 2, 255, 258, 259, 260, **262–84**, 285, 288, 289, 290, 292, 293, 294, 295, 296, 303, 305, 306, 310, 311, 312, 314, 319
Cameron, Ivan 268
Cameron, Mary 262
Cameron, Samantha 266–7, 269
Campbell affair 72, 83
Campbell, Alastair 233, 234, 239, 252, 257
Campbell-Bannerman, Sir Henry 2, 4, 12, **16–26**, 31–2, 33, 43, 56, 70, 244
Campbell, Sir James 16–17
Campbell, James Alexander 18
Campbell, John 83, 175–6, 198–9
Campbell, William 17
capital punishment 169
Cardwell, Edward 18–19, 20
Carlisle, Mark 205
Carlton Club 53, 59, 68, 93
Carr, Robert 180, 181–2
Carrington, Lord 180, 183, 203, 204, 205, 206
Carson, Sir Edward 35, 38, 48, 60
Carter, Jimmy 194
Castle, Barbara 168, 171, 181, 191, 193
Cavendish, Lady Dorothy 136
Cavendish, Lord Frederick 9, 30
Cecil, Lord Hugh 92
Central Policy Review Staff 185
Chamberlain, Austen 2, 16, 45, 52, 53, 58, 59, 60, 62, 67, 72, 73, 89, 90, 91, 92, 93, 95, 96, 125, 128
Chamberlain, Beatrice 89
Chamberlain, Caroline 89
Chamberlain, Clara 89–90
Chamberlain, Dorothy 91
Chamberlain, Ethel 90
Chamberlain, Frank 91
Chamberlain, Hilda 90, 93
Chamberlain, Ida 90, 93
Chamberlain, Ivy 96
Chamberlain, Joseph 2, 10, 21, 23, 43, 59, 66
Chamberlain, Neville 4, 73, 74, 86, 87, **89–100**, 150, 157, 174
Chamberlain, Norman 96
Chanak crisis 68
Charmley, John 110, 118
Cheney, Dick 240
Chinese 'slave labour' 12, 24
Chirac, Jacques 237
Church Times 176
Churchill, Clarissa 129
Churchill, Clementine 110
Churchill, Lord Randolph 9, 10, 101, 128
Churchill, Winston 1, 2, 3, 4, 6, 13, 23, 32, 33, 34, 36, 45, 46, 47, 52, 57, 69, 72, 74, 75, 87, 92, 99, **101–11**, 112, 116, 117, 118,

119, 121, 122, 128–30, 137, 138–9, 140, 141, 142, 150, 151, 199, 207, 212, 246, 262, 315
Citizens' Charter 220
civil liberties 210
Clark, Colin 136
Clarke, Charles 257
Clark, Kenneth 2, 221, 223, 225, 233, 234, 239, 250, 266, 268, 269, 270, 292
Clark, William 131, 132
Clause Four 232
Clegg, Nick 260, 272, 273, 275, 276, 277, 280, 281, 292
Clemenceau, Georges 50, 51, 52
Clinton, Bill 232, 233, 236, 240, 246
Clynes, J.R., 82, 115
coalition government (2010–15) 260, 272–9, 281, 288, 290, 291, 292, 293, 297, 310
Cole, Anne de Vere 91
Collins, Michael 51
Committee of Imperial Defence 13
Commonwealth Immigration Act (1968) 191
Commonwealth preference *see* tariff reform
comprehensive schools 169, 202
Connolly, Cyril 148–9, 157
Constantinople 52
Cook, Robin 231, 234, 240
Cooper, Alfred Duff 99, 262
Corbyn, Jeremy 282, 296, 297, 298, 301, 316
cordite scandal 21, 31
Corrupt Practices Act (1883) 29
Corscaden, Hazel 227
Cote, G.D.H. 136, 159
Coulson, Andy 276
council housing 209
council tax 220
Couve de Murville, Maurice 144
COVID-19 316–17, 318, 319
Crewe, Lord 32, 36, 45
Crick, Sir Bernard 198
Cripps, Sir Stafford 2, 82, 115, 117, 118, 119, 120, 121, 160–1
Crosland, Tony 2, 120, 164, 166, 167, 175, 190, 193, 194, 251
Crossman, Richard 4, 162
Cummings, Dominic 312, 314, 317–18
Curragh mutiny 36
Currie, Edwina 224
Curzon, Lord 35, 45, 49, 52, 53, 61, 62, 63, 68, 69–70, 72
Cyprus 152, 192
Czechoslovakia 96–8

Daily Mail 46, 48, 73, 83, 227, 233, 254, 263, 270, 292, 309
Daily Mirror 152, 221

Daily Telegraph 130, 223, 233, 254, 258, 272, 305, 307, 312, 319
Daladier, Edouard 97, 98
Dalton, Hugh 104, 105, 114, 115, 118, 119, 120, 160, 161, 162–3
Dalyell, Tam 206
Damaskinos, Archbishop 139
Dardanelles 37, 47, 52, 61
Darwin, Charles 80
Davidson, John 69
Davis, David 269–71, 274, 296, 297, 298, 299–300
Dayan, Moshe 133
decolonisation 118, 142, 146, 152
De Gaulle, Charles 107, 139, 144–5, 168, 177
Dehaene, Jean-Luc 223
Devaluation (1949) 161
Devaluation (1967) 165, 167, 190, 215, 222
Devonshire, 8th Duke of 10, 11
Devonshire, 9th Duke of 136
Dickens, Sir Henry 113
Dilhorne, Lord Chancellor 153, 154
disarmament 81, 83, 84, 87, 126, 163, 240
Disraeli, Benjamin, Lord Beaconsfield 9, 19, 59, 146, 225, 246
divorce reform 169
Dixon, Sir Pierson 129
Dobson, Frank 236
Donoughue, Bernard 197
Donovan, Lord Justice 168, 169
Douglas-Home, Sir Alec 2, 4, 13, 98, 103, **148–57**, 159, 165, 178, 180, 244
Du Cann, Edward 178, 184, 203
Dulles, John Foster 131
Duma 26
Duncan Smith, Ian 212, 268, 269, 288, 289, 309, 314
Dunkirk 105–6

East London Ethical Society 77
East of Suez 167
Ecclestone, Bernie 238
Economic and Monetary Union (EMU) 221
Economist, The 29, 201, 265
Eden, Sir Anthony 2, 4, 75, 96, 99, 106, 110, **124–34**, 139, 141, 142, 150, 151, 152, 157, 158, 177, 184
Eden, Jack 124
Eden, Marjorie 125
Eden, Nicholas 125
Eden, Sybil 124
Eden, Sir William 124
Education Act (1902) 12–13, 24, 32, 43
Education Bill (1906) 23, 25
Edward VII 10, 24, 32, 34, 35, 44, 125
Edward VIII 102
Egypt 19, 107, 127, 129, 130–3, 142

Eighty Club 29
Eisenhower, Dwight 109, 110, 131, 132, 139, 141, 142–4
Elcho, Lady Mary 7–8
Elgin, Lord 32
Elizabeth II 262
Employers' Liability Bill (1893) 31
Endicott, Mary 89
Engels, Friedrich 80
Enghien, Duc D' 133
Eton School 6, 64, 124, 135, 143, 148, 149, 150, 153, 262, 263, 264, 267, 268, 304–5, 306, 311
Euro 223, 237, 239, 253
European Coal & Steel Community 176–7
European Exchange Rate Mechanism (ERM) 219, 222, 266
European Free Trade Association 144
European Union/Community 2, 3, 119, 133, 167–8, 185, 211, 212, 218, 220–1, 223, 224, 235, 237, 240, 242, 270, 274, 277, 281–2, 283, 290, 293, 295, 296, 298–300, 304, 307, 312, 315, 316, 317, 318, 319
Eurosceptics 221, 223, 224, 282
Exchange Rate Mechanism (ERM) 211, 219, 266
expenditure cuts 85, 259, 273, 274–5, 278–9, 283, 292, 297

Fabian Society 77, 78, 113, 136
Factory Bill (1893) 31
Falklands War 146, 206, 207, 208, 230
Farage, Nigel 281, 300, 312
Faulkner, Brian 181
Fawcett, Charlotte 304
Featherstone colliery 31
Feiling, Keith 90, 99–100
Fellowship of the New Life 77
Fettes school 228–9
Feversham, Lord 125
financial crisis (2008–9) 255, 258–60
Fit, Gerry 181
Fleming, Ian 133
Foot, Michael 170, 171, 191, 193, 195, 197, 208, 209
Foundation hospitals 239, 242
Fourth Party 9
France, fall of 175
Franz Ferdinand, Archduke 36
Freedom of Information Act 236
Freeman, John 122, 162
free trade 11, 23, 45, 51, 58, 73, 87, 94, 144, 299–300
Friedman, Milton 202
Fry, Christopher 204

Gaitskell, Hugh 2, 118, 121–2, 130, 143, 144, 152, 160, 161, 162, 163–5, 166, 168, 189, 190, 201, 232

324 Index

Galba, Emperor 124
Gallipoli *see* Dardanelles
Galtieri, General Leopoldo 206
Geddes axe 51
General Belgrano 206
General elections: (1832) 225; (1868) 17; (1874)
    9, 19; (1885) 20; (1886) 42; (1892) 10, 30, 42;
    (1895) 24, 31, 42, 78, 79; (1900) 10–11, 12,
    22, 24, 57, 79; (1906) 12, 25, 58, 66, 79–80,
    110, 225, 226; (1910, Jan) 13, 35, 80–1; (1910,
    Dec) 13, 35, 58, 80–1; (1918) 50, 62, 67, 92,
    230, 239; (1922) 53, 82, 114–15, 125; (1923)
    73, 82, 93, 115; (1924) 39, 52, 72, 84, 93, 137,
    186; (1929) 14, 73, 84, 94, 125–6, 149–50, 170;
    (1931) 3, 74, 86, 94, 116, 126, 138; (1935) 74,
    116, 208; (1945) 88, 119, 148, 151, 188, 200,
    234; (1950) 120, 121, 151, 176, 200; (1951)
    110, 118, 120, 122, 129, 151, 162, 177, 183,
    189, 200, 201; (1955) 122; (1959) 143–4, 163,
    177, 200–1, 232; (1964) 165, 178, 190, 201;
    (1966) 166, 171, 179, 228; (1970) 156, 169,
    179, 192, 202; (1974, Feb) 156, 170, 181, 184,
    192, 216, 286; (1974, Oct) 202, 210, 216, 247;
    (1979) 197, 203, 208, 209, 216, 217, 230, 248;
    (1983) 207, 208, 209, 248; (1987) 209; (1992)
    221, 230–1, 232–3, 248–9, 251, 266, 279, 287,
    307; (1997) 209, 224, 225, 232, 233, 236, 237,
    239, 250, 251, 267, 271, 288, 308; (2001) 176,
    235, 239, 252, 253, 267–8, 288, 309; (2005)
    242, 253, 269, 289; (2010) 259–60, 263, 271–3,
    279–80, 289–90, 310–11; (2015) 274, 276, 277,
    279–82, 293, 311; (2017) 297–8; (2019) 300–1,
    316
General strike (1926) 71, 72
George I 1
George V 13, 35, 44, 45, 48, 53, 60, 68, 74, 84, 85,
    94
George, Mary Ellen 40
George, William Jnr 40, 54
George, William Snr 40–1
Gibbon, Edward 101
Gilbert, W.S. 142
Gilligan, Andrew 241
Gilmour, Ian 203, 204, 205
Gilmour, Sir John 149
Giraud, General 139
Giscard D'Estaing, Valéry 192, 194, 205
Gladstone, Herbert 21, 23
Gladstone, Margaret 78, 84
Gladstone William Ewart 6, 7, 9, 18, 19, 20, 27,
    29, 30, 70, 83, 89, 159, 238, 246
Glasgow University 17, 56
Glubb, General John 130
Goebbels, Josef 174
Goering, Hermann 174
gold standard 72, 85, 86
Good Friday agreement 236

Goodman, Lord 171
Gordon Walker, Patrick 166
Gorst, John 9
Gould, Philip 233, 271
Gove, Michael 269, 274, 282, 283, 292, 294, 296,
    297, 298, 312, 313–14
Grandi, Count Dino 128
Granita restaurant 231, 249
Great Western Railway 65
Greater London Authority 235
Greece 49, 52, 109, 139, 144, 275
Greenwood, Anthony 164
Greenwood, Arthur 104, 105, 115, 116
Grey, 2nd Earl 124
Grey, Sir Edward 13, 22, 24, 31, 32, 35, 36, 81,
    124
Griffith-Boscowen, Sir Arthur 68
Griffiths, Arthur 51
Griffiths, James 166
Gromyko, Andrei 152
Grove, Canon John 228
Guardian 4, 207, 257, 272, 276, 297, 307, 314
Guderian, General 105
Gulf War I 220

Hague, William 212, 236, 239, 268, 274, 288, 297
Haig, General Al 206
Haig, Sir Douglas 49
Haileybury House 114
Haileybury School 112, 113
Hailsham, Lord 132, 145, 152, 153, 154, 175, 178
Haldane, R.B. 22, 24, 29, 31, 32, 43
Halifax, Lord 96, 97–8, 99, 103, 104, 105–6, 107,
    128–9, 151
Hall, Viscount 189
Hamilton, Lord George 11
Hamilton, Mary Agnes 80
Hankey, Lord 49
Harcourt, Sir William 16, 20, 21, 22, 30, 31
Hardie, James Keir 26, 78, 79, 80, 81, 158
Hardy, Thomas 136
Harington, General 52
Harkess, James 216
Harrow School 64, 65, 101
Hartington, Lord *see* Devonshire, 8th Duke of
Hastings, Sir Patrick 83
Hatfield House 9, 10
Healey, Denis 164, 166, 170, 175, 193, 194, 195,
    197
Health and Social Care Bill (2011) 276
Heath, Edward 1, 2, 4, 7, 138, 144, 152, 153, 155,
    156, 158, 165, 168, 169, 170, 171, **173–85**, 191,
    192, 193, 200, 201, 202–3, 204, 205, 208–9,
    237
Heath, John 173, 175
Heath, William 173
Hegel, Friedrich 80

Henderson, Arthur 49, 80, 81–2, 84, 85, 86, 87, 115
Henlein, Konrad 96
Henley, Lady 33
Hennessy, Peter 3, 123, 130
Henry V 107
Herriot, Edouard 83
Hertford 9
Heseltine, Michael 2, 205, 209, 211, 212, 219, 220, 223, 224, 226, 306, 309
Hicks Beach, Sir Michael 9
Himmler, Heinrich 174
Hitler, Adolf 51, 96–8, 99, 102, 103, 105, 106, 107, 108, 127, 129, 130, 150, 151
Hoare-Laval Pact 74–5, 127, 138
Hoare, Sir Samuel 74–5, 104, 127
Hobhouse, Emily 22
Hogg, Quentin see Hailsham, Lord
Hogg, Sarah 222
Home Office 31, 125, 169, 191, 290, 291, 292
Home Rule Bill see Irish Home Rule
Home, 12th Earl of 148
Home, 13th Earl of 148, 150
Home, 14th Earl of see Douglas-Home, Sir Alec
homosexual law reform 169
Horder, Sir Thomas 63
Houghton, Douglas 187, 190
House of Lords 3, 13, 24, 25, 26, 30, 31, 32, 34, 39, 44, 54, 58, 68, 70, 103, 104, 122, 142, 151, 152, 156, 169, 187, 189, 207, 232, 236, 276, 309
housing 51, 93, 140, 141, 143, 209, 215–16, 217, 243
Howard, Michael 223, 231, 240, 266, 267, 269, 289, 309, 310
Howe, Sir Geoffrey 203, 204, 208, 211, 218
Howell, David 204
human rights 236, 240, 290, 291, 293
Hungarian Revolution 133
Hussein, King of Jordan 130
Hutton, Lord Justice 241

Imperial Conference 14, 115
incomes policy 181, 194–5
Independent Labour Party (ILP) 78, 79, 81, 82–3, 84, 113, 114, 115, 247
India 6, 24, 72, 73, 78, 92, 102, 103, 115, 118
inflation 122, 142, 143, 170, 180, 182, 183, 194, 195, 202, 204, 208, 210, 211, 218, 225, 232, 234, 235, 279
Ingham, Bernard 211, 257
Inland Revenue Staff Federation 187
Institute of Economic Affairs 202
International Monetary Fund 141, 192, 194, 260
Iraq 224, 227, 240–1, 242, 243, 253, 255, 272, 278, 309
Ireland, Chief Secretary for 9, 19

Irish Home Rule 9, 20, 23, 29, 30, 34, 35, 36, 42, 45, 57, 59–60, 89
Irish Party 9, 20, 30, 43
Irvine, Derry 229, 234
Irwin, Lord see Halifax, Lord
Isaacs, Sir Rufus 45, 46

Jacks, William 57, 60
Jagger, Mick 229
James I 148
James, Henry 136
James, Sir Henry 29
Jay, Baroness 187
Jay, Douglas 161, 164
Jay, Peter 192
Jebb, Sir Gladwyn 131
Jenkins, Peter 171
Jenkins, Roy 2, 29, 31, 33, 34, 38, 45, 55, 60, 69, 72, 74, 94, 95, 106, 107, 164, 166, 167, 169, 170, 175, 190, 192, 193, 234, 236, 306
Jerome, Jennie 101
Jewkes, John 160
Johnson, Boris 257, 264, 269, 282, 283, 292, 293, 294, 296, 297, 300, **303–19**
Johnson, Norma 216
Johnson, Stanley 303, 304
Johnson, Wilfred 303
Jones, George 4
Jones, Jack 195
Jones, Thomas 49, 71
Joseph, Sir Keith 184, 202
Jutland, battle of 125, 186

Keightley, Sir Charles 132
Kelly, Dr David 241
Kenrick, Florence 89
Kenrick, Harriet 89
Kerr, Sir John 222
Keynes, J.M. 51, 85, 95, 136, 138, 180, 185, 202
Khrushchev, Nikita 143
Kidston, Catherine 56
Kidston, Charles 56
Kidston, Elizabeth 55
Kidston, Janet 55–6
Kidston, Richard 56
Kidston, William 56
Kierans, Jean 215, 216
Kilmuir, Lord 140, 142, 145
Kinnock, Neil 209, 221, 230, 232, 233, 236, 248, 266, 279
Kinross by-election (1938) 150, 154
Kinross by-election (1963) 154
Kipling, Lockwood 65
Kipling, Rudyard 65, 73, 136, 199, 312
Kissinger, Henry 192
Kitchener, Lord 37, 47
Knox, Ronnie 135, 136

326 Index

Kohl, Helmut 221
Korean War 118, 121, 122, 162
Kosovo 238
Kreditanstalt 85
Kruger, Paul 22

Labour Electoral Association 77
Labour Representation Committee (LRC) 78–9
Lambton, Lady Lilian 148
Lamont, Norman 220, 223, 225, 266
Land Reform Acts 10
Lansbury, George 84, 87, 115, 116, 174
Lansdowne, 5th Marquis of 38, 44, 45, 48, 54, 60
Laski, Harold 109, 117, 187–8
Laval, Pierre 74, 75, 127, 138
Law, Andrew Bonar 4, 35, 37, 38, 48, 49, 50, 51, 52, 53, **55–63**, 67, 68, 69, 71, 82, 91, 93, 114
Law, John 60
Law, Mary 57, 58, 68
Law, Rev. James 55, 56, 60
Lawson, Daniel 17
Lawson, Dominic 218
Lawson, Nigel 204, 205, 208, 209, 210, 211, 217, 218, 219, 248
Lawson, Sir Wilfred 11
Leach, Sir Henry 206
League of Nations 83, 96, 116, 126, 127
Lee, Fred 190
Lend-Lease 120
Leopold III 107
Lever, Harold 193
Leveson inquiry 276–7
Lewin, Sir Terence 206
Lib-Lab pact (1903) 79
Lib-Lab pact (1977) 194, 195, 203
Libya 277
life peerages 146
Lilley, Peter 223
Lindsay, A.D. 138, 175
Lipton, Marcus 214
Liverpool, 2nd Earl of 6, 34, 210, 262
Lloyd, Elizabeth 40
Lloyd George, David 2, 3, 4, 13, 14, 22, 24, 25, 26, 31, 32, 33, 34, 36, 37–9, **40–54**, 55, 61, 62, 67, 68, 69, 71, 73, 81, 82, 83, 85, 92, 93, 103, 104, 114, 119, 137, 158, 213, 246, 274
Lloyd George Fund 52
Lloyd, John Selwyn 141
Lloyd, Richard 40
local government 9, 32, 36, 66, 91, 92, 93, 94, 140, 195, 198, 201, 210, 217, 242, 288
Locarno treaties 125–6, 127
London County Council 114, 116
London School of Economics 114, 117, 187, 229
Longford, Lord 138, 189
Long, Walter 45, 59
Lough, Thomas 77

Ludendorff, General 49
Lyttelton, Alfred 7
Lyttelton, Edward 7
Lyttelton, May 7
Lyttelton, Spencer 7

Maastricht treaty 221, 223, 225
MacArthur, General Douglas 118
Macaulay, T.B. 101
MacDonald, C.J. 30
MacDonald, David 80
MacDonald, James 76
MacDonald, James Ramsay 2, 4, 39, 71, 72, 73–4, **76–88**, 94, 95, 115, 126, 138, 150, 158, 171, 274
MacDonald, John 76
MacDonald, Malcolm 128
MacDonald, Rev. George Browne 65
Macintyre, Helen 310
Macleod, Iain 2, 146, 152, 153, 154, 156, 176, 177, 178, 180, 191, 202
Macmillan, Catherine 140
Macmillan, Daniel (brother of Harold Macmillan) 135, 136
Macmillan, Daniel (grandfather of Harold Macmillan) 135
Macmillan, Frederick 136
Macmillan, George 136
Macmillan, Harold 2, 4, 5, 130, 132, 133, **135–47**, 152, 153, 154, 155, 156, 158, 164–5, 177, 178, 184, 200, 213, 244
Macmillan, Maurice 135, 136
Macmillan, Nellie 135–6, 137
Macmillan, Sarah 137
Macmillan, Will 136
Macmurray, John 229
mad cow disease 224
Major, Elizabeth 216
Major, Gwen 213
Major, James 216
Major, John 2, 4, 12, 52, 118, 181, 211, 212, **213–26**, 232, 233, 248, 249, 250, 265–6, 267, 280
Major, Patricia 213
Major, Tom 213, 214
Makins, Sir Roger 141
Mandelson, Peter 230, 233, 233, 239, 248, 249, 250, 258
Marconi scandal 45–6
Marlborough, 1st Duke of 102
Marlborough, 7th Duke of 101
Marples, Ernest 141
Marshall Plan 120
Marx, Karl 77, 80, 151, 159, 229, 250, 253
Maudling, Reginald 152, 153, 154, 156, 165, 176, 177, 178, 180
Maurice debate 38, 49–50
Maurice, General Sir Frederick 49–50

Maxwell-Fyfe, Sir David 140
May Committee 85
May, Philip 286–7, 297
May, Theresa 2, 271, 274, 283, **285–302**, 312–13, 314, 316
McKenna, Reginald 32, 36, 47, 69
McNally, Tom 195
Melland, Helen 29
Mellish, Robert 169, 191
Mellor, David 224
Menzies, Robert 131
#Me Too movement 299
Meyer, Sir Anthony 211
Michael, Alun 236
Middleton, Sir Peter 219
Mikardo, Ian 188
Mikoyan, Anastas 160
Miliband, Ed 250, 251, 254, 255, 256, 275, 277, 278, 279, 280, 281, 292
Millar, Ronald 204
Miller, Edric 114
Miller, Violet 114
Milner, Lord 22, 49, 52
miners' strikes 170, 182, 208–9
Mitchell, Sir Derek 155
Mitchell, George 225, 236
Mitterrand, François 205
mixed economy 118, 120, 185, 201
Mollet, Guy 131, 132
Monckton, Sir Walter 132
monetarism 185, 204, 205
Monnet, Jean 106
Montagu, Edwin 14, 33, 37
Moore, John 217–18
Morgan, Rhodri 235–6, 296
Morley, John 3–4, 16, 22, 24, 28, 36, 46
Morris, William 113
Morrison, Herbert 104, 108, 115, 116, 117, 118, 119, 121, 122, 138, 139, 161, 162, 163, 188
Morrison, John 153
Mosley, Sir Oswald 85, 115, 138
Moss, Tom 214
Mostyn-Owen, Allegra 305–8, 311
Moulton, Audrey 187
Muirhead, Anthony 150
Munich Agreement 138, 174–5
Murdoch, Rupert 233, 238, 253, 276
Murphy, Robert 139
Mussolini, Benito 75, 96, 98, 105, 127, 128, 130, 139

Nanney, Ellis 42
Napoleon 133
Nasser, Abdul 130–1, 133
National Government (1931) 73–4, 85–7, 94, 115, 126, 150, 171, 210, 274

National Health Service 45, 119, 121–2, 161, 162, 167, 235, 242, 268, 276, 317
national insurance 34, 45, 53–4, 114, 119, 201, 251
nationalisation 65, 120, 130, 138, 160, 163, 181, 182, 188, 259, 271
naval disarmament 84
Nazi-Soviet Pact 99, 175
Neave, Airey 203
New Party 138
News Chronicle 117
News of the World 276–7
Nigeria 215
Norman, Montagu 69
North, Lord 130
Northcliffe, Lord 38, 48, 92
Northcote, Sir Stafford 9
Northern Ireland 2, 35, 36, 60, 181, 191, 205, 216, 232–3, 234, 236, 237, 254, 282, 283, 297, 299, 315
Norwegian campaign 99, 103
Nott, John 204, 205
nuclear weapons 118, 143, 144, 146, 163, 276
Nutting, Anthony 130, 132

Obama, Barack 259, 277
Observer 155
O'Casey, Sean 136
O'Connor, T.P. 20
Official Secrets Act 210
oil price shocks 180, 182
Olympics (2012) 311, 312
One Nation Group 177
Open University 169, 202
opinion polls 4, 109–10, 132, 142, 143, 144, 153, 155, 156, 164, 165, 169, 171, 179, 183, 195, 196, 203, 206, 207, 210, 220, 221, 222, 225, 231, 233, 237, 239, 241, 249, 252, 254, 255, 256, 259, 267, 272, 275, 278, 279, 280, 281, 282, 292, 297, 301, 307, 312, 316
Orange River Colony 25
Orwell, George 148
Osborne, George 255, 259, 268, 269, 272, 274, 275, 278–9, 282, 283, 285, 292, 293, 294, 295, 296, 306
Owen, David 172, 193
Owen, Margaret 41, 42
Oxford University 2, 28, 112–13, 114, 125, 135, 136, 146, 149, 157, 158, 159, 174–5, 176, 187, 190, 199, 200, 229, 240, 263, 264, 265, 267, 268, 270, 273, 286, 287, 298, 304, 305, 306, 307, 308

Packenham, Frank *see* Longford, Lord
Paisley, Ian 171, 236, 237
Palestine 14, 51, 118
Palmerston, 3rd Viscount 6, 17, 238

328 Index

Parker, John 116, 188
Parliament Act (1911) 13, 35, 45, 58–60
parliamentary salaries 31
Parmoor, Lord 82
Parnell, Charles Stewart 10, 20, 30, 42
Parsons, Charles 227
Patten, Chris 220, 221, 225
Peace Ballot (1935) 95
Pearl Harbor 109
Pease, Sir Alfred 26
Peerage Act (1963) 153
People's Budget 13, 25, 34, 44, 45, 53–4
Peres de Cuellar, Javier 206
Pétain, Philippe 107
Phoenix Park murders 30
phone-hacking saga 276–7
Pigott, Richard 30
Pike, Mervyn 201–2
Pineau, Christian 131–2, 133
Pitt, William, the Elder 37
Pitt, William, the Younger 6, 227
Poincaré, Raymond 71
poll tax 210, 211, 220
Pompidou, Georges 168, 180, 192
Portillo, Michael 223, 224, 268
Portland, Duke of 157
Portsmouth, Lord 32
Potsdam conference 117
Powell, Colin 240
Powell, Jonathan 234, 237, 257
Premium Bonds 141
Prescott, John 231, 232, 234, 241, 254
prescription charges 167
Prior, James 180, 201, 203
privatisation 146, 185, 209, 224, 235
Profumo affair 145, 153, 165
Proportional Representation 235, 236
protectionism *see* tariff reform
Public Ownership *see* nationalisation
Punch 198
Pym, Francis 181, 203, 204, 206, 207

Qatada, Abu 290–1

Ramsay, Annie 76
Ramsay, Bella 76
Raven, Kay 179
Reading, Marquis of 126
Reagan, Ronald 206, 207
Redmayne, Martin 145
Redwood, John 223, 224
Rees, Mervyn 181
Rees-Mogg, Jacob 296
referendums 144, 170, 171, 183, 192, 193, 196,
  223, 235, 236, 237, 238, 247, 52, 270, 273–4,
  275, 277, 279, 281, 282, 283, 293, 294, 296,
  301, 312, 314, 316, 319

Reform Bill (1832) 24
Reform Bill (1867) 17
Relugas Compact 24, 32
reparations, German 51, 69, 83
repatriation, White Russian 140
resignation honours 171, 286
Reynaud, Paul 107
Reynolds, Albert 225
Rhineland occupation 96, 127, 129
Rhodes James, Robert 102, 124, 125, 126, 150
Rhodesia 167–8, 189, 205
Riddell, Sir George 48
Ridgeway, Celia 227
Ridley, Nicholas 218
Ridsdale, Lucy 65
Rippon, Geoffrey 180
Ritchie, C.T. 11
Robbins, Lionel 136, 160
Roberts, Alfred 198
Roberts, Beatrice 198
Roberts, Muriel 198
Robertson, Sir William 49
Robinson, Geoffrey 250, 251
Robley, Annie Pitcairn 57
Roosevelt, Franklin D. 72, 95, 96, 108, 109, 128,
  139, 140
Rosebery, 5th Earl of 10, 16, 20, 21, 22, 23, 30, 31,
  32, 43
Rothermere, Lord 73, 94, 233, 238
Rugby School 90
Rumsfeld, Donald 240
Runciman, Lord 97
Ruskin, John 76, 113
Russell, Sir Charles 30

Saarland plebiscite 126
Salisbury, 3rd Marquis of 1, 2, 4, 6, 9, 10, 11, 13,
  20, 21, 23, 30, 43, 57, 89, 93, 142, 152
Samuel, Herbert 36, 46, 85, 86
Sanders, J.S. 12, 24
Santer, Jacques 223
Scanlon, Hugh 195
Scargill, Arthur 182, 208
Schlesinger, Helmut 222
Schmidt, Helmut 171, 194, 205
school leaving age 51, 167, 202
school milk 202
schools, investment in 10, 42, 169, 202, 235, 242
Schröder, Gerhard 237
Scotsman, The 77
Scottish devolution 196
Scottish independence referendum (2014) 279
Seddon, Ethel 158, 159
Seddon, Harold 158
Shaftesbury, 7th Earl of 225
Sharp, Dame Evelyn 141
Shaw, Bernard 113

Sheffield, Lord 33
Shinwell, Emanuel 82, 87, 160
Sierra Leone 238
Simon, Sir John 36, 87, 95, 104, 115, 126
Simpson, Harry 216
Sinclair, Sir Archibald 104, 105
single currency *see* Euro
Skelton, Noel 126, 149, 150
Skripal poisoning affair (2018) 301
sleaze 224, 238, 239
Smith, Adam 229
Smith, John 222, 225, 229, 230, 231, 232, 233, 248, 249, 260
Smith, W.H. 10
Smuts, General 25
Snow, C.P. 158
Snowden, Philip 82, 84, 85, 86, 87, 94
Soames, Lord 203, 204, 205
Social Charter 221
Social Democratic Federation (SDF) 77, 79
Socialist International 81, 82
Socialist Union 77
Somme offensive 37, 49
Souls, The 7
Spanish Civil War 96, 127
speakership 21
Special Drawing Rights 190
Spectator, The 36, 153, 218, 254, 293, 308, 309
Spencer, 9th Earl 305
spin 239
Spring, Howard 86
St John-Stevas, Norman 203
Stalin, Josef 109, 110, 117, 140, 151
Stamfordham, Lord 69, 70, 72
Standard Chartered Bank 216
Stanley, Venetia 33–4, 36, 37, 102
Stansgate, Lord 152
Starzenski, Count 151
Statute of Westminster 115
stealth taxes 235, 251
Stevenson, Frances 42, 46, 50
Stevenson, Jennifer 42
Stewart, Michael 166, 189, 190
Straw, Jack 234, 240, 253–4, 258
Stuart, James 151
Suez War 127, 130, 131, 132, 133, 141, 142, 163, 167, 177
Sun 186, 202, 233, 253, 285–6
Sunday Express 145
Sunningdale agreement 181
Swann, Sir Michael 246
Sydney-Hobart race 179
Symonds, Carrie 314
Syrian Civil War 277, 282

Taff Vale judgement 26
Talbot, Lord Edmund 67

tariff reform 11, 12, 43, 44, 58–9, 73, 89, 91, 171, 226
taxation 12, 23, 32, 34, 44, 67, 85, 119, 144, 179, 187, 190, 200, 201, 204, 209, 210, 211, 218, 220, 221, 227, 232, 233, 235, 239, 249, 250, 251–2, 255, 257, 259, 266, 271, 272, 274, 278, 279, 280, 298, 312
Taylor, A.J.P. 109
Tebbit, Norman 205, 223
Tennant, Sir Charles 15, 30
Thatcher, Carol 200
Thatcher, Denis 200
Thatcher, Margaret 1, 2, 3, 4, 34, 52, 118, 120, 146, 158, 168, 171, 184, 185, 194, 195, 196, 197, **198–212**, 213, 216, 217, 218, 219, 220, 221, 223, 224, 225, 227, 230, 233, 234, 243, 250, 257, 262, 264, 265, 268, 269, 278, 286, 289–90, 298, 309
Thatcher, Mark 200
theatre censorship 169
Thomas, George 188
Thomas, J.H. 84, 84, 85
Thomson, Peter 229
Thorneycroft, Peter 142
Thorpe, Jeremy 183–4
three-day week 170–1, 183
Times, The 30, 38, 48, 53, 61, 63, 67, 92, 138, 191, 218, 269, 295, 299, 306, 307
Timothy, Nick 291, 292, 293, 295, 296, 297
Tobin, Oscar 114
Tolstoy, Count Nikolai 140
Tomlinson, George 160
top-up fees 239
Trade Disputes Act (1927) 73
Trades Disputes Bill (1906) 26
trade unions 26, 51, 70, 81, 116, 163, 168, 173, 179, 181, 182, 186, 187, 191, 192, 193, 194, 205, 208, 229, 235, 246, 291
Trevelyan, Sir Humphrey 132
Truman, Harry 117, 118
Tweedmouth, Lord 16, 32

unemployment 34, 44, 45, 51, 71, 73, 84, 85, 86, 94, 110, 115, 117, 137, 138, 158, 159, 182, 184–5, 204, 205, 208, 212, 214, 220, 225, 235, 244, 248, 250, 278, 279
unilateral disarmament 163
Union for Democratic Control (UDC) 81
United Clyde Shipbuilders 182
United Kingdom Independence Party (UKIP) 277, 278, 279, 280, 281, 282, 283, 292, 300

Vansittart, Sir Robert 96
Vassal affair 145
Vaughan, Dame Janet 199

330 Index

Vereeniging Peace Treaty 25
Victoria, Queen 18, 20, 247
Vietnam 167, 168

Walker, Peter 203, 204, 207
Wall Street crash 85
Waller, Ian 130
Walpole, Sir Robert 157, 227
Walters, Sir Alan 211
war debts 62, 67
Warwick, Countess of 125
Waterhouse, Ronald 69
Waugh, Evelyn 149
Weapons of Mass Destruction 240
Webb, Beatrice 79, 85, 86, 89, 114
Webb, Sidney 79, 113
Weir, L. Macneill 86
welfare state 26, 34, 39, 45, 53–4, 118, 119, 129,
   160, 201, 282
welfare to work 235, 250
Wellington, Duke of 207
Wells, H.G. 113
Welsh disestablishment 45
Westland affair 209
Wheatley, John 83, 84
Wheeler, Marina 304, 307, 308, 309, 314
Whelan, Charlie 250, 251
Whitelaw, William 180, 181, 184, 201, 203, 204,
   207, 210
Wilkinson, Ellen 108, 117, 118
Willans, Emily 28
Willans, John 28
Willans, William 28
Williams, Francis 87, 91, 121
Williams, Tommy 113
Wilmington, Earl of 157

Wilson, Harold 2, 4, 5, 69, 121, 122, 142, 144,
   146, 154, 155, 156, **158–72**, 173, 174, 178, 179,
   181, 183, 184, 185, 190, 191, 192, 193, 194,
   203, 205, 215, 216, 222, 246, 251
Wilson, Herbert 158, 159
Wilson, Sir Horace 96, 98
Wilson, Jack 158
Wilson, Sir Leslie 68
Wilson, Marjorie 158
Wilson, Mary 159, 171
Wilson, Woodrow 38, 50, 52, 54
windfall tax 235, 250, 251–2
winter of discontent 195, 196, 203
Wolff, Sir Drummond 9
women's suffrage 26
Wood, Sir Kingsley 103
Wood, Richard 201
Worcester, Robert 225
Workers' Weekly 83
Workmen's Compensation Bill 26
World War I 13, 24, 27, 54, 55, 66, 77, 102, 103,
   133, 234
World War II 74, 129, 199, 220, 243
Wright, R.S. 29
Wyatt, Petronella ('Petsy') 309, 310
Wyndham, George 124

Yalta conference 109, 140, 151
Yeats, W.B. 136
Yom Kippur War 170, 182
Younger, Sir George 53, 68

Zaghari-Ratcliffe, Nazanin 312
Zimbabwe *see* Rhodesia
Zinoviev, George 83–4
Zinoviev letter 83–4